FISHER OF KILVERSTONE

Fisher as Captain of the *Excellent* in 1883

FISHER
OF KILVERSTONE

BY

Ruddock F. Mackay

CLARENDON PRESS
OXFORD
1973

Oxford University Press, Ely House, London W.1

GLASGOW   NEW YORK   TORONTO   MELBOURNE   WELLINGTON
CAPE TOWN   IBADAN   NAIROBI   DAR ES SALAAM   LUSAKA   ADDIS ABABA
DELHI   BOMBAY   CATCUTTA   MADRAS   KARACHI   LAHORE   DACCA
KUALA LUMPUR   SINGAPORE   HONG KONG   TOKYO

© *Oxford University Press 1973*

Made in Great Britain at The Pitman Press, Bath

PREFACE

ALTHOUGH much has been published concerning Admiral of the Fleet Lord Fisher of Kilverstone, a number of questions about him still await clear and convincing answers. Some of these questions could already be asked before serious work on this biography began (in 1964); others emerged as the investigation progressed. In particular, Fisher's earlier career extending from his first joining the Navy in 1854 to his role as naval delegate at the Hague Conference of 1899 called for closer examination. Just what part did he play in the technological revolution of the Navy during the nineteenth century? Was he a genius? If so, how did this gift manifest itself in the earlier as well as the later stages of a connexion with the Navy beginning in 1854 and ending in December 1918? Was there anything important to add to previous accounts of his part in naval operations, for example in the second China War or the bombardment (and the occupation) of Alexandria? With regard to his later career, how truly was the Navy of 1914 the creation of Lord Fisher? How far had he contributed to the elements of strength and weakness in the service? To what extent was he personally responsible for the insubordinate antagonism of Lord Charles Beresford and the extraordinary rift in the Navy? As First Sea Lord from 1904 to 1910 did Fisher possess any definite ideas on war plans? Did he, for instance, envisage a close or a distant blockade in the event of a Franco–British war with Germany? Did he seriously intend to launch an amphibious attack on the German North Sea coast or to send a great expedition into the Baltic? How did his hostility to the Army arise and develop? Why did he officially advocate a general staff for the War Office and deny one to the Admiralty? With regard to the Great War, is it true that he returned to the Admiralty in the autumn of 1914 so obsessed with the Baltic project that he concentrated his still-formidable energies on building a great armada for this fantastic enterprise? Yet did he at the same time believe that the submarine was about to dominate all narrow European waters, including the North Sea, to the virtual exclusion of large warships? If he based his conduct as First Sea Lord simultaneously on both principles, should not his sanity be called in question? Yet was it not the case that Jellicoe, with all his caution and knowledge, could only contemplate the idea of Fisher's departure from the Admiralty with dismay? These were some of the questions. A mass of materials, published and unpublished, prospectively contained at least some of the answers.

Inevitably, the present writer is much indebted to the works of Professor Arthur J. Marder. However, it should doubtless be mentioned here that some sources important for Fisher and his times were not available when Marder was collecting material for his volumes on the period ending in 1914. Amongst these sources were the Foreign Office Papers for the Hague Conference of 1899, some personal collections of naval officers latterly acquired by the National Maritime Museum (notably the Slade and Hornby Papers), and also the Bonar Law, Lloyd George, Hankey, and Churchill Papers. The present writer had access to all these, excepting the Churchill archives; and many—probably most—of the relevant Churchill documents have lately been published. Moreover, even so remarkable a researcher as Professor Marder could not be expected to see every document in the collections which he investigated. This applies, for example, to the main collection of Fisher Papers. The present writer, working part time, and an assistant (Mrs. Hazel Edbury) working full time, needed a whole calendar year to arrange and catalogue this collection! On completing their task in September 1968, they found that the Fisher Papers comprised some 6,000 items. An item might consist of a single letter or it might be a large printed volume on naval policy. It is therefore not surprising that some important materials should have escaped previous notice. Likewise, it was only to be expected that some of the relevant Admiralty and War Office records still awaited attention. Again, until 1968, the fifty-year rule stood in the way of anyone wishing to see the Cabinet Papers, including the Papers of the Committee of Imperial Defence. Researchers had to make the best of odd copies which had been (improperly) carried away from meetings by the participants.

Finally, a certain amount of fashionable denigration prompts a brief comment on the historical value of thoroughgoing biography. An aggregation of non-biographical studies, alone, could scarcely provide a full understanding of the Navy during Fisher's lifetime. It is for instance unlikely that the earlier history of British mines and mining could be satisfactorily treated without knowledge of Fisher's private materials on the subject; and these biographical materials in turn lead the researcher to official reports which might otherwise lie buried in the Admiralty records. Similar reasoning applies to many aspects of naval affairs from 1868 to 1915, a period during which Fisher exercised an increasingly pervasive influence.

St. Andrews   R.F.M.

ACKNOWLEDGEMENTS

I am most grateful to the 14th Duke of Hamilton and the 3rd Baron Fisher for doing so much to facilitate the writing of this book; also for the friendly reception which I was always given at Lennoxlove and Kilverstone.

It is likewise agreeable to record my appreciation of the assistance granted by the Court of the University of St. Andrews. Through its Travel Fund the Court helped me with travelling expenses; and, during the academic year 1967–8, provided me with a full-time graduate assistant, Mrs. Hazel Edbury, so that— on behalf of the Department of Modern History and in the interests of scholarship in naval history—I could direct the re-arrangement and cataloguing of the Duke of Hamilton's Fisher Papers. This collection was found to consist of some 6,000 items. Copies of the catalogue, in book form, were sent to the National Register of Archives; the Naval Library, Ministry of Defence; the National Maritime Museum (Dept. of MSS.); the Librarian, Churchill College, Cambridge; Professor A. J. Marder, University of California, Irvine; and Professor Theodore Ropp, Duke University, North Carolina.

Among those who assisted me in writing this book, I wish to mention especially Rear-Admiral P. W. Brock. He read the first three chapters in draft and his detailed comments on these, like his more general views on 'the Fisher era', remain for me an object of delight. I am grateful to Professor Marder for his generous interest and to Mr. H. P. Willmott—a notable source of information. (See the bibliography for details of his unpublished thesis—also the helpful theses of Drs. N. d'Ombrain, H. Moon, and N. Summerton.) Otherwise, I wish to mention Mr. Martin Gilbert, Commander Michael Godfrey, R.N., Mr. Richard Hough, Admiral Sir William James, Mr. Hector Munro, M.P., Mr. Alan Pearsall, Mr. Anthony Preston, Commander H. Pursey, R.N., Mrs. Marjorie Wentworth Reeve, Captain S. W. Roskill, R.N., Professor Donald Schurman, and Mr. Robert Mackworth Young. Miss E. M. Anderson gave valued assistance with the typing of the fair copy.

I also wish to thank the staffs of the relevant libraries and centres of research including the Beaverbrook Library, the British Museum, the Library of Churchill College, Cambridge, the National Army Museum, the National Library of Scotland, the Naval Library (Ministry of Defence), the Public Record Office, the Royal Naval College, Greenwich, and the Library of the University of St. Andrews.

Every effort was made to communicate with holders of copyright in original materials. Where I did not succeed, I hope that my apologies will be accepted. I wish to acknowledge the gracious permission of Her Majesty the Queen to quote from letters of King George V (Fisher Papers); also the permission of the Controller of Her Majesty's Stationery Office to quote unpublished Crown Copyright material in the Public Record Office. My thanks are likewise due to Mr. Mark Bonham Carter (Asquith copyright); Lord Brabourne and the Trustees of the Broadlands Archives Settlement (Battenberg letters); the Trustees of the British Museum (Balfour materials); Lord Cawdor; Mr. Richard Corbett; Lord Esher; Lord Hankey; William Heinemann Ltd. (Publishers), C & T Publications Ltd., and Mr. Martin Gilbert (Churchill copyright); Mr. Hector Munro (Ewart's diary); Lord Jellicoe; the Trustees of the National Maritime Museum and Mr. Alan Pearsall (Bridge, Hornby, May, Noel, Oliver, Richmond and Thursfield Papers); Mr. Anthony Pollen; Lord Selborne; and Mr. A. J. P. Taylor and the Beaverbrook Foundation (Lloyd George copyright). I also wish to thank Vice-Admiral Sir Ian McGeoch for agreeing, as Editor of the *Naval Review*, to my quoting some material from the 1930 volume.

As regards published books, I am grateful to Professor A. J. Marder and Jonathan Cape, Ltd., for allowing me to quote (as agreed) from *Fear God and Dread Nought*; and to Adeline Lady Hankey for permitting extensive quotation from *The Supreme Command*.

R.F.M.

CONTENTS

LIST OF PLATES AND MAP

ABBREVIATIONS

B.E.F.   British Expeditionary Force.

C.I.D.   Committee of Imperial Defence.

C.I.G.S.   Chief of the Imperial General Staff.

D.M.O.   Director of Military Operations.

D.N.C.   Director of Naval Construction.

D.N.I.   Director of Naval Intelligence.

D.N.O.   Director of Naval Ordnance.

D.O.D.   Director of Operations (Division), Naval Staff.

M.L.R.   muzzle-loading rifled gun.

N.D.A.   Naval Defence Act.

N.I.D.   Naval Intelligence Department.

T.B.D.   torpedo-boat destroyer.

IN THE FOOTNOTES AND BIBLIOGRAPHY

Add. MSS.   Additional Manuscripts, British Museum. (See Bibliography.)

Adl.   Admiral.

Adm.   Admiralty Records, Public Record Office.

Ady.   Admiralty.

Anatomy   *The Anatomy of British Sea Power: a History of British Naval Policy in the Pre-Dreadnought Era*, 1880–1905, by Arthur J. Marder.

B.D.   *British Documents on the Origins of the War*, 1898–1914, edited by G. P. Gooch and H. Temperley, London, 1926–38, 11 vols.

B.M.   British Museum.

Cab.   Cabinet Papers.

D.D.F.   *Documents diplomatiques français*, 1871–1914, 2nd Ser., Paris, 1930–55, 14 vols.

D.N.B.   *Dictionary of National Biography.*

D.S.	*From the Dreadnought to Scapa Flow* by Arthur J. Marder. (See Bibliography.)
E.P.	Esher Papers.
F.	Fisher.
F.G.	*Fear God and Dread Nought:* Fisher's correspondence edited by Arthur J. Marder.
(FG)	Indicates that the document is wholly or substantially reproduced in *F.G.*
F.P.	Fisher Papers: the Duke of Hamilton's collection (Lennoxlove MSS.).
G.P.	*Die grosse Politik der europäishen Kabinette,* 1871–1914, edited by Johannes Lepsius *et al.*, Berlin, 1922–7, 40 vols.
J.P.	Jellicoe Papers.
Kilv. MSS.	Kilverstone Manuscripts.
Mins.	Minutes.
N.M.M.	National Maritime Museum.
N.N.	*Naval Necessities:* Admiralty prints compiled by Fisher and bound in 3 vols. (There is a fourth volume at the Naval Library which was never consecutively printed like the other three.)
N.R.S.	Navy Records Society.
P.	printed.
P.R.O.	Public Record Office.
R.C. ii, comp. ii	Randolph Churchill, *Winston S. Churchill,* vol. ii, companion vol. ii.
R.U.S.I.	Royal United Service Institution.
W.O.	War Office.

Where a document is bound—for instance a naval print bound in a hard or paper cover—its title is given in italics. This applies also in the case of an abbreviation such as *N.N.*

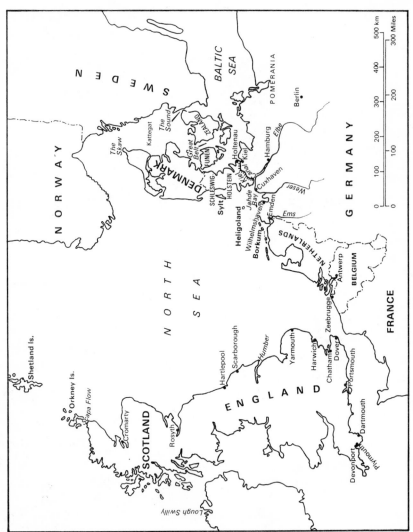

Strategic map of the North Sea

CHAPTER I

FROM CADET TO LIEUTENANT
(1854–1861)

ON 25 January 1841 Sophie, wife of Captain William Fisher, A.D.C. to the Governor of Ceylon, gave birth at Rambodde to her first child who was duly named John Arbuthnot Fisher. The twenty-year-old mother was a formidable person—like a dark, smouldering volcano, to judge by later photographs. Yet even she might reasonably have experienced some dismay had she understood what manner of child she had brought into the world. He would variously be dubbed a genius and a crank, a patriot and a deserter. Some would praise him for clarity of mind and outstanding foresight, others would deem him irrational, even mad. Having been able to claim one King of England as his best friend, he would be judged worthy of hanging at the yard-arm by that same King's son and successor. In the view of the journalist J. L. Garvin, with his wide range of acquaintance and 'prodigious memory',[1] he was the most fascinating of all his contemporaries and 'the least like any other man'.[2]

Jack (as he was always known within the family) had a childhood extending to the age of thirteen. Then he joined the Navy. The main features of his childhood were the robust environment of the first six years, his separation from his parents at the age of six, and the rather uncertain pattern of the next seven years. Although Jack Fisher ultimately left a considerable assortment of memoirs, remarkably accurate in many of their details considering that they were rather casually set down in the last years of a long life, he seems on the whole to have preferred to forget his first thirteen years. In particular he had nothing at all to say about the earliest period, spent on his father's coffee plantation. Captain William Fisher decided to leave the Army in 1841. In due course, Mrs. Fisher gave birth to eleven children all told, of whom seven survived infancy. These seven in order of birth were Jack, Alice, Lucy, Arthur, Frank, Frederic William (born in 1851

---

[1] Esher, ii, 307.   [2] Bacon, i, 228.

and ultimately a full Admiral), and finally Philip (born in 1858 and also a naval officer). It is Frederic William—'Billy' in his young days and 'Uncle Bill' later—who has left an impression of the life led by the young children on the Wavendon estate before being sent away to schools in England.

When I was a youngster Nuwara Eliya was a very wild place, inhabited by a handful of white people who lived in about six houses scattered over a vast semi-wilderness where game, big and small, was plentiful. My father, who was a keen sportsman and a daring hunter, kept a mixed pack of hounds, chiefly used for running down elk. This was done on foot . . . Being the youngest and a mere toddler, I was not able to move very fast . . . What with hunting, swimming, riding and no schoolmaster to worry us, we boys had a glorious time . . . We boys never wore shoes or stockings . . . Our feet were so hard we could walk anywhere without the least discomfort, but when the grass leeches were voracious and bit our legs, mother used to apply Friar's Balsam, which, together with castor oil, were the only names of medicines I knew in those days.[1]

Captain Fisher found coffee-planting a hazardous and financially unrewarding occupation which helps to explain the vicissitudes suffered by Jack and the other children during their time at school in England. Writing from Colombo to an unidentified friend or relative on 30 November 1862, the gallant Captain, then aged fifty-one, summed up his life in Ceylon succinctly enough:

My dear Peg (?),

Jack says you want a letter from me. After 30 years banishment it is very difficult to write one.

I was greatly grieved to hear of your daughter's death but such things we must all bear in our time.

All our children are now away from us. The little fellow 'Toby' [Philip], four years old, lives with Alice [his sister], Mrs. Daniell. They are going to England and take Toby with them. It is cruel work parting with them all—and more so that we are tied down here to provide for them.

Daniell's father is just dead and they are left *very well* off.

I am now Chief Superintendent Police but I fear the man who I am acting for is coming out here again, which will put one out of employment. I have two *good* coffee estates but they are largely in debt and I have to send so much home to the children that I cannot pay much off.

---

[1] Adl. Sir Frederic Fisher, *Naval Reminiscences*, London, 1938, pp. 16–18.

We are both wonderfully well considering I have been 31 years here and my wife 24. I have not a grey hair on my head and can shoot, ride, etc., etc., as well as I ever could. Sophy is 40 but very stout and young looking. I want her to go home with Alice, but she won't and I shall never be able to go. I should like to see you all again but it is hopeless . . .

> Your affectionate
> W. Fisher[1]

Captain Fisher met his death in 1866 in a manner not altogether uncharacteristic—thrown from a horse.

Jack at the age of six was younger than most of his brothers and sisters when sent off to England. His father's straitened financial circumstances help to explain the somewhat dismal record which he left of the years 1847 to 1854.

I entered the Navy, July 12th, 1854, on board Her Majesty's Ship 'Victory', after being medically examined by the Doctor on board of her, and writing out from dictation The Lord's Prayer; and I rather think I did a Rule of Three sum. Before that time, for seven years I had a hard life. My paternal grandfather—a splendid old parson of the fox-hunting type—with whom I was to live, had died just before I reached England; and no one else but my maternal grandfather[2] was in a position to give me a home. He was a simple-minded man and had been fleeced of a fortune by a foreign scoundrel—I remember him well, as I also remember the Chartist riots of 1848 when I saw a policeman even to my little mind behaving, as I thought, brutally to passing individuals. I remember seeing a tottering old man having his two sticks taken away from him and broken across their knees by the police. On the other hand, I have to bear witness to a little phalanx of 40 splendid police (who then wore tall hats and tail coats) charging a multitude of what seemed to me to be thousands and sending them flying for their lives. They only had their truncheons . . .

How can it possibly interest anyone to know that my simple-minded maternal grandfather was driven through the artifices of a rogue to take in lodgers, who of their charity gave me bread thickly spread with butter—butter was a thing I otherwise never saw—and my staple food was boiled rice with brown sugar—very brown?[3]

However, these gloomy memories should not be taken too seriously. The picture had a brighter side. Captain William Fisher may not have been affluent but he stemmed from a line

---

[1] Kilv. MSS., Packet 7.
[2] Alfred Lambe, wine merchant of New Bond Street.
[3] *Memories*, pp. 137–9.

of baronets of the seventeenth and eighteenth centuries, followed by a succession of parsons at Bodmin in Cornwall. He was commissioned through the good offices of Lord Raglan, when Military Secretary to the Duke of Wellington, to meet the dying request of an uncle, also William Fisher, mortally wounded as a Captain at Waterloo. (The nephew would have been only four at the time of the battle.) This background goes some way to explain the fact that Jack's father was not only A.D.C. to Sir Robert Wilmot Horton, Governor of Ceylon, but that Lady Horton became Jack's godmother in 1841. Nor was it forgotten that Captain Fisher had saved the life of the Horton's eldest son. The Governor died during that same year but Lady Horton, who was wealthy, continued after her retirement to Catton Hall in Derbyshire to take a kindly and active interest in Jack and the other members of his family. Jack's memory of his godmother as '*very, very* beautiful'[1] receives support from Byron's lines:

> She walks in beauty like the night
> Of cloudless climes and starry skies;
> And all that's best of dark and bright
> Meets in her aspect and her eyes:
> Thus mellow'd to that tender light
> Which heaven to gaudy day denies.

Fisher remembered Catton Hall with affection. 'I had happy days there. The Trent flowed past the house and I loved being on the river and catching perch.' In the same unpublished memoir Fisher thus recorded the manner of his nomination as a Cadet in 1854:

Lady Horton's neighbour was Admiral Sir William Parker, the last of Nelson's Captains, so she asked him to take me to sea, and he did! Strange to say, another dear old lady took a fancy to me, and she was Lord Nelson's own niece, and she asked Sir William for me, and, curiously, my first ship of war was the *Victory*, Nelson's flagship. She had her sails bent in those days and was kept ready for sea with a regular crew.[2]

Fisher himself seems to have been responsible for some confusion about the date of his entry into the Navy. According to the relevant accounting department his 'First Entry' was on

---

[1] F.P. 5100. Autobiographical MS.—apparently written by the Duchess of Hamilton at F.'s dictation in 1918.
[2] Ibid.

13 July 1854 aboard the *Calcutta* as a Naval Cadet.[1] However, although he was borne on the *Calcutta's* books from the outset, he did enter the service aboard the *Victory* on 13 July and after the customary leave for kitting up he returned (apparently from Catton Hall) 'to Gieve the outfitter at Portsmouth who put him up for the night in an attic at his house in the High Street. Next day he went in a little steamer called the *Sir Francis Drake* to Plymouth. An Admiral Rich and his daughters were in the same ship. They were very kind to the little lonely seasick boy.' He joined the *Calcutta* at Plymouth on 29 July.[2]

For the record, it was at Plymouth, not at Portsmouth, that Sir William Parker was Commander-in-Chief. It was here that Fisher duly delivered his letter from Lady Horton and was invited to dinner by the Admiral. Fisher replied that he thought he had better join his ship (meaning, of course, the *Calcutta*). The Admiral was amused and told the boy to spend the night at his house. According to Fisher:

He told me all about Lord Nelson whom he had served under a great many years. Only his wife was at dinner—he wore tiny little epaulettes at dinner, and the next morning, a Saturday, he sent me off to my ship with the Admiral's Coxwain, and as I stepped on board I had a bucket of salt water over my feet. They were holystoning decks and the white-haired First Lieutenant, with his trousers turned up above his knees and no shoes or stockings, roared at me like a Bull of Bashan and afterwards gave me an orange when he met me outside his cabin in the cockpit. The oldsters among my messmates all had white hair . . . They had been all their lives in a Midshipman's berth—they were failures. Our ship had the failures as the Captain had been tried by Court Martial in his last ship for cruelty—he had flogged all his crew. The Commander was no better—he used to padlock men to a ringbolt and douse them with salt water—any punishment was legal then. I walked the break of the poop with a coil of rope round my neck, as he said I was born to be hung![3]

Another Cadet aboard the *Calcutta*, E. S. B. Kelso, also remembered 'Jacky Stevens', the Commander, as 'a regular old Tartar . . . who used to keep us all moving . . . used to call me

---

[1] Adm. 24/167, f. 88. *Records*, p. 261, gives 13 June, which has often been accepted by writers. *Memories*, p. 137, gives 12 July.

[2] Kilv., Lady F.'s Notebook, entry for 14 July 1907, beginning, 'This morning Jack breakfasted with the King at Buckingham Palace'. Adm. 38/2752, Calcutta's Muster Book.

[3] F.P. 5100. Of course, no firm reliance can be placed on the details of F.'s latter-day stories of this genre.

"Catseyes"—"Fly, Mr. Catseyes", and I flew'. Of his relations with Fisher, Kelso wrote: 'He and I as Cadets were great friends, more so than most lads, but we drifted apart afterwards. He was always very clever and top of us all as Cadets, learning in the Captain's cabin. He was of course very senior to me, but was also very kind to me when we were boys.'[1]

Fisher joined the Navy at a most interesting time in its history. Britain had entered the Crimean War in March 1854 and this conflict may be regarded either as the last of the old wars or the first of the new. From the point of view of the British Navy in particular the ensuing operations in the Black Sea and the Baltic brought home the merits of propulsion by steam rather than wind and sail. Fisher's long naval career thus happened to run parallel, in a very precise manner, to the great technological transformation of the Navy. The Crimean War marks the division between the naval age of sail and the naval age of technology. Recognition that a new type of officer would be required by a revolution in ships and weapons did not come easily. It was not to be expected that men who had devoted years to mastering gradually evolved weapons and techniques would readily accept that, quite suddenly, those weapons and techniques had become obsolete. Sir Charles Walker, for example, has suggested that it 'would not be inaccurate to take the year 1870 as the beginning of the transition from the old type of Naval officer to the new.'[2] But it was the hallmark of Fisher's radical flair that he understood so quickly, at every stage in his career, the threat presented to naval primacy by technical obsolescence; and, far from wishing to comfort himself by trying to preserve a background of familiar objects and practices, he was for ever ready to press forward into the strange, mechanized environment which has since become a commonplace. His willingness to scrap, to seize eagerly on the new, extended beyond things to people. Kelso's experience of enjoying Fisher's charm and friendship, and then being dropped and forgotten, was the earliest known instance of a phenomenon that was often to be repeated, as will in due course appear. It might have consoled Kelso to learn that even Admiral Sir Astley Cooper Key, one of the most sophisticated administrators of the sixties and seventies, was to join him in the class of persons discarded by Fisher! But it

---

[1] Kilv. MSS., Packet 12: letters from Kelso to C. N. Robinson.
[2] Walker, p. 181.

occasions no surprise to find the aged Kelso writing in 1921: 'it's fair to tell you, except as Naval Cadet, I did not like Jacky Fisher!'.[1]

The *Calcutta* belonged to the old Navy. A sailing ship of the line, with 84 smooth-bore, muzzle-loading guns arranged in broadsides on two gun-decks, she had been built of wood in 1831 and was of 2,299 tons burden—about the same tonnage as the *Victory*. Unlike some modernized ships of the line in 1854, the *Calcutta* had no steam-engine. Last coppered in May 1852, she had been recommissioned at Plymouth on 3 May 1854. At this time it was believed that such ships, even without auxiliary screw-propulsion, would still be of some operational value in the Baltic or Black Sea. The ship was still fitting for sea when Fisher joined her in July.

'There were many brutalities when I first entered the Navy', he afterwards recalled. 'For instance, the day I joined as a little boy I saw eight men flogged—and I fainted at the sight.[2] This remark has often been quoted. In fact, the *Calcutta's* log[3] records no floggings on that day, 29 July. Floggings certainly were given on board from time to time but the first such entry after Fisher joined the ship is for 23 September, 7.30 a.m., when a Royal Marine Private, Richard Jackson, received 36 lashes 'for disobedience of orders'. Up to the time when the ship at last sailed from Plymouth on 14 November, the routine was that of a ship of the line in the eighteenth century: the decks were holystoned, the odd seaman was 'discharged run', the crew was 'employed fitting fore and topsail yards and setting up lower rigging' and 'scrubbed hammocks'. Only an entry about 'artificers employed from the Dock Yard' might have raised a question in the minds of men who had served with Hawke, Rodney, or Nelson. Fisher's first voyage took him no further than Falmouth where a second Private of the Royal Marines was given '42 lashes for conducting himself in a drunken, riotous and insubordinate manner'. After returning to Plymouth on 11 December, the *Calcutta* emerged in February 1855 to cruise in the Channel and was based at Spithead for a time. She was moored off Sheerness Dockyard on 9 June and on the 30th she sailed with 'packages for the Fleet in the Baltic'. The ship's log-entries give something of the

---

[1] Kilv. MSS., loc. cit.; Mrs. Rose de Crespigny (*née* Key) to 2nd Lord F., 25 Sept. 1921.
[2] *Records*, p. 10.   [3] Adm. 53/4898.

flavour of the fourteen-year-old Fisher's first voyage on active service:

(30 June, a.m.) 9.30 loosed sails, slipped from lump, and made all plain sail. 10.15 set starboard studding sails & port foretopmast & topgallant studding sails. 10.14 Nore Light Vessel—North.

(1 July, p.m.) 10.20 latitude by Polar Star 54. 12 N.

(2 July, p.m.) 6.30 exercised Boys 2nd class and Novices reefing and furling mizen topsail.[1]

But if routines aboard the *Calcutta* were redolent of Hawke and Nelson, she was sharply confronted with the fact of her own obsolescence when she drew near the advanced base of the Anglo–French squadrons at Nargen island. She was met by the bustling paddle-steamer *Vulture* and towed to the anchorage. Whereas in 1854, when the *Calcutta* was making ready for sea, it was generally believed that sailing-ships of the line would continue to possess some combatant value, by 1855 the campaigns in the Black Sea and the Baltic had proved the superiority conferred by steam-propulsion. As Clowes has succinctly put it, 'sails and wood went out, and steam and iron came in, in 1855.' However, to modify the impression of decrepitude commonly attaching to Napier's fleet of 1854, it is well to note that every vessel of the hastily assembled original squadron, as distinct from reinforcements sent to the Baltic later in the year, did have an engine. Captain Bartholomew Sulivan, who played a very active part in the Baltic campaigns, afterwards testified to the chief weakness at the outset being in personnel rather than ships. He thought that the Russians, who had twenty-five sail of the line to pit against sixteen British in the early weeks, were in a higher state of training, but that 'the advantage of our steam-ships', and especially 'the new screw-frigates', made it possible for the British (with the French) to command the Baltic in 1854. By the time that the *Calcutta*, laden with provisions, clothing, and ammunition, set sail for the Baltic there was no longer any question of using an engineless sailing-ship in a fighting role.[2]

On 25 July, her second day in tow, the *Calcutta* arrived at Nargen, the operational base of the allied fleets in the Gulf of

---

[1] Adm. 53/4899.
[2] N.R.S., *Russian War, 1855: Baltic*, p. 166; Clowes, vi, 473; Sulivan, p. 121—B. Sulivan's evidence before Royal Commission for Manning the Navy (1858).

Finland. Her log records what must have been an interesting event for Fisher:

P.M. 1.15   in fore and aft sails & squared yards: observed the Spires of the city of Reval.

2.30   observed English & French Squadrons at anchor under Nargen Island. Showed number to look-out Blockship.

4.00   cast off from 'Vulture' and came to with B B in 17 fms.[1]

Although every fighting ship sent to the Baltic in 1855 possessed at least auxiliary steam-power, none was yet built of iron. But the beginnings of a gradual revolution in gunnery are reflected in the ammunition supplied by the *Calcutta* to various vessels. Whereas she produced quantities of solid, 68 pounder shot for the *Duke of Wellington* (bearing the flag of Rear-Admiral Richard Dundas) and other large ships of the line, she also distributed supplies of round explosive shell—8-inch, 32 pounder, and 6 pounder. Here is the *Calcutta's* log-entry for a.m. Monday, 30 July: 'Supplied the following mortar boats with Shell and Sweeps, viz.—"Drake" with 100 shell and 2 Sweeps, "Manly" with 60 shell and 2 Sweeps, "Mastiff" with 90 Shell and 2 Sweeps, "Surly" with 59 Shell and 2 Sweeps, "Porpoise" 60 Shell and 2 Sweeps & "Blazer" with 60 Shell and 2 Sweeps.' A few days later these barge-like vessels were to play a prominent part in the bombardment of Sveaborg. This was the most notable operation carried out by the Baltic Fleet in 1855. On Monday, 6 August, the crew of the *Calcutta* could see Dundas putting to sea with several ships of the line, 13 gunboats, and 12 mortar-vessels. On 9 August the British and French mortar-vessels (21 all told) lined up at a range of 3,600 yards from their target and brought their 13-inch weapons into action at 7 a.m. The fortress, which was on a group of islands off Helsingfors (Helsinki), was bombarded by gunboats and mortar-vessels through the day while the ships of the line, drawn up behind them, acted as supply-vessels. Aboard the *Calcutta*, anchored about fifty miles southward of the action, 'heavy firing' could be heard through the later afternoon and on the next day at 12.50 a fire could be seen in the distance to the N.N.E. That morning Dundas had ordered his mortar-vessels to move closer to the forts before renewing the bombardment. As he reported in his dispatch: 'Fires continued to burn without intermission within the fortress,

---

[1] Adm. 53/4899.

and about noon a column of smoke, heavier and darker than any which had yet been observed, and succeeded by bright flames, gave signs that the shells had reached combustible materials in the direction of the arsenal.'[1]

When it is borne in mind that the question of ships versus forts was to recur with mounting importance during Fisher's naval career, it is of interest to discover him within sight and sound, as a Cadet of fourteen, of what must be accounted a successful major bombardment. Admittedly, there was a great expenditure of ammunition; but casualties were astonishingly light, considerable damage was done to military installations (if not to the better-protected forts), and large numbers of Russian troops were pinned down around the Gulf of Finland.

By the beginning of June, the British became aware that the Russians had brought into use new underwater weapons, initially called 'infernal machines' or just 'infernals', subsequently 'torpedoes', and finally (by the 1870s) 'mines'. Seeing that Fisher's reputation as Lieutenant, Commander, and Captain was to be largely based on his expertise in 'torpedoes' it seems appropriate to mention some of the incidents relating to 'infernals' which presumably became common knowledge in the British fleet. It is probable that, during the eight weeks which the *Calcutta* spent at Nargen, Fisher heard details of the first encounters (in June) with the Russian mines: how Captain Sulivan's paddle-steamer *Merlin* had set off two of them when reconnoitring Cronstadt with the French admiral and a large party of allied captains on board; how, a fortnight later, Rear-Admirals Dundas and Michael Seymour persisted in tinkering with 'infernals' which had been raised for inspection; how Seymour proved his expertise by exploding a mine when surrounded by an attentive group of officers on board his flagship; and how Dundas (later on the same day) nearly succeeded in blinding himself by fiddling with a detonator. Here is Sulivan's account of Seymour's mishap which took place off Cronstadt on 21 June:

To my astonishment I found that *Vulture* had exploded an infernal machine in the middle of the fleet . . . Admiral Seymour and Hall got one up, and hauled it over the bows of the gig. How the little slides [trigger mechanism] were not touched is wonderful . . . Then they

---

[1] Adm. 53/4899; Clowes, vi, 493-7; N.R.S., *Russian War, 1855: Baltic*, pp. 184-97; Preston and Major, p. 27.

took it to Admiral Dundas, and again they all played with it; and Admiral Seymour took it to his ship, and on the poop had the officers round examining it . . . Some of the officers remarked on the danger of its going off, and Admiral Seymour said, 'Oh, no; this is the way it would go off,' and shoved the slide in with his finger, as he had seen Stokes do it. It instantly exploded, knocking down every one round it. [A number of people were burned or otherwise injured.] It is a wonderful escape, for pieces of it flew down the main hatchway; and we know that the Russians getting one into a boat exploded it, and killed seventeen men. Admiral Seymour is much less hurt than was first supposed, as he is able to sit up to-day [23rd]; but concussion of the brain is what they fear . . .[1]

Disappointingly Fisher did not comment on these mines in his markedly unsystematic memoirs. But he did refer to the ship's biscuit which was carried in quantity by the *Calcutta* both for her own crew and for the replenishment of the fleet.

A favourite amusement was to put a bit of this biscuit on the table and see how soon all of it would walk away. In fact one midshipman could gamble away his 'tot' of rum with another midshipman by pitting one bit of biscuit against another. Anyhow, whenever you took a bit of biscuit to eat you always tapped it edgeways on the table to let the 'grown-ups' get away.

The water was nearly as bad as the Biscuit. It was turgid—it was smelly—it was animally. I remember so well . . . being sent with the watering party to the Island of Nargen to get fresh water, as we were running short of it . . . My youthful astonishment was how on earth the Lieutenant in charge of the Watering Party discovered the Water. There wasn't a lake and there wasn't a stream, but he went and dug a hole and there was the water.[2]

On 25 August, in the evening, the *Calcutta* prepared to set out for home: '6.30 down topgallant yards and masts; pointed yards to the wind.' Then she was towed off to the northward by the *Vulture* with her belching stack and thrashing paddle-wheels.

After reaching the Nore on 11 September, the *Calcutta* returned to Spithead on the 22nd. With the rest of the ship's company, Fisher was paid off at Hamoaze, Plymouth, on 1 March 1856. By then warlike operations had virtually ceased. The Treaty of Paris was signed on 30 March.[3]

From 2 March, Fisher was borne on the books of a ship possessing greater historical interest than the *Calcutta*. This was the *Agamemnon*. She was of 3,102 tons, had an armament of 91

---

[1] Sulivan, pp. 301–4.   [2] *Records*, p. 8.   [3] Adm. 53/4899.

guns, and was the first ship of the line to be designed from the outset with auxiliary screw propulsion in view. Laid down at Woolwich in 1849, she was launched in 1852. Flying the flag of the energetic and capable Rear-Admiral Sir Edward Lyons, she had done well, by comparison with ships of the line without engines, at the bombardment of Sevastopol on 17 October 1854. She went through the campaign of 1855 in the Black Sea and took part in the capture of Kinburn. When the *Calcutta* paid off in March 1856 the *Agamemnon* was lying at Malta. By April she was at Constantinople. Having apparently been given a spell of leave, Fisher took passage out to the *Agamemnon* and, with two other Cadets, he joined her on 19 May. On the 31st she steamed into the Black Sea and anchored off Kazaten on 2 June; she spent two days 'clearing tugs of baggage belonging to troops' and a further day embarking the troops themselves from various steam vessels. That evening she 'weighed under steam', passed through the Bosphorus on 6 June and by the morning of the 7th she was 'running through the Dardanelles'.

Fisher presumably felt no sense of the momentous when the *Agamemnon*, on the morning of 7 June, at '6.20 passed Gallipoli'. Another eighteen years would elapse before Winston Churchill would even be born.[1]

The troops were disembarked at Spithead on 28 June, the *Agamemnon* paid off on 12 July, and on the next day Fisher, promoted at that time from Cadet to Midshipman, joined the *Highflyer*. Aged fifteen, he was about to enter on a spell of no less than five years on the China station. In the Baltic he had been within sight and sound of warlike activity—close enough to earn the Baltic Medal. He would get a good deal closer to actual fighting in China.

The *Highflyer* was a steam corvette of 21 guns. Her captain could hardly have contrasted more sharply with the hard-bitten Captain Stopford of the *Calcutta*. Fisher afterwards described him as 'about the greatest Saint on earth. The sailors called him, somewhat profanely, "Our Heavenly Father". He was once heard to say "Damn" and the whole ship was upset.' This picture of Shadwell is corroborated by Nathaniel Bowden-Smith who joined the ship in 1859: 'I was appointed acting lieutenant of the "Highflyer", a steam corvette, at Shanghai, commanded by Captain Shadwell, a scientific man, and of a most lovable

[1] Adm. 53/5127–8.

disposition, but he was one of those men too good to be in command of a ship-of-war.'[1] Shadwell's interests lay particularly in the field of naval astronomy and he was elected a Fellow of the Royal Society (1861) in recognition of his published work on that subject. He played a very important part both in Fisher's education and in his advancement in the service. As Fisher remarked, 'he was always teaching me in his own cabin . . . He taught me all I know—I could predict eclipses and occultations and play with the differential calculus all through him.'[2] A large exercise book containing a number of these calculations has been preserved in Fisher's papers.[3]

On the voyage, he recalled:

We towed out four gunboats of 40 horse power to China. They were tiny things in the Ocean! We went far down South in the Indian Ocean to get the westerly winds, and we got more than we bargained for! These little vessels seemed often as if they would be engulfed! And the huge Albatross that never seemed to leave us, hovering over them . . .

In China, the process of western penetration was well under way. The British were playing a leading part in persuading a nation of 200 millions, unshakably convinced of their own superiority but disunited and unable at that time to resist the growing power of western technology, to accept the blessings of free trade and the European outlook. Within a century would come a time for repentance! Fisher in due course came to form an apocalyptic view of the 'progressive' policies which, between 1856 and 1872, he found himself helping to underpin.

When, by-and-by, the Chinese know their power they have only to walk slowly westwards like the locusts in Egypt. No Pharaohs in Europe with all their mighty hosts will stop them. They won't want to fire guns or bombs. They'll just walk along and smother Europe . . . Every fourth Baby born into the world is a Chinese! The Bible Society told me this, that I might subscribe to the Chinese translation of the Bible, and I did![4]

But the situation seemed a good deal more straightforward at the time that Fisher took part in his first operation of war.

[1] Bowden-Smith, p. 25.
[2] F.P. 5100.
[3] F.P. 5413. F. wrote in it: 'Jack Fisher, Esq., H.M.S. Highflyer, Shanghai.'
[4] F.P. 5100.

The first incidents of the Second China War occurred in October 1856. Not only did the citizens of Canton take an independent line in interpreting the Treaty of Nanking; the Chinese authorities also resolutely refused to allow their Emperor to be degraded by contact with the envoys of Britain and the other barbaric nations wishing to establish their merchants in China. The English, dubbed a 'vile race' by the Cantonese, believed for their part in their mission to civilize 'the natives' while teaching them to share in the benefits of international trade.

In charge of the naval operations, focusing from the outset on the Canton River, was none other than Rear-Admiral Sir Michael Seymour who was last noticed inspecting a mine in the Baltic. Little the worse apart from the loss of his right eye, Seymour took vigorous measures against various Chinese forts and junks in the Canton River but after six months no decisive result had been achieved. He waited for reinforcements with a view to eliminating the large numbers of junks which, carrying European 32 pounders and other guns, constantly threatened command of the approaches to Canton from their well-defended refuge in the connecting creeks. It was at this stage that the *Highflyer* joined Seymour's flag.

The *Highflyer* had spent the early months of 1857 cruising in the East Indies. By 13 May she was at Hong Kong. A fortnight later, there was much activity as preparations were made to attack the main Chinese stronghold in Fatshan Creek. On 28 May, while the preliminary step of clearing Escape Creek was being undertaken, the *Highflyer* at Hong Kong 'received on board "Woosoo" (Pilot)' and made an extra issue of spirits to the ship's company. On the 31st she towed the hospital ship *Alligator* to the mouth of the Canton River and anchored. In the late afternoon, she steamed up the Canton River with the gunboat *Staunch* in tow. After nearly two hours' steaming, she anchored again and her boats were manned. The sixteen-year-old Midshipman Fisher was in one of the boats. These were now towed away by the *Staunch* to the rendezvous whence, in combination with a flotilla of gunboats, they were to make their attack early the next day.[1]

The Battle of Fatshan Creek was duly fought on 1 June. Flying his flag in the paddler *Coromandel* (which Fisher would fleetingly command only three years later) Seymour steamed up Fatshan

[1] Adm. 53/6826.

Creek, followed by the gun-boat *Haughty*. From these vessels, landing parties were put into boats and Seymour personally led a successful attack on a commanding fort. Commodore Henry Keppel with a force of gunboats then approached the hundred or so strategically placed junks which awaited him. The gunboats were accompanied by boats from the *Highflyer*, *Calcutta*, and a number of other vessels. The gunboats went aground while under fire from the junks. The boats were ordered to attack. Casualties were suffered but the junks were boarded before they could reload. Despite increasing danger, as the supporting gunboats were left behind out of range, the boats went on to attack and take a second line of junks. The Chinese abandoned their vessels and fled across the paddy fields. The British landed in pursuit and ranged as far as Fatshan, seven miles away.[1] Fisher long afterwards recalled Captain Shadwell's striking appearance during this affray: 'I saw him go into battle with a tall white hat with a gold stripe on the side of it, a blue uniform Post Captain's tail coat, a yellow waistcoat, white trousers and a white umbrella, and he cheered us on to attack the enemy waving his umbrella! And we got there all right. It was a piratical stronghold up the Canton River.'[2] The following passage in *Records* also fits the Fatshan action: 'Once the Chinese guns were firing at us, and as the shell whizzed over the boat we all ducked. "Lay on your oars, my men," said Shadwell; and proceeded to explain very deliberately how ducking delayed the progress of the boat— apparently unaware that his lecture had stopped its progress altogether!'[3]

After their success, which has been fairly described as a 'brilliant feat of arms',[4] the British were left in untroubled command of the river as far up as Canton. The next major step was to be an amphibious attack on Canton itself; but there was a pause until reinforcements, including a French squadron and British Marines, had assembled. During this period of six months, there were frequent signs of preparation aboard the *Highflyer*, such as the carpenters making and repairing ladders, and the sail-makers 'making slings for landing party's blankets'. An

[1] Clowes, vii, 105–7; N.R.S. *Second China War*, pp. 204–8; Preston and Major, pp. 42–4.

[2] F.P. 5100. This account, taken down early in 1918 to F.'s dictation, contains the specific reference to the Canton River. Bacon, i, 13, places his 'baptism of fire' in June 1859; other writers have tended to follow suit.

[3] *Records*, pp. 13–14.   [4] Preston and Major, p. 44.

interesting point which emerges from the ship's log is that Fisher first performed the duties of officer of the watch on 8 October when he was a Midshipman of sixteen and a half. From then onwards he regularly kept the morning and first dog watches. The other watch-keeping officers were Lieutenants Charles H. Smith and Henry Huxham, and Arthur E. Dupuis, Acting Mate. No other Midshipman was performing this duty, which could be testing—even at anchor up the river—as the following log-entry for one of Fisher's watches sufficiently illustrates: 'A.M. 9 Mustered at Quarters. Exercised Field Piece Party, firing at a Target with Rifles. 10.30 Man fell overboard, let go life buoy. Sent boat and saved the man.' This occurred on 21 December. On the 24th, with Fisher again officer of the watch: 'Mustered Landing Party in heavy marching order.' When the landing party, consisting of two lieutenants and 109 men together with launch and pinnace, was collected by the gunboat *Bustard* on the 28th, Fisher evidently went with this body. (Shadwell had gone off in the *Staunch* during Fisher's watch the previous morning. The former commanded the gunboats during the bombardment which began on the 29th.)

The *Highflyer's* landing party took part in the escalade and capture of the city of Canton on 29 December. Though the action was by no means as fierce as the Battle of Fatshan Creek, Fisher could be said to have fully earned the Canton clasp which, in due course, he was to wear on his China Medal.[1]

On 12 January 1858 the landing party returned to the ship and on the 24th Fisher reappeared as officer of the watch. However, he did not occupy this role when the ship was actually under way at sea. For example, after the *Highflyer* had returned to Hong Kong in February, she sailed in March for Shanghai. Shortly after steaming through the Lyemoon Passage she was confronted with 'very thick and threatening weather' and anchored off Tamtoo Island. Fisher took over during the first dog watch, but did not officiate while the ship was under way.

The *Highflyer* was moored off Shanghai from 28 March 1858 till 10 June 1859.[2]

In the spring of 1858, Seymour sailed for the Peiho River in order to carry Lord Elgin, the principal British envoy, in the

---

[1] Adm. 53/6826; N.R.S. *Second China War*, pp. 228–32, 269, 275, 280; Clowes, vii, 114n.

[2] Adm. 53/6827–8.

direction of Pekin. There ensued a successful action by gunboats against the Peiho forts; and when the Chinese authorities decided to subscribe to the Treaty of Tientsin in June, it seemed as if the war was at an end. Meanwhile, Seymour had left Shadwell in the *Highflyer* as the senior British naval officer at Shanghai. It was here that Mr. and Mrs. Edmund Warden offered hospitality to British naval officers. Fisher subsequently wrote a series of high-spirited letters to Mrs. Warden[1] whose husband was manager of the P. & O. Steam Navigation Company offices at Shanghai. Sixteen of these letters were preserved. Nearly 80 years later, Fisher's son bought them for £21. As Fisher himself never kept a diary, these 'China letters' remain the earliest biographical material in Fisher's own hand, apart from the large exercise book mentioned above.[2]

The first letter from Fisher to be kept by Mrs. Warden is dated 15 June 1859. At that time the general situation was that, despite spasmodic skirmishing, a certain amount of trade was being done at Canton and elsewhere. However, it had been agreed with the Chinese that the Treaty of Tientsin was to be ratified by the representatives of Britain, France, and the United States on the one hand and the Chinese government on the other, at Peking, by June 1859. Unfortunately the Chinese were reluctant to permit contamination of their capital by the foreign diplomats. Having failed to exclude the British gunboats in May 1858, they had since busied themselves in reconstructing the Peiho forts and placing formidable obstructions in the channel. In order to clear the way for the allied envoys Rear-Admiral James Hope, who had recently replaced Seymour as Commander-in-Chief, arrived off the mouth of the Peiho on 17 June. He advised the Chinese to let the British and French representatives proceed upstream. The Chinese stalled. Hope (whom Fisher afterwards remembered as a stately, awe-inspiring man) demanded from the Chinese definite intimation, by 8 p.m. on 24 June, that the obstructions were about to be removed. If not, he would 'proceed to remove them, using force if necessary'.

Up till then, Fisher had found it a 'jolly' expedition, in 'beautiful weather'—'just like May in England'. On the way up to the Gulf of Pecheli he wrote to Mrs. Warden: 'We saw the Admiral in the *Chesapeake* on the 13th. It was great fun, we beat him sailing with a gunboat in tow. At last he got up steam and

---

[1] Kilv. MSS., Pkt. 32 (*FG*).   [2] F.P. 5413.

beat us and left his own two gunboats to make the best of our passages.' On the 18th, with the squadron at anchor off the Peiho in a half-gale and rain, instructions from the Admiral reached the *Highflyer* which sounded a more serious note. 'He has just sent orders down to make a lot more scaling ladders,' Fisher reported, 'so I suppose something is up. This is horribly disgusting work. We are all but *battened* down and it is blowing and raining, and the old "hooker" is turning herself inside out.' But on the 23rd, the eighteen-year-old veteran of Fatshan and Canton was confident enough. 'We are just going to take the forts!' Apparently Admiral Hope had much the same idea despite the fact that a frontal assault on the forts would be involved.

The main action took place on 25 June. The *Highflyer* and the other larger vessels remained at anchor outside the bar. Nine gunboats, a gun-vessel, and a sloop were to bombard the forts after the first obstruction had been penetrated. Fisher was initially assigned to the gunboat *Banterer*. She formed part of the first division of gunboats, commanded by Captain Shadwell, which was to engage the fort on the north bank. A second division was to bombard the more extensive line of fortifications on the south bank.

Admiral Hope hoisted his flag in the gunboat *Plover*. At the outset he aimed to penetrate the first barrier with a third group of gunboats, including the *Plover*. These four vessels would anchor close to the second (apparently impenetrable) obstruction. Owing to lack of room for manoeuvre between the two barriers, the channel being only 200 yards wide, the first and second divisions would have to line up outside the first barrier. The next step was to try to silence the forts. Once this had been achieved, about 350 Marines, a division of seamen, some army sappers and miners, and a small body of French seamen would land on the south side of the estuary. The state of the tide would leave them with about 500 yards of ground—mainly mud—to cross before capturing the nearest part of the southern fortifications.

In fine weather, with the temperature rising to 74 °F., and a strong tide, the bombarding force moved into position during the morning. The *Banterer*, on the extreme right of her division (presumably somewhat further upstream than the second division) ran aground, but was well placed to fire at the northern fort. On the south side of the channel another gunboat was like-wise stranded; she was badly positioned and virtually eliminated from the ensuing action. The two outer divisions lay at a range of approximately 1,000 yards from the forts.

The first barrier was penetrated by 2.30 p.m. The Admiral with his four gunboats moved up to the second barrier thus closing the range of both the inward section of the southern forts and of the northern fort to less than 500 yards. At 2.40 'the forts opened a simultaneous fire of not less than between thirty and forty guns, of calibres from 32-pounders to 8-inch.' Hope thereupon 'directed the ships to engage'.[1]

Nathaniel Bowden-Smith, who had recently been transferred from the *Highflyer* to the *Chesapeake*, provides an interesting comparison between the battle of 25 June 1859 and the successful forcing of the same position in May 1858.

I was told off for the landing party, and on the appointed day the gunboats steamed in and gallantly attacked the forts on both sides of the river, the landing party of bluejackets and marines being placed in junks and ships' boats and towed into a position out of range. I noticed that the Chinese fire seemed much more effective than it had been in 1858, and that some of our vessels were getting a good deal knocked about, but towards five o'clock the fire seemed to slacken, and the signal was made for the landing party to make for the shore and take the batteries by assault, and . . . I had no doubt in my own mind that we should be successful and carry the position as we had done the previous year; but really a considerable change had taken place since 1858. Not only was the Chinese fire much more accurate, but they had also dug some wide ditches across the approach to the forts, and these trenches were filled with soft mud . . . We made a dash for the shore as soon as the signal was taken in . . . but the fire was tremendous, and immediately men began to fall; however, I pressed on with the rest, never doubting for a moment of our ultimate success, when just after crossing the second trench I felt a sudden shock and fell down, and then discovered that my left arm was useless . . .[2]

To this account, it needs to be added that at 4.20 p.m. Hope had sent for Shadwell to come aboard the *Cormorant*. This gun-vessel was now the flagship in place of the disabled *Plover*. The badly wounded Hope handed over to Shadwell 'the more immediate command of the squadron'. Shadwell also directed

---

[1] Kilv. MSS., Pkt. 32, F. to Mrs. Warden, 28 June 1859; N.R.S. *Second China War*, p. 395 (original dispatch being in Adm. 1/5712); Adm. 53/6828, log of *Highflyer*.

Bowden-Smith, pp. 27–8.

the landing. This, incidentally, took place at 7.20, not at 5, as indicated by Bowden-Smith. Fisher's version of the battle, written for Mrs. Warden on the 28th, can now be read against the foregoing background of events.

I don't know whether I can give you a description of it, I feel in such a state of excitement . . . In the *Plover*, the next gunboat to ours (*Banterer*), 26 . . . were killed and wounded out of 36 men and officers, the Admiral being one of them. Rason, her Commander, was smashed to atoms. So was McKenna, the Military Secretary, and all the Admiral's Staff nearly. In the last part of the action I was the only one left to carry the orders about . . . We had a hard fight for it, but what could we do against such a fearful number of guns? and us poor little gunboats inclosed in such a small place, not much broader across than the length of our ship . . . The old Admiral behaved splendidly after he had part of his thigh and leg shot away. He had a cot slung to a pole and was carried about in a boat from the *Plover* to the *Cormorant* to encourage the men . . .

My poor old Skipper keeps his pecker up. I was with him all day till he was wounded in the mud and then I brought him out to the ship . . . I had to fling all my arms away coming back from the forts and was nearly smothered once, only one of our bluejackets was kind enough to haul me out. You sank up to your knees *at least* every step, and just fancy the slaughter going 500 yards in the face of that fire of about 30 pieces of artillery right in front of you and on each flank. It was dreadful, horrible work but, thank God, I came out all right . . . They had horrid fire-balls firing at us when we landed. I saw one poor fellow with his eye and part of his face burnt right out. If a piece struck you, it stuck to you and regularly burnt you away till it was all gone . . . The Chinamen fought like anything . . . They had fearful advantages, no doubt. I expect the Admiral will either die or go home very shortly. He never suspected the place was so strong . . .

I am glad to say I have just received your letter . . . I thought you had forgotten all about me. I had three fellows to look after in the *Coromandel* wounded, the old Skipper, [Acting Lieutenant C.E.] Buckle of the *Magicienne* [paddler], and a Midshipman of the *Fury* [paddler]. I never smelt such a horrid smell in my life as on board the *Coromandel* bringing the wounded out yesterday afternoon. Abaft the mainmast it was nothing but blood and men rolling about with arms and legs off, nearly all roundshot wounds . . .[1]

On the 26th Fisher returned on board the *Highflyer* in the afternoon, as did Captain Shadwell, 'severely wounded in the foot'.[2] Fisher wrote that neither of them had eaten for thirty-six

[1] Kilv. MSS., loc. cit. (*FG*).   [2] Adm. 53/6828.

hours and that he himself was 'regularly done up'. Adding on the 30th to his letter to Mrs. Warden, Fisher said that he had to go back near the forts on the 28th to try to recover some of Shadwell's papers and belongings. The forts now presented a grisly aspect because, on the night of the attack on the 25th, the Chinese had come out 'and hauled what fellows they could find out of the mud and cut their heads off and stuck them on the walls'.

A little insight into Fisher's personality and attitudes is afforded by his remark to Mrs. Warden that his letter to her about the battle was 'larger than the one I wrote to my Mother'. Fisher had never seen his mother since he was sent away from Ceylon at the age of six and he appears to have suffered from a sense of grievance on this account. However, there was also an obvious clash of personalities between the two. Particularly as he grew older, Fisher was prone—as will be seen in due course— to sever communication with friends and relatives alike if they failed to comply with his wishes. But as a young officer he seems to have been scarcely touched by this domineering tendency. He certainly craved affection. This comes out clearly from his letters to Mrs. Warden.

The British squadron withdrew from the Peiho estuary on 3 July. The losses amounted to three small ships: the gun-vessel *Cormorant* (4 guns) and the gunboats *Lee* and *Plover* (each 2 guns). The British casualties amounted to 89 killed and 345 wounded; the French had 4 killed and 10 wounded. Fisher was a witness of the help given by the American Commodore Josiah Tattnall in towing boat-loads of the wounded from the scene of the battle, in respect of which he made his famous remark that 'Blood is thicker than water'.[1] In the light of his disagreeable experience during the attack, it may seem curious that Fisher should have later emerged as an over-enthusiastic advocate of amphibious landings. But he acquired a healthy distrust of the practice of pitting ships against forts and was imbued with the advantages of landing by surprise—on some remote shore, if available.

In the autumn, the *Highflyer* visited Japan. Fisher wrote accounts of visits to Tokyo which are certainly high-spirited but contain no really memorable observations. He was already pre-paring for his examination, to be held on 25 January 1860 (his nineteenth birthday), for promotion to Mate. 'I am working

[1] Kilv. MSS., loc. cit., 28, 30 June 1859; Clowes, vii, 128, 130–1.

like a horse', he wrote on 24 September; and on 3 November:
'I am working like a young elephant for that horrible 25th
January, 1860. I think I shall go mad if I don't pass . . . The
worst of it is the old Skipper has made up his mind that I shall
pass a very brilliant examination. I should much prefer him to
think I couldn't pass and then to pass all serene.' The exercise
book, containing problems in mathematics and astronomy,
worked out by Fisher between September 1857 and the end of
1859, testifies to his mode of preparation. Swiftly, surely,
immaculately, the equations, substitutions, and deductions
flowed from his pen. For example he proceeded 'To determine
the Horizontal Parallax of a heavenly body by observations
taken at two distant places on the same meridian . . .'. And
elsewhere he answered the question 'At what time will the star
Regulus pass the meridian of a place in Lat. 22 N. and Long.
60 W. on February 28th 1859 and at what distance N or S of the
zenith? . . .'.[1] By December it was known that Shadwell was to
go home by the mail steamer from Hong Kong on 15 January.
'The Captain has advised me to remain in the ship,' Fisher
reported, 'and he sent for me in the cabin and said he should have
much pleasure in bringing my conduct, while he had been in the
ship, to the notice of the Admiral . . . I can hardly realize the
fact of the old buffer going. I'd give anything for him to stop.'[2]

However, Fisher's fortunes did not suffer through Shadwell's
departure. He wrote from Hong Kong on 5 February 1860:

I went up on the 25th January on board the *Cambrian* before the
three Captains, and they gave me a regular bounce out. It took altogether three days and, as I told you last mail, I had the satisfaction of
getting a *first-class* certificate. Well, I came on board the *Chesapeake*
and handed in my certificate. After a short time the Admiral[3] sent
for me and told me he was very pleased to see I had passed such a
good examination, and that as a reward for it and on account of old
Shadwell's report of me, he should take me as his Flag Mate, and that
he would take care to look out for me always . . . I have nothing to
do with anyone in the ship except the Admiral himself, and, no mistake, he keeps me going. He hardly takes off his boots without sending
for me and informing me officially of it . . .

A less agreeable side of Fisher, more in evidence in later life, is
revealed in his comment: 'It is very jolly in one way. I can give

[1] F.P. 5413.   [2] Kilv. MSS., loc. cit., 14 Dec. 1859 (*FG*).
[3] Hope.

some of these Lieutenants a good snubbing sometimes. They dare not say anything to me, because the Admiral has given strict orders that no one is to interfere with his Staff on any pretence what-sum-dever.'

But, all in all, Fisher was a remarkable young officer and he left the following durable impression on Midshipman Day Bosanquet[1] of the *Chesapeake* who wrote in 1921 as follows:

I can clearly call to mind [Jack Fisher] joining the *Chesapeake* . . . a delightfully happy good-looking boy liked by everyone and full of life and energy.

Sir James Hope, the Commander-in-Chief, took to him at once, and appreciated him immensely. Sir James put him in charge of the signals under the flag lieutenant G. A. Douglas, Albert Markham [of the *Camperdown-Victoria* disaster in 1894] and I being the two juniors. [Fisher] soon took the place of the flag lieutenant in every-thing connected with the signals, and he was remarkable for knowing everybody and exercising a strong influence (strange for one so young) upon those with whom he came in contact . . . [He was] at that time a wonderful mathematical genius. Oborn, the naval instructor, who himself had a gift for imparting knowledge, carried on the good work which Shadwell started, and when Fisher's time came for his examination for lieutenant he passed . . . without realizing its difficulty . . . Sir James Hope appointed him to the command of the *Coromandel* (the C.-in-C.'s yacht) and sent him from Hong Kong to Canton in command of that ship so that he actually commanded one of Her Majesty's Ships at the age of 19 years. He returned to Hong Kong with the *Coromandel* in a few days enormously pleased with himself.

I remember the intense enthusiasm which he displayed in every-thing he attempted and he was easily the most interesting midship-man I ever met . . .[2]

Fisher's pleasure in his brief spell of command was in no way diminished by the fact that he was able to cock a snook at old shipmates aboard the *Highflyer*, in particular Lieutenant F. R. Purvis whom he held in great detestation: 'I forgot to tell you', he wrote to Mrs. Warden on 4 April 1860, 'that the Admiral gave me *command* of the *Coromandel* for four days . . . We passed close by the old *Highflyer* on our way up and down. Old Purvis and all the fellows up there could hardly believe their eyes.'[3]

---

[1] Ultimately a full Admiral and C.-in-C., Portsmouth.
[2] Kilv. MSS., Pkt. 35, Adl. Bosanquet to 2nd Ld. F., 26 Sept. 1921.
[3] Kilv. MSS., Pkt. 32 (*FG*).

Promotion from Midshipman to Acting Mate on 25 January increased his daily rate of pay from 1s. 9d. to 3s. 8d. A second promotion from Mate to Acting Lieutenant on 29 March brought a further increase from 3s. 8d. to 10s.[1] He was one of the last officers to be appointed as a Mate; the Navy List issued on 20 March 1861 shows him (retrospectively) as an Acting Sub-Lieutenant from 25 January 1860.

On his promotion to Acting Lieutenant at the end of March 1860, Fisher was transferred from the *Chesapeake* to the *Pearl* (screw, 21 guns). The plan was for Fisher to join the *Furious* (paddle-sloop, 16 guns) at Shanghai, a couple of months later. Thereupon, he would be made available as naval A.D.C. to the Honourable Frederick Bruce, the British Minister, who was expected to go up north to liquidate any outstanding diplomatic questions. (The resistance of the Chinese government to the wishes of the British and French had officially ceased in October 1859.)

Just after joining the *Pearl* Fisher wrote to Mrs. Warden: 'The old Admiral was so kind to me when he gave me my commission. He said he was very sorry indeed to part with me, but that it was for my own benefit, and that I might depend upon his keeping an eye upon me.' Fisher enclosed for Mrs. Warden's edification a copy of a letter from Rear-Admiral Hope in the *Chesapeake* (at Hong Kong) to Captain Oliver Jones of the *Furious*, dated 30 March 1860:

I have appointed Mr. Fisher to act as a Lieutenant in the *Furious*. He is at present in the *Pearl* for a passage and will not join you till superseded . . .

When Shadwell went away I asked him to mention to me anybody he was interested about, and he named Fisher, for which I took him into this ship. He passed a very good examination, for which reason I promoted him; in fact, he was the first in that respect on the station.

He is sharp, well conducted, and anxious to do his duty, so that I think you will like him.[2]

Fisher proved wonderfully adept at handling a varied assortment of senior officers during his long spell on the China station. He found John Borlase, Captain of the *Pearl*, 'such a rough old fellow, so different to old Shadwell. He is one of the regular old school.' Borlase, incidentally, was then aged 45 and Shadwell 46. Fisher was writing by 13 April: 'I feel quite confident now in

[1] Adm. 24/167.   [2] Kilv. MSS., Pkt. 32, 30 Mar. 1860.

keeping watch . . I shall feel quite confident when I go on board the *Furious* . . . they are all jolly fellows. I shall be very sorry to leave them, only I know it will be better for me to be in the *Furious*.' Four days later he was able to report, 'Captain Borlase (the Captain of this ship) wants to keep me on board here altogether . . . The old Skipper on board here and myself are great friends. I like him very much. I am tremendously lucky. I manage to get good friends everywhere, somehow or another.' But a stiffer exercise in the art of making friends and influencing people was not far ahead. 'All the fellows here say that the Captain of the *Furious* is an awful character.'[1]

The day of confrontation appears to have been 12 June. At 8 p.m., according to the log of the *Furious* (at Shanghai): 'Joined Acting Lieut. J. A. Fisher.' According to the log, it was not only her eccentric Captain that presented difficulties aboard the *Furious*. A wooden paddler of 1,286 tons, she was credited with the following characteristics: 'Ship sails fairly with a leading wind, but becomes very leewardly when close hauled. She stays very well, but wears badly (especially in heavy weather) and takes a great deal of room to turn. Her steaming qualities are poor, going full speed ahead, on account of the bad condition of her boilers.'[2]

Fisher certainly found the process of adjusting his relations with the *Furious* and her Captain rather difficult. After a fortnight he reported: 'She (the *Furious*) is such a horrid old tub and not at all comfortable, and Oliver Jones, the Captain of her, is an awful scoundrel. There has been one mutiny on board of her already through him, and he has very cunningly managed to get none but acting Lieutenants . . . he knows we are all young and don't want to risk a court-martial just after we have received our commissions.' From this account, and also the fact that Jones had escaped from the half-pay list by joining a naval brigade during the Indian Mutiny as a volunteer, one might suspect that Hope had made a blunder in sending Fisher to the *Furious*. But Fisher's latter-day dictated reminiscence goes some way towards explaining the Admiral's action:

When I was a young Lieutenant I got moulded by another ferocious fearnought! He was a consummate sailor, a wonderful linguist, a master of words, skilled in all the arts of navigation and surveying, and raised a regiment of native cavalry which he led with distinction

[1] Kilv. MSS., Pkt. 32, 4, 13, 17, 21 Apr. 1860 (*FG*).   [2] Adm. 53/6946.

in the Indian Mutiny and got the unstinted admiration of the great cavalry leader, Sir Hope Grant. This man led me a dog's life! As a lieutenant he used to send me up to the maintop in my tail coat and epaulettes after I had been dining with him, when shifting topsails or some other evolution—he being 'three sheets in the wind' as the sailors say! He was a rich man and had unparalleled champagne and a French chef. He might tyrannize us but he fed us![1]

However, Fisher found that even this formidable eccentric could be managed. 'I believe I was the only officer he did not put under arrest. For some reason I got on with him, and he made me the Navigating Officer of the ship.'[2]

By August 1860 a joint British and French expedition was ready to tackle the Peiho forts and recover the prestige lost in June 1859. Admiral Hope remained in command of the British naval forces. He had made a remarkable recovery from his wound. In February he had taken Fisher for a seven-mile- an-hour walk! 'He kept me at almost a run the whole way', Fisher wrote. 'You would never think, to see him walking, that he had a hole in his thigh you could shove both fists into.'

Since the previous action, Hope had also improved his tactical ideas. On his return to the forts, a frontal assault was avoided. Fisher aboard the *Furious* helped on 1 August to cover an unopposed landing at the mouth of the Pehtang River, nine miles north of the Peiho. On 21 August the troops attacked the northern forts while gunboats provided a supporting bombardment from the river. Although the Chinese seem to have fought as spiritedly as before, they were overwhelmed by this well-planned combined attack. The *Furious* remained outside the bar, close enough for Fisher to follow the progress of the operation. There is no indication that he was called upon to play an active role. However, in due course he became entitled to wear the Taku as well as the Canton clasp with his China Medal. Of course, no medal or clasp was awarded to those who endured the much more testing action of June 1859 because it did not result in victory.[3]

January 1861 found the *Furious* gripped fast in drifting ice not very far from the scene of the conclusive action of the previous August. However, a log-entry of 9 February marks some im-

---

[1] Kilv. MSS., Pkt. 32, 25 June 1860 (*FG*); F.P. 5100—cf. *Records*, p. 15.
[2] *Records*, p. 15.
[3] Clowes, vii, 132–5; Kilv. MSS., Pkt. 32 (*FG*); Adm. 53/6946; *Records*, p. 251.

provement in this unenviable situation: '5.50 p.m. Went ahead and astern as requisite to break through the ice. 6.20 Stopped. Banked fires.' Fisher afterwards recalled that Jones kept his ship in the Gulf of Pechili, despite the onset of Arctic conditions, precisely because he had been ordered to get out.

I never knew a man who so hated Authority. I forget how many degrees below zero the thermometer was, and it was only by an unprecendented thaw that we ever got out. And with this intense cold he would often begin at four o'clock in the morning to prepare for battle, and hand up every shot in the ship on to the Upper Deck, then he'd strike lower yards and topmasts (which was rather a heavy business), and finish up with holystoning the decks, which operation he requested all the officers to honour with their presence.

However, to judge by the ship's log this somewhat idiosyncratic officer was not an enthusiast for flogging. At Cape Town in June 1861, on the way back to England, there was a bout of disrating —probably in consequence of giving shore leave to the ship's company—and a member of the sailmaker's crew was given 18 lashes; but even here there was a humane touch: '30 lashes remitted during good behaviour.'

The *Furious* had left Hong Kong in March and sailed by way of Batavia to Cape Town. At that port, Captain Jones received orders from the Commander-in-Chief 'to touch at Ichaboe Island and annex it to the British Crown'. The order was thus worded:

On your arrival you will in the presence of any persons on the Island, gathering guano[1] or for other purposes, hoist the British Flag (Union Jack) on a Staff and saluting the same from Her Majesty's Ship 'Furious' with twenty-one guns, declare the Island to be annexed to the British Crown . . . You will receive a Staff and Flag from the Naval Yard at this Port for the purpose herein mentioned.

The *Furious* reached Ichaboe on 19 June. In order to provide precise information about this latest addition to the jewels of Empire, Captain Jones landed Fisher on what he afterwards described as 'a desert island' to make a survey. Details of this are still to be seen amongst the latter's personal papers.

On 20 August the *Furious*, bearing 'forty cases of presents to her Majesty from the Tycoon of Japan', arrived at Portsmouth. The next day Fisher's application to be examined for Lieutenant

---

[1] Manure derived from sea-fowl.

—having completed the required period of five years from the date of becoming a Midshipman—was forwarded to the Admiralty by the Commander-in-Chief, Portsmouth. On 27 August Oliver Jones's recommendation was likewise sent up. The originals of such communications to the Admiralty during the nineteenth century were normally destroyed by a process of weeding, carried out after a lapse of time. This was the case with Jones's letter of the 27th. But, as usual, both the application and the recommendation can still be traced in the appropriate index and they support Fisher's recollection of the 'transcendental certificate' written by Captain Jones: 'He was sparse in his praises; but he wrote of me: "As a sailor, an officer, a Navigator, and a gentleman, I cannot praise him too highly." '[1]

[1] *Records*, pp. 15–17; Adm. 53/6947–8; Adm. 1/5756; F.P. 5414; IND. 12495; *Memories*, p. 146.

CHAPTER 2

A GUNNERY AND A TORPEDO MAN
(1861–1869)

'If you are a gunnery man you must believe and teach that the
world must be saved by gunnery and can only be saved by gunnery.
If you are a torpedo man you must believe and teach the same thing
about torpedoes . . . You are missionaries. Show the earnestness, if
need be, the fanaticism of missionaries.'
[Fisher reiterated this advice to qualifying classes of gunnery and
torpedo lieutenants, *c.* 1874. Kilv. MSS.; G. Bowers to second Lord
Fisher, 16 July 1921.]

FROM the time when the *Furious* paid off on 30 August until his
appointment to the *Excellent* on 17 January 1862, Fisher was
without employment. As an Acting Lieutenant he was not
entitled to half-pay.[1] In November 1861 he completed the
qualifying examination for Lieutenant and on the 16th the
following communication was addressed to the Commander-in-
Chief, Portsmouth, by the Secretary of the Admiralty:

I have the honour to bring to your notice the highly creditable
examination passed by Mr. J. A. Fisher, Acting Lieutenant of H.M.S.
'Furious'; this officer obtained high first class certificates in seaman-
ship and gunnery, and has now passed in navigation under the
Regulations laid down in Circular 286, obtaining 963 numbers out
of 1,000, being the highest numbers yet obtained by any candidates
who have voluntarily passed under the 5 years system.

This brilliant performance in navigation won for him the
Beaufort Testimonial, an annual prize comprising books and
instruments. This marked a triumphant ending to his earlier
education in the Navy; for Fisher had been one of the last Naval
Cadets to enter under the old system, whereby the young officer
was sent at once to sea where he picked up what he could from
his Captain or Naval Instructor. From 1854 onwards Cadets
received consecutive schooling aboard stationary training ships
before being sent to sea.

[1] Adm. 24/167.

Fisher was confirmed as a Lieutenant, the promotion being backdated to 4 November 1860.[1]

Fisher's parents, stranded in Ceylon, followed the progress of their first-born with gratification. A few months after the Peiho action Fisher wrote to Mrs. Warden: 'I am a regular hero, it appears, in Ceylon, and my deluded mother thinks I had as much to do as Admiral Hope'; and presumably in response to news about the Beaufort Testimonial, Captain Fisher took up the pen: 'I wrote you a few lines to tell you *how pleased* I am at all you have been doing and I am *sure* you will continue to prosper.' He continued pathetically that he had written to Frederick Whimper, husband of Jack's Aunt Kate, to thank him for letting Jack have £20 to tide him over—presumably during the recent period when he held no appointment. 'If I had known you wanted it,' continued Captain Fisher, 'I would have tried to send it to you but I am so distressed for money I don't know when it will end. I have no crop at all this year and my estates will have cost £2,000 which is a clear loss.'[2]

With two married aunts in England, and with Lady Horton's town and country houses open to him, Fisher was possibly a good deal better off than his parents; but he was doubtless relieved to return to the Navy's pay-roll on 17 January 1862. This was the beginning of his long and distinguished connexion with the *Excellent*.

The *Excellent* was the Navy's principal gunnery school. In a wider sense, it was also a highly important experimental establishment which was to play a key role in the impending technical transformation of the Navy. Fisher joined the gunnery school as an instructor at the very beginning of what might be termed the scientific era at the *Excellent*. This era is commonly associated with the name of Astley Cooper Key, but he did not take over command of the establishment till June 1863, by which date Fisher had departed for a spell aboard the *Warrior*. However, Key's predecessor was a genuine gunnery expert and Fisher learnt to love the *Excellent* under his command.[3]

Captain Richard Hewlett commanded the first gunnery ship at Devonport. In 1857 he became Captain of the *Excellent*. (The

---

[1] Kilv. MSS., Pkt. 41; IND. 12495; Adm. 24/153.
[2] Kilv. MSS., Pkt. 32, 27 Nov. 1859; Pkt. 7, 14 Jan. 1862.
[3] Kilv. MSS., Pkt. 6, F. to Mrs. Whimper, 20 Mar. 1863.

ship herself, which was still the central unit in the establishment, was a three-decker moored at Portsmouth for purposes of gunnery instruction since 1830.) Hewlett gave evidence in 1858 before the first Committee on Rifled Cannon. Fisher joined the *Excellent* at a time when the revolutionary Armstrong breech-loading guns were being pitted against the more conservative muzzle-loading Whitworth type in a series of experiments. Hewlett and his staff seem to have preferred the Armstrong guns. In this they were premature, although they were ultimately justified by long-term experience and technical advance.[1] However, the Admiralty decided to abandon breech-loading in 1866 and, despite the improvements made to breech-loading guns abroad, allowed an excessively long time to elapse before reconsidering the whole matter.

Not only was the *Excellent* developing into an élite establishment by the time of Fisher's original appointment there. It was the practical expression of a deepening interest amongst service officers generally in the technology of warfare. This interest had been otherwise expressed by the foundation of the United Service Institution two years earlier. (Significantly 1860 also saw the establishment of the Institution of Naval Architects.) Yet, just as the Navy was embarking on its great technical transformation, the financial means for effecting it were about to be even more strictly limited. Between 1835 and 1861, expenditure on the Navy had roughly trebled. But from the time that he became the Liberal Chancellor in 1859 Gladstone persistently fought to reduce the service estimates and thus to lower taxation. This policy achieved limited success in the 1860s. Disraeli as Chancellor and then Prime Minister proved as keen an economizer as his rival and between 1868 and 1884 the Navy descended into what have been, on that account, termed its 'Dark Ages'. Fisher was to play a part in bringing this state of things to an end, as will be seen in due course. Although it has been said that the British Navy was not outstanding for its inventiveness during this period, the progressive élite of the service (in which Fisher established himself by 1869) kept up a remarkably high level of activity in the face of persistent lack of funds. Of course, Disraeli and even Gladstone did not oppose the principle of British naval supremacy. But they were able to keep up appearances at remarkably

[1] Oliver, pp. 53–4.

low cost owing to the absence of serious foreign naval competition until the 1880s.[1]

Few details have survived regarding Fisher's first spell of service at the *Excellent* (January 1862 to March 1863). Some, at least, of the account supplied by Bacon[2] really belongs to Fisher's second appointment on the staff of the *Excellent*, after he left the *Warrior* in March 1864. For example, he did not receive his first-class gunnery certificate till March 1866 and was not paid the appropriate allowance until November 1866.[3] However, Fisher's success during his first term of service in the *Excellent* is strongly indicated by his reference in a letter of March 1863 to 'my beloved "Excellent" '[4] and also by his appointment to the *Warrior* at the end of March 1863. As he remarked in his memoirs:

The 'Warrior' was then, like the 'Inflexible' in 1882 and the 'Dreadnought' in 1905, the cynosure of all eyes. She had a very famous Captain, the son of that great seaman Lord Dundonald, and a still more famous Commander, Sir George Tryon, who afterwards went down in the 'Victoria'. She had a picked crew of officers and men, so I was wonderfully fortunate to be the Gunnery Lieutenant, and at so young an age I got on very well, except for skylarking in the wardroom, for which I got into trouble.[5]

There are various stories about Fisher's cultivation of his vocal powers as a young officer. By the time he reached the *Warrior*, he was able to make an indelible impression in this regard. Some forty-seven years later, a seaman who had served in the *Warrior* at the material time wrote: 'I had in mind you standing on the Main Hatch with a voice like a lion drilling the whole of the quarters and the landing parties. You gave us some rare rousing ups, which I think was not lost on myself.' According to the same witness, 'it was a saying amongst the crew of the "Warrior" that they had the smartest Gunnery Lieut. in the service.'[6]

The *Warrior* was the first British ironclad warship. Laid down in May 1859 and completed in October 1861, she was the

---

[1] *Studies in International History*, ed. K. Bourne and D. C. Watt, London, 1967—see the essay by C. J. Bartlett, pp. 189–208.

[2] Bacon, i, 25–7.

[3] Adm. 24/167; cf. Bacon, i, 26. Likewise Bacon states that Fisher 'served three and a half years in the *Warrior*' when in fact he served in her for exactly one year.

[4] Kilv. MSS., Pkt. 6, F. to Mrs. Whimper, 20 Mar. 1863.

[5] *Memories*, p. 146.

[6] F.P. 2048, W. Mitchell to F., 12 Mar. 1910; F.P. 1842, ibid., 8 Dec. 1905.

British answer to the developing French lead in that type of vessel. Her construction marks a decisive severance from the traditions and assumptions of British naval shipbuilding. Not only did she imply the increasing reliance of naval power on technical expertise and industrial productivity; she also ushered in an era, continuing to the present, where a warship was expected to reach obsolescence within ten years of her completion. In the Age of Sail, which had extended up to the year when Fisher joined the Navy, the ship of the line had in some cases lasted for fifty years or more without becoming obsolete. Fisher, brought up under sail and educated in the old manner, had emerged at the age of twenty-two as a technical expert aboard the Navy's most modern ship—arguably the most revolutionary ship in British naval history.

The *Warrior* was of 9,215 tons and during her steam trials she reached 14·08 knots. As Parkes has written: 'The basic conception in the design of the *Warrior* provided that she should be able to overtake and overwhelm any other warship in existence.' This was Fisher's ideal when, some forty years later, he was at the height of his influence on the construction of large warships. Described as a frigate and fully rigged, she actually achieved 13 knots 'under all plain sail and stunsails'. Fisher was, of course, particularly concerned with her armament of 40 guns. There were changes from time to time, but while Fisher was aboard the *Warrior* appears to have had, on each broadside along the main deck, four 110-pounder Armstrong breech-loading guns and thirteen 68-pounder Whitworth smooth-bore guns; while on the upper deck were two more of the Armstrong guns, one at the bow and one at the stern, and four 70-pounder breech loaders. Largely due to the sanguine expectations of Captain Hewlett and the staff at the *Excellent*, it had been intended to replace all the smoothbores with breech-loading 110-pounders as they became available. But in 1861 the Select Ordnance Committee discovered, as a result of further tests, the somewhat devastating fact that the 68-pounder smoothbores were much more likely to penetrate armour plating. Hewlett, who deserves some credit for his advocacy of the principle of the ironclad, had a happier influence on the nature of the *Warrior's* protective armour than on her armament. She carried a belt of 4½-inch wrought-iron plating backed by 18 inches of teak.[1]

[1] Parkes, pp. 16–24; 12; Oliver, pp. 53–4.

The *Warrior* spent August and September cruising off the northern coasts of Great Britain. 'At Leith', wrote Fisher, 'I went up to spend a day at Linlithgow at Sir James Hope's who was my great friend in China . . . We leave [from Invergordon] on Tuesday morning for Kirkwall in the Orkneys and then Lough Swilly . . . I think we shall get to Liverpool about the 21st of September and leave for Lisbon soon after.[1] The voyage to the south occupied most of the winter and, as will be seen below, Fisher made reference to the Schleswig-Holstein affair which exposed Britain's inability to intervene in Europe against a military power (in this case Prussia under Bismarck) without being sure of a continental ally. (This set-back marked the end of Palmerston's attempts to manipulate the balance of power in Europe and for a decade Britain largely isolated herself from European affairs.) Fisher wrote to his aunt from Portland on 15 March 1864:

After three months travel here we are . . . For the last month until the present time I have had quite enough to do. There are only 5 Lieuts when all together and 3 of them are and have been hors-de-combat. We left for Madeira on the 15th Dec. . . . two very wild and unpleasant days in the Bay, rolling on the average 18° each way . . . a week in Madeira . . . balls and dinners the whole time . . . we had to cut and run for Gibraltar. We took our time going there, every day manoeuvring or firing shot and shell at a target and all sorts of outlandish things. Directly we got into Gibraltar, there was a telegram came out ordering us home to England on account of Schleswig-Holstein, and just as we were on the point of starting, out comes another, telling us to go to Lisbon where we arrived on the 15th January . . . what with all sorts of drills and firing and King's balls and Ministers' dinners, the time went very quick and pleasantly. While there, the Admiral[2] inspected all the ships and I am glad to say we came out A.1. The Admiral was awfully civil to me and said he had hardly ever in his life seen a ship in such splendid gunnery order and that he should bring my conduct to the notice of the Admiralty, in consequence of which when we arrived home I got a special letter of thanks from the Admiralty.

I feel very anxious about my Mother and should you hear anything of her, would like very much to hear it as I never get my letters until some time after the mail comes in. I felt poor Grannie's death very much . . . I am so glad that I saw her before we left England . . .

---

[1] Kilv. MSS., Pkt. 6, F. to Mrs. Whimper, 8 Aug. 1863.
[2] Rear-Admiral Sydney Dacres, C.-in-C. of the Channel Squadron, 1863–6.

Alice and Lucy are very good correspondents but they go on the principle of quality, not quantity . . .

We are ordered to be ready to go anywhere at 48 hours notice, but I don't think myself there is much chance of a row . . .[1]

His assessment of the diplomatic situation was accurate enough in so far as Britain, though near the height of her power, had been revealed as incapable of effective intervention on the continent. On the personal side, it is interesting to read of his affection and concern at this stage for his mother and other members of the family. His brother Frederic William left an account of how, in the summer of 1863, Jack organized his nomination to join the Navy through Captain Shadwell (with whom Fisher continued to correspond for many years). 'Billy' was twelve years old at the time.

We usually spent our holidays with Lady Horton, at Catton Hall . . .

One summer we were taken to Seaview, in those days a charming little fishing village in the Isle of Wight. With us was my eldest brother, Jack, who was then a lieutenant of the *Warrior*, our first sea-going ironclad.

One day when we were all bathing on the beach, a boat came ashore from a man-of-war. On seeing us, one of the officers who manned her called out: 'By jove, there's Jack Fisher and all the little fishes!'

To my delight these officers invited us to have tea with them. Whilst listening to the conversation I was so fascinated that my elder brother noticed it. 'How would you like to join the Navy?' he suddenly asked me, making my heart palpitate so violently that my eager 'I'd love to' almost stuck in my throat. When I had fully recovered my speech I said that I did not care a bit what would happen to me, so long as I got away from that awful school [at Lichfield where he, together with his older brothers Arthur and Frank, was constantly beaten by an irascible clergyman].

Being very serious about it, I was puzzled when a roar of laughter greeted my final remark, and I wondered if the whole thing had been only a leg-pull [a distinct possibility where Jack was concerned] until, on the following day, my brother took me with him to see Captain Shadwell, who at the time was the captain-superintendent of Haslar Hospital . . . Shaking with excitement and fear until I thought my knees were about to give way. I listened to the conversation, and stuttered answers to a few questions I was asked.

When I heard that I was nominated, and that, after another term at Lichfield, I was to go to North Grove House at Southsea to be

[1] Kilv. MSS., Pkt. 6. The Admiralty's letter of appreciation is logged in IND. 12543.

educated for the Navy, I felt like running out of the office, in order to jump and shout with delight.

He was, in the event, very happy at Southsea and came sixth out of forty-five candidates for the Navy examination.[1]

Another letter to 'Aunt Kate' Whimper brings out Jack's fatherly care for his small brothers. This was written in 1865—the only year, apparently, when all the brothers and sisters were ever together. Indeed, according to Frederic Fisher they all assembled on only one occasion and that was to have a photograph taken. Fortunately, this has survived. (See Pl. 1.) Philip, otherwise 'Toby', had been taken by his married sister Alice to England at the age of four and, by 1865, he was seven. In March, Fisher reported: 'I took Toby to school on Saturday to Reading —such a delightful place, quite in the country . . . I hope to get a telegram tonight to say that Billy has passed all right. I feel quite sure that he has; he comes up in full uniform tomorrow afternoon.' The arrangement was that, in due course, Aunt Kate would see that 'Billy' caught an early train from Paddington in order to join the *Britannia*. (This three-decker was moored in the Dart from 1863. When she was condemned in 1869, her replacement was given the same name. The second ship remained the school for Cadets until the Royal Naval College was completed in 1905.) In a postscript Fisher thoughtfully asked Aunt Kate whether she would 'look out Mr. Billy doesn't damage his uniform as he will only have one suit with him and I want him to go on board a "swell".'[2]

Yet Fisher himself was soon to marry and have children; and they were brought up, apparently, 'in complete ignorance of their father's brothers and sisters'[3]—excepting only Frederic William ('Billy'). Some explanation of this conundrum will be attempted at an appropriate moment.

Fisher first met his future wife, Katherine Delves-Broughton, in 1862 when he was on the staff of the *Excellent* (not during his service in the *Warrior* as Bacon has implied).[4] The year seems firmly fixed by a letter which Fisher wrote to her from the S. Atlantic on 19 April 1872:

 . . . I am so pleased with all you tell me about Billy. I do so greatly hope that I shall see him when I get home. I can hardly realize that

[1] Adl. Sir Frederic Fisher, *Naval Reminiscences*, pp. 33–4.
[2] Kilv. MSS., Pkt. 6, F. to Mrs. Whimper, 24 Mar. 1865.
[3] *F.G.* i, 99.   [4] Bacon, i, 34.

1. Fisher with his brothers and sisters in 1865. Back row (left to right): Frederic, Frank, Lucy, Arthur, Jack. Sitting: Lindsey Daniell, Philip Fisher, Alice (Mrs. Daniell) with two of her three children. (All three died from accidental poisoning in Ceylon the next year)

he is now the same age as I was when you first saw me. My darling, that was my great mistake in life not marrying you when I first met you and when I was really very much in love with you. We should both have been 21, quite old enough . . . and I should have been very much better in every way . . . and I should have done professionally as well . . .[1]

A few passing references in private correspondence show that Fisher was linked with the Delves-Broughtons by 1865. Probably, he became engaged to Katherine during that year. Meanwhile, he had left the *Warrior* at the end of March 1864 and returned to the focus of his professional affections.[2]

After a spell of leave, Fisher was appointed by an Admiralty Minute of 3 June for his second term of service in the *Excellent*. Almost at once, he was put in command of the *Stork* which was one of the tenders attached to the *Excellent* for instructional or experimental purposes. She was a *Dapper* class gunboat, built to meet the requirements of the Crimean War. Armed experimentally with Lancaster guns (forerunners of the rifled gun), she had taken part in the bombardment of Sveaborg. Her normal armament was one 68-pounder smooth-bore gun and two 24-pounder howitzers. Of 232 tons, she was 106 feet long, equipped with a 60 horse-power reciprocating engine and a single screw (maximum speed 8 knots), and was designed to bear a complement of 36 officers and ratings.[3]

Aboard the *Warrior*, Fisher did not officially become a 'Gunnery Lieutenant' until 4 November 1863 (three years from his date of confirmation as a Lieutenant). He then received an extra shilling a day in addition to the usual ten shillings for a Lieutenant. While commanding the *Stork* he was paid an additional half-crown a day.[4]

By the time of Fisher's service in the *Stork* (16 June 1864 to 2 November 1866), his 'beloved "Excellent" ' had developed into a greater experimental establishment than when he had coined the phrase in March 1863. On 30 June 1863 the command of the *Excellent* had passed from Captain Hewlett to Captain Astley Cooper Key. Combining vision with caution, derived from great knowledge and varied experience, Key was the leader of the rising élite of scientifically minded officers in the 1860s. He

---

[1] Kilv. MSS., Pkt. 6.
[2] Kilv. MSS., Pkt. 6, F. to Mrs. Whimper, 14 Sept. 1864 or 1865; 24 Mar. 1865.
[3] Preston and Major, pp. 27, 197–8.   [4] Adm. 124/153.

had played a notable part in operations known to Fisher—the bombardment of Sveaborg and the capture of Canton. An enthusiast for steam propulsion since the early 1840s, Key had commanded the Steam Ordinary at Devonport from 1860 to 1863. In a position somewhat like that of a latter-day Director of Naval Equipment, he had ably controlled experiments at a time of controversy and flux in the sphere of ship-design. His work in the *Excellent*, which continued till he became the first Director of Naval Ordnance at the Admiralty in September 1866, clearly represented an important influence on Fisher's development as a technical expert. For this reason, and also because Fisher himself would one day become Captain of the *Excellent*, some extracts from Philip Colomb's classic life of Key must here be quoted.

. . . The four ironclads, *Warrior, Black Prince, Defence* and *Resistance*, forming the first instalment of that class of ship, were complete and at sea, and were well reported on. In those ships a supposed balance had been struck between steam-power and sail-power; between the $4\frac{1}{2}$-inch armour-plate and the 68-pounder gun. The second instalment, the *Minotaur, Northumberland* . . . was in course of completion, and several wooden line-of-battle ships cut down and coated with armour—in cases $5\frac{1}{2}$-inch—were also in hand. All these were also designed under the idea that some balance between offensive and defensive powers existed. It was only beginning to dawn on us that there could be no balance, because no conclusive experiments could be tried . . .[1]

The fourth instalment was the *Royal Sovereign* [completed in August 1864], Captain Coles's turret ship, which it was contended would sweep away and supersede all before her by inaugurating an entirely new system of mounting guns on board ship.

The real condition of things was that there was a crowd of inventors, designers, and manufacturers, all let loose with their inventive and constructive powers in the highest state of activity, each of them intent on his own point, and none of them under such control as could harmonise their work with that of others . . . There was an immense public opinion clamouring for, and forcing on, the adoption of each nominal advance in offensive and defensive power, and those who clamoured loudest had least thought out the nature of an excessively complex problem.

There was really only one person competent by his position to control the whole of this seething mass of rivalries, and to turn the

---

[1] Colomb, one of the most reflective officers of his day, had reached the rank of Commander in 1863. He was ten years older than Fisher.

rushing and foaming streams into designed channels, and that was the captain of *Excellent*.[1]

The stereotype of the Victorian naval officer, nimble on the field of sport or in a sailing boat, but instantly comatose when invited to study any complex subject, doubtless had some basis in reality. But a man of this type would scarcely have found his way on to the staff of the *Excellent*. Yet even this élite found it difficult to dispense with all the outdated practices slowly perfected during the centuries of sail-powered British predominance. For example, cutlass drill continued to take up much time which could have been more fruitfully used elsewhere. The bizarre but impressive variety of the work falling under Captain Key's direction is thus described by Colomb:

Apart from guns and their mountings, and the trials of armour-plates, we have fuses, rockets, sights, friction tubes, bolts for armour-plates, fire screens, obsolete gear, cartridges, shell boxes, shot plugs, shrapnell shell, fixed floating batteries, small arms, hollow shot, muzzle disparts, pistols, magazines, hand-spikes, photographs, submarine guns, breech-loading rifles, shell extractors, case and grape, boats' magazines, explosive bullets, high-angle fire, sponge and worms, shot supply, cutlasses, gun drill, steam launches, submarine attack, life-saving, gunnery books, electricity, light-balls, lighting decks in action, bugle signals, protecting rudders, manoeuvring powers of ships, special gunboats, armoured decks. Such a list as this gives some slight idea of the enormous catalogue of subjects which came under his ken, and the progress or condemnation of which fell under Captain Key's influence . . . He was always for the medium course—he was always for simplification; for the weeding out of what was obsolete; and for the endeavour to make one thing do the duty of two . . .[2]

Fisher was hardly to prove a man for the medium course; but in respect of simplification, the elimination of obsolescence, and rationalization of expenditure, there was much common ground between Key and Fisher (as a mature officer). Fisher was never slow to recognize his own superiority over his fellows but in 1870, at least, he still found himself able to 'look up' to Key and admitted that the latter was one of the senior officers who could exert 'professional force' over him.[3]

---

[1] Colomb, pp. 324–6. See also Oliver, pp. 55–7.
[2] Colomb, p. 364.
[3] *F.G.* i, 69.

Fisher spent April and May of 1865 undergoing instruction at the Hythe School of Musketry. He does not seem to have found the course very rewarding from a professional point of view.

I found myself in a small Squad of Officers, my right hand man was a General and my left hand man a full Colonel. The Colonel spent his time drawing pictures of the General . . . When we were examined *viva voce* we each had to stand up to answer a question (like the little boys at a Sunday School). The General was asked to explain the lock of the latest type of British Rifle. He got up and stated that as he was neither Maskelyne and Cooke nor the Davenport Brothers (who were the great conjurers of that time) he couldn't do it. Certainly we had some appalling questions. One that I had was, 'What do you pour the water into the barrel of the rifle with when you are cleaning it?' Both my answers were wrong. I said, 'With a tin panniken or the palm of the hand.' The right answer was *'with care'*![1]

In later life, Fisher was excessively prone to attribute stupidity to the Army. His experience at Hythe seems to have done little to educate him in a contrary direction. 'All the same', he averred, 'I had a lovely time there; the British Army was very kind to me and I loved it.'[2] Needless to say, he was duly awarded his 'Hythe Certificate' by the War Office (5 July).[3]

Fisher's marriage to Frances Katharine Josephine Delves-Broughton took place on 4 April 1866. They were both aged twenty-five—she being a few months his elder. Her father had been Rector of Bletchley. There was a seventeenth-century baronet in her ancestry to complete the balance between her background and Fisher's. During her engagement she insisted (as a cousin long remembered) 'that Jack would *certainly* rise to the top of the tree' and she resolved never to stand in his way.[4] She proved her devotion throughout a long life. Unfortunately none of her letters to Fisher appears to have survived (though she preserved well over a hundred of his letters to her). However, there is enough evidence to show that she was not only a good wife and mother, but also much liked as a hostess and an effective support for her husband in his service career. She was not an intellectual but showed that she could entertain successfully up to the level of royalty. Fisher for his part was deeply in love with her. This experience evidently awakened in him religious feelings which were not much in evidence before. He passed through a

---

[1] *Records*, pp. 17–18.   [2] Ibid.   [3] IND. 12559.
[4] F.P. 1666, Walter Campbell to Lady F., 2 Mar. 1904; *F.G.* i, 61.

potent Christian phase which seems at times to have disturbed his wife by its intensity. In later years he veered towards an Old Testament standpoint with the God of Battles as a leading feature.

Early in November 1866 Fisher was transferred from the *Stork* to the main establishment—without loss of pay because he now received the full 3s. 6d. in virtue of the first-class gunnery certificate which he gained the previous March. Apart from his obvious ability as a Gunnery Lieutenant, no reason for his retention at the *Excellent* is extant. At first, he was still exclusively concerned with gunnery; it was not till some time in 1867 that he turned his attention to 'torpedoes' with important consequences for his naval career. It was when he came ashore from the *Stork* that he first made contact with another remarkable young officer, just over a year younger than himself, whose career followed a similar course in many respects. This was Arthur Wilson—confirmed as a Lieutenant from 11 December 1861. Both men established themselves as experts in a wide range of naval equipment and techniques; they both had a special connection with torpedoes; each of them became Controller of the Navy; Wilson succeeded Fisher as First Sea Lord in 1910; he came close to succeeding him again during the Great War; and they both maintained an official connection with the Admiralty till 1918. In professional knowledge they came near to being on a par, though Wilson's abilities lay particularly in naval tactics and, ultimately, fleet-handling, while Fisher's lay more in the sphere of administration. In character and temperament, the two men contrasted sharply. Where Fisher was dynamic and volatile, Wilson represented the essence of Victorian self-restraint. Like a member of a monastic order, he came near to self-abnegation. The service was, apparently, his only love. With the utmost diffidence, he accepted the award of the Victoria Cross. Although he came to know Wilson's obstinacy and lack of vision, Winston Churchill was to pay him this ultimate tribute: 'He was, without any exception, the most selfless man I have ever met or even read of.'[1]

When he first met Fisher, Wilson was completing the qualifying course for Gunnery Lieutenant. It is clear from what the latter wrote long afterwards that Fisher had already developed a vivid lecturing style.

[1] Adm. 24/167; Bradford, pp. 20–2, 87–90; W. Churchill, i, 66.

The principal thing I remember of him at the time was a very characteristic lecture he gave us on his experience as a Gunnery Lieutenant in a seagoing ship. He had served a commission as Gunnery Lieutenant of the *Warrior*. The main point of his lecture consisted in the cunning devices he professed to have used for getting the men he wanted for drill out of an unwilling Commander as the claims of paint work and polish were paramount in those days. His methods chiefly consisted in the artful use of judicious flattery.[1]

Already, then, battle had been joined (or renewed) in the emergent steam-Navy between the paint-work school, apparently represented aboard the *Warrior* by Commander Tryon, and the scientific progressives, already spear-headed in this instance by Fisher. Tryon was himself an active thinker in such spheres as signalling, tactics, and strategy, so he was doubtless much less obstructive than most officers of his rank. More than thirty years were to elapse before the spirit of the *Excellent* began to predominate in the service as a whole.

The year 1867 marks a crucial stage in Fisher's career. It was then that he began to take a systematic interest in electricity and mines. What may be described as his 'torpedo' phase lasted till 1876. Not much of this phase has been closely investigated before and a number of inaccuracies and misconceptions have in consequence become established in the existing accounts. In particular, it must be realized that when a British naval officer of 1867 referred to a 'torpedo' he did *not* mean a Whitehead torpedo running under its own power. He meant either a mine or a spar torpedo (otherwise 'outrigger' torpedo)—the latter being an explosive charge on the end of a pole projecting from a small boat. Seeing that by 1869 Fisher, despite his youth and junior rank, had already emerged as an authority on 'torpedoes' it is clear that some general account must be given of their state of development in 1867.

Admiral Sir Cyprian Bridge left in his memoirs a useful account of the place of mines, spar torpedoes, and electricity in the Lieutenants' gunnery course which he took in the *Excellent* in 1867.

. . . It may be mentioned that I was the first officer in the Navy to be examined in submarine mining, counter-mining, and torpedo work . . . I confess that I was sorry to discontinue my connection with the 'Excellent', as I was greatly interested in gunnery and the

---

[1] Kilv. MSS., envelope 'Chapter I', Wilson to Cecil, Ld. F., 18 Apr. 1921.

other matters connected with it. Great changes were being made. Electricity was being brought into naval use; submarine warfare was beginning to be regarded as a practical possibility of the future; protection of ships with armour and means of attacking the armour were matters of daily experiment. We still adhered to the same old principles and methods. Ships still carried boarding pikes and tomahawks. The cutlass-drill, though less elaborate than it had been, still took a long time to learn . . .[1]

While the indications are that Fisher was to some extent concerned with instruction in electricity and mines at least by the summer of 1867, the ex-seaman of the *Warrior* (whose recollections of Fisher have been quoted above) makes it clear that the latter was still expending much time and energy on more primitive subjects of instruction. 'There was no mistake', Mr. Mitchell wrote to Fisher in 1905, 'about your earnestness in making all you had to do with smart . . . You were very kind to me and took some pains to smarten me up . . . I believe that from you I received a training that has considerably helped me through life . . . I can remember as yesterday yourself on the lower deck of the "Excellent" and I one of a class that you were passing through handspike drill.' In 1910 the same correspondent recalled: 'You also passed me through the first in Gunnery and Cutlass in the "Excellent" granting me V.G.I in both.'[2]

Up to the end of 1866 the Navy had taken little interest in mining which had been the business of the Royal Engineers. The initiative in suggesting that the Navy might be interested in sending officers and specialist ratings on a course of instruction in 'torpedoes' appears to have come from Professor Frederick Abel who was Chemist at the Royal Laboratory, Woolwich, from 1854 to 1888.[3] After consulting the Captain of the *Excellent*, Rear-Admiral Key (Director of Naval Ordnance) wished to take up the idea but, in February 1867, the Board of Admiralty refused to write officially to the War Office because of 'several instances' of their 'distinct proposals' receiving no official answer from the said office! Fortunately, the War Office now suggested to their Lordships that a class, 'to include a Gunnery Lieutenant if possible', should be sent to Woolwich. Lieutenant H. C. Kane

[1] Adm. Sir Cyprian Bridge, *Some Recollections*, London, 1918, pp. 210–11.
[2] F.P. 1842; 2048.
[3] Frederick A. Abel (1826–1902) was an F.R.S. (1860) and an accomplished musician. He was knighted in 1883; K.C.B., 1891; and 'almost every branch of technical science was enriched by his labours.' (*D.N.B.*)

(a future D.N.O.) was selected and at the same time appointed to the staff of the *Excellent*. He began his course at the end of March.[1] In May, the War Office offered a further course at Woolwich. Late in the month, a scheme of instruction at the *Excellent* received Key's endorsement. The War Office suggested that all 'torpedo' instruction should in future be given by the Royal Engineers at Chatham but Key was successful in establishing the principle of separate instruction in the *Excellent* and *Cambridge* (Devonport). Fisher, who had clearly become involved in the new course at the *Excellent*, was a member of the last class of naval students to be sent to Woolwich. This was in October 1867.[2]

Fisher applied himself to the course with characteristic energy and, according to Abel, 'he distinguished himself most highly' amongst those who attended. In later life, Fisher became the most voluminous printer of official memoranda that the Navy has ever known;[3] and he apparently saw no reason to doubt the usefulness of a printed version of Abel's course! By January 1868 it was ready for printing. The main text of the small book extended to 128 pages. Its title was *A Short Treatise on Electricity and the Management of Electric Torpedoes* and it was printed by E. Annett, Paradise Street, Landport. At the time when Fisher was preparing his manuscript, there were not many precedents to guide him as to procedure. There was a marked flavour of private enterprise about the whole undertaking. (The first official gunnery manual, as it happened, was not issued to the Navy until 1868.) Rear-Admiral Key's role is not entirely clear but when Captain Arthur Hood (his successor in the *Excellent*) forwarded an advance-copy with his blessing on 14 April, the D.N.O.'s report expressed no surprise. The implication of this and a minute by a civil servant is that Key was privy to the whole affair and had obtained authority for the book to be printed from Rear-Admiral Sir John Hay, Bart., F.R.S., M.P., then holding the office of Fourth Sea Lord. Key, in fact, thought that there was

---

[1] A. K. Wilson thought that Kane was also directed to compile the Navy's first torpedo manual (Kilv. MSS., env. marked 'Chapter I'; also Bradford, p. 47, and Sayer, p. 27). I can find no evidence to support this version. In the preface to his *Treatise*, F. thanks Kane for his 'valuable and ready co-operation'.

[2] IND. 12600 (digest—see 59–8); 12591 (Fisher); 12593 (Kane); Adm. 1/6000.

[3] Information received from Lt.Cdr. P. K. Kemp, a former Admiralty Librarian.

no obvious case for keeping the work confidential and advised that, unless Abel reported to the contrary, the book should be published by Annett and that the Admiralty should buy enough copies to supply the *Excellent*, as well as two copies for 'every ship in commission'.[1]

Hood's opinion was that the book would be 'exceedingly useful' in aid of Fisher's 'first object', namely 'to enable the Student Lieutenants of the "Excellent" to obtain in a concise form the information required to assist them whilst undergoing the course of Instruction in Torpedoes'. Key thought that the *Treatise* was 'a very valuable contribution to the Science of Naval Warfare' and endorsed Hood's view that it should be made generally available to seagoing officers. Key was aware that much of the information had originated from Abel. The latter may perhaps have been slightly disconcerted by the sudden appearance of the *Treatise*. In his report of 24 April he remarked that he and his assistant Mr. E. O. Brown had been preparing since the previous summer 'a somewhat more comprehensive Manual of electric Torpedo Service' but had refrained from printing it until he had completed further investigations. 'Pending the completion of this work', he considered that the Treatise was 'well suited to serve as an instruction book for the Courses in Torpedo Service at the" Excellent" and "Cambridge" '. Elsewhere he commented:

The first part of the Book (Chapters 1–10) is a concise, clear and for the most part very correct account of some of the most important fundamental principles of electrical science, compiled as Mr. Fisher states from Works on Electricity; and is well adapted to aid those going through a course of instruction in the employment of electrical Torpedoes.

The remainder of the book exclusive of the Appendix and of a short account of the experiments with outrigger torpedoes conducted at Portsmouth, consists in substance of the notes of my course of instruction in electric Torpedo Service, and gives a clear outline of the more important points connected with the system of constructing, firing and testing Torpedoes which has been worked out in this Department, and which are described in full detail in the Report of the Committee on Floating Obstructions, very shortly to be submitted to the Secretary of State for War.

---

[1] The sources for the correspondence and minutes relating to the *Treatise* are given below. See p. 49, n. 1.

He thought that the book contained a good deal of information which ought to be kept confidential and that copies should be restricted to the two gunnery ships.

From the point of view of originality, Fisher's most notable offering was contained in an eight-page appendix entitled 'Firing Guns by Electricity'. This foreshadowed the scheme of director firing adopted more than thirty years later. In the *Treatise* Fisher introduced his proposal thus:

> The following appears to the Author to be a simple method of carrying on Independent or Broadside Firing by Electricity, from the maintop (or any other desired position) under certain [later changed by Fisher with a pen to 'all'] circumstances, and has been elaborated in order that *the delivery of the Fire by the Officer at the Director should be instantaneous on his sights being aligned* . . . There is nothing either to prevent the resumption of the ordinary methods of firing at any instant, nor, if any of the ordinary methods of firing are being practised, is there anything to prevent their being instantly superseded by the electric system.
>
> The arrangements which were made to carry out this system of electric firing from the battery of heavy guns on board H.M.S. 'Excellent', and which met with perfect success, will now be described . . .

Abel was favourably impressed by the practical details of Fisher's scheme. 'The arrangements for applying my electric Tubes and Battery to the firing of guns on board ship, which Mr. Fisher describes in the Appendix, originate with him; they appear to me likely to work very effectively and afford additional proof of the success which has attended Mr. Fisher's study of the application of electricity to explosive purposes.' Key's comments (8 May) registered his continuing faith in the practice of linking the director to the guns by means of speaking tubes but he thought that Fisher's scheme would prove appropriate when the ship was rolling. Hood was asked to report and did so on 13 May with his usual lucidity:

> With regard to the plan proposed by Lieutenant Fisher for firing by electricity, it certainly has this very considerable advantage—it enables the Officer working the Director to fire the guns when the sights are exactly on with the object, instead of conveying the order to do so to the Officer in the battery, which necessitates a loss of time between the order being given and the fire being delivered; when a ship is rolling quickly, it must therefore be left to the judgment of the Officer at the Director to select the proper moment for giving the

order 'fire' . . . I am quite satisfied that the method proposed by Lieutenant Fisher will cause the fire to be more efficiently delivered than can be done by order, provided always that you can depend thoroughly on the efficient working of the whole apparatus. It has been tried in the 'Excellent' and has answered perfectly . . .

However, when the scheme was referred to the Ordnance Select Committee, which came under the War Office, it met with summary rejection (3 June) for the following reasons:

1. Although no gun can be fired until it is primed, there would be constant danger of its being fired when primed before everyone was clear.

2. A gun not primed would lose its shot altogether.

3. A considerable length of wire would be necessary to meet the entire range of a gun's training and would be much in the way.

4. There would be constant liability to have the circuit broken in which case all the guns are silenced for the time.

5. Electric tubes at present fail in a greater degree than ordinary ones and are less fit for general service.

> (Signed) H. Heyman
> Lt. Col. & Secretary
> for President.

Fisher's reactions to this rejection seem to have escaped the record. But it is probably sufficient to note that, at least as early as 1871, he was ascribing stupidity to the leading 'soldiers of the Queen'. As will be explained in the next chapter, the Admiralty did not attach any degree of finality to the arguments of the Ordnance Committee.

With regard to the main body of the *Treatise*, it is necessary to remove a misconception which has arisen about Fisher's opinion of the Whitehead 'locomotive' torpedo. Some of his 'Preliminary Remarks' (pp. vi and viii) have been interpreted as a prophetic reference to the Whitehead torpedo.[1] No doubt such statements as 'There can be no doubt that the Electric Torpedo is destined to play a most important part in future wars' and 'Ships as at present constructed are powerless against its attacks, supposing them to get within its destructive area' do suggest knowledge of the Whitehead torpedo. (The weapon was first given an official test at Fiume in December 1866 and some

---

[1] E.g. *F.G.* i, 63. Hough, p. 53, follows suit.

account will be given below of how the news about it was received at the Admiralty.) But a close reading of the text of the *Treatise* can leave no one in doubt that when Fisher referred to an 'Electric Torpedo', he meant an electrically detonated mine. After devoting his first sixteen chapters to electricity, he takes up consecutively the subject of the 'torpedoes' themselves. In Chapter XVII (p. 88) he discusses 'self-acting Electric Torpedoes':

> In very dark or foggy weather, when it would be impossible to fire the Torpedoes by observation, they explode through the circuit being completed by the shock of impact with the enemy's vessel . . . If there is reason to believe by some private signal that a friendly vessel is entering, the electrical circuit can be permanently interrupted at the shore end, and made good again when she has passed.

In other words, he is concerned with defence of harbours by observation mines which, as he goes on to explain in more detail, can be set to go off on contact when thought desirable.

Fisher was soon adding copious marginalia to his personal copy of the *Treatise*. Amongst these is the following note in red pencil (p. 119) which, partly from the mention of the Harvey torpedo and partly from evidence given below, may be ascribed to the year 1869: 'Now tell them of Harvey's divergent Torpedo & read letter to Adl. Key. Disadvantages of Outrigger Torpedoes. Advantages & Disadvantages of Whitehead Locomotive Torpedoes.'

Otherwise, some characteristic notes pencilled inside the front cover deserve reproduction:

1. Not to touch any of the gear . . . Mr. May will report when you come in.

2. With regard to the books, only to have them during the course, not to take notes in them, and all notes & information supplied supposed to be confidential. Only 30 allowed—damit.

3. With regard to the system of instruction . . . this book only an abstract of the course, a series of rough notes thrown together in their right order. Impossible for anyone to learn from it. Never intended for the instruction of the ignorant.

4. Mode of instruction. Take a paragraph or two, read it. You won't perhaps understand it. Then explain by illustrations from common life & look several ways at it . . .

5. Length of course depends on the stupidity of the class . . .

Even at this early stage of his career, Fisher believed in the educative value of a jolt to the nervous system. Under the heading of 'First Principles' (of electricity) he wrote (p. 2): 'N.B. Give them all a shock of Sand Battery.'[1]

The *Treatise* undoubtedly represents a landmark in Fisher's naval career. From March 1868 onwards he was writing technical reports on suggestions, within the sphere of 'torpedoes' and electricity, which had been submitted to the Captain of the *Excellent*. The first of these reports concerned the proposal of 'a Hawser or Cable with insulated wires connected with Torpedoes for River Defence' and there was no hint of uncertainty in Fisher's comments dated 18 March: 'There is nothing at all to be said in favour of this proposal. It is not practical, and extremely limited in its electrical application. The objections will now be stated . . .'[2]

In May 1868 he wrote some 'Remarks on that portion of von Scheliha's work on "Coast Defence" relating to torpedoes'. In retrospect, the most interesting remark stems from the position which he had adopted in the *Treatise* (p. viii) regarding 'the special advantages of electric over mechanical Torpedoes', including 'Greater Safety. For mechanical Torpedoes do not possess the power of selection, and consequently are as dangerous to friend as to foe.' This apparently unobjectionable preference for observation mines, fired by observers stationed ashore, was to hinder the development of a really effective British mine. As will be made clear, this view retained its plausibility until the Russo–Japanese War, and it was by no means the view of Fisher alone. But after 1905 he came to regard the submarine, possessing 'the power of selection' and much else, as a weapon which rendered the mine (and possibly surface-vessels) obsolete. So it is of special interest to notice, from 1868 onwards, his persistence in condemning 'mechanical' mines—not only because he thought electrical detonators superior to mechanical ones but especially because the latter, being contact mines, did 'not

---

[1] F.P. 5459. This is F.'s personal copy of the *Treatise*. Hood's letters to the Admiralty about the book and its appendix on firing guns by electricity, together with the minutes by Key, are in Adm. 1/6045. The reports by Abel and the Ordnance Select Committee are in Adm. 1/6073.

[2] F.P. 5415. This hard-backed exercise book is an important source, hitherto unpublished. It contains F.'s copies of his reports and papers on professional subjects, 1868–71. The originals (also unused till now) in some cases survive in the Admiralty archives at the P.R.O.

possess the power of selection'. Regarding von Scheliha's book, he wrote:

About 100 pages of the book relate to Torpedoes. Of these, but 30 pages are devoted to electric Torpedoes. However interesting the subject of mechanical Torpedoes may be, yet as it is quite certain they will never again be used (for this 'opinion' indisputable reasons can be given if required) it is not worth while to dwell upon that portion of 'von Scheliha' which treats of them.[1]

As will be made sufficiently evident, this confident prognostication was to prove unfortunate.

Fisher's abilities are better represented by his report of a visit in July to the Royal Engineers' 'torpedo' establishment at New Brompton near Chatham. Captain Hood had instructed him to consult Captain R. H. Stotherd, the chief instructor in telegraphy and an expert on mines. Fisher was to report on Stotherd's adaptation of an American 'portable sound telegraph equipment'; also on any features of torpedo instruction and of the electrical equipment used by the Royal Engineers which might profitably be adopted by the *Excellent*.

According to Fisher, the portable telegraph would 'enable messages to be transmitted between a ship and her boats, when placed in electrical communication'. Using a manipulating key, an operator could send messages 'by a simple adaptation of the Morse system of telegraphy'. An inexperienced operator 'was able after ¼ of an hour's study to carry on a rapid conversation with another operator at an electrical distance of 4 miles'. From the tone of his extensive report Fisher discovered a kindred spirit in Stotherd—and indeed the Royal Engineers represented one branch of the army which he continued to respect in later years. Fisher worked out a number of improvements in the device from the point of view of a ship communicating simultaneously with a number of boats and the boats sending messages direct to each other. The tactical object in view seems to have been observation of an enemy port, though action against mine defences and possibly the conduct of landings could also have been envisaged. However, the feature of the report which foreshadows a very characteristic side of a great naval administrator is the nature of the practical recommendations. Better examples of Fisher's cost-consciousness and businesslike approach will soon be given, but

[1] F.P. 5415.

this earliest instance (emanating from a Lieutenant of twenty-seven years) should not be omitted:

... The cost of the instrument would be under £3. I would suggest therefore that Messrs. Siemens of Woolwich be directed to supply four of these instruments . . . and that Mr. Hooper be directed to supply a mile of his wire . . . on three reels, each of them to admit of being shipped between the thwarts of a boat (so as to revolve) and that he should, if practicable, so coat the insulation as to allow of the wire floating when paid out (NOTE. Try Clarkson's material) and that Messrs. Silver of the Telegraph Works, North Woolwich, be directed to supply a Mathieson's portable Telegraph Battery (12 cells in a box complete), cost about £5, for use with the above instruments.

If the above gear is supplied to the 'Excellent' a full trial can be given to it before adopting it generally in the Navy.

Fisher supplied much other technical comment but its flavour has doubtless been sufficiently indicated.

Turning to the subject of torpedo instruction at Chatham, Fisher developed a theme which he was to reiterate in the 1870s: the need to provide for research by the instructing staff.

From the large number of every sort of instrument at their disposal, and the apparently unlimited and ready supply of *any description* of fitting which they may happen to require, but chiefly owing to the comparatively undivided time at the disposal of the instructional staff, it ought not to be long before we are completely outstripped by the Royal Engineers in everything connected with the management of Torpedoes.[1]

Before passing on from this report of 28 July 1868 it will be useful to note a few points from his detailed account of the 'system of torpedoes' being prepared for the defence of Chatham and other ports. The mines would be fired either by contact or by an observer stationed on shore. Fisher thought that the Chatham type of circuit-closer was 'much too sensitive for the defence of open Harbours'. This remark related to the current policy of leaving the Engineers to provide the mine defences of the ports. The Navy wanted only to lay and dismantle, with maximum expedition, temporary mine defences for open anchorages and to be able to destroy the mine defences of an enemy.

Although Fisher had so far had nothing to do with the development of the Whitehead torpedo, he would come across detailed

[1] Ibid.

information on the subject during his visit to Germany in August 1869. So it is now appropriate to summarize the knowledge of the torpedo acquired at the Admiralty by that date.

On 11 January 1867 the Foreign Office transmitted to the Admiralty a report from Fiume of an official trial, held on 21 December 1866, 'at the "Stablimento Technico and Foundry", under the direction of Mr. Robert Whitehead, Chief Manager and Civic Engineer . . . of a new invented Marine Torpedo by Colonel Luppis of the Imperial Royal Navy now in Pension'. The trial was held before an Austrian commission consisting of naval authorities and engineers. The torpedo, continued the report,

has to completely destroy any Vessel of War passing, or at Anchor, by its contact when so directed, and launched from the shore or from a Vessel afloat; the Machine is self-propelled with necessary force, and has speed under water's surface, at some 6 feet depth, less or more, so as to be perfectly invisible to the Enemy . . . I am able to learn that the Experiment, so far as concerns Speed, Depth of Water and Direction, was most satisfactory . . . I am not able to give Your Lordship[1] any particulars of the Form, Force, Speed, etc., of the Torpedo, for Mr. Whitehead, the able Mecanick, keeps all to himself, it being his head work and personal labour; the publick were kept off the Works at some distance.

The informant, one C. T. Hill, remarked: 'I hear also that the parties interested are most sanguine of complete success, and intend making an exorbitant demand on the Imperial Royal Government for possession of the Secret; the amount however I fear is too high (£300,000) for the Imperial Govt. to meet, and so the parties will have to look elsewhere for a Purchaser.'[2]

As D.N.O., Rear-Admiral Key appears to have received this (and doubtless other) information with his usual blend of open-mindedness and scepticism. In August 1868, Vice-Admiral Lord Clarence Paget, Commander-in-Chief in the Mediterranean, wrote to the Admiralty that, although 'beset' by reports of foreign inventions, he thought he should draw the attention of their Lordships to the Whitehead Torpedo. He had been told that the Austrian government had paid £20,000 'for the simple possession of the secret'. Whitehead had indicated to him that he wished to offer the invention to H.M. Government. Paget retailed a description of an underwater tube and a torpedo.

---

[1] H. M. Ambassador in Vienna.   [2] Adm. 116/135.

'Attached to the torpedo is a trigger and line communicating with the Spot on deck from which the Commanding Officer is guiding his Ship, and when the object aimed at is on, he discharges the missile.' Key's reaction (17 September) to this communication, although cautious, proved decisive: 'This is not a new idea. I much doubt the possibility of the machine making a straight course for even a cable's length,[1] but it is easily tested and I recommend a trial of it, when Mr. Whitehead makes his proposition.'[2]

The upshot was an interview in November when Whitehead achieved the provisional conversion of Rear-Admiral Key. 'I consider', wrote the latter in a minute, 'that if the results are confirmed—and he produces very conclusive evidence regarding them—the invention is one of the *very highest importance* to any maritime power.' A committee of three officers of the Mediterranean Fleet (including Lieutenant H. C. Kane, now of the *Caledonia*) went to Fiume and reported favourably on the weapon —long since freed from the aforementioned firing lanyard—in August 1869.[3]

Fisher was meanwhile closely concerned, as before, with questions relating to gunnery as well as mines. By September 1868 he had devised a '24 pounder rocket tube' which received Hood's blessing. Trials had been successful; a couple of modifications were needed. 'When these slight alterations are made', wrote Hood to the Admiralty, 'I consider this rocket tube will be in all respects suitable for the Naval service.' Sir John Hay (4 September) ordered that the invention should be notified to the War Office as a matter of urgency. This appears to have led to the quiet asphyxiation of the proposal.[4]

Fisher may not have had much knowledge of the Whitehead torpedo before 1869 but his reputation as a technical expert is indicated by his being selected in that year to attend a remarkable ceremony in Germany. The King of Prussia was to inaugurate Heppens, hitherto a fishing village, as a naval port for the North German Confederation. (It became familiar in later years under the name of Wilhelmshaven.) Fisher's inclusion in a very select official party was announced in May. On 12 June he embarked aboard the *Minotaur*, normally the flagship of the Channel Squadron but specially detached for the visit. According to the somewhat imprecise report in *The Times*, the ship was 'to

---

[1] 200 yards.   [2] Adm. 116/135.   [3] Ibid.   [4] Adm. 1/6046.

sail from Spithead for the Baltic [*sic*] with Admiralty officials on board, to be present at the official opening of the German port of Heppell [*sic*]'.

The ceremony duly took place on 17 June. The words spoken by William I on that little-noticed occasion—just over a year before Prussia humbled the armies of France—are not without interest:

My late lamented brother long ago originated the plan of constructing a harbour for vessels of war on the German coast. Now we have achieved it through the co-operation of my Federal ally, the Grand Duke of Oldenburg. Had it not been for his patriotic feelings the execution of the work would have been impossible. I look forward with cheerful confidence to the further development and to the future of our young German navy.[1]

Fisher met the King of Prussia. At lunch he sat next to him but one. Moltke and Bismarck, wearing helmets and greatcoats like the rest, were there—Fisher was even the recipient of a pithy comment from Bismarck on the long-windedness of the Burgomaster. (The comment was presumably in English because Fisher admitted his inability to master German or French.) Fisher also remembered that during lunch the King asked him why he had been sent and whether he was the only one who knew about 'torpedoes'. At the stage of compiling his memoirs, Fisher thought he *was* in fact the only one! But he is not likely to have said or even thought it at the material time. He afterwards remembered that 'telegrams kept coming to Bismarck, who would get up and draw the King aside.' Von Roon he thought 'very débonnaire, and Moltke was like an old image, taciturn and inscrutable', but he talked English as well as Fisher did. 'I never can make out', Fisher reminisced, 'why I didn't get a German decoration. I think perhaps they thought me too young. However, I had the honour of an empty sentry-box placed outside the little inn where I was staying; and if I had been of higher rank there would have been a sentry in it.'[2]

This seems as good a juncture as any to remark on the inaccuracy of some of the personal claims made by Fisher in his memoirs. These two volumes were largely dictated by Fisher, in his usual buoyant spirits, mainly during 1918 and 1919; and

---

[1] Adm. 167/1, Ady. mins., 14 May, 9 June 1869; *The Times*, 12 June, 19 June 1869.

[2] *Memories*, pp. 229–30; *F.G.* i, 78.

these characteristic exaggerations, at least partly aimed at amusing his immediate audience, should not attract undue censure.[1] But some definition should doubtless be given to these inaccuracies so that the usefulness of the memoirs can be estimated. It should at the same time be repeated that Fisher's memory remained on the whole very good and, apart from matters connected with his own reputation and achievements, he usually comes close to the truth on matters of fact. For example, his dates—even the early ones—are hardly ever more than one year out. Here, then, is the version of the technical side of his visits to Heppens and (two months later) Kiel which Fisher published in *Memories* (pp. 230–1):

On the occasion of my visit I imagined and reported what Heppens would become, and so it did . . . So far as I know, the present[2] German mine is nearly what it was then, and the sea-gulls rested on the protuberances as they do now, for I went to Kiel Bay to see them . . . I recommended the adoption of these German mines, and it's a pity we didn't. They hold the field to this very day. However, the First Sea Lord of that date didn't believe in mines or torpedoes or submarines, and I was packed off to China . . .

As it happens, Fisher's report (addressed as a letter to Captain J. G. Goodenough of the *Minotaur* and dated 19 June 1869) has miraculously survived the 'weeding' which has devastated many of the Admiralty files relating to the nineteenth century.

Sir,

I have the honor [*sic*] to report to you for the information of their Lordships the result of my visit to Heppens in H.M.S. 'Minotaur'.

There was nothing whatever at Heppens in the way of Guns or Torpedoes upon which a report could be made with the exception perhaps of a small ironclad ram built in 1863 by Arnaud of Bordeaux for the Confederates, but purchased by the Prussian Government . . . but I accidently found out that a Committee on Torpedoes, consisting of two Naval Officers and one Engineer Officer have for some months been carrying out experiments at Kiel, and devising an elaborate system of torpedo defences for the protection of all their harbours and coasts.

I was informed by Captain-Lieutenant Kykbusch that in July or August they were going to have some large experiments at Kiel with Torpedoes containing not less than 1,000 lbs. of Powder which are to

---

[1] F.P. 5100–3; see also 5286 for an interesting account of how *Memories* and *Records* were compiled.

[2] 1918.

be placed at various distances from two or three ships which are to be filled up solid in order to make them as strong as possible and the Torpedoes are to be exploded under all the circumstances likely to occur in war . . .

I heard that a private application had been made by the Russian Government to allow one of their Officers to attend the experiments . . . Colonel Walker, the Military Attaché at Berlin offered to obtain me an order to visit the great arsenal at Spandau and Tegel near Berlin where all the gunnery experiments are carried on but I found I should not have had time to get back to the Ship before she sailed.

I heard also that Admiral Jackmann proposes to have some ramming experiments at Kiel . . .

In conclusion I would respectfully suggest for their Lordships' consideration that an application should be at once made through Colonel Walker for permission for me to visit Kiel in order to witness any Torpedo experiments that may be going on, and I submit that it would be of advantage if I visited Tegel and Spandau on my way back . . .[1]

On 3 July this report came before a meeting of the Board of Admiralty attended by Childers, the First Lord, Admiral Sir Sydney Dacres, the First Sea Lord, and Vice-Admiral Sir Spencer Robinson, Controller of the Navy. They decided to ask the Foreign Office to seek permission for Lieutenant Fisher to attend the 'proposed torpedo experiments' at Kiel. It is perhaps worth adding that, a week earlier, Admiral Dacres—roughly handled in Fisher's memoirs for supposed lack of interest in 'torpedoes'—had minuted on the latter's report: 'Lieutenant Fisher to be thanked for the interesting account.' The Controller took up Fisher's suggestion that he should go back to Germany; and Dacres wrote: 'I quite concur as it will be the cheapest plan of gaining experience of the effects of firing large charges.'[2]

On 2 August Fisher, at the early age of twenty-eight, was promoted to Commander.

On the 11th, in accordance with his instructions he duly met Captain Vincenz of the Prussian Navy at Kiel. He was to watch the expected monumental explosions there; then he was to go on to the arsenal at Spandau and the gunnery establishment at Tegel near Berlin.

The visit to Kiel proved distinctly anticlimactic. As Fisher put it in his long official letter of 21 August:[3] 'Captain Vincenz

---

[1] Adm. 1/6087.   [2] Adm. 167/1; 1/6087.
[3] Adm. 1/6088. There is a copy in F.P. 5415.

informed me that there never had been nor were there likely to be for some time yet any Torpedo experiments at Kiel of the magnitude suggested by the Foreign Office communications . . . I assured myself of the accuracy of Captain Vincenz's statement during the three days I was living with the Prussian Officers at Kiel.' However, he made a brave recovery from this daunting set-back; if he witnessed no monumental explosion, he managed to produce a massive report!

But [he continued] I trust their Lordships after a perusal of my report will not regret having sent me, and I earnestly hope they will be pleased to consider favourably the suggestions I have deemed it my duty to make, more especially with regard to Torpedoes.

In view of his remark in *Memories* quoted above ('I recommended the adoption of these German mines') particular interest clearly resides in what he did actually have to say on this subject. Elsewhere in *Memories*[1] he even specified that it was 'the Hertz German Submarine Mine' that he had seen on that visit to Kiel and he went on: 'That same Hertz mine in all its essentials remains still [1919] "The King of Mines", and if only in those years immediately preceding the war we had manufactured none else, instead of trying to improve on it, we should have bagged no end of game.' Indeed, after painful demonstration of the ineffectiveness of the British mines, the Royal Navy resorted to making an exact copy of the Hertz-type mine in 1917.

According to Fisher's account in August 1869 Vincenz, who was head of the Prussian Torpedo Department, took him first to Holtenau where there was a torpedo establishment. Fisher was unimpressed by the conduct of experimental underwater explosions there, but he saw merit in the Prussian arrangements for mooring heavy mines. Concerning the independent contact mines he wrote: 'They had in store at Holtenau about 100 Mechanical Torpedoes precisely similar to those used in the American War. Anything striking against one of the projections . . . breaks a small glass tube inside containing sulphuric acid which thus escaping mixes with a powder surrounding it, thereby causing a flame which ignites the charge.' This is not a description of the famous horn designed in 1868 by Dr. Albert Hertz. The horn enclosed carbon and zinc plates together with a bichromate solution contained in a sealed glass tube, this tube

[1] p. 130.

being in the outer part of the protuberance. When the glass tube was broken the horn was transformed into a battery producing a sufficient current to set off the electric detonator of the mine itself. The great virtue of this device was that its firing energy was stored chemically rather than electrically. It did not go flat.[1] In fact it seems quite certain that Fisher was not shown a Hertz horn on this occasion, though he did see one some five years later, as will appear in due course. But in his report he put forward an argument about independent, as distinct from electrically fired observation mines, which makes it clear why he was not greatly interested when he did subsequently see a Hertz horn.

> Kiel is especially easy of defence by Torpedoes and Captain Vincenz informed me confidentially of their number and position. He is going to make use of a large number of mechanical Torpedoes but as he is not going to put them down anywhere in or near the passage for fear of blowing his own Ships up, I don't much see what will be their use for it is not likely the enemy is going out of his way on purpose to be blown up. In fact it is difficult to conceive the circumstances anywhere in which mechanical Torpedoes can be applied with advantage; they can certainly be put down in conjunction with booms, chains and sunken Ships and other passive obstructions, but . . . it is through the *apparently* open Channel left for your own Ships that the enemy will come, which ceases really to be open to your own Ships the moment a mechanical Torpedo is put down in it.

As long as Fisher adhered to this opinion, already indicated in the *Treatise* (p. viii) and his comments on von Schelila's book, the design of Dr. Hertz's horn would not be likely to attract his interest.

Being so convinced an advocate of observation (as distinct from contact) mines, Fisher was intrigued by the complicated technique evolved by the Prussians for determining which mines in a defensive field should be set off to destroy a ship passing over the said field. It involved 'four people doing their duty to a second'; two observers to take a cross-bearing and two other operators in the control room. In Fisher's words: 'It is as if Nasmyth's Hammer were to be constructed on purpose to crack walnuts . . . The great principle to be observed in any method of firing Torpedoes by observation is this: the instrument should be exceedingly simple in its construction without requiring any

---

[1] Cowie, pp. 26–7.

refinement in its management.' Fisher's passion for simplification was indeed an essential ingredient of his organizational flair. He submitted an alternative to the Prussian scheme which, rather characteristically, amounted to one very big bang. He wanted the mines, presumed to contain 1,000 lb. of powder, moored in groups of six. Then a single operator, using 'a rough and simple instrument', would be able to set off the whole group with sufficient accuracy; and, as he put it, 'the much greater moral effect produced by the explosion of such a group as opposed to the explosion of a single Torpedo is not to be lost sight of'.

Already conditions of financial stringency had accustomed Fisher to argue his case from the economic viewpoint; also notable is the theme of immediate readiness for war:

The principle I have sketched out above appears so simple and unanswerable that I would not have mentioned it but that (strange to say) almost everyone connected with Torpedoes is elaborating most refined and elegant methods of firing by observation, methods which I am quite confident (after careful study of them all) will most certainly fail when the rough practice of War comes, and it is found out 'too late' that the head Torpedo man cannot be everywhere at once. The usual objection against arranging the Torpedoes in groups is the increased expense entailed thereby, but when it is remembered that a 1,000 lbs. Torpedo does not cost more than a few rounds from a 9 inch Gun (putting aside altogether the cost of the Gun) and when it is remembered also that one such Torpedo will cause the strongest Ship in the World to sink in two Seconds this argument of increased expense should have no weight. If the time and money now spent elaborating such plans as I have alluded to above were devoted to the two questions of mooring and the effect of large charges (1,000 lbs.) against real submarine structures, the advantage to the Country would be very great, for it is absolutely essential that these two points should be decided if Torpedoes are to be applied to the best advantage.

Until the effective range of guns defending the British home ports had been greatly extended beyond what it was in 1869, defences consisting of observation mines had much to be said for them. As Fisher had pointed out in the *Treatise* (p. viii) and elsewhere, the electrically detonated observation mine was in principle a dual-purpose weapon: in good visibility, it permitted selection between enemy and friendly vessels; in poor visibility, it could be set to go off on contact.

However, it must also be said that mine defences of ports were not primarily a naval responsibility. In February 1868

Rear-Admiral Key strongly resisted a War Office proposal to hold all torpedo instruction, naval as well as military, at Chatham; and the basis of his argument was that the Army was essentially concerned with defensive mining whereas the Navy was concerned with the offensive aspect.[1] Fisher soon took up a similar tale. This suggests that he might well have taken more interest in independent contact mines, whether of a 'mechanical' or an electrical type, during his visit to Germany in August 1869. In a letter written the previous August to Captain Stotherd of the Engineers he had explained the matter thus:

> Your Torpedo work is mainly defensive, ours on the other hand is purely offensive; (when the Navy acts on the defensive affairs should be very desperate indeed) and for this reason I maintain that what we require thoroughly to understand is the rigging up of extempore Torpedoes for use from Torpedo boats or on an emergency barring with Torpedoes the passage of a river or narrow channel, and it is most essential that we should have a thorough practical knowledge of the best methods of removing or disabling Torpedo obstructions. When it is urged by some that this is an insufficient return for the labour we necessarily have to undergo to obtain an understanding of electricity, etc., it will be sufficient answer to say that it requires more electrical knowledge to rig up an extempore Torpedo or a small system of Torpedo defence than to manage an extensive and elaborate system of Torpedo defence such as you are perfecting at Chatham.[2]

As far as Fisher's report of 21 August 1869 is concerned, he was confirmed in his hostility to independent mines by an incident which occurred towards the end of his visit to Germany. He went to the gunnery establishment at Tegel where Dr. Werner Siemens showed him 'a beautiful invention': 'he has lately been able to produce such a light from the Dynamo-Electric Machine as to be able to distinguish objects on a pitch dark rainy night at 3,000 yards.' In Fisher's opinion, 'The value of this invention for warlike purposes cannot be overrated especially as regards Torpedoes, as it does away *to a great extent* with the necessity of self-acting arrangements.' In other words, there was now less need for mines which could be set to explode on contact. (The first major British warship to be fitted with a searchlight was the *Minotaur* in 1875.)[3]

---

[1] Adm. 1/6073.
[2] F.P. 5459. Holo. copy by F. inserted at end of the book.
[3] Parkes, p. 62.

A notable item in Fisher's comments on the arsenal at Spandau is a reference to the fuses in use there. This emphasizes his characteristic desire to achieve economy and greater efficiency through standardization: 'As far as I could see, they only use two Fuzes where we burden ourselves with 9 of sorts. I feel convinced that time Fuzes might be almost entirely abolished with great advantage to the Navy and an immense saving to the Country.' Also striking is a reference to the discipline of the workmen in the arsenal:

I cannot conclude this brief description of my visit to Spandau without bringing to their Lordships' notice the remarkable discipline maintained amongst the workmen; they never ceased work for a moment, never by any chance spoke to one another and did not apparently take the slightest notice of strangers like myself walking about.

In general: 'It was instructive to notice the great extent to which the Prussians apply electricity, and is one example among many of how much more alive they are than ourselves to the requirements of modern Science.'

During his brief stay in Berlin, 'some very cordial friends' took Fisher to 'a very exclusive Military Club' where he had the singular experience of lunching with William I's illegitimate brothers. 'They were the counterparts of the King,' thought Fisher, 'marvellously like him.'[1]

Another interesting encounter was with a Captain Hassenpflug who had recently been in the Austrian Navy and had served from February 1868 as a member of the Torpedo Commission examining the Whitehead torpedo. This officer had subsequently joined the Prussian Navy. He proceeded to oblige Fisher by lending him 'privately' (as Fisher duly reported to their Lordships) his papers relating to the work of the Austrian Torpedo Commission from July 1867 onwards. Fisher copied them out 'verbatim'—either they were in English or a translation was provided—and he embodied them in his report of 21 August. Although this lengthy section of Fisher's report may have conveyed some details about the Whitehead torpedo which were of interest to the Admiralty, their Lordships were bound to rely mainly on the forthcoming 'Report of Committee of Officers appointed by Vice-Admiral Sir Alexander Milne[2] to witness experiments with Mr. Whitehead's locomotive Torpedo at

---

[1] F.P. 5103.   [2] C. in C., Mediterranean.

Fiume'. Indeed the date of completion of this very favourable report was 7 August, though it was not forwarded by Milne (from Gibraltar) till 2 September.[1] In his own report of 21 August Fisher, having made clear his strong preference for Harvey's towed torpedo, proffered a brief general comment on 'Whitehead's Locomotive Torpedo'. This is of interest for at least two reasons: it shows that at this stage Fisher was still far from being an enthusiast for the Whitehead torpedo; but it also demonstrates to advantage the critical faculty which Fisher did possess but which was sometimes inoperative during the later stages of his naval career.

Although this Torpedo has been said to prove effectual as far as 2,000 feet in any required direction, it must be remembered that Mr. Whitehead's successful experiments have taken place in

> Smooth water
> Without any tide
> At a fixed object
> From a stationary Vessel

and that, once started, his Torpedo is beyond control and will blow up any one it comes across.

In addition to this it is extremely delicate to handle and manipulate and requires extreme care to prevent any clogging of the Pneumatic Apparatus.

But at the same time it must be conceded that it is a wonderful invention.

Near the end of September the report of the experiments at Fiume (dated 7 August) duly reached the Admiralty and was favourably received by the Board. Dacres minuted: 'Mr. Childers. This is a most excellent report on Whitehead's torpedo.' But it is interesting to see the questions raised by Captain Arthur Hood (who had recently left the *Excellent* to succeed Key as Director of Naval Ordnance). The D.N.O.'s long, clearly reasoned minute of 1 October evidently reflects Fisher's reservations at several points. The Committee's view on the accuracy of the torpedo had been formed under the 'most favourable' conditions. Experiments should be held where the attacking and attacked vessels were moving. Would the torpedo be damaged if delivered from a vessel that was rolling or pitching? He disagreed with the Committee's view that the torpedo would assist 'defence of narrow passages' especially where the amount of navigation

---

[1] Adm. 116/135. See p. 53 above.

rendered 'fixed floating torpedoes' impracticable. Hood suggested that attacking vessels would try to enter such channels at
top speed. In line with Fisher's argument for electrical observation instead of mechanical contact mines, the D.N.O. continued: 'I consider that large ground torpedoes exploded by
electricity would be a far more efficient mode of defending
narrow passages, and if properly arranged the navigation of
friendly vessels would not be interfered with.' While Hood urged
the necessity of further experiments, he said nothing to discourage adoption of Whitehead's torpedo. He envisaged a fast,
manoeuvrable type of vessel to deliver the torpedo—'such vessels
would be most formidable in action with iron clads, presenting
from their low freeboard a very small target.' In conclusion, he
urged the desirability of getting Mr. Whitehead to bring some
of his torpedoes to England for a series of trials.[1]

It is quite well known that a committee comprising Captain
William Arthur, Captain Morgan Singer, and Lieutenant A. K.
Wilson did conduct a series of trials in the Medway in the late
summer of 1870 and that the result was the adoption of the
Whitehead torpedo by the British Navy. Amongst British naval
officers, those who had played the most active part in bringing
this about seem to have been the two D.N.O.s of 1867–70,
namely Key and Hood, while there is every indication of open-
minded encouragement from Dacres as First Sea Lord and
Spencer Robinson as Controller. Milne (First Sea Lord, 1866–8
and 1872–6) also took a favourable view of the weapon in his
forwarding letter of 2 September 1869 from Gibraltar (enclosing
the Fiume report of 7 August).[2] Fisher, in the concluding section
of his report of 21 August 1869, did advocate extensive experiments with various types of torpedoes, including the Whitehead.
It is quite likely that this section of his report helped to shape
Hood's attitude. This is the full extent of Fisher's positive contribution to the British adoption of the weapon.

However, while it must be admitted that Fisher brought back
from his second visit to Germany no remarkable insights on the
technical aspects of mines or other 'torpedoes', yet his long
report of 21 August did on balance mark a substantial contribution both to the Admiralty's general policy regarding
'torpedoes' and to his own career in the service. In his introductory section Fisher listed the various subjects which he would

[1] Ibid.   [2] Ibid.

cover in the report: Prussian 'torpedoes', the visit to Spandau, the visit to Tegel, and the proceedings of the Austrian Torpedo Commission. He then wrote:

> And in conclusion I have brought before their Lordships the only plan by which a real and steady progress will be made in the management of Torpedoes, which will prevent this Country being unprepared in case of War and will avoid the strong probability (which at present exists) of our being outstripped by other Nations in the practical manipulation of ELECTRIC TORPEDOES; and in order to gain their Lordships' especial attention to the plan I have proposed, I beg to state that it is worth more than all the rest of my report put together.

This was a fair assessment. Seeing that Fisher's 'Concluding Observations' clearly foreshadow the appointment of the Admiralty Torpedo Committee of 1873–6, and that they appear to have had a considerable formative influence on naval policy with regard to mines and torpedoes, they deserve extensive quotation:

> Although the Prussians are far behind us at present in their knowledge of the management of Torpedoes, it will not be for long. For with their accustomed determination they are not sparing either money or time in elaborating a perfect system; and in order that we may not be left behind all other Nations not only in preparation (which we are already) but in actual knowledge (in which as yet we are *far ahead* of everyone) I beg to submit the following points for their Lordships' consideration as being worthy of adoption, observing that the French and Americans have, I believe, quite recently adopted them in extenso.

>> That a special Committee should be formed of four officers of the Royal Navy, Royal Engineers and the Chemical Department at Woolwich Arsenal, and I respectfully suggest that they should be
>> Captain Morgan Singer, R.N.
>> Lieutenant Anderson, R. Engineers
>> Lieutenant Kane, R.N.
>> E. O. Browne, Esqre., of the Chemical Dept.,
>> Woolwich.[1]

>> I take the liberty of mentioning these names on account of all these Gentlemen having a thorough knowledge of the subject

---

[1] This recommendation of a committee attracted marginal marks and underlining when it was read at the Admiralty.

already (though perhaps in different ways) and I know them to be especially suited to an investigation of this sort.

The *sole* duty of this Committee should be to establish the Theory and Practice of Torpedoes. They will make experiments, elaborate plans for the defence of all our Coasts and Harbours, and not only elaborate the plans, but to a certain extent prepare the Torpedoes. They would also have to decide upon the best *Offensive* Torpedo, whether 'Outrigger', 'Harvey's' or 'Whitehead's', or perhaps a combination of some of them, and having done so they would have to decide upon the number of them required, the Vessels, etc. They would also have ample employment in devising methods for rendering the Enemy's Torpedoes harmless, etc., and numerous other points might be mentioned which as yet have hardly been thought of.

For these purposes the Committee should have the disposal of a certain sum of money, and a certain number of men, and should have a small Vessel of their own where, during certain periods of the year, instruction should be given to Officers carefully selected from the Navy and the Engineers.

It is only by some such scheme as this that any real progress in the application of Torpedoes will be made. What is principally wanted is the undivided attention of a few really clever men with a lump sum given them annually to do what they like with. At Chatham, even, the Torpedo Department is mixed up with that of Photography, Chemistry, Army signalling, etc. . . . And in the *Excellent*, under present circumstances, it would be perfectly impossible to spare an Officer entirely for this branch of study.

As one reason among many for giving a fixed sum in money at the commencement of each year for Torpedo purposes, I wish to point out the delay, inconvenience, and I might almost say annoyance experienced in getting Torpedo stores at present . . . after all, instead of getting the things we require, we are at the mercy of the Controller's Department at Woolwich, who, even if they be Electricians, cannot be expected to feel the same interest in getting the full value for the money as we should.

I wish further to bring to their Lordships notice the utter inadequacy of the present annual supply of Torpedo gear *for anything like real work*, for to instruct over 100 officers during the year, besides carrying on small Torpedo experiments to the best of our ability and when time permits, we are allowed annually about £60 of Torpedo gear, equivalent to about 15 rounds from *one* of the *Hercules*' Guns.

It was indeed true that the United States Navy had formed a special corps to deal with the offensive as well as the defensive aspects of mines and torpedoes. On 21 August Hood drafted a minute on the implications of this development and the Board of Admiralty wrote to the War Office on 13 September (after reading Fisher's own report) suggesting the appointment of a joint committee. It was to consist of the Hydrographer of the Navy, an officer of the Royal Engineers, and Commander Fisher. The suggested terms of reference included the 'defence of each Naval, and of the principal Commerical, ports by torpedoes'; also the 'value of the schemes' which had been 'proposed for offensive operations with the aid of torpedoes'. The War Office took some time to reply and before its letter of acceptance was finally penned on 28 October their Lordships of the Admiralty had decided to substitute Captain Morgan Singer for Fisher as a member of the proposed committee.[1]

Judging by a couple of brief minutes in the Admiralty files[2] Dacres secured Childers's agreement to this substitution on 24 October. In *Memories* (p. 130) Fisher stated that he had an interview with Dacres 'a few days' after his visit to Kiel. No doubt, such an interview did take place, though it may well have been in October. In any event, Fisher in later years built up one of his favourite stories out of his exchange with the First Sea Lord; it appears in one of his prints of late 1903[3] and is repeated in *Records* (p. 177):

It is an historical fact that the British Navy stubbornly resists change.

A First Sea Lord told me on one occasion that there were no torpedoes when he came to sea, and he didn't see why the devil there should be any of the beastly things now!

This was a propos of my attracting the attention of his serene and contented mind to the fact that we hadn't got any torpedoes at that time in the British Navy, and that a certain Mr. Whitehead (with whom I was acquainted) had devised an automobile torpedo, costing only £500, that would make a hole as big as his Lordship's carriage (then standing at the door) in the bottom of the strongest and biggest ship in the world, and she would go to the bottom in about five minutes.

Fisher always enjoyed a good story—whether as raconteur or (which is in his favour) as listener. However, particularly after entering on his grandiose period round about 1900, he harboured little respect for the niceties of historical scholarship unless they happened to serve either one of his schemes of reform or the

---

[1] Adm. 1/6128; 1/6130.   [2] Adm. 1/6130.   [3] F.P. 4940.

interests of his reputation. In *Memories* (p. 130) there is another exuberant though otherwise contrasting travesty of the interview with Dacres:

As quite a young Lieutenant, with extraordinary impudence I told the then First Sea Lord of the Admiralty that the Hertz German Submarine Mine, which I had seen a few days before in Kiel Harbour, would so far revolutionise sea warfare as possibly to prevent one fleet pursuing another, by the Fleet that was flying dropping submarine mines in its wake; and certainly that sudden sea operations of the old Nelsonic type would seriously be interfered with. He very good humouredly sent me away as a young desperado, as he remembered that I had been a lunatic in prophesying the doom of masts and sails, which were then magnificently supreme . . . [p. 151:] I have remarked elsewhere how the First Lord [*sic*] of that date did not believe in mines or torpedoes, and I left for China as Commander of the China flagship.

It will be seen that Fisher was indeed progressive over the matter of masts and sails; but he does not seem to have pronounced on this subject till March 1871.

Fisher's views on his life and prospects in the autumn of 1869 are indicated in a letter which he wrote to his wife in December 1870 and also by an item in his memoirs which agrees well enough with that letter:[1] he was very happily married with two young children; he was absorbed in his technical work and in its wider applications; and he hoped to go to the Admiralty as Assistant Director of Naval Ordnance rather than to the *Ocean* (then on the China station) as Commander. It appears from the same sources that Captain F. Beauchamp Seymour, Private Secretary to the First Lord at the material time, played some part in having Fisher sent to the *Ocean*—in the interests of the latter's naval career. Although Fisher was invariably successful in his various seagoing roles, the real focus of his interest from 1862 onwards was the *Excellent*, with the Admiralty emerging as a serious rival by 1869. Apart from Seymour, the persons responsible for the switch were Dacres and Childers, as may be seen from a minute addressed by the First Lord to the First Sea Lord on 24 October 1869: 'I have no objection to Comr. Fisher being appointed to Ocean, and his nomination to the Torpedo Committee being cancelled.'[2]

Finally, before leaving the subject of Fisher's early connexion

---

[1] *F.G.* i, 70; *Memories*, p. 140.   [2] Adm. 1/6130.

with mines and torpedoes, some account must be given of current views on naval tactics. Otherwise it can hardly be understood why, in his report of 21 August 1869, Fisher deemed 'Harvey's divergent Torpedo' to be '(all things considered) apparently far superior' not only to the suicidal outriggers but also to the Whitehead. As Fisher explained with the aid of a diagram, Harvey's scheme was that the attacking vessel would tow, on the end of 100 yards of rope extending from each quarter, a torpedo weighing about 2 cwt. when charged and ballasted. There would be a cork buoy 40 feet astern of, and sustaining, each torpedo. With the towing vessel advancing at 6 knots, the two torpedoes would swing out until the tow-ropes each formed an angle of 45° with the line of advance. 'Now', continued Fisher warming to his theme, 'if the enemy can be made to come any-where in the 100 yards between the Torpedo Ship and the Torpedo, he will be blown up. In the case of suddenly coming across a friend, it is only requisite to stop the Ship or let go the towing hawser when the Torpedo will at once sink to a depth of 40 feet where it will remain suspended by the buoy.' Among the advantages he adduced in favour of Harvey's torpedo are these: 'They cannot explode without being in actual contact with the enemy'; 'You never need approach the enemy's Vessel nearer than 70 or 100 yards' as compared with the 'training and nerve, needed for the run-in with an outrigger; there was a margin of manoeuvre of 70 yards when attacking; and (an attribute always attractive to Fisher) the Harvey torpedo represented 'Cheapness and Simplicity'. It could be 'used from any Ship whatever without any special fitting, though of course the smaller and faster the Vessel the better; but still, even in the case of the most unhandy vessel they may be of great use. For example, you are ramming a Ship and by her superior handiness you just miss her. Then Harvey will blow her up.'

Of course, the question which presents itself to a twentieth-century mind is: Why would the enemy not settle the issue by gunfire long before 'Harvey' could 'blow her up'?

The crux of the matter—and indeed of the state of naval tactics generally—is the effectiveness of gunfire. It is clear that there was much curiosity, at least amongst such officers as attended meetings at the Royal United Service Institution (henceforth R.U.S.I.) about the accuracy of gunfire and thus the tactics which should be used in fleet and single-ship actions.

In 1872 Commander William Dawson complained: 'The Navy does not record, or recording, does not publish to its Officers, any of its gunnery experiences. We are, therefore, driven to the War Department for official naval intelligence, scraps of which are given in those "Extracts of Artillery Proceedings".' However, there was a fairly general consensus amongst naval officers between 1866 and 1880 that gunfire alone was unlikely to prove conclusive in an encounter between fleets of steam-driven ironclads. There was only one example of this kind of action available for analysis and this was the Battle of Lissa (fought between the Austrian and Italian fleets in the Adriatic as a somewhat irrelevant by-product of Bismarck's anti-Austrian designs).

In April 1867 Commander Philip Colomb gave a lecture at the R.U.S.I. entitled 'Lessons from Lissa'. Fisher became interested in the transactions of the Institution round about this time and from the drift of his remarks (1869) about 'Offensive Torpedoes' it is reasonable to conclude that he had read Colomb's printed lecture and the following discussion. Everyone interested in naval affairs had in any case been impressed by the sinking of the (unhappily named) *Re d'Italia* by the Austrian flagship. The decisive weapon on this occasion was the ram. Gunfire had no important effect. Admittedly, numerous would-be rammers had scored nothing better than a grazing blow (though the fading of Italian enthusiasm just before the moment of impact had perhaps contributed to the general impression of elusiveness). During the discussion at the R.U.S.I., Commander Dawson inferred from the number of narrow escapes from ramming that the Harvey torpedo might prove to be the weapon of the future.

However, the actual ramming of the *Re d'Italia*, perhaps inevitably, produced more effect on opinion than the less tangible features of the battle. (For the record, the ramming vessel—a sturdy steam-frigate of 5,130 tons—delivered the *coup de grâce* by the imaginative device of backing away from her adversary. The plug having been thereby removed, the *Re d'Italia* instantly sank.) This victory for the ram continued to exercise a marked influence on naval construction and tactical thought for at least thirty years; and its influence will shortly be seen in Fisher's pamphlet on 'Naval Tactics', written in the Far East in 1871.[1]

[1] *Journal of the R.U.S.I.* (1868), pp. 119–20, 124; (1872), pp. 12, 377; (1873), pp. 231–4; (1876), pp. 260–2; (1880), pp. 57–9. Parkes, p. 176; Lewis, pp. 141–2, 581–3.

CHAPTER 3

CHINA REVISITED AND THE
VERNON REBORN (1869–1876)

ONCE it had been decided at the Admiralty, in October 1869, that Fisher was to go to sea he seems, according to his memoirs, to have hoped to go to the flagship in the Mediterranean; but he remarked from the Olympian standpoint of 1919 that his 'life-long and good friend Lord Walter Kerr' was 'justly preferred' for the post. (Kerr was two years older than Fisher and ultimately pulled off the notable feat of reaching the top of the naval ladder just ahead of the latter. Having thus forestalled a much-disconcerted Fisher as First Sea Lord in 1899, he was then repeatedly harassed by Fisher until the latter eventually succeeded him in 1904.) Fisher admitted, in retrospect, that his draft to China (1869–72) 'turned out trumps'. As he put it, 'the Admiral got softening of the brain, and I was told that when he got home and attended at the Admiralty I was the only thing in his mind; the only thing he could say was "Fisher!" '.[1]

Fisher was appointed Commander of the *Donegal* on 8 November. She was one of the last wooden ships of the line and had been designed for auxiliary screw propulsion. Reliefs for ships on the China station, including the *Ocean*, were to take her out and turn her over to the crews they relieved. Shortly before his eventual return to England Fisher wrote to his wife from the China station and described his feelings on commissioning the ship on 25 November 1869:

Two years ago to-day since we commissioned the *Donegal* and in 17 days more it will be two years since we said 'goodbye'. I often try to think that I never can again feel so miserable as I did then. Everything then was as black as it could be; it was the first time we had really parted, and such a distant station, and such an exceptionally disagreeable way of starting, not in one's own ship, and over 1,200 people were packed on board anyhow, and, most of all, I did not feel that I knew my work, and so my mind was never at rest. I was constantly picturing myself as utterly failing in my work and having to

[1] *Memories*, p. 140.

come home on half-pay, much to everyone's surprise, and I could fancy so many fellows rubbing their hands at it: 'He could drill 'em very well on the Common [Southsea], but he had never been out of Portsmouth Harbour in his life, so what could you expect?' 'The *Excellent* ought to be done away with,' etc., etc. . . .[1]

However, these gloomy heart-searchings were hardly apparent to one J. T. McDonnell[2] whose memory retained, long afterwards, the following details:

. . . I first saw 'Jacky' standing on the poop of the old liner giving instructions to the assemblage of drafts as they arrived from the several depot ships and barracks. His orders were like peals of thunder, given in a good gunnery style. His arrangements were complete in every detail, there was not the least confusion with all these men who were mustered on the dockyard jetty . . . So thoroughly had all the little details been thought out that by supper time . . . everything was working as if the ship had been in commission for years . . .

The passage to China around the Cape was taken up by drills, drills, drills, exercises of every description, so that when the crews arrived at Hong Kong they were very efficient in all kinds [of] gunnery, rifle, and sail drill exercises . . . I believe of the 1,300 on board, Jacky could call everyone by name—not only call them by name, but could tell them where they were born and what religion they were supposed to be . . . in all my after [i.e. subsequent] 40 years service I never came across the equal of the 'Ocean's' ship's company for efficiency . . .[3]

Despite his activity as Commander aboard the *Donegal*, Fisher found time and energy to finish preparing the manuscript of the second edition of his book. This was published by Griffin & Co. of Portsmouth in 1871 under the title: *A Treatise on Electricity and the Construction and Management of Electrical and Mechanical Torpedoes*. This revised and enlarged work ran to 293 pages in its printed form; the Preface is dated April 1870 aboard the *Donegal* at Singapore. Admiralty approval of the new edition having been obtained in June 1869, Fisher arranged before leaving England for the proofs to be read by H. B. Stewart, who had succeeded Fisher as Senior Lieutenant of the *Excellent* on the latter's promotion to Commander, and W. J. L. Wharton who was then Flag Lieutenant to Sir James Hope. Otherwise,

---

[1] F.P. 1437 (*FG*).

[2] A rating in 1869, he rose to warrant rank as a Gunner in 1878 and was commissioned under Fisher's scheme of 1903.

[3] Kilv. MSS., Pkt. 41, J. T. McDonnell, Lt. Cdr. R.N. (Rtd.) to 2nd Ld. F., 18 Oct. 1921.

the publication of the book was arranged by correspondence between Fisher and Henry Boys, who had succeeded Hood as Captain of the *Excellent* on 12 July 1869.[1] In April 1870 Fisher wrote to Boys:

I have finished the Torpedo Book and have sent it to Griffin by this mail, with orders to send it to you directly the proofs are ready . . . I hope that you will be pleased with the book, and that you will let me know what you think of it when you get time to write. I have found it a very difficult business on account of having so much other work to do. I hope you will prevent any alterations being made because I believe there is nothing wrong, but more especially on account of the liability to disarrange other parts of the book, as one portion depends so much upon another.

I hope the 'Excellent' is flourishing; I can never feel so much interest in any ship as I do her. We are getting on famously well on board here; I have an idea that we shan't be much behind the 'Marlborough' when we have been a year in commission. Captain Hewitt [W. N. Hewett, V.C.] I like immensely. We hope to turn over to the 'Ocean' at Hong Kong about the first week in May. I shall be very glad when the time comes, for 1,200 men and such a large number of officers are not very easy to handle, although I am very glad indeed that I have gone through it, for I have learned more about discipline and organisation in the last 5 months that I ever expect to do for the rest of my time in the service . . .[2]

Fisher's diplomatic reference to Captain Hewett receives equivocal support from his letters to his wife. The transfer from the *Donegal* to the *Ocean* having taken place at Hong Kong in May, the homesick Fisher wrote on 13 June: 'I can't get used to the separation at all and feel every day to get worse instead of better.' These feelings were associated with Fisher's most intense religious phase and over the next two years his wife was kept fully informed on this subject. Hewett, however, did not share Fisher's convictions and his attachment to the Communion Service, as the latter explained to his wife in a letter of 9 December 1870.

I am so glad to be down at Hong Kong, as there is always Sacrament every Sunday at 8 a.m., to which I can go without interfering with my work in the ship, and I intend to go every Sunday without fail while we are here, for I so seldom get the chance anywhere else,

---

[1] Adm. 1/6087; 24/153; F.P. 5415. A copy of F.'s book is held at the Naval Library.

[2] F.P. 1. This item consists of a number of typescript copies of F.'s letters to Boys.

and when very occasionally we have it on board there's always an unpleasant feeling about it, as there are seldom more than 3 or 4 take it, so that one is in a certain kind of way held up to a certain kind of unpleasant public observation. The Captain never comes, and yet I see he feels he ought to come and he offers a sort of unpleasant kind of resistance to it, such as coming and asking me what the bell is tolling for and what the Chaplain is doing, etc., etc., which is not at all agreeable, as he must know of it, for the Chaplain always asks his leave before giving notice of the Communion. Now mind, darling, you don't mention anything of this; perhaps I ought not to have told you, as it may make you dislike Captain Hewett, but we all have our faults and he has very few, and we get on very well indeed together, only I wish I could feel he knew more than I did. It's a bad feeling on my part, I know, but I can't help feeling always that he could never tell me that I am wrong, and so I can't look up to him like I could to Goodenough or Admiral Key or Captain Wells or a dozen others I might mention, and I know he feels himself that he hasn't that professional force over me that he ought to have.[1]

On 11 December Fisher was writing again in similar vein, this time incorporating his views on Vice-Admiral Sir Henry Kellett, the Commander-in-Chief, China, who flew his flag aboard the *Ocean*.

I feel so very angry with the Admiral; I heard him half whispering to Mrs. Smith one of those blackguard sort of things that Mr. Martin Smith is in the habit of saying, asking her what Doctor she had in her confinement and how it went off . . . I struck in as well as I could so as to avoid her having to answer . . . He is always so very proper whenever I have been present before, and this time he hadn't the least idea I heard, but I believe he's a most wicked old wretch. He is always so extraordinarily civil to me that I am in great fear of Captain Hewett being jealous. He's constantly saying before Captain Hewett and a lot of people that as long as he has me by him to take care of him, he doesn't care what happens, and he asks me confidentially about things he speaks to no one else about at all. He hasn't a spark of religion about him, never goes to Church by any chance, and this together with his being an Irishman makes me distrust him.[2]

Against this background of religious preoccupation, it is of particular interest to read the following revelation, in a letter to his wife of 13 June 1870, of his feelings about his mother who was still living in Ceylon:

I heard from my Mother by this mail; she contemplates coming to see me as it only costs £14 she says, but I am going to write and tell

[1] *F.G.* i, 71.   [2] Ibid., p. 72.

her, it will cost her *at least* £2 a day living here and besides that I shall have very little time to see her . . . I am in a horrid fright of my Mother some day turning up unexpectedly when we are settled down somewhere; I'm sure we couldn't live together. I hate the very thought of it and really, I don't want to see her. I don't see why I should as I haven't the very slightest recollection of her.[1]

Yet some six years previously he had written to his Aunt Kate: 'I feel very anxious about my Mother and should you hear any-thing of her, would like very much to hear of it as I never get my letters until some time after the mail comes in.'[2]

Certainly, Fisher's antipathy towards his mother seems to date from round about the time of his marriage. Before this event, he was affectionate towards his brothers and sisters and continued to be so at least into the 1870s. While there is evidence that he was annoyed by his mother's tendency to look to him for financial assistance—on at least one occasion she drew money from his agent without specific consultation[3]—and while he may well have felt that other members of the family were not accepting a fair share of the burden, it is doubtful whether this goes to the heart of the trouble. After 1870 Fisher's proclivity for destroying old personal relationships, whether with friends in the Navy or with close relatives, becomes gradually more marked. For example, in 1875 Fisher's elder sister Alice (by then a widow of thirty-three) proceeded to marry her first cousin, Commander F. A. Sargeaunt. Up to this time, Fisher had shown every sign of being fond not only of his sister but also of his cousin, Sargeaunt. However, once he learnt that marriage was in the offing he vehemently declared his opposition on general grounds to the union of first cousins, and issued a warning to the effect that, if his views were disregarded, he would never speak again to either of the offending parties. Mrs. Alice Sargeaunt's grand-daughter is able to vouch for the fact that this threat was literally fulfilled.[4]

Of course, such behaviour might be interpreted simply as that of a strong-willed individual bent on securing his own way; an ample capacity for hating as well as loving is already indicated, for instance, in the letters of 1859–60. But it seems at least a

[1] Kilv. MSS., Pkt. 6.

[2] Ibid., F. to Mrs. Whimper, 15 Mar. 1864.

[3] F.P. 1437.

[4] Information from Mrs. M. F. Wentworth Reeve, CBE, TD, JP. Although she never spoke with her great-uncle she did on one occasion stand near him—when he was lying in his coffin before his public funeral in July 1920!

reasonable hypothesis that Fisher's experience of being sent away from Ceylon at the age of six, while the younger children stayed with their parents, had some long-term effect. Highly emotional and craving female affection, he was clearly much affected by the early years of his marriage. They brought much happiness—also spiritual and emotional disturbance. The financial trouble associated with his mother does nothing to explain his severance of relations with his sister, Alice. Nor, in the case of his mother, can the financial factor—irritant though it was—have been completely decisive. For example, two months after complaining about his mother drawing money direct from his agent, Fisher was proposing to his wife that they should give away '£18 5s. od. a year in charity'. This, he wrote, would amount to 'just a shilling a day and 1/20' of his pay; 'and this', he added, 'is the VERY LEAST that we ought to give.' Other evidence shows that he did in fact make a number of gifts to charity.[1]

Despite his latter-day ability to dominate individuals and groups, it will appear that Fisher was occasionally to display a curious unwillingness to take a decisive stand and even to accept responsibility. Possibly, his early separation from his family left him with a residual sense of insecurity even when he was at the height of his prestige and power. But, notwithstanding, his dominant characteristics were overflowing energy, aggressiveness, and zest for life.

December 1870 found Fisher chafing at his remoteness from the Admiralty where there had been some possibility of the post of Assistant Director to Naval Ordnance falling vacant. He understood from Hewett that Beauchamp Seymour (who seems to have understood Fisher very well) was determined to keep him in the *Ocean* till she paid off. Fisher recognized that this was probably for his own good; yet he continued to fume at the possible check to his ambitions. He wrote to his wife that 'the mere fact of being at the Admiralty gives one a great lift in the Service, as one gets to know all the bigwigs so intimately. I feel quite sure that it is a most horrid mistake being so far away from England—one either gets forgotten or else it's too far off to send for anyone even if a good billet does offer.'[2]

[1] F.P. 1437, F. to Mrs. F., 25 Nov. 1871 (*FG*); Kilv. MSS., Pkt. 6, F. to Mrs. F., 25 Jan. 1872 (*FG*).
[2] *F.G.* i, 70.

In fact, quite apart from his being evidently marked out as one of the most promising officers in the Navy, there was no likelihood of Fisher's continued existence being forgotten at the Admiralty. It has already been mentioned that he had sent the manuscript of the second edition of the *Treatise* to England in April 1870. The arrangement was that the first copy actually printed would in due course be sent to the Admiralty for their Lordships' approval.[1] Then, having taken up his post as Commander of the *Ocean* in May, Fisher not only played a great part in bringing the ship up to a high standard of efficiency; he also proceeded to bombard the Admiralty, through the normal service channels, with information about his various technical activities. At Hong Kong on 23 June he wrote to his commanding officer with their Lordships in mind.

The successful removal of the upper deck of the 'Dunmail' by means of Electric Torpedoes was attended with such a certain amount of difficulty as to lead me to bring the circumstances to your notice in the hope that they will prove interesting to their Lordships and be of service to those who are now engaged in perfecting the management of Torpedoes at home.

The British ship 'Dunmail', carrying a cargo of the estimated value of £70,000, was wrecked close to the Lyemoon Pass and within sight of the anchorage of Hong Kong on the 6th May. She struck upon a rock (which dries at low water), was back off from it, and sunk in about 12 fathoms. As the value of the cargo was so great, it was considered the best course to give up the idea of saving the ship, which would have occupied a considerable time, and to devote all efforts to the recovery of the cargo before any further deterioration took place.

For this purpose it was found indispensable that the whole of the upper deck should be removed as, besides the difficulty of obtaining access to the hold on account of the stowage on the upper deck, it was found that the lives of the divers were constantly endangered through portions of the cargo suddenly rising up when they were between decks and jamming them there.

He went on to give details of the various explosive charges which proved most effective at that depth and the various means

[1] 600 copies were printed. On the initiative of Captain Hood, 100 of these were interleaved so that Gunnery Lieutenants, retaining their copies, could make notes beside the text. The officer, according to the D.N.O., 'will be constantly adding to the value of the book by the addition of such incidents or ideas on the various points treated therein as may come before him'. Adm. 1/6184. Hood's minute of 15 Aug. 1871.

which were employed to keep the water out of the electrically fired 'torpedoes'. In the end, 'the remainder of the upper deck was completely removed without the slightest damage to the cargo or a hitch of any kind.' Fisher's own satisfaction with this performance was enhanced by an appreciative letter written to Hewett by the ship's insurance agents at Hong Kong on 30 June. So much cargo would 'probably not' have been saved, in the opinion of the agents, if it had not been for 'the exertions of Commander Fisher and the divers' and 'had the Salvage been dependent on our local resources only'.

Fisher rounded off his own report with a clear indication to the Admiralty of the focus of his current interests: 'If this letter meets with your Lordships' approval, I hope on a future occasion (should time and opportunity present themselves) to offer some more submissions for their Lordships' consideration on subjects connected with the management of Torpedoes.' The Board did not reply directly to this feeler, but an official letter of thanks was sent for Fisher's 'very interesting report of the Torpedo Experiments made by him in removing the upper deck of the British ship "Dunmail" '.[1]

Needless to say, Fisher did not wait for their Lordships' letter to catch up with the *Ocean* at Nagasaki on 16 November before harnessing his extraordinary energies to further work on 'torpedoes'. However, by the autumn he was turning his attention back in the direction of gunnery, in which field he made a more valuable over-all technical contribution, despite a period of reduced interest during 1873–8, than in the sphere of 'torpedoes'. This technical contribution was, in any case, a minor one compared with his work as an administrator. It was on the organizational rather than the purely technical side of the Navy that Fisher's real proclivities lay. But as a young Commander in 1870, he was only just reaching the rank and status that would enable him to emerge in such a role.

In the previous chapter reference was made to Fisher's suggestion (printed as an appendix to the first edition of the *Treatise* on 'torpedoes') for 'Firing Guns by Electricity'. Although this suggestion was duly rejected by the Ordnance Select Committee, the successive D.N.O.s, Rear-Admiral Key and Captain Hood, continued to attach importance to the idea.

[1] F.P. 5415 has copies of Fisher's report, the letter from the insurers, and the Admiralty's letter of appreciation dated 10 Sept. 1870.

This can be seen from the alternative firing arrangements provided aboard the epochal first-rate warships *Thunderer* and *Devastation* which were laid down in June and November 1869. As Parkes has written, the *Devastation* (completed, well ahead of the *Thunderer*, in 1873) was, with 'her quasi-monitor hull, turret armament and its distribution, absence of masting, twin screws and huge coal supply', fit to rank in her day as 'even more of a wonder ship than the *Dreadnought* of 1906'. It will soon be seen that Fisher was fully in agreement with the 'absence of masting'. Moreover, provision was made aboard the *Devastation* for firing the guns by electricity from the conning tower, when required.[1] It was mentioned in the previous chapter that Key favoured adoption of Fisher's scheme to provide an optional method of firing while Hood was inclined to depend on it entirely. However, Key's view was evidently accepted by Hood when he went to the Admiralty in the summer of 1869. In sum, it seems fair to credit Fisher with at least a share in the original thinking which resulted in this notable technical development.

While the *Devastation* was being built, Fisher was already installing a system of electrical firing aboard the *Ocean*. This leaky, fully rigged, timber-hulled ironclad, with her main armament of 7-inch and 8-inch M.L.R.s arranged in broadsides, was a far cry from the *avant-garde* design of the *Devastation*.[2] Nevertheless, Bacon seems to be correct in stating that she was the first British warship to be fitted with electrical firing.[3] Fisher wrote to his wife from Amoy on 4 December 1870:

> You will be glad to hear that I have just finished another most tremendous letter to the Admiralty which will puzzle Captain Hood immensely, I feel sure. Don't say anything about it, it's pointing out an awful lot of humbug in the way all our guns are arranged on board ship. I have been having a very great success with the electric firing and introduced a lot of new dodges.[4]

Fisher's letter to the Admiralty was dated 1 December and began as follows:

> By a recent circular their Lordships have authorized the firing of ships' guns by electricity and they have detailed the stores which may

---

[1] Parkes, pp. 195–8.

[2] The *Ocean* was the only British ironclad ever to double the Cape of Good Hope under canvas. Having sailed to China in 1867 she was not docked till her return to England in 1872 (Parkes, p. 58).

[3] Bacon, i, 40.   [4] *F.G.* i, 69.

be demanded for that purpose. I therefore submit the experience we have had in firing the 'Ocean's' guns according to this plan as offering fresh proofs of its efficacy and I hope that the observations I may make will be worthy of their Lordships' attention.

Then followed details of how they 'ensured the guns being accurately laid for direction and elevation when not using the sights; also the means taken to evade the use of Moorsom's director' which Fisher thought 'quite inadequate to present requirements'. He gave 'six reasons' for using 'the standard compass instead' when directing the fire. He remarked, for example, that 'one has not to be running about from one side of the deck to the other as in using Moorsom's director for each broadside but the firer always remains in one central fixed position'; and 'being carefully adjusted in gimbols, it is always horizontal and so the eye is kept quietly on the horizon. But in using the Moorsom's director the eye is one moment upon a big wave to be the next instant directed to heaven.' He claimed that his methods had been rewarded in practice 'with complete success for the target was covered with every broadside'.[1]

McDonnell's recollection of this strenuous period was that

The first two years of the 'Ocean's' commission was a very hard one—continuous exercises—also really very happy. Jacky was a perfect organizer. The minutest detail was thought out, and he was always ready to learn himself . . . [Fisher held field days ashore at Kowloon.] Jacky would often invite military officers to see the ship's company carry out these exercises and it would astonish them to see the proficiency to which they (the ship's company) had been trained in Company and Battalion movements.[2]

In these exercises ashore can be discerned the origin of Fisher's concept of the British Army as a seaborne force; his close interest in the details of operations carried out by small military forces implies his conviction of their relevance to naval strategy. The most important of these exercises is described by notes in Fisher's hand entitled 'Abstract of the Landing Party of H.M.S. "Ocean" by the Commander-in-Chief at Kowloon, on Jan. 26, 1871'.

509 Officers and Men were landed. The organization was as follows:—

> 6 companies of blue-jacket small-arm men.
> 1 company of Marines.
> 2 field gun crews . . .

[1] F.P. 5415.   [2] Kilv. MSS., Pkt. 41.

The men were landed in gaiters and carried haversacks and bamboo water bottles; their blankets were made up so as to be carried as knapsacks . . .

The Admiral and his staff were received in line with a general salute; after which he went round the ranks and inspected the men individually. He also exercised the scaling ladder and stretcher parties . . .

The object of the first portion of the programme was to show that all the seamen and boys were acquainted with the rifle, cutlass, and sword bayonet exercises; and that they could march in line and could wheel by companies with facility although on broken ground.

The second portion of the programme consisted of the following movements:[1] Two companies were thrown out skirmishing, two companies as their supports, and the remainder of the bluejackets formed the reserve; the Marines acting as the main body . . . The whole force then retired across a bridge in contact with a supposed enemy. The main approach to the bridge was defended by electric mines which were laid down by the shelter trench party as the retreat was being effected . . .

REMARKS

The ground at Kowloon is well adapted to show out to advantage all those movements which would probably be required in actual practice, being rugged and broken in places, possessing a moderate amount of cover for skirmishers with good commanding positions for artillery and in some places offering employment for scaling ladders. The shelter trench party were found to be sufficient to throw up an epaulement in three places for the field guns . . . and laid down the electric mines in the concluding movement. These mines were placed in a series and were exploded by Dynamo Electricity when the main body of the enemy was supposed to be about to cross the bridge . . . The Field Battery was placed on a commanding height which was considered to be the key of the position . . . The stretcher party were constantly employed carrying in men (supposed to be wounded) from the line of skirmishers, a small field hospital having been extemporised in rear of the position.

The skirmishers, supports and reserves were moved by signal . . .

The application of spare field gun limbers for the supply of spare ammunition proved very successful. One was stationed in rear of each company of skirmishers and was always dismounted when not in motion so as not to attract the enemy's attention. When in motion they were instructed always to move at the double. A couple of picks and shovels sent with each limber allowed them to throw up a little earth as protection when no natural cover presented itself. A dozen

---

[1] Six in number.

small cartridge cases went with each limber to facilitate the supply of ammunition. These were thrown to the Petty Officers of the companies as the limbers passed them. The Petty Officers then distributed the ammunition to their respective sections.[1]

All this goes some way to explain why McDonnell wrote, so long afterwards, that in forty years of subsequent service he 'never came across the equal of the "Ocean's" ship's company for efficiency'. The Commander-in-Chief held a somewhat similar opinion; on 15 January 1871 he had written a favourable report of an inspection of the *Ocean* and the relevant digest volume records the official letters of appreciation—'Capt. W. N. W. Hewett, Comr. J. A. Fisher & Lt. I. Cole praised for state of "Ocean" on inspection by Sir H. Kellett.'[2]

Fisher pursued the subject of seaborne landings in a detailed paper entitled a 'Rough plan of organization of the China Squadron for an attack on the Corea' compiled in July 1871.[3] This was a minute account of the ships, gunboats, and hired junks required for the operation, together with the organization of the landing force consisting of 600 seamen with 6 field guns, 500 marines with 6 field guns, and a number of coolies. 'The Coolie Force should consist of 1,100 men. They will be for commissariat purposes, also to aid in dragging the field guns and carrying the spare ammunition and to serve with the field hospital and in conveying wounded and sick to the rear. They should be divided into 7 distinct parties . . .' It is clear that Fisher's interest lay in the precise organization of the vessels and forces involved rather than in the reasons for landing at all or even in the precise form of the operation. For example, the organization of the gunboats strongly implies that the initial landing will be contested, but this is never actually stated. However, the plan is impressive in its Teutonic thoroughness: the 'deep draught' of every gunboat is given to the inch and the exact details of armaments and distribution of men in boats is readily available at a glance from carefully prepared tables. Fisher even makes an attempt to improve on the contemporary techniques for getting men and guns ashore:

The steam launches, boom boats and cutters of the Squadron should be formed into a division by themselves and organized both

[1] F.P. 5415.
[2] IND. 18101, No. 85a; 18085. Kellett's report of 15 Jan. 1871 has been weeded.
[3] F.P. 5415.

for landing the men and for acting on the offensive. Four rafts should be constructed of casks and spars similar to those used in the Indian troop ships for disembarking the men. The rafts would be of great advantage. The landing can be effected closer to dry land and the boats, from being clear of men, are more easily handled and freer to act on the offensive. These rafts offer great facilities for landing the field guns, as broad planks laid from the edge of the raft to the shore will probably get over the usual difficulty experienced in landing on mud shores, as the weight of the gun falling from the bows often causes it to bury itself entirely, when not only is there great difficulty in extricating it, but it takes considerable time after getting it on shore to render it free from dirt and fit for use. Should the rafts from any cause (such as a very strong tideway) be found impracticable, it is estimated that the boats would land the seamen, marines and guns in one trip, if properly arranged, provided they had been previously practised at getting in the boats. (See detailed arrangements for this on next page.) The field guns would offer the chief difficulty in this case . . .

Fisher was clearly concerned to benefit from his unpleasant experience at the Peiho forts in 1859, to which he made explicit reference. However, he evidently failed to discover grounds on which this evidence of capacity for operational planning could be sent to the Admiralty. But there remained the 'torpedoes'. These were never far from his mind and on 27 August he completed a paper headed 'Reporting Torpedo Operations'[1] which duly went to the Admiralty and probably had considerable effect in determining his more immediate future.

Fisher had already submitted in January 1871 an account of a series of experiments but there is no trace of this communication in the Admiralty indexes—perhaps because he sent the material directly to Hood. At Chefoo on 27 August Fisher began a letter which was, in due course, well received by their Lordships.[2]

Sir,
 In continuation of my letter of January last, I beg to submit to you for the information of the Director of Naval Ordnance several experiments I have made with

   I Towed Electric Torpedoes.
   II Outrigger Electric Torpedoes.
   III Extempore Electric Fuzes.

[1] F.P. 5415. The fair copy has been weeded from the Admiralty files but it is recorded in the indexes.

[2] IND. 18101. '*Commr. J. A. Fisher.* Report on Torpedo experiments. Praised for his zeal and ingenuity.' 29 Oct. 1871.

He went on to explain that the first type of 'torpedoes experimented upon are in principle those of Commander Harvey, but their shape and mode of firing appear to differ sufficiently to merit attention.' He drew attention to the fact that 'the necessarily few experiments', though 'constructed by the ship's artificers in 24 hours' diverged like Harvey's 'and that such Torpedoes have been exploded at will by Electricity although the towing rope containing the electric wire was subjected to almost a breaking strain.'

On 19 July he practised attacks on the *Ocean* at anchor with a torpedo towed by a steam launch, and 'also practised on Junks under weigh'. Later, he towed torpedoes from the *Ocean* at 4½ and 5 knots; he also gave details of various electrical tests aiming to increase the reliability of the torpedoes as regards detonation. As in his report of 21 August 1869, he emphasized the 'peculiar advantages of firing at will by Electricity' though, of course, it was the Harvey torpedo which he had in mind in August 1871 rather than the electrical mine.

The Torpedo can be fired when perhaps actual contact with the enemy is missed and as these Torpedoes could carry somewhere about 500 lbs. of gun cotton without being too unwieldy for use from ships, the Torpedo might be exploded with destructive effect at some little distance from the enemy. Again this mode of firing makes it absolutely safe against your own ships. This cannot be said to be equally the case with mechanical or even electric Torpedoes when acting by percussion. *The fact of contact is so liable to damage in the former case the safety arrangements and in the latter case the circuit-closing apparatus.*

So here again is to be seen the trend of thought which probably influenced Fisher's attitude when the Hertz fuse was actually offered to the Admiralty in 1874.

The outrigger experiments performed in June and August likewise entailed electrical detonation. As usual the attacking boat was liable to be abruptly lifted from the surface by the explosion, dropped, and then drenched by the fall of water. These hazards, to say nothing of those involved in closely approaching an enemy in the first place, were obviously considerable; but they were (according to Fisher) insufficient to discourage the Torpedo Corps recently established in the American Navy. 'The 1st Lieutenant of the U.S. corvette "Alaska", who has been attached till lately to the Torpedo Department at Washington, informs me that all their vessels now carry

Mechanical Torpedoes which can be used either from their ships or their steam launches in the form of outrigger torpedoes.' Fisher testified to his strong preference for electrical over mechanical fuses by giving details of 835 tests which he had carried out on extemporized electrical fuses. Not surprisingly, he remarked in a private letter to Henry Boys dated 22 August: 'I find it very uphill work carrying on those matters, for of course the ship must be the principal object of my affections, and I find her uncommon *exigeante*.'[1]

This kind of technical activity seems to have persisted through most of the *Ocean's* commission. F. G. Olliver (a Midshipman and then a Sub-lieutenant aboard the *Ocean*) long afterwards remembered Fisher's electrical firing and the Harvey-type torpedoes. 'He worked out an arrangement by which *all* the guns on the broadside (12) could be laid on the target and fired simultaneously by day and night. He also constantly experimented with rough made torpedoes towed from the after yards of the ship.'

The same witness testified to Fisher's agreeable relations with the junior officers. 'He was very kind to some of us youngsters, frequently taking us for walks in Japan.' In general, as J. T. McDonnell remarked of the same commission, 'He was clever himself and he liked clever people around him.' On the side of personnel, an important point remembered by McDonnell was that Fisher 'was really the Warrant Officers' and Seamen's friend, and no officer that I have ever met better understood human nature.' Fisher's interest in and understanding of the lower deck was to prove a valuable ingredient in a career frequently occupied with questions of *matériel*.[2]

In sum, despite Fisher's restlessness aboard the *Ocean* and his craving for closer contact with the Admiralty and the *Excellent*, this spell of two years in the Far East represents a crucial stage in his advance towards maturity as a naval officer. This can best be illustrated by focusing attention on two papers of a more general character than those which have already been reviewed. These deal with 'Naval Tactics' and 'Gunnery, Ammunition and Administration'.

The earliest surviving version of the paper on 'Naval Tactics' is dated 23 March 1871 at Hong Kong.[3] Fisher's latter-day

[1] F.P.I. (*FG*).   [2] Kilv. MSS., Pkt. 41.   [3] F.P. 5415.

account of how he came to write this paper was published in *Records* (p. 211):

When I was 'sore let and hindered' in the days of my youth as a young Lieutenant, a cordial hand was always held out to me by Commodore Goodenough. He was killed by the South Sea Islanders with a poisoned arrow. Being on intimate terms with him, I sent him, in 1868, a reasoned statement proving conclusively that masts and sails were damned as the motive power of warships.

Alongside this may be set the following which occurs in Fisher's biographical manuscript:

About 1867, 50 years ago that is, I wrote a letter to Commodore Goodenough saying that sails were doomed—propulsion no longer above the deck but below it—the Engineer was the coming man! Commodore Goodenough without my knowledge printed my letter and circulated it—he was afterwards murdered by cannibals in the South Seas. I was sent for to the Admiralty by the First Sea Lord and bastinadoed! But they put a printed copy of my letter in the Admiralty Library![1]

The printed version is indeed still to be seen in the aforesaid library (now the Naval Library, Ministry of Defence); and it includes the following brief preamble which confirms 1871 as the true year of composition:

The following observations seem to me so worthy of circulation that I have caused them to be printed, to be attached to a memoir which I am preparing on Naval Tactics.

June 20th, 1871   J. G. Goodenough,
                                   Captain, Royal Navy.

Fisher's latter-day disclaimer of any active desire to have the paper printed is hardly borne out by an introductory note on a second manuscript copy of 1872, apparently prepared with a further printing in view:

This paper was written a considerable time ago [probably in fact only a year] and was somewhat widely circulated by a friend to whom it was sent. It met with such approval and provoked so much discussion that the Author ventures to give it a more extended circulation. Although through the kindness of numerous friends he has been made well aware of its many shortcomings, yet the writer thinks it best and more honest to submit the paper as it originally appeared.[2]

---

[1] F.P. 5101.   [2] F.P. 5415.

The interest shown by other naval officers in the paper (which does not seem in fact to have been reprinted) is indicated in a lecture given on naval tactics by Commander Cyprian Bridge at the Royal United Service Institution in February 1873: 'Though there are not wanting Officers who have bestowed upon NAVAL TACTICS much thought and patient study; still, it cannot be denied, that the consideration of the art, has not occupied the minds of the great body of Naval Officers in general.' He referred, however, to 'Captain Goodenough, Commander William Dawson, and Commander Fisher' as 'students of tactics' and acknowledged Philip Colomb as the leading British thinker on the subject. Bridge still envisaged a Lissa-type engagement with the opposed squadrons passing through each other and suffering no decisive damage, though he thought that some shots would hit their target and some success would be achieved with divergent or outrigger torpedoes. Immobilized ships might be 'conveniently disposed of by one of Mr. Whitehead's torpedoes'. He continued: 'My friend Commander Fisher, in a most interesting little pamphlet, quotes the opinion of a distinguished French Admiral, that "the armour-plated navy recognizes no fundamental order of battle." ' Bridge could not accept such a verdict. He thought that the *peloton* (or group) would permit both bow-fire and broadside-fire. He advocated *pelotons* arranged *en échelon*, but did not wish to see this made obligatory.[1]

Turning to a consideration of the contents of Fisher's paper, one may at once remark that, while he forcefully argued that '*Masts and sails should be done away with*', he was not original in this. According to Colomb, even the relatively cautious Captain Key, when serving in the *Excellent* in 1863–6, 'did not see clearly how sails were to be retained' aboard the ironclad of the future. 'He did not even then think them of propulsive advantage to the ship.'[2] But characteristically, Fisher during his long spell at the *Excellent* had absorbed the various items of advanced thought then current. Thus, the abolition of masts and sails had become part of his naval philosophy. This eclectic approach does not reduce the interest of 'Naval Tactics' as a summary of Fisher's thinking on the subject; indeed the value of the paper as an indicator of the current state of tactical thinking, to say nothing of proficiency, is thereby enhanced. The paper also touches on a

[1] *Journal of the R.U.S.I.* (1873), pp. 227–35.
[2] Colomb, p. 375.

number of important points connected with the question of tactics and therefore merits extensive quotation.

NAVAL TACTICS

The following observations are made chiefly with the view of drawing attention to the two following points:

I. The substitution of a shorter and simpler system of Fleet Tactics than we have at present.

II. The adoption of a system of tactics for actions between single ships.

The English, French and Russian Navies have elaborated ingenious systems of tactics—more especially the French. The principle which guides the manoeuvres of a battery of field artillery appears to be the basis of them all.

To be a master of all the combinations laid down in the signal book (as well as of the exact course, speed and helm to be given to each vessel in order to attain her required position in all of these numerous formations, and the avoidance of collisions with other ships, moving with great speed and in diverse directions) is to suppose the captains of our ships to be men of such nerve and self-confidence as could only have been acquired by a long service in squadrons of exercise and great familiarity in the handling of large ships. Now what would usually be the case, and especially should war break out, leading to the commissioning of a large number of new ships?

But a small proportion of the Captains and Officers would have exercised in a fleet of iron-clads; and there never can be but a small proportion of Captains, as only the seniors are appointed to the large iron-clads; and these we don't have in reserve against an eventuality for they go on to either the Admirals' List or situations (such as Steam Reserves or Dockyards) from which it would be most impolitic to remove them on the breaking out of a war.

With the latest alterations, there are no less than 43 distinct evolutions, differing in character and which require to be explained in the signal book by means of diagrams . . .

There are only two formations, as a rule, which we require in the presence of the enemy:

I. THE LINE ABREAST   (Ready to attack or be attacked; that is ready to ram or be rammed.)

II. THE LINE AHEAD   (From which, in any required direction or situation, the above formation can be attained.)

See what simplicity and efficiency would at once be gained by only having these two movements to practise and remember. No one says that our present formations are difficult to understand or practise; but they are too numerous and unnecessary . . .

Lord Nelson's practice should still hold good: have if possible one undeviating mode of advance. Make the first attack together and by order, after which every Captain should be his own master, and must follow out, to the best of his ability, those principles of 'single-ship tactics' which we will presently sketch out . . . our plans have this great advantage over those of Nelson, that they are not dependent upon winds or sails.

As to the manner in which 'Line Abreast' or 'Line for Action' should be formed from 'Line Ahead' or vice versa, there is little to be said . . . To attain either of these formations in any other direction or situation, there can be nothing simpler or easier than for each ship upon the hauling down of the signal to make the best of her own way to her new place . . .

It would be of advantage were squadrons to be exercised at avoiding collisions in the following manner. Let buoys be dropped marking a circle of half a mile radius (or according to the size of the squadron). Let the ships enter this circle at a speed of 6 knots in line abreast and then disperse with orders to continue at that speed within the circle for an hour. Such ships as decreased speed or overstepped the circle (being obliged to do so to avoid collision) to be considered as badly handled and treated accordingly. In course of time as the ships were more perfectly handled, the speed should be increased or the circle narrowed.

There can be no doubt that once having engaged the enemy, there will be no more manoeuvring as a fleet. It will be all single-ship fighting. This appears evident from the following considerations: the whole order of the fleet will be disarranged by some ships passing through the enemy unhurt and unchecked in their course; by some becoming entangled with the ships of the enemy; whilst others, managed with better judgement, will be preparing for the return charge, having stopped and turned immediately on the enemy avoiding their impact.

The signal book will then be practically useless. In fact the use of signals at such a time would be fraught with danger. They would fetter the action and diminish the responsibility of the Captains . . .

It may be asked, why is there more necessity now than in former days for the course which should be followed in engagements between single ships? In answer to this, we observe that though there were no written instructions on the point, there were traditional rules which were felt to be even more binding. There was the attainment of the weather gauge (thus keeping in your own hands the choice of time

for the action); the damaging of the enemy's spars as you bore down
. . . there is much more necessity now than in former days for principles and rules to guide single ships when in action, for there are no
precedents to go by as was formerly the case, and instead of guns
alone being the means of attack, we have now Ramming, Torpedoes,
Top Mitrailleuse, etc., etc.

We suggest four modes of attack by single ships and we place them
in the order they would be used:

    I. The Bow Gun Attack.
   II. The Ramming Attack.
  III. The Torpedo Attack.
  IV. The Broadside Guns.

Ramming is now almost universally acknowledged to be the
great mode of attack and the guns are considered as auxiliaries. This
view prevails to a much greater extent both with the French and
Americans than amongst ourselves, especially amongst the senior
officers . . .

Fisher went on to quote the 'very distinguished French Admiral'
whose views on the 'armour-plated navy' requiring no 'fundamental order of battle' were to excite the disapproval of Cyprian
Bridge. The French Admiral held that while gunfire had improved its effectiveness 'when able to strike in a normal direction',
it was 'utterly powerless' to prevent an onslaught by ramming.
Fisher continued:

With regard to the attack by the heavy bow guns, we wish to urge
that if ramming does now occupy the important position we have
assigned to it above, then it follows as a matter of course that the bow
guns should be of the very largest calibre the ship can carry, for it is
the bow instead of the broadside which will chiefly be fronting the
enemy, and that the broadside armament should be reduced if
necessary should there be any question as to weight of ammunition,
etc., being too great.

These bow guns, which in all first class iron-clads could we presume
be at least 18 tons weight, should be loaded with battering charges
and chilled projectiles and should not be fired till within a short
distance of the enemy, as in addition to their then increased effect, it
is just probable that the smoke and effect of the projectiles will cause
a few moments' indecision on the part of the enemy which may make
all the difference in ramming, between a graze and sending him to the
bottom.

The Harvey's Torpedoes towing well out on each quarter are with
the view of catching the enemy, supposing you miss him in ramming
even by as much as a hundred yards.

The broadside guns previously loaded with battering charges and chilled projectiles and concentrated on the beam should be fired by electricity (so that the broadside may be simultaneous and instantaneous at the desired moment) first, when passing the enemy, having just missed ramming him; and secondly as, in sharply turning your ship for a fresh attack, the enemy comes on with the points of the sights of your other broadside.

Briefly recapitulating what we have sketched above, each ship should be guided by the following rules after the first encounter of the two fleets. You will know which ship you have to engage. The Admiral will have made this plain beforehand. The bow guns and broadside guns are all prepared; the torpedoes suspended over each quarter, ready to be dropped at any moment. You make full speed for the enemy.

    I.   Give him the bow guns.
   II.   Ram him if possible.
  III.   One electric broadside as you just graze him.
  IV.   One of the torpedoes should now catch him.
   V.   Hard a starboard (or port) and give him the other electric broadside.
  IV.   Finally the torpedo on the opposite quarter may strike him.

. . . .

The success of naval actions would be half ensured were a few principles followed in the construction of ships dictated by common sense and which no shipbuilding or other theories can subvert. We will briefly state three of them.

    I.   The object in the construction of the ship should be to make her *unsinkable* and to *protect her vital parts*. Never mind the guns or the men. Regiments don't move about surrounded by 6 inch armour. Therefore, instead of a thin coat of armour all over the ship, lay it on thick at the water line and well below the water line. Let the bottom and sides of the ship under water be composed of an infinite number of small water tight cells, thus more like a beehive in its construction under water, for this is the only true defence against torpedoes.

   II.   *Masts and sails should be done away with.* The weight and room they now represent should be taken by coal . . . A paper might be written to prove the actual waste of coal caused by masts and sails in squadron sailing, due to the frequent stoppages and alterations in speed, and it may almost be asserted as a general rule that the cost of refitting exceeds the value of the coals which would have been used in the year's cruise had steam alone been used. It is always a great argument on the side of the masts and sails to ask where would you be should the engines break down. But it is proposed to make universal what now obtains in some of the latest designs of iron-clads, viz. two screws and four engines . . .

III. Extreme rates of speed should not be aimed at. The corresponding expenditure of room in engines and boilers is then out of all proportion to the amount of coal that can be carried. And as handiness is now of the first importance since ramming has become the first mode of attack, no vessel should exceed 280 or 300 feet in length.[1]

It appears worthy of consideration whether a small vessel of the 'Staunch' class [gunboats of about 230 tons and 7½ knots] might not with great advantage be attached to every large iron-clad. Their small size, extreme handiness and powerful armament would under certain circumstances enable them to afford invaluable assistance.[2]

This is the end of the paper in its printed form. It shows that Fisher was fully abreast of the tactical ideas of the day. His usual penchant for simplicity imparts a characteristic flavour to the whole. The paragraph about high-speed exercises points to the future: such evolutions were to be a feature of Fisher's remarkable shake-up of the Mediterranean fleet between 1899 and 1902.

The remarks on ship-construction bear testimony to Fisher's growing interest in a subject which was in due course to occupy much of his thinking. A feature of the 1860s had been the controversy about the merits of mounting guns in turrets rather than in broadsides. In the immediate background to Fisher's paper is a report issued in March 1871, by a Special Committee, on the design of the *Devastation*. In 1869 Reed had seized an opportunity (arising from the new First Lord's interest in turrets) to put forward the revolutionary design embodied, with Barnaby's judicious modifications, in the *Devastation* and the *Thunderer*. A violent public controversy over the design then ensued. The Special Committee (reporting after Reed had been succeeded as Chief Constructor by Barnaby) was able to express confidence in the design which corresponded quite closely with Fisher's above-quoted views. However, it is notable that, as a gunnery expert, he does not come out as an advocate of guns mounted in turrets with unimpeded axial fire. He is at one with

[1] The *Ocean* was 273 feet and the *Devastation* 285 feet in length.
[2] F.P. 5415.

Reed and other progressively minded experts in demanding the abolition of masts and sails, but he rests his argument on his favourite ground of simplicity, and especially economy, rather than the requirements of gunnery. In conformity with Reed's views as expressed in the design of the *Devastation*, he assumes that ramming is the principal tactical requirement and that the ships must therefore be relatively short and tubby in the interests of handiness. His emphasis on unsinkability shows understanding of the currently emerging trend in that direction. The gun, despite its inaccuracy, was increasing in destructive power and compelling naval constructors to provide ever-heavier belts of armour. Inevitably, belting along the whole length of a ship would shortly have to give way to protection of the 'vital parts'. Thus the concept of a ship consisting of a heavily protected citadel and 'soft' or lightly protected ends was about to prevail. Reed had adopted double-bottoms; also subdivision of the hull. These measures were primarily to afford protection against 'torpedoes'—as Fisher says in his paper.[1]

In sum, 'Naval Tactics' is a very respectable statement of opinion, coming from a naval Commander soon after his thirtieth birthday on a remote station in the supposedly complacent year of grace 1871. The original version is followed by a postscript judiciously omitted from the printed paper. As it fairly exemplifies Fisher's exuberant sense of comedy and emphasizes his contempt for outworn traditions, it is here reproduced in part:

Note. One argument in favour of masts and sails, much relied on, [retails] the advantages they afford in the shape of gymnastic exercises for the crew. The best way to meet such an absurdity as continuing masts and sails for gymnastic purposes is to propose another absurdity.

Proposed Routine in Ships of the New Class

7.50   Sound the Officers' call. Man duty cutter, ready for squaring funnels after evolution.

7.55   Clear watertight cells. (This corresponds with the old pipe, 'Clear lower deck'.)

8.00   Evolution as follows:
        Forecastlemen, grease top up, and climb the torpedo outrigger pole. *Note*. The last man should be obliged to eat a pound of Boatswain's tallow.

[1] Parkes, pp. 126–36, 188–202, etc., for technical background.

Fore and Maintopmen. Shin up the funnel stays, go down the funnel, and out through the smoke doors. *Note.* The last man should be directed to stand on his head for half an hour.

Mizen Topmen. The flying trapeze between funnel and ensign staff. All those boys that don't break their necks to be caned. . .

Note. The Officers should be invited to encourage the men at their exercises by swallowing sword blades, eating wine glasses, etc. To preserve the old traditions, the Captain should invariably dance the hornpipe on the conclusion of morning prayers, before the men separate for the work of the day . . .[1]

Not long after thus expressing his feelings, Fisher wrote a revealing letter to Captain George Tryon who had just gone to the Admiralty as Private Secretary to the First Lord. He referred to his service under Tryon when Commander of the *Warrior.* 'I never felt so much zeal as I did in her and you put it into me.' He enclosed 'a few papers' which he had 'written at odd times lately'; and, evidently hoping that Tryon would pull strings on his behalf, he continued:

I am getting horribly tired of being a sort of upper housemaid, devoting severe thought to the cleaning of paintwork and, by way of relief to the mind, investigating the correctness of Midshipmen's watch bills or (still more interesting) following the trail of a missing bucket. If it's not much trouble I wish you would forward the papers to Admiral Hornby [Flag-Captain to Dacres when Fisher was in the *Warrior* and, in 1871, Rear-Admiral commanding the Flying Squadron and then the Channel Squadron] as I think he might like to read them.

I shall be so glad to get home again. The China station has lost all its ancient glories—no fighting, no looting, no death vacancies . . .[2]

It is not clear how close a relationship Fisher had already established with Hornby. However, from about 1870 Hornby began to keep a great number of the letters he received from naval officers, and it can readily be inferred from this correspondence that he did much to encourage Fisher in his radical approach to naval affairs. On 15 September Fisher wrote to Hornby from Nagasaki:

I received your letter today and feel very much flattered by your thinking my few remarks on Naval Tactics worthy of comment . . .

[1] F.P. 5415.

[2] N.M.M., Hornby Papers, PHI/132, F. to Tryon, 31 May 1871. This was passed on by Tryon to Hornby, presumably with a copy of 'Naval Tactics', etc. It represents F.'s earliest extant communication with Hornby. The Hornby Papers are an important source for F. as Cdr. and Capt., hitherto unpublished.

I am now venturing a paper on the necessity that exists for some superior *naval* officer to rearrange and be responsible for the disposition of the space on board men of war, so as to make the most of the room with the great end in view of increasing their coal carrying power . . . regardless of the fact that our ships are six times bigger than in the days of Benbow and have entirely changed their nature, you will still see the same old things in the same old places . . .

I have heard that the Admiral Superintendent superintends the fitting of a ship but that the highest powers always object to a man who does more than superintend the plans sent down. His only road to fame is by putting in an extra water-closet or bath for someone who never had either before . . .

My heart is full of things in the Service which appear to want capsizing, but I am afraid to tell you for want of being taken for a strong member of the Commune. But in regard to the Navy the words of Jeremiah to my mind apply with peculiar force: 'The prophets prophesy falsely, the wise men talk foolishly and the people love to have it so.' . . . [1]

Elsewhere in the letter, Fisher expressed boredom with his Commander's role (at the age of thirty-one!), though not as freely as in writing to Tryon (above). But his distaste hardly meant that the paintwork of the *Ocean,* with her black hull and white superstructure, suffered from neglect. Here is McDonnell's memory of the 'evolution' of painting ship:

Every man of the both watches [was] provided with painting pots improvised out of bully tins. To each part of ship men were stationed for painting. When the ship went into harbour after being at sea, perhaps a week or ten days, immediately anchor was dropped the whole of both watches would by order scramble over the ship's side, and in half an hour the ship would be painted from stem to stern.[2]

It now remains to give some account of the second paper of a general character produced by Fisher. Entitled 'Gunnery, Ammunition and Administration',[3] it was written during the Ocean's homeward voyage from the China station. Fisher was simultaneously working on a supplementary torpedo book, which was finally published at the Stationery Office in 1873 under the title of *Addenda to the Second Edition of the Treatise on Electricity and Torpedoes.* But he believed that the paper on 'Gunnery, Ammunition and Administration' was of particular

---

[1] N.M.M. PHI/132.   [2] Kilv. MSS., Pkt. 41.
[3] F.P. 5415.

value, as he explained to his wife in a letter written at sea on
25 January 1872 (his thirty-first birthday):

. . . my time will be pretty well taken up in getting the men up to
the mark for paying off . . . I have been busy writing, partly at my
new book, about which you must not be too sanguine, and partly at
what I think is a very good pamphlet upon things in general in the
Navy, and gunnery in particular. I am thinking of sending this
pamphlet to Admiral Key and asking his advice about printing it
anonymously, as it pitches into certain people pretty hard, or whether
I should put my name to it . . . I think it's the best thing I have ever
written, but a fellow can never judge well of his own writings. That
article I wrote on 'Naval Tactics', which I didn't think much of,
seems to have been made a great deal of . . .[1]

In fact, 'Gunnery, Ammunition and Administration' was a
less readily acceptable composition than 'Naval Tactics'. While
the latter provides a readable epitome of the advanced naval
thinking of the day (except on the question of end-on fire), the
'Gunnery' paper is discursive and, at times, inflammatory. It
does not seem ever to have been printed. This may have been
due to the judicious advice of Admiral Key but there is no direct
evidence on this point. However, the paper is by no means devoid
of interest. It conveys many of Fisher's views on broad matters
of policy and shows how already, in 1872, his life-long interests
had taken distinct shape, to say nothing of his talent for controversy and interdepartmental strife. It begins in thoroughly
characteristic style:

Si vis pacem, para bellum

A Memorandum on the desirability of further simplifying the
practice of Naval Gunnery.

Also a few considerations leading to the adoption of a more simple
system of Naval Ammunition.

And some observations upon the present tendency to ignore Naval
Officers in the Administration of the Navy.

Fisher went on to list as many as fourteen methods of firing
the guns then in use and, echoing a criticism voiced in his report
of 21 August 1869, he remarked: 'there are no less than ten fuzes
used in the Naval Service, (see page 97, Gunnery Manual,
1868), besides three special fuzes since introduced for use with
the 7 in. M.L.R. gun. But it should be acknowledged that we

[1] Kilv. MSS., Pkt. 6 (*FG*).

have only to consider three of these in dealing with heavy ordnance.' Moreover, there were '13 natures of rifled guns and at least 14 modes of firing each of them; and for each of our heavy guns we have 5 or 6 species of projectiles, 3 kinds of fuzes, and 3 descriptions of powder charge.' This was just the sort of confusion most likely to rouse Fisher's ire.

Now it cannot be maintained in the face of the above facts that either guns, gunnery or gunners are all that are to be desired. The guns are unnecessarily diverse, the gunnery is too diffuse and in consequence the gunners are too often in a dilemma.

There is much to lead one to think that one prevailing cause of diversity of guns and ammunition lies in the fact that each new chief of a department at Woolwich feels impelled to show his fitness for his appointment by the introduction of some new fuze, projectile, gun or carriage. It has just taken 3 volumes of closely printed matter to explain the things made in one department alone! And the writer naively observes in the preface that he has not waited for all things to be settled as experience tells him that this would be to wait indefinitely.

With the aid of hindsight, it can be seen that the mid-Victorian period extending to 1889 (the year of the Naval Defence Act) was specially conducive to experiments. On the one hand, the Navy was in the throes of an unprecedented technical revolution when all the pre-Crimean techniques were being questioned or replaced, but when selection of the best new technique had usually to depend on the costly method of trial and error. On the other hand, in the context of (effectively bipartisan) economy in government expenditure such a method of technical development was bound to be long-drawn-out. This was a situation inevitably frustrating to a man like Fisher with a passion for rationalization and simplification. But in the mid-Victorian period, with no serious naval challenger on the horizon, the Navy was afforded a unique opportunity to carry out an extended process of trial and error. Ruthless simplification was only too likely to prevent the emergence of the best technical solutions.

It is, however, a marked feature of the technical papers produced by Fisher during his formative period that he constantly presupposed the possible imminence of war. That is one reason why the Navy turned to him as tensions and dangers mounted at the beginning of the twentieth century; and secondly his ability to simplify and rationalize in the interests of economy became a political asset as defence costs rose ever more steeply. In his paper on 'Gunnery' (1872) he was again urging simplicity with a view to immediate readiness for war.

The degree of refinement at which we have arrived is absurd. There is an especial manner of charging the gun for almost every circumstance.

If the enemy is an iron-clad having thick armour—use the Palliser shot. If it is not so very thick—use the Palliser shell. If he is of Wood and at some distance from you—use the common shell fitted with Pettman's fuze with full charges. But if he is close—use the double shell with the general service fuze. If you are bombarding a town or attacking an earthwork—use the common shell and battering charges with the time fuze at its whole length; but if at a moderate distance, use the double shell. If the enemy attacks you by boats or should he expose his men—you are to use Shrapnell shell with a full charge and time fuze, so fitted as to burst about 160 yards in front of them. But if the enemy approach you under these circumstances within 500 yards, then you must fire case shot with reduced charges . . .

But we ask seriously: would it be possible for the Captain of a ship in the heat, excitement and uncertainty of an action to discriminate as to the thickness of his antagonist's armour? Or even whether the approaching enemy is or is not an iron-clad? Is it right at such a time to torment him with doubt and indecision as to whether he shall use 22 lbs. of powder or 14 lbs? whether he shall use double shell and chance it? or whether he shall use common shell but perhaps throw away victory by it?

But imagine the confusion on the gun deck incident to a continued change of projectiles and charges! When the right projectile was [near] to the muzzle, there would be delay for the proper charge of powder belonging to it to arrive from the magazine and vice versa. In the course of a few more years of peace and provided no check be placed on the ingenuity of the manufacturing departments, we might probably arrive at such a pitch of refinement and exactness as would enable the powder to be legibly addressed to the care of the exact projectile to which it belongs . . .

We have the same unnecessary multiplicity of guns. As a vessel of 200 tons, the 'Staunch' [of the second series of *Dapper* class gunboats] has proved herself capable of carrying a 12-ton gun with ease and safety in a heavy breeze in the Channel, there can be no question about vessels more than twice that size doing so, especially as the necessity of a turntable in small vessels for carrying heavy guns seems to be now generally admitted.

At all events if circumstances such as the position and size of the hatchways, want of beam, etc., etc., compel the use of so many different natures of guns in the Navy, let them be kept as much as possible together. In the numerous vessels of the 'Dwarf' class [a highly successful class of gun-vessel used on all foreign stations during the period 1868–88], carrying only four guns, we have no less than three different natures of guns—different too in every particular. There is one 7-in. M.L.R. gun with Woolwich rifling, one 64 pr. M.L.R. gun with shunt rifling, and two 20 pr. breech loading guns rifled on the polygrooved system.

Is it possible to adduce a more striking example than this of the necessity of some reform?

It may here be remarked that the adoption of a uniform armament for the *Dreadnought* in 1904–5, in so far as this departure derived from Fisher's initiative, was largely due to his desire for rationalization along lines very similar to those indicated in this paper of 1872. It will be shown later that the salvo-spotting advantage did not specifically weigh with Fisher at the design stage. In 1872, Fisher continued:

The guiding principle in the construction of a ship of war should be that she is a floating gun carriage and until that principle is insisted upon to the last degree, we shall continue to see the absurd spectacle of guns being measured for their ships instead of laying down ships to carry a particular class of gun.

It is quite a chance a ship being exactly suited to her guns. Nearly all could carry a much heavier armament so far as strength is concerned. In proof of this we may mention a dozen vessels off hand, such as those of the 'Warrior' class, the 'Ocean' class and nearly all the larger vessels of the period, which originally carried guns of 5 tons weight where now they all carry guns of $6\frac{1}{2}$, 9 and 12 tons weight without any signs of weakness. Let us get rid of the multiplicity of guns . . .

But to return to our subject, it appears quite feasible to determine upon some one charge, projectile, fuze and mode of firing as the rule; and if on consideration it appears desirable for some peculiar purpose (about any which we are rather sceptical) to retain some portion of the varieties of ammunition now in use, let it clearly be retained as exceptional and treated so in practice . . .

Let us consider whether the Palliser shell fitted with the base percussion fuze invented by the late Lieutenant Boxer, R.N., would not meet all requirements and therefore permit the other 5 descriptions of projectiles [for the 7-inch gun] to be dispensed with in the Naval Service.

It will be tedious, but to be exhaustive let us compare the Palliser shell as fitted above with each of the other projectiles . . . Comparing the Palliser shot and shell, the case stands thus: the shell is more accurate owing to its greater length and also owing to its radius of gyration being longer; and where penetration is effected the damage it causes [is] very much greater . . . Now on comparing the common shell, we observe that it contains more than three times a larger bursting charge than the Palliser shell . . . But on the other hand we have great reason to suppose that the destruction they would each effect would be very unequal, owing to the much smaller pieces into which a chilled shell divides on explosion.

The double shell has been used with considerable accuracy beyond 2,000 yards and is certainly a most formidable projectile against a wooden ship . . . It would be especially formidable against earthworks, as each shell with so large a bursting charge and burying itself before explosion would act the part of a mine. If an exceptional projectile is to be retained, this appears to be the one. If the double shell is accurate beyond 2,000 yards as reported by the late Ordnance Select Committee (see their Report 3858, 4.8.65) what can at all events be the advantage of retaining the common shell which also can only be used against wooden ships? We cannot think with those who believe that future naval actions will be decided, even if commenced, at greater ranges than 2,000 yards.

This last statement may come as something of a jolt to those accustomed to expect Fisher to display extraordinary vision in technical matters. However, much technical advance would have to take place before, some thirty years later, Fisher himself would play a leading role in showing the Navy that fleets should train to engage at ranges considerably greater than 2,000 yards.

With regard to the projectiles, it remained for Fisher to consider shrapnel shell and case shot.   *165369*

They are neither of them effective against ships but are intended for use against boats or men exposed. These two eventualities are in these days of steam and shelter trenches so very remote so far as ships are concerned that the ammunition supplied for this special purpose for use from the boats' guns and field guns will probably be deemed sufficient . . .

After a digression about over-refinement in the theory and practice of naval gunnery, Fisher systematically discusses the subject of charges. His reference to the nature of war is characteristic and a pointer to his ability to grasp the possibility of total war:

. . . At present there are usually three [charges] for each gun. The breech-loading guns of necessity have only one charge . . . We are decidedly of opinion that the battering charge should be retained in the service and the others discarded. A non-professional mind might have some reason to conclude that instead of invariably hitting the enemy as hard as we possibly could, we were in the habit of so adjusting our powder charges that the effect of them should be equal at all distances. And this idea would only be in accordance with that Quixotic conference at St. Petersburgh (into which the wily Russians beguiled us) which bound us never to use explosive bullets in war, and which always reminds one of two single stick players who commence with a distinct understanding not to hit hard but invariably end by breaking the sticks over each other. War cannot be successfully carried on upon homeopathic principles.

Turning to fuses, Fisher stated that the '2 inch or 9 seconds fuse gives a range of 3,000 yards which appears to be amply sufficient for ship purposes'. He saw no reason why this fuse could not be lengthened to four inches 'so that the same fuze would then be applicable for all distances whatever'. The design of the existing four-inch fuse was faulty. Time fuses were impractical for firing at ships. 'By the time the shell was fitted with the required length of fuze, the conditions would certainly have altered. Ships will always move with such rapidity now that there will probably be only time for broadsides.'

He went on to restate his advocacy of electrical instead of independent firing of the guns. Bearing in mind that the '100 or 200 guns of the ironclad squadron' had to do the work previously done by '3,000 guns', a wasted shot had become a serious matter. It was a common experience, when practising independent firing at more than one target, to find gunners aiming at the wrong target. 'This is due to the narrow ports which so greatly restrict the view and also to the eye of the firers not being high enough. But if these difficulties are experienced in ordinary practice when firing at fixed targets, what may we expect in the heat of action and when the targets are moving at the rate of 10 or 11 knots?' But electrical firing brought all the guns 'under the personal and immediate control of the Captain of the ship', thus minimizing the danger of shots being fired at one's own ships. 'A naval war would introduce a rare simplicity in most affairs but in nothing more than in the mode of firing the guns.'

Fisher then took up the subject of Woolwich and the control enjoyed by the War Office over naval ordnance and supplies. In a private letter of 22 August 1871 he had already intimated his feelings to Captain Boys of the *Excellent:*

It always makes my blood boil when I remember the studied and deliberate manner in which the Navy is ignored at [Woolwich, Shoeburyness and Chatham], especially at Woolwich and least at Chatham, and it takes its origin from the Admiralty being made subordinate to and dependent on the War Office for almost any species of warlike store, from a 35-ton gun to a boarding pike and a common shovel. I have been assured that had the Duke of Somerset [First Lord, 1859–66] remained at the Admiralty a few weeks longer, he would have got possession of all the gun wharves and magazines, and this would have been the first step towards the Navy occupying its rightful position.[1]

Fisher was in due course to expend much energy in attempting to remove these matters from the control of the War Office and his hostility to the Army clearly became ingrained long before all ordnance stores finally came into Admiralty hands in 1909. Meanwhile in his paper of 1872 he wrote:

With regard to the alterations in ammunition which we have sketched out, we can prognosticate the indignant chorus of the Heads of Department at their weekly meeting at Woolwich. What! Alter our patterns and hieroglyphics and manufactures because the Navy forsooth wish it so! No! Perish Woolwich! . . .

Woolwich almost exists for the use of the Navy. Most of the manufacture, at all events the most expensive portion of it, is on account of the Navy. But is the Navy in any degree represented there? Is there a single Naval Officer amidst that vast assemblage of Military Officers at Woolwich who *practically* determine what guns we shall carry, what carriages we shall use, what fuzes shall be supplied to us, and how we shall stow our powder on board? Surely we who shall have to do the fighting with these things ought to have some share, a very considerable share, in the superintendence of these manufactures!

Fisher inveighs with equal passion against 'a growing tendency to oust the Naval Officer from any position which can be held by a civilian. He has been taken away from the superintendence of the victualling yards and also from the great naval hospitals, and we are threatened with his removal from all dockyards.'

Underlying his advocacy of naval officers running the administration of the Navy was Fisher's concern about what might be

[1] F.P. 1 (*FG*).

termed the infrastructure of the service. He grasped in a peculiarly modern way how essential was this infrastructure to the
fighting of a naval war in the age of technology:

To sum up the whole matter, if our Admirals and Captains are
competent to fulfil their highest [duty] that of fighting their country's
battles, and if to them is still entrusted the honour and safety of this
kingdom, then surely, to them ought to be entrusted the minor though
important duties of superintending all the means which compel
success.

No amount of courage and daring, no amount of talent and
endurance, will be of avail to avert that great and national disaster
which must ensue where the house is divided against itself.

This the Navy assuredly will be if this pernicious and humiliating
system of civilian superintendence is perpetuated. This is not the
opinion of a humble few neither is it a precocious young officer who
is holding forth. Read the opinions of our most distinguished Admirals, and especially that of Sir William Martin, Sir James Hope,
and Sir Sidney Dacres. Sir Sidney Dacres speaks with peculiar
authority on the matter of the victualling yards and hospitals, as
having been superintendent of the principal ones at a most important
time.

Here are some questions for consideration. Are we the principal
defence of England? Is it true and do Parliament really believe what
they state in the preamble of the Articles of War, that it is the Navy
'whereon, under the good Providence of God, the Wealth, Safety,
and Strength of the Kingdom chiefly depend'? If so, it behoves them
to see that the efficiency of the Navy is not impaired through so noble
a profession being conducted too much on the principle of a merchant
office.

Having thus declared his interest in the general administration
of the Navy, Fisher reverted to the Army–Navy relationship,
this time considered from the viewpoint of national policy. While
it is quite true that the shortcomings and comparative inefficiency
of the Army were in due course to be painfully revealed, especially during the South African War, and although Fisher was
actually to contribute to the reform of the War Office in 1904–5,
it is fair to say that his influence on Army–Navy relations is
chiefly remembered as a disruptive one. Because the subject was
ultimately so important for national strategy before and during
the Great War, it is of special interest to see Fisher's attitude
already defined in broad terms as early as 1872. In his above-
quoted letter to Captain Boys, written in August 1871, Fisher

had dwelt with great indignation on the admittedly provocative references to the Navy contained in *The Soldier's Pocket Book* by Colonel Sir Garnet Wolseley, then Assistant Adjutant-General. Virtually the same extracts are angrily deployed in the paper on 'Gunnery, Ammunition and Administration'. One or two examples will suffice.

Page 38 . . . It is bad enough that the sea transport of the Soldier should be entirely subject to Admiralty control but that only entails difficulty on General and Staff Officers and discomfort on the men; but to allow the Navy to interfere with the store vessels may be ruin to the undertaking . . .

Page 91. Under existing regulations, the transport of troops by sea is unfortunately for the Army entirely subject to Admiralty control.

Some thirty-five years later, the Committee of Imperial Defence would be subjected to diatribes along the lines of the following commentary penned by Fisher in 1872:

In the face of such sentiments as these and considering that for the future they are to be inculcated upon every young military officer from his first entry into the service, can we look forward to the hope [of] that unity of action between the Navy and the Army which is absolutely essential to *their* (not *our*) success? Owing to our insular position, the Army cannot move one step (except in actual defence of our shores) without the Navy. They have always been (and must continue to be) dependent on the Navy for their very existence, for we have ever formed their base of operations and protected and supplied it.[1]

It may be remarked that Fisher was at this early date apparently prepared to admit that the Army might have a legitimate role 'in actual defence of our shores'.

This brings to an end the series of papers written by Fisher during his second spell of service in the East. They clearly represent an important phase of his development, as well as clarifying the basis of the good opinion held of him in high naval circles. They are of special interest in being composed by him unaided and in being devoted to broad subjects. Although a number of his later professional memoranda will deserve notice, the papers written aboard the *Ocean* have been extensively reproduced here because they emanated from a period of consecutive thinking by an unassisted individual. Moreover, these earlier papers are arguably more thorough and systematic than some of the later ones. Also, as Fisher rose to more responsible positions, the

[1] F.P. 5415.

memoranda associated with him were often the product of team-work under his direction.

In January 1872 the *Ocean*, on her return voyage to England, called at Trincomalee and Galle. Fisher apparently met his mother as well as his brother Frank, but tantalizingly (and perhaps significantly) the letter which gave an account of the former has not been preserved. On 16 January Fisher wrote to his wife from Galle: 'I hope you will receive a letter from Colombo in which I told you all about Frank and my Mother.' He made no further reference to his mother but dilated upon Frank: 'I am so delighted with Frank and very proud of him.' (Frank was taking his examinations for the Ceylon Civil Service a year early.) 'I said "Goodbye" to him last night at Colombo and we were both quite upset by it. It seems so odd that such a short time should have made us such good friends.'[1]

Brotherly enthusiasm persisted during the rest of the voyage home. In April Fisher wrote to his wife from the South Atlantic:

I am so pleased with all you tell me about Billy [Frederic]. I do so greatly hope that I shall see him when I get home . . . I am so pleased with Billy's letter to me, there's something very pleasant about it, I can hardly think I shall like him as much as Frank, who to me is a perfect specimen of a man. I fell completely in love with him and so I think would you. He has a sort of bold careless proud way about him which is very captivating.[2]

But this captivation evidently wore off with time. Fisher's children were brought up in ignorance of their uncles and aunts, except for Frederic ('Uncle Bill'); and the affectionate relations existing between Fisher and Frederic—at least in these early years—were not translated into objective assessment of his subsequent deserts.[3] As for Fisher's mother, the only additional surviving evidence seems to be contained in a note written by Fisher's son for Admiral Bacon: Mrs. William Fisher died on 27 January 1895, in London (he thought). 'I believe Father did make her an allowance.'[4]

By the time that the *Ocean* had reached Sierra Leone (9 May) Fisher was expounding to his wife the extent of his immediate ambitions.

[1] Kilv. MSS., Pkt. 6.
[2] Kilv. MSS., Pkt. 6, F. to Mrs. F., 19 Apr. 1872 (*FG*).
[3] *F.G.* i, 99; McKenna MSS., 3/5, Bridgeman to M., 10 Nov. 1910.
[4] Kilv. MSS., Pkt. 38, 2nd Ld. F. to Bacon, 15 Feb. 1929.

. . . I expect you will be very disappointed with me for not having written a book or something of the kind during our way home but I have not had so much spare time as in the 'Donegal' and besides I have been doing these miscellaneous sort of papers.

All these fellows I meet at each place we go into always say, 'Of course you will be promoted directly you get home.' 'Oh! There's no doubt about it' and so on. But I daresay you remember that it was just the same thing for about 2 years before I was promoted to Commander. In my heart I think I ought to be promoted for that new Torpedo Book and on account of all that Sir Henry Kellett has written of me, but I don't like to say this as there are 270 fellows on the list above me and only about 50 below me and so it sounds very presumptuous . . .

It is quite true that Fisher already contrasted, with his particular array of formidable if potentially disturbing qualities, with his most gifted contemporaries. Some of the latter possessed at least equal knowledge and judgement in technical matters; and some of them were better endowed with qualities of leadership, or with tactical and strategic flair, and were therefore more likely to succeed as fleet commanders. But Fisher not only scored heavily in the technical field and possessed powers of leadership well above average in many respects. He also possessed unrivalled drive and energy, a capacity for ruthless action, and a hatred of anyone or anything standing in the way of his schemes for rationalization. Soon, a grasp of the importance for naval reform of public relations, together with a love of intrigue, would manifest themselves, endowing him with a combination of characteristics which was remarkable if not entirely agreeable. In view of his feeling (resurrected subsequently in his memoirs) that he deserved earlier promotion than he was given, it is appropriate to compare him with some of his ablest contemporaries in this respect.

One point of interest in the list below is the very early promotion to Commander and Captain of two outstanding officers, namely Key and Hornby, long before Childers completed the retirement scheme for unemployed officers in 1870. Likewise, it comes perhaps as something of a surprise to find, in the later part of the century, Battenberg and Jellicoe being promoted comparatively late (although early enough by twentieth-century standards). Despite his complaints—private at the time but ultimately published to the world—Fisher seems to have been very fairly treated!

	Born	Age when promoted Commander	Age when promoted Captain
A. C. Key	1821	24	29
A. W. A. Hood	1824	30	33
G. T. P. Hornby	1825	25	27
F. W. Richards	1833	26	33
Lord Walter Kerr	1839	29	33
J. A. Fisher	1841	28	33
A. K. Wilson	1842	31	37
Lord Charles Beresford	1846	29	36
W. H. May	1849	32	38
Prince Louis of Battenberg	1854	31	35
J. R. Jellicoe	1859	31	37

By December 1871 Fisher had already been earmarked by the Admiralty for a new post to be created in the *Excellent*. Captain Hood wrote a memorandum for the Controller on 'the future instruction of Naval Officers in Electricity and Torpedo Management' in which he argued that torpedoes were daily becoming more important. He developed at length the case for separate instruction at Portsmouth instead of accepting Chatham as the only school for the two services. Although the naval course now occupied as much as five weeks in every quarter of the year, it was still the responsibility of the Senior Staff Officer of the *Excellent* who was mainly engrossed in gunnery. (That is, the organization was much the same as it had been when Fisher was appointed Senior Staff Officer in October 1868.) What with lectures and practical work, such as that with the Harvey torpedo which was 'constantly carried out in the gunboats attached to the Gunnery Ships' *Excellent* and *Calcutta*, a full-time instructor in electricity and torpedoes was required. He should be assisted by a Staff Officer of the *Excellent*, a Gunner, and some seaman gunners. 'The Chief Torpedo Instructor should under the Captain of the *Excellent* have entire charge of everything connected with the course of instruction in the subject, both theoretical and practical, and should conduct all experiments, and be in frequent communication with the Chief Instructor at the School of Military Engineering at Chatham.' His rank should not be below that of Commander and the appointment should be for three years. Provision should be made in the estimates for the requisite stores. Hood continued:

The point of primary importance to ensure success is the selection of the Officer to fill the position of Chief Instructor; he must be thoroughly conversant with the subject in all its branches, and should possess great zeal and ability. Commander Fisher, now serving in the 'Ocean' and who will probably arrive in England about the end of March, is without doubt the Officer best fitted in every way for this appointment; he has thorough knowledge of the subject, has paid great attention to it during his absence from England, and possesses considerable ability and zeal.

He said that Captain Boys agreed with these recommendations. Dacres minuted: 'I do not concur in all the views expressed by the Director of Naval Ordnance, but I am prepared to approve of the substance of the plan, namely to appoint [an] official instructor for Torpedoes in "Excellent".' Seeing that Fisher duly took up the appointment in September 1872, about two months before Dacres left the Admiralty, it may be presumed that the First Sea Lord's reservations applied to the amount of torpedo instruction required rather than to the choice of the instructor.[1]

To judge by Fisher's own letters to his wife, she appears to have been much impressed by the unrelenting torrent of religious matter which she received from her husband, and perhaps somewhat perturbed by the prospect of a reunion with the author. Neither the selections from these letters of 1871–2 published by Professor Marder nor the less extensive extracts printed by Admiral Bacon[2] convey the sheer extent of the religiose material contained in the letters, especially those written during the last six months before the *Ocean* reached Plymouth in June 1872. There is page after page of self-accusation and guilty self-examination, as well as some hints of a sense of insecurity. Indeed, Fisher himself had feelings of revulsion about these letters:

I hope that you can remember that I never by any chance read my letters over again so I fear there are many mistakes [which was not actually the case], but whenever I read them over, they have always disgusted me so that I feel inclined to tear them up and quite hate

[1] Adm. 1/6201. Hood's memo. of 6 Dec. 1871; Dacres's minute of 18 Dec.
[2] *F.G.* i, 76–85; Bacon, i, 43–6.

sending them to you, they always seem to me afterwards so hum-
bugging and namby-pamby.[1]

Such robust and (on the whole) typically self-confident passages
as that describing his own performance in a severe gale off the
coast of South Africa come as a considerable relief after some of
the aforesaid religious material:

Now it is all over, I am rather glad that we have had this gale,
although it's rather a nasty spirit that leads me to say it, but it gave
me an opportunity of coming to the front again, and I think I did
very well . . . She once rolled 41 degrees over to one side. I was up in
the foretop at the time, helping to furl the fore-topsail.[2]

Both Fisher and the ship appeared to be in extremely good
shape on arrival at Plymouth on 5 June. 'Captain Fisher[3] looks
younger and better than ever', a friend telegraphed to Mrs.
Fisher. 'His ship is a perfect yacht.'

Fisher himself wrote jubilantly to his wife: 'All my naval
friends appear to have collected here. Almost every Captain and
Commander here is a great friend of mine. I do feel such a
humbug—they all make me out such a marvellous fellow!'[4]

The seal was set on Fisher's time as Commander of the *Ocean*
when the ship paid off at Devonport Dockyard on 22 June. The
Admiral Superintendent, William King-Hall, wrote to the
Commander-in-Chief, Devonport:

I deem it my duty to report the very satisfactory manner in which
H.M. Ship 'Ocean' has been stripped and put out of commission,
reflecting the greatest credit on Captain Hewett, Commander
Fisher, her Officers, and Men . . . The crew have shewn that whilst
in the most perfect discipline, they are most contented, active and
cheerful, proving the 'Ocean' to fulfil all the conditions entitling
her to be called a British man of war, in its most comprehensive
meaning . . .[5]

From 22 June until 19 September, Fisher was on half-pay. His
subsequent appointment to the *Excellent* in charge of torpedo
instruction lasted for just over four years.

Immediately before taking up this post Fisher wrote on
18 September to Hornby (still commanding the Channel

---

[1] Kilv. MSS., Pkt. 6, F. to Mrs. F., 5 Mar. 1872.
[2] Kilv. MSS., Pkt. 6, F. to Mrs. F., 3 Mar. 1872 (*FG*).
[3] Commanders were normally addressed as 'Captain'.
[4] F.P. 1438, Wm. Ross to Mrs. F., 5 June; Kilv. MSS., Pkt. 6, 9 June 1872 (*FG*).
[5] Kilv. MSS., Pkt. 6. A copy.

Squadron) who had evidently been in receipt of one of Fisher's outbursts of reforming zeal. 'It was with great pleasure that I received your letter yesterday and found no "wigging" in it. I was rather afraid you might think me too radically inclined', Fisher admitted. He intimated that he would send Hornby 'some more papers when copied out'. His friendly correspondent and prospective commanding officer Captain Boys might not have enjoyed reading the ensuing paragraph:

> The present condition of the 'Excellent' is lamentable and in my humble opinion is entirely due to the absence of any real talent from the top to the bottom of the staff of the ship. But this, of course, Sir, I say to you privately. I have told Captain Hood the same thing. There cannot be the least doubt as to the necessity of a much higher school than the 'Excellent' for the study of scientific gunnery; with such a splendid chief as Admiral Key I think there is much hope in the future at Greenwich . . .[1]

While this contemporary document contains at least a profession of humility, this is not strikingly evident in the account contained in Fisher's autobiographical manuscript: 'I originated the *Vernon*, the Torpedo School of the Navy. There was terrible obstruction! The First Sea Lord's argument was impregnable! There were no torpedoes when he came to sea and he didn't see why there should be any now!'[2]

However, he somewhat modified this version when compiling his published memoirs.[3] As has been indicated, his exuberant accusation could not be fairly levelled at Dacres; and judging by a minute of December 1875 on the proposed separation of the *Vernon* as an independent command, Admiral Milne (First Sea Lord from November 1872 to September 1876) did nothing but welcome the project.[4]

The *Vernon* had been laid down in 1831 to the design of Sir William Symonds. Originally a 50-gun frigate she was but a hulk when moved to Portsmouth in 1872 so that she could be fitted as the torpedo school; but she still retained the graceful lines for which she had been celebrated. From September 1872 Fisher was, of course, mainly occupied by running the torpedo courses in the *Excellent*. From the outset, he was given an officer as assistant, namely Lieutenant George S. Parker, who had been in the *Excellent* since the end of 1870. Otherwise he was involved

---

[1] N.M.M., PHI/132.   [2] F.P. 5101.
[3] Cf. *Memories*, p. 140 and *Records*, p. 177.   [4] Adm. 1/6336.

in planning for the establishment of the school aboard the
Vernon (as a tender to the *Excellent*) when her conversion was
completed in the spring of 1873; and probably even more of his
time was taken up by the completion of the *Addenda to the Second
Edition of the Treatise on Electricity and Torpedoes*. As was mentioned
above, this extended to 298 pages. It was therefore slightly
longer than the second edition of the *Treatise*. While the first
edition of 1868 had not mentioned the Whitehead torpedo, and
the second edition of 1871 included only a brief note of a non-
committal character (p. 184), the *Addenda* (pp. 232–3) gave some
more information together with favourable comment. The
Preface to the *Addenda* is dated January 1873 at Portsmouth but
a letter from Fisher to Boys (who remained as Captain of the
Excellent till May 1874) indicates that Fisher did not finish
writing the book until the end of February 1873. This same
letter, written on 18 February when Fisher was visiting the
Admiralty, pin-points the date at which he first obtained any
detailed knowledge of the Whitehead torpedo for which he
emerged as such a keen enthusiast: 'I think I shall finish the book
about Monday or Tuesday at latest, and then Captain Hood
proposes I should go with Singer to be initiated into the Whitehead secret.'[1]

By 26 February Fisher was writing again to his commanding
officer. Apart from his reaction to the Whitehead, it is of interest
that Fisher was apparently informed about the appointment of
the Admiralty Torpedo Committee though not officially consulted; also that he was edging his way towards the separation
of the *Vernon* from the *Excellent* as an independent command.

I have sent you the official letter with respect to the Whitehead
Torpedo. It is certainly a most wonderful invention! As far as I can
gather from Captain Singer,[2] I shall be about a fortnight over it.
On Tuesday week we go down to Sheerness to have some sea trials
with it, and also that I may understand the working of the launch
fittings.

I asked Parker to draw up and submit to you a list of gear required
for the 'Vernon' as I fancy there should be no time lost in demanding
them if we are going to begin on April 1st. What do you propose we
should do with regard to the officers' messing, or rather I mean the
luncheon for the class, as I expect the wardroom of the 'Excellent'

---

[1] Sayer, p. 28; copies of 2nd ed. of *Treatise* and *Addenda* at Naval Library;
F.P. 1.

[2] A member of the Torpedo Committee of 1870. See also pp. 64 and 66 above.

will object to their gear being transported backwards and forwards to the 'Vernon'.

I have met with very great difficulties about the book. They are so very dilatory and the stationery office have been very obstructive about pushing it on.[1]

It is very inconvenient my being away just now as I should have wished to have seen you myself with respect to the fittings of the 'Vernon', and I know that if we don't get all the things now we certainly shall not get them hereafter.

Captain Singer is very much in favour of Captain Aynsley being the President of the Torpedo Committee, as he says he is very well up in the subject . . . If you approve perhaps you would suggest it independently to Captain Hood. I was very much impressed by what Singer said; if you do take any steps, it should be at once, as I fancy the matter will be settled almost immediately. I have not mentioned it to Captain Hood, thinking it best to leave it to you and Captain Singer.

I mentioned casually to Captain Hood yesterday that I thought I should receive some sort of definite instructions, or some definite position, on turning over to the 'Vernon'; but I will reserve my ideas on this subject till I see you, as I couldn't explain in a letter as clearly as I should wish what my views are.[2]

In fact, Captain Morgan Singer seems to have emerged as the obvious choice for President of the Torpedo Committee. Fisher was personally impressed by him and derived considerable profit from his fortnight at Sheerness. On 8 March he was writing to Boys:

I took advantage of one afternoon that Singer had to go on with some powder experiments to get him to explain to me the management of Boulange's and Naves-Lewis's Ballistic Chronoscopes, and Noble's Chronoscope. If you have not seen them, they are well worth an afternoon's study when you come up to see the Whitehead run, and Singer explains them so very clearly that one has no difficulty in understanding them . . . I shall try to get back on Wednesday if I can, but I want if possible to take the Whitehead to pieces and put it all together by myself (if I can) before leaving.[3]

The Committee on Torpedoes was appointed in May 1873 and was to sit at the Royal Naval College, Portsmouth. After some changes in its composition, the committee, consisting initially of five and ultimately of seven members, completed its final report in July 1876. The official letter advising Singer of

[1] The book was published by H.M.S.O.   [2] F.P. I.   [3] F.P. I.

the terms of reference mentioned that Boys was to be an ex-officio member of the committee and added: 'Commander Fisher is to give his assistance to the Committee, when he is not employed on instructional duties.' This committee was of considerable importance for the development of British torpedoes and, seeing that Fisher was associated with it throughout its existence, the subjects assigned to it for investigation are relevant to this biography:

(1) The most efficient manner of protecting vessels, both at sea and at anchor, from the attacks of offensive torpedoes of the various natures known; viz., the Whitehead, the locomotive torpedo invented by Lay, and Von Scheliha, the Harvey torpedo, and the Outrigger torpedo.

(2) The best means to be adopted for operating efficiently against an enemy's vessels, under various conditions, with the various offensive torpedoes known.

(3) The best mechanical or practical system of arranging impromptu means for naval torpedo attack or defence.

(4) The most efficient manner of clearing a passage through the torpedo defences of an enemy, and of destroying booms and other submarine and floating obstructions.

Fisher's old acquaintance from Chatham, Lieutenant-Colonel Stotherd, R. E., and also Professor Frederick Abel, joined the committee in June 1873.[1]

It may therefore be said that Fisher's strong recommendation, in his report of 21 August 1869, that a torpedo committee should be appointed, had borne fruit. Of course, responsibility rested with the Board of Admiralty now led by G. J. Goschen, with Sir Alexander Milne (who seems to have been genuinely interested in torpedoes) as First Sea Lord. It should also be remembered that Hood was the Board's chief professional adviser on torpedoes over the whole period from July 1869 to May 1874. However, despite his subordinate role, Fisher can be credited with considerable influence on the form taken by this sustained inquiry. The membership of the committee conformed largely to the kind of representation suggested by him in 1869, including his original choice of a president, and the representation of Woolwich and Chatham. Both establishments were in the outcome represented by their leading experts. It can also be seen

[1] Adm. 116/158, 'Preliminary Report of Admiralty Torpedo Committee, 15 Oct. 1873.'

that the scope and method of investigation followed quite closely the guide-lines originally suggested by Fisher. It was obviously felt by Hood and the Board that Fisher was more fruitfully occupied in furthering current instruction in torpedoes than as a full member of the committee, but there are sufficient indications that Fisher kept continuously in touch with the work of the committee.[1] His assistance was requested particularly in connection with the third subject of study mentioned above, namely extemporized methods of attack and defence. Clearly, his persistent efforts in this field when Commander of the *Ocean* proved handsomely relevant to this aspect of the committee's work.[2]

In view of what has already been said about the Royal Navy's failure to develop an effective contact mine, it is tantalizing to read the following passage in the Preliminary Report of October 1873:

Defence of a Port by extempore Submarine Mines . . . a satisfactory method of defence by means of submarine [electrical observation] mines has been determined; it only remains to be ascertained to what extent the stores of a ship can be made available, and what are the best means of utilising them to effect the same object . . . Experiments have already been made at the Naval Torpedo School with submarine mines and their appliances extemporised out of ship's stores; the Committee . . . propose to continue them in conjunction with the Head of the School, in order to determine the best means of defending a port with such appliances, and to ascertain what forms of firing battery and electric cable are most suitable for Naval purposes.

Mechanical means of Ignition. A good mechanical mine is very essential for Naval Torpedo operations. Among the more important uses of this mine may be mentioned the great facility it would give a Fleet, possessing a number of them, of sealing up a port, either partially or wholly, so as to make it dangerous of egress or ingress by enemy's vessels.

With a view, therefore, of obtaining reliable data on this point, the Committee propose to make experiments with the following . . .:—

1 Abel's primers.
2 Singer's improved Mechanical Torpedo.
3 The instantaneous fuse.

This series of experiments will probably enable the Committee to report definitely whether any and what Mechanical Torpedo is suitable for general service, or admissible on board ship . . .[3]

[1] Adm. 116/158; 116/163; 116/164; F.P. 1.
[2] Adm. 116/158, p. 12.   [3] Ibid.

There is little evidence to show whether or not Fisher himself
had become more open-minded on the subject of 'mechanical'
mines; but it is certainly clear that the committee was at this
stage heading in the right direction. The immediate sequel
deserves a modest place in British naval history.

In April 1874 a German initiative brought a visit to the *Vernon*
by a civilian, ultimately of considerable repute as the originator
of the most effective category of mine used in the Great War.
This was none other than 'Dr. Albert Hertz, Electro-Tech-
nologist of the German School'. According to Hood's minute of
the 9th, the visit was to be on a reciprocal basis. In exchange for
informative hospitality in the *Vernon*, 'a British Naval Officer of
experience would be allowed to visit and obtain every information from the torpedo establishments at Wilhelmshaven and
Kiel, proceeding there at the most favourable time for witnessing
experiments.' According to the German authorities, 'everything
should be laid open' to the British officer selected. It will come
as no surprise to the reader to learn that this officer turned out
to be Fisher.

On 16 April Fisher wrote his report of the two days which
Hertz and a German attaché spent in the *Vernon*. First they
investigated the organization and staffing of the School. It is
clear from the next section of Fisher's report that the visitors
were well informed about his own special interests.

They then went very closely into all the details connected with our
extempore torpedoes, and in compliance with Dr. Hertz's particular
request, he witnessed the whole process from beginning to end of
preparing and laying out an extempore mine and circuit closer, and
went through the testing and then saw the mine exploded by the
Steam Pinnance making contact with the circuit closer. He afterwards
asked to see the arrangements for clearing a channel through hostile
torpedoes, and at his request a countermine was prepared and laid
out.

Fisher stated that Hertz told him about the German torpedo
organization. This was on much the same scale as the British. In
Germany, mines were exclusively a naval responsibility. Hertz
mentioned that 'some very interesting torpedo experiments were
going to be carried out at Wilhelmshaven and Kiel.' 'I did not
receive any fresh information from him beyond a description of
an electro-contact mine and a new species of frictional machine,
but he informed me that he had brought some things over to

show me which I should have an opportunity of seeing in London.' It will shortly become apparent that the 'description of an electro-contact mine' comprised the Hertz horn.

Impressed by Hertz's technical knowledge, Fisher did not doubt that the German would submit a very detailed and accurate report of what he had seen in the *Vernon*.

The nature of the 'things' which Hertz had brought with him is described in a minute of 20 April appended by Hood to Fisher's report. After visiting the *Vernon*, Hertz had appeared at the Admiralty with details of his 'electro-contact submarine mine'. This had been generally adopted in Germany; 'the plan is simple,' wrote Hood, 'very much cheaper than is the plan at present adopted for supplying electro-contact mines in this country, and is stated to work in a very efficient manner.' Forty years on, there would be no lack of survivors from mined British vessels to confirm that the claim was fully justified! The items actually handed to the Admiralty by Hertz consisted of 'a portion of the circuit closer adopted in Germany and of their platinum and wire fuses'. In other words, a specimen of the famous horn does not seem to have been included. Hood suggested that the exhibits should be sent to Fisher but they seem in fact to have been railed to Portsmouth for examination by the Torpedo Committee.[1]

Although Hertz certainly presented both Fisher and the Admiralty with descriptive details of the horn, it is hardly necessary to repeat that this device was not adopted by the Royal Navy, until the humiliating experiences of the Great War inexorably wrought a wholesale conversion. It has not previously been revealed that the Germans exerted themselves to persuade the British to accept it—in gratitude for services rendered by the *Vernon*!

The surviving evidence does not, however, prove that Fisher was chiefly responsible for the rejection of the Hertz mine in the 1870s. The burden of this initial rejection should probably be placed on the Torpedo Committee; there is nothing definite to show that Fisher actually influenced the committee against the mine. On the other hand, there can be no doubt that during his visit to Germany he had every opportunity to appreciate the virtues of the weapon and that, as D.N.O. and Controller, he showed no more interest in it than he did subsequently as First

[1] Adm. 1/6314; 1/6294.

Sea Lord. Although there is no very satisfactory direct evidence, all the indications are that Fisher agreed with the findings of the Torpedo Committee on this subject in its final report.

Meanwhile, in July 1874, Fisher had duly paid his visit to the German establishments in return for opening the secrets of the *Vernon* to Hertz. The precise wording of his report on the 'Hertz electro-contact mine' is unfortunately not available because his official letter has been weeded from the Admiralty files. The letter must have run to some length, to judge by the relatively extensive summary in the Admiralty digest volume. Although inevitably skeletal, the summary in the digest deserves reproduction. (The date assigned to Fisher's report is 22 July.)

He states that the greatest possible courtesy was shown him and apparently the fullest information afforded him.

He visits Kiel and Wilhelmshaven. He reports on Mechanical and Electrical Submarine Mines. The Hertz electro-contact mine and submarine mines with circuit closers. On the Leclanché battery, Siemens' instruments for firing mines by observation, and on White-head's torpedo which is to be purchased . . . The Harvey torpedo is not approved owing to the great practice required to work it success-fully and the danger to friendly ships in action . . . Commander Fisher reports on the defences of Kiel and Wilhelmshaven, and upon the organization of the Torpedo Corps on shore and afloat, and he remarks that the German system of defence by submarine mines and their modes of torpedo attack and defence are as yet in the experi-mental stage, but they are working so steadily and carefully, another year will place them in the very first rank with respect to submarine defence and torpedo attack.[1]

The implication certainly is that Fisher did not go much further than furnish a technical account of the 'Hertz electro-contact mine'. As in 1869, he was impressed by the diligence and exactness of the Germans and in the concluding section of his report he seems to have been mainly concerned to impart to their Lordships a sense of urgency on that account.

The story of the Hertz horn may now be pursued as far as the final report of the Torpedo Committee. This was signed on 28 July 1876 at the Royal Naval College, Portsmouth, by Captains M. Singer, R. M. Blomfield, H. Cleveland, and F. Brandreth (who had succeeded Boys in the *Excellent*); by Professor F. A. Abel, Commander W. H. Hall and Lieutenant-Colonel R. H.

[1] IND. 18166 (digest—see 59.8).

Stotherd.[1] Understandably, the report laid stress principally on 'Offensive Torpedoes', especially of the Whitehead variety, and on the protection of ships against this menace. On the question of close blockade of the enemy's ports the Committee had already, at this early stage of Whitehead development, reached conclusions similar to those officially entertained between 1903 and 1914. They had 'no hesitation in expressing their opinion that none of our large vessels could remain for any length of time during war off an enemy's port without the imminent risk of destruction by Offensive Torpedoes'.[2] How then, would it be possible to implement the strategy of blockade which had served the country so well in the past? This (implied) question brought the committee back to the subject of contact mines. It is noteworthy that they now conceived of these mines as offensive weapons.

In the event of war with any great maritime power, the first consideration in naval strategy would be, as heretofore, to confine the enemy's ships to his own ports. A well considered system of mechanical mines, which could be readily laid down before the chief military ports of the enemy, would materially supplement the efforts of the Blockading Squadron and admit of a reduction in its size. The Committee would therefore urge the consideration of the most convenient mode of effecting this, so that it may be ready for adoption when required.[3]

This enlightened recommendation goes far to exculpate the committee for the eventual crisis over ineffective British mines in 1914–17. Although the committee failed to accept the free gift of the Hertz design, it did urge the importance of 'mechanical' mines and encouraged further investigation in this sphere. The reasons for dissatisfaction with the Hertz fuse do not emerge, though the final report does make reference to foreign fuses: 'Various forms of electric fuzes are used by foreign nations for submarine mining service . . . The Danes employ a fuze similar to Ebner's, and the Germans, who commenced with Abel's

[1] Stotherd visited the German torpedo establishments in August 1874 on behalf of the War Office. The Admiralty readily agreed with this arrangement because Fisher's visit in July had been one month ahead of the German experiments. Stotherd's full report, printed and including details of the Hertz horn, is in W.O. 33/27. He makes it clear that the horn was not fitted in mines until after the war of 1870–1.

[2] Adm. 116/163, p. xxx.

[3] Ibid.

mining fuze, have now adopted low-tension fuzes.' There is no comment on these items of information.[1]

As far as mines were concerned, Fisher's persisting interest in electrical detonation by an observer rather than by contact is indicated by a note elsewhere in the report on various fuses which had been sent to the committee for their inspection: 'Arrangement proposed by Commander Fisher for using platinum-silver fuses in submarine mines.' This had been passed on to the War Office Torpedo Committee; in July 1875 the latter had expressed preference for an alternative proposed by a Captain Armstrong, R.E.[2]

Before leaving the final report of the Torpedo Committee, it is pertinent to notice its general conclusion on the subject of mines and torpedoes:

> The Committee have fully considered the effects which Stationary and Offensive Torpedoes are likely to have upon the operations of future naval warfare. The tendency of Stationary Torpedoes is to increase the difficulties hitherto experienced in invading the seaboard of an enemy, whereas Offensive Torpedoes will also play a most important part in future *ocean* warfare. The Committee recognise the introduction of the latter as specially inimical to the manoeuvring of large squadrons, and as having a tendency to reduce to one common level the Naval Power of the greatest and the most insignificant nations.

This warning, together with the implications drawn for the future of close blockade, testifies to the reflective qualities of the committee. The opinion that mines would help to prevent invasion was to hold good for many years. Yet Fisher would accept this verity on odd occasions only; usually he was against laying mines because they would restrict the offensive manoeuvres of British squadrons and, it will be seen, he tended to believe that the enemy's mines could easily be swept. As an enthusiast for the Whitehead torpedo he continued to back a weapon which, on balance, tended to favour Britain's enemies. Of course the committee was far from arguing that, because torpedoes would not improve Britain's naval position, she should not develop them. In Fisher's case, it is his enthusiasm for such a dangerous development, as distinct from a cool acceptance of its necessity, which is characteristic. Not for nothing would he become known as 'Radical Jack'! As long as the drive associated

---

[1] Ibid., p. xvii.   [2] Ibid., p. 149.

with his love of change was submitted to criticism, the results would be mainly good. Only when he rose at last to the top of his profession were such safeguards reduced at times below the level of effectiveness.

Already during his time in command of the *Vernon* Fisher was becoming a controversial figure. In 1873, he promoted more general awareness of the current state of torpedo development through a course for senior officers. Nathaniel Bowden-Smith, who was last noticed at the unsuccessful attack on the Peiho forts (and was in fact badly wounded there) underwent the course of 1873 as a newly promoted Captain. He later remembered that although Fisher 'had some flag officers and several senior captains in the class, he kept us all interested and amused with his clever lectures'.[1] Admiral Tarleton, a visiting Sea Lord, was impressed by one of his lectures in October 1873 and there are other indications that he continued to stand well with the Board of Admiralty. Just before Gladstone's government gave way to that of Disraeli in February 1874, Fisher visited the Admiralty and (as he confided to Boys) received 'a very kind message' from the First Lord, Goschen. Admirals Milne, Tarleton, and Beauchamp Seymour, as well as the Parliamentary Secretary of the Admiralty 'all expressed themselves as very favourably inclined' towards him.[2] However, Fisher handled less tenderly the susceptibilities of the officers connected with the Torpedo School, as emerges from a letter written to Fisher's son by Graham J. Bower in July 1921:

. . . I was one of the Lieutenants qualifying as gunnery and torpedo lieutenants who received instruction in torpedoes from your father when he was in command of the *Vernon* and even in those days controversies had begun . . .

Your father was always terribly in earnest about any subject or question he took up. His advice to us was always the same. 'If you are a gunnery man you must believe and teach that the world must be saved by gunnery and can only be saved by gunnery. If you are a torpedo man you must believe and teach the same thing about torpedoes. But he is terribly in earnest. The man who doubts or who is half hearted never does anything for himself or his country. You are missionaries. Show the earnestness, if need be, the fanaticism of missionaries.[3]

[1] Bowden-Smith, p. 79.
[2] Kilv. MSS., Pkt. 9; F.P. 1, F. to Boys, Feb. 1874.
[3] Kilv. MSS., envelope marked 'Chapter I'. Bower left the Navy as a Lt. in 1884.

Here indeed is one of the principal keys to an understanding of Fisher's career. Already his mind has been seen working on about as high a level of systematic analysis as he ever attained. This level might be described as very respectable but falling well short of genius. His thoroughness in the sense of attention to the small details of organization has also been seen at something near its zenith. He certainly strained every nerve and concentrated his maximum energy in the effort which resulted in his promotion to Captain (on 30 October 1874) at the age of thirty-three. It will be seen how, on the whole, his thinking became less scientific, less systematic, with the passing of the years. But his energy remained quite exceptional and he tended to invest progressively more of it in the gift so tellingly recorded by Bower. This was the gift of personal persuasion. It will be seen that Bower in 1921 was not a fully committed Fisherite; yet the passage of half a century had not erased the impact of Fisher's face-to-face indoctrination of the young lieutenants at the *Vernon* so long before. As an advocate, Fisher was well-nigh irresistible. This was true where he sought to convert an individual or a small group rather than a wider audience. He could often succeed on paper but with nothing like the regularity resulting from personal interview. This flair, perhaps comparable with Churchill's but less intellectual (as may be seen by comparing their respective modes of argument in correspondence), helps to explain the extraordinary degree of dominance ultimately asserted by Fisher over perhaps three out of four First Lords from 1904 to 1910. It is what underlay Bacon's remark that 'it was on his extraordinary magnetic influence that the success or failure of the reforms he was about to introduce [in 1904] largely depended.'[1]

Bower did not comment directly, when writing to Fisher's son, on the provocative aspects of Fisher's personality. His willingness to ride roughshod over convention and anyone who stood in the way of his schemes of the moment was clearly beginning to emerge and is sufficient explanation for a certain amount of hostility. However, the analysis which Bower offered of the clash of ideas is worth summarizing. He thought that the clash was fundamentally between the doctrines of matériel and personnel. Those loyal to the latter standpoint held that the man was more important than the weapon. But Fisher believed

[1] Bacon, i, 227.

that 'the gun or the torpedo or the ship was all important.'
Bower continued:

> The truth in my judgement is that both are important. Your father
> with his energy and earnestness held by the material school and it
> must be said that he had justification for earnestness. It is difficult to
> realise now how low our material had fallen. I had a few years before
> been employed slave cruising on the East Coast of Africa. The
> catridges supplied for the revolvers would not go off; or if they did,
> burnt like squibs.

It is ironical that the defective British mines of the Great War,
after all the sound and fury of Fisher's age of reform, were to be
described by Fisher himself as 'squibs'. As for the wartime gun, it
duly roared impressively and—thanks in some measure to
Fisher—it lobbed its projectiles accurately enough on to its
target; but the shells failed to penetrate properly on the supreme
day of trial. Yet while these facts show that Fisher's passion for
matériel ultimately fell short of complete consummation, they
are far from proving that it was misguided. It may rather be
argued that they show how desperate was the need for a reformer
who put technical effectiveness first, and would be 'ruthless,
relentless, and remorseless' in its pursuit. But, as has already
been indicated, Fisher was also intensely interested in people—
if not as ends, certainly as means.

By the time that Bower qualified in 1876, the argument was
revolving mainly around the methods used by Fisher to mobilize
public and political support for the accelerated development of
the torpedo branch. This approach was not entirely unprecedented: for example, Captain Coles was much in the public
eye when campaigning for turrets during the 1860s. But the
flavour of deliberate showmanship was new and was to remain
an important device in Fisher's repertoire.

> The controversy was raging in the *Vernon* when I joined the school.
> Your father was very much in earnest about the school and wished
> to make it not merely a teaching school but a school of research. To
> do this he wanted money and support, and he used to get politicians
> and journalists down and give them a show of all the magical tricks
> which the school could produce. But the old school men hated these
> shows . . . Here you find the two schools in conflict: your father
> would never have secured all he wanted had he not secured the sup-
> port of the Press and Parliament. On the other hand the introduction
> of the Press and politicians has landed the service in the degradation

of the propaganda and publicity departments . . . Men of all ranks court the Press and the politicians to the detriment of discipline and efficiency.

Bower's letter illustrates another persistent theme in Fisher's career, namely economy:

Now your father was all for the latest and best material which he held to be the cheapest in the long run . . . Whilst your father always wanted the best material and was determined to get it, he was always opposed to extravagance. [He recalled an incident in the *Vernon* when Fisher opened a large box lying on an instrument table] and disclosed a wondrous assortment of brass screws and strings and other things which formed part of a mysterious instrument of some sort.

He said 'You fellows would be puzzled to know what this is. It is a circuit closer or what the Royal Engineers call a circuit closer. It costs £7 10s. and will ruin any nation that adopts it. We can make one as good ourselves for less than a shilling.'

And so they did. They made a very good circuit closer from a preserved meat tin.[1]

It has already been seen that as early as 1868 Fisher was complaining about the lack of time for research in the *Excellent* as compared with Chatham. In November 1873 he took up officially the need for an increased complement for the *Vernon* mainly on the ground that it was impossible for the existing staff to cope with teaching and examining, and at the same time to do 'any continuous experimental work'. He listed seventeen items awaiting attention for lack of staff. The first two, underlined in red, were 'Electric steering and countermining apparatus' and 'Electric and mechanical torpedo gear extemporised from ship's stores'. These items were heavily backed up by a final paragraph, also in red ink, to this effect: 'The first two items on this list are of extreme importance, but, though every effort has been made, hardly any progress has been made in them during the past 7 months on account of instructional work occupying the whole force of the establishment—180 officers and men having been under instruction.' Other items on the list which deserve mention are 'Experiments with Foreign Electric Fuzes', 'Extempore Electrical and Mechanical Fuzes', and 'Various forms of mechanical mines'. Even if the staff of the *Vernon* did not have time to investigate these subjects very much before Hertz's visit

---

[1] Kilv. MSS., envelope marked 'Chapter I'.

six months later, there can hardly have been a total lack of interest in what he had to offer![1]

Boys seems to have thought that Chatham and Woolwich were the proper establishments for research on torpedoes. In his covering letter, he agreed that the *Vernon*'s complement should be increased, but in the event of their Lordships deciding 'that instruction in the management of torpedoes, etc., is the chief duty for which Commander Fisher is appointed, and that the experimental work is supplementary, I am of opinion that reduction can be made in Commander Fisher's submission'. At the Admiralty, Hood agreed with the latter view and the Board sanctioned a modified increase of complement. Milne emphasized the need to match the progress of torpedo instruction in the United States but made no comment on the issue of research.[2]

The question of increasing the staff of the *Vernon* having been settled for the time being, Boys (who had succeeded Hood as D.N.O. in May 1874) suggested to Fisher that yet another edition of the *Treatise* on torpedoes was required. Fisher replied most reasonably:

I am very strongly of opinion that the Admiralty Torpedo Committee should prepare the new Torpedo Book. With the mass of valuable information they have now collected and taking into consideration the unequalled personal experience of Mr. Abel, Captain Singer and [Lieutenant W. H.] Hall, the book would be so very easily and very completely prepared, and prepared in this manner would be so very authoritative, as much so as the Gunnery Manual is in respect to gunnery, etc. Indeed, the report of the Committee on Naval Electrical Stores is almost a new Torpedo Book in itself.[3]

In August 1875 the matter was pursued on an official level. Writing to Brandreth (Captain of the *Excellent* since May 1874) Fisher restated the view that a manual should be jointly prepared. It should be based on the experiments and reports not only of the Admiralty Torpedo Committee but also the other bodies which had been investigating various aspects of the subject, such as the War Office Torpedo Committee, Naval Electrical Stores Committee, and the Military Ports Torpedo Defence Committee. He suggested that the 'section of the Admiralty Torpedo Committee which has belonged to most

[1] Adm. 1/6256, F. to Boys (holo.), 20 Nov. 1873.

[2] Ibid., Boys to Ady., 12 Dec. 1873; mins. of 29 Dec. and 7 Jan. by Hood and Milne.

[3] F.P. 1, F. to Boys, 3 Dec. 1874.

of the above named committees' should prepare the official manual. As he put it,

> The circumstances are now very different to those under which the present Torpedo Book was compiled in as much as a number of officers are now well qualified to participate in the preparation of a work of this nature and I venture to submit for consideration that it is undesirable (if it can be avoided) that a text book for the Service of such vast and growing importance as Torpedoes should appear as emanating from one Officer.

In any case he thought it unlikely that he could prepare a new book in good time without neglecting the experimental and instructional work of the Torpedo School. Fisher's well-reasoned presentation of the case prevailed. In accord with his recommendations, the first *Torpedo Manual for Her Majesty's Fleet* duly appeared in two volumes, including a contribution from Fisher, in 1876 and 1877.[1]

In his same letter to Brandreth (13 Aug. 1875) Fisher pressed once again the need for an increase in the complement of the *Vernon*. He considered that 'in addition to the Officer in charge of the Naval Torpedo School, another Officer of some *standing and experience*' was 'urgently required' on account of the greater numbers of officers and men under instruction as well as the 'number of experiments constantly in progress'. Moreover, the officer in charge would inevitably be away from the School from time to time. This implied some danger to those under instruction. 'Fatal accidents have occurred at the French, German, Austrian and American Torpedo Schools through insufficient or inexperienced superintendence.'

This submission received support from Brandreth and from Admiral Elliott, the Commander-in-Chief at Portsmouth. At the Admiralty, the post of Second Sea Lord was now held by Vice-Admiral Hornby. He thought that a Commander should be sent to the *Vernon* to assist the officer in charge. In his minute of 27 August, he also commented on the idea (which seems to have been aired only in conversation) that the *Vernon* should become a separate command: 'And in view of the increasing importance and magnitude of the subject of Torpedo Management, I think it quite true that the "Vernon" should be separated from the "Excellent" and kept as a separate establishment under

---

[1] Adm. 1/6336, F. to Brandreth (Capt. of *Excellent*), 13 Aug. 1875; F.P. 1, F. to Boys, 7 Jan. 1876.

the D.N.O., Lieuts. being allowed to take up Torpedo instruction separately from Gunnery.' Milne signified general agreement on 2 October. At about the same time the names of the 'Naval Torpedo Manual Committee' were issued: Captain Singer (President), Captain Fisher, Lieutenant W. H. Hall (who later directed the Navy's first intelligence department), and Professor Abel.[1]

By November 1875 the Admiralty was asking for a detailed up-to-date account of the work of the *Vernon* which Fisher duly supplied. It is perhaps worth remarking that, as far as the documentary evidence goes, it was the Admiralty that took the initiative over separating the *Vernon* from the *Excellent*. Bacon seems to have absorbed Fisher's latter-day version which light-heartedly claims all the credit.[2] However, there is no reason to doubt that, behind the scenes, Fisher exerted influence on Captains Boys and Brandreth, as well as on the Second Sea Lord, Vice-Admiral Hornby.

A minute written by Admiral Milne on 2 December 1875 implies that Fisher would have been appointed the first Captain of the *Vernon* in its independent role if he had not signified that he wished to go to sea. When the *Vernon* was commissioned on 26 April 1876, the Commanding Officer was Captain William Arthur (of the Whitehead committee of 1870). Second in command was Commander A. K. Wilson (also a member of the 1870 committee) with whom Fisher had latterly struck up a friendly though basically professional correspondence. It is a point of interest apparently unknown to Wilson's biographer, and presumably to Wilson himself, that the First Sea Lord's initial reaction (Dec. 1875) to the problem of replacing Fisher was to write: 'Comd. Wilson from all the information I can obtain is best qualified to fill his place . . . Wilson should be ordered home from *Raleigh*' (then on the coast of India). However, it was evidently decided that, in the interests of continuity and future development in the *Vernon*, Fisher should be retained for a few months in an advisory capacity; and a Captain senior to Fisher was therefore selected to take command of the establishment.[3]

In April 1876 Fisher was officially advised of his forthcoming

[1] Adm. 1/6336, 13 Aug. 1875, etc.
[2] Adm. 1/6336; Bacon, i, 53; F.P. 5101 (quoted above).
[3] Adm. 1/6336; Bradford, p. 46.

supersession as head of the Torpedo School and of his continuance there for the time being as an adviser. He was also informed of their Lordships' appreciation of his services in the *Vernon*. Even though Fisher's achievements are to an extent overshadowed by the failure (either then or in the long term) to adopt the Hertz horn, they must still be rated as considerable. The emphasis on electricity led quickly on to such developments as searchlights (in which Fisher had, as noted above, been much interested since 1869) and internal electric lighting in warships. Fisher undoubtedly provided, as a Commander and junior Captain, an impetus towards modernization of the Navy unequalled by anyone of comparable seniority and rank. On the other hand, this contribution must be kept firmly in perspective. Through the 1860s and 1870s there were many other highly capable, if more orthodox, naval officers working scientifically for the improvement of weapons and techniques. Moreover, from the mid-sixties to the mid-seventies, at least, the various Boards of Admiralty led on the professional side by Milne and Dacres seem to have been sensible and open to new ideas. Despite the stringent economy associated with Disraeli and Gladstone, they carried the Navy forward into the unfamiliar world of technology.

As a parting shot, Fisher rounded off his service in the *Vernon* with yet another of his papers on naval reorganization. Having been involved during October and November in an unsuccessful attempt to salvage the *Vanguard*[1] (the first British capital ship to be sunk by collision), he returned from Dublin to the *Vernon* and set his hand to a memorandum on 'Torpedo Defence', dated 8 December 1875. The covering letter to Brandreth reads:

Sir,

I have the honor to submit for your consideration the accompanying observations on the recent French Ministerial Decree (forwarded for my information) which determines the organization of the French system of Torpedo Defence.

I have also ventured to make a few remarks upon our own organization and I have offered some suggestions for the Torpedo Defence of our Mercantile Harbours and the Coast generally.

I am, Sir,

Your obedient Servant

J. A. Fisher

Captain Addl. for Torpedo Service.

---

[1] F.P. 1, F. to Boys, 26 Oct., 1 Nov. 1875.

There follow fourteen pages of foolscap in Fisher's own hand, supplemented by extracts from American reports copied out by a clerk. The key points, as far as Fisher was concerned, were:

The chief merit of the French system is that there is no divided responsibility . . . It is entirely in the hands of the Navy . . . The Torpedo Defence of the English Naval Arsenals is, at the present time, in the hands of the Royal Engineers but the Navy provides Officers, Seamen, steamers, and boats for laying down the mines and electric cables etc. There is a general opinion that this arrangement is not altogether satisfactory to either Service.

He also drew attention to the fact that no provision had been made for torpedo defence of the 'mercantile harbours', as distinct from 'the five great military ports', nor for such defence of 'any portion of the coast'. In France, retired naval officers were to be trained to take charge of this aspect of torpedo defence. In Germany, where the Navy was likewise in sole charge of torpedo defence, 'plans for the defence of the whole coast' had been drawn up (according to a report by Colonel Stotherd, R.E.). For the British Navy, Fisher suggested the following scheme which carried less than complete conviction with Milne:

It is believed that the coast as mercantile harbour defence might be easily, efficiently and cheaply organized under the direction of retired naval officers who would command the various local Torpedo Corps consisting of the resident seafaring population [Milne: ? ?] who would be enrolled as a portion of the Naval Reserve and who as far as practicable should employ their own boats and gear. [Milne: 'How is this possible?'] The postal telegraph department could furnish the needful electro-technical knowledge of which very little would be necessary. Old sailing men of war [Milne: 'Where are they?'] could be fitted up as moveable torpedo depots and might be utilized in the winter as Naval Reserve drill ships. All the mines, etc., would be prepared by the officers and men of the Naval Torpedo School on the same system as the Germans keep all their Torpedoes ready for almost instant use . . .

In his concluding section Fisher stressed 'the daily increasing importance' of the locomotive torpedo 'as a cheap, readily applied, and almost resistless weapon' under the circumstances of the day. He went on to pay a compliment to the Royal Engineers—despite his general prejudice against the Army. As the minutes of the First and Second Sea Lords, and of the D.N.O., were soon to testify, this compliment also pointed to the weakness in Fisher's case.

The Royal Engineers of this Country are unsurpassed in ability and in the power of adapting themselves to any circumstances. They were the first in this country (in conjunction with Professor Abel) to recognize the value of the Electric Torpedo [i.e. mine]. They saw their opportunity and seized it. Too much credit cannot be given them for so doing; but as Admiral Porter [of the U.S.N.] irresistibly argues: *Torpedo Practice* [as distinct from the theory of the subject] *must of necessity fall to the Navy.*

Fisher's paper was taken seriously by the Admiralty and subjected to close examination. On 15 February 1876 the Commander-in-Chief, Portsmouth, was asked to 'convey their Lordships' thanks' to Captain Fisher 'for the able paper submitted and inform him that some of his proposals will be considered'. As a letter of the same date from the Admiralty to the War Office indicates, the former wanted reassurance 'as to the state of preparedness of the necessary material for the defence of the Military Ports'; and called 'attention to the importance of some steps being taken in regard to the defences of the Commercial Ports'. Reference was made to 'the confidential agreement arrived at by the War Office and the Admiralty' which defined the responsibilities of the two departments for the defence of the 'Military and Commercial ports'. But more important, Fisher evidently engendered some heartburnings on the subject of divided, or rather ill-defined responsibility. The upshot was an emphatic reaffirmation of the prime responsibility of the Army! There is a substantial file which bears the following epitome: 'Decision in September 1876 that the War Office shall take charge of the defence of the ports at Home and Abroad, the Admiralty supplying the necessary vessels and boats.' One of the objections to Fisher's scheme was that Britain lacked the powers of conscription possessed by Germany and France; and the officers and men needed for effective implementation of the scheme would inevitably represent a considerable burden on the naval estimates.[1]

In October, the Admiralty decided to send a committee of

[1] Adm. 1/6336. Covering letter from C.-in-C. Portsmouth, 24 Dec. 1875; mins. by Boys, Milne, and Hornby, 21, 22 Jan. and 1 Feb. 1876; Ady. to W.O., 15 Feb. 1876 (copy). Adm. 116/175, 'Submarine Defence of, and Mining Practice at, Military Ports at Home and Abroad'.

four to Fiume to report on 'a new small sized Torpedo, designed and constructed by Mr. Whitehead'; also on 'any other description of Torpedo Mr. Whitehead might be willing to exhibit'. This select body was led by Captain Singer, and otherwise included the Superintendent of the Royal Laboratory at Woolwich (a Colonel of the Royal Engineers), Mr. T. E. Miller (Chief Engineer, R.N.—an interesting appointment to such a committee at that date), and Fisher. The committee reached Fiume on 2 November and witnessed trials of the small torpedo on 6–8 November. This torpedo was the forerunner of a famous class: 14 feet long; 14 inches maximum diameter. (The torpedo in service during the early and mid-1870s was 16 inches in diameter.) A table of results included in the report shows eight deflections of less than 40 feet out of twelve runs at 200 yards, and seven deflections of less than 200 feet on eleven runs at 830 yards. 'The running was exceedingly steady, with respect to the depth attained, and the deflection was due to gradual curving in the course, not to erratic movements.' Adjusted to run at a depth of 10 feet, the torpedo 'did not vary from this depth more than 6 inches at 200 yards range'. The speed was 'about 17 knots for 830 yards and 20·5 knots for 200 yards'—a dramatic advance on the 9·5 maximum speed of the 16-inch torpedo. The committee agreed that the inaccuracies experienced at 830 yards would be satisfactorily reduced and that the torpedo would achieve the performance claimed by Whitehead: 'over 16 knots for 830 yards and over 20 knots for 200 yards'.

The committee was also impressed by a larger torpedo (extreme length 19 feet 3 inches and maximum diameter 15 inches) from which much of the inaccuracy seen in the experimental 14 inch torpedo had been eliminated. This was 'the weapon with which most Foreign Governments' were supplied. The committee gave details and remarked that it was 'highly satisfactory' and 'a most powerful weapon, admirably adapted for use in ships fitted with submerged tubes or for Vessels whose principal aim is the Torpedo, but not so suitable as a smaller Torpedo, for use in ordinary ships from above water, on account of its length, weight and general inconvenience of handling'.

Whitehead had already supplied 15-inch torpedoes to Russia, France, Denmark, Sweden, and Germany (the largest batch) and the first four powers had ordered more. Austria and Italy had already taken delivery of the 14-inch weapon. The Germans already possessed 'a special Torpedo Vessel'. This was 'unarmoured, of about 900 tons, double screw and fitted to eject the [15-inch] torpedo from submerged tubes in line with the keel, both forward and aft'.

Finally, it should be mentioned that the committee showed considerable interest in an arrangement for controlling the depth of mines. It 'could be applied to both electrical and mechanical Mines but appears especially adapted for use with the latter, as it would greatly enhance their value: for a channel defended by mechanical Mines, thus fitted, could be at will opened to friendly ships, by causing the Mines to sink to a depth greater than the draft of the Vessels.' The mines could be brought back to operational depth at will. So here is a clear indication that the committee still saw grave objections to mechanical mines in general—that is, objections similar to those stated by Fisher in 1869.

The report was completed and signed in England on 20 November. Captain Singer noted at the foot: 'Captain Fisher was obliged to leave England before signing; he however concurs in the foregoing Report.'[1]

[1] Adm. 116/164.

CHAPTER 4

SEAGOING CAPTAIN (1876–1882)

By 1876 the Bosnian revolt against the Turks followed by Turkish atrocities in Bulgaria had led to declaration of war against Turkey by Serbia and Montenegro. The whole Eastern question was thus revived. As usual in such circumstances, the British government was ultimately concerned about the course of action which would be taken by Russia. If the latter penetrated to the Mediterranean British communications with India would be threatened. (India's importance to Britain is illustrated by the fact that she had just replaced Germany as Britain's greatest export market.) In May 1876 Disraeli expressed his interest in the Balkan crisis by having the Mediterranean Fleet sent to Besika Bay.

In November Fisher was suddenly appointed Captain of a ship in the aforesaid fleet, namely the *Pallas*, a corvette-ram of 3,794 tons (four 6-inch and four 8-inch M.L.R.). The *Pallas* had possessed some notable features at the time of her construction (1863–6): she was the first British warship designed primarily as a ram and the first to have compound engines. She was a characteristic creation of Reed's, being short, tubby, and very handy. But an accumulation of timber in the Dockyards resulted in her hull being made of wood, not iron, as Reed had wished. Consequently a survey of 1875 had found her hull to be in a state of general decay; also her boilers were in a shaky condition.[1]

In his memoirs, Fisher confused some details of his hurried journey out to the *Pallas* in 1876 with his appointment to the same ship, still in the Mediterranean, early in 1879.[2] Here is one of Fisher's versions of this abrupt affair of November 1876:

The British Fleet was near Constantinople. The First Lord of the Admiralty sent for me at noon and asked me when I could start. I

---

[1] Parkes, pp. 98–101.
[2] *Memories*, pp. 141–2. The story about going out in a collier may be dated November 1876 by a reference to 'the Science of Navigation as practised on board your collier' in a letter from Evan MacGregor to F., 22 Dec. 1876, Kilv. MSS., Pkt. 7.

said I would catch the 2 p.m. train, and I went night and day by train to Naples, thence by steamer to Malta, nipped on board a collier that was steaming out of harbour at the moment, though the Captain of the collier greatly objected, and so got there quick . . .[1]

This was only a temporary appointment, occasioned by the sickness of Captain H. H. Beamish. Fisher assumed command of the *Pallas* on 3 December. She was then at anchor with the Fleet in Besika Bay. On 29 January 1877 Fisher was ordered to proceed from Greece to Malta and hand the ship back to Beamish. Shortly afterwards, he took passage back to England to take up an appointment as Flag-Captain to Admiral Key, Commander-in-Chief, North America and West Indies. While in the *Pallas* Fisher had seen enough of the Mediterranean Fleet under the command of Vice-Admiral the Hon. Sir James Drummond to induce him to write as follows, on 6 March, to Vice-Admiral Hornby, who had succeeded Drummond in the Mediterranean:

I am not sure that you will have heard of my appointment to the 'Bellerophon'. I am not overjoyed, as I am told I ought to be, for I had set my heart on remaining a few months at least under your Flag in the certainty of learning a good deal, more especially in the way of Fleet manoeuvring. No one in the Mediterranean had the faintest notion of it as far as I could make out but as the terror of your name is making them read up the manual and combine their information like Mr. Potts of the 'Eat and Swill Gazette', you may possibly be agreeably surprised; but I venture to warn you that one of the Captains can't see a large arm chair 5 yards off and another has an inverted cranium which frequently causes him to understand signals upside down.

I suppose there never before were such opportunities as we had at Besika Bay[2] for tactics, landing men and exercise aloft, but practically nothing was ever done, and I feel dreadfully disgusted in going home having learnt nothing whatever and astonished at the apathy in all quarters, especially amongst the Lieutenants whose ignorance and want of interest in the service struck me as very great.[3]

There are three or four points in this letter which call for comment. First, it seems rather surprising that Fisher should not be keen to serve under Key, though it is understandable that, his interest having been switched to fleet tactics by his experience in the Mediterranean, he should have preferred service under

---

[1] F.P. 5100.   [2] Near the entrance to the Dardanelles.
[3] N.M.M., PHI/120.

Hornby. Being of an even more scientific disposition than Fisher was himself, Key had been ashore almost continuously since his distinguished service in the Second China War. Most of his appointments were of a type interesting to Fisher: Captain of the Steam Ordinary at Devonport, Captain of the *Excellent*, Director of Naval Ordnance, and, latterly, the first Admiral President of the Royal Naval College, Greenwich. (He had been elected a Fellow of the Royal Society in 1868.) Secondly, Fisher's account of the tactical inefficiency of the Mediterranean Fleet receives some support from Bowden-Smith's memoirs. Bowden-Smith, who was then Captain of Drummond's flagship (and still on friendly terms with Fisher), appreciated a side of Drummond which apparently earned him little credit with Fisher, describing him as 'my charming admiral, one of the most courteous and pleasant men I have ever met, with whom it was a real pleasure to serve'. Fisher's conception of command at sea was somewhat different to Drummond's, as he would shortly make clear on joining the *Bellerophon*! Bowden-Smith brings out well enough the easy-going atmosphere in the Fleet at Besika Bay.

Of course, we often weighed for a few days at a time to carry out evolutions, but were nearly always in touch with our Consul at Chanak, in the Dardanelles, through which the Admiral received telegrams. As the fleet was now assembled, and a war with Russia appeared possible, I asked permission of the admiral to submit my views as to the formation in which a fleet should attack an enemy in the event of an outbreak of hostilities, and having obtained his consent, I submitted them in writing; but . . . I will merely state that they were to the effect that the 'line ahead' was the only formation.[1]

In fairness to Bowden-Smith, it should be added that his subsequent remarks show him to have been well abreast of the current literature on naval tactics. He rejected—doubtless correctly—the 'peloton' formation which had become a fashionable topic of discussion. But it seems clear enough that his 'charming admiral' did not number fleet-tactics among his leading interests.

Thirdly, the continuity of Fisher's interest in 'landing men' may be noticed—also the fact that these landings would have been in the vicinity of the Dardanelles. Finally, his remark about

[1] Bowden-Smith, p. 92.

the apathy and ignorance of the Lieutenants induces particular reflection. The shortage of really capable admirals some thirty years later will be a matter of importance for this biography when, in due course, the problem of finding a replacement for Fisher at the Admiralty in 1906 is considered.

Fisher's spell in command of the *Bellerophon*, the flagship of Vice-Admiral Sir Astley Cooper Key, lasted from April 1877 to June 1878. According to Joseph Honner, who was then senior Midshipman aboard the *Bellerophon*, the news of Fisher's appointment was received aboard the ship with 'something like consternation'. The ship had been undergoing a refit in the dockyard at Bermuda, the previous Captain had left the ship nearly three weeks before Fisher's arrival (9 April), and the level of efficiency on board was not high. Addressing the assembled ship's company, Fisher duly promised them three months of hell! At the end of this discomforting period, he would reappraise the situation. If he was not satisfied, the rule of Satan would be reimposed.

He was as good as his word. It was drills and exercises all the time. The officers were however a fine lot and the men had been a picked crew, so they quickly responded to the lead given by the Captain. At the end of three months the ship was as efficient as any in the Service at that date. Then Captain Fisher with characteristic energy and versatility threw himself heart and soul into the amusements of officers and men.[1]

Another informant quotes Admiral Moresby's statement in his book *Two Admirals* (p. 319) that, at this time, 'Fisher's humour was inexhaustible.' By way of illustration, he embarks on the following anecdote:

In the early seventies torpedo work was in its infancy, Whitehead torpedoes were unknown in the service. We used towing charges such as the Harvey torpedo and outrigger charges—latter consisted of a charge of guncotton at the end of the lower boom and in the Bellerophon the circuit came aft to the poop from whence the Captain would fight his ship.

On one occasion of our going out for target practice he invited from Bermuda the principal military officers to attend. As usual in those days they came off in their scarlet tunics which had much lace etc.

The starboard lower boom was rigged out and the military officers were assembled in the starboard dickey or rather the fore part of the

---

[1] Kilv. MSS., Pkt. 41. Cf. (needlessly) edited version in Bacon, i, 55–6.

poop. A fairly fresh breeze was blowing and the Captain turned the ship to bring the wind on the starboard bow and he did it cleverly for his purpose. He explained the idea to them to run alongside the enemy and explode the charge on contact and told them to watch the end of the spar. They did.

I was his ADC. He beckoned me to go with him to the lee side of the chart house and pressed the key.

A huge volume of water rose. The speed of the ship and force of the wind were well judged and the column of water fell on top of the military officers and drenched the poor devils to . . .[1]

Unfortunately, the narrative here breaks off; but it extends far enough to illustrate Fisher's liking for practical jokes! It also suggests that his poor relations with the Army during the critical pre-war years were not entirely due to the shortcomings of the military.

As aboard the *Ocean*, and subsequently, Fisher was particularly kind and agreeable towards the younger midshipmen and was in general accepted as a friend by the lower deck, despite the rigorous discipline he maintained. This receives support from the reminiscences of F. C. Alton who served in the *Bellerophon* as Captain's Clerk. On joining the ship, Fisher announced (along the lines indicated above) that she was shortly to be brought up to a point of favourable comparison with the smartest ship in the Mediterranean. After a few months, he ruled that this object had been achieved. 'This pleased the Ship's Company—they had not at first known how to take their new Captain but soon learned his forcible ways and how he wished things done, and it was not long before they were very proud of their Captain. His ways appealed to them for the bluejacket loves a strong man in command.'[2] These activities are reflected in a letter written by Fisher to his wife during this commission.[3] This is dated 22 September 1877 at Halifax where the Commander-in-Chief was based during the summer and early autumn (normally spending the rest of the year in the West Indies). Fisher was still at the time of writing preoccupied with discipline aboard the ship and his zest for ship-board life is implicit in his remark that 'as captain one can't take part in all the small things which go on in the ship and these really are at the bottom of discipline, smartness and

[1] Kilv. MSS., Pkt. 35: sheet headed 'Clystlands'. The rest of the letter, probably written to the 2nd Ld. F. in 1921 by Adm. Sir Gordon Moore, is missing.

[2] Kilv. MSS., Pkt. 40, Alton to 2nd Ld. F., 17 Aug. 1921.

[3] F.P. 1441.

everything else.' He thought at the time (as did Honner in retrospect) that the ship's company were 'a very good lot of men'; they were 'very willing and cheerful' and, he considered, 'very comfortable'. According to Parkes, 'Old Billy', as this popular ship was called, had very poor accommodation for the officers. Nevertheless, she was one of Reed's most successful creations, still holds the record (fourteen years) for a flagship's accumulated service on any one station, and was always a sought-after billet.[1]

Further on in his aforementioned letter to his wife, Fisher touched on his relations with Admiral Key: 'Brand (Adl. Seymour's Flag Lieut.) write to me that Sir H. Yelverton [First Sea Lord] is very bad again since his return from Homburg but the Admiral [Key] has not heard a word yet and I don't think it at all certain that he will go to the Admiralty. He will be most bitterly disappointed if he doesn't go.'[2]

There is no hint here of the rift which occurred between Fisher and Key in the mid-1880s. Admiral Key's daughter, Rose (later Mrs. de Crespigny), well remembered in later life how, from the time that Fisher came under her father at Portsmouth (1864–6) she heard her father's 'opinion of him often repeated: that he was bound for the "top", "one of the finest brains in the Navy" —and so on—"with an inexhaustible capacity for hard work" '. When the Keys were on shore at Halifax and Fisher commanded the *Bellerophon* 'his spirits were inexhaustible, a born optimist in little as well as great things, and he then developed a most extraordinary passion for dancing which I believe he never grew out of. He would come to the schoolroom, or the verandah, or the lawn, it did not matter where, and we would dance for any length of time to his own whistling!' Fisher's displays as a dancer were, from this time onwards, a feature of ship-board entertainments and were ultimately in demand on regal occasions. Mrs. de Crespigny also remembered that his 'other great passion' was for sermons. 'He attended morning and evening service mainly for the sermons, which he would discuss afterwards with great animation.' In his letter to his wife of 22 September 1877, Fisher likewise records: 'I didn't go ashore early as there was no

---

[1] Parkes, p. 107. 'An exceedingly handy ship under steam' was Fisher's verdict on her 'General Handiness'; 'but under sail not to be trusted near the land or in any difficult position' (Adm. 53/11158).

[2] Yelverton was succeeded by Admiral G. C. Wellesley in Nov. 1877. Key had to wait till Aug. 1879 to realize his ambition.

communion. The Admiral and his people came off as usual to Church and I had 4 of the Ward Room Officers to lunch which is a great bore but one must entertain; then I went to afternoon church at the Bishop's Chapel, back to the Admiral's to tea, and then with Miss Key and the governess to Evening Church.' He commented on the sermon, but the morbid note often struck by his religious communications from the *Ocean* was noticeably absent. To all appearances, his religion had ceased to oppress him by the mid-1870s. It remained an important part of his life, but by 1877 his drift towards a kind of Old Testament approach was probably incipient.[1]

By the beginning of 1878 the position in the Near East was threatening and was soon to affect Fisher personally. Hostilities between Russia and Turkey had begun the previous April. In January 1878 the Russians advanced to Adrianople and the British government sent Hornby with the Mediterranean fleet up the Straits to Constantinople. Anti-Russian war fever swept through England and the word 'jingoism' was added to the language.

In May both Key (who was now a full Admiral) and Fisher were recalled to England. Urgent steps were taken to place a Particular Service Squadron on a war footing in the Channel. On 7 June Key hoisted his flag aboard the *Hercules* (8,680 tons; completed in 1868). Fisher was once again his Flag-Captain. The *Hercules* was an enlarged and improved version of the *Bellerophon*. However, with a main armament consisting of three calibres of gun, she represented the confusing multiplicity of charges and projectiles of which Fisher had complained so bitterly in his gunnery paper of 1872.

By 18 June this squadron, truly representative of the Navy's era of experiment, had assembled at Portland. It consisted of '6 broadside masted armour-clads [including *Hercules*]; 1 sea-going mastless armoured ship [*Thunderer*]; 6 coast defence armoured turret ships [*Prince Albert*, etc.]; 1 unarmoured masted frigate; 2 river and 2 coast defence gunboats; and 1 despatch vessel'. Sorting out this 'sufficiently incongruous' array into two main groups, Key conducted manoeuvres and thus brought to fruition a recommendation he had made on the subject nine years before.[2]

---

[1] F.P. 1441; Kilv. MSS., Pkt. 40, Mrs. Rose de Crespigny's memoir.
[2] Colomb, pp. 407-8.

By far the greatest convulsion experienced by the higher command of the squadron was, however, caused by the prospect of an inspection by the Queen. This culminating event was planned for 13 August. Amid all the details, the Queen's dislike of the sound of gunfire was not overlooked. As soon as the Royal Standard was sighted aboard the approaching but relatively distant Royal Yacht, the Royal Salute was to be fired—'so that Her Majesty may not be inconvenienced'. No doubt Fisher contributed to the success of the occasion. In the event Key received 'an expression of the gratification' which the Queen had 'experienced in inspecting the ships and vessels assembled under his orders at Spithead'.[1]

Fisher's lack of seniority as a Captain was still making it difficult for him to obtain command of a ship of his own. On the termination of his appointment aboard the *Hercules* (21 August 1878) he became Captain of the frigate *Valorous* but (as he communicated to Hornby) he was only in the role of *locum tenens*.[2] From 13 September, he was without employment.

Now that Fisher had four children to support (a second daughter, Dorothy, having been born in 1873 and a third, Pamela, in 1876),[3] he was finding it difficult to meet his financial obligations. On the one hand, his pay had gone up from £7 a week as a Commander to about £12 as a Captain; but on the other he had to meet more insistent demands on his pocket in virtue of his relatively high rank. For example, in his above-quoted letter of September 1877 he gave his wife the following analysis of his position:

My weekly bills this week came to £5 1s., which I think is my limit of economy. This includes servants' wages, postage and everything. This leaves £7 for other expenses; my pay is as nearly as possible £12 a week. I can see I get done in various small ways, to the extent of perhaps 10 shillings a week, but unless I did the marketing myself I can't well avoid it, without its being rather infra dig. Every now and then there come these balls or a subscription, such as the Seaman's Club at Bermuda, and these are the things which exhaust one's money. I see that Philip has drawn £50 from Bosanquet and there is the £40 at the store for his uniform, etc. I hope he will content himself with that.

As the reference to his brother Philip (a promising young naval officer) shows, Fisher had accepted the role of head of the family

---

[1] Adm. 1/6451.   [2] N.M.M., PHI/123, 16 Aug. 1878.
[3] Beatrix and Cecil had been born in 1867 and 1868 respectively.

in the widest sense. However, in this case, at least, the drawings presumably represented a loan rather than a gift. In the same letter, Fisher remarks: 'I have had the banker's book by this mail; all dividends have been paid in all right.' So, although his wife lived with her children in France during his North American appointment, as an economy measure, it is clear that Fisher was no longer completely reliant on his naval pay. The general impression left by all the surviving evidence of this type is that, while both Fisher and his wife exercised the most careful economy throughout their marriage, they were able to maintain appearances consonant with his progress through the more senior ranks. Cecil Fisher, for example, was duly educated at Charterhouse and Magdalen College, Oxford.

However, the period from 13 September 1878 to 9 January 1879 represents the longest spell of unemployment in Fisher's career as a naval officer and his sense of relief and gratitude can readily be imagined when, apparently at the request of Sir Geoffrey Hornby, he was offered a command in the Mediterranean.[1] Had it not been for his somewhat necessitous circumstances at the time, Fisher might well have lacked enthusiasm for this appointment. The ship in question, now near the end of her commission, was none other than the *Pallas*! Her condition had been poor in 1876 and had not improved with the passage of a further two years. According to Bacon, the armour-plating adhered to the hull thanks only to a chain cable passed under the bottom.[2] The Midshipmen of the *Pallas* were duly furnished with anecdotes about Fisher's interest in developments below the water-line: ' "Jacky" used to nose about the orlops and holds of the "Pallas" all the way home fearing that the bottom would fall out of her before they reached England.'[3] It says a good deal for Fisher's ability both as an officer and a showman that, at the end of the ship's commission, the Secretary of the Admiralty wrote (12 July 1879) as follows to the Commander-in-Chief, the Nore:

With reference to your report of inspection of the 'Pallas' on the 1st instant, I am commanded by my Lords Commissioners of the Admiralty to signify their direction to you to express to Captain Fisher and the officers of that ship the great satisfaction with which

[1] Kilv. MSS., Pkt. 7, Hornby to F., 5 Jan. [1879].
[2] Bacon, i, 61.
[3] Kilv. MSS., Pkt. 40, A. Trevelyan Taylor to 2nd Ld. F., 1 Sept. 1921.

they have received the report of the admirable condition of the vessel and the efficiency of her officers and crew.[1]

Before the commission of the *Pallas* was thus brought to a successful conclusion, Fisher had derived considerable instruction from his appointment. His previous ambition to serve under Vice-Admiral Hornby was fulfilled. Clowes has described Hornby as 'a great student of professional history; he had a wonderfully clear head, and a scientific mind; he was a natural diplomatist, and an unrivalled tactician; and to a singular independence and uprightness of character, he added a mastery of technical detail, and a familiarity with contemporary thought and progress that were unusual in those days among officers of his standing.'[2] Fisher's own account of Hornby, with special reference to the few months of his service under him in the *Pallas*, is to be found in *Memories* (pp. 142–3):

I found Admiral Hornby's fleet at Ismid near Constantinople [29 Jan. 1879] and Admiral Hornby sent a vessel to meet me at Constantinople. He had heard from Malta that I was on board the tramp. That great man was the finest Admiral afloat since Nelson. At the Admiralty he was a failure. So would Nelson have been! With both of them their Perfection was on the Sea, not at an office desk. Admiral Hornby I simply adored. I had known him many years; and while my cabins on board my ship were being painted, he asked me to come and live with him aboard his Flagship, which I did, and I was next to him always when at sea. He was astounding. He would tell you what you were going to do wrong before you did it; and you couldn't say you weren't going to do it because you had put your helm over and the ship had begun to move the wrong way . . . He couldn't bear a fool, so of course he had many enemies. There never lived a more noble character or a greater seaman. He was incomparable.

To judge by the log of the *Pallas*[3] there were exercises involving 'steam tactics with Fleet' in February and early March; also some firing at a target. By this time the Russians were at last withdrawing from Adrianople and on 13–14 March Hornby moved the Fleet down to Gallipoli, performing manoeuvres *en route*. Fisher wrote to his wife from Gallipoli (at the head of the Dardanelles):

We arrived here yesterday in a tremendous snow storm and blowing hard, and had a most difficult movement to perform but we

---

[1] Kilv. MSS., Pkt. 7, a copy.   [2] Clowes, vii, 291–2.   [3] Adm. 53/11068.

did it all right, and the Admiral seems very pleased with the 'Pallas'. We are going to Constantinople tonight to stay with the Sultan, and a swell dinner on Monday night. We are to go to the Dolma Belche Palace which is the finest the Sultan has, and we are to go to another Palace for the dinner . . . I am delighted to go to Constantinople, as I wanted much to see it again, for I have hardly any remembrance of it . . . There is no idea of how long we stay here, but I expect it will not be for very long.[1]

The dinner took place on the 17th. It is interesting to compare the respective accounts of the event (both of which have been published *in extenso*) given by Fisher and Sir Geoffrey Hornby. Fisher (who was confessedly without much interest in buildings) concentrated on the appearance and peculiarities of the people present while Hornby spent more time noting the physical surroundings as can be seen from this:

We had a most quiet dinner at the Yildiz Kiosk. The room was in the shape of a wide cross—the sidebays being separated from the aisle, in which the table was laid, by very pretty and light marble pillars, formed of four brownish columns each, the rest of the room being white and gold. In each corner of the dining-space was a very handsome glass candelabrum, about 10 or 12 feet high, and a large glass chandelier hung over the centre of the table. The silver plate on the table was fairly handsome; the candelabra represented trees, with deer, sheep, etc., at their roots. There were large and high masses of artificial flowers on stands between, and the whole effect was good.

Out of about thirty people dining, the British naval party consisted of ten officers, including four Captains. According to Fisher, the Sultan was 'a little man with a hook nose, very black beard and whiskers cut close, and looking very delicate and care-worn, but with a most sweet smile when he spoke.' The Chief Interpreter and the Grand Vizier made constant 'humble reverences to the Sultan when spoken to' and the servants 'trembled, or pretended to do so, when they approached the Sultan with the various dishes at dinner'. (Indeed, there was small reason for them to pretend! For the gentle host was none other than the redoubtable 'Abdul the Damned', who had emerged as Sultan after dark and clandestine deeds had engineered the removal, some two years earlier, of two of his sublime predecessors; and, as Lord Blake has written, though 'destined to be one of the worst tyrants in Turkish history', he was 'greeted with singularly misplaced enthusiasm in Turcophil quarters'.) Fisher's own view of the Sultan is thus epitomized: 'He spoke very low and softly always and took all our fancies very much.'[1]

It is still a matter for dispute whether or not the presence of Hornby's squadron went far to deter the Russians from occupying Constantinople. However, the Sultan, having proposed the health of his guests at dinner, was at some pains to reinforce his gratitude afterwards. He had them all presented to him individually in his drawing room, and as Fisher recorded:

> Then he made us another speech, and said he could never forget the services rendered to him by the Fleet and it was a real pleasure to him to have us in his drawing-room, and he begged that we would sit down and smoke a cigarette with him, which we did; and then presently, after some conversation with the Admiral, translated by the Grand Vizier, who also appeared to be trembling, we were bowed out.[2]

Fisher had time to visit St. Sophia before the squadron sailed for Besika Bay, but he was not greatly impressed—though possibly a little more than he had been by Athens some two years earlier. (He then wrote: 'I went all over Athens yesterday with Seymour and cannot understand what people rave about when they go on about the beauties of the Acropolis, etc., etc. I have been disappointed in all I have seen abroad, excepting perhaps St. Peter's at Rome.')[3]

On 19 March the fleet passed down the Dardanelles to Besika Bay. While the *Pallas* was at anchor, two of Fisher's Midshipmen were reported lost ashore, namely C. E. Munro and Alfred Douglas-Hamilton.[4] Fisher was afterwards said to have regretted the possible loss of Munro, 'a clever youngster who had promised well, but the other young devil was no loss—small as a rat, with a voice like a bosun's mate, and more oaths than one of Cromwell's troopers'. However, the two youngsters were back with the ship by the time she sailed for Piraeus on the 21st. During April and May she was in dock at Malta. It is of interest that Fisher, who is commonly said to have played no ball-games, apparently

---

[1] Egerton, pp. 310–11; F.P. 1444, F. to Mrs. F., 18 Mar. 1879 (*FG*); R. Blake, *Disraeli*, London, 1966, p. 595.

[2] F.P. 1444.

[3] Ibid., Kilv. MSS., Pkt. 6, F. to Mrs. F., 24 Jan. 1877 (*FG*).

[4] The latter subsequently became the 13th Duke of Hamilton.

used to play fives with Douglas-Hamilton during this spell at Malta.[1]

Having sailed for England on 9 June, Fisher paid off the *Pallas* at Chatham on 24 July. Meanwhile at the end of May he had already been designated president of a committee to revise the gunnery manual. The first meeting was held on 14 August.[2]

The original *Manual of Gunnery for Her Majesty's Fleet* came out in 1868. In this connexion it is appropriate to mention here the survival, among Fisher's papers, of a draft memorandum of 1867–8, anticipating the first manual. It is headed 'A Proposal to write a Work on the Theory and practice of Naval Gunnery' and its substance is as follows:

There can be no doubt that a work on this Subject is urgently needed. The only authorities on the subject at present are:—

> 'Naval Gunnery', by Sir Howard Douglas, 1860.
> Holley's 'Ordnance and Armour', 1865.
> Simpson's 'Naval Gunnery', 1865.

The first mentioned Work is to a great extent obsolete. It contains no mention whatever of armour plated ships or Muzzle Loading Rifled Guns nor does it in any way answer the requirements of modern Science.

'Ordnance and Armour' by Holley is almost entirely confined to the manufacture of Guns, systems of rifling, and experiments against armour plates up to 1864 . . . It is the work of a Civil Engineer who necessarily and confessedly could not bring either professional or practical experience to bear on the working of the Guns on board ships . . .

Simpson's 'Naval Gunnery' is a valuable work on smooth bore Ordnance . . .

It seems to be a pity that a work on Naval Gunnery should not be undertaken by Naval Officers, not only on account of its intimate connexion with their profession, and its increasing importance, but also that the Navy may not be indebted either to Military men or Civilians for a Work which undoubtedly could be undertaken by many Naval Officers . . .

Being then deeply impressed with the conviction that such a book is wanted, that it should be written by Naval Officers and that the Senior Officers cannot afford the necessary time and labour, we propose to undertake the task—provided we can obtain countenance and

---

[1] Kilv. MSS., Pkt. 41 (signature of informant illegible) for the fives; otherwise Pkt. 40, A. Trevelyan Taylor, 1 Sept. 1921 and Adm. 53/11068.

[2] IND. 18254 (Fisher).

support from our superiors. We have undertaken the matter conjointly as we think that by such a course we shall obviate to a great
extent one sided views, that we shall be able to make the work more
complete, and at the same time by only two being engaged in it be
able to keep clear of the delays and disagreements usually consequent
on any number of persons being associated in a work of this kind . . .[1]

Whether this memorandum exerted any influence remains an
open question. It probably antedates the first edition of the
Treatise on torpedoes.

The 1868 edition of the gunnery manual extended to 173
pages. A second edition of 317 pages was issued in 1873. Fisher's
committee produced the third edition. This ran to 543 pages and
was issued by the Stationery Office in 1880. In retrospect 1879,
the year of the third edition's preparation, may be seen as
climacteric in more than one respect germane to this study.

Economically, 1879 was a bad year for Britain. While it
marked a depression which was by no means confined to the
United Kingdom, it represented the first substantial jolt to
confidence in the continued predominance of British industry
and trade. In the same year, Germany adopted a comprehensive
system of protective tariffs, thus setting an example inimical to
universal free trade; this example was soon followed by other
great powers and the threat of serious industrial competition
became more marked. Although public interest in the effectiveness of the fighting services had receded, the Near Eastern crisis
of 1876–9 had promoted a degree of governmental concern for
the safety of overseas bases and coaling stations. In September
1879 this concern was expressed in the form of a royal commission, headed by a recent Colonial Secretary, Lord Carnarvon,
'to enquire into the defence of British possessions and commerce
abroad'. While the principal long-term threat to the British
Empire lay in the overland Russian advance towards India, the
Russians were now apparently intent on building up a strong
fleet. Another threat to the British trading complex lay in the
recent increase of French expenditure on new naval construction;
in 1878–9 France spent as much as Britain—about one and a
half millions. As yet the so-called 'Liberal Alliance' between
France and Britain continued its shadowy existence. Notwithstanding, British naval supremacy could no longer be taken for
granted. The Admiralty had to face the emergence of two

---

[1] F.P. 5415. The name of Fisher's collaborator does not appear.

possible maritime enemies in France and Russia. The 'Fisher era', with its mounting stresses and drastic solutions, had entered upon its slow but ultimately alarming gestation.

The *Gunnery Manual* of 1880 should be set against these barely discernible murmurings in the European background. In the technical sphere of gunnery itself, a major revolution was actually under way. The European powers had committed themselves to main armaments of breech-loaders some time previously. The Admiralty has often been reproached for its undue conservatism in adhering so long to muzzle-loaders; but in so far as breech-loading had been downright dangerous to the gun-crews of the 1860s and improvements in technique continued through the 1870s, there was something to be said for allowing other countries to make the necessary experiments, as long as no serious challenge to British naval supremacy could be perceived. In August 1879 Sir Cooper Key became First Sea Lord; and in that month a party of officers was sent to Meppen to witness the trials of the latest breech-loaders produced by Krupp. The report made clear the great superiority of these weapons over their muzzle-loading equivalents and the Board quickly decided in favour of long breech-loaders for future battleships. The lucid Introduction to the *Gunnery Manual* of 1880 reflects this decision.

A remarkable increase in the knowledge of facts connected with Gunnery has taken place within the last few years. This has made it evident that the powers of ordnance can be greatly developed, and will necessitate a complete revolution in our armaments, entailing great changes in the guns, systems of mounting, and ammunition.

Besides the question of actual armaments, other matters relating to naval gunnery, such as firing at sea, etc., are also in a tentative and undeveloped stage . . .

Full details of the most prominent systems of breech-loading have been given, as the proposed introduction of breech-loading guns makes this of great importance, the system to be adopted for the service guns about to be manufactured not yet being decided, and the necessary information not existing in any English work.

The Manual of 1873 did not contain any information relative to the mounting of ordnance, but the importance of the subject necessitated its discussion in this edition . . .

Because of the key discovery that slow-burning large-grain gunpowder would develop sustained pressure in a gun and thus dispatch a projectile with greater velocity, extended treatment was given to this subject. Otherwise, the provision in the *Manual* of a systematic comparison of the strength of the British and foreign navies is worthy of remark. In August 1879, Key had entered office 'with a navy not superior to that of France alone, either in ironclads or in cruisers; and with no general feeling either in Parliament or in the country that this was not as it ought to be'.[1] Gladstonian retrenchment and public disinterest in the Navy continued to predominate until the scare of 1884. On the side of public education, Thomas Brassey (Civil Lord of the Admiralty from 1880 to 1884) published *The British Navy* in five volumes in 1882–3, but this had little evident effect on public opinion. However, a step in this educative direction had already been taken in the *Manual* of 1880: 'As a knowledge of the leading particulars of the various classes of ships of our own and foreign navies is both useful and interesting to naval officers, and only to be found scattered through various works, a part of the Manual has been devoted to "Ships and Armour".' In view of the fact that Fisher passed in to the Admiralty a paper (31 October 1879) on 'Recent European Ironclad Ships', it is reasonable to attribute to him the aforesaid section on 'Ships and Armour'.[2]

Before preparation of the *Manual* had been completed, Fisher was appointed to the *Northampton*, due to be commissioned on 25 September. Then, wrote Fisher to Hornby, 'we go for an experimental cruise. We don't leave England till the end of November. I am to be kept on at the Gunnery Book.' He enclosed an 'outline of the Great Gun portion' so that Hornby (still in the Mediterranean) could collect criticism from any 'Gunnery Talent' available.[3]

Meanwhile, Fisher was on very good terms with the leading officers in the service. When he dined at the Navy Club, W. H. Smith (First Lord in real life and the model for Sir Joseph Porter in H.M.S. *Pinafore*) was 'very *empressé*' and Hood (now in his last year as Second Sea Lord) 'came up and said, "Well you are being buttered down well by everybody."' Wellesley (soon to give way to Key as First Sea Lord) assured Fisher that the Admiralty appreciated him; the (First Lord's) Naval Secretary said that he deserved a ship of his own. Shadwell, now Admiral

[1] Colomb, p. 428. See also Parkes, p. 307.
[2] IND. 18254 (Fisher). The paper has been weeded.
[3] N.M.M., PHI/120 (a), 15 Sept. 1879.

President at Greenwich, persisted in introducing Fisher 'to all the old Admirals as "his boy", and adding in a stage whisper, "the best boy I ever had" '. The First Lord referred to Fisher in his after-dinner speech. Key was also in evidence: 'Sir Cooper was in the chair and made an awful mess of his speech.'[1]

Indeed, it is probable that the years 1876 to 1882, occupied mainly with seagoing appointments and therefore representing a break in Fisher's career as an administrator, saw him at a peak of unalloyed popularity. His good relations with the lower deck seem to have been maintained; and the following letter from Lady Jane Ely, dated at Osborne on 8 February 1878, testifies to his success on a more exalted social level:

My dear Captain Fisher,

   The Queen was speaking of you yesterday, so I repeated again to Her Majesty what you had said about your appointment, and the Queen said no one deserved it more and said she liked you, and that you were much respected and looked up to in your profession, and so popular. Pray remember me to Mrs. Fisher, and

Believe me

Yours truly

Jane Ely.

This shows that Fisher met and impressed the Queen at least as early as 1877; and seeing that he knew of his appointment to the *Bellerophon* before returning to England in March of that year,[2] it seems likely that the meeting was in 1876. Lady Ely's letter implies that the Queen may have influenced Fisher's selection for the *Bellerophon*.[3]

Mrs. Fisher and the family apparently remained on the continent, for continuing reasons of economy, during the summer of 1879. Fisher lived with them for a time at Bruges[4] and Mrs. Fisher was still there when he took up his next appointment in September. This was in command of the *Northampton*, flagship of Vice-Admiral Sir Leopold McClintock, who was about to take over the North American station. Fisher's eldest child Beatrix, now aged twelve, had not been well and, all in all, Mrs. Fisher

---

[1] F.P. 1445, F. to Mrs. F., 17 July 1879 (*FG*).
[2] N.M.M.. PHI/120, F. to Hornby, 6 Mar.
[3] F.P. 2 (*F.G.* i, 96—but the date is February, not July).
[4] *Memories*, pp. 152–3.

does not seem to have relished the prospect of her continuing exile. 'I do hope', Fisher wrote from Portland on 4 November, 'that you will keep up your spirits and I hope you may be able to bring Beatrix over to Southsea before we go on December 7th.'[1]

The *Northampton* was a brand-new ship of 7,360 tons. She occupies a place in the history of construction as the first ship to be completed with a submerged armoured deck at both ends, and subdivision, instead of a continuous armoured belt. Laid down in 1874 she thus corresponded somewhat to the ideas which Fisher had adumbrated in 'Naval Tactics' in 1871. This was true also in so far as the *Northampton*, and her sister the *Nelson*, were the first armoured ships in which thicker belt armour and heavier guns were provided at the expense of protection for the guns. Fisher apparently commented favourably on the water-tight compartments as rendering the ship 'practically unsink-able'.[2] However, the *Northampton* failed completely to meet his demand of 1871 that 'masts and sails should be done away with.' In fact, with a ratio of sail area to tonnage more generous than that provided aboard the *Bellerophon*, she came near the end of the line of fully masted ships. In sum, she is reckoned to have been one of the least useful products of the Barnaby era. Barnaby thought of her as an armoured cruiser rather than a battleship, and as a natural successor to the *Bellerophon* on the North American station. But with a top speed of 14 knots (slightly less than that achieved by 'Old Billy') she was not fast enough for her intended role and contrasted with Fisher's later con-ception of an armoured cruiser which could catch the fastest marauder.[3]

On the whole, Fisher's service in the *Northampton* could be described as a repeat performance. There was the usual shake-up on commissioning followed by pranks and jollity on the station. Admiral John Moresby, the explorer, was then Captain in charge of the dockyard and establishments at Bermuda and some of the Captains in the squadron would bring him game and mutton from Halifax in return for his hospitality. He later recorded that Fisher expressed his appreciation in the form of a live sheep tossed into his garden as the flag-ship was putting to sea. However,

---

[1] F.P. 1446.
[2] Kilv. MSS., Pkt. 40, Adl. Sir George Egerton to 2nd Ld. F., 9 Nov. 1921.
[3] Parkes, pp. 239–40, 243.

he considered that, as a practical joker, Fisher was outdone by another Captain then serving on the station, one William Kennedy. For instance, Kennedy invited to dine with him two men who had recently quarrelled. On opening their napkins, they each found a pistol thoughtfully enclosed! Kennedy was also on record as saying that anyone serving with Fisher required 'the temper of an angel and the hide of a rhinoceros'. Nevertheless, Fisher's officers and ship's company apparently settled down to enjoy his rigorous and sometimes theatrical regime, and genuinely regretted his departure. This was true of his initially harassed Commander, Wilmot Fawkes (who was to prove important to Fisher in 1900–2); and one of the Midshipmen afterwards testified that 'all the Gunroom asked to go with him' when he was called back to England.[1]

While Fisher was on the station, Philip (his favourite brother according to Bacon) was in the vicinity as a Lieutenant aboard the *Atalanta*, a training-ship for ordinary seamen. Philip, who had recently served aboard the royal yacht, was much liked by Queen Victoria and, being keen to have a second spell of service aboard the *Atalanta*, he succeeded by indirect means in enlisting the Queen's support. He was duly reappointed to the *Atalanta* which foundered without trace near the West Indies in 1880. The *Northampton* was one of the ships employed on the melancholy task of searching for survivors. The only indication of Fisher's reaction at the time of the disaster is the following scrap in a letter of 5 May 1880 written at 'The Farm', Bermuda, and addressed to Admiral Hornby: 'We are very anxious about the "Atalanta". I regret to say my young brother is on board her. I do trust she is only dismasted.'[2]

The same letter (to Hornby) is also of interest in showing Fisher well abreast of the current discussions at the Admiralty which soon led to the laying-down of the *Collingwood* (12 July 1880). In general, she embodied in updated form the leading features of Key's ideal, unrigged battleship of 1866 and, as the first of a whole class of similar vessels (known subsequently as the 'Admiral class'), she marks the end of the era of experimental construction. She was the first British ship with a main armament of breech-loading guns mounted in elevated barbettes, as distinct

[1] Bacon, i, 64–72; Moresby, *Two Admirals* (1909), pp. 391–2. Kilv. MSS., Pkt. 40, A. Trevelyan Taylor to 2nd Ld. F., 1 Sept. 1921.
[2] Bacon, i, 69–70; N.M.M., PHI/120.

from the old type of heavy turret. In his letter of 5 May, Fisher was already writing:

> I am more than ever sure that the barbette armament is the correct thing, the gun to be provided with a Whitworth metal umbrella.
>
> <div align="center">Advantage of Barbette
(<i>incontestible</i>)</div>
>
> 1   All round fire.
> 2   Height out of water.
> 3   Weight in centre line of ship.

He went on to define his view of guns in relation to torpedoes: 'Not that I believe in guns as opposed to the Whitehead Torpedo when that weapon of the future is taken in hand con amore. We tried to fire it ahead and gave it up, but the Danes go on trying and they make it answer even when going 14 knots through the water.'

If he approved of the *Collingwood*—the prototype of the ship of the future—there was some irony in Fisher's appointment in January 1881 to the command of the *Inflexible*. Although this extraordinary ship possessed a number of striking features, ranging from a sophisticated protective system to electric light, she was already obsolete in certain important respects before her final completion on 18 October 1881. She was fitted with full brig-rig (for peacetime cruising only) and armed with four monster muzzle-loaders, mounted in turrets placed *en échelon* on a central citadel. These guns were consequently positioned relatively close to the water and possessed severely limited arcs of fire. However, she was undoubtedly regarded as the Navy's most powerful ship at that time and, remembering the six years which Fisher had spent as a Captain without a full commission in an independent command, it comes as no surprise to find him writing to his wife from the *Northampton* at Antigua on 14 January 1881:

> My own darling heart,
>
>   You may fancy my joy this morning at the following telegram from the Admiralty to Sir Leopold [McClintock]: 'Lord Northbrook has selected Captain Fisher for the *Inflexible*. Send him home immediately, if you have no objection, and name a successor.' The Admiral is, I think, very sorry at my going away, and so say all the officers, and I really think they all mean it . . .

Fisher expected to reach Plymouth by mail steamer on 12 February, but he asked his wife, then at Wiesbaden, to remain there for a time. This was not, apparently, so much for the usual reasons of economy but because (as he put it) 'I must be most careful in all I do, because they have paid me a most wonderful compliment, I think, and I am sure to be more awfully envied and watched, so I want to show that I put duty in the first place.'[1]

Not least among the remarkable features of the *Inflexible* was the length of time taken to build her. Laid down in February 1874, she was launched in April 1876 but not completed till 18 October 1881. Fisher was borne on the books of the *Duke of Wellington*, a tender at Portsmouth, from 30 January until the *Inflexible* at last commissioned on 4 October. Almost as soon as the ship was completed, Fisher set out for the Mediterranean where the Commander-in-Chief was his old friend Sir Beauchamp Seymour. The latter, writing on 19 October in his usual gossipy style to Admiral Hornby, complained:

Jack Fisher will I suppose pass the winter in Southsea, so as to enable 'Miss [Beatrix] Fisher to paint his cabin'.[2]—vide newspaper. It makes me very angry for it shows such utter want of determination on the part of Key. I believe that John Hay would have bundled the 'Inflexible' out had he been first Naval Lord. However, if we are indirectly ruled by women at the Admiralty, it cannot be expected to go otherwise than it does.[3]

In fact, there were scant grounds for suspicion that Fisher would encourage delay. On 15 November, Seymour (at Malta) was in a position to inform Hornby:

We have got the 'Inflexible' into the dock. *I wish she had never been built.* She is a much stronger ship than the 'Duilio' [one of her Italian rivals] but too much has been attempted in her. You know I have always advocated the retention of masts and sails, and thus if I have a prejudice it is in their favour. Well, if I had my own way I would remove the masts and all their gear from her tomorrow . . .

She is well officered and manned above the average. Fisher is quite indefatigable, his Commander [Albert B. Jenkings] is a Muff . . . One has to keep one's eyes open with Mr. Jack Fisher and George

[1] *F.G.* i, 95.
[2] The painting phenomenon, in which Mrs. F. participated, was witnessed on 12 August by Prince Henry of Prussia, younger brother of the future Kaiser William II. (Adm. 53/12093 and *F.G.* i, 104).
[3] N.M.M., PHI/120 (b).

Tryon. The first wants everything belonging to other people and the other is about as wideawake a customer as you know him to be . . .[1]

The equipment of the ship included the mariner's compass devised during the 1870s by Sir William Thomson (later Lord Kelvin) and advocated by Fisher from 1878. In *Records* (pp. 21–2) Fisher also retailed a story to the effect that he converted the 'old fossil' who was Admiral Superintendent of Portsmouth Dockyard in 1881 to Swan's incandescent lamps and that these were consequently installed in the *Inflexible*. However, an official report on electric lighting, written in 1883, makes it clear that 'the Brush arc lamp system was fitted in the "Inflexible" '; this system, 'though it unfortunately caused the death of a stoker, has given great satisfaction'. But the report indicates that Swan's system was emerging as superior by 1883.[2] When the ship was working up, Thomson himself was on board. An electrical leakage having been reported, Fisher took the opportunity of discussing it on the spot with the great scientist. The latter was in the process of diagnosing 'a nasty little leak, but not likely to be dangerous to life' and was waving a deprecating finger, when he suddenly sprang into the air. The case for reducing the voltage in lighting systems aboard ship was thereby instantly reinforced.[3]

Internally, the *Inflexible* was more complicated than any other ship in the Navy and Fisher had to devise a system of direction-signs for the benefit of the ship's company. Initially, benighted ratings were wandering from one compartment to another, unsure whether they were heading forward or aft. As he wrote in *Memories* (pp. 155–6):

The 'Inflexible' in 1882 was a wonder. She had the thickest armour, the biggest guns, and the largest of everything beyond any ship in the world.[4] A man could crawl up inside the bore of one of her guns. Controversy had raged round her. The greatest Naval Architects of the time quarrelled with each other. Endless inventions were on board her, accumulated there by cranks in the long years she took building . . . There were whistles in my cabin that yelled when the boiler was going to burst, or the ship was not properly steered . . .

In March 1882 the *Inflexible* was stationed in Villefranche harbour as guardship while Queen Victoria was at Menton. Fisher duly re-established himself as a favourite. Poor Gladstone

---

[1] Ibid.   [2] Adm. 116/237.   [3] Bacon, i, 77.
[4] Actually, the *Duilio* mounted four 17.7–inch guns against the *Inflexible's* four 16-inch.

might well have envied this happy flair which was commemorated in April by the gift of a 'print in remembrance of the *Inflexible* having been stationed' at Villefranche 'as Guard Ship during Her Majesty's residence in Mentone'. This memento was supplemented by 'a Photograph of Princess Beatrice—from the Queen'.[1]

Meanwhile Fisher had been busy in the role of torpedo expert. On 22 March he sent off to Vice-Admiral Seymour a 'Memorandum for Sir Cooper Key in answer to his question as to the advisability of fitting underwater torpedo tubes in ironclads, and observations on the Whitehead torpedo generally'.

The *Inflexible* not only possessed two 14-inch torpedo carriages above water. She was the first armoured ship to be fitted with submerged tubes at the bow and she carried two second-class torpedo boats which could be lowered for night attack. There were also two other experimental contraptions for launching torpedoes which proved a great nuisance, but at least Fisher could not complain (as in earlier years) of lack of equipment! After giving details of a variety of experiments carried out since 1 January, he submitted the following recommendations:

1   Fixed tubes should be fitted underwater in all vessels (ironclads included) for firing the Whitehead torpedo ahead in a line with the keel, a single tube below and behind the ram as in 'Dandolo' for ironclads and two tubes parallel with the keel as in 'Heligoland' for unarmoured vessels.

2   Mr. Whitehead's system of Hydro-pneumatic impulse must be employed.

3   Mr. Whitehead's 15 inch torpedo should be used for this system of discharge ahead.

4   Mr. Whitehead should fit the whole apparatus complete, supply the torpedoes, run them from the ship at her maximum speed, and then turn over the whole of the arrangements complete after trial, thus following the same course as is pursued in the not more important matter of ships' engines.

5   Astern firing tubes should be fitted as in the Danish *Tyen*.

6   No more Whitehead torpedoes or apparatus connected therewith should be manufactured by the Government, as they can be obtained by contract from Mr. Whitehead, more quickly, certainly as cheap, decidedly more efficient, and we always then know that we have the latest results of Mr. Whitehead's ingenuity and experience.

[1] F.P. 4, H. Ponsonby to F., 10 Apr. 1882.

In the subsequent commentary on his recommendations, he referred to 'the torpedo, the most fatal of all weapons' in the same striking and somewhat misleading way that he would assert thirty-one years later: 'The submarine is the coming type of war vessel for sea fighting.' *Under what operational circumstances* and *when* would these prophecies be fulfilled? However, he was certainly on firmer ground in his appraisal of the ram:

> The object of discharging the torpedo ahead is to entirely avoid the use of the ram which is a most dangerous method of attack, because it is a matter of almost pure chance whether the ramming vessel does not herself get rammed, and it must never be forgotten that previous practice in peace time at ramming is impossible and experiments with gunboats, etc., are misleading, for it requires quite a different order of nerve to manipulate a first-class ironclad.

But, as far as 'vision' and foresight are concerned, it should not escape notice that he had accepted the ram as the prime weapon in 1871; and that in 1882, despite his position as an acknowledged gunnery expert, he placed the torpedo ahead of the gun. Although the torpedo certainly had a future, it was largely in a context quite unforeseen by Fisher for many years; and as far as fleet-strategy was concerned, the gun was on the point of re-asserting its primacy. He was often abreast of the most percipient naval thinking of his time, but rarely ahead of it. His forte was to collect and sift advanced ideas; then—above all—to act on them.

Enlarging on his highly controversial sixth recommendation that no more Whitehead torpedoes should be manufactured in England, Fisher commented: 'our torpedoes are never tried beyond 200 yards range, we know nothing of their actual speed and accuracy at 600 yards. A special range with smooth, clear, tideless water is required which Mr. Whitehead possesses at Fiume, and we nowhere have.' He rounded off characteristically: 'Mr. Whitehead has always been ahead of us, is now ahead of us, and always will be ahead of us; his torpedoes go faster than ours and are more accurate. They must be because the rudder is abaft the screw; no one supposes a ship would steer as well with the screw behind the rudder.'[1]

At the Admiralty Fisher's recommendations, together with comment from the *Vernon*, duly found their way into the hands of the D.N.O., Rear-Admiral Frederick A. Herbert. His com-

[1] Adm. 116/224.

ment on Fisher's last point about the rudder was brief: 'This is the system which we now carry out.' He agreed with Fisher's recommendations numbered 2 to 5. (He had already suggested purchase of two 15-inch torpedoes for trial.) On point 1, he did not see much virtue in submerged tubes for firing ahead from armoured vessels because 'the effective range of ram and torpedo approximate so nearly that, given the opportunity of using either, many would probably prefer to use the former unencumbered with any thoughts of possible danger to his own ship from over-running the torpedo or any mishap in its discharge.' However, he was awaiting 'trials with bow tube of *Polyphemus* at high speeds'. Otherwise, he roundly condemned complete reliance on Whitehead (item 6):

I entirely disagree with this proposition. Independent of the points of cost and efficiency, I think it would be a great mistake to rely upon Foreign manufacture for such an article, because if we bought a large number at once we should lose the benefit of improvements now made annually, and if only a small number were purchased at a time, on a sudden outbreak of war the market would be closed.

In any case, it was generally considered that the Woolwich torpedo was better than Whitehead's for above-water discharge —'the two torpedoes have had a much more extended trial in "Vernon" than "Inflexible".'

Sir Cooper Key, as First Sea Lord, assessed the needs of the moment in the following succinct manner:

1 Submerged tubes should not be fitted in future, except in torpedo vessels, for firing ahead.
2 Where impulse of discharge is necessary, the Hydro Pneumatic impulse should be adopted in future.
3 Some 15-inch torpedoes should be obtained from Mr. White-head for trial and if satisfactory the pattern should be followed by Royal Laboratory for use in ships firing torpedoes ahead.
4 There can be no doubt that it is essential to continue manu-facture of torpedoes at Woolwich—for obvious reasons unneces-sary to dilate upon.
5 It is very *necessary* for the reliability of the torpedoes issued to the Fleet that a proper range should be established for testing them.
6 And it is essential that torpedoes intended for being fired from above water should be tested from above water before final adjustment and issue to the Fleet.[1]

1 Ibid., mins. of 24 and 28 Apr. 1882 by Herbert and Key.

The impression produced by the whole transaction is that, as a Captain aged forty-one, Fisher had produced a technical memorandum embodying some useful points but marred by one technically dubious and one generally unwise recommendation. In terms of professional judgement, he did not on this occasion show himself superior to the D.N.O. of the day—let alone the First Sea Lord.

However, there can be no doubt as to Fisher's exceptional activity aboard the *Inflexible*. The ship's log testifies to frequent visitations by Seymour who was clearly full of interest in the torpedo experiments, including an exercise at Malta in April involving the *Inflexible's* two torpedo boats. In May the ship went back into dock. Fisher profited by an opportunity to visit the French naval port of Toulon. Although his report has not survived, a summary in the appropriate digest, to date 6 May, can be given:

Notes by Captain Fisher, H.M.S. *Inflexible*, on French Fleet and Dockyards, forwarded. Particulars respecting anchors, armour, conning towers, electric lights, ironclads, ordnance, torpedoes and torpedo gunboats, etc., enclosed. Printed copy enclosed. Copy sent to C.-in-C. Mediterranean and their Lordships. Thanks conveyed to Captain Fisher.[1]

Later in the month the Fleet sailed for Crete. While in Suda Bay on 6 June, Seymour received orders to proceed to Alexandria. A critical situation was developing in Egypt. At last the moment was approaching when the big guns of the experimental mid-Victorian Navy would fire in earnest; and Fisher in the *Inflexible* would be prominently involved.

During the 1870s British interest in Egypt, hitherto a French sphere of influence, steadily grew. Once the Suez Canal had been completed (1869) and Disraeli had purchased 45 per cent of the canal company's shares (1875) Britain, though reluctant to annex Egypt unilaterally, was unwilling to leave France in control of the new route to India. However, the Khedive Ismail ran into debt, the British and French jointly took over financial control of the country, and this quite soon led on to an extension of control. Under British and French pressure, the Sultan installed Tewfik as Khedive. The fellah officers of the Egyptian army became restive under economies imposed by the Anglo–French condominium and in 1881 they revolted under one of

[1] Adm. 53/12093; IND. 18314—52 France.

their colonels, Arabi Pasha. It is now generally accepted that Arabi was leading a genuine nationalist movement against foreign interference, including Turkish overlordship. The French, fearing a pan-Islamic threat to their whole position in North Africa, were bent on forcible suppression of Arabi. On 25 June 1882 the Sultan offered Egypt to Britain as a free gift but the anti-imperialist Gladstone (having succeeded Disraeli as Prime Minister in 1880) rejected this solution out of hand. Accepting the need to restore Anglo–French control, he hoped to obtain sanction for military intervention from the Concert of Europe. Meanwhile, in May, the activities of the Egyptian nationalists led to the British and French Mediterranean Fleets being strongly represented off Alexandria in order to discourage attacks on the European community there.

Fisher derived limited satisfaction from this virtuous exercise in international co-operation. On 11 June there were riots in Alexandria destructive of European life—fifty killed and more than sixty wounded, including the British consul. On the following day Fisher wrote in disgust to his wife:

We appear to be playing a most ridiculous part here. Last night a gunboat came out ordering us to go five miles further in, or fifteen miles from the shore, on account of a disturbance ashore. What the good of that 5 miles was no one can make out, as we were equally out of sight of the Alexandrians. Then at 7 a.m. we were ordered to go out again five miles, as things were more peaceable, we suppose! It really is too absurd. The only advantage of our laying out here is that it's very economical.[1]

The beginning of July found Seymour, flying his flag in the *Invincible*, anchored in the harbour of Alexandria together with other ships of shallow draft. His interest was focused on the various forts overlooking the harbour where Arabi's soldiers were mounting guns and strengthening the earthworks. Against a background of political crisis at home the French, despite their former interventionist tendency, ended by withdrawing from the scene altogether! Meanwhile, when Seymour reported to London that the forts were becoming a threat to the fleets, the Liberal government came to a decision—troubled, muddled, and momentous—that Seymour should bring about a cessation of work on the forts, by persuasion if possible, but if not, by force. The nationalists were determined to resist despite the inadequacy

[1] *F.G.* i, 105.

of their equipment and training. Thus, once France and Italy had backed away, it followed inevitably that a government headed by Gladstone found itself responsible for the military occupation of Egypt. The Prime Minister and a large number of radical politicians aimed at an early withdrawal from Egypt; but other Liberal ministers saw continued occupation as a strategic necessity and, what with the 'new imperialism' growing in strength at home and the Russians continuing to rouse alarums abroad, the British took many years to escape from the Egyptian coils.

On 10 July Seymour made dispositions of immediate concern to Fisher. If 'the Military Governor of Alexandria' refused to allow the British to disarm the principal forts, the squadron would attack at 5 a.m. on the following day, 11 July.

> There will be two attacks:
>
> 1   From the inside of the harbour, in which the *Invincible*, *Monarch*, and *Penelope* will take part.
> 2   By the *Sultan*, *Superb*, *Téméraire*, *Alexandra*, and *Inflexible*, from outside the breakwater . . .
>
> The *Inflexible* will move down this afternoon to the position off the Corvette Pass assigned to her yesterday, and be prepared to open fire on the guns in Mex Lines in support of the in-shore squadron when signal is made . . .

Painted black and white with buff funnels (except for the *Alexandra* and *Téméraire* which were white all over)[1] the squadron celebrated the strenuous rite of sending down top-gallant masts and rigging in bowsprits. By the evening of the 10th the ships—wildly diverse in their design—had moved into their assigned positions. Seymour, with the inshore squadron, lay only about 1,000 yards north of the Mex Lines, while the *Inflexible* was a good two miles to the northward of Mex but little more than a mile west of the Lighthouse battery.

Against the ninety-seven heavy rifled guns of the British squadron, the Egyptians could oppose only forty-four comparable weapons in addition to an interesting array of virtually useless smooth-bores. With their defective gun-mountings and poor-quality powder, as well as conspicuous and ill-protected magazines, the defenders lacked most of the essential assets

---

[1] Parkes, p. 224.

except for a fair degree of fighting spirit. So Seymour's simple but flexible plans were to prove adequate to the occasion.

Here is Fisher's considered but informal impression of the whole episode in a hitherto unpublished letter written to Hornby on 24 October:

. . . The subject naturally divides itself into three heads: (1) The bombardment, (2) the Navy ashore, (3) the Military party.

The bombardment—speaking after much reflection—was a great success but it was a great stroke of luck. The luck was all on our side. No shell from their 18 ton guns entered any of our ships' ports nor hit the deck covering the *Inflexible's* citadel which would have been pierced as brown paper at that angle of descent, and we have ¾ of a ton of gunpowder in the citadel when loading that might have exploded and with it the ship. On the other hand we had the luck to explode the magazine of their best worked fort (Ada) and one of our 8 inch shell was found unexploded, the fuse blown out, in the midst of their principal powder magazine, lying harmlessly amidst 300 tons of gunpowder. However, that was not luck. It would have been luck if we had possessed efficient fuses. Thanks, however, to Sir John Adye [Director of Artillery, 1870–5], Sir Frederick Campbell and Woolwich Arsenal, and our supineness in the Navy in not cutting ourselves free and getting all we want by open competition, that magazine did not explode. The failure of our fuses was shocking. I believe now the Ordnance Committee are to invent a fuse. Why not ask them to invent a new kind of perambulator! The thing ought to be put up to public competition—they did that when they wanted a good rifle; they had I think about 2,000 sent in.

We are in the same predicament about our guns. The Egyptians had Krupp guns with a range of 8,600 yards as measured by Wilson of the *Hecla*. We have nothing to compare with it. We shall have but we have them not (afloat). Why is this? Because we couldn't have long guns because we wouldn't have breech loaders. If the Navy had been free to buy in the market and had not been under the heel of Woolwich, we should long ago have had steel breech loaders. Now Woolwich is going to begin at steel when steel is becoming obsolete and it's time to take to wire.[1] However, I am getting off the bombardment. Please excuse the digression but it makes my blood boil when I reflect how Admiral Boys ruined us by pandering to Sir John Adye and Sir F. Campbell. Sir Cooper Key when he was D.N.O. got us the gun wharves and would have got everything, but he went, and after that it was a case of 'trim sails'. Broadside ships are a relic of the

---

[1] In 1884 the Superintendent of the Royal Ordnance Factory finally admitted the obsolescence of the Woolwich guns.

past. The guns are so powerful and so few, we ought to be able to fire all of them: therefore in all ships (no matter how small) they ought to be on central pivots, central or echelon barbettes.[1] This was noticeable at Alexandria. To see the *Alexandra, Superb* and *Sultan* fighting at half power and with stern anchors, springs, etc., with a chance of fouling their screws, even to get their half power to fight on account of the small training given by their broadside ports.

Our shooting was not all that could be desired. You will remember that it admits of arithmetical demonstration that the firers of our guns should be 620 times better than in the year 1854. This I humbly think one of the most burning questions connected with the Navy. A *corps d'elite* of great gun marksmen, to be sought for and exercised with as much solicitude and with as certain a prospect of great reward as a Prima Donna. The other lesson of the bombardment was the want of light guns in the armament of our ships but especially in the *Inflexible.* The niggers ran out like rabbits after we had fired, knowing it would be a long time before we fired again. We should have kept them down with a light armament, besides the great advantage of their serving as range-finders for the big guns. I much prefer the Hotchkiss machine gun to the Nordenfelt; the man who aims, fires in the case of the Hotchkiss; in the Nordenfelt No. 1 aims, No. 2 fires. I took the liberty of asking Admiral Herbert if he ever would hit a snipe if another fellow had to pull the trigger!

Then again it is such a great disadvantage firing a shell, which the Hotchkiss does and the Nordenfelt don't. You see where it hits. We fired tons of Nordenfelt bullets at Alexandria. The Lord only knows where they went to. However, the Khedive told me he found some in his bed which was a precious long way from the Egyptian gunners that we were firing at.

The sailors ashore behaved admirably. We had a very rough time of it, the first few days of the occupation of Alexandria. Like St. Paul we were troubled within and without: no transport, of course, no commissariat, nothing. However with . . . 1,200 men at first, gradually increasing to 2,700, we handed over the concern to the military who thought 5,000 too few, and General Alison told us, and I really think with truth, that we had done splendidly. We marched the sailors round like the army in the theatre, and like we humbugged Sir Sydney Dacres with the division of cutlass men (who retired down one ladder and came up another, a fresh set of faces aft), so we humbugged the Egyptians into magnifying us into an army, for Arabi might have eaten us without salt. It was the multitude of things we had to do which was so harassing. The brigades, Police, Commissariat,

---

[1] Key's administration was meeting these requirements, and many others, in the emergent 'Admiral' class.

spare ammunition; looking outside for Arabi and looking inside after his friends and the Khedive's Ministers, all nominees of Arabi in constant communication with him, and the line of fortifications round the city 5 miles in length with many a weak point, and our ridiculously small force quite knocked up from want of sleep. But it all went off all right, chiefly attributable to our having plenty of officers with the men, and the officers knowing their men and calling them by their names, and this struck me as being one of the great differences between us and the Army.

The Marines fully deserve all the praise they have received but from all I have heard the Indian contingent bears the palm for completeness of organization, endurance and fighting qualities generally. They never seem to have been adrift for anything and actually sold their grub and forage to our people . . .[1]

If the 'Fisher era' was still a number of years off, several of its dramatis personae were already to be found aboard the British ships involved in the action of 11 July. Apart from Fisher himself, there was Captain A. K. Wilson (in command of the Torpedo Depot Ship *Hecla* which supplied shells to the bombarding squadron). Amongst prospective swimmers in 'the Fish-pond' were Lieutenant C. L. Ottley of the *Monarch* and Midshipman R. H. S. Bacon of the *Alexandra*; and Lieutenants Percy Scott, Prince Louis of Battenberg, and J. R. Jellicoe were on the scene soon after the bombardment. The future anti-Fisher school was strongly represented by Lord Charles Beresford (who made a name for himself on the 11th as commander of the composite gun-vessel *Condor*), Lieutenant the Hon. Hedworth Lambton, and Lieutenant F. C. D. Sturdee of the *Hecla*. However, there was no such rift in the naval lute of 1882. After the bombardment, Fisher was put in command of the Naval Brigade and, on his recommendation, Beresford was appointed under him as Provost Marshal and Chief of Police. In November, Fisher, who subsequently received the C.B. for his services at Alexandria, regretted that Beresford had not been awarded at least a C.M.G.[2]

During the bombardment and subsequent service ashore Fisher was involved in several incidents, besides those communicated to Hornby, which deserve mention in their chronological sequence. On the 11th many shots were fired at the *Inflexible* but only two hits of any real significance were made.

[1] N.M.M., PHI/120 (b).
[2] Bennett, p. 86; *F.G.* i, 113.

These hits illustrated the efficacy of her protective arrangements, namely sub-division of the unarmoured ends and submerged armoured deck. Thus, a glancing hit on the port quarter near the water-line caused a leak in the breadroom, above the protective deck, but there was no flooding outside that compartment. Secondly, a 10-inch Palliser shell from the comparatively close and bothersome Lighthouse battery penetrated the unarmoured side below the water-line aft, struck the convex armoured deck, and flew upwards, base first, to stamp the word 'Palliser' in reverse on the bitts situated on the upper deck. This projectile killed the ship's Carpenter and mortally wounded a Lieutenant directing a 20-pounder mounted on the superstructure.[1] As regards the shooting of the squadron, that of the *Inflexible* and the *Téméraire* seems to have been the most impressive.[2]

Although the bombardment succeeded in producing the final withdrawal of Arabi's forces from the forts on 13 July, rioting was now widespread in Egypt and Arabi was soon threatening to destroy the Suez Canal. On the 14th, Fisher landed 'to take possession of the forts and city and [he wrote to his wife] the two following days were the most anxious ones I have ever spent in my life, as our force was quite inadequate'.[3] Troops from Malta and Cyprus began to arrive on the 17th. Meanwhile orders had been sent to Seymour to retain command of all the forces at Alexandria. The Admiralty telegraphed: 'The primary object of employment of forces on shore is police protection of place and it is essential for political reasons to avoid appearance of military occupation.' On the 17th Seymour therefore appointed senior naval officers to various key appointments in the city, including Fisher to command a 'Naval Brigade' consisting of seamen and Marines.[4] At about the same time Arabi Pasha issued a proclamation in the following terms:

The Khedive has imprisoned the Ministers at Alexandria through the medium of the English soldiers in order that they may be instruments in their hands to serve their ends . . .
The defence of our reputation, of our religion and of our Country is obligatory according to the Moslem law and faith. Irreconcilable war exists between us and the English and all those who prove traitors to their duty and their Country will not only be subjected to the

---

[1] Parkes, p. 257; Bacon, i, 81–3. [2] Parkes, pp. 257, 315.
[3] *F.G.* i, 107. [4] Adm. 116/34.

severest punishment in accordance with martial law but will be for ever accursed in the future world.[1]

Until the arrival of an expeditionary force under Sir Garnet Wolseley on 16 August the position of the British forces seemed precarious, but Arabi failed to profit by his opportunities to mount a counterattack.

On 26 July, Fisher and A. K. Wilson hit on the idea of using the railway to support reconnaissance. Major-General Sir Archibald Alison, who commanded the troops, was 'much taken with' the 'ironclad truck armed with gatlings' shown to him by Fisher and Wilson and (wrote Wilson) 'this led up to the idea of mounting a heavy gun in the same way. I had some trouble in persuading the Admiral to let me try, as of course, in duty bound, he foresaw all sorts of dangers and difficulties.'[2] The upshot was a reconnaissance in force beyond Malaha Junction late in the afternoon on 5 August. The operation as a whole was commanded by General Alison who rode in 'the Naval armoured train' with Fisher and his 'Naval Brigade' (which consisted of only 200 men). The train comprised:

1   Two empty trucks.

2   Truck carrying 40-pounder gun mounted on slide, with pivots and racers laid down; breeching secured to bolts in the truck.

3   Ammunition waggon for 40-pounder, protected by iron plates and railway iron.

4   Machine-gun truck, carrying one Nordenfelt and one Gatling gun. Truck protected by iron plates and sandbags.

5   Engine protected by iron plates and sandbags.

6   Torpedo truck, protected by iron plates, and carrying materials for destroying rails or bridges, and electro-contact torpedoes for use against trains.[3]

7   Field-gun truck, carrying two 9-pounders.

8   Portable steam crane to lift 10 tons.

9   Machine-gun waggon, with one Gatling gun, and protected embrasure to the rear.[4]

---

[1] Adm. 116/35.

[2] Bradford, pp. 69–70.

[3] Thus was born, apparently, the precursor of the anti-tank mine. Cf. Cowie, p. 28.

[4] Adm. 116/36. Enclosure with Fisher's report of 6 Aug.

A second train carried about 700 Marines. The equivalent of two battalions of troops also took part in the operation. Fisher afterwards reported to Seymour:

> . . . On arrival at the broken rails at Malaha Junction, we disembarked the two 9-pr. Naval guns (using the portable steam crane for that purpose) . . . In pursuance of the General's orders, we opened fire with the 'Hecla's' 40 pr. . . . directly the enemy opened with his artillery. This gun, under the personal directions of Captain Wilson, of H.M.S. 'Hecla', made most excellent practice during the whole engagement.[1]

Fisher did not report the fact that, while supervising the relaying of the track by seamen and marines, he happened to stand too close to Wilson's truck and 'was knocked down by the concussion of the gun and stunned for a time'.[2] The line was nevertheless 'most expeditiously relaid' and, Fisher reported, 'we proceeded in the armoured train to some distance beyond the junction, to the place where we had broken up the rails some time back.' It was too late in the day to restore this section.

> The heaviest fire from the enemy appeared to be now directed on the right flank of the Marine Battalion. The Naval guns were at this time doing good service, and, I believe, prevented the enemy making use of his reinforcements, which were now being brought up by trains from his rear. Towards dusk the General gave orders for the re-embarkation of the men and guns, which was conducted with great steadiness and order, and we continued firing till the 40-pounder was out of range.

Seymour covered Fisher's report with a letter of 8 August which ended as follows:

> The Major-General in command speaks in the highest terms of the conduct of the officers, seamen, and marines engaged under the orders respectively of Captains John A. Fisher, of the 'Inflexible', and A. K. Wilson, of the 'Hecla', Lieutenant William L. Morrison, who commanded the guns engaged on our left, and of Lieutenant-Colonel Tuson, of the Royal Marine Artillery. They all seem to have behaved with the utmost coolness and gallantry. I am assured by the General that the exertions of the seamen in dragging the field guns through heavy sand under a hot rifle fire were most conspicuous.

---

[1] Ibid., Fisher's report.
[2] Kilv. MSS., Pkt. labelled 'Stopford's Orders', 'Certificate for Wounds and Hurts'.

Arabi's forces engaged in this clash were thought to number about 2,000 with 6 guns and 6 rocket tubes. Seymour reported that they were 'supposed to have suffered severely' and that some of the prisoners taken by the British were badly wounded. The British losses amounted to two killed and about twenty wounded.[1]

Most of the Naval Brigade re-embarked on 11 August. On the 16th General Wolseley arrived at Alexandria with the expeditionary force. In furtherance of the General's plans, the Navy moved to secure Port Said and Ismailia. A Naval Brigade was to use the railway on 13 September—which turned out to be the day of Wolseley's crushing victory over Arabi at Tel el Kebir; but much to his own disappointment, Fisher was not fit to go with them. Having returned to the *Inflexible*, he was struck down with a severe attack of dysentery on 22 August. On the 29th Fisher was writing prematurely to his wife that he was 'perfectly well again'; but the medical treatment meted out to him may help to explain the persistence of his disagreeable ailment. Sedgewick, Fleet Surgeon aboard the *Inflexible*, 'having had a great experience of dysentery in the East Indies and China, had learnt by experience that the only way to cure dysentery is to poison the patient with ipecacuanha. The remedy [wrote Fisher] was 50 times worse than the disease; the sickness was simply indescribable.' In fact, he did not shake off the trouble for at least another four years.[2]

On 2 August, a Captain George Clarke, R.E., whom Fisher had met at Bermuda in 1881, had arrived at Alexandria with orders 'to make a detailed report on the defences, and the effects of the fire of the fleet upon them'. In 1904 Fisher would insist on the need to appoint this brilliant but somewhat indiscreet officer to the post of Secretary of the Committee of Imperial Defence. By 1906, he would be equally anxious for his dislodgement. Owing to Fisher's illness, the two men did not meet in 1882; but Fisher, who managed despite his ailment to submit some detailed reports of his own on the same subject, experienced a distinct foretaste of his subsequent irritations with Clarke. On seeing a preliminary draft[3] of Clarke's report in December, Fisher wrote to Seymour (now Lord Alcester):

---

[1] Adm. 116/36; Clowes, vii, 340–1.

[2] Clowes, vii, 341–5; Bacon, i, 88; *F.G.* i, 108–9, 111.

[3] 'The text occupied nearly one hundred printed foolscap pages, and all was finished on February 13.' Sydenham, p. 32.

A Captain Clarke, R.E., has sent in an official report about the bombardment in which he does his best to minimise what the ships did. There are two glaring inaccuracies in his report. He states that there were no rifled guns ever at Marabout, but you will remember you sent Wilson down with the Khedive's people to have them dismounted. Then he says the Egyptian magazines were very ill-provided . . . I believe this report will in due course come to you, in which case I trust you will call on Wilson and Younghusband to report on it, as I believe it to be a very one-sided affair . . .[1]

There can be no doubt at least that, as Clarke wrote in his memoirs, 'most of the magazines were recklessly exposed'. As for the rifled guns, it seems possible (from what Fisher wrote to Lord Alcester) that they were removed before Clarke examined Marabout.

Clarke looked through his report when he was composing his memoirs in the 1920s. It still appeared to him to be 'exhaustive'. Reflecting on the disastrous Dardanelles affair of 1915, he thought that 'the Carden plan and its ready acceptance at Whitehall by Mr. Churchill and the advisers whom he was moulding to his will would have been impossible if this information had been studied.' He had warned against the disadvantages of ships attacking forts and had stated: 'The effect of the fire of modern guns on earthworks had been, on the whole, immensely overrated.'[2]

In point of fact, Fisher's conclusions did not fundamentally differ from Clarke's. On 1 August the Admiralty wrote to Seymour asking for a statement about the bombardment. On the 5th Seymour circularized his Captains, asking seven questions. Fisher replied from the Naval Brigade Headquarters (in the Khedive's palace) on 7 August; and to judge by marginal scoring it was only Fisher's response which received close attention at the Admiralty.[3] In answer to a question about the effects of 'heavy shell-fire on earthworks and masonry', Fisher wrote: 'The earthworks have sustained very little damage from our shell, and could be easily and rapidly repaired . . . Masonry has, on the other hand, suffered considerably, whole buildings being demolished by one shell.'

Despite the onset of dysentery Fisher compiled a further report,

[1] *F.G.* i, 113, 20 Dec. 1882.
[2] Sydenham, pp. 32-4.
[3] Adm. 116/208. Enclosures with Seymour's report dated 10 Aug. 1882.

dated 26 September, which embodied his detailed conclusions about the bombardment.[1]

Further Observations on the Bombardment of the Forts at Alexandria

Although several reports have been submitted on the subject of the bombardment . . . a few points of some interest still remain to be discussed.

The marked features of this engagement between ships and forts are—

(a) The magnitude of the armaments on both sides.
(b) The complete success of the ships.
(c) The causes which so greatly favoured that success.
(d) The erroneous views which this success may possibly engender . . .

It will probably be conceded that the plan of attack left little to be desired. As far as practicable the positions of the ships were so arranged as to enfilade the batteries, and the intention of the Commander-in-Chief that the forts should be reduced seriatim was in the main adhered to. These two principles of a flank attack and a concentration of fire are of an equal force afloat as ashore.

When ships pass and repass a line of forts, each gun of the enemy in succession deliberately delivers its fire; the ship is unable to fire at each gun of the enemy, because her guns cannot be loaded quickly enough. The enemy thus acquires confidence, and the ship is more injured than she otherwise would be . . . the advantage is thrown away of the unsteadying effect produced on the unengaged guns' crews of the enemy in seeing each battery successively demolished.

It is however to be noted that it may more often be the case for ships to be forcing a passage past a line of forts, as in the case of Admiral Farragut at New Orleans, or the passage of the Dardanelles, when rapidity of movement on the part of the ships past the forts would be the principal element of success, and when probably an attack by night would place the ships more on an equality with the forts as to difficulty in knowing the range.

It is this difficulty of ascertaining the range with exactness, and the still greater difficulty which exists in every ship of conveying the distance of the enemy to the captains of the guns which makes our gunnery practice so uncertain. If a good range-finder could be devised for use on board ship, a great want would be supplied.

If it is not an improper expression to make use of, the luck was all on the side of the ships at the bombardment of the forts at Alexandria;

---

[1] Adm. 116/208, 'Further Report (No. 3) by Captain J. A. Fisher, R.N., of H.M.S. "Inflexible", respecting the Bombardment of the Forts at Alexandria', forwarded to Admiralty by Seymour on 5 Oct.

the enemy possessed sufficiently powerful ordnance in their heavy rifled guns to produce on board most of our ships . . . destructive effects . . .; but though their men were most courageous they were not at all expert, and this offers one more illustration of the really vital importance of specially selected and specially trained marksmen as captains of our guns . . . Much has been done of late years to improve the shooting of our men as a whole by the introduction of prize firing and a more extended course of target practice in the gunnery ships; but what is urgently needed is a small special body of marksmen . . .

Another piece of good fortune favoured the ships in that the enemy, though well provided with artillerymen, made no use of the large number of mortars mounted along the whole line of his fortifications —some of them of large calibre. Vertical fire is perhaps the greatest danger to which ships are exposed in engaging forts manned by skilled artillerymen provided with accurate range-finders.

The absence of three other great disturbing causes, namely, stationary mines, hostile torpedo boats, and machine gun fire, enabled the ships to choose and maintain the most effective positions for damaging the enemy, and prevented that loss of superior officers which otherwise would probably have occurred, judging from the conspicuous positions they occupied, due probably to the difficulty they had in seeing anything from their respective conning towers.

A European enemy would have certainly employed torpedo boats and machine guns, and his system of defence would probably have prevented ships taking up an enfilading position by rendering such a position unapproachable through the agency of mechanical torpedoes . . .

It would certainly seem desirable that all captains of ships should be supplied with a confidential book giving plans and information respecting the principal military seaports of the world. A considera-tion of the best or the various methods of attacking such fortresses might usefully employ the time of a combined Naval and Military Committee. In the case of Alexandria our information was most meagre . . .

So far as the batteries of Alexandria are concerned, it has been clearly shown in previous communications that though a number of the enemy's guns were disabled by our fire . . . yet the principal cause of our success was the havoc made amongst the enemy by the *débris* of the embrasures and masonry when struck by our projectiles. Embrasures appear to be a mistake, and the great value of parapets constructed of rammed sand, as opposed to stone or stiff earth, has been already commented on in referring to the long resistance offered by Fort Omuk-Kubébé and the battery at the Hospital Point.

In the case of both these forts just mentioned, the practice we made against them was very good, our projectiles apparently lodging just on the muzzles of the enemy's guns, round after round in succession, and a careful examination afterwards showed that the practice was quite as good as it appeared to be.

Now if the practice from those rifled guns at Omuk-Kubébé and the Hospital Fort had been equally accurate, the 'Inflexible', for one, would certainly have been hit by them nearly every round, and great damage must have been caused . . .

One point which has to be borne in mind when ships engage forts is that the ship has to hit the gun or the crew; the fort has only to hit the ship. From this appears to flow the conclusion that a ship intended to engage shore batteries ought to have a great number of comparatively light guns so as to increase her chances of hitting and to prevent the guns' crews having time to rally between the long and awful pauses of heavy gun firing . . .[1]

Another remarkable point to be noted during the bombardment was that all the broadside ships were fighting at half power . . . The conclusion which appears to follow from this is that guns should be mounted on central or échelon barbettes, so as to admit of concentrating the whole power of the ship on an enemy, whether ship or fort. Even down to our smallest vessels this principle should guide their armament, the masts and sails being considered a secondary point . . .

Unless the Naval Force employed in a bombardment is of overwhelming force, the Admiral has to consider that his supply of powder and projectiles is limited . . . whereas the enemy can, as was the case at Alexandria, have enormous supplies of ammunition and spare guns and carriages ready to hand.

This was undoubtedly a valuable report. It represents Fisher near his peak; and it shows how expert he really was, at least in the middle 1880s, on the subject of ships attacking forts. It is also relevant to the agonized arguments and discussions in which Fisher would be involved before the naval attack on the Dardanelles in 1915: the problem of exact range-finding from the ships, the possible effects of 'stationary mines', the apt summary that 'the ship has to hit the gun or the crew; the fort has only to hit the ship.' There is even the reference, by way of example, to 'the passage of the Dardanelles'. On the other hand, this document also illustrates the limitations of historical precedent, even where the technological factors have not changed out of recognition. The example of 1882, well analysed, might have provided a

---

[1] It took about two minutes to reload and fire one of the *Inflexible's* big guns.

useful starting-point for an appraisal of the prospects in the Dardanelles in 1915. But having, for instance, pointed to the need to consider the effect of mines, the paper of 1882 can of course tell nothing about how many mines the Turks of 1915 would lay, or where they would lay them, or whether the mines would fire efficiently on contact. In October 1916 the Chairman of the Dardanelles Commission would ask A. K. Wilson whether Fisher had ever expressed 'an opinion favourable or the reverse on the practicality' of knocking out the Turkish forts. Wilson replied:

I do not think he ever expressed an opinion against the practicality; but, like everybody else, he had certain doubts. We all had doubts, because there were so many uncertain factors. We did not know the exact extent of the Turkish preparations; we did not know the exact extent of their ammunition supplies; we did not know exactly what mobile guns they could bring up. All these questions were matters that nobody could tell us about . . .[1]

Despite these imponderables, what Fisher did know from his past experience at Alexandria and his personal acquaintance with the Dardanelles was that a naval attack on the latter, without troops, would be a decidedly hazardous affair.

[1] Cab. 19/33, Dard. Comm., p. 275.

CHAPTER 5

THE *EXCELLENT* AND THE ADMIRALTY (1883–1897); AMERICAN EPISODE (1897–1899)

FISHER's illness was not entirely lacking in consolation. The Queen was concerned and sent solicitous messages, for example through Admiral Sir William Dowell, then commanding the Channel Squadron. The latter wrote to Mrs. Fisher: 'The Queen made most kind inquiries about Captain Fisher's health and desired me to convey to him from her, her great regret at his illness and her hopes that he will soon recover.'[1] Moreover, the following early record of the future Edward VII's friendly interest in Fisher, which was subsequently so important to the latter, is worthy of notice:

Dear Madam,

I am desired by the Prince and Princess of Wales to convey to you the expression of T.R.Hs. sincere regret at Captain Fisher's illness— and to ask you kindly to let me know for their information how he is progressing.

T.R.Hs. greatly hope that he is getting well through his very untoward illness and the Prince of Wales wishes me to add that he trusts when Captain Fisher is convalescent he may have an early opportunity of seeing him in London.

T.R.Hs. return to Sandhm. on Saty . . .[2]

On a more professional level, Lord Northbrook (the First Lord of the Admiralty) urged Fisher to give up his command and come home for the sake of his health—'We can get many *Inflexibles*, but only one Jack Fisher.'[3] But Fisher was very reluctant to leave the ship. On 24 October he wrote from Malta to Hornby (soon to be Commander-in-Chief, Portsmouth):

Yesterday I received your most kind letter with the offer of Lordington and I do most sincerely thank you and Lady Hornby for

[1] F.P. 1453, 22 Nov. 1882.
[2] F.P. 1454, Col. Arthur Ellis to Mrs. F., 23 Nov.
[3] Bacon, i, 89.

your more than kindness in thinking of me and I do most thoroughly appreciate it. Some old gentleman wrote in a book that one of the pleasures of being ill was finding out who his friends were and I quite agree with him.

I think I am all right now. I have an occasional twinge in the internal regions but with care, going to bed with the chickens, and such like precautions and avoiding Sir Beauchamp's banquets, I trust to keep all right and I am sure I shall have your approval in sticking to the ship while I can. I dare say any other conjuror would manage this box of tricks just as well but it requires some practice; and with a new Commr., Staff Commr., Chief Engineer, Carpenter, etc., I should not have enjoyed being away from the ship, though the temptation to go home was very great and the Admiralty made it so pleasant that the general opinion out here (shared even by Sir Beauchamp) is that I must have softening of the brain to have foregone the pleasure of going home . . .[1]

Financial reasons also made Fisher reluctant to give up his command. However, although he was finally invalided home in November, he remained on the books of the *Inflexible* till 31 December. He carried with him a valued memento in the form of a letter of condolence from the ship's company of the *Inflexible*, written during the early part of his illness. It convincingly testifies to the good relations which he continued to enjoy with the lower deck. His popularity with the ratings was a feature of his career as a whole and contributed to the morale of the fleet which had ultimately to face the testing conditions of 1914–18.

H.M.S. 'INFLEXIBLE'

27 August 1882

Sir,

We, the ship's company of H.M.S. *Inflexible*, take the earliest opportunity of expressing to you our deep sorrow and sympathy on this sad occasion of your sickness, and it is our whole wish that you may speedily recover and be amongst us again, who are so proud of serving under you. Sir, we are all aware of the responsible duties you had to perform, and the great number of men you had to see to during your long stay on shore at Alexandria, which must have brought the strongest to a bed of sickness; but we trust shortly to see you again amongst us and on the field of active service, where you are as much at home as on your own grand ship, and at the end may you receive your share of rewards and laurels, and your ship's company will then feel as proud and prouder than if it was bestowed on themselves.

[1] N.M.M., PHI/120 (b).

Sir, trusting that you will overlook the liberty we have taken in sending this to you,

We beg to remain,

Your faithful and sympathizing ship's company,

INFLEXIBLES.[1]

Fisher indicated his own reaction to this remarkable tribute when he wrote to his wife: 'I have been much touched by the men sending me such a nice letter. There's no doubt we are very good friends with each other. I am going to have it framed one day as being one of the most valued things I possess.'[2]

Fisher continued to be plagued with dysentery. Consequently it was not until 6 April 1883 that he was appointed to his last command as a Captain. Twenty-one years after he first went there to be trained as a Gunnery Lieutenant he became the commanding officer of his 'beloved "Excellent" '.

Queen Victoria was said to have harboured a feeling of resentment against the Navy because the Admiralty had refused to make the Prince Consort an Admiral of the Fleet[3] but she continued to show a marked liking for Fisher which was expressed in January 1883 by an invitation to stay at Osborne. A similar annual invitation was issued subsequently whenever he was in England. Fisher was anxious about how his ailment would fit in with protocol during his stay, but on 22 January he was able to report to his wife:

Darling Heart,

I am all right. Two cups of tea and bread and butter, and a very comfortable sofa and a delightful sitting room out of my bed room, deliciously quiet, have all combined to renovate me. I am let off the knee breeches which is a weight off my mind! The rooms I have are called 'Baron Stockmar's' . . . these were his rooms.

We do not dine till 9 o'clock, my proper time to go to bed! . . .

A fortnight later, on 5 February, he wrote again from Osborne:

The man-in-black has just been in to my room to say I am to dine with the Queen. No one else here. Isn't it awful! Sir John Cowell[4] told me the Queen put me off coming last night as she wished to have a good opportunity of talking to me! Sir John Cowell met me at the Pier and I walked up with him and Major Edwardes . . . I had a

[1] Bacon, i, 92.   [2] *F.G.* i, 109, 29 Aug.
[3] Bacon, i, 80.   [4] Major-General and Master of the Household.

little talk with Lady Ely who enquired after you and Beatrix . . .
[The] barber came into my room as white as a sheet just now, having
lost his way and gone into someone's bed room—perhaps a maid of
honour's! No time for more.[1]

In March Fisher's late Commander-in-Chief, Lord Alcester,
was also invited to Osborne and wrote to ask Fisher about dress
and the routine generally. Fisher sent a full and helpful reply,
including such items as: 'She talks to one a good deal more than
I expected'; 'She is sometimes silent for a little time, preparing
her next subject of conversation, and I believe the plan is to
remain silent also'; 'The Princess [Beatrice] always sits next to
her, and the most comfortable place is next the Princess, as she
is so very pleasant and helps on the conversation.' On a delicate
point of protocol:

I would suggest your asking Ponsonby[2] if you are to kiss the Queen's
hand on first seeing her. I ought to have done so, but they did not
warn me about it, so when she put her hand out I was all adrift. I
think you will find her very glad to see you and very pleasant, judging
from the manner she spoke of you . . . The Queen is uncommon
particular about medals, etc., being put on the right way.[3]

When Fisher took up his post in the *Excellent*, he mustered
sufficient energy to administer a characteristic shake-up. He
cleared out of the establishment numbers of pensioners who took
up space better occupied by personnel under training. Up till
this time, smooth-bore guns were apparently still used for firing
practice. These were replaced by quick-firing guns. According
to the historian of the *Excellent*:

This period [1883–6] may be considered to mark the 'revolution'
in Naval Gunnery, particularly as regards training. It was no longer
considered heresy to decry in the smoking room what was then known
as the 'Forty Years' Routine'. Though Fisher was all his life an advocate of progress and reform, and equally strongly an opponent of
conversatism and tradition, the change of feeling was not entirely due
to him. Credit must be given to the progressive Staff Officers of the
day, who gradually introduced a new system of training.[4]

Amongst this capable staff were Charles C. Drury, then
Commander and later Fisher's successor as Second Sea Lord

[1] F.P. 1455; 1457.
[2] Maj.-Gen. Sir Henry Ponsonby, private secretary to the Queen.
[3] *F.G.* i, 115.   [4] Oliver, pp. 76–7.

during the innovation of the new scheme of naval education; Lieutenant Frank Younghusband, who had been Gunnery Lieutenant of the *Northampton* and then the *Inflexible* under Fisher; the ingenious Lieutenant Percy Scott; and Lieutenant J. R. Jellicoe, who joined the junior staff of the *Excellent* in May 1884, after catching Fisher's eye during the qualifying course for gunnery. The first Experimental Officer had already been appointed in 1882 to 'supervise gunnery fittings of ships preparing for commission'; Jellicoe participated in this work during 1885–6 as Assistant Experimental Officer. While Captain of the *Excellent* Fisher also began his close and important connection with Sir William Armstrong, gun manufacturer at Elswick, and with his expert on gun-mountings, Josiah Vavasseur. The adoption of breech-loading guns necessitated the design of a new type of mounting. Trials of Vavasseur mountings were held aboard the tender *Kite* in January 1883 and again in April (when Fisher took over command of the *Excellent*). Good results were obtained then; also during further trials in May and June.[1]

Fisher was still suffering severely from his ailment during 1883. On 28 August he wrote to Hornby: 'I am still on the flat of my back so please forgive a letter in pencil.' Despite his recurrent illness, Fisher was already involved in the polemical activities which were to play so considerable a part in the subsequent history of the Navy:

I send you the concluding part of the Naval Battle of Dorking [presumably a cautionary tale about naval preparedness] in case it has not caught your eye. Old Barnaby [Director of Naval Construction] has been to cross-examine me, thinking I wrote it; but four or five people wrote it, so they will never find out. The Secretary of the Admiralty [Fisher's friend, Captain George Tryon, who was Permanent Secretary, 1882–4] has gone to Scotland. He spent an hour with me the day before he left, but I hadn't an opportunity of saying a word to him!

Fisher said that his doctor had advised him 'to go North for some weeks' so he planned to stay with a cousin in Northumberland. He would apply for leave through Hornby (who remained Commander-in-Chief at Portsmouth till 1885); 'Lord Northbrook sent me a very kind message so I think I shall get it.'[2]

[1] Oliver, pp. 71–2, 76, 142–3; Patterson, pp. 21–2.
[2] N.M.M., PHI 120 (b).

His expectations were fulfilled. On 30 September he wrote again to his Commander-in-Chief:

Your letter of enquiry has just arrived and I have the honor to report as follows:

1   On the first day of my leave I was 10 stone 8 lbs. Now I am 11 stone 2 lbs.

2   *Then*, I did not much care to eat, *now*, I demolish three square meals a day.

3   Nothing but water once passed my lips, now rare old port in prodigious quantities courses through my veins and reminds me that my grandfather died of the Gout.

4   When last I saw you, no occupation was pleasing. Now each morning the wily trout in the neighbouring stream I lure to destruction with the insidious fly. I regret, however, to say that I am much humiliated by my daughter catching two fish to my one.

I really am quite well and never remember feeling better. The air here is so delicious and bracing. We are about 20 miles from Newcastle, just on the edge of the moors. Sir W. Armstrong has asked us to his place near Rothbury; we are to spend the day there tomorrow. Everything done by hydraulic power or electricity, I believe. You touch a button and all the plants in the greenhouse slowly revolve like the beautiful young lady in a hairdresser's window in Oxford St. I will endeavour to recount all the wonders when I return to Portsmouth . . .

I hope it will not be considered very improper my being absent when their Lordships pay their official visit to Portsmouth . . .[1]

These letters to Hornby show how close Fisher's relations with the Admiral had become; likewise an exchange of cards at New Year, 1883, which illustrates Fisher's buoyancy and resilience, even in ill health. Lady Hornby's card reads:

> To little Jack Fisher
> I am a well wisher
> For the year that is come, eighty three,
> So with my good wishes
> I send him some dishes
> Of Apples, and hope they'll agree.

---

[1] Ibid.

She received the following reply:

> *Ode to Lady Hornby from a Half Pay Officer on*
> *receiving from her a present of apples.*
>
> With regard to the apples
> My genius it baffles
> To describe in an adequate way
> How intense the delight
> When I took the first bite
> And felt there was nothing to pay.
>
> The thanks of Jack Fisher
> To his friendly well wisher
> These verses are meant to convey.
> Her prayers may she offer
> For the good of his coffer
> And his speedy return to Full Pay.
>
> Each amiable wish
> That came with that dish
> Is returned with affection sincere.
> May the Heavens above
> Send her gallons of love
> And I wish her a Happy New Year!
>
> January, 2, 1883.

It is also noticeable that Fisher's previous friendly allusions to Sir Cooper Key—for example in a letter to his wife of the previous October ('I have no doubt Admiral Key will get me a home appointment if it's possible')[1]—peter out about this time. In 1876 Hornby had attempted to form a compact with Beauchamp Seymour and Sir Cooper Key, as the only officers then fit for selection as First Sea Lord, to refuse office unless reform of the Admiralty was promised. He wanted the Board to be freed from much of the burden of day-to-day administration, so that more time would be available for considering major problems and preparing seriously to meet the eventuality of war. Hornby revived the proposal when a change of First Sea Lord appeared imminent in 1879 but Key would not commit himself (though he offered to make way for Hornby as First Sea Lord). As Colomb points out, the great issue at that time should clearly have been the comparative weakness of the fleet rather than the

---

[1] *F.G.* i, 112.

organization of the Admiralty, but mere parity with France alone was, politically and generally, accepted as satisfactory at that time. However, Admiral Sir John Hay (the former Lord of the Admiralty) directly raised the issue of naval strength in the House of Commons, though without obvious effect, in 1881; and Lord Henry Gordon-Lennox followed suit early in 1882. But it was not until 1884 that discontent with the strength of the Navy blew up into a public scare. Meanwhile it would seem that, by 1883, Fisher was already in active association with the opponents of the moderate policies pursued by Key. To some extent, Fisher's own experience of office is forecast by Colomb's remarks on the fate of the latter Admiral:

A First Sea Lord, however, who enters the Admiralty without leaving many personal friends behind him in the active service, is better off than was Sir Cooper Key, whose popularity was so widespread, and his personal friendships so warm. It is not to be denied that, speaking generally, he was less popular with the navy on leaving the Admiralty than he had been on entering it; and yet he did not escape that taunt that 'the bunch of keys' got all the good things.[1]

In so far as Fisher himself was probably regarded in many quarters as a member of 'the bunch of keys', a letter written in 1921 to Fisher's son by Key's daughter (covering a memoir of Fisher which has been used above) is enlightening. She refers to her early acquaintance with Fisher and continues:

My recollections of him will always be pleasant and affectionate. At the same time I must in honesty say something arose in later life that came between him and his friendship for my father. The latter was always quite unaware—as were we all—of the cause, but although he attended my father's funeral [in 1888], he had rather markedly avoided intercourse with him after he retired from the Admiralty. It extended to Lady Fisher also. When he was asked [presumably by Colomb] to contribute to my father's memoirs, he refused.[2]

It must be concluded that Fisher, like many other officers in 1884, considered that Key should have threatened resignation in order to hasten the programme of construction. In retrospect, it is perhaps somewhat easier to accept the case made out for Key by his biographer. During Key's tenure of office, the revolution in gunnery associated with the adoption of breech-loaders

---

[1] Colomb, p. 415. See also pp. 412, 428, and 443–6. Also Egerton, pp. 192–6.
[2] Kilv. MSS., Pkt. 41, Mrs. de Crespigny to 2nd Ld. F., 25 Sept. 1921.

was set on foot; despite the doubts occasioned by the emergence of the torpedo boat, the Board started to lay down a homogeneous class of battleships in 1882 (the 'Admirals'); the Foreign Intelligence Committee (forerunner of the Naval Intelligence Department) was established in 1882; and in the same year the Controller was restored to a seat on the Board. When Key went to the Admiralty in 1879, mere parity with France was generally accepted; when he left office in 1885 British superiority over the strongest potential enemy had been re-established. Given the tepidity of public interest up to 1883 and (according to Parkes)[1] the agreement of both political parties to delay any open discussion of the disturbing (unpublished) report of the Carnarvon Commission, the achievements of Key's regime seem very considerable. As Parkes has written: 'The seven years during which Cooper Key was at Whitehall proved to be one of the momentous periods for the Navy and the turning point in its material progress.'[2]

However, there was a worsening of the international climate in 1884. This favoured the agitation for a bigger Navy associated with W. T. Stead and 'The Truth about the Navy' articles. In August H. O. Arnold-Forster (who was to become Parliamentary Secretary of the Admiralty in 1900) went to see Stead at the offices of the *Pall Mall Gazette* and convinced that early exponent of sensational journalism that the Navy was at a dangerously low ebb. Meanwhile Stead had formed a connexion with Reginald Brett (later the second Viscount Esher) who was private secretary to Lord Hartington, Gladstone's Secretary of State for War. Brett supplied Stead with political information and had latterly attempted to ameliorate relations between the journalist and Gladstone;[3] but it is not clear that he contributed anything substantial to the articles. He was always more interested in the Army than in the Navy and the latter service hardly figures in his correspondence and journals during the period 1885 to 1903. According to Stead's later account of Fisher's career:[4] 'He was recommended to me as the ablest officer to be found ashore or afloat. I sought him out, and we speedily became close friends. I used to meet him, as he said, like Nicodemus, at night, in all sorts of out-of-the-way places.'

[1] Parkes, pp. 324, 328.   [2] Ibid., p. 286.
[3] Esher Papers, 5/2 and 2/6.
[4] 'Lord Fisher' in the *Review of Reviews*, Feb. 1910.

While Fisher never evinced any particular aversion for intrigue, he was certainly prudent to cover his tracks in this affair. But the evidence in the Esher Papers lends no support to the supposition that Brett and Fisher met at this time.[1] It seems quite likely that it was Rear-Admiral Hoskins[2] who advised Stead to consult Fisher. In his article of 1910, Stead wrote that an Admiral said to him at the time of the 'Truth about the Navy' campaign that Fisher was the one serving officer who was comparable with Nelson. 'I have forgotten who the Admiral was, but I think it was Hoskins.' The following letter, written by Stead to Brett on 18 September 1884, shows that Hoskins was certainly involved:

I have fired my shot and I hope it will do some execution. I only reproved myself that it was not discharged many months ago. I submitted proofs to Admiral Hoskyns [*sic*], who says it is very good and fair, only too favourable to our first class ironclads . . . I think I shall put the thing through, unless England is really doomed, which I don't believe.[3]

It is difficult to make out much more about Fisher's role in the affair.[4] His close interest in comparative strengths has already been shown to date from 1879. However, when he wrote to Hornby on 29 June 1884 it was not the over-all weakness of the Navy which was chiefly bothering him at that time. He was then on extended sick leave and making the first of a long series of continental visits for the sake of his health. He (and apparently his family) were then about to leave the German spa of Homburg for Ragatz in Switzerland where he would take 'another course of waters'. He admitted: 'I am not so strong as when I came here but I hope Switzerland will set me up again.' He went on to criticize Admiralty policy but confined his remarks to the lack of tactical training for ships in commission.

Egypt seems to have quite disorganized our Mediterranean Squadron. The ships are never at sea together, no tactics, nothing.

[1] The style of a letter and a telegram from Fisher to Esher, both dated 9 Nov. 1903, imply that the two men did not know each other well before that date. (Esher Papers, 10/41.) They possibly met in Aug. 1891. (Whyte, ii, 32.)

[2] Anthony Hiley Hoskins, Junior Naval Lord (1880–2) and First Sea Lord (1891–3).

[3] Esher Papers, 5/2.

[4] See also Stead's earlier account in the *Review of Reviews*, July 1897. This gives details of his interviews with Key and Alcester, and shows that many senior officers in active service were consulted.

The officers up the Nile and the ships' companies disorganized . . .
I suggested to Sir Cooper that it would be quite worthwhile to send a
shoregoing squadron complete to Egypt, Admiral and all.

I think there ought to be an Act of Parliament against the new
fashion of sending the Mediterranean ironclads on independent
cruises . . .[1]

However, Fisher was certainly well qualified to supply Stead
with much of the information he needed.

Stead's optimism about the effect of the articles was justified;
indeed, the immediate outburst of public anxiety surpassed his
expectations. By 22 October he was writing to Brett: 'I have just
seen W. H. Smith. He asks Gladstone tomorrow, What are you
going to do about Navy? . . . Smith is very much alarmed,
chiefly at the temper of the French.' Smith, in accord with the
demands voiced in Stead's articles, said that the Conservatives
would press the government to 'push on ironclads, lay down fast
cruisers, buy torpedo boats and make guns'.[2]

The success of the 'Truth about the Navy' campaign can only
have reinforced Fisher's conviction that, in the type of parliamentary democracy which began to emerge after the Reform
Act of 1867, judicious feeding of information to the press provided an indispensable means of influencing naval policy. The
atmosphere was never again the same after the scare of 1884.
Once Stead had published his articles, it became a matter of
public concern that Britain was only a little ahead of France in
numbers of ships, that both France and Italy were superior in
armament (the 'Admirals' having been delayed by painful slowness in the production of their breech-loaders), that Chili and
Brazil had acquired ironclads superior to British cruisers in the
Pacific and South Atlantic; that the Royal Navy was short of
personnel. The age of international rivalry now embraced warships; and the Navy itself was aroused. The 'bully of the Admiralty', Sir Edward Reed, was invited to give a paper at the
Royal United Service Institution on 26 November 1884 to
answer the incendiary question, 'What are the most urgent
measures that should be taken for increasing Her Majesty's
Navy?' Needless to say, he performed the task with vehemence
and relish. During the subsequent discussion, the pent-up feelings of the attendant naval officers were released. 'For the last
fourteen years the Navy has been starved', Captain Gerard Noel

[1] N.M.M., PHI/120 (b).   [2] Esher Papers, 5/2.

stated. 'We ought to have had at least one million of money yearly added to the Navy Estimates. In this I am sure all naval Officers will agree, and', he added, 'especially the Naval Lords of the Admiralty.' Captain Philip Colomb commented: 'We have ever since 1870 been dealing with the Navy at starvation point, and then we have, every one of us, come to the conclusion that the starvation point is the proper condition for the British Navy.' Arnold-Foster, the original begetter of the press campaign, also had his say. Aged only twenty-nine at the time, this energetic, cock-sure young man registered the changing spirit of the times:

> Now I do not think that the people of this country quite know what war would mean. They knew what it meant to some extent at the beginning of the century . . . I have a great respect for the French, but I believe that if they make war it will not be with kid gloves on. [The British public] should be made to realize the importance of Colonel Maurice's statement that nine wars out of ten come like a bolt out of the blue, without any declaration of war at all.[1]

If civilization in some of its aspects was retreating, the 'Dark Ages of the Navy', at least, were at an end. In December Lord Northbrook announced a programme of increased construction: in addition to the previously approved expenditure, £3,100,000 would be spread over the following five years. Also, an extra £2,400,000 would be spent on Naval ordnance and coaling stations.

Although this increase in naval expenditure had stemmed largely from disturbing comparisons with the strength of the French Navy, a new crisis in relations with Russia soon brought home to the Admiralty the fact that the newly allocated funds would take time to produce ships. In the course of their steady advance towards the Afghan frontier, the Russians had already occupied Merv in February 1884. By the beginning of March 1885 the Admiralty was facing the distinct possibility of war with Russia and an attempt was made (in a memorandum of 16 March) to list the measures to be taken at the outbreak of hostilities.[2] When the Russians duly attacked and took the village of Pendjeh on the Afghan frontier (30 March) the Gladstone government took a surprisingly firm stand and it was suggested

---

[1] Marder, *Anatomy*, pp. 120–2; F. Manning, pp. 162–3; Parkes, p. 328; *Journal of the R.U.S.I.* (1884), pp. 993–1040.
[2] Cab. 37/14.

that an expeditionary force should be sent through the Dardanelles to divert Russian troops from the approaches to India.
However, the Turkish attitude to passage of the Straits proved
highly problematical; no means of injuring the land-bound
giant offered other than to follow the precedent of 1854 and send
a fleet into the Baltic. Meanwhile, the slowness of British naval
mobilization, under a system where ships were to an extent
concentrated in the Mediterranean but otherwise scattered
across the globe, was painfully revealed. The aforementioned
Admiralty document of 16 March reveals the sense of revolution
induced by this genuine crisis in naval affairs: 'Owing to no
naval war with a first-class Power having occurred since the
early part of this century, there is no previous experience available to assist in laying down the steps to be taken on the eve of
such an event; the whole subject must therefore start afresh.'[1]
Small wonder, then, that orders issued on 25 March to commission all the warships theoretically available at home took some
three months to produce a seagoing force! Vice-Admiral Hornby
was appointed to command this second Particular Service
Squadron. Fisher, appointed as his Flag Captain, had behind him
experience of a similar role in 1878. Seeing that the squadron was
destined for the Baltic, Fisher's health had presumably improved.[2]

On 8 June Fisher was appointed to command the venerable
ironclad *Minotaur*, flagship of the largely dormant Channel
squadron from 1867 to 1885. Throughout this period of time
she served (as Parkes has put it) as 'senior flagship with a unique
record of pomp and ceremony which she carried with impressive
presence'. (It will be remembered that Fisher took passage in
her in 1869 to attend the ceremonial inauguration of Wilhelmshaven.) Another familiar veteran which put to sea with the
squadron—and was doubtless subjected to baleful rather than
nostalgic scrutiny by Fisher—was the *Hercules* (flagship of Key's
squadron of June 1878). None of the breech-loading battleships
had yet been completed, so inevitably Hornby's squadron
presented the grotesquely diverse and individualistic aspect
inseparable from the passing experimental era. From that time
onwards, classes of ships would be the rule.

[1] Ibid.
[2] He afterwards attributed his complete recovery from dysentery to a series of
summer visits to Marienbad in Bohemia. Recommended by a 'waltzing angel',
the first of these visits took place in 1886. (*Memories*, p. 157.)

During June the Russians evinced willingness to settle the crisis by negotiation and the tension subsided. However, from 20 June to 20 July, Hornby (like Key before him) carried out manoeuvres and a genuine effort was made to impart warlike reality to the proceedings. Hornby's official letters testify to Fisher's activity in planning and recording the exercises and special mention was made of the assistance given by Lieutenants J. R. Jellicoe and F. T. Hamilton.[1] The emphasis of the manoeuvres was on torpedo boats carrying Whitehead torpedoes. Booms and mines were among the protective devices; also torpedo nets. Fisher doubtless enjoyed his role as chief-of-staff to Hornby whose zeal for warlike efficiency attracted him so strongly; and the Commander-in-Chief, for his part, reported: 'I feel much indebted to Captain Fisher for this valuable record [enclosed and subsequently printed], as well as for many suggestions made by him to extend the instruction which the gathering of so many ships afforded to officers.'[2]

In September 1885 Fisher was occupied with torpedo-boat exercises at Weymouth and (as he intimated to Hornby on the 20th) he was better pleased to be there than at Portsmouth for the trials about to be conducted aboard the gunnery tender *Bustard;* 'as there is a possibility of the muzzle of her gun blowing off, I agree with the great Thomas Dibdin that "there's a sweet cherub that sits up aloft that looks after the like of poor Jack" and brought him to Weymouth.'[3] Not so very long afterwards, the 'cherub' abruptly withdrew his favours. On 4 May 1886 Fisher and a party of experts, including Vavasseur (representing Armstrong's), were on board the *Collingwood*—at last under going her gunnery trials off the Isle of Wight. She was armed with four 43-ton breech-loading 12-inch guns, mounted in barbettes. A scaling charge was fired from one of the after guns. The gun was then loaded with a firing charge and a 720 lb. shell filled with water. The expectant onlookers were rewarded by the disintegration of the last eight feet of the barrel. The neighbouring structure of the ship was damaged but fortunately there were no casualties.[4]

---

[1] Hamilton was Second Sea Lord during Fisher's spell at the Admiralty in 1914–15.

[2] Print in Naval Library: *Manoeuvres and Operations of the Particular Service Squadron,* n.d. but presemably 1885.

[3] N.M.M., PHI/120 (b).

[4] *Brassey* (1886), pp. 367–8.

Understandably, this brusque experience did little to prejudice Fisher in favour of the type of gun which had burst. His immediate object was to persuade the Admiralty to scrap the ten existing guns of the Mark II (*Collingwood*) type within fourteen months and replace them with the stronger Mark V which was double-tubed to the muzzle. However, he accepted speedy chasehooping to the muzzle of the Mark II guns as a stop-gap measure and he succeeded in convincing the First Lord that both remedial steps were necessary. In fact, it appears that the 12-inch guns of the *Collingwood* never were replaced, presumably on the grounds that the chasehooping (which brought the weight of each gun up from 43 to 45 tons) was a sufficient remedy. However, even if they failed of their objective, the methods used by Fisher to secure the suppression of the Mark II guns are not without interest for this biography.

Although as Captain of the *Excellent* he bore special responsibility for the testing of guns for the Navy, he was definitely subordinate to the Director of Naval Ordnance. His attempt to bring Lord Ripon (fleetingly First Lord in Gladstone's abortive 'Home-Rule' government of 1886) round to his point of view involved concealment from the D.N.O., Rear-Admiral John Hopkins, and the production of private letters from two of the ordnance experts involved in the case without their knowledge or consent. Thus, on 10 May, he was writing to Ripon:

I think I am only doing my duty to you in sending for your *private* perusal the enclosed letters from Noble and Maitland, and trust you will forgive me for taking such an active part in this business . . . Will you please return them to me, and may I beg you to consider them as quite confidential? . . . I am on difficult ground with Admiral Hopkins in this business, which is another reason why I beg you to allow this conversation to be confidential. I am writing very hurriedly but I do not like to delay for fear of your committing yourself to some other course which this correspondence may keep you from . . . I should not have interfered at all, but that I saw the *really serious* breech defect was being evaded and had evidently not been brought under your notice as its importance deserved . . .[1]

In later years Fisher came nearer perfection in concealing his subterranean activities; but in a letter of 20 May to Hornby (now in influential retirement) he had to admit that a slip had occurred on this occasion!

[1] Kilv. MSS., Pkt. 9, copy.

Since I saw you yesterday I have had a confidential letter from a friend connected with the War Office to tell me and warn me that the authorities at [the] War Office have discovered that I am the sole author of this row about the 43 ton gun of Collingwood type and I am to expect a hot time of it. I mention this to you to show why I don't want to get into any more hot water just at present.

Elsewhere in the same letter, Fisher's apprehension of 'more hot water' is explained. He had evidently furnished Hornby with material useful for the latter's campaigns for a stronger Navy. Referring to this informative communication, Fisher wrote: 'If you can make quite sure not to let Lord R[ipon] have any clue as to writer or recipient of letter, I think you would be doing the Navy a great service by reading him the letter. But do not leave him a copy as there is evidence on every page which would enable the Admiralty ferret to detect where from and who to.'[1]

Disconcerted by the War Office's discovery of his role, Fisher now began to worry about the use which Ripon might make of the letter from Noble, sent to him by Fisher on 10 May. (Obviously, Noble's letter was critical of the Mark II gun which had been manufactured, against the advice of Armstrong's, by the Woolwich factory; whereas Colonel Maitland's letter was presumably a defence of the said factory of which he was Superintendent.) So on 26 May Fisher was writing to the First Lord:

I have just heard confidentially that an effort will be made to induce you to produce whatever evidence you may possess as to the defective construction of the Collingwood type of gun! And I am writing this to beg you not to let any allusion to Noble emanate from you and I feel myself under a solemn pledge of secrecy to him as regards his private opinions expressed to me . . .[2]

A final surviving record of the progress of this complex transaction is a letter from Fisher to Ripon dated 29 May. Clearly, the First Lord had returned Noble's letter and Fisher was by now in a position to deem it 'a subject of sincere congratulation for the service that you have had the firmness to carry your point in getting rid of these Mark II' guns of the *Collingwood* type. He hoped that the *Collingwood, Colossus,* and *Conqueror* would all be given Mark V guns.[3]

[1] N.M.M., PHI/120 (b).   [2] Kilv. MSS., Pkt. 9, copy.   [3] Ibid.

In the event, Lord George Hamilton replaced Ripon as First Lord in August, on the change of government (Lord Salisbury having for the second time succeeded Gladstone as Prime Minister); and in May 1888 Fisher was complaining to Hornby that the *Collingwood*'s guns still had not been replaced.[1]

There can be no question, at least, that the reigning system of providing ordnance and ammunition for the Navy represented a serious danger to the efficiency and preparedness of the service. Since the Crimean War the provision of all ordnance, whether for the Army or Navy, had fallen to the War Office and naval ordnance stores were a charge on the Army Estimates. The justification for this extraordinary arrangement was purely financial: it prevented duplication of productive capacity. However, from 1879 onwards the complications of the Navy's conversion to breech-loading guns, with their appropriate mountings, broke down the system. As has been said above, provision of large breech-loaders by Woolwich proved scandalously slow and inefficient during the early 1880s and seriously delayed the commissioning of the 'Admiral' class and other new ships. Fisher's appointment as Director of Naval Ordnance, effective from 1 November 1886, has to be seen against this background. Already in 1879 a joint military and naval Ordnance Committee had been formed to initiate and supervise gunnery experiments; but this did not alter the fact that, from 1881 to 1887, only a third of the sums requested by the Admiralty actually appeared in the Army Estimates.[2] On the other hand, it should be emphasized that it was not the fault of the War Office that naval ordnance was charged to the Army Estimates. In 1868–9 and 1880–2 the Admiralty resisted the attempts of the War Office to transfer financial responsibility. Only in December 1882 did the Admiralty accept the principle of payment for gun-mountings out of naval funds—and with payment went control over designs.[3] Already on 8 October 1886 Fisher knew of his selection as D.N.O. and he attributed the appointment to Hornby: 'I sent you off a telegram directly I received Lord George's letter asking me to be DNO and the wording of his letter makes us believe quite firmly that it is your influence which has planted me at the Admiralty and we feel accordingly, and I hope it may be a success.'[4]

[1] N.M.M., PHI/120 (c).   [2] Bacon, i, 97.
[3] Adm. 116/267.   [4] N.M.M., PHI/120 (b).

Hamilton's Board comprised Admiral Sir Arthur Hood, Vice-Admiral Sir Anthony Hoskins, Vice-Admiral William Graham (Controller and thus Fisher's immediate superior), and Captain Lord Charles Beresford, with E. Ashmead Bartlett as Civil Lord and A. B. Forwood as Parliamentary Secretary. Hamilton was to hold the office of First Lord for six years—an exceptionally long term. He afterwards considered himself extremely fortunate in the 'application, ability', and 'experience' of Hood, Hoskins, and Forwood. However, he harboured very mixed feelings about Beresford—'the weak spot in my team' who had 'an uncontrollable tongue' and a penchant for leaking information to the press.[1] Notwithstanding, Beresford did achieve something of value during his brief term as a member of the Board.

Although appointed as 'Junior Naval Lord',[2] Beresford was an M.P. on half-pay at that time. From the first month of his appointment (August) Beresford, fortified by his aristocratic background and the reputation he had won for himself in Egypt and the Sudan, set out to revolutionize various aspects of naval policy and administration. In particular he wished to build a true naval staff on the basis of the existing Foreign Intelligence Committee. Already on 27 August, exactly three weeks from the installation of the Board, he was writing to Hornby: 'I am so aghast at the danger we incur from our present state of utter unpreparedness of a *plan* if we go to war that, if I do not carry something when I bring it forward, I shall resign and stump the country on the matter.'[3]

Below the Board level, the Admiralty was manned by quite a constellation of able and progressive officers. Apart from Fisher as D.N.O. (from November), there was Captain W. H. Hall (a member of the Torpedo Committee of 1873–6 and from 1882 head of the Foreign Intelligence Committee), and Captain R. N. Custance (Hall's assistant and already a keen student of naval strategy). Finally, the brilliant naval architect William White was Director of Naval Construction—a post which he was to hold till 1902. He was the 'right man in the right place', wrote Fisher on White's appointment in 1885.[4]

[1] Hamilton, pp. 88–9, 108.

[2] That is, Fourth Sea Lord; the titles 'Senior Naval Lord', etc., were used officially until Fisher had the popular alternative 'First Sea Lord', etc., officially restored in 1904.

[3] N.M.M., PHI/120 (b).   [4] F. Manning, p. 183.

It is, perhaps, difficult to say which need was the more pressing: that for a better provision of ordnance or that for a strengthened naval staff. Beresford succeeded in his aim in so far as the Naval Intelligence Department (N.I.D.) was established in February 1887, with Hall[1] as its first Director (D.N.I.). However, possessing as yet only two divisions—Intelligence and Mobilization—the Department did not number the preparation of war plans as one of its acknowledged functions. The limit of Beresford's achievement is indicated in a letter written by Custance to Hornby on 9 January 1888:

Hall is, as you know, quite in the van of naval thinkers and he has done wonders by sheer force of character and of *knowing*, and the extraordinary thing is that he has been able to do so much, but he has been aware for a long time that he has not sufficient standing to hold his own. The strongest proof of this being that his pay has been cut down. Fancy the pay of D.N.I. being less than that of D.N.O. or Director of Transports. This is equivalent to saying that the whole is *less* than its part.[2]

If Custance (despite his earlier career as a gunnery specialist) did not ascribe overwhelming importance to the work of the D.N.O., Fisher was blissfully free from any such tiresome reservations. On 26 November 1886, less than a month after taking over from Hopkins, he was writing to Hornby:

Dear Sir,

I am getting on like a house on fire! I asked for a list of things I was not allowed and have got them all but one. Then I declined to do any work until I got a new room with *two* windows, the First Lord's carpet, a red leather chair and a shorthand writer. I've got 'em all. Then I declined to write on any paper except that allowed to Cabinet Ministers. I'm writing to you on it now! Finally I have pointed out that the whole building revolves round the DNO's department. If you haven't got the guns, what's the use of building the ships? And if you haven't got the ships, what's the good of entering boys and Naval Cadets . . . This is the house that Jack built!

I shall write further by and by. As yet I have worked daily till 8 p.m. at the Admiralty, but as the Yankees say I'm going to simmer down next week.

A full reply to your questions later on. This simply to report that I am kicking everybody's shins just to let them know that I am here.

[1] His elder son (b. 1870) became Adl. Sir Reginald Hall, well known as D.N.I., 1914–18.

[2] N.M.M., PHI/120 (c).

I planked the D.N.C., the Engineer in Chief[1] and the Director of Dockyards for signing papers for the Controller in his absence which I ought to have signed. I think they like me all the better for it.

> 'Your wife, your dog and your walnut tree,
> 'The more you beat them the better they be.'
> Yours very truly, and just now in a great hurry,

J. A. Fisher[2]

The recipients of Fisher's shin-kicking seem to have been prepared to accept this treatment as being in a good cause, at least for a period of some years. But such treatment could hardly be expected to pay dividends indefinitely; and it comes as no great surprise to find that, some twenty years after his stormy inauguration at the Admiralty, the circle of his naval friends and admirers was markedly diminished. However, through the later 1880s and into the 1890s Fisher and White, certainly, appear to have worked harmoniously together on the whole. This partnership was to be a crucial feature of Fisher's term of office as Controller (1892-7).[3]

The importance of securing for the Navy control over the provision of its own ordnance was accepted at the Admiralty shortly before Fisher became D.N.O. and an interdepartmental committee was formed in the autumn 'to consider the question of the transfer to the Admiralty of Naval Armaments'. However, Fisher was a member of the Committee, together with his predecessor as D.N.O., Rear-Admiral Hopkins. In its report of 11 November 1886, the committee assumed 'that the provision of money required for Naval armaments, including guns and ammunition and all warlike stores and equipment, shall, in future, be taken upon Naval Votes'. The Admiralty would annually notify the War Office of their probable needs before the preparation of the service estimates, 'in order that the War Office may state the extent to which the requirements of the Navy can be met from the Government Establishments'. However, 'it will be understood that the private trade may be resorted to by the Admiralty, not merely for articles which the War Office cannot supply within the required time, but, on due notice to the office, for any articles which can be obtained, by the requisite dates, more cheaply from the private trade.'

---

[1] James Wright.   [2] N.M.M., PHI/120 (b).
[3] F. Manning, pp. 241-2, 268-9, etc.

Interchangeable stores should 'for the present' be purchased by the War Office, but the others were to be ordered by the Admiralty.[1]

The indications are that Fisher wished to see this report put speedily into effect but the Board minutes indicate recurrent misgivings about the additional cost to the Navy. Moreover, by early 1887 Fisher himself, to judge by his minutes, had come to share these misgivings. He pointed out that the existing system provided the Navy with the best ordnance available while the Army was prepared to accept the remainder. All would be well if the Admiralty were furnished with sufficiently frequent and regular information to be able to check the provision of naval ordnance at every stage of manufacture and supply. As an ideal solution to the problem, at once ensuring greater efficiency and avoiding the new charge on the Navy Estimates, Fisher suggested a separate Ordnance Department and, not altogether surprisingly, he secured the enthusiastic endorsement of the Board. On 26 March 1887 the Admiralty wrote to the War Office:

On the whole, after very careful deliberation, my Lords are decidedly of opinion that the best if not the only solution of this difficult problem is to establish an Independent Ordnance Department, common to both army and navy, which should be responsible for the efficient supply of all war matériel for both services.

At the same time, the Admiralty set out in considerable detail all the difficulties involved in the proposed transfer of financial responsibility for naval supplies—a consummation much desired by the War Office.[2]

In view of the attitude taken up by the Admiralty (which hardly emerges from Fisher's latter-day account in *Records*),[3] it is not surprising that negotiations dragged on into 1888. On 3 January 1888 Fisher wrote to Hornby: 'I have all along been pegging away for a separate Ordnance Dept. common to both Army and Navy with its own Estimates and its own independent Parliamentary Head, and I believe in a few years we shall have

---

[1] Adm. 116/267.   [2] Adm. 116/283.

[3] Pp. 54-5. 'I came to the definite conclusion that the Ordnance of the Fleet was in a very bad way, and the only remedy was to take the whole business from the War Office. . . . The result, after immense flagellations administered to the Director of Sea Ordance, was that the whole business of the munitions of war for the Navy was turned over to the Admiralty. . . .'

it.' However, on 27 June 1888, the matter was settled for the time being on the basis of the Navy paying for its own ordnance, although the War Office continued to provide storage facilities and staff. It was not until Fisher was First Sea Lord with Jellicoe as his D.N.O. (1905–7) that the Admiralty secured a degree of direct control over the design of naval guns. Only then was the Navy prepared to pay for its own staff of trained inspectors to control the process of manufacture.[1]

At some stage of the proceedings, Lord Salisbury acted as chairman during a meeting between the Admiralty and War Office.[2] Although (according to Fisher) the Prime Minister 'slobbered over' his brother-in-law, Colonel Henry J. Alderson, (who was Director of Artillery at the War Office) and showed little apparent interest in Fisher, he remarked on Fisher's performance *vis-à-vis* Alderson when nominating him as naval delegate to the Hague Conference of 1899.[3] Whether Fisher 'fought' Alderson to get control of the gun-wharves or merely to avoid charges to the Navy Estimates is unclear! However, Fisher did succeed some two years later, 'in getting all the gunwharves at Portsmouth, Devonport, Chatham, Malta, Hong Kong and Bermuda transferred bodily to the Admiralty'.[4]

In view of Fisher's equivocal role with regard to control over ordnance, it is easy to agree with Jellicoe's view (of 1928) that Fisher's principal achievement as D.N.O. was to hasten the equipment of the Navy with quick-firing guns. These guns assumed particular significance in the 1880s on account of the French and Russian emphasis on building commerce-raiders and especially torpedo-boats. (By 1890 the French 'Jeune Ecole' went so far as to threaten unrestricted torpedo-boat attacks on unarmed merchantmen at night.)[5] From the point of view of providing British battleships with an effective secondary armament and of producing suitable weapons for torpedo-boat 'catchers', it was of obvious importance that, by the later 1880s, the Elswick 4·7-inch gun could fire a shot every seven seconds.[6]

---

[1] Adm. 116/283; Patterson, p. 39.

[2] *Records*, pp. 54–5. Neither the First Lord nor the Secretary of State for War were members of the interdepartmental committee of Nov. 1886; but both these ministers signed the agreement of 27 June 1888 (E. Stanhope having succeeded W. H. Smith at the W.O.).

[3] *Records*, p. 55.

[4] N.M.M., PHI/120 (c), F. to Hornby, 7 Aug. 1890. 'The DNO has been in a hot place lately . . . I have hardly a kick left in me.'

[5] Marder, *Anatomy*, p. 87.   [6] Parkes, p. 345.

Jellicoe wrote that, when Fisher was D.N.O.,

> he followed up the work carried out while Captain of *Excellent* in the way of bringing in the 4·7 and 6″ QF guns and mountings. That was certainly the most important work then carried out and he pushed it with all his vigour. I was his assistant in the *Excellent* (as Asst. Experimental Officer), and at the Admiralty [from Sept. 1889] I was in closest touch with all that work. His association with Vavasseur (for mountings) and Noble (for guns) was very close and all-important in its results.[1]

Meanwhile very soon after Fisher became D.N.O. he was granted a high-level assistant in the form of a Director of Torpedoes. This post was offered to Captain A. K. Wilson. He accepted; but on arriving at the Admiralty in March 1877 he was disconcerted to find his title neatly modified to Assistant Director of Torpedoes! Fisher had emerged as 'Director of Naval Ordnance and Torpedoes'. 'It is rather as if they had offered me a situation as cook and then made me scullery-maid', was Wilson's reaction.[2] On this basis began an often renewed official association between Fisher and Wilson which was to be finally terminated under much more extraordinary circumstances in 1915.

Wilson was to 'advise and assist the Director of Naval Ordnance on all torpedo matters', including 'all experimental and instructional work carried out by the Torpedo School Ships "Vernon" and "Defiance" '; to 'watch the progress of the expenditure in the manufacture of Torpedoes and torpedo material by Woolwich or Private Firms, especially as regards time of completion'; and (*inter alia*) to 'prepare programmes when required for Submarine Mining practice and manoeuvres'. Under this regime, efforts were made in the *Vernon* to develop an independent mine but proved abortive. Needless to say, the Hertz horn was not adopted; instead a battery was linked to an over-sensitive mercury circuit-closer which was never rendered serviceable. However, Lieutenant C. L. Ottley (ultimately Fisher's D.N.I.) devised an automatic sinker which allowed mines to be laid at preselected depths.[3]

Between Fisher and Beresford (who had greeted Fisher as 'old fellow' in 1882[4]) relations remained harmonious. They co-operated in a grand propaganda exercise in June 1887; Fisher

---

[1] Kilv. MSS., Pkt. 38, Jellicoe to Bacon, 6 Oct. 1928.   [2] Bradford, p. 107.
[3] Adm. 1/6896 A; Cowie, p. 28.   [4] F.P. 6.

had various displays put on at Portsmouth and Beresford produced 120 Members of Parliament 'to see for themselves how the
money they voted was spent.'[1] However, Fisher was shrewd
enough to steer well clear of involvement in the ructions which
led up to Beresford's resignation from the Board in January
1888. Implying some resemblance between Beresford and
General Boulanger, then cutting a figure as a champion of discontent in France, Fisher wrote to Hornby on 2 November 1887:

Lord Charles Boulanger has circulated the draft of a speech he
proposes to make his constituents in which he wants 5 more ironclads
and a heap of other vessels, etc., etc., and this I think is causing
annoyance to his colleagues. He asked me to read it before he sent it
round, but I declined, knowing what happens to the fender when you
come alongside with too much weigh on![2]

With Custance, destined to be Beresford's chief helpmate in
the anti-Fisher agitation of 1907–9, Fisher was also on good
terms. Custance was to write many years later to Professor A. J.
Marder:

You ask, What was the root cause of England's submission to the
hobgoblin whose name was Fisher? May I suggest that it was largely
due to the absence of that education which is being slowly supplied by
Greenwich . . . Fisher was the product of the 19th century navy and
of the superficial education from which we all suffered—of the
examination system which pushed to the front men with very superficial education. Owing to the long peace these men were not weeded
out by war as they should have been. Stated very shortly this may
perhaps be an explanation of what will always be a curious
phenomenon.[3]

In view of this long-pondered verdict, a letter which Custance
wrote to Fisher in December 1887 is entertaining to read. Fisher
had been offered a chance to leave the Navy, at great financial
advantage, by joining the armament and shipbuilding firm of
Sir Joseph Whitworth & Co. Ltd. (then headed by Lord Rothschild). Custance wrote to the future 'hobgoblin':

My dear Captain Fisher,
    I think after our conversation this morning I ought to write and
emphasize the view that you should not accept Lord R's offer. You

---

[1] *The Times*, 9 June 1887 (Bennett, p. 140).
[2] N.M.M., PHI/120 (b).
[3] Marder, *Anatomy*, pp. 389–90.

would be giving up a certainty to begin life again on altogether new lines. The strain of doing this would be very severe, and would arise not only from picking up new work, but also from the anxiety attendant on competition with rival firms. You must remember that there would be against you difficulties greater than those encountered by Noble. You are older than he was; you would have to compete with established firms; Armstrong was behind Noble at the commencement to help him along; Rothschild could not give you the same assistance; your health is not so good. You would go to Sheffield simply to make money, the position would not compare with that of an Admiral in war.

On the other hand you are certain of employment in the Navy until you retire, and you will have sufficient income to live on comfortably. Your son is provided for, and I have no doubt you will be able to save sufficient for your daughters.

If you accept this offer and your health gives way as Grenfell's did, you will be in a worse position than you are now in, because there would be no other appointment open to you, whereas in the Navy there are numerous easy billets. I have written freely, being convinced that to do one's duty to the country is the greatest satisfaction a man can have and that honourable poverty has no drawbacks for a man who has done such.

Yours very truly

R. N. Custance.

You must remember that the present is a most inopportune time for throwing up D.N.O.[1]

The unwitting irony of Custance's advice is compounded by that of Fisher's hero and supporter, Sir Geoffrey Phipps Hornby, now an Admiral of the Fleet, who wrote solicitously on 13 December:

My dear Jack,

It is always wise to advise a man to do what his wife approves, but I don't profess to be wise, and feel strongly that the balance of reasons, public and private, are for your going to Whitworth's. First, the public ones.

It is most desirable to have more than one great gun manufacturing firm from wh. the Army and Navy can get their weapons; and what we want especially, the thing that is most difficult to get, is thorough and honest articles . . .

---

[1] Kilv. MSS., Pkt. 9, 'Monday', but n.d. F. weeded from his main collection of papers (lately kept at Lennoxlove) nearly all items emanating from his latter-day opponents. The relatively small collection at Kilverstone apparently escaped these attentions.

Now I believe that in Noble we have a man who gives such work from Elswick; and if you boss the other establishment we should get like worth, tho' I hope on different designs, from the new factory.

On the other side it may be said that it will be difficult to replace you as D.N.O. So it will. Still designing is higher work than administration; and tho' there are plenty of idiots from whom a successor may be chosen—say the great Bosanquet[1] or such-like—still you may have a word to say in it, and may shove Wilson in.

Now as to the private claims. I think your children have the first claim for consideration. What can you do for them by remaining in the Service? If your son was in it, it would be different; but as it is he may find the Indian climate too much for him;[2] if so, you will have means wherewith to start him in England, and probably some opening too. As to your girls, I don't think much of London life . . .

Lastly, as to your health, I don't think it is your strongest point. As a manager in such a firm you could ease yourself, when you felt the work too hard for the liver, easier than you can with the continuous pressure of Admiralty work.

Therefore I am all for you accepting the new work, and may you be successful in it.

Yours very truly,

G. Phipps Hornby.[3]

In his memoirs, Fisher attributed his decision to stay in the Navy to the persuasions of Lord George Hamilton. By then he had little desire to remember the advice received from Reginald Custance!

Both Beresford and Hornby—the latter continuing to receive information from Fisher—did much to stimulate the public agitation culminating in the Naval Defence Act of 1889. At the Admiralty, a confidential report was drawn up on the needs of the Navy for war against France and for war against France and Russia in combination. A considerable shipbuilding programme was recommended, including eight first-class and two second-class battleships; this was to be spread over five years. At about the same time (July 1888) a report was drawn up by 'the three admirals', William Dowell, Vesey Hamilton, and Sir Frederick

---

[1] Presumably George S. Bosanquet: Rear-Adl. Jan. 1887; rtd. as Vice-Adl. in 1894.

[2] Cecil was at Oxford with a view to entering the Indian Civil Service. He did join it in 1890.

[3] Kilv. MSS., Pkt. 9.

Richards, on the naval manoeuvres. This report, by exceeding its brief, proved a powerful lever.[1]

On 16 November Fisher attended an important meeting in the First Lord's room at which White presented alternative designs of the proposed first-class battleships. 'It would have been impossible to bring together men more representative of naval opinion or who could have spoken with greater authority.'[2] Besides the Lords of the Admiralty, White and Fisher, there were the 'three admirals', together with Vice-Admiral J. K. E. Baird (C.-in-C. Channel Squadron) and Captain Lord Walter Kerr. The result was that Hood (First Sea Lord) deferred to the views of the majority, in so far as seven battleships (the *Royal Sovereign* class) were projected with high freeboard and guns mounted in raised barbettes. Hood, still preferring the greater protection afforded by the turret-ship, secured construction of one more battleship of this type. The barbettes allowed the *Royal Sovereigns* to work their guns in a seaway (whereas turret-ships sat lower in the water) and their high freeboard likewise permitted a higher speed in a seaway.

Fisher was also to be concerned with the actual construction of the *Royal Sovereign* in its final stages. She was laid down at Portsmouth on 30 September 1889 as part of the programme embodied in the Naval Defence Act. This provided for the battleships (eight first-class and two second-class) together with a large number of cruisers and torpedo-boats, to be built by 1894. Fisher's connexion with the preceding campaign may be inferred from a letter which he wrote to Hornby earlier in the year—complete with one of his favourite journalistic maxims:

> We owe you a deep debt of gratitude for pegging away [in *The Times* and at public meetings] as to the increase of the Navy. It promises to bear good fruit but the pressure must be maintained up to the last moment. One of my proverbs has come out well: '*Re-iteration is the secret of conviction.*' People do talk such humbug about a thing being judged on its merits, etc. 'Importunity is the secret of success.'[3]

It was at about this time that the suggestion of a Ministry of Defence began to be publicly discussed. In 1889 Field-Marshal Sir John Simmons advocated it as a means of settling interdepartmental disagreements, for example about the relevance

---

[1] Cab. 37/22, no. 24 (Ady. report of July 1888); Parkes, pp. 351–2.
[2] Manning, p. 242.
[3] N.M.M., PHI/120 (c), 26 Jan. 1889.

of fortifications to a possible invasion.[1] In view of Fisher's advocacy of a single service minister in 1903 and his subsequent bitter opposition to the idea during Haldane's term at the War Office, it is interesting to discover an account of his attitude to it in 1889–91. Cyprian Bridge, who first became friendly with Fisher in 1869 or thereabouts, wrote in 1921 to Fisher's son:

Whilst he was still Director of Naval Ordnance I became his colleague as Director of Naval Intelligence, our respective offices being in the same part of the building. Though officially he was not concerned in it, he was greatly interested in the agitation started by some people who knew little or nothing of the Navy or of its history, to set up what was to be called a 'Ministry of Defence'. This was to mean in practice putting the Admiralty under the War Office—a silly and indeed mischievous suggestion which your father helped us, who foresaw its dangers, to defeat.[2]

The notion of a Ministry of Defence would not strike Fisher as at all 'silly' or 'mischievous' in 1903—because he then hoped that the Army would be subordinated to the Navy! If there had been a more favourable reception for the proposal in 1889, the country would have been spared much of the inter-service squabbling which was subsequently to absorb so much of Fisher's energy.

However, Fisher was certainly not short of drive as 1889 came to an end. Jellicoe, who from September was his assistant dealing with new guns and mountings, found that the flood of work often kept him busy till 11 p.m.; and Fisher's own vitality, fortified by a recent visit to Marienbad, is sufficiently evident in this letter to Hornby of 19 December:

. . . You enquire after my 'girder strength'.[3] I can best reply by a French proverb

'Si on n'a pas ce qu'on aime
'Il faut aimer ce qu'on a.'

---

[1] Schurman, pp. 48–50. In a letter to Esher of 19 Nov. 1891, Gen. Lord Wolseley wrote: 'I have for the last twenty years urged the propriety of having only one War Minister and of placing the Army and Navy both under him.' Esher Papers, 5/5.

[2] Kilv. MSS., Pkt. 41, 2 Apr. 1921.

[3] On 2 Dec., Hornby had written to *The Times* criticizing, amongst other things, the supply and quality of the Navy's guns: 'We are told that we have the best guns in the world; that one of them, a 110-ton gun, "is somewhat deficient in girder strength, and has developed in other directions indications of weakness" . . . The First Lord rightly esteems himself fortunate in his Director of Naval Ordnance. . . . But does he follow [his] advice?'

When the general public ask me that question in the Club and the streets I reply in old English

'Ask no questions and you'll be told no lies.'

When the High Authorities ask me for information I ask them

'What do you want to prove?' and the data can be selected accordingly.

When the Foreign Naval Attaché is inquisitive I say to that

'We don't want to fight
'But by jingo if we do
'We've got the ships
'We've got the GUNS
'And we've got the money too!'

and that all our arrangements are calculated on the old British basis, that one Englishman is equal to three Frenchmen.

As the bluejacket sentry said, 'You'll get me 'ung if you let anyone know what the undersigned has written to you.'

In very violent haste, overwhelmed by foolscap,

Believe me, Sir,

Yours very truly,

J. A. Fisher.[1]

By dint of his seniority as a Captain, Fisher was promoted to Rear-Admiral on 2 August 1890. During that year he drew up a memorandum on 'English and Foreign Guns'[2] which summarizes the way in which the fleet was armed with breech-loading guns during his term of office as D.N.O. He attributed the difficulties experienced during the 1880s to the abolition of the Ordnance Select Committee on 7 December 1868, leading to ten years without proper control of experiment and development in the field of naval gunnery. Only since the appointment of the Ordnance Committee of 8 July 1879 had development been able to get painfully under way once more.

To give some idea of the magnitude of the task which has been accomplished in re-arming our fleet with breech-loading guns, the following figures are quoted:— On March 31, 1881, there was not a breech-loading gun in the fleet, and in 1885 there were only 507 guns mounted, while on December 31, 1889, we had 1,293 actually

---

[1] N.M.M., PHI/120 (c).

[2] Printed in *Notes for Navy Debates, 1896–97*, pp. 149–51 (at Naval Library). This was F.'s first major compilation of Admiralty prints. These prints were immediately available whenever a favourable explanation of some aspect of naval policy was required for political or other purposes.

mounted in our ships, exclusive of all natures of quick-firing guns. It may be confidentially asserted that such a gigantic work could not have been accomplished by any other nation in so short a time and with so much success.

According to the Admiralty's information, the British guns were superior to those in every other navy except the German. The German guns were on a par with the British, and possibly superior in one category. Unfortunately foreign accidents and failures were kept quiet while British mishaps were 'advertised with as much persistence as Pears' soap'. Not only was this damaging to British prestige and to morale in the fleet; it caused the loss of large orders to the British armament manufacturers. Foreign agents admitted that they could get best value by placing their orders in Britain but they could not face criticism at home, based on the strictures to which British manufacturers were subjected by their own press.[1]

Fisher thus showed himself well aware of the advantage of large capacity in the private armament factories, even if this meant supplying weapons to possible enemies.

Towards the end of his time as D.N.O., Fisher began to concentrate on the problem presented by the large force of French torpedo-boats stationed in or near the Channel. His connexion with the 'torpedo-boat destroyer' is commonly dated from his advent as Controller in 1892, but this expression is used in a paper written by him as D.N.O. in February 1891. The paper is entitled 'Increase in French Torpedo-boat Harbours and Distribution of Torpedo-boats in the Channel and on the French Coast, with Suggestions as to the best way of meeting these Tactics'.[2] It is avowedly based on information prepared by the D.N.I. (Bridge) and is the first instance of Fisher proposing a new type of vessel for a particular strategic purpose.

He stated that there were thirteen French torpedo-boat stations in the Channel. While a watch on Brest and Cherbourg might be attempted, the British cruisers would be exposed to attack from 'the outlying torpedo-boat stations in their rear'. The threat to merchant-shipping receives specific notice:

In the event of a war with France it would be absolutely necessary at any cost either to destroy the torpedo-boats and, if possible, the stations of Boulogne, Calais, and Dunkirk, or so to watch them as to paralyse the torpedo-boats.

[1] Ibid.   [2] Ibid., pp. 111–14.

So long as torpedo-boats from these stations have a free range they would practically deny all passage of the Straits of Dover by night to merchant ships, and except in very clear weather, even to men-of-war.

He also remarked on the 'vital question raised by Sir G. Tryon as to making our ports safe against torpedo attack'.

To counter the French torpedo-boats, the British possessed torpedo-boats; also torpedo-gunboats. The French had 80 first-class boats available for operations in the Channel; the British had 49.

Further, France is building 35 more boats, whilst we have none in hand or in prospect. In addition to these torpedo-boats the French have for years past been constructing larger vessels in the 'Bombe' class (315 tons), and the 'Haute mer' boat of 150 tons.

The 'Bombe' class were designed as torpedo-boat catchers or destroyers: and our first torpedo gunboats ('Rattlesnake' class)[1] were designed to over-match the 'Bombe' class as well as to be capable of more extended service.

However, neither the *Rattlesnakes* nor the larger *Sharpshooters* (of about 750 tons) were fast enough to catch torpedo-boats, though the *Sharpshooters* could usefully substitute for cruisers as the 'eyes of a fleet' or dispatch vessels. Fisher then went on to indicate the characteristics which should be possessed by a torpedo-boat destroyer.

Since torpedo-boats necessarily have a limited range of operations, a moderate coal supply and radius of action suffices for the torpedo-boat destroyer. The armament may also be of a lighter character than that appropriate to the torpedo gunboat, and inferior sea-keeping qualities and accommodation are permissible.

These views did not prove altogether far-sighted in so far as the early destroyers (240–600 tons) proved too small for operations outside the Channel. However, Fisher was on the whole correct in his further specification that the T.B.D. 'should be considerably larger than a torpedo-boat, so as to have superior sea-going qualities, together with a more powerful quick-firing gun armament'. Compared with the *Sharpshooters*, the T.B.D.s should be handier; should be less conspicuous in outline; should have shallower draught so that a Whitehead torpedo, set at normal depth, might pass under; and should be cheaper. He therefore proposed a vessel of about 300 tons, costing about

---

[1] 570 tons.

£30,000 compared with £60,000 for a *Sharpshooter*. Its duties would be 'Channel protection'; 'hunting down the enemy's torpedo-boats, and watching their stations'; and doing the lion's share of watching Cherbourg and Brest 'when the ordinary torpedo-boats could not be depended on to keep the sea, and large cruisers would have to keep off at night on account of torpedo-boats'.

In Fisher's view it would be much better to build vessels of this type rather than more torpedo-boats; 'the role of the latter is more offensive than defensive, *and as our real line of defence lies on the French side of the Channel*, and France has no trade against which the boats could act, it appears to be expedient to build a larger class of vessel.'[1]

Thus Fisher had already, in February 1891, prepared the way for one of the leading features of his term of office as Controller. However, there is nothing to show whether he knew that, after leaving the Admiralty in May 1891, he would come back as Controller and a member of the Board as soon as February 1892. A letter of 14 April 1891 addressed to Hornby indicates Fisher's more immediate preoccupations. On 21 May he would become Admiral Superintendent of the dockyard at Portsmouth.

I think I shall make a good job of it at Portsmouth Dockyard as I know most of the 'Dockyard mateys' by their Christian names and there's 'honour among thieves'.

I shall come and see you directly I come down and unfold my deep laid scheme for making the Leopard change his spots (I mean the Dockyard matey) . . .

[P.S.] Do you know why an alchemist is like Neptune? Because he is a-seeking (a Sea-King) what never existed.[2]

The postscript typifies one of Fisher's brands of humour. While this kind of offering appealed to many people, others found it lacking in subtlety! For example, Violet Asquith at a later date likened Fisher's continuous sallies to a string of jokes culled from Christmas crackers.[3]

Fisher contributed in notable fashion to the speed with which the *Royal Sovereign* was completed.[4] Laid down on 30 September 1889, she was to be completed (like her six sisters) in three years —a short time compared with the four to seven years required for recent battleships. Fisher himself had helped to clear the

---

[1] Ibid.   [2] N.M.M., PHI/120 (c).   [3] Bonham-Carter, p. 253.
[4] Bacon, i, 104–5, for an account of his methods.

crippling delays in the supply of guns; William White had contributed fundamentally by reorganizing the dockyards since
1885. By 4 October 1891 Fisher was still thinking in terms of
three years for the *Royal Sovereign:* 'We are going to hoist (I hope)
Sir George Tryon's flag in the Royal Sovereign on Sep. 30, 1892,
3 years to a day from the time she began to be built.'[1] However,
the Admiralty saw advantage in accelerating this ship so that she
could undergo trials ahead of the *Empress of India* and the rest of
the class. With Fisher's drive at the dockyard, she was completed
in May 1892. The total time from keel-laying to commissioning
was two years and eight months—a record.[2]

As a result of the Naval Defence Act and the improvements in
organization to which reference has been made, Britain's naval
position had been transformed. On 29 December 1891 A. J.
Balfour (who had recently become First Lord of the Treasury
and was beginning to take a serious interest in defence) wrote to
the First Lord of the Admiralty about Britain's comparative
strength. The Board admitted, he understood, that Britain was
still not a match for France and Russia combined, though the
outlook seemed to be improving. 'I suppose the command of the
sea turns upon the relative strength and numbers of the *battleships*
engaged.' Hamilton supplied corrected comparative figures
which showed a comfortable margin of British superiority, based
on the assumption that 'only a small proportion' of the building
programmes of France and Russia would actually be completed.
'We build 50 per cent quicker than either France or Germany',
he added.[3]

Once the *Royal Sovereign* and the other N.D.A. battleships
started coming into commission (1892–3), it could be seen that
White had designed 'the finest group of fighting ships afloat'.
They 'sat the water with majesty and distinction'.[4] But despite
the success achieved during Lord George Hamilton's administration of 1886–92 in bringing Britain up to the Two-Power
Standard (announced by the First Lord in March 1889), there
was to be no reversion to the relaxed conditions of the 1870s. As
an Admiralty report of 1890 had put it, 'when, unhappily, a
game of international "beggar my neighbour", so to speak, is
being carried on, England is the one country in Europe which
can not afford to give it up, and the surest way to check the

---

[1] PHI/120 (c), F. to Hornby.   [2] Parkes, p. 357.
[3] Add. MSS., 49778, ff. 13–14; 19.   [4] Parkes, p. 356.

epidemic would seem to be to make it clearly evident that she meant to maintain a recognised relative standard of superiority, as being necessary to her existence as a nation, come what may.'[1]

It was in these circumstances of insecure naval supremacy that Fisher, aged fifty-one, first became a Lord of the Admiralty on 2 February 1892. As was duly noted in various newspapers, he seemed admirably qualified for the post of Controller. The *Daily News* of 16 November 1891 had announced his appointment thus:

In selecting Rear-Admiral Fisher, C.B., to succeed Vice-Admiral Hopkins as Controller of the Navy the Admiralty have made an excellent choice. Admiral Fisher, who gained considerable reputation at Alexandria by his skill in handling the ironclad train which was designed by him, is regarded throughout the service as an officer of exceptional ability. While Director of Naval Ordnance he was mainly instrumental in bringing about reforms to which the Navy is indebted for its most effective system of armament . . . As Controller of the Navy, Admiral Fisher will have scope for the exercise of his many qualifications, and all who have served under him express satisfaction with the appointment as likely to promote the efficiency of naval administration, and place the system of supply, so far as he may be responsible for it, on a throughly sound basis.

On the whole this latter expectation was realized during Fisher's tenure of this post (from February 1892 to August 1897). His main spheres of activity were: the innovation of 'destroyers';[2] the general adoption of water-tube boilers; and the acceptance by the Liberal government of the Spencer programme of shipbuilding.

The subject of destroyers may be taken first. In March 1892 Fisher appointed a committee which duly produced a recommendation for a torpedo-boat destroyer along the lines adumbrated in his paper of February 1891. Alfred Yarrow, the ship-builder and engineer, and William White, who continued as D.N.C. and Assistant Controller until 1902, both came prominently into the picture. Yarrow contributed information about the latest, fast French torpedo-boats. White also derived first-hand knowledge of them from a visit to Cherbourg. Fisher apparently assumed that the British torpedo-boat destroyers

---

[1] *Notes for Navy Debates*, p. 148: memo. on 'Proportion of Cruisers to Battleships' by Adls. Sir W. Dowell, Sir F. Richards, and R. O. FitzRoy.

[2] Fisher is usually credited with authorship of the term 'destroyer' *tout court* (e.g. Bacon, i, 110). But cf. F. Manning, p. 323, who ascribes it to White.

should be built in the Royal Dockyards but White, whose previous experience included two years at Elswick, put forward irresistible arguments for ordering the vessels from private builders expert in the construction of torpedo-boats. Tenders were invited. Some firms offered designs of vessels of 300 to 400 tons. Fisher commented that the Board wanted boats of about 200 tons—which seems unfortunate. A speed of 27 knots was the minimum acceptable. He accepted the designs of Yarrow and Thorneycroft and asked Yarrow to quote for a tubulous boiler. (After some years of development, Yarrow had first installed one of his water-tube boilers in a torpedo-boat in 1887.) The first two 'destroyers' were launched by Yarrow and their trials were held in 1893-4. On 28 October 1893 the *Havock*, fitted with locomotive boilers, reached 26·78 knots—a world record.

However, the *Hornet* with her water-tube boilers attained 27·6 knots, and she once reached 30·5 knots on the measured mile. There followed a number of '27-knotters'. Launched during 1894-5, they were all under 300 tons. Most of them had water-tube boilers but they were too small and too lightly built to achieve their designed speed in anything of a seaway. There followed the larger and more seaworthy '30-knotters'. The first batches (designed by different private firms) were launched in 1896 and many of them served right through the Great War. However, they were still very uncomfortable for their crews and, with their displacement of about 350-400 tons, they could not maintain high speeds except in fine weather. But the French 'mosquito fleet' now presented much less of a threat than it had done. It was soon realized that the destroyer had inherited the offensive role of the torpedo-boat.[1]

While acknowledging Fisher's major share in the early evolution of destroyers, it is appropriate to mention his reliance on the technical expertise of William White. As Frederic Manning has pointed out, the partnership was a remarkable one. Fisher and White were both 'imaginative and ambitious' but were otherwise 'entirely dissimilar in mind and in character'. While Fisher loved innovation 'for its own sake', White supplied the necessary brake of informed criticism. Although the Controller's department 'was scarcely large enough to contain two stars', there was no serious conflict between them during Fisher's term of office. As

---

[1] Marder, *Anatomy*, p. 168; Barnes, pp. 101, 123-9; F. Manning, pp. 323-4; March, pp. 24-6; T. D. Manning, pp. 32-42; Parkes, p. 377.

Manning remarks, 'White was at the summit of his career' and Fisher 'was astute enough to profit by his criticism and to share in his success'.[1] It has been seen how White was closely associated with the origins of the destroyer. This is true also of the controversial adoption of water-tube boilers.

Subsequently, Fisher was always quite ready to accept responsibility for what was regarded by his critics as an impetuous, ill-timed, and costly decision. Lord George Hamilton (who gave way to Lord Spencer at the Admiralty in August 1892) afterwards wrote of it as 'a fiasco which might have been catastrophic, but which was entirely due to precipitate action'.[2] Before giving further consideration to this matter, some of Hamilton's discriminating reflections on Fisher, largely based on acquaintance during the years 1886–92, merit quotation here; also his contrasting appraisal of Lord Walter Kerr who was to beat Fisher to the First Sea Lord's post.

There were two distinguished officers . . . with whom I had very close personal relations and to both of whom I was in the past greatly indebted for the help which in times of stress and embarrassment they afforded me. Although they were the antithesis of one another in character and demeanour, each well represented a certain tone and school of thought of the Navy. Kerr was the embodiment of accuracy, moderation and reliability. During the latter part of his career, when at the top of his profession, his decision or ruling upon any disputed question, either personal, disciplinary or administrative, was accepted without cavil by the whole Service. Cautious in making changes or reforms, he never went back upon his work nor stultified his previous utterance by pyrotechnic capitulations. For five years he was my head Naval Secretary and a rock upon whom to rest. He was as good afloat as he was in Council, a splendid specimen of disinterested loyalty and devotion to the highest demands of duty.

Fisher was a wholly different personality—strong, ambitious and go-ahead, and he made a rare splash in naval and other circles. When controlled, he was an invaluable public servant; when uncontrolled, he was apt to be dangerous from his love of the limelight and the ease with which he became obsessed with the fad of the moment. He was a great humorist and delighted to draw picturesque descriptions of his past work, always adorned with very strong and amusing expletives and Biblical quotations; but he would be the first to laugh at anyone who appraised him by his own recitals. I knew him as Captain of the *Excellent*, then Director of Naval Ordnance, then Superintendent of

---

[1] F. Manning, pp. 379–81.   [2] Hamilton, p. 134.

Portsmouth, and finally as Controller of the Navy. All these promotions, which he well deserved, were made whilst I was at the Admiralty, and in these posts he did exceptionally good service . . .

[Taking account of his later career] Fisher did some very valuable work for the Navy, but he was in no sense an unfailing success. Some of his changes have worked well, some badly; but in most cases they have been marred by the precipitancy with which they have been forced through . . .[1]

In Hamilton's view Fisher deserved the chief credit for the 'extraordinary feat' whereby, with the help of the 'mechanical genius' Vavasseur, the British Navy was re-quipped with breech-loading guns between 1884 and 1892. From being 'the most backward Navy in Europe' in that regard, the British emerged 'at least two years ahead of any nation both as regards the quantity and quality of new guns'. But by way of contrast he cited the 'precipitate' adoption of water-tube boilers. He had himself, with the agreement of Hopkins (then Controller) intervened to secure the trial of water-tube boilers in the torpedo-gunboat *Speedy* and the experiment 'was a complete success'. After one further trial Fisher (with Spencer as First Lord) went straight ahead with Belleville boilers for the big cruisers *Terrible* and *Powerful*. Owing to the peculiar stresses produced in the tubes of these boilers there ought, according to Hamilton and other critics, to have been a longer period of intensive experiment in Britain before large-tube boilers were generally adopted. Hamilton commented: 'This elementary precaution was ignored, and as a consequence for years to come the steaming incapacity of our cruisers was a naval byword.'

Indeed, a violent public and parliamentary controversy, known as 'the Battle of the Boilers', raged through the later 1890s. In 1900 a committee was set up to inquire into the matter and recommended in an interim report that no more water-tube boilers should be installed. However, it seems clear that this advice was itself hasty and ill informed. After a short period of paralysis the authorities accepted that water-tube boilers were better than any alternative then available; but the Belleville type, adopted by Fisher, was finally rejected in 1902.[2]

Fisher therefore remains open to criticism for the difficulties

---

[1] Hamilton, pp. 132–3.

[2] Hamilton, pp. 133–5; Adm. 116/869, report of boiler committee printed in June 1900; Parkes, pp. 392–3; *Anatomy*, p. 420.

and breakdowns experienced over a period of several years. On the other hand, there was no lack of discussion at the Admiralty. White advocated large-scale adoption of the boilers, though he did tell the Boiler Committee of 1892 that the French viewed their large-scale adoption as a gamble. However, the French were insuring themselves by putting 'a great many boilers' into any one ship. In September 1892 H. J. Oram[1] presented a detailed report on a visit to various ports and establishments in France. A. J. Durston, the Engineer-in-Chief, then advocated a trial. Mr. J. Williamson, the Director of Dockyards, sounded a note of caution and Sir Ughtred Kay-Shuttleworth, the Parliamentary and Financial Secretary, commented: 'The Director of Dockyards' minute is full of good reasons against too hasty or general adoption of French tubulous boilers.' But he accepted the case for experiments with Belleville boilers as proposed by Durston who was supported by Fisher and the Boiler Committee (Dec. 1892). Lord Spencer approved.[2]

Belleville boilers were ordered and put into the torpedo-gunboat *Sharpshooter*. Trials were conducted for 23 months from 7 February 1894; the ship's Chief Engineer reported in great detail and considered that the advantages of the boilers decidedly outweighed their disadvantages. However, in November 1893 Durston had already proposed that Belleville boilers be fitted in the large new cruisers *Powerful* and *Terrible*. Fisher approved and it was done. Although the Engineer-in-Chief and his staff appear to have been convinced of the desirability of this move, there can be no doubt about Fisher's backing and approval. To this extent, the charge of precipitation would appear to be well founded.[3] But while a number of breakdowns did occur, it is important to remember that the old type of cylindrical boiler also gave plenty of trouble, besides not measuring up to the requirement for higher speeds. During the 1890s the shortage of British engineers versed in the mysteries of large-tube boilers led to shortcomings in operation and repair work. But there can be no question that, in the long term, tubulous boilers produced higher speeds, saved weight, used less fuel, and were easier to repair.[4]

It now remains to summarize Fisher's influence on the level of naval expenditure during the years 1892–7. His was essentially

---

[1] A future Engineer-in-Chief; then Senior Engineer Inspector at the Admiralty.
[2] Adm. 116/869.   [3] Ibid.   [4] Ibid.; Parkes, op. cit.

a supporting role. The dominant administrative figure of these years was the formidable Admiral Sir Frederick Richards who joined the Board as Second Sea Lord in May 1892 and succeeded Sir Anthony Hoskins as First Sea Lord in November 1893. (Among Fisher's other naval colleagues on the Board were Walter Kerr, 1892–5, and Captain Gerard Noel, 1893–7, who was to become one of his numerous bitter enemies of the next decade.) In November 1893 Richards at once pressed the case for a large shipbuilding programme, especially for battleships and destroyers. The French had recently moved into alliance with Russia and both countries were threatening the British Empire: there was trouble with the French as ever, in Egypt, and latterly over Siam, while the Russians continued to advance overland towards India. In naval terms, the British would be in serious difficulties by 1898 if they did not build against French and Russian ships already on the stocks. Public agitation for clear-cut supremacy over France and Russia had already been stimulated by the visit of the Russian Baltic Fleet to Toulon in October 1893, and by December there was much excitement generated in the press and at meetings about British inability to command, or even to remain in, the Mediterranean. Meanwhile Fisher was very much at the heart of the deliberations which began at the Admiralty in November. While White was, as usual, the principal fount of technical expertise, Fisher was both the head of the constructing department and a member of the Board; and his previous interests and experience naturally tended to place him at Richards's right hand in the ensuing struggle with Gladstone and his Chancellor of the Exchequer, Sir William Harcourt. A compilation of relevant printed documents[1] bears the stamp of Fisher and testifies to his intense interest in the proceedings; so do letters written by him in 1893 to the youthful Austen Chamberlain and to Lord Spencer.[2] The lively account in *Records* (pp. 50–1) seems quite accurate:

> Sir Frederick Richards and myself were on the very greatest terms of intimacy. He had a stubborn will, an unerring judgement, and an astounding disregard of all arguments . . . However, he had one great incapacity. No one could write a more admirable and concise

---

[1] Adm. 116/878, 'Programme of New Construction', P. 15 Nov. 1895—mostly represented in *Notes for Navy Debates*. The detailed information was largely supplied by White.

[2] *F.G.* i, 119; *Anatomy*, p. 200.

minute; but he was as dumb as Moses. So I became his Aaron. The moment arrived when that magnificent old patriot, Lord Spencer, had to choose between fidelity to his life-long friend and leader, Mr. Gladstone, and his faithfulness to his country . . . Mr. Gladstone would not have [the increased programme]. Sir Frederick Richards and myself, in quite a nice way, not quite point-blank, intimated that the Sea Lords would resign. (My bread and cheese was at stake, but I did it!) Lord Spencer threw in his lot with us, and conveyed the gentle likelihood to Mr. Gladstone; whereupon Sir William Harcourt and Sir Henry Campbell-Bannerman were alternately turned on the three of us (Lord Spencer, Sir F. Richards and myself) sitting round a table in Lord Spencer's private room . . . Sir William Harcourt always started the conversazione by insulting Lord Spencer (quite in a friendly way); then he would say to Sir Frederick Richards, 'I always thought that one Englishman was equal to three Frenchmen, and according to this table of ships required, which has been presented to the Prime Minister, it takes three Englishmen to manage one Frenchman.' Old Richards would grow livid with anger; he wanted to say, 'It's a damned lie!' but he couldn't get the proper words out!

He had an ungovernable temper. I heard him once say to one of the principal Officers in his ship: 'Here; don't you look sulky at me, I won't have it!' . . .

Dear Lord Spencer was pretty bad in his want of lucid exposition; so I usually did Aaron all through with Sir William Harcourt, and one of the consequences was that we formed a lasting friendship . . .

Campbell-Bannerman was a more awkward customer.

But it was all no use. We got the ships and Mr. Gladstone went.[1]

Confronted by a cabinet now agreed on the need for a big programme, Gladstone terminated his illustrious parliamentary career on 1 March 1894. His refusal to accept the reality of the Franco–Russian naval danger was justified by events; but on seeing the young Kaiser sailing through his assembled fleet at the opening of the Kiel canal in 1895, he uttered the untypical but prophetic remark: 'This means war!'[2]

On 12 March naval estimates for £17,366,100 were presented, with provision for laying down the 7 first-class battleships demanded as a minimum by the Sea Lords. There would also be laid down 6 second-class cruisers, 36 destroyers, and 2 sloops. Further details of the five-year programme would be released at the beginning of each year.[3]

---

[1] This version is corroborated by a letter written by F. to Esher in 1907. (*F.G.* ii, 144–5.)

[2] P. Magnus, *Gladstone*, London, 1963, p. 429.   [3] *Anatomy*, p. 204.

In May 1894 it was intimated that Fisher was about to be made a K.C.B. Richards assured Mrs. Fisher: 'None of his innumerable friends and admirers can rejoice more sincerely in this fresh tribute to his worth than I do.' And some three years after Fisher had completed his term at the Admiralty, Richards (then in retirement as an Admiral of the Fleet) wrote to Lady Fisher: 'I always recognise the immense advantage I had as 1st Sea Lord, in having such a colleague for Controller of the Navy for the best part of the time I held office.' His good opinion was not, however, to extend to Fisher's later career.[1]

As long as Fisher remained under firm control and was subjected to effective criticism, he did good work without any perceptible loss of his popularity in the service. Yet, of his colleagues on the Board during his time as Controller, Richards and Noel would be actively working against him by 1903, and Walter Kerr would be politely neutral; Hoskins would by then be dead and Bedford apparently uncommitted. Of the Directors of Naval Intelligence, Cyprian Bridge would be distinctly critical of Fisher by 1904; Lewis Beaumont (Fisher's Commander in the *Bellerophon*, 1877–8, and D.N.I., 1894–9) would try in 1903 to forestall Fisher's return to the Admiralty as First Sea Lord (as did Noel).

Noel's diaries for 1894–7[2] indicate good social relations with Fisher: 20 February 1894 'Dined with Fishers. Met Lord and Lady Kelvin and Mr. Chamberlain'; 28 July 'I played tennis at Admiralty with Fishers'; 12 May 1895 'Called on Calthorpes, Fishers and Beaumonts'; 20 June 1895 'Free and I dined with the Fishers'; 17 January 1896 'Present Miss Fisher 2.0.0. Stamps 0.4.0.'[3]; 28 April 1897 'I dined with Richards. All Admiralty there to meet Lambton.'[4] It is also a remarkable fact that Noel's friendship with Fisher's brother Frederick, which was firmly established by the 1890s, survived the anti-Fisher animosities of the following decade without apparent strain.[5] As for those who had been with Fisher at the Admiralty when he was D.N.O. and were still active in the Navy after 1900, Custance was a friend

---

[1] F.P. 1467, 22 May 1894; 1514, 13 Feb. 1900.   [2] N.M.M., NOE/32.
[3] Beatrix, Fisher's eldest daughter, married Captain Reginald Neeld on 26 Jan.
[4] Captain the Hon. Hedworth Lambton, Private Secretary to the 1st Lord, 1894–7, maintained friendly relations with F. till 1906, when he emerged as a leading opponent.
[5] N.M.M., NOE/1 (b) and NOE/5.

till at least 1899 and was hostile by 1901; Beresford maintained tolerably friendly, though increasingly unstable, relations with Fisher till 1904. Direct personal clashes were to occur with Beresford, Noel, and Custance, but this does not seem to apply to Richards, Bridge, and Beaumont. The main explanation for their change of attitude to Fisher must be sought in the new scheme of entry and education of officers introduced in 1902— apparently an issue of policy rather than of personality. But it is difficult to discard the impression that Fisher, as Controller, had implanted a measure of distrust for his unfettered judgement. He subsequently destroyed most of the letters from those distinguishable as enemies, but he allowed some from Lambton—of whom he had been exceptionally fond—to survive. In a very friendly letter of 11 July 1900 Lambton (Captain of the *Powerful* from 1897 and now back in England after distinguished service in South Africa) wrote:

I wonder what you think of Belleville boilers. I wish I could be happy about them—but I fear they are frightfully extravagant and no doubt beastly dirty. *Terrible* could not steam 13 knots from Las Palmas to Cape! True, it was bad management on part of engineers, but that could not have happened with good Scotch boilers. Thank goodness foreigners have followed our lead.[1]

This, coming from what was then a friendly source, may be set alongside the criticisms which have already been noticed. Fisher had been correct in seeing the water-tube as the coming type of boiler, rather as he was ultimately in some sense justified in calling the submarine of 1907 'the Battleship of the future'. Undeniably he showed imagination and flair in these assessments; but in practical judgement and timing he was not reliable. These characteristics would be emphasized in the strategic sphere once he became a commander-in-chief abroad.

Fisher had been promoted to Vice-Admiral in May 1896. On 24 August 1897 he hoisted his flag in the *Renown* as Commander-in-Chief, North America and West Indies. As D.N.O. Fisher had supported the Controller (Hopkins) in directing White to design two second-class battleships—a category for which White had no use. Intended for service on the China and Pacific stations, they eventually proved a fair example of false economy.[2]

---

[1] F.P. 42. When writing to the Prince of Wales in 1904, Lambton ironically dubbed Fisher 'festina lente'. (F.P. 138.)

[2] Parkes, p. 366.

When Fisher came back to the Admiralty as Controller he was an enthusiast for 'the lightest big gun and the biggest secondary gun' which brought him, rather surprisingly, into alliance with Bridge (D.N.I.)—an alliance which was disrupted by Fisher's marked change of view on the armament of battleships some dozen years later. The *Renown*, with her 10-inch guns and rapidly diminishing value as a fighting ship, was the result of this enthusiasm of 1892. Fisher was so much enamoured of this fast but lightly armed battleship that the Navy narrowly escaped being saddled with a class of six! Completed in January 1897, she permitted Fisher to offer Lord Spencer 'a trip' in the West Indies when he would 'be most comfortable and treated like a Royal Prince'.[1]

Very soon after hoisting his flag, Fisher received a letter from George Goschen who had succeeded Lord Spencer as First Lord on the change of government (July 1895). This indicates that Fisher was on as good a footing with this First Lord as with his two predecessors and had no wish, while out of sight, to be out of mind. On 27 August 1897 Goschen wrote:

We were all very pleased with your photograph . . .

Thanks for the extracts. The same day as I received yours about the United States, I had a very alarming letter about the feeling in Germany. We are not loved.[2]

In case I should not write to you again let me once more say goodbye and assure you that it has been a great pleasure to me to work with so able, loyal, and successful a Controller as I, like my predecessors, have found you to be.[3]

The themes already noticed in dealing with Fisher's time as a Captain at sea reappear in reminiscences of his first spell as a Commander-in-Chief: bustle, emphasis on smartness and speed of evolution, interest in and kindness towards the midshipmen and younger officers. Associated with his access of personal power was something of the aura of the eastern potentate which was to mark his reign at the Admiralty. Officers were told that they had to be 'first in everything—or look out', and the dilatory or unfortunate were earmarked for sudden removal and ignominious homeward conveyance. The most interesting

---

[1] Parkes, p. 370; *F.G.* i, 137.

[2] The Kaiser's telegram of support for President Kruger on 1 Jan. 1896 had led to reciprocal ill-feeling between Britain and Germany.

[3] F.P. 29.

development was Fisher's encouragement of officer-specialists to give him their ideas for the future enhancement of naval efficiency. Such invitations would be a prominent feature of Fisher's remarkable command in the Mediterranean (1899–1902).[1]

As indicated above, Fisher also provided a hint of his erratic proclivities as a strategist. Britain's colonial rivalry with France led up to the Fashoda crisis in the autumn of 1898. Fisher's command was somewhat remote from the area of the main operations, which were expected to be in home waters; but he perceived a connexion in the person of the unfortunate Albert Dreyfus. This gallant Captain was unjustly imprisoned for treason on Devil's Island in 1894. By 1898 the famous *affaire* was convulsing French society. In the event of war with France, Fisher planned to send a strong force of warships to Devil's Island (800 miles south of Barbados), cut the cable to France, kidnap Dreyfus, and land him secretly to spread dissension in France. Fisher communicated this plan to Captain W. H. Henderson, then Commodore at Jamaica.[2] Five cruisers and five smaller vessels (the *Renown* being excluded) were earmarked for this extraordinary enterprise. Henderson later denied having seen other plans which, according to Bacon, Fisher had issued for an 'instant attack' on Miquelon and various French possessions in the West Indies. 'Every detail was carefully worked out, both for sea and land, as to troops, transports, and naval escorts, with the General, Lord William Seymour, at Halifax', writes Bacon. This raises a question about the allocation of the available warships. However, Bacon certainly agrees that Fisher intended to kidnap Dreyfus. 'It is impossible to say what would have happened', he remarks, 'but, at all events, the idea was a bold one and it required a fertile brain to conceive it.' No doubt the same could just as well be said of the scheme for a preventive attack on the German fleet (1904) and that for a major landing in the Baltic during the Great War. In the realm of strategic commentary, such words as 'fertile', 'bold', 'creative', and 'imaginative' are sometimes readily interchangeable with 'wild', 'hare-brained', 'suicidal', and 'crazy'![3]

However this may be, Fisher had, during the years 1884–97,

---

[1] Bacon, i, 115–17.

[2] Adl. Sir William Henderson—'Busy William'—became the first editor of the *Naval Review* in 1913.

[3] Bacon, i, 118–20; *F.G.* i, 348–9; *Naval Review* (1930), p. 192.

contributed importantly to the transformation of the Navy. Thanks to this strengthening and modernization the public could, in 1898, face with confidence the possibility of war with France; whereas, in 1884, British superiority over that country had been a matter for dispute.

CHAPTER 6

FROM THE HAGUE TO
THE MEDITERRANEAN
(1899–1902)

In March 1899 Fisher was still eighteen months short of the termination of his command in the West Indies—'this lovely station'—when he received a telegram from Goschen to say that he had been selected by the Cabinet as British naval delegate at the forthcoming Hague Conference. Moreover, he would then succeed to the command-in-chief in the Mediterranean—'*the* tip-top appointment of the Service', as Fisher observed in a letter to his daughter, Beatrix.[1]

The reasons for sending Fisher to a conference assembled to limit armaments and mitigate the horrors of war cannot be appreciated without some knowledge of the background. During the 1890s France and Russia had emerged as military allies and comprised a combination opposed to the Triple Alliance of Germany, Austria–Hungary, and Italy. Britain, seeking to maintain the *status quo* in the Near East against Russian encroachments, had since 1887 been linked through the 'Mediterranean agreements' with the Triple Alliance. In 1895, however, William II launched a campaign for a large German Navy and in January 1896 he sent his famous assurance of support to President Kruger, thus expressing the strength of German feeling against Britain and her ubiquitous Empire. Having faced the unpalatable fact that British naval power precluded German intervention in South African affairs, the Kaiser declared in 1897: 'The trident must be in our fist.' The Kaiser through Tirpitz, his new Navy Minister, induced the Reichstag to meet the cost of a large navy; and under the Navy Law of 1898 a seven-year programme of construction was begun. Hitherto, the German Navy had been small, though of excellent quality. As far as Britain was concerned the immediate consequence was indirect. The shipbuilding of France and Russia, her obvious rivals under the Two-Power Standard adopted in 1889, was

[1] *F.G.* i, 139.

stimulated by the German Navy Law. However, Sir Frederick Richards concluded that Britain now needed more than a bare naval equality with France and Russia.[1]

Meanwhile, Britain's colonial rivalry with France continued. It was no more than a portent of future developments that the French tended, at the time of the Fashoda crisis, to reflect that the upper Nile meant less to them than the recovery of Alsace-Lorraine. However, in 1897, Russia and Austria–Hungary agreed to suspend their rivalry in the Near East. Thus the besetting British problem of how to meet a hostile combination of France and Russia in the Mediterranean was decidedly eased. But Russia now threatened the British position in the Far East. With the Russian occupation of Port Arthur it looked as if, instead of being open to the trade of all nations, China was about to be partitioned. Because the Germans were also pursuing a forward policy in China, Joseph Chamberlain proposed an alliance with Germany to resist Russian ambitions in that area. But Britain could offer no inducement to Germany to compensate her for the risk of war on her frontiers with Russia—and thus, probably, war with France as well.

Therefore, when Fisher in the *Renown* was heading for England and the Hague Conference, Britain was still strong at sea in terms of the Two-Power Standard, but what with the new German programme and the emergence of stronger Japanese and American fleets, the future was very uncertain. Fired by imperialist sentiment, British public opinion still preferred to bear the cost of a supreme Navy rather than to seek relief in alliance. Yet a note of desperation was also discernible in the British press. In 1897–8 the idea of preventive war was already being canvassed. One journalist provided the stuff of future Fisherisms by recommending that, if European powers continued to build large navies, 'an ultimatum should be sent to them by some modern Pitt, and, if not attended to, British fleets should be sent to destroy them in foreign ports and dockyards, à la Copenhagen and the Basque Roads.'[2]

The Russian proposals for the scope of the Hague Conference had been set out in a memorandum issued in January 1899 by Count Muraviev, the Foreign Minister. The main subjects were (1) limitation of armaments, (2) mitigation of the horrors of war, and (3) arbitration for the settlement of international

---

[1] *Anatomy*, p. 299.   [2] Ibid., p. 313.

disputes. Russian motivation was naturally much discussed by the press in Britain and elsewhere. One source of this motivation was a very remarkable book published in Russia at the time. This was *The Future of War* by Ivan Bloch. It has been said that in 1914 there was universal expectation of a short war and that consequently there was no general preparation for a war of peoples extending over years. But Bloch devoted no less than six volumes to a detailed and prophetic account of huge armies of conscripts locked in struggle both sanguinary and indecisive. No end could come to this great European war until the industrial infrastructure of one side or the other had collapsed owing to the exhaustion of the whole population. As a sequel, Bloch forecast bloody revolution. His argument was particularly relevant to Russia, the backward giant governed by a rigid and inadequate autocracy and yet, in the course of belated industrialization, acquiring an urban proletariat already subjected to Marxist influences. In a vague way, the Tsar Nicholas II and his Foreign Minister understood the applicability of Bloch's warning. However, the other powers pointed to a more immediate explanation of Russia's interest in the conference—the hope of avoiding the adoption of quick-firing field guns by her chief European rival, Austria–Hungary.

The British government had a vested interest in the international *status quo* and, superficially, the Russian proposals suited British interests. However, as the Admiralty pointed out, 'it will be found to be quite impractical to come to any agreement as to the meaning of the term "effectifs actuels", or to ensure that the terms of any agreement arrived at would be carried out.' Their Lordships also opposed restrictions on new explosives and weapons: such measures would penalize 'the more highly civilized' nations and, in any case, control would prove impracticable. With regard to arbitration, however, the government was anxious that something should be achieved, thus overruling the Admiralty which thought that Britain, being well prepared for any emergency, would be penalized by any delay imposed on the would-be combatants by arbitration agreements. The Admiralty also opposed 'the various proposals to regulate the conduct of war' on the rather absurd grounds that 'such an arrangement would be almost certain to lead to mutual recriminations.'[1]

[1] *B.D.* i, 224–6; Dugdale, iii, 76; *G.P.* xv, 229.

The British delegation, led by Sir Julian Pauncefote (who had recently succeeded in negotiating an arbitration treaty with the United States), arrived at the Hague on 17 May. Fisher, with some forty-five years of naval service behind him, was the senior officer at the conference and, as his old acquaintance W. T. Stead enthusiastically reported, prominent in his white top-hat he was 'almost instantly acclaimed as the heartiest, jolliest, and smartest delegate at the Hague'. He was at a peak of physical vitality; 'at the first evening party at the British Legation, Admiral Fisher, although close upon sixty, danced down every-one else in the ballroom.' Moreover, 'the precedence which he obtained from seniority was nothing to that which he won by the charm of his manner, the frank heartiness of his conversation, and the genuine, unmistable earnestness with which he applied himself to the task that he had in hand.'[1]

Indeed, the contrast between Fisher's restrained diplomatic performance in the formal sessions of the conference, and his torrential and frequently lurid conversation during the intervals between them, is the most remarkable feature of the two and a half months which he spent at the Hague. His diplomatic adroit-ness was well illustrated in connexion with the 'Russian proposal for the non-augmentation of military armaments and budgets'. This (as Pauncefote reported) was opposed by Colonel Schwarz-hoff, the German military delegate, 'in a speech of great force and ability'. No other representative of a major power offered to speak, so Pauncefote saved the proposal from immediate and humiliating rejection by proposing 'two small committees of naval and military experts'. When the naval committee met, it was at once proposed to leave the question of limitation to a future conference. The voting was seven for and seven against. Fisher (despite his complete scepticism) voted *against* the motion. The Russian delegate naturally appreciated this assistance towards the face-saving formula then adopted, namely that the delegates should refer the proposals to their governments for further consideration. In his report of 26 June, Fisher suavely wrote:

It may be added that it is fully understood by all the Delegates that no hope is entertained of any of the Russian proposals being accepted. The Russian Naval Delegate thanked Sir John Fisher for supporting his proposal, as it had prevented an immediate unfavourable decision,

[1] F.O. 83/1704; F.P. 5477, W. T. Stead in the *Daily News*, 29 July 1899.

and afforded time for his explanations receiving the consideration which he thought was due.[1]

Fisher was equally flexible when 'the interdiction of asphyxiating shell' was brought before the naval sub-commission. Despite his well-known view that war should be made as terrifying as possible, he voted officially for prohibition of gas-shells 'on the distinct understanding', as he reported, 'that the vote was unanimous. It was obvious that if asphyxiating shell were adopted by any one nation, other nations could not avoid their use.' Just as Schwarzhoff had obligingly saddled Germany with the odium of the virtual rejection by the conference of arms limitation, so in the case of gas Fisher had only to wait for Captain Mahan, the famous historian and American naval delegate, to oppose prohibition of gas-shells. He thus ensured that the Admiralty's policy prevailed without giving offence to any other delegation.[2]

By skilful public conduct combined with private vehemence, Fisher mesmerized Stead, although the journalist was then as zealous for the success of the peace conference as he had ever been for the supremacy of British sea-power. Writing for the *Daily News*, Stead described Fisher's performance thus:

In the debates he took very little part. He believed much more in getting things done than in obtaining credit, or posing as a champion of this, that, or the other cause. At the very opening of the Conference he was one of the few delegates who believed that something would be done, and who was resolute that so far as he was concerned it would be done . . .

No one in the Conference co-operated so heartily as Admiral Fisher with the Russians. Some of his colleagues indeed, declared that he was more Russian than the Russians in his anxiety to bring about international arrangements for the arrest of the break-neck competition in shipbuilding which has been going on for some time past . . .[3]

Nor did Pauncefote hesitate to commend Fisher and the military delegates. According to his final report to Lord Salisbury (31 July 1899): 'The important part of which they took in the deliberations of the Conference and the great technical knowledge, as well as sound judgement, which they displayed will

---

[1] F.O. 83/1702. Also F.O. 83/1703 for holo. draft of F.'s memo. of 26 June.
[2] F.O. 83/1702.   [3] F.P. 5477.

have been apparent to your Lordship from the Reports of Proceedings.'[1]

However, there was another side to Fisher's activities at the Hague. This was in his unofficial talk where he expressed himself very forcibly at times. Such informal communications gave rise to a French report: 'Les procès-verbaux ne donnent pas une idée de ce qui se passe. Le plus intéressant de beaucoup a lieu entre les séances.'[2] As far as Fisher was concerned, the most favoured and attentive audience was provided by the German naval delegate, Captain S. Siegel. When Fisher explained the reasons for his selection as British delegate, he did not refer to Lord Salisbury's memory of his wrangles with General Alderson.[3] On 28 June Siegel reported as follows:

> He told me he had been chosen as Delegate to the Conference because his views on sea-warfare and its exigencies were known . . . he acknowledges but a single axiom: Might is right.
>
> He had left the Minister Goschen in no doubt as to his views when he received his new appointment and he had left him free to choose another Admiral to command in the Mediterranean if he did not agree.
>
> In the event of war in the Mediterranean he would not hesitate for an instant to brush aside, without orders, any equivocal agreements reached about arbitration and mediation, if he was persuaded that the political and military position of his country called for this.
>
> The impression which I have received from my sundry conversations with the Admiral may be summarized as follows:
>
> 1 England holds more than ever the fixed conviction that her position in the world, her power and her prosperity depend on the fleet, and that everything must be done to make the fleet as strong as national policy requires.
>
> 2 Currently the fleet has attained a strength that is equal to all demands. It suffices on its own to crush a combination of all other states . . . The fleet is perfectly capable of protecting all British trade.
>
> 3 England is firmly resolved to employ with all cunning and ruthlessness, in case of need, the instrument of war which she possesses in her fleet according to the principle: Might is Right.[4]

It was with just such a voice that the Kaiser and Tirpitz yearned to be able to speak! Their jealousy of British naval power found expression in the new German Navy Law of 1900.

[1] F.O. 83/1703.
[3] Cf. Records, p. 55 and see p. 192 above.
[2] D.D.F. xv, 314–15.
[4] G.P. xv, 229–30.

In so far as Pauncefote contributed positively to the one tangible achievement of the conference, the establishment of the permanent Court of Arbitration at the Hague, it is of interest that Fisher, who knew that Goschen was a 'determined opponent' of the proposal, worked in the lobbies against it. In this, he found himself in accord with Count Münster, the principal German delegate.[1] The Germans, of course, were in a similar position to the British, being extremely proud of the speed with which they could mobilize their forces and therefore not favouring the delays implied by arbitration. However, with Pauncefote and others working for arbitration, Münster found himself isolated in the formal sessions and the Kaiser grudgingly decided to accept the proposal on an optional basis.

Fisher's 'charm' and 'the frank heartiness of his conversation' (as reported by Stead) succeeded with Count Münster. Towards the end of the conference, on 17 July, the latter sent to the German Chancellor a long dispatch and his comments on the various delegations attracted a number of characteristic marginalia from the Kaiser. The English, wrote Münster, saw the conference as a bad joke (the Kaiser: 'correct'); and he illustrated the point by retailing a conversation with 'the splendid Admiral Sir John Fisher' who described the president of the conference, the Russian Baron de Staal, as the 'president of that nonsense'.[2]

Another feature of what Fisher afterwards termed his 'very animated conversations' at The Hague should be mentioned.[3] According to his account in *Records* (pp. 55–6) he 'made great friends' with both Siegel and Colonel Gross von Schwarzhoff; 'and', he wrote, 'I then imbibed those ideas as to the North Sea being our battle ground, which led to great things between 1902 and 1910.' Stead, too, made a good deal of these 'animated conversations' when he came to write a eulogistic article in the *Review of Reviews* of February 1910 to mark Fisher's retirement from the Admiralty. Stead's account is coloured with Fisher's phraseology of the post-1904 period.[4] However, it corresponds well enough with Siegel's above-quoted report, and seeing that it contains so much of Fisher's philosophy of war, as well as some of his favourite slogans, its tenour is worth giving here.

---

[1] Dugdale, iii, 76; *G.P.* xv, 229.
[2] *G.P.* xv, 357. In *Records*, p. 55, F. claims de Staal as 'a great friend'.
[3] *F.G.* ii, 453.
[4] For a letter using language almost identical with that in the article, see *F.G.* ii, 51 (22 Feb. 1905).

Stead wrote that Fisher believed—mistakenly, he thought—
'that nations are deterred from going to war by fear of the
atrocities which accompany conflict.'

He was a bit of a barbarian, who talked like a savage at times, to
the no small scandal of his colleagues at the Hague. 'The humanising
of war!' he declared. 'You might as well talk of humanising Hell!
When a silly ass at The Hague got up and talked about the amenities
of civilised warfare, and putting your prisoners' feet in hot water and
giving them gruel, my reply, I regret to say, was considered totally
unfit for publication. As if war could be civilised! If I am in command
when war breaks out I shall issue as my orders:

> 'The essence of war is violence.
> Moderation in war is imbecility.
> Hit first, hit hard, and hit everywhere.'

In later years, wrote Stead, Fisher would reiterate his view
of deterrence:

He exclaimed impatiently, 'I am not for war, I am for peace! That
is why I am for a supreme Navy. Did I not write in your autograph
book at The Hague, 'The supremacy of the British Navy is the best
security for the peace of the world'? My sole object is peace . . . If
you rub it in both at home and abroad that you are ready for instant
war with every unit of your strength in the first line, and intend to be
first in and hit your enemy in the belly and kick him when he is down,
and boil your prisoners in oil (if you take any!), and torture his
women and children, then people will keep clear of you.

The implication that Fisher declared these views in a formal
session of the conference should be treated with considerable
reserve.

Stead, of course, was yet another 'great friend' of Fisher's. The
Admiral was always ready to take pains over handling an influential journalist who could promote his overriding aim: the
maintenance of a supreme British Navy. Indeed, Fisher had no
objection to peaceful means, such as deterrence, provided that
no obvious risks were entailed. On the other hand, he deemed it
unnecessary to tell Stead everything he had said to Siegel!

At the conference it was said of Fisher (according to Stead's
contemporary report) that ' "when he has made up his mind as
to the point he wants to reach, he is a man who gets there every
time"; and (Stead added) he has "got there" this time without
a doubt.'[1] If Fisher's aim was to make the Kaiser strain yet

[1] F.P. 5477.

harder to seize 'the trident', through jealousy of British naval power, he may well have succeeded! However, in a highly personal sense, Fisher was very conscious, at about the time of the Conference, that he had not 'got there'. On 8 October 1898 he had communicated the following agreeable sentiments to Sir Frederick Richards: 'Mr. Goschen writes very sadly at the thought of your going, and I feel quite miserable . . . I hear from outsiders that Walter Kerr has been arranged for to sit in your red chair, and no doubt he is the best man that can be selected, and personally I shall be very glad, as I think he is the most worthy to follow such a giant.'[1] Richards, in the event, was specially promoted to Admiral of the Fleet and stayed on for a time as First Sea Lord. However, during 1899 it was decided to make a change after all and Kerr was in fact selected to take Richards's place. An Admiralty civil servant named Charles Walker (who was appointed Fisher's private secretary in June 1902) heard of Fisher's reaction to the news. The charming modesty and self-effacement pervading the above-quoted letter, to Richards, were not evident to Walker's informant. Walker afterwards wrote:

While there is no doubt J.F. had always aimed at being First Sea Lord, it is equally true to say that at times it seemed to him as if he would miss it. In 1899 when Lord Walter Kerr was appointed to succeed Sir F. Richards, it was believed that J.F. was bitterly disappointed. He was only 16 months younger than Lord Walter and would be well over 63 when the latter retired. I was told at the time that after the appointment was made known Jacky shook his fist and said, 'I will get there yet in spite of them.'[2]

As he sped to the Mediterranean in the *Renown*, Fisher was fiercely determined to make his command a memorable one. There can be no dispute that he achieved this aim. The next two years were to find him at the peak of his powers and in his most creative vein. He had recently emerged from a long spell of administration at the Admiralty. Then he had taken advantage, under the relaxed circumstances of the North American station, of the opportunity to focus on the seagoing use of the ships and equipment which had emanated from the Controller's department during the past decade. He had already on the American station begun sifting such progressive ideas as he could collect

[1] *F.G.* i, 138.
[2] Kilv. MSS., Pkt. 9, 'Some Recollections of Jacky Fisher' (*FG*).

2. Vice-Admiral Sir John Fisher aboard his flagship, the *Renown*

from the seagoing officers. Now, he was about to make an impact where it was badly needed: on the attitudes of the seagoing personnel of Britain's principal battlefleet. It would be misleading to suggest that the Mediterranean Fleet had never been energetically and instructively commanded in recent times— by Hornby, for example. But there seems to be an unshakable consensus that the 'brightwork' school was, on the whole, predominant in the fleet between the bombardment of Alexandria and the South African War.

The future Lord Hankey, then a Captain of Marines aboard the *Ramillies* (flying the flag of Sir John Hopkins till July 1899), had been writing home critically about 'the great fetish "brass and paintwork" '. On 5 September he wrote from Aranci Bay in Sardinia: 'The new Admiral—Fisher—has just joined the fleet; he is said to be a tremendous scoundrel.' Interestingly, he added: 'He has got Siamese blood in him.' The appellation 'the Asiatic', directed at Fisher, is usually associated with Beresford; but the latter did not hoist his flag aboard the *Ramillies* till 12 January 1900. Fisher had been concerned, earlier on, that dysentery was affecting his liver and it may be that his yellowish complexion was a legacy of his illness.

At the outset, Fisher tactfully allowed Noel to complete his cruise and take the fleet back to Malta. However, Hankey wrote perceptively: 'I fancy the new Admiral, of whom the executive branch can say nothing too bad, is going to shake them out their fools' paradise a bit . . . [he] is very keen on dancing, and in spite of the great heat and the scarcity of ladies is giving a dance next Saturday.' In due course he reported: 'I had not seen Admiral Fisher before; he is a queer looking cuss, but very affable, and he capered about all the evening like a junior snotty.'[1]

The galvanization of the fleet began with a cruise to the Levant beginning in late September. In his memoirs Hankey reflected:

It is difficult for anyone who had not lived under the previous régime to realize what a change Fisher brought about in the Mediterranean Fleet, and by example and reaction throughout the Navy. Naval personnel always was, and always will be, keen and full of enthusiasm. In the pre-Fisher era, however, this keenness was often wasted on comparatively unworthy objects. Before his arrival the

---

[1] Roskill, i, 39, 47.

topics and arguments of the officers' messes (where shop, interspersed with much badinage, was the rule, and a wise rule) were mainly confined to such matters as the cleaning of paint and brasswork, the getting out of torpedo nets and anchors, and similar trivialities. After a year of Fisher's régime these were forgotten and were replaced by incessant controversies on tactics, strategy, gunnery, torpedo warfare, blockade, etc. It was a veritable renaissance and affected every officer in the Fleet.[1]

As usual, Fisher's dynamism was an important ingredient in his success, but it was hardly a sufficient explanation. On the contrary, Fisher was successful in reforming so many old habits, without engendering harmful opposition, precisely because he went out from England eager to listen and to learn. If some of the younger and more gifted officers like Commander R. H. S. Bacon of the *Empress of India* and Lieutenant H. W. Richmond of the *Canopus* 'literally felt born again',[2] it was not so much because the prophet had descended to reveal the truth but because their own ideas were welcomed and adopted for experiment in the fleet. In the first instance, these suggestions related to torpedo tactics. However, the story of gunnery in this, Britain's principal fighting force, throws light on the nature of Fisher's achievement.

In September 1899 it could fairly be said that no individual bore a greater responsibility for the state of gunnery in the Navy as a whole than Fisher himself. His early interest and technical expertise in the subject, up to 1872, has been duly noted above. It has been related that he was president of the committee which produced the Gunnery Manual of 1880; also that he was the leading naval witness concerning the bombardment of the forts at Alexandria in 1882. At Portsmouth from 1883 to 1885, he turned his attention towards the guns themselves rather than the procedure for firing them at sea. This was logical enough. There was little to be said for worrying about the efficiency of shooting at sea until the mighty task of equipping the Navy with breech-loading guns had been accomplished. The well-deserved tributes to what Fisher achieved in this respect as D.N.O. (1886–91) have been duly noted. However, he continued to bear some general responsibility for what was done in the D.N.O.'s department during his years as Controller (1892–7). The fact that he did not serve at sea before taking up this post

---

[1] Hankey, i, 19.   [2] Bacon, *From 1900 Onward*, p. 24.

may explain his apparent lack of interest in the seagoing use of the breech-loaders which he had done so much to supply. In this context, it will be helpful to quote from the latter-day recollections of Admiral Sir William Henderson (who has been noticed as Commodore in the West Indies during the Fashoda crisis). While he must be regarded as a witness markedly hostile to Fisher, it must also be remembered that he was editor of the *Naval Review* from 1913 and he may fairly be rated a lover of accuracy.

Fisher was Captain of the *Excellent* and D.N.O. from April 1883 to May 1891, practically 8 years, during which he was the moving spirit of the Gunnery Department. Much was done during that time to improve weapons; the new armaments of the 1889 programme ships were designed and provided . . . but nothing whatever was done to provide for their fighting use though their range and accuracy was much increased; it was a materialistic period. It is true to say that up to the beginning of the nineties, the fighting organization of ships was identical with the smooth bore gun and sailing ship period, though even then we had director firing.

When I took command of the *Edgar* [a cruiser launched in 1890], a most up-to-date ship in all respects in the earlier days of 1894, I found this to be the case, although she complied with the gunnery regulations as they existed; and at once I had to set to work to make her a more efficient fighting instrument by introducing an extempore system of range finding, communications and fire control. I also devised a system of target practice of my own which at least gave some training to the gun layers and sight setters; these I carried out each quarter with the exception of the prize firing quarter when I had to fall in with the regulations. Every captain recognised the necessity of these changes, I made no secret of what I was doing. In 1897 Percy Scott in the *Scylla* by adapting an electrical instrument that had long been set up either in the *Vernon* or the *Excellent* for nerve rapidity tests, provided a real training test for gun layers and sight setters; the gunnery schools had done nothing.[1]

This account is substantially corroborated by Percy Scott, except that he omits from his memoirs the suggestion that Fisher himself shared responsibility for the stagnation in gunnery. In May 1896 Scott, the chief originator of the coming reformation in that crucial field, was appointed Captain of the second-class cruiser *Scylla* in the Mediterranean. He subsequently wrote:

It was six years since I had left the Mediterranean, and I expected to find great improvements in the routine in gunnery and signalling.

[1] *Naval Review* (1930), p. 191.

To my surprise everything was just as it had been; no advance had
been made in any way, except in housemaiding the ships. The state
of the paintwork was the one and only idea. To be the cleanest ship
in the fleet was still the objective for every one; nothing else mattered.[1]

Jellicoe, who was Commander of the *Ramillies* (flagship of the
Mediterranean Fleet) from 1893 to the end of 1896, afterwards
recorded a similar view of the state of gunnery: 'Gunnery
efficiency in the modern sense was I fear non-existent . . . fire
control was unheard of, as was long-range practice.'[2]

Improvements began gradually to make themselves felt in the
time of Fisher's predecessor, Sir John Hopkins; he was Commander-in-Chief from late 1896 till June 1899 (when Rear-
Admiral Gerard Noel took over command on a temporary
basis). Hopkins adopted Scott's suggestion that night-signalling
could be improved through competitions and a striking advance
resulted. Even if, to judge by the memoirs of Bacon and Hankey,
Hopkins failed to enthuse the fleet as a whole, Scott recorded:
'I found that he had ideas of fleet manoeuvres, gunnery and
signalling far in advance of any other Admiral with whom I had
served.'[3]

In gunnery, the great reformation began with the *Scylla* being
sent on an independent cruise to Crete in 1898. Scott asked
Hopkins for permission to experiment with means for improving
the accuracy of shooting. Hopkins agreed. Memorable amongst
Scott's innovations was the 'Dotter' which trained the gunlayer
to maintain continuous aim despite the rolling of the ship.
Canvas targets on which the holes could be seen, supplied a need
voiced elsewhere in the service. He also fitted telescopic sights.
According to A. E. M. Chatfield, then Gunnery Lieutenant of
the new battleship *Caesar*, the 'Dotter' and the 'Loader' (another
practice-machine devised by Scott in 1900) were received 'with
something akin to horror by the old seamen' who feared the
implied competition of constant practices with the imagined
needs of brightwork. However, encouraged by his Commander
(the future Admiral Sir Charles Madden) Chatfield consulted
Scott and adopted telescopic sights for the *Caesar*. Meanwhile,
Hopkins had offered in December 1898 to present a cup for the
ship scoring most hits in a competition organized by Scott. The
latter did the preliminary work.

[1] Scott, p. 73.   [2] Patterson, p. 29.
[3] Scott, pp. 73–9; Padfield, pp. 75–8.

But [wrote Scott of Hopkins] he met with too much opposition from the senior officers in the Fleet to carry it through, and, unfortunately for the Navy, his time as Commander-in-Chief was nearly expiring. Had he remained a little longer on the station, I feel sure that we should have seen introduced under his command all the improvements in gunnery for which we had to wait six long years.[1]

The delay was due to the fact that the Admiralty took more than three years to produce an improved 'Dotter' and six years to adopt Scott's type of target. There was a similar time-lag before the instruments which Scott wanted for long-range firing were made generally available.[2] However, though Scott himself returned to England in June 1899, he left Chatfield, for one, imbued with his ideas. When Fisher arrived and made it clear that progressive ideas were welcome, and when the *Caesar* duly used Scott's telescopic sights to win a firing competition in 1900, Chatfield was probably not surprised to receive a summons from the Commander-in-Chief. 'He expressed his approval of my work and told me of his intention to shake up the Fleet in many ways, especially in gunnery. I felt embarrassed by his confidences, but, telling my colleagues, they were elated at the prospect of a new broom to sweep away the many remaining cobwebs.'[3] It would appear that Scott's 'Dotters' were soon improvised and brought into use in the Mediterranean Fleet.[4] Telescopic sights were adopted.[5] Hankey, who did not altogether admire Fisher's style of leadership at that time, was nevertheless able to report from Aranci Bay, Sardinia, on 16 June 1900:

We have at last had some gunnery experiments of a useful character. I dare say you remember how continually I have railed against the Navy for their want of long-range firing. Well, at last, the present Admiral (whom nearly all naval officers revile because he goes on lines of his own—fools, they hate anyone not hide-bound by their own ridiculous traditions!), who took the advice of the much derided 'New Navy', including, I am happy to say, our Gunnery-Lieutenant Webb, carried out a practice at 6,000 yards, a most valuable and in every way instructive lesson . . . Really, I have hopes that, if the voice of calumny doesn't succeed in driving Fisher out of the Mediterranean, there is some chance for the Navy yet. He is the only Admiral (except Charles Beresford and 'Jerry' Noel and a few others) who doesn't care a fig for the Admiralty and tradition, and dares look facts in the face as they are. He has already done incalculable good

[1] Scott, pp. 81–8; Charfield, p. 33.   [2] Scott, pp. 85 and n., 89, 161.
[3] Chatfield, p. 34.   [4] Hankey, i, 16.   [5] F.P. 4702, p. 26.

out here, and may do more, if he can keep afloat with the awful mill-stone of naval prejudice trying to sink him.[1]

The 'Fisher era' had dawned; and already Hankey had touched on one of the crucial questions concerning this period of reform. The question is: could Fisher have carried through his reforms (which he originated in the Mediterranean) without generating the bitter dissension associated with his later career? As members of Fisher's youthful elect, Commander Bacon and Lieutenant Richmond saw little objection to Fisher's appeal to 'the New Navy'.[2] Chatfield, however, to judge by his memoirs, thought that this unconventional procedure carried the seeds of disruption as well as of hope. Looking back from the eminence of an Admiral of the Fleet, who had recently been First Sea Lord from 1933 to 1938, Chatfield wrote:

> Fisher had a practice of consulting young officers which was proper enough in itself. But, regrettably, he spoke to them in a derogatory way about their superiors. It was his ruthless character and his scorn of tact that led to violent criticism, and enmities that shook the Service, reducing the value of his great work. Fisher's greatness was not then realised. There were many who hated him, and he hated them. His was not the method of leading smoothly but of driving relentlessly and remorselessly. He prided himself on this policy, and boasted of it and of his scorn of opposition.
>
> Whether the Navy could ever have emerged from its old ways in time for the Great War without his forceful acts is difficult to estimate, but in my opinion it could not. He was the leader the young technicians wanted. At our end of the scale he helped us, devoured our ideas, and stimulated us with his own, while at the other end his record was one of ruthlessness, creation of enemies and the splitting of the Navy into two parties as far as a great and fundamentally loyal Service can be split.[3]

The term 'megalomania' was ultimately applied to Fisher, mainly by his enemies but also on occasion, by persons of level judgement usually well disposed towards him—for example, Hankey and Asquith. However, as Commander-in-Chief in the Mediterranean he recognized this predisposition and tried to control it. In letters to his wife about successful manoeuvres in 1900 and 1901 he reiterated: 'The only thing now is to look out

---

[1] Hankey, i, 16.
[2] Bacon, *From 1900 Onward*, pp. 23–4; *F.G.* i, 153; Roskill, i, 41–2.
[3] Chatfield, p. 34.

that the "foot of pride" does not come against me!' 'We are going on splendidly, but I must take care of the "foot of pride".' 'We had a great day yesterday . . . Really splendid . . . *But we must look out for the "foot of pride"*!'[1] Fisher's erratic and finally devastating relationship with Beresford may be placed against this background.

Beresford, now a Rear-Admiral, hoisted his flag aboard the *Ramillies* as Fisher's second-in-command on 12 January 1900. Some indication has been given above, particularly in connexion with Lord George Hamilton's administration, that Beresford was always liable to prove a difficult subordinate. While he possessed exceptional gifts of leadership and would in due course show himself to be in many respects an outstanding fleet-commander, he was also possessed of somewhat excessive self-confidence, based on his proven gallantry and aristocratic background; and he was often enough the soul of indiscretion. Intellectually, he was inferior to Fisher. Having spent his time in seafaring, politics, love-making, and other spirited pursuits, he lacked the technical knowledge which Fisher derived from a lifetime of natural interest and a succession of relevant appointments. However, amidst a good deal of gaseous volubility, Beresford showed himself reflective, imaginative, progressive, and basically sensible. Although Fisher proceeded to handle him erratically and thereby laid up a store of trouble for himself in the future, it will be seen that he derived much benefit from Beresford during his Mediterranean command.

It would seem that Fisher was intent, from the outset, on making Beresford toe the line. He was soon presented with an opportunity which he utilized in the most unfortunate way possible. Hankey, who had been so much encouraged by Fisher's new-broom approach, and remained on balance much impressed by his over-all achievement in the Mediterranean, afterwards explained how, as an officer of the *Ramillies*, he was affected by this initial incident. (He did not get to know Fisher personally until 1906, and not at all well until he went to the Committee of Imperial Defence in 1908.) In 1900, Hankey wrote:

my prejudices were rather against Fisher, since a deplorable feud had started between him and my own chief, Beresford, whom I held in the highest esteem and affection. This feud was destined to spread

[1] *F.G.* i, 161; F.P. 1571, 1577.

to the whole Navy and eventually to affect the Supreme Command in later years. Fundamentally, so far as I could judge, there was at that time no serious difference of professional opinion between the two Admirals. Beresford always spoke well of Fisher's activities and abetted him to the best of his power . . . Beresford, who had been in Parliament for some years, had his political friends, with whom he no doubt maintained correspondence. This alone was rather calculated to arouse suspicion in a man of Fisher's temperament, engaged as he was in drastic innovations . . .

The difficulties began soon after Beresford hoisted his flag. Before taking a squadron to sea he wished to refresh his memory in the elements of the craft. To do this he adopted the expedient of landing with his own galley's crew, early in the morning, before breakfast, on the naval parade ground at Corradino Heights, Malta. The men were spread out to represent ships in a fleet, and were manoeuvred in line ahead, line abreast, quarter-line, and so forth, as though they were ships. One day the Commander-in-Chief sent a signal demanding to know why the Rear-Admiral was landing men without first obtaining his authority. The signal was sent in plain language (not in code) and was read on every signal bridge in the fleet. This public affront caused great indignation on board the *Ramillies* and was naturally resented by Beresford. Although appearances were maintained, it was some time before the bitterness aroused subsided, and the incident was seized on with delight by Fisher's numerous critics. The vendetta, manifesting itself sometimes in odd ways, was never really dropped.[1]

Presumably quite insensitive to the harm he had done, Fisher proceeded to rub more salt into the wound. Chatfield, having also commented on the Corradino incident, goes on to describe the sending of an even better-known signal to Beresford:

A few months later the Fleet was returning to Malta at the end of the first summer cruise. Admiral Fisher always led in first in the 'Renown', and walked up to the 'Barracca', a vantage point whence he could watch every ship come into the difficult and narrow harbour and turn round 180 degrees before securing bow and stern to her buoys. It was a fine test of the nerve and skill of their captains. Rapidity in every task was the order of the day. Charles Beresford was a fine seaman and anxious that his division should be smarter than the others. His Flag-Captain [R. S. Lowry], unfortunately, was not one of the best ship-handlers. When the 'Ramillies' came in, she had to secure to two buoys in Bighi Bay, the outer anchorage, a fairly easy task. He made a mess of it, got his ship stuck across the harbour and

----

[1] Hankey, i, 20.

delayed the entrance of the second division. 'Jacky' lost his temper and signalled to the [Rear-]Admiral second-in-command:

'Your flagship is to proceed to sea and come in again in a seamanlike manner.'

Everyone present tried to dissuade him from making such a signal to his second-in-command, but to no avail. It was made, and started a naval feud of far-reaching consequences. News of it spread throughout the Service and was a lamentable example of bad leadership. It was not the last.[1]

Apparently, this habit of reprimanding the second-in-command by open signal had begun even before Rear-Admiral Noel had handed over to Beresford. Noel responded in kind, terminating with the somewhat daunting intimation 'I am on my way to see you in my frock coat and sword.'[2] However, there seems to have been no definitive breach between Fisher and Noel till 1904, or thereabouts.

These incidents point to the limitations of the largely admirable educative work done by Fisher during his term of command. Through giving at Malta a number of vivid and stimulating lectures on a wide range of naval themes to officers of the fleet, and through offering prizes for essays on tactical and strategical subjects, he provoked constructive thinking to an extent quite without precedent. In retrospect Admiral Sir Sydney Fremantle believed that, over-all, Fisher's 'great claim to fame is that he succeeded in making us *think*'.[3] Yet, paradoxically, a leading criticism of Fisher from 1905 onwards would be that he was unduly autocratic. In line with this criticism, Beresford was to succeed in 1909 with the charge that Fisher had failed to establish a Naval War Staff at the Admiralty. Yet while commanding in the Mediterranean Fisher would urge 'the Increasing Necessity for a General Staff for the Navy to meet War Requirements'.[4] How much light is shed on these contradictions by Fisher's Mediterranean activities?

There can be no doubt that Fisher sought and stimulated suggestions of improvements from any source. On the other hand his own dislike of *regular* consultation with his principal subordinates also emerges clearly from the record. In March 1900 he appointed Captain George King-Hall as his Chief of Staff. Although Fisher basically looked on King-Hall as a useful

---

[1] Chatfield, p. 41.   [2] Bennett, p. 235.
[3] *D.S.* i, 28.   [4] F.P. 90.

tool for dealing with routine-matters,[1] King-Hall seems to have been given a chance to demonstrate any strategic ability he might have.[2] But already on 15 March he was writing in his diary, with regard to the inadequate supply of coal: 'Charles Beresford, anxious to stir up everyone at home on this and other matters. Sir John, who is working towards the same object, not anxious C.B. should know too much.' By 25 November 1900, the position of Beresford had not changed. That of King-Hall himself had received clearer definition.

Fisher a difficult man to have anything to do with. Fear he is shifty. His views as to my duties much modified. He is a difficult man to bring to the point. However, I find lots to do. I think it is a pity the C-in-C does not take me into his confidence in some little measure. It is the same with Beresford; he tells him nothing, and won't let him do anything.[3]

This view of Fisher's treatment of Beresford is endorsed in a letter of 3 March 1901 written by Hankey to his sister from Suda Bay in Crete: 'Admiral Fisher, who is most vindictive, seizes every opportunity to show his dislike of Beresford, and refused to give him any ships to play with on this cruise, although several are cruising independently in the vicinity.'[4]

In these circumstances, it is rather surprising to find Fisher writing on 3 June 1900 to Captain Fawkes (formerly his Commander in the *Northampton*, now Captain of the *Canopus* in the Mediterranean, and soon to return to an influential post at the Admiralty): 'I'm quite delighted with the captains and the way they handle their ships, and C.B. also is most amenable and attentive, and don't mind his signals from the C.-in-C.!'[5] Evidently Fisher believed that he had discovered an effective technique for subjugating proud and potentially insubordinate senior officers. It is a remarkable fact that Beresford, who was wont to quarrel with anyone from royalty downwards on a point of honour, could bring himself to list no fewer than twenty items standing to Fisher's credit during his command:

Has made radical alterations in Mediterranean naval strategy, approved by Admiralty.

Unceasingly directs attention to the fact that the fleet wants more cruisers, destroyers and auxiliaries, and that they must be *practised in peacetime*.

---

[1] *Anatomy*, p. 395 n.; *F.G.* i, 218. [2] King-Hall, pp. 314–16.
[3] Ibid., pp. 316–17. [4] Roskill, i, 56–7. [5] F.P. 41.

Has got additional destroyers and torpedo-boats sent out from England.

Has increased stocks of coal at Malta and Gibraltar.

Has represented the imperative necessity for building a breakwater at Malta.

Has made representations as to the status of the Suez Canal in war.

Has represented defenceless condition of Alexandria.

Has made out detailed war scheme for the fleet, with orders for every senior officer.

Has drawn up complete instructions for destroyer and torpedo-boat flotillas.

Has developed a private scheme of information which makes him independent of Admiralty as regards movement of French and Russian ships.

Has the movement of every foreign war vessel, transport and cable ship telegraphed to him.

Keeps [training] Cruiser employed all the year round instead of only for six months.

Has made the fleet a 15-knot one without breakdowns, in place of a 12-knot one with breakdowns.

Has instituted practices for officers and men such as they will be required to perform in war.

Has exercised destroyers being towed by a cruiser, and battleships towing one another.

Has practised rigging boom defence across mouth of a harbour to protect ships coaling or disabled in war.

Invited his officers to give their opinion on cruising and battle formations, with excellent results.

Has instituted long range target practice.

Has introduced a challenge cup for heavy gun shooting, and a scheme for ships to fire in company when manoeuvring.

Has carried out fleet exercises based on war possibilities, ignoring past traditions.[1]

It is clear that Beresford was often enthusiastic about Fisher's doings, not least because the latter in a number of cases acted in accordance with Beresford's own suggestions. Beresford reinforced Fisher's own concern about the strength of the Mediterranean Fleet in the event of war and about the state of its gunnery. He raised such important and forward-looking points as the advantages of French nucleus crews over British care-and-maintenance parties for ships in reserve, the comparative slowness with which the fleet was being equipped with radio, the

---

[1] N.M.M., Beresford's notebook—Bennett, pp. 235-6.

merits of a Naval War College for the training of senior officers, and the need to improve conditions on the lower deck—notably victualling and leave. The precise extent of Beresford's influence on the stream of demands and suggestions flowing from Fisher to the Admiralty is difficult to assess, but it was certainly considerable.[1]

Nevertheless, the underlying tension between Fisher and Beresford persisted. The latter's penchant for working the press upset Fisher, who was himself operating (more stealthily) in the same field, and he communicated his irritation to Lord Charles. King-Hall noted on 22 October 1901: 'Beresford the night before detained me for half an hour, more or less, having a hit at C.-in-C., ending up by saying he was an Asiatic!'[2]

The principal common interest uniting Fisher and Beresford in unstable alliance was the strength of the Mediterranean Fleet in relation to its probable tasks in war. Yet Fisher is remembered as the far-seeing man who concentrated naval strength to meet the Germans in the North Sea. It is rather paradoxical that, from 1900 to 1902, he was exerting himself to build up strength in the Mediterranean! With the doubtfully welcome assistance of Beresford, Fisher succeeded in bludgeoning a reluctant Admiralty into raising the numbers and quality of the battle-ships, cruisers, and destroyers on the Mediterranean station.

Of course, the international scene changed a good deal between 1899 and 1904. The Anglo–French *entente* denoted the end of a colonial rivalry which had been a source of contention since the 1880s. By late 1904 the Russian Navy had suffered at the hands of the Japanese and the German Navy was nearly equal to the French. However, when Fisher assumed command in the Mediterranean, his position was difficult. He had barely joined the fleet when the South African War began (Oct. 1899). The early reverses inflicted by the Boers on the British Army suggested that the Navy might also be found wanting. European opinion was hostile to Britain and in March 1900 the Russians proposed to France and Germany combined intervention to save the Boers. As Commander-in-Chief in the Mediterranean Fisher bore great responsibilities. He had to prepare detailed plans, with Admiralty approval, for fighting either France alone or Russia and France together. He had constantly to assess the adequacy of his fleet in this context. But the fact remains that it

[1] Bennett, pp. 230–1, 236–7. [2] King-Hall, p. 322.

was Reginald Custance (D.N.I., 1899–1902) who first emphasized the German danger.

As late as 7 July 1899 Fisher had written to his wife: 'Half
Moon Street sounds excellent for lodgings, as it is near Custance.
He lives there, and I shall want to see him very often.'[1] By the
beginning of 1901 Fisher evidently knew about Custance's opposition to his demands for reinforcement of the Mediterranean in
peacetime—as distinct from the Admiralty's plan to send more
ships when an emergency arose.[2] When Fisher proposed arrangements for the visit, in April 1901, of the First Lord and others to
Malta he intimated to Fawkes, now Naval Secretary, that he did
not wish to accommodate Custance at Admiralty House.[3] Nor
did the actual discussions, which revolved round the question of
strength in the Mediterranean, do anything to diminish Fisher's
incipient hostility to Custance.[4] Custance for his part began
during 1901 to regard Fisher as a threat to the proper distribution of the Navy. From December 1900 onwards the D.N.I.
had 'on various occasions' drawn their Lordships' attention to
the German Navy as 'the most formidable force' which Britain
would 'have to meet in the future'.[5] In a minute of 14 September
1901 he commented on Fisher's demands:

The wants of the Mediterranean Fleet have been repeatedly
pressed upon the attention of their Lordships by the C.-in-C. The
Home Fleet has had no such advocate, but it is believed that the
manoeuvres have shewn that the necessity of practice and frequent
exercise together of its battleships, cruisers and destroyers is important, if it is to be on a par with the formidable German force which is
being rapidly developed in the North Sea.[6]

Both Lord Selborne (First Lord since November 1900) and
Walter Kerr refused at this time to look beyond the Franco–
Russian danger, though Kerr had two months earlier criticized
Fisher for exaggerating 'the hostile intentions of France and
Russia, who he seems to credit with being always on the watch
to fall upon him without any provocation and at a moment's
notice.'[7] It must be said on Fisher's behalf that the French fleet
at Toulon, under Admiral Alfred Gervais, attained an exceptional level of efficiency during 1901–2—even if disaster was

[1] *F.G.* i, 143.   [2] *F.G.* i, 187.   [3] F.P. 64, 25 Feb. 1901.
[4] Kilv. MSS., Pkt. 9, Sir Charles Walker's 'Recollections' (*FG*).
[5] Add. MSS. 50287, Arnold-Forster Papers, 'Notes on a Visit to Wilhelmshaven':
Custance's minute of 5 Nov. 1902.
[6] *Anatomy*, p. 463.   [7] Ibid., pp. 463 and 404.

about to overtake the whole French service in the form of the Pelletan administration. However, such considerations did little to reconcile Custance to Fisher and his strategic views. The D.N.I. addressed to Cyprian Bridge (now Commander-in-Chief on the China station) a number of observations, beginning on 17 October 1901:

> The War Course at Greenwich is turning out a great success under [Captain H. J.] May's efficient leading. There is no doubt a great deal of mental activity now displayed in regard to tactics which may, I hope, be productive of good. Fisher is very active in the Mediter-ranean, but much of the advantage which should be derived from it is lost on account of his want of grasp of fundamental principles and desire to run himself to the front at any price. It is a depressing and melancholy spectacle.[1]

Having presumably elicited a sympathetic response from Bridge, Custance warmed to his theme. On 3 January 1902 he wrote: 'Fisher has made a great effort to get into the Admiralty as Second Sea Lord, but has, I trust, been defeated. The way in which he takes in most people is extraordinary, seeing how super-ficial and time-serving he is.'[2] And on 11 May: 'After pounding away for a long time, the German menace has been at last brought partially home . . . The worst thing I know is the advent of Fisher with all his wild superficial ideas. No man has less grasp of principles. Beresford is as mischievous as he can be, but is losing prestige rapidly.'[3]

These remarks show that Fisher had succeeded in converting a friend into an embittered enemy. However, it is clear that even Custance was willing to ascribe some value to Fisher's educative activity in the Mediterranean and this merits further considera-tion here. Beresford's contemporary opinion was that Fisher 'deserves the lasting gratitude of the Country for instituting essays and utilising the brains of his officers for solving the new problems which new circumstances have created'.[4] Moreover, despite his subsequent feud with Fisher—extending fairly con-tinuously from 1907 to his own death in 1919—Lord Charles decided to include in his *Memoirs* (published in 1914) an appre-ciation of Fisher's contribution in this sphere:

> Among the excellent practices introduced by the commander-in-chief, was the writing of essays by officers upon a given subject—the

---

[1] N.M.M., BRI/15.   [2] Ibid.   [3] Ibid.   [4] Bennett, p. 236.

interchange of ideas being of much educational value; and perhaps of hardly less utility, was the exercise in composition. Many naval officers evince marked literary ability; but there is always a proportion who find accurate expression a difficulty . . . [Fisher] invited, with excellent results, officers to formulate their opinions upon cruising and battle formation.[1]

A process of cross-fertilization took place. Fisher attempted to carry out some realistic exercises in the autumn of 1899 without prior consultation or discussion on any scale. Dissatisfied with these manoeuvres, he decided to prepare for further exercises in 1900 by assembling the Captains, Gunnery Lieutenants, and other recommended specialists of the fleet at Admiralty House, Malta. He delivered 'one of his breezy lectures' and said that he would welcome suggestions from any officers in the fleet. Suggestions came in. Fisher appointed a committee, including Commander Bacon, to submit to him a programme for the summer manoeuvres. Bacon commented in his memoirs that Fisher

was a living winnowing machine. He welcomed suggestions from all who possessed ideas. These he assimilated, separated the wheat from the chaff. The majority of our Admirals never consulted any officer under the rank of a Post Captain; and few even unbent to this extent. Fisher was just the opposite; rank and age to him had no meaning so far as gathering information was concerned. All grist was welcome at his mill. Moreover, he always gave full credit to those who helped him; he never pretended that all his schemes originated in his own brain; he was most magnanimous in acknowledging assistance. As a result of his request I sent him a screed about the use of torpedo craft both for attack and defence of a fleet. I scribbled it out one morning and then had qualms as to whether it was worth while to send it along. However, I did so, and the decision I made that morning probably altered the whole of my career, for Sir John immediately sent for me; and, for the remainder of the time that I was on the Station, he kept me hard at work on his various schemes.[2]

Bacon left the Mediterranean in June 1900 on his promotion to Captain. His appreciation of Fisher's educational methods may, however, be applied the whole of the latter's time in the Mediterranean, with the caveat that Fisher remained autocrat of the fleet and was less generous to Beresford than to the lesser mortals.

[1] Beresford, *Memoirs*, pp. 466–7.
[2] Bacon, *From 1900 Onward*, p. 24.

After a combined naval and military exercise in the spring, when 5,000 men were landed at Malta, Fisher took the fleet on two series of manoeuvres during June–July and August–November.[1] In June he offered a fifty-guinea gold cup as a prize for an essay on a tactical subject, such as attack and defence by torpedo craft. This met with a good response, including entries by Bacon and Hankey which both earned favourable mention.[2] On Fisher's conduct of the exercises Hankey comments:

One thing he did was to increase the speed of the fleet. All exercises were carried out at a much higher speed than formerly, and woe to the captain and fleet engineer of the ship that could not maintain its speed. All the 'chiefs' were shaking their heads at the probable effects on engines and boilers, which they said were being rattled to pieces. Yet the speed was always maintained during the three years that 'Jacky' Fisher remained on the station, and some of the ships of that day were commissioned fifteen years later in the war of 1914 and cruised all over the world. This increase of speed for tactical exercises was a complete repudiation of the calumny that Fisher lacked nerve. But an even stronger refutation was his habit of steaming in fleet formation at night without lights, when he sometimes took great risks.[3]

While driving the fleet hard during manoeuvres Fisher did not neglect the matter of entertainment. Greece, Sardinia, Majorca, Fiume, and Zara (Zadar) were all visited. In connexion with the sumptuous entertainment given by the Austrians at Trieste, Hankey remarks: 'It was characteristic of Fisher that he gave lavish entertainments in return, sending the bill to the Admiralty afterwards without having first received their permission.'[4] In September the fleet went up to Constantinople. Fisher took Lady Fisher and his unmarried daughters Dorothy and Pamela (who otherwise lived at Admiralty House, Malta) with him in the *Renown*. He wrote to his son, Cecil: 'We had a most successful visit to Constantinople. I had three solemn interviews with the Sultan [Abdul Hamid] and he treated us in a right royal way. He gave me the highest order of Osmanieh, set in brilliants, and Mother the 1st class of the Chefeket, and D. and P. the 2nd class.'[5]

After completing the year's manoeuvres Fisher delivered lectures which summarized lessons learnt and listed subjects deserving further attention. Unfortunately, the notes of these

---

[1] *F.G.* i, 155–6; F.P. 4178–9. [2] Roskill, i, 53. [3] Hankey, i, 15.
[4] Ibid., p. 18. [5] *F.G.* i, 160.

earlier lectures were 'inadvertently destroyed'[1] but there is no reason to doubt that any of them failed to stimulate. All commissioned officers were now welcome to attend and comments were recorded such as: 'These lectures stretched the mind to the fullest conceivable extent. They were also humorous.'[2] Fortunately, an assortment of notes for lectures given between December 1901 and May 1902 was preserved and subsequently printed. These notes will be considered in due course as they form a background to the cardinal reforms of 1904–5. Meanwhile it will be chronologically convenient to treat Fisher's relationship with the Admiralty and with certain journalists who were then writing about naval affairs.

Fisher has been credited with 'burning patriotism'. Certainly, in terms of his wish to become First Sea Lord, it was not to his personal interest to engage in a struggle with the Admiralty over the strength of the Mediterranean Fleet.

In the background were the following events. In the early 1890s the British position in the Mediterranean had seemed weak and some publicists advocated immediate withdrawal. The Admiralty held to something of a compromise, planning to concentrate the Mediterranean and Channel Squadrons at Gibraltar in the event of war with France (or with France and Russia). During the Fashoda crisis, faced by the French alone, the Admiralty ordered Hopkins to concentrate the Mediterranean Fleet at Malta while the Channel Fleet sailed for Gibraltar. Just before handing over command of the Mediterranean Fleet to Fisher, Noel wrote to the Admiralty suggesting that the point of concentration for the two fleets should be at Gibraltar, but that a strong detachment should be based on Malta to fight the Russians if they issued from the Black Sea. Fisher strongly supported Noel in a letter of 1 November 1899. On 19 February 1900 the Admiralty replied, accepting and amplifying this strategy. British cruisers would watch Toulon and the combined battlefleet, under Fisher's command, would be ready to advance and engage the Toulon fleet.[3]

Dissatisfied with the strength of the Mediterranean Fleet, whether before or after reinforcement, Fisher mounted a two-pronged attack on the Admiralty (where Goschen continued to

---

[1] F.P. 4702, p. 7.
[2] Vice-Adl. Humphrey Hugh Smith, *An Admiral Never Forgets*, London, 1936, p. 127.   [3] *Anatomy*, pp. 210, 326–7, 396–8.

preside until October 1900). Officially, he began with a show of restraint. On 28 April 1900 he referred to the Board's directions of 19 February and remarked: '*Their Lordships are limited by their resources in making this appropriation, which I fear is inadequate* to carry out the requirements of February 19th.' 'Their Lordships of course appreciate that newly commissioned vessels joining the Fleet will not be so efficient or so reliable as those instructed or practised beforehand by the Commander-in-Chief.' With regard to cruisers and small craft, he confined himself to observing: 'I understand their Lordships are proposing to send the total number it will be possible to appropriate to the Mediterranean Station, so it's no use harassing them for more.'[1]

However this letter did not wholly represent Fisher's plan of action. Harassment of their Lordships was envisaged at least as early as 20 February 1900. On that day Fisher wrote from Malta to J. R. Thursfield, naval correspondent of *The Times*, whom he had carefully nursed since 1897:[2]

We are all greatly dreading a relaxation of Naval Shipbuilding in the next Estimates. This will be truly fatal. I fear from all I hear Sir M. Hicks Beach[3] has terrorised the Admiralty, the only man he feared (Sir F. Richards) having left. We require a great increase of battleships to take the place of those old obsolete dummies now counted in our strength, *misleading both the Nation and the Navy*, and also an increase *in all classes of cruizers* and MORE ESPECIALLY DESTROYERS.[4]

A more recent journalistic acquaintance than Thursfield was the inflammatory navalist Arnold White. Resembling in appearance the lately deceased Prince Bismarck[5] and given to blatant indiscretion, he was capable of producing convulsions of opinion, somewhat in the tradition of W. T. Stead. Fisher claimed him for his own; faithful unto death, White would receive the last letter (almost certainly) to be signed by Fisher's hand.[6] In July 1900 the proofs of an article written by White, 'Shall Britain be "Ladysmithed"?', reached Fisher. It was duly published in *Cassell's Magazine* the following September. Fisher's reaction to the proofs was enthusiastic. He thought it was 'the most eloquent and graphic exposition' he had ever read. 'If you ask me what is

[1] F.P. 59.   [2] *F.G.* i, 137–9.
[3] Chancellor of the Exchequer, 1895–1902—'a perfect beast, without a single redeeming feature that I ever found out', wrote F. in *Records*, p. 51.
[4] N.M.M., THU/1.   [5] Dewar, p. 69.
[6] F.P. 3717, F. to White, 7 July 1920.

the "kernel" of the whole question, I reply that it lies in your "Belshazzar" words, "Preliminary failure in Naval War means the ruin of the British Empire." ' The article supplied him with one of his favourite phrases, to the effect that a naval disaster caused by unpreparedness would be 'irretrievable, irreparable, eternal'. 'You must keep on telling the people the same thing,' Fisher insisted in his reply of 17 July, 'and of course this is the secret of advertisement.' This exhortation bore fruit the following summer.[1]

It was soon brought home to Fisher, however, that White's enthusiasm was outrunning his discretion. On 8 January 1901 the Admiral wrote:

> In the first place I must again entreat you to keep our correspondence and any peculiar phrases I may use as your own private property, for I have been paid the compliment of a letter from Lord Goschen, as he now is, to say that there is a strong Mediterranean flavour in your writings, and that you might even be supposed to have read all the public and private letters I have been writing to the Admiralty ever since I assumed command of this great fleet . . .[2]

By this time Goschen was no longer writing as First Lord of the Admiralty. In November 1900 he had been succeeded by the Earl of Selborne. Fisher had lost no time in adapting himself to the change. On 1 December he wrote to Selborne:

> You very kindly invite me to write to you privately and I presume as freely as I did to Mr. Goschen, and if so I am confident you will find it advantageous, and, if at times I express myself very strongly, I hope you will forgive me and kindly remember that I have the rope round my neck, and if we don't beat the French I shall be hung or shot like Admiral Byng! I have been told that I only believe in myself and no one else! All I know is that if you do not believe in yourself, no one else will! and I humbly venture to think I have set forth impregnable arguments to establish the following points:
>
> 1 Success in war depends upon the concentration of an overpowering force upon a given spot in the shortest possible time . . . the attacking power has the privilege of selection . . .
> 2 The Mediterranean is of necessity the vital point of a naval war, and you can no more change this than you can change the position of Mount Vesuvius, because geographical conditions,

---

[1] *F.G.* i, 157 and 350.
[2] F.P. 1744 (copy). The original letters from F. to Arnold White are at Kilverstone.

Sebastopol and Toulon, and the Eastern question, will compel
the Battle of Armageddon to be fought in the Mediterranean.

3   Therefore, I have reiterated *ad nauseum* in official and private
letters that, owing to the suddenness possible and desirable in
naval war (see point 1, above), the Mediterranean Fleet should
be more nearly on a war footing than at present in destroyers,
cruisers, and auxiliaries, in all of which we are criminally
deficient. I say 'criminal' because a naval disaster is irretrievable, as you cannot extemporise destroyers, cruisers, and
battleships like you can the component parts of a military
force . . .

4   *We want more ships of all classes*, with all their adjuncts in the
shape of officers, men, etc. Last year, or rather I mean in this
year's Estimates, *there is not a single destroyer to be built!* Probably
the answer is that turbine propulsion will give us a new type,
but 'half a loaf is better than no bread', and we never can afford
like small nations, or indeed any nation, to wait for experiments
and cease building, because the existence of the British Empire
absolutely depends on our Navy . . .[1]

This, in essence, was Fisher's case for strengthening the
Mediterranean Fleet. He pressed it on Selborne during the next
six months, together with the point (included in the initial letter
just quoted) that

to send out to an Admiral on the outbreak of war the mass of fresh
vessels now contemplated is to lay on him a burden he should not be
called on to bear at such a time. He must have a practised Fleet to
ensure success, and provided with its proper quota of accessories
during peace, so that he may try and prove them and use them to
advantage.[2]

This last argument was a compelling one. Unfortunately, it was
to carry insufficient weight in Fisher's own dealings with Beresford from 1906 to 1909. In 1909 the Admiralty offered as one of
its reasons for denying Beresford a unified command in home
waters 'the sensitivity of international relations'.[3] But in his
letter of 1 December 1900 Fisher used a sharply contrasting
argument: 'When relations with France and Russia are strained,
the measures that prudence dictates will not be taken for fear of
precipitating matters.' In other words, he insisted on concentration of his whole force under his sole command in time of
peace.[4]

<hr>

[1] *F.G.* i, 167–8.
[3] *D.S.* i, 194; also 41–2.
[2] Ibid., p. 169.
[4] *F.G.* i, 168.

Fisher's relationship with the new First Lord was to prove crucial both for himself and for the Navy. Born in 1859, Selborne was a Liberal Unionist. Before going to the Admiralty in November 1900 he had been colonial under-secretary. Possessed of good administrative ability, he was open to new ideas. When he became First Lord the Navy Estimates were about double those of 1892; yet in January 1901 he had to inform his ministerial colleagues that Britain was scarcely maintaining her naval lead over France and Russia. If the latter powers completed their building programmes, they would have a total of 53 battleships by 1906, thus drawing level with Britain. Moreover, in recent years three new navies had 'sprung into existence', namely those of the United States, Germany, and Japan. Selborne declared that, if the United States developed their full potential, Britain could hardly hope to apply the Two Power Standard to the United States and France combined. Therefore Britain should aim at a clear superiority over France and Russia. Even then, naval expenditure would continue to rise. Already in December he had written to the Chancellor of the Exchequer that he could see 'only one possible alternative' to this prospect. This was the conclusion of a formal alliance with Germany.[1]

This, then, was the background to Selborne's early official connexion with Fisher. While he was never entirely uncritical in his attitude towards the Admiral, Selborne was evidently intrigued from the outset by the latter's unusual characteristics and their possible relevance to Britain's naval and financial predicament. However, Fisher's campaign to strengthen the Mediterranean Fleet constantly irritated the First Lord's principal advisers at the Admiralty and rendered uncertain the attitude of Selborne himself. One event assisting Fisher's attempt to win over Selborne to his views was the appointment in November 1900 of Wilmot Fawkes (a Rear-Admiral from the beginning of 1901) as the First Lord's Naval Secretary. He has been noticed as Fisher's Commander in the *Northampton*. Since then, Fisher had found him a useful connexion when serving, from 1897 to 1899, as Goschen's Naval Secretary and he had maintained cordial relations with him subsequently.[2] From December 1900

---

[1] Monger, pp. 10–12.

[2] *F.G.* i, 140–1, 162–3; F.P. 4–6 (copies of letters from F. to Fawkes, Oct.–Nov. 1900, when Fawkes was about to leave the Mediterranean Fleet in which he was a senior Captain).

onwards, Fisher supplemented his verbal assault on Selborne with a series of letters, often of similar tendency, to Fawkes; and it was to Fawkes that he threw out a feeler in the autumn of 1901 about the possibility of his own return to the Admiralty as Second Sea Lord.[1]

In the middle of January 1901 Fisher made a special effort to shake the Admiralty. On the 16th he wrote privately to Selborne:

At the same time as this letter I am sending an official letter N. 100/426 dated Jan. 16 1901 by way of being a sort of 'clearing up' paper, bringing together the various communications which have been made to me by the Admiralty with my submissions thereon, so as to make quite sure that no misunderstanding exists between the Admiralty and the Commander in Chief in the Mediterranean in the event of war, and I have asked for certain information and made various proposals which I hope will not be thought unreasonable. I bear your excellent remarks in mind as to 'thorough' and 'caution', but as someone has observed though 'slow-and-sure is good, *sure-and-*READY is better'![2]

The lengthy official letter of the 16th terminates with a summary of the principal points therein contained:

(a) It is desired that a list, and afterwards weekly corrections, may be sent to the Commander-in-Chief of the Mediterranean Station, of the names of the vessels forming the intended reinforcement of the Mediterranean Fleet, together with the names of probable Captains as regards vessels of war.

(b) The same in regard to hired mercantile cruisers, despatch vessels, and other Fleet Auxiliaries, as regards the names of vessels only.

(c) That the provision of permanent Fleet Auxiliaries for the efficient peace training and exercise of the Fleet may be hastened . . .

(d) That the stock of coal on the Mediterranean Station may be brought up to war standard as speedily as possible . . .

(e) That the reinforcements for the Mediterranean Station may if practicable be concentrated during peace (and organised under the Flag Officer who will bring them out) at one of the home ports ready for an immediate organised start at a few hours notice . . .

---

[1] *F.G.* i, 210–11.
[2] F.P. 59. The rest of the letter is extensively reproduced in *F.G.* i, 182–3. However, the final para. is not printed; this shows that No. 88, dated 13 Jan. 1901 (about the need for young admirals), *F.G.* i, 180–1, was almost certainly never sent to Selborne.

(f) That the necessity of Alexandria being required as a Naval Base in the Eastern Mediterranean may be immediately recognised . . .

(g) That it may be recognised that the alteration of our policy towards Turkey *has practically brought Sevastopol to the mouth of the Dardanelles,* and the acquisition by France of Tunis *has brought Toulon to Bizerta,* which is every day becoming more strongly fortified and more approaching the conditions of a first class Naval Base.

(h) That *the only chance of a French success lies in an immediate offensive* . . .

(i) The number of Fleet Auxiliaries mentioned in Admiralty Secret Letter M/0595 of 24 May 1900 *seems inadequate* . . .

(j) No submission is made to increase the number of cruisers and other vessels for the reinforcement of the Mediterranean Fleet in view of their Lordships' statement that '*all that is possible has been appropriated.*'

(k) But in view of the above statement it is respectfully submitted whether the relative standard of British Naval strength *should not be immediately raised.*[1]

On 16 January Fisher wrote also to H. O. Arnold-Forster who was now Parliamentary Secretary of the Admiralty:

Our frontiers are the coasts of the enemy and we ought to be there 5 minutes after war is declared ready to take the offensive, preventing the newly mobilised vessels of the enemy coming out for their commissioning trials, masking his torpedo flotillas, throwing a shell or two into Marseilles and Toulon at night, harassing Algeria, etc., but the tables will be turned if we don't mind. It will be the French Admiral throwing himself in overwhelming numbers on Malta before the Mediterranean reinforcements of some 70 vessels have joined the Mediterranean Squadron! However I won't weary you with any more and please consider these remarks as quite for your own private eye as I fear I am already in rather an antagonistic position, and as Lord Selborne has the whole case fully before him and I have complete confidence in his and your doing all that is proper, or else putting someone in my place who would be satisfied with things as they are! . . .

I won't hide from you that I am called a 'Radical enthusiast', 'Gambetta', and several other names indicating a very bad opinion of me! But I believe I have the whole Mediterranean Fleet at my back in all the opinions I have expressed . . . I don't want to share the fate of Admiral Byng.[2]

[1] F.P. 60.   [2] F.P. 61.

As was frequently the case when Fisher was determined to impose his point of view, he had suited the letter to the man; and in due course Arnold-Forster came out strongly in his support.[1]

Nor was the First Sea Lord forgotten. On 17 January Fisher wrote in tactful vein to Lord Walter Kerr[2] notwithstanding his concurrent activity in undermining the latter's reputation with Thursfield. On 8 January he had written to Thursfield: '*Between ourselves*, there's no question that we have missed in the last few years that clear, broad old back of Sir F. Richards set against the wall!' He added: 'What good stories I could tell you, were I able to break through the sacred confidence of official letters, to illustrate Nero fiddling while Rome was burning!' However, on 29 January he found a way round this 'sacred confidence' by enclosing for Thursfield a slip removed from the latest *Navy List*. This showed what, in Fisher's view, was 'occupying the attention of the Sea Lords' namely: 'Addendum, p. 670, 4. Cuffs of the full dress coat. The Regulations for the cuffs of the Flag Officer's Full Dress Coat are undergoing further consideration.'[3]

Selborne had apparently already decided to pay an official visit to the Commander-in-Chief, Mediterranean.[4] However, Fisher's direct onslaught on the Admiralty, supported by a campaign in the press, persuaded the First Lord to expedite the visit. In March 1901 he took with him Kerr, Custance, and Fawkes. Fisher supplied spectacular pageantry and illuminations in the Grand Harbour of Valetta. The upshot of the discussions was a promise to raise the number of Fisher's destroyers from 16 to 24. That Fisher was not much mollified by this concession is evident from his letter of 22 May addressed to Lord Rosebery, a politician still of the first rank who had recently paid a visit to Malta:

We are in a dangerous and serious position in the Mediterranean . . .

Believe me, *what we want is a more rigorous administration at the Admiralty. That is the root of the whole matter.* They are lost to a sense of proportion: they can see a pin but they can't see a mountain! because their eyes are fixed on the floor of petty details as to what coloured socks we shall wear and a new collar for an Admiral's full-dress coat! . . .

Of course, Walter Kerr had grounds for believing that it was Fisher who lacked a sense of proportion and was exaggerating

---

[1] Add. MSS. 50288, A.-Forster to Selborne, 26 June 1901.
[2] F.P. 62.   [3] *F.G.* i, 180, 186.   [4] Bacon, i, 141.

the claims of the Mediterranean over those of the Channel.[1] However, Fisher proceeded in his letter to Rosebery to deploy the following version of the recent Admiralty visit to Malta:

I enclose for your private eye a portion of a letter I wrote to Lord Selborne on his first taking office. Not one single thing had been done since that date, notwithstanding reiterated letters from me, until, like related in the second epistle to the Corinthians, the 10th Chapter and the 9th verse (I quote because I know it by heart!), they say 'his letters are weighty and powerful, but (perhaps) his bodily presence is weak and his speech contemptible': let us go out to Malta and flatten him out! So, after getting on for nearly two years representing the inefficiency that may prove the death of the Empire, they come out—*three to one*—and there are fierce words, but again, to quote Scripture: 'The words of the men of the Mediterranean were fiercer than the words of the Admiralty', and they were beaten all along the line! but delay goes on. Lord Selborne is attending to coaling stations, which are no concern of his, as regards garrisons; Lord Walter Kerr is attending to our socks and coats; and the Director of Naval Intelligence is occupied with the strange case of Mr. Jekyll and Mr. Hyde in arranging a 'Fleet' return for Sir C. Dilke in the House of Commons and showing the disposition of our ships on paper as being out here and at home at the same time.[2]

In Custance's opinion, Fisher had distorted and misconceived the danger represented by the Russian Black Sea Fleet. Fisher had argued that his position would be weakened if the Russian, squadron issued from the Black Sea whereas in the D.N.I.'s view 'it is ardently to be desired that it should come out in order that it may be engaged and rendered incapable of further mischief.' The Admiralty's information was that the said Russian squadron was in a deplorable condition.[3]

It thus proved in the end to be the gentlemen of the press who tipped the balance with regard to the Mediterranean Fleet. In May 1901 the French, apparently in all innocence, announced that the whole of their battleship force would hold manoeuvres in the Mediterranean in July. This induced Arnold White and Robert Yerburgh, the President of the Navy League, to repeat a visit of the previous summer to the Mediterranean Fleet. (On each occasion they went as guests of Beresford.) A good deal of collusion with Fisher, and doubtless Beresford, resulted in White

---

[1] *Anatomy*, pp. 400–4.   [2] *F.G.* i, 193–6.
[3] *Anatomy*, pp. 405–6.

writing to the latter.[1] White asked whether it was true that Fisher's fleet was below its full combat strength. On 10 June Beresford replied:

It would be most improper and prejudicial to discipline if I were to give you details as to why I am so anxious at the want of strength and proper war organisation of the fleet in the Mediterranean. I have communicated my views in strong and clear Anglo-Saxon language to the properly constituted authorities. My duty and business out here as second-in-command are simply to obey orders to the best of my ability . . .

Through White's agency this letter was printed for the enlightenment of readers of the *Daily Mail* on 21 June.[2] On 4 July Arnold-Forster wrote to Fisher that Beresford, whose patriotic activity of 1887 he remembered with admiration, had now 'set an example which he would be the very first to condemn if followed by any Officer of seaman under his command'.[3] Meanwhile on 3 July a reduction of Lord Selborne's salary was moved in the House of Commons! The First Lord, for his part, deplored the hypothesis that the French and Russians would 'act as pirates, and, with a perfectly clear political atmosphere and without any warning' mobilize and concentrate their squadrons undetected and fall upon the Mediterranean Fleet 'at its peace strength unawares and unreinforced'. But such parliamentary utterances failed to silence the navalists. White declared in an article in the *National Review:* 'We present to the French and Russians a temptation almost irresistible in the weakness and deficiencies of our main fighting fleet.'[4]

In the early stages of the agitation, Kerr lost no time in linking Fisher with an article in the *Fortnightly Review.* 'The mischievous article', he minuted, 'is a rechauffé and in many instances in identical terms, of the views expounded to the Board by the C.-in-C. on the occasion of their recent visit to Malta.'[5]

Fisher received news of these developments without much optimism. Towards the end of June he wrote to his wife:

I have a letter from Fawkes to say there is much turmoil—it was all those articles appearing about the Mediterranean Fleet, especially

---

[1] F.P. 1748, F. to White, 9 June 1901; King-Hall, pp. 318–20 (Diary, 9 June, 21 July); Bennett, pp. 231–2.
[2] Bennett, pp. 232–3.   [3] Add. MSS. 50288.
[4] *Anatomy*, pp. 408–11; Bennett, pp. 232–3.
[5] *Anatomy*, p. 409 (min. of 12 June).

as they had so many of my views and phrases in them. I really have not had time to study them carefully, but I have no doubt it is correct what he says, and can't help it for it is all quite true, and I have never disguised my views or opinions, and I told Lord Selborne so when he was at Malta, and that I should be a traitor if I did disguise my views, considering the safety of the Empire is at stake! So I can't help it whatever may happen.

I don't believe myself that any good will come of all the newspaper and magazine articles because the Government have got a majority of 130 in the House of Commons . . .[1]

And to Fawkes he wrote on 27 June: 'So far as I am personally concerned, it will be of course obvious to you that I have nothing whatever to gain by kicking the shins of the Admiralty! so that the articles (of which, by the way, I have only seen a portion) are certainly not written in my interest! and only serve to aggravate instead of smoothing and facilitating.'[2]

On 29 June Fisher could still discern no cause for personal celebration. Arnold White, he wrote to his wife, was a 'scoundrel'; contrary to his 'distinct request', White had published in the *Daily Mail* 'a sort of journal of my day's work'. 'I believe', Fisher continued, 'that scoundrel Beresford is at the bottom of it; he tells me he has written to Mr. Balfour about me and that if I am superseded he will resign also, etc., etc.'[3]

However, a few days later Fisher learned that the Channel Squadron was to become an integral part of his fleet in the annual manoeuvres. This changed his attitude towards White; by 17 July the latter had been promoted from the rank of 'scoundrel' to that of 'true patriot'.[4] Ten days later Fisher was reporting to his wife: 'Almost every single point has been conceded and there is no question about it that this recent agitation has done in a few days what I have been incessantly writing about for two years nearly.' Arnold White had 'done wonders'.[5] Indeed, there now ensued a steady strengthening of the Mediterranean Fleet which continued into 1903.

Meanwhile, on 25 July, Arnold White was writing from Hampstead to Lady Fisher. He had discovered an area of comparability between her husband and Jesus Christ!

Sir John Fisher's *silent* devotion to country is what appeals so strongly to my imagination. There is a Spanish proverb 'He who

---

[1] F.P. 1538, n.d.   [2] *F.G.* i, 197.   [3] F.P. 1550, 29 June 1901.
[4] F.P. 1555.   [5] F.P. 1565.

would be a Christ must expect crucifixion.' It would have been so much easier for the Commander-in-Chief to have let things slide, to have drifted with the tide, to have said 'aye' to official optimism at home. Because he has done none of these things he has stirred up a nest of hornets. Curiously enough I find that his deadliest opponents are the Jesuits. Of their subtlety and unscrupulousness I will not speak, and I only mention the fact in order to explain confidentially to you the reason for things that will appear in the papers about Protestantism and the Fleet. A very important conference of Protestants is being held today in order to consider the best means of counteracting the Jesuit manoeuvres of Lord Walter Kerr's friends . . .[1]

Fisher thought this letter 'very interesting'. He added: 'I quite agree about the Jesuits and Roman Catholics.'[2] However, he was correct in believing that he had at least one friend in high places. 'There is no doubt', he wrote to Lady Fisher on the 27th, 'about my being "tabooed" by the whole Admiralty except I think Lord Selborne, as his two letters were very cordial, and he has done two or three things I have telegraphed to him about!'[3]

During the twelvemonth previous to the agitation of 1901 Fisher, who turned sixty during that time, began to contemplate the possibility of retirement. In 1900 Josiah Vavasseur, now aged sixty-six, was a leading director of Sir W. G. Armstrong, Whitworth & Co. The Vavasseurs were childless. They privately resolved to arrange for Fisher's son Cecil to benefit directly, and thus for Fisher himself to benefit indirectly, from their considerable fortune. Cecil Fisher returned to England in 1900 for eighteen months' furlough, having completed ten years in the Indian Civil Service. Unaware of the Vavasseurs' intentions regarding himself, he wrote to his father on 25 June 1900:

I am going down to Kilverstone[4] with Mr. Vavasseur on Monday for 1 night. He has bought the place outright, and is only regretting that he did not buy 'Shadwell Court' too, the adjoining property of the late Sir T. Buxton, of 13,000 acres, just sold to an Australian for £111,000! He seems to be rolling in money now, and bought a little picture at Christie's last week for 500 or 600 guineas. He took me to see it beforehand and then took me to lunch at the Junior Carlton.[5]

Fisher wrote to Cecil on 6 September: 'Give my best love to Mr. and Mrs. Vavasseur, and ask him to let us know should he

[1] F.P. 1564.   [2] F.P. 1566, F. to Lady F., 31 July, 1901.
[3] F.P. 1565.   [4] Near Thetford, Norfolk.   [5] F.P. 1531.

at any time hear of a bargain near Bury St. Edmunds in the shape of a few acres of land and nice cottage with good garden.'[1] Fisher evidently reverted to the idea of a country retreat, but Cecil would not accept this as a serious proposition; 'you know you will not be unemployed for the next five years at least', he wrote in March 1901. In similar vein he reported on 20 May: 'I went to the Academy today. I overheard 2 Naval officers talking. One said "I suppose Fisher'll be home soon." The other said "Yes, in a year. I saw Ld Walter the other day and he looked very weary; the work is too much for him." So you see which way the wind blows.'[2]

Shortly afterwards Cecil met the twenty-seven-year-old Winston Churchill. Already, in a speech in the Commons on 13 May 1901, Churchill had displayed that sweeping military imagination which was to prove so attractive in due course to Cecil's father. On 9 October Cecil wrote to his mother: 'I went up to Gisbourne on Saturday and met Mr. Winston Churchill, and Raymond Asquith, and the young Lord Lytton, son of the man who was Viceroy of India some 20 years ago. I thought all three very interesting, and all I think will make their mark. Churchill talks as if he were a radical Home Ruler, but he is not.'[3]

By the autumn of 1901, Fisher was concerned not so much with the faded possibility of becoming First Sea Lord as with his chances of returning to the Admiralty in any capacity whatever. He threw out a preliminary feeler to Fawkes on 17 September[4] and followed this up with a definite question on 29 October. He inferred from the complex of probable retirements and promotions that Vice-Admiral Archibald Douglas might vacate the post of Second Sea Lord early in 1902. Was there any chance of his emulating Lord Alcester by going from the Mediterranean to become Second Sea Lord? He added, less plausibly: 'Having been ten years at the Admiralty, I think I could hit it off without treading on anyone's toes!'[5]

However, this approach made some headway at the level of the Naval Secretary. On 3 December 1901 Fisher wrote to Fawkes: 'Very many thanks for your kind letter of Nov. 27, and the mental note you have made of my wishes. I know I need not have said anything, but that "expert" Gamble having "risen"

[1] *F.G.* i, 160.   [2] F.P. 1543, 1544.   [3] F.P. 1579.
[4] F.P. 76.   [5] *F.G.* i, 210–11.

me as to Bedford getting to the top so soon, made me send you a few lines on the impulse of the moment!'[1]

At this uncertain juncture Philip Watts, then designer and general manager of Armstrong & Co's warship-building yard at Elswick, Newcastle upon Tyne, wrote to say that he expected to succeed Sir William White as Director of Naval Construction in January 1902. (Watts was a strong believer in powerful ships and would exert material influence on the design of the *Dreadnought* and her successors.) Writing from Elswick on 17 December 1901, he continued:

> I remember quite well when I was in the 'Inflexible'[2] your promising to make me D.N.C. when you became Controller, and thought of it more than once when White broke down. I suppose it may come yet, i.e. I may be working with you at the Admiralty, if you should come back there in another capacity. I trust it may be so! . . .
>
> I cannot imagine you 'on the shelf'; rumour says you will succeed Lord Walter Kerr. But if not, how would you like to take up *trade*? When Sir Andrew [Noble] was so ill after his bicycle accident, you were mentioned as one who might be able to come in and manage this concern! Sir Andrew now looks like pulling round but he is still very shaky . . .[3]

Fisher evidently received further communications from Elswick and Cecil reported that 'several people at the U.S. Club said to Uncle Bill that they had heard' about his brother going to Elswick.[4] Fisher's version, for the benefit of Arnold White, was headed 'STRICTLY PRIVATE'. This was hardly a dependable safeguard. White stated in 1923 that when Fisher enjoined him to 'burn and destroy', he took him to mean 'publish as widely as possible but don't give me away!'[5] However, confidentiality was so much emphasized on this occasion that White seems to have restricted publicity. Fisher wrote:

> Now I am going to say something to you *very private* apropos of your kind offer to help me at any time in the Parliamentary line! Quite unknown to me, when Sir Andrew Noble, the head of the great Elswick firm, was nearly dying lately, the Directors very kindly unanimously proposed to invite me to take his place with his perquisites (that is, Dictator with £10,000 a year!). Although Sir A. Noble has made a wonderful recovery, and the matter is in abeyance at present, it may still come off later on . . . *Please don't mention a word*

[1] F.P. 81.   [2] He went in her as an assistant naval constructor in 1881.
[3] F.P. 84.   [4] F.P. 1580.   [5] *F.G.* i, 355.

of this to anyone, as Noble, who is a lifelong friend, is very sensitive naturally, and I have heard nothing direct except through the indiscretion of two of the Directors. But it's a place I should revel in, and I should immediately set to work to revolutionize the naval fighting by building on speculation a battleship, cruiser, and destroyer on revolutionary principles—oil fuel, turbine propulsion, equal gunfire all round, greater speed than any existing vessels of their class, no masts, no funnels, etc., and I should build them all in 18 months and sell them for double their cost and 'stagger humanity'—and put up the Elswick shares 50 percent! *Now, don't quote any of the above: it's copyright,* and I don't want it to get out![1]

Sir Charles Walker afterwards recalled, 'J.F. said the post and salary (£10,000) nearly tempted him, so small did his chances then seem of getting back on the Board.'[2] However, Lord Selborne very soon came to the point of decision. Writing on 9 February 1902, he offered Fisher the succession to Admiral Douglas as Second Sea Lord. Examination of the letter shows that the First Lord had carefully weighed the risks inherent in this offer against the prospective advantages.

I have received the King's permission to make you this offer, but in making it I want to make an observation or two to obviate any possibility of misunderstanding in the future. I much hope that you will come, because I believe there is a great deal to be done in connection with the personnel, and that we can do much together for the good of the Navy, but I make no promise as to your succeeding the present First Naval Lord when his time is up. I reserve complete freedom of choice of his successor for myself or my successor when the time comes.

My second point is that, if we ever differ, as in the natural course of events we probably occasionally shall, no one off the Board must ever know of our differences. Each member of the Board has his eventual remedy in resignation, a remedy which a wise man reserves for some special occasion only. But so long as we do not resign, our solidarity to the Service and the world outside must be absolute.[3]

Fisher had risen to the rank of full Admiral in November 1901 and the appointment of so senior an officer as Second Sea Lord was distinctly unusual. Fisher himself certainly looked on this post as a stepping-stone. Having accepted it, he began at once to prepare plans for the general future of the Navy. Only a

---

[1] *F.G.* i, 185; but the date should be 28 Jan. 1902, not 28 Jan. 1901. (The year was not written on the original which is at Kilverstone.)
[2] Kilv. MSS., Pkt. 9 (*FG*).   [3] *F.G.* i, 222.

fraction of this effort was directed to the educational reforms falling within the province of a Second Sea Lord. On 25 February 1902 Fisher sent to Selborne three papers, all of which demand close attention and remembrance:

1 'On the Increasing Necessity for a General Staff for the Navy to meet War Requirements'.
2 'The Strategical Distribution of Our Fleets'.
3 'The Engineer Question'.[1]

Probably the most substantial criticism made of Fisher as First Sea Lord is directed at his failure to establish a fully effective Naval Staff at the Admiralty. Yet, in the first of the above-mentioned papers he wrote, in his own hand, as follows:

A study of the paper herewith on the Distribution of the Naval Strength of the Empire; a study of the one subject of Commerce Protection in War; a study of the tactical exercises (past and proposed) of the Mediterranean Fleet during the past $2\frac{1}{2}$ years; a study of the previous history and calibre of Flag Officers in command of Fleets and of their Staff; a study of these four subjects alone, without numerous others in all minds (such for instance as the limitations of British gun fire absolutely imposing a broadside action!); a study of the above subjects alone lead[s] to the absolute conviction that we must have a very much larger department than the present Intelligence Bureau at the Admiralty with its associated small though excellent Greenwich College Class for Strategical Instruction. We have a magnificent model to work upon and to guide us! The Great German General Staff, the admiration of the world and the organizer of the greatest victories of modern times is absolutely applicable in its ideas and its organization to meet all the needs of the Navy. It is essential that our 'Fighting' Admirals should also be 'Thinking Admirals' . . .[2]

Yet it seems quite possible that Fisher had not thoroughly considered this suggestion from a practical viewpoint. The notion of the War College at Greenwich sharing the functions of the N.I.D. is at variance with the admired example of the German General Staff. In practice Fisher as First Sea Lord would prefer the informal and advisory service provided by the War College to a unified and responsible Naval Staff. Meanwhile, Fisher's short-lived advocacy of a general staff in the German style owed much to the influence of Captain Prince Louis of Battenberg.

---

[1] All three papers are in F.P. 90.   [2] Ibid.

Born in 1854, Prince Louis was high on the Captains' list when he took the new battleship *Implacable* out to the Mediterranean in the autumn of 1901. Already in January 1901, when he was an Assistant Director of Naval Intelligence at the Admiralty, Fisher thought him one of 'perhaps the two best officers in the whole British Navy'—Captain W. H. May being the other.[1] Battenberg, for his part, was an old friend of Fisher's Chief of Staff, King-Hall; and on 15 April 1900 he wrote from Frogmore House, Windsor, to King-Hall as follows: 'As to *Renown* she should not be the flagship; in fact, she ought to be in China. We want the biggest and best in the Mediterranean; J.F. of course, won't part with his "yacht", but it is quite wrong.'[2]

However, from the time of his joining the Mediterranean Fleet in October 1901, Prince Louis was taken into Fisher's confidence. From then until the onset of the Home Fleet controversy in 1906, Battenberg accounted himself 'a firm believer in the genius of John Fisher'.[3]

During the early months of 1902, Fisher plied Battenberg with memoranda about desirable naval reforms and invited his comments. Following a conversation on 9 February, Fisher sent him a paper listing various 'probable and improbable' enemies. At the head of the list came 'War with France'; and then came 'War with the Dual Alliance (France and Russia)'. War with Germany alone does not appear on the list; 'War with the United States' takes fourth place. However, the Triple Alliance and 'a German–American Alliance' do appear as possible enemies. Fisher wished to discover from Battenberg whether 'all these cases have been considered in careful detail and all the minutiae elaborated'. He asked Prince Louis to let him have his comments in view of his 'considerable and unique experience at the Admiralty as Second-in-Command of the Intelligence Department'.[4]

In his extensive reply of 11 February Battenberg referred to the 'great strides' made by the department under Custance's leadership. To the pre-existing mobilization and foreign intelligence

---

[1] *F.G.* i, 176.

[2] Kerr, p. 138. George, Prince of Wales, also admired the *Renown's* seagoing qualities. On 25 Oct. 1905 he wrote to F.: 'I must say your old ship is one of the most beautiful ships I have even been on bd., she is absolutely steady and no vibration whatever at 13 knots.' (F.P. 186.)

[3] Kerr, p. 217: Battenberg to Thursfield, 23 Jan. 1907.

[4] *F.G.* i, 223.

divisions had been added the 'Defence Division'. This dealt
with 'the Plans of Campaign' and 'Strategy for Peace and
War'. Previously, the D.N.I. had been 'forced to do all this
personally'. The Admiralty seemed reluctant 'to lay down for
guidance any very precise plan of action, beyond the Secret
Instructions' normally issued to senior officers abroad, but
'Home Operations' came 'under immediate control of the
Admiralty'. To prepare for war against 'improbable' as well as
'more probable combinations' would be 'a gigantic labour';
indeed, in Battenberg's opinion it would be 'wholly beyond the
powers of our small "General Staff" as now in existence in the
shape of the N.I.D.—that is if thoroughly done'. However, under
Custance the N.I.D., 'backed up by the Naval Lords', had
'invaded every department of the Admiralty' and had 'had its
say' upon all matters of importance.

Still the Department is carefully labelled 'purely advisory' and if
the Civilian Element *can* 'short-circuit' it, it occasionally does so. The
time has come when the head of this department (the title is a mere
detail) should be given such a position that his views—or rather the
well digested, focused opinion of the many and versatile brains at
work in his 'shop'—cannot be lightly brushed aside or ignored. He
should be a member of the Board, second only to the First Sea Lord
(the Commander in Chief), but that Officer's first assistant. *Preparation for War* in every particular should be his charge . . .

However, Battenberg argued, the basis of a naval general staff
already existed.

The War Office is accused of copying many things from the Germans—from Army Corps to caps—but not one thing which is applicable to our conditions. The Navy has copied only one thing—the best
of all, but the one and only thing the Army has not copied: the true
'Organizer of Victory', the 'General Staff'. The N.I.D. as now constituted is modelled exactly on Moltke's great creation: its three
main divisions have their exact counterpart at Berlin. We thus have
the skeleton ready to hand—it only wants clothing, and placing on a
higher pedestal. Quite recently we have added to it indirectly by the
establishment of the 'War Course' at Greenwich, already crowned
with excellent results. It is to be hoped that the next step will be the
completion of the structure by the establishment of branches afloat,
in the shape of the 'Admiral's Staff'—at present, oddly enough,
represented by Paymasters and Clerks. It is hardly necessary to point
out that if Moltke found it necessary to have trained disciples attached

to the Generals, it must be still more necessary in the case of Admirals scattered over the Globe.[1]

This throws much light on the origins of Fisher's own paper 'On the Increasing Necessity for a General Staff for the Navy'. However, Fisher's enthusiasm for a War College antedated Battenberg's arrival in the Mediterranean. He had written to his wife on 20 July 1901: 'I have had another great point conceded by Admiralty in the establishment of a Naval War College which I urged ferociously when they were at Malta. I feel sure Lord Selborne was convinced but the others would not have it at any price and now it is announced!'[2]

Once Fisher was in the saddle as First Sea Lord, he ensured that the N.I.D. remained purely advisory and he farmed out the drafting of war plans to the War College. In any case his interest in strengthening the Naval Staff was somewhat superficial. Predominating over it was his preoccupation with the calibre of the existing Admirals. He wrote to Selborne in May 1902: 'More and more it is forced on one how much depends nowadays on the Admiral. The ablest and largest staff no use in the critical emergencies that require instant decision and absolute self-confidence, and no doubt these qualities can be trained.'[3] Likewise, in his above-quoted paper of 25 February on the 'Increasing Necessity for a General Staff' he soon digresses from this subject to the education of Admirals before sending them to a seagoing command. But he does touch on the selection and training of the Admiral's staff. Then he warms to the theme of his 'naval Von Moltke'.[4]

In Fisher's correspondence with Selborne prior to Battenberg's arrival in the Mediterranean, this strategical and tactical genius is placed at the head of the War College.[5] In his paper of 25 February 1902, Fisher adopts Battenberg's belief that the officer should be placed higher in the service, without seeing how intolerable this 'Moltke' would be for any First Sea Lord:

It seems quite clear that no subordinate of the Board but a member of the Board of Admiralty must direct this brain power of the Navy; that he must give his whole time and mind to it; that he must be absolutely unfettered and untrammelled by any administrative or executive functions whatever, in a word he must be a Von Moltke, and as Von Moltke was co-existent with Von Roon, the great Minister

---

[1] F.P. 4203.   [2] F.P. 1559.   [3] *F.G.* i, 241.
[4] F.P. 90.   [5] *F.G.* i, 213–15.

of War, so also there should be no difficulty in having an additional Member of the Board of Admiralty who would in no way trespass on the great and almost overwhelming administrative and executive functions of the First Sea Lord, even if relieved of this vital portion of his almost superhuman task . . .[1]

In the event, as First Sea Lord, Fisher decided to rely basically on his own 'brain power'; but it remains a curiosity that he came so near to accepting the principle of a true Naval Staff. Moreover, writing to Fisher on 25 February, Battenberg suggested what proved in the end to be the correct approach to the problem, namely that the First Sea Lord should be Chief of the Naval Staff. But Prince Louis himself did not implement this principle when he himself became First Sea Lord.[2]

The second of Fisher's papers of 25 February concerns 'The Strategical Distribution of Our Fleets'. This contrasts with the first paper through being substantially his own work. Battenberg's comments on his scheme are dated 29 January and are confined to the following:

> Your proposal as to abolishing stations has taken my breath away, and I will only observe that:—
>
> 1   I agree that the appearance of a squadron is more effective than a single ship kept tied to the place.
> 2   Per contra, local knowledge and mutual understanding between Admirals and others must count for something.[3]

Nor, to judge by Fisher's letter to Beresford of 27 February, did the scheme of redistribution, which closely resembles that of November 1904, owe anything much to that Admiral.[4] However, this is not to suggest that the general idea of such a redistribution originated entirely in the brain of Fisher. The journalist G. W. Steevens, for example, in his book *Naval Policy* published in 1896, had emphasized the wastage of manpower involved in the many small naval vessels scattered about remote parts of the world. For example, as many as 1,600 trained sailors, who might be urgently required to man the fleets at home, were to be found in Australian and Pacific waters aboard craft 'too weak to fight, and too slow to run away'.[5] But it was Fisher who took effective action. Looking at the problem from a Mediterranean standpoint he wrote to Rosebery of 10 May 1901:

---

[1] Ibid.   [2] Kerr, p. 144; *D.S.* i, 266.   [3] F.P. 86.
[4] *F.G.* i, 233.   [5] Preston and Major, pp. 163–4.

. . . all round the compass we have no friends. It is truly a case of 'Splendid isolation', but that being the case, surely we ought to consider the fundamental principle of war, which is to concentrate your force on the vital point of the war! *We are weak everywhere and strong nowhere!* . . . Because in the days of Noah we did the police duties of the world at sea, we continue to do them still and have vessels scattered over the face of the earth according as they settled down after the deluge! Of what earthly use is it cutting off the legs and arms of your enemy in China and elsewhere if he pierces your heart in the Mediterranean![2]

The scheme of this fundamental and overdue reform—which would tread heavily on the toes of officers aspiring to the proscribed commands—assumed the following shape in Fisher's submission of 25 February 1902:

It will of course be admitted that our Fleets should be so grouped and so disposed during peace as to be ready for instant war.

When vessels are isolated and distributed all over a station, that fleet is not ready for war, putting aside the unavoidable deterioration that invariably takes place in solitary vessels away from the Flag.

There is no obligation except that of tradition and sentiment to have these stationary, isolated vessels on any station, because in these days of steam and electricity an Admiral can quickly have vessels where required when the necessity arises. Any number of cases can be quoted in support of the above statement if so desired, notably in the West Indies, East Indies, China and both Coasts of Africa.

It is admitted that Esquimalt cannot be held in case of war with the United States, even if it were desirable, which it is not. Of what use, then, is a Pacific Squadron? And even if reduced to, say, a single vessel—of what use is that vessel?

Similarly the South East Coast of America. There is no object in having any vessels permanently on that station.

The following suggestions are made for *Efficiency* and *Economy*:
Have 5 Fleets—

1   The Home Fleet.
2   The Atlantic Fleet.
3   The Mediterranean Fleet.
4   The Cape Fleet.
5   The China Fleet.

Commencing for facility of explanation with the last named:—
The China Fleet to include Australia.
The Cape Fleet to include the East Indies and the East Coast of Africa.

[1] *F.G.* i, 190–1.

The Mediterranean Fleet to include the present Channel Fleet.

The Atlantic Fleet to be the present Cruiser Squadron augmented to 12 Cruisers and to include the North American Station, the West Coast of Africa, with an occasional visit to the South-East Coast of America.

The Home Fleet to consist of all the Naval Force reserved for service in the Channel, North Sea, Ireland, etc., etc., in case of war.

The rule to be that these are all bona fide Cruising Fleets organized for war, and that at whatever loss of prestige to Consuls and minor interests none but the fighting vessels should compose these Fleets.

It will be a terrible anxiety to an Admiral on the outbreak of war to get "Partridges', 'Magpies', 'Redbreasts' and 'Pigmies' into a place of safety, for they can neither fight nor run away! . . .

The waste of officers (especially) in the smaller class of vessels is out of all proportion to the fighting requirements of the Fleet. A vessel like the 'Espiegle' just passed through Malta to China takes a Commander and three Lieutenants, and she is of absolutely no fighting value whatever in case of war, on account of low speed; but she absorbs 113 men in her complement. The battleship 'Formidable' of 15,000 tons, with a complement of 777, has 7 Lieuts. against 3 in the 'Espiegle' of 1,000 tons . . .

The shores of the Mediterranean equally with those of other Naval Stations are infested by importunate British Representatives, whose ideas are bounded by their own jurisdiction, but a deaf ear has been invariably turned to their entreaties for visits of solitary men of war and no evil consequences have resulted. This procedure has enabled several detached squadrons to be formed to make periodical cruises under the orders of Senior Officers who will command squadrons in war, with the result of great credit and experience to those officers and much benefit to the Service, observing also that the visits of these squadrons of ten to six ships each produce a much greater effect than the continued and enervating stay of solitary ships at various ports.

In connection with the proposed nomenclature and disposition of the five great Naval Divisions, the following remarks may be thought worthy of consideration:—

The Atlantic Fleet of twelve or more cruisers might be the germ or skeleton of the commerce protecting Fleet.

The Channel Fleet might have its title altered with advantage, as the name is now misleading, and might be mischievous in leading the uninformed public to suppose it formed part of the 'Home' Fleet and thus cause panic by its absence from the Channel when relations become strained. In view of the approaching completion of docks and dockyard and protected harbour at Gibraltar, its headquarters might be fixed there and its name altered from 'Channel' to 'Gibraltar' Squadron . . .[1]

This is very similar to the scheme which Fisher began to implement soon after becoming First Sea Lord in October 1904.[2] It is commonly believed that the scheme of 1904 was aimed at Germany; and it will in due course be seen that anti-German considerations did begin to influence the scheme soon after Fisher's advent. Nevertheless, up to the time of becoming First Sea Lord, Fisher adhered to the intention of redistributing the fleets according to his ideas of 1902; and it is clear that these ideas were centred on the Mediterranean rather than the North Sea. While the growth of the German Navy was certainly noticed by Fisher, an examination of his published letters of 1901–2 will show that he placed little more emphasis on Germany as a possible enemy than on the United States.[3] The strong Mediterranean assumptions underlying his strategic thinking early in 1902 can best be understood by examining his lecture notes of that date. For example:

Some answers to recent questions as to why the Mediterranean is the strategic vital centre of the world.

(a) France is the principal opponent of England at present.
(b) France in the Mediterranean occupies geographically and, by nature, the advantageous strategic position.
(c) France in the Mediterranean is close to her principal resources, while England has, as yet, only Malta with one dock for battleships . . .
(f) In the Mediterranean France has an ally emerging from the Black Sea, and that ally practically in possession of the Dardanelles. New port at Bourgas. The Baltic freezes, the Black Sea does not . . .
(g) The strategic conditions of the Mediterranean rest on its geographical conditions, and you can no more move the vital naval strategic spot elsewhere than you could move Mount Vesuvius.[4]

Especially significant are the extracts from Mahan which Fisher included in his lecture notes. Printed under the heading

---

[1] F.P. 90.   [2] Cf. N.N. i, 215–16 (P. 11/04).
[3] F.G. i, 163, 166, 179, 189–91, 221, 223–4, 259–61.
[4] F.P. 4702, *The Mediterranean Fleet, 1899–1902*, p. 22 (P. 10/02).

'Considerations Governing the Disposition of Navies', these extracts show how Fisher derived much of his thinking on the subject from the American historian. Here are some of them, in Fisher's order of printing:

Hence appears the singular strategic—and because strategic, commercial—interest of a narrow or land-locked sea, which is multiplied manifold when it forms an essential link in an important maritime route.

To this consideration is due the supreme importance of the Mediterranean in the present conditions of the communications and policies of the world. From the commercial point of view it is much the shortest, and therefore the principal, sea route between Europe and the Farther East . . . From the military standpoint, the same fact of shortness, combined with the number and rivalry of national tenures established throughout its area, *constitutes it the most vital and critical link* in an interior line between two regions of the gravest international concern.[1]

The Mediterranean therefore becomes necessarily the centre around which must revolve the strategic distribution of European Navies . . .

The Mediterranean will be either the seat of one dominant control, reaching thence in all directions, owning a single mistress, or it will be the scene of continual struggle.

The Home waters and their approaches will be the scene of national defence in the strictest and most exclusive sense; *but it will be defence that exists for the foundation, upon which reposes the struggle for, or the control of, the Mediterranean.* The distant East . . . will be the offensive sphere; but the determination of the result, in case of prolongation of war, will depend upon the control of the Mediterranean . . .

Geographically, Great Britain is an intruder in the Mediterranean. The habitual distribution of the warships of the United Kingdom must provide for a decisive predominance here, upon occasion arising, over any probable combination of enemies. Such provision has to take account not only of the hostile divisions within and without the Mediterranean, *but of movements intended to transfer one or more from or to that Sea from other scenes of operations* . . .

Every consideration emphasizes the importance of the Mediterranean . . . Reinforcements sent by the Cape, whether west or east, can always be anticipated at either end of the road by the Power which holds the interior line.[2]

---

[1] F. notes that the italics are his and 'emphasize points made familiar by frequent reiteration' in his lectures.

[2] Ibid., pp. 80–4. The dots indicate omission of further material on the same subject.

Traces of this mode of thought are clearly discernible in Fisher's paper 'The Strategical Distribution of the Fleet', printed in November 1904.[1]

How, then, did the small but growing German Navy fit into Fisher's strategic picture? On 29 November 1901 he suggested to Thursfield that Britain should form an anti-German alliance with France and Russia or with France alone.[2] Moreover, after his return to the Admiralty as Second Sea Lord he will be found attending closely to the German threat. But even then he seems to have believed that Mahan's reasoning held good. Command of the sea largely depended on control of the Mediterranean; this was the basis of British strategy against any European opponent. Thus when, in 1903, public demand for a North Sea base made itself felt, Fisher was not associated with it.

In so far as Fisher based much of his reasoning about redistribution on the generalizations of a naval historian, it is pertinent to ask what he meant by his well-known declaration that 'History is a record of exploded ideas.' This dictum originated in a lecture about naval leadership: 'Those who rise in peace are men of formality and routine, cautious, inoffensive . . . Hawke represented the spirit of war, the ardour, the swift initiative, the readiness of resource, the impatience of prescription and routine, without which no great things are done!' Having thus appealed to historical example, Fisher at once continues:

History is a record of exploded ideas! In what sense? Conditions all altered! The wind formerly determined the course of action.

Now it is only the mind of man! One man and the best man is wanted! Not a fossil!

Fleets and ships were formerly days coming into action. Now only minutes. (Two Fleets can be alongside each other in twenty minutes from first seeing each other's smoke!)

Formerly Sailors' battles, now Officers'.

At Trafalgar, Nelson walking up and down the quarter-deck, and having a yarn with his Flag Captain (Hardy), at the zenith of the action! It was the common sailors only who were then at work! How different now! *The Admiral everything!*[3]

Even if he does not develop it very impressively, Fisher's argument seems to be that strategy and tactics need constant reassessment in the light of changing technology. To this extent,

---

[1] *N.N.* i, 215–18. See p. 313 above.   [2] *F.G.* i, 218.   [3] F.P. 4702, pp. 14–15.

his dictum about history is unobjectionable, even if it did not save him from over-reliance on Mahan! However, his enthusiasm for that historian gained him credit with Lord Esher who wrote on 1 November 1901 to the ex-Liberal leader, Sir William Harcourt: 'You will not find the *Sea Power in History* clash with your notions about the navy. Fisher, who is perhaps the best of our seamen, thinks this book is a classical work. So it has the approval of an expert.'[1]

The third paper which Fisher sent to the First Lord on 25 February concerned the main problem awaiting him at the Admiralty in 1902. Although Fisher had not, before 1901, aspired at any stage of his career to become Second Sea Lord, he had often been concerned with professional education and training; and already, when Controller, he seems to have been interested in the problem of the naval engineers.[2] By the end of the nineteenth century, the engineers were much discontented with their position of inferiority to the officers of the executive branch. Fisher's proposed solution comprised two principles. The first was a common entry of executive and engineering cadets into the service; the second was provision for 'interchangeability' of the two types of officer. Of these two principles, the first was sound but the second was inappropriate. The idea of 'interchangeability' (which will be defined later) ran counter to a fundamental tendency of the times. An accelerating expansion of technology was tending to impose narrower specialization, not least in the field of engineering. Therefore, while some of the opposition to Fisher's scheme was due to sheer social conservatism, much of it was based on a valid objection. In his paper of 25 February 1902 Fisher put the case thus:

All must now admit we have been slow to appreciate the alteration in the status of the Engineer, consequent on the abolition of masts and sails.

The deck officers have no longer what really was an all absorbing task in becoming proficient in handling a ship under sail. Men's lives aloft were absolutely dependent on the skill of the Officer of the Watch —a brace improperly touched with the men on the yards, the helm perhaps only touched the wrong way . . . brought such odium that the laziest and most thick-skinned felt compelled to be sailors . . .

---

[1] Esher, i, 312.
[2] See, for example, F.P. 5469, an album of press-cuttings (with index) for 1891–7.

These qualities no longer required on deck are acquired now and required now (but both in lesser degree) amongst the engines and boilers . . .

This alteration in training so essential for the efficiency of the Navy can be readily brought about by following precisely the same method as was employed to make the navigation of His Majesty's ships more efficient, a plan attended by the most signal success as the Hydrographer will testify, for never has the British Navy been better navigated than in the present time. The method then pursued to attain the present excellent results was gradually to stop the entry of the old Navigating Class and increase that of Naval Cadets, and for officers so elected (and in view of the advantages and extra pay there has been no lack of candidates) to take up navigating duties as Sub-Lieutenants, and as Lieutenants and as Commanders, following on to the Captain's List and the Flag List in the usual course.

Such a plan is suggested with a feeling of absolute confidence in its ultimate success in regard to the engineering duties of the Navy. This course is not proposed on account of the present engineer agitation . . . The general good and efficiency of the Navy renders it imperative that the entry of Engineer Students as at present arranged should be gradually stopped and the entry of Naval Cadets gradually increased in like proportion, and that instruction from the moment of entry into the College at Dartmouth should in a large measure, *at least half the time*, be devoted to engineering. That like Gunnery, Torpedo and Navigating as at present, there should be Engineer Officers, Sub-Lieutenants, Lieutenants and Commanders, and going on perhaps to the Captains' List and the Flag List, but the pay in view of greater responsibilities (the extra pay, that is) should be such as would perhaps induce officers to prefer remaining in the Engineer Class.

The present College at Keyham would serve the same purpose as the 'Excellent' and 'Vernon' for qualifying and requalifying Engineer Officers.

The Artificer-Engineers would require to be largely increased . . . this excellent class of Engine Room Warrant Officer already has proved itself the backbone below . . .[1]

This memorandum subsequently appeared in an Admiralty print of July 1902 together with other materials relating to the proposed new scheme of education and training.[2]

---

[1] F.P. 90.

[2] Add. MSS. 50299, *New Admiralty Scheme 1902–1903*, pp. 6–8. The prime collection of such Admiralty prints is held by the Naval Library at the Ministry of Defence; but where copies have been found in other locations, reference has normally been made to these in the footnotes to suit the possible convenience of researchers.

In his covering letter of 25 February 1902 Fisher informed Selborne that he had been prompted to send him the three papers at once because he was 'delighted' by the First Lord's recent parliamentary statement.[1] (In this, Selborne had indicated that such matters as the distribution of the fleets should be periodically reconsidered. He had also displayed interest in naval education and declared that 'important as the matériel of the Navy is, the personnel is much more important.') Secondly, wrote Fisher, he thought that early action might possibly be taken on the subjects treated in his enclosures, so he had decided to submit his views at once.

In the third place the enclosed suggestions are not those of a solitary person, namely the Commander-in-Chief in the Mediterranean, but they are shared by all the principal officers of the Fleet. At least I have met with no dissentient. I, of course, admit their kind partiality for their Admiral, but this would not go to the length of absolute suppression of their own convictions.

Lastly, it appears to me that I can legitimately and properly send you direct, as Commander-in-Chief of the Mediterranean, these enclosed papers, when possibly, owing to the 'Distribution of business' of the Admiralty . . . it might not be equally proper or judicious to do so.

In any case I feel sure you will impute no other motive to me than a desire to give you the best assistance I can.[2]

In addition to what has already been mentioned, Fisher had plied Selborne with his ideas on ship-construction. Replying, in his letter of 19 December 1900, to a question from the First Lord he had insisted:

The Golden rule to follow is not to allow ourselves to be 'out-classed'. The French are going to build vessels of 14,865 tons (practically 15,000 tons), and that means that our new battleships must be of considerably larger displacement, and we must certainly exceed them in speed, for, if we do not, we give them the option of refusing or bringing on an action! . . . I will give you my experience of the value of speed in battleships (an experience which impressed me immensely!) when I was Commander-in-Chief in North America. I on one occasion 'mopped up' all the cruisers one after another with my flagship the battleship *Renown* . . . *Whatever type the French have, we must go one better*, and that is a principle which will always keep us safe, and if we built as quickly as we ought to build, we ought always to commence

---

[1] *Hansard*, 4th Ser., vol. ciii, App. I.   [2] F.P. 90.

after they are well advanced and have the more powerful vessel afloat beforehand. *What I beg to impress on you,* as the result of much thought on all the plans of battle we have elaborated, and as a result of our operations out here, is that speed is almost the first desideratum in all types from battleships downward to meet the game that England must play in a naval war . . .[1]

In this early communication may be glimpsed the *Dreadnought* and, more clearly, the *Invincible*. Fisher's contentious emphasis on speed is here related to conditions in the Mediterranean. In construction, priority for speed implied limitation of armament or armour, or limitation of both. Transposed from the setting of the Mediterranean to the misty conditions of the North Sea, the relative advantages of speed would be open to question. On the side of building policy in general—whether it was better for Britain to lead in design or follow quickly with an improved version—it has been seen that, in December 1900, Fisher still held to the traditional approach. Of course, the validity of this approach depended on Britain continuing to be able to build more quickly than her rivals. It is hardly possible to specify just when Fisher decided that Britain should lead in battleship design. It will be remembered that, in his above-quoted letter of 28 January 1902 to Arnold White, he said that he would, if he went to Elswick, 'immediately set to work to revolutionize the naval fighting by building on speculation a battleship, cruiser, and destroyer on revolutionary principles'. As he put it in a lecture not long afterwards:

The chief and overwhelming reasons against building small Battleships, or Battleships of lesser speed than the fastest Foreign Battleships afloat, are those given long ago by Admiral Gervais (when Chief of the French General Naval Staff)—that one very strong and faster Battleship will certainly overcome two, or possibly three, less strong and slower though cheaper vessels; also, that the one large vessel effects a great economy in officers and men as compared with, say, the two or three smaller and cheaper vessels.[2]

From December 1901 he urged on Lord Selborne the advantages of oil fuel;[3] and in a lecture of early 1902 he expatiated on this subject.[4]

In view of the subsequent 'battle cruiser' controversy, it is interesting to find that, in a lecture of 1902, Fisher stated: 'It is a

[1] *F.G.* i, 173–4. [2] F.P. 4702, p. 89.
[3] *F.G.* i, 220. [4] F.P. 4702, pp. 18–19.

cardinal mistake to assume that Battleships and Armoured Cruisers have not each of them a distinct mission.' The latter, he said, were essentially intended to outpace and eliminate enemy cruisers.[1] Here again, French vessels were envisaged as opponents: 'When the French get vessels of the type of the "Jeanne d'Arc" and "Montcalm" class to sea, we shall have a difficult task to deal with them effectually.'[2] At the same time, the protection of British commerce was receiving much of Fisher's attention. He believed, contrary to his later views, that large numbers of small cruisers would be needed.[3] He illustrated the need by quoting Lloyd's—'186 Cruisers required for protection of commerce'.[4]

However, not long afterwards he thus enunciated the principle which he had glimpsed aboard the *Renown* on the North American station: 'In regard to Cruisers, the fact has been overlooked that no number of unprotected or unarmoured or smaller type of Cruisers can cope successfully with even one thoroughly powerful first-class Armoured Cruiser. An infinite number of ants would not be equal to one armadillo! The armadillo would eat them up one after another wholesale!'[5] Although Fisher remained anxious about commerce protection till the end of his time in the Mediterranean,[6] he had already hit on the expedient which, in the form of the *Invincible* and *Inflexible*, was to triumph over Spee's raiding cruiser squadron at the Battle of the Falklands. A few fast armoured cruisers (known from 1911 as 'battle cruisers') partly obviated the need for large numbers of light cruisers to guard the trade routes; but Fisher undoubtedly went to an extreme in believing (by 1904) that light cruisers were about to become obsolete as a type. They were still needed as 'eyes of the fleet' and for blockade duties, apart from the requirements of the mitigated problem of commerce protection.

The seeds of the costly confusion about the role of the battle cruiser in a fleet were sown in 1902: 'The Armoured Cruiser of the first-class is a swift Battleship in disguise. It has been asked that the difference between a Battleship and an Armoured

---

[1] Ibid., p. 89.

[2] F.P. 4198, 'Notes on the imperative necessity of possessing fast armoured cruisers and their qualifications', *c.* Feb. 1902.

[3] F.P. 4702, p. 49.   [4] Ibid., p. 18.   [5] Ibid., p. 75.

[6] F.P. 95, F. to A. K. Wilson, 16 Mar. 1902; F.P. 4196, 'Notes for Successor', May 1902, pp. 14–15.

Cruiser may be defined. It might as well be asked to define when a kitten becomes a cat!'[1] This comes close to a direct contradiction of his statement, just noticed, about the two types of ship having 'each of them a distinct mission'.[2]

On 27 February 1902 Fisher wrote to Beresford, who had just returned to England and the House of Commons, to communicate to him some of his burgeoning ideas. 'Consult Thursfield before you make out your speech', Fisher advised the headstrong Rear-Admiral. '*Indeed, I should ask him to revise your speech were I in your place.*' This letter was headed '*Private. No one to see this except your own self !!!*' Beresford would have been much intrigued to read the following communication, also dated 27 February, which still reposes among the papers of J. R. Thursfield: 'I send you an *exact* copy made by Lady Fisher of my letter sent this day to Lord Charles Beresford. As you will see I ask him to consult you. I beg you not to let even him (Lord Charles) have the faintest idea I have sent you the enclosed but I want you to keep his head straight . . . don't let Beresford know you have enclosed . . . he might not like it. . . .'[3] Thus did Fisher combine the 'peculiarly frank method of address', approvingly noted by Bacon, with delicate and devious manoeuvres![4] However, as Bacon elsewhere remarks, the Admiral's activities did focus on the interests of the service; and when he walked at Malta, almost daily, accompanied by his wife or one of his daughters, he would often stay silent—'Always thinking out, always scheming for the good of the Navy'.[5] Despite his sackings of inefficient officers from the Mediterranean Fleet and despite his uncomfortable, if valuable, legacy of Commander-in-Chief's inspections, another of Bacon's generalizations may here be remembered: 'Every ship to which he was appointed feared his coming only one degree less than they lamented his leaving.'[6] Fisher's eldest daughter Beatrix, aboard the dispatch vessel *Surprise*, wrote to Cecil Fisher about their father's departure from Malta on 4 June 1902:

I must write and tell you about Father's sendoff; it was simply splendid . . . We had a dinner on board *Renown* the last night at Malta, the 3rd. Admiral Domvile [the new Commander-in-Chief]

---

[1] F.P. 4702, p. 75. [2] Ibid., p. 89.
[3] N.M.M., THU/1, including the copy of F. to Beresford.
[4] Bacon, i, 93-4. [5] Ibid., p. 242.
[6] Ibid., pp. 129-30, 241; Chatfield, pp. 35-6, 66.

arrived about 6 . . . After dinner all the officers of the Fleet were invited and nearly all must have come . . .

After Admiral Domvile had left they began singing Old Lang Syne and Goodbye Dolly Grey, and then danced the Lancers, Father with the old Chief Engineer of the Dockyard . . .

Next morning the *Surprise* was surrounded by boats—Captains, etc., coming to say goodbye to us [that is, Lady Fisher, Dorothy, Pamela, and Beatrix and Reginald Neeld] and to the Renowns. At 12 o'clock, as the gun fired, off went the *Renown* full-speed. She was doing 17 knots and went out like a Torpedo Boat with the largest Admiral's flag that has ever been flown. *Royal Sovereign* followed, then *Surprise* and *Hussar* and *Dryad*, all going full speed. As we passed the ships they cheered over and over again, drowning the bands and salutes, Auld Lang Syne, etc.—the soldiers on shore cheering too. You never saw anything so lovely as the *Renown* as she fired the parting salute to the Governor with the sun shining on the smoke . . . They say over a thousand copies of Father's photo were bought by blue-jackets last week . . .[1]

On 8 June, she wrote again to her brother from Milan.

. . . Last night the *Renown* [at Genoa] gave a dinner (the wardroom officers) . . . and then *quite* to everyone's surprise the men had assembled on deck and sang 'Goodbye Dolly Grey' which is the popular song everywhere now . . . they sang 'Goodbye *Jacky* we must leave you' instead of Goodbye Dolly. Poor Father got quite speechless and no one could say anything much and this morning he had to ask for no more cheering as he couldn't stand it, so he just slipped quietly on shore . . .[2]

[1] Kilv. MSS., Pkt. 1, 6 June 1902.   [2] Ibid.

CHAPTER 7

THE REFORMATION OF THE NAVY
(1902–1905)

TOWARDS the end of his Mediterranean command, Fisher looked forward with satisfaction to the prospect of working with Selborne at the Admiralty. He wrote to Arnold White:

I must confess to you that I think it shows a very Christian spirit in Lord Selborne and his colleagues to invite me into the fold, considering the way I have embarrassed and pestered them during the last three years and they have written me such cordial letters that I am most anxious to do all in my power to get things straight without unnecessary friction. It's plain to anyone that Lord Selborne has got his head the right way by his parliamentary statement. Never before has such a document been so outspoken or so revolutionary! and he deserves great credit for it . . .'[1]

Fisher was now embarking on an active examination of the whole problem of the entry, education, and training of naval officers and men. A series of investigating committees from 1870 onwards had agreed in condemning the system of semi-education of Cadets aboard the *Britannia* and especially the second stage of their instruction aboard a seagoing ship.[2] These committees had made their recommendations to little practical effect, though Goschen had announced in 1896 that a college would be built at Dartmouth. The shell of the main building having been completed, King Edward VII laid the foundation stone on 7 March 1902. A German Admiral representing the Kaiser at the ceremony heard the Chaplain pray that, having passed through the college, the Cadets would uphold 'the honour of their great calling' and defend their sovereign's cause 'faithfully, even unto death'.[3] However, it was not expected that the college would be ready for occupation until 1905 and it was open to Fisher to determine the details of the system of entry and education. In

---

[1] F.P. 1755, 1 Mar. 1902.
[2] Adm. 116/862–3; J. S. Corbett's article 'Education in the Navy', *Monthly Review*, Sept. 1902.
[3] Pack, p. 139.

the previous chapter, it was seen that he advocated a common entry and similar instruction for intending executive and engineer officers in a paper of 25 February 1902. This proved the most important feature of the scheme which, thanks to the determination and energy of Fisher, was actually adopted towards the end of the year.

The idea of a common entry did not originate with Fisher; indeed, Sir John Colomb (an ex-Marine and prominent writer on defence) had been advocating this principle for some twenty years.[1] In the Mediterranean Fisher habitually began his working day at 4 or 5 a.m. and, considering the attention he paid to newspapers and current literature on naval matters, it is likely that he noticed a report of Colomb's statement in the Commons on 8 March 1900: 'At present we are keeping up an artificial and expensive system, which produces two distinct branches of officers. I cannot see why all officers should not go through the same course of training up to about twenty-one years of age.'[2]

Fisher's ideas about the kind of instruction to be given to the Cadets were derived, at least in part, from such sources as an article in the *National Review* of June 1900 written by his subsequent critic, Rear-Admiral C. C. Penrose Fitzgerald. An extract from this article was subsequently reproduced by Fisher, including these passages:

> The Navy has made great strides in the direction of becoming a mechanical profession since Sir Geoffrey Hornby's day . . . 'Jack' finds his general utility impaired because he is not a mechanic . . . Unless our Executive [Branch]—both officers and men—receive a more mechanical training than they do at present, they will be gradually ousted by the engineers and artificers . . . a complete revolution in it, from the day the boys are first entered from the shore, is absolutely necessary . . .[3]

Just when Fisher, in March 1902, was casting about for more detailed suggestions, there came into his hands the first of Julian Corbett's articles in the *Monthly Review* on 'Education in the Navy'. These articles, in their turn, owed much to the collaboration of Lieutenant H. W. Richmond who noted in his journal: 'I gave him copious notes to shew how things stood at present.'

---

[1] *The Times*, 2 Jan. 1903, p. 8.

[2] *Hansard*, 4th Ser., vol. lxxx, p. 441. G. Noel kept a relevant newspaper cutting (N.M.M. Noel Papers).

[3] *N.N.* iii, 87–8.

He also suggested that Cadets should spend four years at Dartmouth.[1] Corbett's articles marked the beginning of a long connexion between Fisher and the gifted naval historian. Fisher asked Captain Christopher Cradock, then commanding a cruiser in the Mediterranean Fleet, for his opinion of Corbett's first article which was devoted to criticism of the existing system. Cradock found it rather irritating;[2] but the second article, published in April, was very well received by Fisher and Cradock fell into line. This article suggested some broad features which were actually embodied in the scheme; and Cradock made a number of detailed suggestions which were commended by Battenberg in a letter to Fisher of 26 May.[3] Of special interest is the following reference to interchangeability in Battenberg's letter:

As regards promoting the Commander ('E'), and giving him command of a ship, I am afraid I must adhere to my views expressed in my notes of a former date. But that in no way invalidates the scheme. By all means make him a Captain, but find employment for him in the engineering line—only make it clear at the beginning that this is so, and state the compensating advantages in large extra pay and 'stone frigate' which will appeal to the 'missus'.[4]

It was Fisher's adherence to the principle of engineers commanding ships that proved the most contentious element in the educational reforms; but his reasonable attitude at the preparatory stage is illustrated by his printing Battenberg's letter unabridged, together with other critical material, in the introductory section of the *New Admiralty Scheme* in July 1902.

Meanwhile, at the beginning of June, Custance was bemoaning the imminence of Fisher's reappearance at the Admiralty. On the 3rd he wrote to Cyprian Bridge: 'Fisher arrives next week. Heaven only knows what he may not attempt to run. Any wild cat scheme finds a supporter in him. It is much to be feared that we are on the eve of a phase of court interest. Fawkes is playing up to them for all he is worth, and I fear the advent of Battenberg in Fisher's train.'[5]

It was indeed the case that Fisher lost no time in re-establishing

[1] N.M.M., RIC/1/6, 13 Apr. 1902.
[2] F.P. 99, Cradock to F., 9 May 1902.
[3] Add. MSS. 50299 (Arnold-Forster Papers), *New Admiralty Scheme 1902–1903*, pp. 14–22.
[4] Ibid., pp. 14.   [5] N.M.M., BRI/15.

good relations with the King[1] and that he came to depend on his support during the stormy times ahead. It also transpired that Prince Louis succeeded Custance as D.N.I. in November and duly exercised a material influence on Admiralty policy—an influence at once moderate and constructive. He did much to help Fisher place his reforms on a sound basis. Hankey, who served in the Intelligence Department under both Custance and Battenberg, found the latter a 'most inspiring chief' compared with the mistrustful though capable Custance.[2] Fisher himself described Battenberg's appointment as 'a great triumph'.[3]

There can be little doubt that Fisher's naval colleagues on the Board of Admiralty viewed with misgiving the idea of such a fundamental change in their profession as that swiftly described in some hundred pages of print by Fisher. He arrived at the Admiralty on 10 June 1902: '. . . at 10 minutes to 12 I said "how d'ye do" to Lord Selborne. At 5 minutes to 12 he gave me practically *carte blanche*, and at 12 I was read in at the Board, and five minutes after, I commenced operations in my room at the Admiralty in sending the first pages to the printer of the preamble of the new schemes of training, entry, etc. . . .'[4]

This first instalment was entitled 'A Brief Summary of Reasons and Proposals for altering the present System of Entry and Training of the Officers and Men of the Navy' and it emerged from the printing press on 2 July. Determined, doubtless, that a substantial reform should at last be effected, but sounding the note of caution often heard in his dealings with Fisher, Selborne had a covering slip affixed to each copy of the print: copies were restricted to individual members of the Board, were to be treated as '*very confidential*', and would serve as a basis 'for discussion' after the summer holidays.[5]

A description of Fisher's methods of work as Second Sea Lord was subsequently recorded by Charles Walker. He had met Fisher during the latter's time as Controller and was appointed his private secretary in 1902. Fisher intimated to Walker—as he had done to King-Hall, his Chief of Staff in the Mediterranean —that he didn't mean to keep a dog to bark himself. Nevertheless, Walker at first underestimated the scope of the work thereby

---

[1] *F.G.* i, 249.   [2] Hankey, i, 23.
[3] Walker, 'Recollections', op. cit.
[4] *F.G.* i, 272: F. to Cecil F., 10 Apr. 1903.
[5] Add. MSS. 50299, *New Admiralty Scheme.*

assigned to him and was alarmed to see a heap of 'the more important papers' steadily piling up on Fisher's desk. It emerged that Fisher expected to be verbally informed of matters of real significance; otherwise he devoted virtually the whole of his 'demonic' energy to his schemes of reform. 'I never met anyone who could dispose of papers at the rate he could', wrote Walker, who assessed his experience of working under Fisher as 'all too short' and 'most valuable'.[1]

By 14 November Fisher was writing to his son: 'I've got through the biggest part of the big scheme I have been working on since June 10th last, and Lord Selborne seems very pleased; but I think the rest of my colleagues look on me as a sort of combined Robespierre and Gambetta!'[2] The First Sea Lord, Lord Walter Kerr, was impeccably loyal to his colleagues and altogether a man of very high character—the 'preux chevalier' of the service according to Lord George Hamilton.[3] However, he partook of the conservatism of the average naval officer; and the latter took a somewhat exalted view of the stature of the executive branch, as indicated by Bacon's story about an officer commanding on the West Coast of Africa who declined to read the Bible without first doffing his uniform jacket. While he wore it, he could acknowledge no superior power![4] By way of contrast, it is perhaps worth recalling that, as Commander of the *Ocean*, Fisher used to work in the coal-lighters with the men and jolly them through the filthy task of coaling ship—'black as a sweep'.[5] But though there may have been some underlying feeling amongst the Sea Lords that the proposed common entry would taint the glory of the executive officer with the oil, grime, and heat of the engine-room, it is probable that much of the anger generated in the Board Room arose from reasonable objections to 'interchangeability'. After all, how reactionary and obstructive was Lord Walter Kerr? In June 1901 Selborne thought Kerr's opinions on current strategy 'quite as good as Fisher's and Beresford's';[6] and even in January 1905 he still placed Kerr 'in the same flight' with Fisher, Wilson, and Beresford.[7] Lord Selborne's own intelligence and perceptiveness

---

[1] Walker, pp. 36–7; also his 'Recollections', op. cit.; *F.G.* i, 248.
[2] *F.G.* i, 264.   [3] *D.N.B.*, Lord Walker Kerr.
[4] Bacon, *From 1900 Onward*, p. 87.   [5] Bacon, i, 42.
[6] Add. MSS. 50288, Selborne to A.-Forster, 26 June 1901.
[7] Add. MSS. 49708, Selborne to Balfour, 16 Jan. 1905.

are not in doubt, and if Kerr had been stupidly conservative in opposing Fisher's first major reform, which Selborne favoured, the First Lord would scarcely have continued to rate him so highly. Therefore, when Fisher emerged from a heated session of the Board and remarked, 'My dear Walker, I did not think admirals could have been so rude to one another',[1] it is not unlikely that the genuine bugbear of 'interchangeability' was the cause. However, before tracing Fisher's handling of this subject, some account must be given of the Selborne Memorandum of December 1902.

On 15 December Fisher cautioned Arnold White ahead of the Memorandum's publication:

The Naval Rip Van Winkles (N.B.: *that phrase is copyright!*) have dubbed it 'a d——d revolutionary scheme!'. So it is! and perhaps they are going to vilify me and identify it as my work alone, so as to discredit it! It would be disastrous to the prestige of the scheme if it were in any way otherwise than what it is, which is *the unanimous decision of the whole Board of Admiralty*, and therefore I send this line of caution, in case your kindly feelings might entice you to mention my name in association with the scheme, as then the enemy would blaspheme at once![2]

The reference to unanimity is probably accurate; it will be noticed shortly that interchangeability was almost completely eliminated from the published document. This was dated 16 December and made public on Christmas Day. The title was 'Memorandum Dealing with the Entry, Training and Employment of Officers and Men of the Royal Navy and of the Royal Marines'.[3]

A historical introduction summarized the impact on the service of science and technology. Development had been 'comparatively slow for the greater part of the last century' but during the last fifteen years had gone ahead 'with startling rapidity'.

In the old days it sufficed if a Naval Officer were a seaman. Now he must be a seaman, a gunner, a soldier, an engineer, and a man of science as well . . . the character of the Naval Officer has remained unimpaired, and character is of more value than knowledge. Now, however, as always, the highest type of Naval Officer is that wherein great professional knowledge is added to force of character. The danger within the Navy itself is lest insufficient importance should be attached to the results of study . . .

---

[1] Walker, 'Recollections', op. cit.   [2] *F.G.* i, 267.   [3] Cd. 1385.

The strength which its unity gives to the Service can hardly be over-estimated, yet in respect of this matter a strangely anomalous condition of affairs exits. The Executive, the Engineer, and the Marine Officers are all necessary for the efficiency of the Fleet; they all have to serve side by side throughout their career; their unity of sentiment is essential to the welfare of the Navy; yet they all enter the Service under different regulations, and they have nothing in common in their early training. The result is that the Executive Officer, unless he is a gunnery or torpedo specialist, has been taught but a limited amount of engineering, although the ship in which he serves is one huge box of engines; that the Engineering Officer has never had any training in executive duties; that from lack of early sea training the Marine Officer is compelled, sorely against his will, to remain comparatively idle on board ship . . .

In order to repair these deficiencies, the Admiralty had decided that:

1. All Officers for the Executive and Engineer branches of the Navy and for the Royal Marines[1] shall enter the Service as Naval Cadets under exactly the same conditions between the ages of 12 and 13 [instead of 14 to $15\frac{1}{2}$];
2. That these Cadets shall all be trained on exactly the same system until they have passed for the rank of Sub-Lieutenant between the ages of 19 and 20;
3. That at about the age of 20 these Sub-Lieutenants shall be distributed between the three branches of the Service which are essential to the fighting efficiency of the Fleet—the Executive, the Engineer and the Marine.

The result aimed at is, to a certain point, community of knowledge and lifelong community of sentiment . . .

Both at the time of the publication of this 'New Scheme' and subsequently, there was much curiosity and some doubt about the possibility of senior engineer officers moving into executive posts and commanding ships. In item 3 quoted above, the position seemed clear enough, and there was another section of the Memorandum which confirmed separation from the age of twenty onwards. But just how were recruits for the engineering specialization to be obtained? Here, the position was problematical:

As far as possible each Officer will be allowed to choose which branch he will join, but this must be subject to the proviso that all branches are satisfactorily filled . . . for entrance to the 'Britannia',

[1] Inclusion of the Marines was soon found to be impracticable.

preference will (other things being equal) be given to those boys whose parents or guardians declare for them that they will be ready to enter either of the three branches of the Service.

The possibility of a shortage in one of the three specializations, especially engineering, was inherent in the circumstances of the time. Apart from the common distaste for engineering on social grounds, ultimate career prospects were clearly vital for any officer considering the engineer branch. The Memorandum stated that the rate of promotion would be the same for engineer as for executive officers. It proceeded:

> The ranks of Engineer Officers will be assimilated to the corresponding ranks of Executive Officers and the Engineer Officers will wear the same uniform and bear the same titles or rank, e.g., Sub-Lieutenant (E), Lieutenant (E), Commander (E), Captain (E), and Rear-Admiral (E). The Engineer branch will receive additional pay, and, although it is proposed to make the division into the various branches definite and final, every endeavour will be made to provide those who enter the Engineer branch with opportunities equal to those of the Executive branch including the same opportunity of rising to Flag Rank.

The end of the final sentence suggested that there might be interchangeability after all, at least for some engineers. Fisher obviously hoped to avoid any future conscription of officers for engineering by holding out hopes of equivalent promotion, irrespective of specialization, right to the top. For this reason, he would have preferred to retain interchangeability for Commanders (E). He later had the following comment typed in the margin of a print of 1906: 'It was the original intention and was the only sound basis to have complete interchangeability, but in deference to a strongly expressed desire not to fetter unduly future Boards, the separation into three branches was reluctantly acquiesced in . . .'[1]

Fisher did not readily accept his defeat over interchangeability though his efforts to reverse it were unfortunate. Able men and potential allies like Sir George Clarke began to attack the principle from 1903,[2] while Fisher himself tended to exchange the arts of persuasion for the less agreeable methods of the despot.

---

[1] 'The New Admiralty Scheme', with unbound prints at Naval Library. Elsewhere (e.g. F.P. 4752) there are copies with the marginal note printed (P. 2/06).

[2] N.M.M., THU/1, F. to Thursfield, 4 Oct. 1903.

Selborne sympathized with Fisher's view of the problem. In response to inquiries about the implications of the Memorandum, he had the following letter of 9 January 1903 published in *The Times*:

In reply to the inquiries you have made, I have to say that the words of my Memorandum, to the effect that the division of the Sub-Lieutenants into the three branches—Executive, Engineer, and Royal Marine—shall be definite and final, mean exactly what they say as regards the intention of the present Board.

The point could not be left doubtful. Either there will be interchangeability hereafter between the three branches or there will not. Either an Engineer Officer, for instance, will be able to rise to the command of a ship or squadron, or he will not.

These are questions which time and experience alone can answer, and the Board, in framing the present scheme, had to be prepared for either event . . . The announcement made that the division will be definite and final can apply only to the principles by which the present Board must be guided . . . and leaves a future Board perfectly free to relax the rule if it thinks fit . . .[1]

In a debate of 8 May 1903 in the House of Lords, Selborne made his personal feelings plain:

Are the Officers who have taken the Engineer branch to be interchangeable with the Executive branch? As the scheme now stands they will not be interchangeable . . . If it had been decided that they were to be interchangeable, and the cadets had come into the college on that understanding, no Board of Admiralty could have gone back on that decision . . . Nevertheless, I fully believe and hope that they will be made interchangeable, and that Engineers as a special branch will disappear altogether, and that specialised Engineer Lieutenants will be only known by the letter E after their name.[2]

H. W. Richmond joined the D.N.O.'s staff at the Admiralty early in 1903. He called on Fisher to thank him for his recent promotion to Commander; and he carried with him materials embodying a scheme for improved instruction in navigation, prepared by his friend, Commander H. F. Oliver. Fisher having expressed curiosity, 'this bundle of papers I gave Jacky. He thanked me and said he would read them and let me know what he thought; and next day I was sent for—told they were exactly what he wanted.' A committee would be speedily appointed,

---

[1] F.P. 4752, 'New Admiralty Scheme', P. 2/06.
[2] Printed in *N.N.* iii, 65 and other prints.

including Oliver and Richmond. The latter noted: 'Oliver is delighted, naturally. It really is wonderful to have a man at the head of affairs who can take up a matter as Fisher has, and who is so absolutely approachable and ready to listen to suggestions and act on them.'[1]

Having been associated with the origins of the new education scheme and having been thanked by Fisher for his subsequent 'missionary work',[2] Richmond participated also in the work of Fisher's education committee. On 28 April he attended a meeting convened by Fisher for presentation of a 'progress report', including the syllabus for the college at Osborne.[3] Dartmouth could not receive Cadets till 1905 and at the end of January 1903 Fisher had set on foot the swift preparation of Osborne for educating the first and second years of the new-style entrants.[4] The King had decided not to use his mother's cherished residence at Osborne and allowed the main building to become a military hospital. Through Esher's good offices the stables were made available to the Navy and Fisher insisted that conversion be completed by August, so that the first Cadets could enter in September.[5] Richmond's account of the 'progress' meeting gives an impression of Fisher's drive as a chairman:

The big meeting in the old Board Room on the 'New Scheme' the other day was distinctly amusing. Jack Fisher as Chairman, Arnold-Forster Vice Chairman and among those present Evan Macgregor,[6] Capts Wemyss[7] and Hood, Ruck-Keene, Sir John Durston, Prof Ewing[8] and Ashton[9] the new Head Master of Osborne . . . Naturally enough Fisher did the talking, using his usual formula 'Now to begin at the end'. It's perfectly sound. First we see what we want and then we work back and get it. People are too apt to begin at the beginning and worry and wrangle over small details which obscure the main issue, with the result that instead of a big scheme being produced, a result is obtained which is the patchwork of many small ideas sewed together.[10]

---

[1] N.M.M., RIC/1/6, journal, 26 Mar. 1903.

[2] Ibid.

[3] F.P. 4730, 'New Admiralty Scheme', 2nd progress report, P. 6/03, 18 pp.

[4] *F.G.* i, 276.   [5] Lee, ii, 20; *F.G.* i, 276.

[6] Permanent Secretary of the Ady., 1884–1907, and a friend of F.'s since the 1870s.

[7] Rosslyn E. Wemyss, first Capt. of Osborne; estranged from F., 1908; First Sea Lord, Dec. 1917–Oct. 1919.

[8] James Alfred Ewing, having held chairs in engineering and physics, was the first Director of Naval Education, 1903–16.

[9] Cyril Ashford.   [10] N.M.M., RIC/1/6, journal, 3 May 1903.

However, at one stage of the meeting Fisher failed to carry complete conviction. According to the printed minutes he declared:

First of all, the scheme of training should be so arranged that every officer entering the Navy could aspire to the command of ships and squadrons. It followed as a natural consequence that there must be complete interchangeability between all branches; therefore, the plan of education would have to be arranged accordingly.[1]

In support of this pronouncement, Fisher quoted a long letter written to him by Beresford on 14 April. This had already been reproduced in the 'First Progress Report'[2] and was a favourite item for reprinting during Fisher's subsequent conflict with Beresford.[3] Beresford wrote that, during 'three recent visits to the United States', he had assiduously inquired about the success of the American version of interchangeability 'by which deck officers have charge of the engines'. (Indeed, the American scheme went a good deal further than that envisaged by Fisher.) 'I regret the opposition in this country to the present scheme', wrote Beresford. 'I am certain such opposition is unfounded and unsound, and if still in the House of Commons I could have knocked the bottom out of it.' (In view of his later opposition to Fisher's scheme, it may be noted that Beresford's letter focused on deck officers in the engine-room and did not mention engineers commanding ships. However, in a press-interview, published on 1 January 1903, Lord Charles had supported this possibility also.)[4]

Richmond was rather taken aback by this part of Fisher's address:

He sprung one surprise on us, for which I confess I was not prepared and have not yet digested, though I may, namely that Engineer Lieuts, or rather Lieuts (E) of the future, are to be entirely interchangeable with the other Lieuts and rise to command of ships and fleets. It is a broad big idea; and, if feasible, an excellent one; but certain provisos are necessary. Your Lieut (E) *must* keep up his acquaintance with work on deck. He must not be, like the present Engineer, entirely below: and how he is to be a good working Engineer as well as a good deck officer—and it's no use making him a Captain if he isn't a good deck officer—seems rather difficult . . . As regards the Lieut (E), the idea—Jack's idea—is that he is the

---

[1] F.P. 4730.   [2] F.P. 4729, P. 6/03, 122 pp.   [3] See *N.N.* iii, 81 etc.
[4] *N.N.* iii, 82–6. See also Beresford, *The Betrayal*, pp. 9–17.

counterpart in every way of the Lieut G, T or N. I hope it's not too Utopian . . .[1]

Fisher's growing intolerance was illustrated at this time by an incident arising from the concurrent reorganization of gunnery and torpedo courses for Lieutenants. Captain G. le C. Egerton (who had served under Fisher as a Lieutenant aboard the *Northampton*) was in command of the *Vernon* and he did not accept the proposition 'that Torpedo Lieutenants could be made in three months'. Four years later Egerton told King-Hall that 'Fisher beckoned him out of the Council Chamber and led him into his room, then shook his fist at him, and almost spat at him, saying: "If you oppose my Education Scheme I will crush you." Fisher was beside himself with rage.'[2] The minutes of the relevant committee suggest a consequent diplomatic illness: 'Captain Egerton of H.M.S. "Vernon" was precluded by ill-health from attending all the meetings of the Committee.'[3] After moving to Portsmouth as Commander-in-Chief in August, Fisher apparently conducted a vendetta against Egerton for a time but was successfully resisted.[4]

However, what with the new education scheme for officers together with improved training and prospects of ratings, there can be no question that Fisher had swiftly achieved a number of much-needed reforms. As Walker records, the year 1903

witnessed an activity at the Admiralty which had never before occurred in times of peace. Reform after reform connected with the personnel of the Navy was brought about by Sir John Fisher with bewildering rapidity. Engineer officers were given semi-executive titles, commissioned rank was opened to that most deserving class of warrant officers, warrant rank was instituted for stokers through the new grade of mechanician, and an establishment for boy artificers was started to supply the Navy with engine-room artificers . . . and from this time onward fighting efficiency afloat became the aim and object of every ship.[5]

Meanwhile, it is surprising to find Fisher writing to his son as early as 14 November 1902 about his wish to leave the Admiralty, at least for a time: 'Tyrwhitt says Lord Selborne is extremely reluctant to let me go now, but he admits I'm entitled to Portsmouth and that he can't expect me to play second fiddle

---

[1] N.M.M., RIC/1/6, 3 May 1903.   [2] King-Hall, p. 327.
[3] F.P. 4732, 'New Admiralty Scheme', 3rd progress report (P. 6/03) p. 20.
[4] King-Hall, loc. cit.   [5] Walker, pp. 42–3.

here for 2 years after having played the first fiddle for so long.'
Tyrwhitt (whose appointment as Naval Secretary had been
influenced by Fisher) intimated that the First Lord was 'determined' to have Fisher back as First Sea Lord, if he was still in
office when Lord Walter retired.[1] Apart from his desire to be
'first fiddle', Fisher valued the Commander-in-Chief's facilities
for entertaining at Portsmouth. As at Malta, he would be
entitled to the highest rate of table money. Indeed, in both
appointments he utilized these advantages to the full. His proclivities as a host emerge from an account of his reception at
Lagos of officers of the Channel Squadron before the combined
manoeuvres of August 1901:

> The two chief figures of this meeting, Fisher and Wilson, presented
> a remarkable contrast: the latter self-restrained, reserved, silent and
> thoughtful, but watchful and attentive, with everything about him
> denoting a simplicity of life and habit; while Fisher loved to contrive
> a dramatic effect about everything he did. His flagship, the *Renown*,
> had been specially fitted for him, and carried a fore top-gallant mast
> to fly his flag higher than anyone else's; he had a special barge, which
> was said to have excited the envy of the German Emperor; the furni-
> ture and decorations of his cabin were more like those of a luxurious
> yacht than of a man-of-war, and he now greeted the strangers to his
> fleet with a frank and easy air of hospitality as if their entertainment
> was all that he had on his mind.[2]

While on holiday at Marienbad in July 1903, Fisher was 'very
busy hatching' with a view to taking over as First Sea Lord about
a year later. Anticipating the political demands for economy
with which he would be faced, he assured Thursfield: 'We can't
go on with such increasing Navy Estimates and I see my way
very clearly to a *very great reduction* WITH INCREASED EFFICIENCY!
That sounds nice and will *I* think come true! but the Reform
will require the 3 R's: Ruthless, Relentless, Remorseless.'[3]

However, soon before going to Portsmouth, Fisher was
travelling by train from Plymouth to London; and he pencilled
a note to his son, outlining what seems to be a different approach
to the problem of economical defence. This would produce the
agreeable result of maintained Navy Estimates and a massive
cut for his old *bête noire*, the Army!

---

[1] *F.G.* i, 266.   [2] Bradford, pp. 160–1.
[3] N.M.M., THU/1, 5 July 1903.

I've got a new big scheme hatching next year which I think will put everything in the shade which has been done in the past. I am interesting some very influential people in it—Sir E. Grey, Sir C. Dilke and the Editor of the Monthly Review and many others, but it must be kept a great secret at present as its whole success will depend on its bursting on the public as a complete, well-thought-out scheme. My idea is 23 millions only for the Army, 37 millions for the Navy, and a threepenny income tax. That will fetch the British Public and the Army will be a Lord Lieutenant's army, each county providing its own military force à la militia and a small expeditionary army for extraneous purposes and an Indian Army working in conjunction with the Expeditionary Army.[1]

The background to this remarkable proposal is as follows. The estimates of the Army had overtaken those of the Navy during the 1860s. In 1895–6 the position was reversed; the Navy cost £19,724,000 against £18,460,000 for the Army. By 1904–5, the last year before Fisher became First Sea Lord, the Navy Estimates were £36,830,000 against Army Estimates of £29,724,000. However, in a debate of February 1903 Sir Charles Dilke asserted that the annual cost of all the land forces of the Empire was above £50,000,000. During the South African War, the Army Estimates for 1901–2 attained the figure of £92,542,000— without producing particularly brilliant operational results.[2] What with recent invasion scares, Fisher was haunted, by 1903, by the spectre of a general demand for an Army large enough to repel a major landing. If the public ceased to place complete trust in the Navy, demand for an Army of continental proportions might prevail. This would result in a disastrous diversion of funds from the Navy.

Already, when preparing his original print of July 1902 on the education scheme, Fisher had reproduced some extracts from one of his Mediterranean lectures, dated as early as 1899, under the title 'The War Reserve for the Navy is the Army'. Recognizing that this brain-wave might not achieve instant popularity with the Army, Fisher had a cautionary slip inserted in the print: 'If this proposal is favourably entertained, *it is essential for its successful adoption* that not one word should be said in regard to it, either to *anyone* at the War Office or in any other quarter whatsoever, until the plan has been elaborated in

[1] Kilv. MSS., Pkt. 1. Undated but received by Cecil in India on 14 Sept. 1903.
[2] Halévy, p. 157 and n.

connection with all the other schemes treated of in this Print.'[1] This shows how seriously Fisher took this idea which, in turn, illuminates his whole approach to inter-service relations and national defence policy.

In Fisher's view, it was the Navy which was indispensable to the defence both of Britain and the Empire. The Army should be assigned limited roles, especially amphibious ones. Thus, the Navy Estimates could be held steady while the cost of defence as a whole fell. It may therefore be appreciated how antipathetic Fisher was to the claims of the War Office, examined during 1903 by the newly established Committee of Imperial Defence, that a considerable home-based army was needed to guard against invasion. When preparing the *New Admiralty Scheme* Fisher intended (pp. 39–41) to base the 'Training of Men and Boys' on the principle that, with as many as 1,200 to 1,500 seamen entering annually, only potential specialists should be trained at the gunnery schools. Besides these specialists there would be 'a large number of men, or rather "items", which will act as "Heavers of wood and drawers of water" '. These would be occupied in carrying ammunition and various other labouring tasks. In fact, as he had explained in his 'War Reserve' lecture of 1899, their work could just as well be performed by soldiers:

No matter how exhaustively the question of reserves of men for the Fleet in war is examined, or how closely we consider and provide for schemes for getting efficient men quickly on the outbreak of war, there will be found nothing approaching in either rapidity of supply or in the efficiency of the men (for the purpose required) than the good old system adopted in the time of Nelson (and long before his time) of embarking portions of the Army to supplement the crews of the Fleet. Thus, in the Mediterranean a plan has been worked out to commission at once a battleship and a cruiser, if such were in Reserve, with the aid of an infantry battalion from the garrison at Malta, without waiting for any officers or men from England for the purpose . . .

Nothing can get over the fact that if the Fleet is predominant no invasion of our shores can take place, and no Colony of ours can be seriously threatened . . . A study of Mahan's works has made this quite convincingly plain to all sea officers, but apparently neither the civilian nor the military mind has, in a general way, taken in the full significance of the memorable words of Mahan describing Nelson's

[1] *New Admiralty Scheme*, Appendix A.

work with the Mediterranean Fleet, when Nelson had never put foot ashore for two years!

'Nelson's far-distant, storm-beaten ships, upon which the Grand Army never looked, stood between it and the dominion of the world.' . . .

It has also been most convincingly pointed out that no more excellent system of increasing the efficiency of our military force could possibly be devised than the frequent embarkation of troops in the Fleet in our annual manoeuvres and mobilizations. This should be practised to the utmost practicable extent, because nothing will better fit the troops for the only purpose for which the Army will ever be required in war, which is for rapid military expeditions for the capture of the enemy's strategic points and Colonies . . .

It is therefore suggested, with implicit confidence in its success and on the firm basis of the teachings of history, that the only way, and the effective way, of making the Navy predominant is for the Army to be its reserve for war, and so be ready instantly to provide the men we require . . .

The details have been carefully considered, and there are no difficulties in the way . . .[1]

In this revolutionary fashion did Fisher seek to apply to national defence policy as a whole the principles of greater economy, combined with greater efficiency, which were to characterize his forthcoming naval reforms. In the light of these proposals, his willingness to undertake apparently extraneous service on the War Office Reconstitution Committee becomes readily comprehensible.

Fisher's appointment to Lord Esher's committee was arranged at Balmoral at the end of September 1903. The Prime Minister, A. J. Balfour, was reconstructing his cabinet. He and Esher were staying with the King and, on or about the 24th Esher was trying to escape from his threatened appointment as Secretary of State for War. 'So I made my counter proposal', wrote Esher. In the first place, someone else should shoulder the ministerial responsibility which was always anathema to Esher; otherwise, Balfour should 'appoint Commissioners to carry out the W.O. changes—the Commissioners to be myself, Fisher, and Brackenbury'. Fisher was now summoned to Balmoral. He appears to have arrived on 28 September, by which time Esher, and probably also Balfour, had left. The King told Fisher that he wished him

---

[1] *New Admiralty Scheme*, App. A; reprinted in F.P. 4928, papers for the use of the War Office Reconstitution Committee, late 1903.

to serve on the proposed committee which stemmed from the inquiry of the Elgin Commission into the early stages of the Army's effort in the South African War. Fisher lost no time in expounding to the King his somewhat idiosyncratic views on national defence. According to his own later account:

King Edward once upbraided me for my violence and said to me 'Will you kindly leave off shaking your fist in my face!' His Majesty was sitting down in a secluded seat at Balmoral and I was walking up and down in front of him explaining an Army and Navy Co-operative Society by which the Army would be a Reserve for the Navy—like Nelson had the 69th Regiment on board at the Battle of Cape St. Vincent.[1]

By dint of intensity and personal magnetism, Fisher succeeded in impressing King Edward and by 4 October he was writing to his wife: 'You can't think how very friendly the King is. He has kept me pretty busy writing out various memoranda, which I hope won't get me into hot water later on, but His Majesty promises that no other eyes than his own, the Prince of Wales and Lord Knollys shall see them.'[2]

These memoranda included various items, along the lines indicated above, dealing with defence policy in general and the role of the Army in particular. Several of these short papers were printed at Portsmouth for the benefit of Lord Esher's committee —and others. Among them was 'A Brief Précis of the Principal Considerations that Must Influence Our Future Naval and Military Policy'. This contains what appears, at first sight, a surprising suggestion to come from Fisher, namely a single minister for defence. His opposition to the idea in 1889 has been noticed above. However, by October 1903 Fisher could prescribe a healthy role for such a minister. His aim would be to limit service expenditure to '60 millions sterling instead of 84 millions sterling, combined with a Navy 30% stronger and an Army 50% more effective'. This would clip *'eightpence off the income tax!'* Fisher continued:

Naval and Military requirements must be considered together. It must be *One Service*, and not two great Departments fighting independently with the Treasury to see what they can get, and the Treasury saying if we give so much to one we must take if off the other!

[1] Esher, ii, 16, 21; *F.G.* i, 285; F.P. 5101.
[2] *F.G.* i, 287; but the date should be 4, not 5 Oct.—the letter was written on the Sunday.

We are therefore led irresistibly to the conclusion with which we started that the War Office must be reorganized on such lines as will ensure most intimate joint Naval and Military action; and the natural question that arises is—can this imperative requirement be met by any other method than a single Cabinet Chief, as in Austria? Can the Cabinet Committee of Defence be relied on to perform this function? . . .[1]

As soon as Fisher inferred, a few years later, that a talented War Secretary (Haldane) wished to become Minister of Defence, he reverted to bitter hostility to the idea. His hope of permanently subordinating the Army to the Navy explains his initial eagerness, in October 1903, to join Lord Esher's committee. However, he was to have some uncomfortable moments before he was actually appointed to the committee.

Arnold-Forster, the new Secretary of State for War, had worked harmoniously with Fisher at the Admiralty in 1902–3. When Balfour wrote to the minister on 4 October suggesting 'a small committee' to assimilate the organization of the War Office to that of the Admiralty, and consisting perhaps of 'Esher, Admiral Fisher and Sir John French', Arnold-Forster at once replied, 'I like your suggested Committee immensely.' Moreover, he wrote on the 14th: 'I think Sir John Fisher should be designated as Chairman. His rank, experience and great force of character will fully justify this.'[2] For his part, Balfour had had little direct contact with Fisher thus far; but Selborne had been keeping him informed about the Admiral, even if the First Lord's enthusiasm was less unqualified than Arnold-Forster's. 'He is not infallible', wrote Selborne, 'but he *is* clever and as full of fiery energy as Joe' (that is, Chamberlain).[3] But the plan to appoint Fisher to the Esher committee disconcerted the First Lord. He heard of it only when he arrived at Balmoral on 3 October. As he afterwards told Balfour, Fisher 'and the King appeared to have arranged it all before I came, and I lay low'.[4] Fisher had previously urged on Selborne the importance of his naval assignment at Portsmouth. In view of the First Lord's evident dislike of his prospective diversion of effort to the affairs of the War Office, it comes as no surprise to find the Admiral

---

[1] F.P. 4928 (P. 10/03?).
[2] Add. MSS. 50335, 4, 5, 14 Oct. 1903.
[3] Add. MSS. 49707, f. 141, 6 Sept. 1903.
[4] Ibid., ff. 142–3, 20 Oct.

writing an agitated note to J. S. Sandars, the Prime Minister's private secretary, on (or about) 21 October:

Private.

Dear Mr. Sandars,

I did not have time to show you the letters from the Admiralty but I wish to impress upon you that it was a direct direction from Lord Selborne to decline as he implied I could not hold my present appointment *but this is for your private information only.*

Yours truly,
J. A. Fisher.

Tell me if you disagree with print I gave you.[1]

It was not only Selborne who had given Fisher cause for reflection since the Balmoral episode. In what Fisher described as 'a most urgent letter', Battenberg had pointed out that the Admiral would 'cause endless ill-feeling and bitterness amongst the soldiers' if he served on the committee—a great pity in view of the constructive work that Fisher could do for the Navy. Drury, the new Second Sea Lord, and W. H. May, the Controller, had written to the same effect. Fisher therefore asked Arnold-Forster to 'pitch' him 'overboard' and to inform Balfour accordingly.[2] However, Arnold-Forster was insistent that Fisher should serve! In a forceful letter of 16 October, he had already written to Balfour: 'It having been suggested that the Admiralty procedure might with advantage be adopted, it is reasonable and indeed essential, to include in the Committee one member who has a recent acquaintance with the Board of Admiralty. I am quite certain that no name will command as much confidence with the public as Sir John's . . .'[3] A telegram from Balfour to Selborne did not modify the latter's attitude. Battenberg had already told Selborne that Fisher was looking to the First Lord to 'get him out of it'. Selborne's view was that as Fisher 'had run himself on this rock alone he must haul himself off it alone, if he wished to do so'. He reiterated 'that the Board would expect him to do all his work at Portsmouth' if he did serve on the committee, and he proceeded to inform Fisher in this sense. Fisher, on 22 October, found the tone of this communication

[1] Add. MSS. 49710, f. 14. N.d., but *F.G.* i, 289 indicates *c.* 21 Oct.

[2] *F.G.* iii, 13–14, 17 Oct.

[3] Add. MSS. 49722, f. 72.

'rather nasty'. However, a compromise was achieved when Balfour suggested that the meetings of the Esher committee should be held at Admiralty House, Portsmouth.[1]

In the event, Fisher's contribution to the constructive achievement of the committee seems to have been comparatively small—hardly sufficient to compensate for the animosity which grew between himself and the soldiers chiefly involved. Even before starting work with Esher in November, Fisher was embroiled over the proposed appointment of General Sir Henry Brackenbury as a member of the committee. He insisted that no recent member of the War Office staff could command public confidence and that all 'the old gang' should be evicted from the War Office. Buckingham Palace witnessed some heated exchanges. Referring to Fisher's expressions of view on Brackenbury, Arnold-Forster recorded in his diary for 26 October: 'There was trouble at the Palace.' 'There was a great palaver.' The next day Esher (who originally nominated Brackenbury) found Fisher embattled with General Kelly-Kenny, the Adjutant-General, who supported Brackenbury; 'there they all were, arguing and discussing anew', wrote Esher. 'It is unedifying.'[2]

Finally, Sir George Clarke, then Governor of Victoria, was chosen as the third member of the committee, after being strongly backed by Fisher. Last noticed at Alexandria in 1882, Colonel Clarke had subsequently been secretary of the Colonial Defence Committee and of the Carnarvon Commission. He had also been in touch with Fisher and kept him posted on his maritime approach to national strategy.[3] So far, so good. However, unbeknown to him, in early October Clarke had stood on the edge of Fisher's enmity, and was in danger of missing his successive appointments to the Esher committee and to the Committee of Imperial Defence (1904). At Balmoral Selborne had mentioned to Fisher that Clarke was writing to him against the new education scheme on account of its tendency towards 'interchangeability'. Fisher wrote at once to Thursfield, who was friendly with Clarke, asking him to advise Clarke to

¹ Add. MSS. 49707, ff. 142–7, Selborne to Balfour, 20, 21 Oct. 1903; Kilv. MSS., Pkt. 37, Selborne to F., 21 Oct. 1903 (copy); F.G. i, 288–9, F. to Sandars, 22 Oct.
² Add. MSS. 50335, A.-Forster to Balfour (copy) 16 Oct.; diary, 26 Oct.; Esher, ii, 29.
³ F.P. 5469, offprint of 'Fixed Defences and the British Empire' in Royal Engineers' Journal, Apr. 1892; Add. MSS. 49710, f. 10, Clarke to F., 31 Aug. 1903.

drop this line of criticism as being 'inimical to his interests'. Clarke did apparently let the matter rest, at least until 1905; and by the end of December 1903 he was to be found at Portsmouth, working harmoniously with Esher and Fisher. 'Clarke is *excellent*', Esher enthused to Balfour. 'All on the right lines—and *fat* and comfortable!' This was a misleading report. While possessing considerable strategic and political capacity, Clarke was nonetheless inclined to be hypercritical, interfering, and tactless. In due course, he would join the ranks of Fisher's opponents.[1]

The report of the Esher committee was issued in four parts during February and March 1904. Fisher deserves a share of credit for the celerity of the operation; he also provided advice, as expected, on the application of Admiralty principles to the new Army Council. However, Sir John Dunlop fairly attributes 'the great changes' effected by the committee largely to Esher himself and to Lieutenant-Colonel G. F. Ellison, secretary to the committee. Esher contributed heavily to the development of the C.I.D. while Ellison dealt with the Army's staff organization. Clarke concentrated on the financial aspect. As a consequence of the report, the post of Commander-in-Chief was abolished in the interests of unified military administration; the posts of Chief of the General Staff and Director of Military Operations (D.M.O.) were among the new creations; and a General Staff was prescribed—coming fully into effect in 1906.[2] However, having recommended a General Staff for the War Office, Fisher was unfortunately to deny the Navy the advantages of a similar arrangement at the Admiralty.

To cite once again Sir John Dunlop, Fisher's main contribution to the committee's work consisted of 'cheerful and all-embracing' advocacy of navalization. His ebullience is illustrated by one of the Admiralty House prints sent to the Prime Minister. In this, Fisher attacks the regimental system and attributes to Kitchener, then Commander-in-Chief in India, insistence on

assimilating Naval and Military Practice in regard to the interchangeability of Officers. He maintains that it is not possible by any other means whatever to obtain efficiency, and he says efficiency is

---

[1] *Naval Review* (1930) p. 335; Sydenham, pp. 207–8; N.M.M., THU/1, F. to Thursfield, 4 Oct. 1903; Add. MSS. 49718, f. 46, Esher to Balfour, 30 Dec.

[2] Dunlop, pp. 204–12; Hamer, p. 234.

the first and *only* consideration, and that sentiment must go to the devil, like it has had to go in giving up masts and sails, in giving up the Roman phalanx, and giving up flaps to trousers, and taking to what the sailors call 'fornicating breeches'.[1]

At the head of this print, he wrote for Balfour: 'I had no idea Esher was going to have this printed and I have asked him to suppress it—some of the details are totally unfit for publication!' However, the drift of Fisher's views was duly apprehended by the military and much resentment against the committee arose from the precipitate sacking from the War Office, in February 1904, of Kelly-Kenny, the Duke of Connaught, Ian Hamilton, and W. G. Nicholson.

While he continued to accept the committee's recommendations, Arnold-Forster told Balfour that he had 'a very sincere regard for General Nicholson and his work' as Director of Military Intelligence. However, 'the Committee' was 'quite agreed that he ought to go too'. Fisher seems to have been at the bottom of this particular removal. Nicholson was anathema to the Admiral on account of his role in the invasion inquiry of 1903. It was he who conducted the War Office's case, explaining to the C.I.D. the supposed possibility that the Navy might not be able to prevent an invasion of Britain (by the French). By 7 December Fisher was forcibly impressing on Esher that 'there must be an entire "clear-out" of the present military gang at the War Office, root and branch, lock, stock, and gunbarrel! Apparently Nicholson, the D.M.I., is the dominant conspirator . . . Nicholson hopes to hang on under the new régime by damning every possible successor!'[2] By 10 February 1904, as the future Field-Marshal Henry Wilson noted, the Esher 'Triumvirate' was 'appointing officers to billets here, there, and everywhere, quite regardless of anyone'. The next day, Wilson was discussing the situation with Nicholson when Brigadier-General Grierson came in to say that '*Esher*' had ordered him to come and 'take over Nick's office'. Lord George Hamilton was amongst the leading politicians surprised at the 'extraordinary lack of consideration thus shown to a group of our most distinguished generals'. He tried to discover from Arnold-Forster, without success, why Nicholson (whom he considered 'an absolutely first-rate official') had been axed with the rest. 'Nick'

---

[1] Add. MSS. 49710, ff. 98–9.   [2] *F.G.* i, 292.

himself 'flushed crimson with anger' when it was suggested that he had indicated readiness to leave the War Office. Thus originated a feud between Fisher and Nicholson which was to flavour Army–Navy relations for several years, especially between 1907 and 1909. Nicholson could not be kept out of the War Office. He was back there by 1905; and in 1908 he became the first holder of the title 'Chief of the Imperial General Staff'. He proved himself a disagreeable antagonist for Fisher at the C.I.D. and had the ultimate satisfaction of sitting as a member of the Dardanelles Commission in 1916. He made his mark on 13 October 1916 as the official minutes testify:

Lord Nicholson. With regard to Lord Fisher's sudden departure [from the Admiralty in May 1915], is it not extremely unusual in your experience for a high official to leave a high appointment which he has held, without being relieved?

Commodore C. F. Lambert [4th Sea Lord]. Most unusual—unprecedented.[1]

At the time of the invasion inquiry of 1903, Nicholson seems to have been animated by departmental considerations. Fisher was certainly correct in assessing the real danger confronting Britain as starvation rather than invasion. However, his conduct of a vendetta against Nicholson did little to improve the situation. This merely encouraged the latter to retreat further into his defensive departmentalism, seeking to safeguard the existence of the Army from the aggressive navalism of Fisher.[2]

However, Fisher derived some profit from his membership of the Esher committee. He was afforded opportunities for impressing some leading politicians, as well as the King, thus strengthening his position as a prospective reforming First Sea Lord. On 23 February 1904 Arnold-Forster noted in his diary:

Went to see the King at 11.30. He kept me an hour talking over every kind of subject . . . The King highly praised the work of the Esher Committee, and I could only cordially agree. He was impressed by Clarke, and of course immensely by Fisher . . . He is anxious that the Committee should be dissolved as soon as possible, and not sit on for consultative purposes, as was at one time proposed. Esher and Fisher he says are in favour of dissolution, Clarke against. He thinks

---

[1] Cab. 19/22, Dard. Comm., p. 239. Other refs. for above section: Add. MSS. 49722, ff. 113–15, A.-Forster to Balfour, 13 Jan. 1904; Callwell, i, 55; Hamilton, pp. 300–1.

[2] H. R. Moon's thesis on 'The Invasion of the United Kingdom' gives much information on the interdepartmental struggle.

the Army will grow restive if a Committee which is irresponsible goes on too long . . .

He spoke of Fisher and the Admiralty. Thought there would be opposition to him in some quarters. 'Some people thought he (J.F.) went too fast, but it would be very wrong if he were not to be utilized.' I could only agree most cordially, and say I thought it would be a calamity if the abilities of our ablest man were not fully utilized for the benefit of our greatest Service.[1]

It was indeed the case that opposition to Fisher was already gathering strength in some naval quarters. Pre-eminent among the retired admirals opposed to the new education scheme was Sir Frederick Richards who still enjoyed the deep respect of many serving officers. Vice-Admiral Sir Lewis Beaumont, who had been with Fisher in the *Excellent* in 1873, had been his Commander in the *Bellerophon*, had done much to help him when he was ill in 1883, and had been with him at the Admiralty in 1894–7, was (according to King-Hall's diary for 15 October 1903) 'endeavouring to prevent Fisher from returning as First Sea Lord'.[2] Very soon after this, Sir Gerard Noel—'eminently gifted' according to Fisher in 1901—was similarly employed. In March 1903 Noel rounded off his command of the Home (reserve) Fleet by conducting some manoeuvres. He had Selborne, Tyrwhitt, and Fisher on board and saw a good deal of the latter. Shortly after coming ashore Noel 'bicycled to Hurlingham Court and saw Sir F. Richards'; and he had a 'long talk' with the same admiral at the United Service Club in July. On 23 October he met his old friends, the Beaumonts.[3] Some eight years later he wrote to Lord Selborne:

You may perhaps remember an interview I had with you at the Admiralty before I left to take up the China Command in [January] 1904. I firmly believe that had you then listened to the protest I then made against Fisher's coming to the Admiralty as First Naval Lord— a protest which was backed by the opinions of practically all the most reliable men in the upper ranks of the navy—we should not have been brought into the deplorable and even perilous position we now hold in the world.

Lord Selborne's terse reply on that occasion discouraged further correspondence. However, it is clear enough that many capable, if conservative, officers already by the beginning of 1904

[1] Add. MSS. 50336, ff. 161–3.
[2] F.P. 5206 for Beaumont in 1883; King-Hall, p. 324.
[3] *F.G.* i, 181; N.M.M., NOE/32, Noel's diary.

regarded the prospect of Fisher's advent as First Sea Lord with considerable apprehension.[1]

Fisher received no firm invitation to return to the Admiralty till 14 May 1904—two days after the dissolution of the Esher committee. Up to that date, the most remarkable feature of Fisher's command at Portsmouth had been the development of his interest in submarines. Already before his arrival, R. H. Bacon, now Inspecting-Captain of Submarine Boats, was busy at the port conducting manoeuvres with the original five (British-built) Holland boats; and he had already sent to the Admiralty a report dated 31 May 1903, embodying various conclusions about the role of the submarine.[2] In this report of 31 May Bacon (who, according to a note by Fisher was 'acknowledged as the cleverest officer in the Navy')[3] suggested the potential of the submarine in helping to prevent invasion, in providing more effectively than fixed minefields for the defence of ports, and in various offensive roles. The idea that the submarine would supplant the defensive mine appealed to Fisher—with unfortunate results, as will be seen. But the reference to an offensive role was certainly well founded. Towards the end of his Mediterranean command, on 1 April 1902, Fisher had remarked:

Arrangements by which Submarine Boats can be towed at high speed in almost any weather, and with any sea, are believed to be feasible; and if these arrangements for so doing can be perfected (about which there seems but little doubt), then we shall have another revolution in strategy and tactics, and the Offensive will again regain the ascendency, as such vessels will largely alter the present conditions of Blockade and of Harbour Defence.[4]

Thus, from the outset, one is confronted with the mixture of vision and confusion inherent in Fisher's thinking about submarines. On the one hand, he outdid (for example) Bacon in imagination, seeing at once the offensive potential of the submarine as its most remarkable feature; and he was in the forefront in realizing that this carried far-reaching implications for strategy and tactics. On the other hand, his reasoning was confused in detail; and it is this defect in his approach which explains

[1] N.M.M., NOE/5, Noel to Selborne, 14 July 1912 (copy); undated reply, received on 16 July.

[2] Adm. 1/7725; *Anatomy*, pp. 363–6. See also Jameson, Ch. 4 and Bacon, *From 1900 Onward*, Ch. 3.

[3] F.P. 4194.   [4] F.P. 4702, p. 73, note.

some of the obvious shortcomings of the Navy in 1914. In this instance, he is correct in arguing that, if the range of submarines can be increased, a new offensive weapon will exist. But, at the end of the quoted paragraph, he seems to argue, also, that harbour-defence submarines will make close blockade impracticable. In so far as the existing small submarines were much better suited to such defensive functions than to offensive operations at a distance, it was the defensive aspect of strategy that was strengthened. It was quite illogical to include 'Harbour Defence' with the other prospective submarine activities which were going to allow 'the Offensive' to 'regain the ascendency'.

Nor should the degree of originality in Fisher's view of April 1902 be overstressed. The French had been conducting a series of submarine trials which, by 1901, had already stimulated much speculative writing in the British press. Indeed, the *Sunday Times* went so far as to question the wisdom of continuing to build 'great and powerful battleships' when an enemy might destroy them with 'a boat'.[1] At the Admiralty, the imminence of operational submarines was not received with joy. A. K. Wilson (who had succeeded Fisher as Controller in 1897 and was then finishing his term of office) wrote a minute in January 1901 recommending that 'this underhand method of attack' should be outlawed by international agreement. He recognized that the traditional British discouragement of submarines would no longer delay their development; but he argued, logically enough, that Britain should avoid accelerating the development of the submarine 'in order that the means of trapping and destroying it may develop at a greater rate than the submarines themselves'. However, Lord Walter Kerr was less conservative. He argued that Britain should not deny herself the offensive potential of submarines. Evan MacGregor advocated 'unostentatious progress' rather than the attitude of Canute.[2]

When Fisher, in September 1903, found Bacon conducting further submarine manoeuvres at Portsmouth, there was nothing 'unostentatious' about his enthusiasm for these new craft. However, his immediate interest in the submarines was much stimulated by his concurrent preoccupation with the role of the Army and with Nicholson's arguments that defence against invasion should be counted as one of the Army's functions. Bacon's forecast of the submarine's effectiveness in that very

[1] Jameson, p. 78.   [2] Ibid., pp. 76-7.

role came apropos. On 11 November 1903 Balfour presented to the C.I.D.—which was his own creation—his lucid 'Draft report on the possibility of serious invasion'.[1] On the 12th Esher arrived at Admiralty House to start work with Fisher on reform of the War Office. Fisher assembled the various memoranda which he had already written about restricting the role of the Army and, for printing purposes, he covered them with a letter he had written to Esher on 19 November. This letter included the following:

> I expect the Prime Minister and the Secretary of State for War must have pretty good ideas now crystallised as to how the Army should be constituted. Let us ask them for this at once. If they haven't got it, let us tell them we must have it because, as I said at starting, you cannot organise an administration without clearly knowing what you are going to administer![2]

Up to this time Fisher does not seem to have corresponded directly with Balfour, but on 5 December he wrote to Sandars to say that, on Esher's suggestion, he wished to invite the Prime Minister to stay at Admiralty House and see some submarine exercises. 'Arnold-Forster is staying with me from Friday to Monday and he seems thoroughly in accord with our [War Office] proposals.'[3] Balfour was too much preoccupied with the danger of war between Russia and Japan to be able to go to Portsmouth but Arnold-Forster came. He pleased Fisher by proposing for the Army 'an immediate reduction of 300,000 men'.[4] At this juncture Fisher may not have seen Balfour's draft report on invasion but, doubtless, through Esher, Sandars, or other contacts, he had some knowledge of the Prime Minister's views. He therefore set to work and produced a paper entitled 'Invasion and Submarines'.[5]

---

[1] Cab. 3/1/18A.   [2] F.P. 4928. These prints were bound in Dec. 1903.

[3] Add. MSS. 49710, ff. 57–8.

[4] Add. MSS. 49707, ff. 152–80, Selborne–Balfour correspondence; F.G. i, 292.

[5] F.P. 4940 (Dec. 1903). He himself later noted on a section of this print (F.P. 4942), separately entitled 'The Effect of Submarine Boats': 'Written by Sir John Fisher when Commander-in-Chief at Portsmouth, October 1903'. However, Appendix C of the whole print 'Invasion and Submarines', refers to 'the month before last (October 1903)' which indicates Dec. 1903 as the time of writing. Typically, when preparing this print for inclusion in *Records* (pp. 176–9), F. scored out from 'The Effect of Submarine Boats' (F.P. 4942) a para. beginning: 'During last October, (1903), our representatives . . .' As far as he was concerned, the document could now be dated Oct. 1903! See Esher Papers 10/41 for a letter from F. to Esher, n.d. but definitely Dec. (ref. to Balfour not coming), for confirmation that 'Invasion and Submarines' was written in that month.

The print begins with an 'Explanatory Statement': 'The primary object of the enclosed remarks is to make clear that the Submarine Boat has made Invasion impracticable, and this being so, that it follows the Army requires to be reconstituted because Invasion has apparently been hitherto a governing condition in arranging its strength . . .'

After this introductory section comes the principal memorandum, 'The Effect of Submarine Boats'. Many years later, Sir George Clarke recalled his close acquaintance with Fisher at the time when the Esher committee was operating:

I now had special opportunities for noting his remarkable qualities, and his genius for picturesque language, which carried him far and won him the reputation of being a master of the science of the sea . . . To Ministers and others who might know nothing of naval affairs, his breezy, picturesque and always positive language, implying profundity of thought which was not there, was irresistible.[1]

Allowance must certainly be made for the indelible effect on Clarke of his personal clashes with Fisher in 1906–7 when reading the above appraisal. It is an incomplete assessment, taking no account of Fisher's drive as an executive or, indeed, his grasp of basic reality which tended, in the long run, to assert itself despite a barely penetrable smoke-screen of indiscreet and sometimes wild talk. But Clarke's comments may be borne in mind when reading the following extracts from 'Invasion and Submarines'. Fisher evidently enjoyed himself when composing the section on 'The Effect of Submarine Boats'!

These remarks can only be fully appreciated by those who have witnessed the Flotilla of Submarine Boats now at Portsmouth practising out in the open sea.

It is an historical fact that the British Navy stubbornly resists change. For instance, masts and sails were obsolete 40 years ago, and they haven't even yet quite left us.

I remember when I was a young Lieutenant the First Sea Lord of the Admiralty telling me that he never washed when he came to sea and he didn't see why the devil the Midshipmen should want to wash now! This was apropos of an application for a Midshipmen's wash place in a large new ship then building, where there was ample room for it.

Another First Sea Lord also told me on another and later occasion that there were no torpedoes when he came to sea, and he didn't see why the devil there should be any of the beastly things now! . . .[2]

---

[1] *Naval Review* (1930), pp. 336, 508.

[2] See pp. 51–67 above for an examination of this story.

This Whitehead torpedo can be carried with facility in Submarine Boats, and it has now attained such a range and accuracy (due to the marvellous adaptation of the gyroscope), that even at two miles range it possesses a greater ratio of vitally injuring a ship in the line of battle than does the most accurate gun . . .

During last October, (1903), our representatives at Whitehead's Torpedo Factory at Fiume in Austria saw some foreign specimens, (notably a Russian torpedo) run accurately for 3,000 yards at $24\frac{1}{4}$ knots, and we are on the eve of getting greater results than these . . .

But the whole pith and marrow of the whole matter lies in the fact that the Submarine Boat which carries this automobile torpedo is up to the present date absolutely unattackable . . .

Now for the practical bearing of all this and the special manner it affects the Submarine Boat and the Army and the Navy—for they are all inextricably mixed up together in this matter.

As regards the Navy it must revolutionize Naval Tactics . . .

It affects the Army because, imagine, even one Submarine Boat with a flock of transports in sight loaded each with two or three thousand troops. Imagine the effect of one such transport going to the bottom in a few seconds with its living freight. Even the bare thought makes invasion impossible! Fancy 100,000 helpless, huddled up troops afloat in frightened transports with these invisible demons known to be near. Death near—sudden—awful—invisible—unavoidable! Northing conceivable more demoralizing!

It affects the Army and Navy conjointly because how could there possibly be any bombardment of any place (fortified or not) with Submarines present, or even, if suspected of being present? . . . It affects the Chancellor of the Exchequer because over half a million sterling a year is now being thrown in the gutter by the up-keep of stationary mines in our military and mercantile ports . . .

It affects the existence of the Empire because just as we were in peril by the non-adoption of the breech-loading gun until after every Foreign nation had it . . . so are we in peril now by only having 20 per cent of our very minimum in Submarine Boats because we are waiting for perfection! . . . We strain at the gnat of perfection and swallow the camel of unreadiness! We shall be found unready once too often!

Note:—It may possibly be said in reply that we are building Submarines to the utmost extent of our existing manufacturing capabilities—but it only requires a sufficiently large order to be given to make it worth while to set up fresh plant—an order for 25 more Submarines would cost less than one Battleship. Which is the more pressing? . . .[1]

[1] F.P. 4940 is the complete print (except for some of App. C. which has dropped off); F.P. 4942 consists of 'The Effect of Submarine Boats' only and was used for *Records*, pp. 176–9.

Most of the basic ideas in this paper are to be found in Bacon's above-mentioned report of May 1903. Fisher's contribution is largely in terms of vivid presentation. The submarine's ability to prevent invasion is, of course, much exaggerated; but during his term as First Sea Lord, Fisher would supply only too tangible a demonstration of his belief in this capability by his excessive orders for small coastal types which were virtually useless in the Great War. A serviceable 'overseas' submarine was simply not available in 1904.[1]

On 29 December 1903 Fisher dispatched the print, complete with three appendices, to Sandars. The latter duly passed it on to the Prime Minister. Balfour may well have derived amusement from a cautionary remark in Fisher's covering letter: 'Sir Evan MacGregor (Secretary of the Admiralty), a devoted friend of mine, was staying here when I wrote it, and he was simply aghast at the thought of Lord Selborne or my late colleagues hearing of it!'[2] Howbeit, Balfour's natural interest in defence was aroused by the paper and on 3 January 1904 he dictated a personal reply:

My dear Admiral,

I have read with the deepest interest your 'private and secret' Notes on 'Submarines' . . . It is unnecessary to tell you how heartily I am in sympathy with your observations on the relation between Submarines and Invasion; indeed, my paper on Home Defence, which I think was shewn you, is largely based upon the considerations to which you refer . . . I was not aware of the extraordinary efficiency of the modern Whitehead as demonstrated in Appendix B of your Paper. It is very disquieting, and becomes positively alarming when supplemented by your observations on the superiority of foreign torpedoes . . .[3]

Balfour then proceeded to question Fisher's unqualified enthusiasm for submarines, including their potential offensive role, as expressed in Appendix A of the paper. Here Fisher, without evident tenderness for the incipient *entente cordiale*, declares:

The great advantage of Submarine Boats is that, although of great defensive value, they can through their large radius of action become

---

[1] Jameson, p. 106. For information about the construction of the early types, see also Bacon, *From 1900 Onward*, pp. 68–9 and *N.N.* ii, 446–7.

[2] *F.G.* iii, 17–18.

[3] In App. C. Fisher asserts that Woolwich Arsenal is producing torpedoes markedly inferior to those 'in course of manufacture at the factory at Fiume to which we have access at any time'.

offensive. Thus, the Malta Submarine Boats could be off Toulon towed there by armoured cruisers in 2½ days and if the French were unprepared they would be put into the harbour like ferrets, and out would have to come the French Fleet like rabbits (to be fought by our Fleet) or be sunk in their own harbour!

Prophetic words indeed! Unfortunately it was to be the British Grand Fleet that was, in 1914, to play this fugitive role owing to the Admiralty's failure to supply Scapa Flow with fixed anti-submarine defences!

Fisher's vision attracted the following comments from Balfour at the end of his letter of 3 January:

I am very little consoled by an observation which occurs on page 3 of Appendix A, where you point out that the Submarine may be used for offensive, as well as for defensive purposes. On the whole, this seems to me to be greatly to our disadvantage. I take it that Portsmouth for instance is more accessible than either Brest or Toulon, and the game you propose to play at the latter could be played by the French even more effectually at the former.

> Forgive these hasty notes, and
> Believe me,
> Yours ever,
> Arthur James Balfour.[1]

Fisher replied to this final comment on 5 January with an answer which probably seemed adequate to him at the time, in so far as he was soon to put its argument into practice at the Admiralty: 'I note your anxiety about Portsmouth being treated *à la* Toulon! The whole and complete answer is "instant readiness for war". . . The vital importance of instant and vigorous initiative is the primary condition of naval warfare and it defends you from everything, SUBMARINES INCLUDED . . . *all our weapons must be tried* . . .'[2]

Some nine years later, as a result of renewed correspondence with Balfour on this subject, Fisher would realize—in advance of probably all other high-ranking officers—that unrestricted attacks on commerce by submarines were virtually inevitable in a major war. It is therefore tantalizing to find, enclosed with his letter to Balfour of 29 December 1903, a print entitled 'The French Naval Estimates for 1904'. Here, the French Minister of Marine demands overseas bases for 'torpedo boats and

---

[1] Add. MSS. 49710, ff. 71–3 (copy).   [2] *F.G.* i, 294.

submarines', not only to prevent attacks on French possessions but also 'to harass the trade routes of the enemy'.[1] But at that date Fisher and Balfour did not perceive, as they did in 1912–13, that submarines were too small to be able to capture merchant vessels in accordance with the accepted rules of war; and therefore they did not pass on to conclude that, notwithstanding the diplomatic disadvantages, a hard-pressed belligerent would probably disregard the said rules.

The submarine exercises continued at Portsmouth during 1904. In March A. K. Wilson (now Sir Arthur Wilson and Commander-in-Chief of the reconstituted Home Fleet) was conducting submarine manoeuvres when the *A1* was rammed and sunk by a merchant vessel. This, together with other accidents at home and abroad, led to the adoption (by 1906) of such stringent safety-precautions that submarine manoeuvres were divested of any reality. Wilson, who was still most anxious to discover effective countermeasures, wrote to Noel on 22 May 1904: 'The most effective way of dealing with the submarines, namely running into them, was barred by the dangers, both to the destroyers and submarines. Charleton and Bacon are carrying out further trials in working destroyers against submarines and we have a great deal to learn yet.'[2]

Unofficially, suggestions concerning anti-submarine projectiles were made at about this time and publicized by *Brassey's Naval Annual* but there seems to be no evidence that Fisher was actively interested. In the event, the Navy entered the Great War without hydrophones or depth-charges.[3]

The *A1*, developed by Captain Bacon in conjunction with Vickers, Sons, and Maxim, had been one of Fisher's favourite showpieces. The Admiral had been very busy entertaining politicians and journalists with this and other exhibits. Sir George Clarke later recalled this activity. Crediting Fisher with 'unrivalled' talents as a showman, he commented: 'He spared no trouble, looked into all details himself, and rehearsed when necessary.' Thus was the country 'skilfully prepared to expect a "crusade of Reform" '.[4] This mobilization of support was crowned in February 1904 by the visit to Admiralty House as Fisher's guest, of King Edward. Seeing that (as has been mentioned) none of Lady Fisher's letters to the Admiral have

[1] Add. MSS. 49710, f. 68.   [2] N.M.M., NOE/5.
[3] Jameson, pp. 89–91.   [4] *Naval Review* (1930), p. 336.

survived, but that her agreeability as a hostess and her constancy in supporting her husband were well known, it is appropriate to make use of her account of the royal visit. She wrote to her son on 25 February:

The King's visit has come and gone and passed off without the slightest hitch. H.M. arrived in time for lunch on Friday the 19th. . . I cannot tell you how perfectly charming he was, so genial, so kind and pleased with everything . . . Father had a bathroom, W.C. and lavatory built for the use of the 2 best bedrooms and dressing rooms. (Formerly there was nothing accessible of this sort without going up the back stairs!!) . . .

Next to the King's sitting room is a small sitting room . . . This was for the Secretary, Captain Ponsonby, and in this a telephone was put and on the King's own writing table 2 buttons to press, one to call Secretary and one the servant who always sits outside his door. What was our consternation when a message came: the King wants a *hand bell!* . . . One was found somehow, but before it arrived the tele-graph buttons had been discovered. They had been covered by some papers . . .

All my department was very satisfactory: *excellent lunches* and *dinners* and waiting. I put down all this to our having done the whole thing with *our own usual staff*—no strange chef from London to upset the house. Our Cook is first rate and so delighted to have it all to do. The King sent for her before he left and gave her a brooch . . . We were about 26 to 29 at lunch every day and 18 to 20 at dinner . . .[1]

By the spring of 1904, therefore, Fisher had prepared for his era of reform by securing the personal support of the King, which indeed never failed him, and to a considerable extent that of the leading politicians and the press. The principal remaining uncertainty was his relationship with Selborne. The First Lord was never fully reconciled to Fisher's work on the Esher committee and seems to have disliked the treatment meeted out to General Nicholson.[2] Nor is it clear how much Selborne knew about Fisher's latest plans for the Navy. Since the Admiral's accession to the Esher committee the flow of suggestions to the First Lord had been diverted in the direction of Sandars and the Prime Minister. In January 1904, for example, it was with Sandars that Fisher discussed the proposed redistri-bution of business at the Admiralty. The object here was to strengthen the powers of the First Sea Lord in order to obviate

---

[1] Kilv. MSS., Pkt. 1.   [2] *F.G.* i, 300, 318–19.

opposition to his reforms on the part of other members of the Board.[1]

However, on 11 May Selborne wrote tersely to the Prime Minister: 'Lord Walter Kerr's time is up at the end of September. Do you agree to my recommending Fisher to the King as his successor?'[2] On the 14th, Selborne informed Fisher that the King had approved his appointment.[3] He also sent him two memoranda, the first giving details of the proposed new distribution of business and the second discussing several aspects of naval policy—some of which had been considered by Lord Walter Kerr and the Board. The first memorandum met Fisher's wishes; by an Order in Council (which was issued in August) wide powers were to be given to the First Sea Lord when Kerr was replaced in October. The second treated a number of points in which Fisher had already expressed interest: long-range firing; scrapping of obsolete vessels; more destroyers and submarines; mobilization; nucleus crews; two-year commissions; the training of potential flag officers and selection of their staff; and development of the war course. Redistribution of the fleets was also mentioned, albeit in rather cautious language: 'The organisation, composition and training of our smaller foreign squadrons requires much revision.'

However, what was made abundantly clear in the first paragraph of the memorandum was that economy was to be the essential basis of Admiralty policy. This cannot have come as a surprise to Fisher. Nevertheless, in view of his reputation as an 'economist', the point needs to be made that he did not voluntarily advocate financial stringency. In fact, he had not yet abandoned his attempt to maintain the existing level of naval expenditure at the expense of drastic cuts in the Army. However, the unpalatable view of the Chancellor of the Exchequer that both services must face limitations was now embodied in Selborne's opening paragraph:

1. *Economy of Estimates.* It is quite certain that the Navy Estimates have for the present reached their maximum in the present year. In 1905–1906 not only can there be no possible increase, but it is necessary, for the influence of the Admiralty over the House of Commons and for the stability of the national finances, that we should show a substantial decrease.

---

[1] Add. MSS. 49710, ff. 115–19, F. to Sandars, 30 Jan. 1904, enclosing relevant notes by Evan MacGregor.

[2] Add. MSS. 49707, f. 221.　　　　*F.G.* ii, 95.

On certain items, spending would have to increase. Therefore cuts must be sought in new construction, repairs, and perhaps stores and reserves. Under the heading of naval works, Chatham Dockyard would have to be extended as far 'as the present serious state of the finances makes possible'; but there was no hurry about developing Rosyth.

Selborne listed the numbers and types of ship to be laid down during the two years 1905–6 and 1906–7: 5 battleships, 8 armoured cruisers, 8 scouts, 28 destroyers, 20 submarines, 6 auxiliary vessels. He remarked:

In the autumn we shall have the material wherewith to decide whether we cannot make a further alteration of the programme and further postpone a part of it in consequence of what has occurred in the war between Japan and Russia. It is most important for the stability of national finance and credit that we should do so if we can.[1]

Russian losses in the war with Japan were clearly crucial in relation to the Two-Power Standard and to Fisher's schemes of redistribution and ship-building. However, ultimate Russian victory was still generally anticipated by British political and service leaders, Fisher apparently not excepted;[2] and it was not until 1905 that the full extent of the change in Britain's naval position could be assessed. For the moment, Fisher was more interested in his own prospective position at the Admiralty. He was so suspicious of Selborne that he wrote about him privately in a manner normally reserved for his principal bogey men, such as General Nicholson. On 16 May Fisher discussed his role with Selborne for 'two solid hours'; and on the next day he reported on the outcome to Esher who was now entrenched as his intimate confidant: 'The die is cast! I accepted yesterday on the understanding I commenced work on October 21st (Trafalgar Day!) Nothing like a good omen!'[3]

In another note to Esher of about the same date, Fisher quoted Selborne as remarking to some third party that Fisher's appointment as First Sea Lord was 'simply unavoidable'. By way of

---

[1] N.R.S. *F.P.* i, xvi–xx; Monger, p. 168.

[2] Lord Newton, *Lord Lansdowne*, London, 1929, p. 307.

[3] *F.G.* i, 316. Nelson had figured in the Mediterranean lectures but now, on the brink of his reforms, F. was even more conscious of the great national hero. He had three compilations printed on the subject, including 'Nelson: a sketch by one who served under the last of Nelson's captains'. A note in one of them indicates the date of composition: 'This letter has been made public to-day (21st May 1904).' (F.P. 4946; also 4945, 4947.)

retaliation Fisher was considering whether to hold back his reforms until a change of government (which was always a distinct possibility during 1904–5). He added:

4 days ago Selborne told a friend of mine (*you can imagine this is pretty secret*) that he was afraid of me and so was going to make certain appointments to anticipate anything I might be up to! In fact, to checkmate me, *and he has done it . . .*

Treat your enemy as if he was one day going to be your dearest friend, and your friends as if your bitterest enemy (Solomon).[1]

Lewis Beaumont, writing to Noel on 26 June, provides some support for Fisher's account: 'Drury tells me that Lord Selborne, he believes, is not so very keen about *new* schemes as he was and that the Cabinet are setting their face against expenditure at the rate of the last few years.'[2]

This throws some light on Selborne's references, in his memorandum of 14 May, to some of the listed possible reforms having received 'great attention' from Lord Walter Kerr who had brought them 'nearer and nearer to solution or perfection'.[3] The First Lord's intention was, presumably, to impress on Fisher that he should work within the guide-lines indicated in the memorandum. There was certainly no likelihood of Lord Walter embarking on a crusade of reform. While he scrupulously avoided reference to Fisher and his schemes, he described his post as 'this unpleasant job'.[4] On 22 September his view was similar: 'The ceaseless worries and bothers tell on one in time and at this moment I welcome the prospect of freedom from them.'[5]

Before getting down seriously to the herculean task of drafting his schemes in some detail, Fisher made further efforts to persuade the government to reappraise 'the Indian Frontier Bogey and the 100,000 men wanted', to cut the Army at once by 60,000 men, and thus 'get nearly threepence off the income tax'. Unable to sleep, he addressed these injunctions to Sandars at 4 a.m. on 29 July. Obviously, he would soon have to finalize his proposals for the Navy. If nothing drastic could be done about the Army, he would have to work within the limits prescribed by Selborne.[6]

---

[1] *F.G.* i, 316. This undated letter and the foregoing one of 17 May are in Esher Papers 10/41.

[2] N.M.M., NOE/5.   [3] N.R.S. *F.P.* i, xvii.

[4] N.M.M., NOE/5, Kerr to Noel, 10 June 1904.   [5] Ibid.

[6] Add. MSS. 49710, ff. 150–2 (*F.G.* iii, 23); also 49710, f. 141, F. to Sandars, 10 June: 'That damned North West frontier of India is what your Master is suffering from! For God's sake ask him to drop it!' See also *F.G.* i, 318 and 320–1.

The fact that Fisher did not welcome a cut in the Navy Estimates is illustrated, in a minor key, by his concurrent request that his salary as First Sea Lord should be raised by £800! In a letter of 11 September to Esher—the first of many to be signed 'Yours till death'—he summed up the case which he had been pressing: 'As I want to entertain my brother officers as First Sea Lord, I asked for my pay, as a special case personal to me, to be made up to £3,400 a year on account of my giving up an appointment of £4,000 a year to suit them.'[1] Selborne did not welcome such an exception to the rule, but—apparently without Fisher's knowledge—he did raise the matter with Balfour early in June.[2] Selborne having subsequently conveyed to Fisher the objections of the Treasury, Fisher replied on 8 July 'it would be an immense advantage if I could freely entertain my brother officers of all ranks to the same extent I do here and did in the Mediterranean.' He added: 'There seem to me also some other cogent reasons peculiar to myself, but I really don't like to urge them.' After Selborne left the Admiralty in 1905, Fisher revived his plea and Balfour eventually accepted it.[3] However, by October 1904 Fisher had been somewhat mollified by being appointed the King's principal A.D.C., a position carrying £365 a year as well as 'giving access to the King at any time'.[4]

An interesting feature of Fisher's correspondence with Esher during the summer is his reiterated conviction that he would be better placed with the Liberals in power. He had been in touch with Haldane for some time, particularly since early 1903.[5] After a visit from the future War Secretary, he wrote to him on 3 May 1904 in the following highly confidential terms:

. . . So I ask you to keep all to yourself, or at the very most disclose and discuss in the most secret terms with the other two friends you named, but please don't ask me to be present or assist. The present Prime Minister has stood by me against 'all hands'! I could not even have the appearance of being in collusion with his political enemies.[6]

---

[1] *F.G.* i, 328.

[2] Add. MSS. 49708, f. 1, 3 June 1904.

[3] Add. MSS. 49711, ff. 60–3, F. to Selborne, 8 July 1904 (copy); f. 59, F. to Balfour, 26 July 1905; ff. 133–42, draft memo. by Balfour, 4 Dec. 1905.

[4] *F.G.* i, 328–9; ii, 66n.

[5] Searle, p. 229.

[6] F.P. 4933 (Admiralty House print). See also *F.G.* i, 314–15 for a slightly edited version without the addressee's name.

Fisher's selection as First Sea Lord was published on 20 June. By 20 August one of his erstwhile friends (Cyprian Bridge) was writing to another (Gerard Noel): 'I look with dismay upon the loss of W. Kerr's honesty and straightforwardness in a place where both are much wanted.'[1] Indeed, Fisher's deviousness has already been often enough remarked. But he himself was, at this creative stage, far from depressed! 'I've got the preamble of my new scheme ready!' he exulted to Esher on 28 July. With rare panache, the preamble began:

ORGANIZATION FOR WAR

'IF THE TRUMPET GIVE AN UNCERTAIN SOUND, WHO SHALL PREPARE HIMSELF TO THE BATTLE?'

(St. Paul, I Corinthians XIV, 8.)

The object of the following remarks is to make clear what has now to be done to organize and prepare for war.

What are the two great essentials?

I.   FIGHTING EFFICIENCY.

II.   INSTANT READINESS FOR WAR.

To get these two essentials an immense deal is involved! It is believed they can both be got with a great reduction in the Navy Estimates!

This reduction combined with a very great increase in the fighting efficiency of the Navy involves great changes and depends absolutely on one condition:—

THE SCHEME MUST BE ADOPTED AS A WHOLE!

Simply because all portions of it are absolutely essential—and it is all so interlaced that any tampering will be fatal!

The whole scheme must emerge next Christmas morning from the Board of Admiralty (as did the new scheme for the entry and training of officers and men) like Minerva from the head of Jupiter—fully developed, full grown, complete, and armed like Minerva against all objectors! and this is possible!

The country will acclaim it! the income-tax payer will worship it, and the Navy will growl at it! (they always do growl at first!)

BUT WE SHALL BE THIRTY PER CENT MORE FIT TO FIGHT AND MORE READY FOR WAR!

and in time when we get rid of our redundancies in useless ships and unnecessary men it will probably be 30 per cent cheaper!

---

[1] N.M.M., NOE/5.

Though foiled in his attempt to have the Army reduced, Fisher did not on that account fail to define—with an eye to future estimates—the relative importance of the two services: 'If the Navy is not supreme, no Army however large is of the slightest use. It's not *invasion* we have to fear if our Navy is beaten.

'IT'S STARVATION!'

He then proceeded to outline the major reforms which have become so well known: redistribution of the Fleet, the scrapping of impotent vessels, two-year commissions in conjunction with reorganized reserves and nucleus crews. He also announced a radical approach to ship-construction:

The New Navy to be absolutely restricted to four types of vessels being all that modern fighting necessitates.

   I.   Battleships of 15,900 tons. 21 knots speed.
  II.   Armoured Cruisers of 15,900 tons. 25 knots speed.
 III.   Destroyers of 750 tons, and 4-inch guns. 36 knots speed.
 IV.   Submarines of 350 tons. 14 knots surface speed.

Beside high speed, the main innovation indicated for the first two types of ship was the provision of uniform armament: '16 10-inch guns of a new type' for the battleships and sixteen 9·2-inch guns for the armoured cruisers. It was soon found that 36 knots was a technical impossibility in a destroyer of the prescribed small tonnage. Submarines of more than twice 350 tons would be needed for effective operational use in war. The implied proscription of all light cruisers was actually applied to all Fisher's building programmes until the matter was reconsidered in June 1907. However, such defects were not evident to the amateur Lord Esher who duly registered the likely effect of the printed version upon intelligent laymen and politicians by writing on 24 August: 'You have captured the first position, and of course you will win all along the line. I have never read anything better than the "Preamble". It is a new *gospel* and *magnificent!*'[1]

However, as indicated in the previous chapter, most of the scheme had been well matured and it is impressive in its

[1] F.P. 134. F.'s print, F.P. 4932, appears in edited form in *N.N.* i, 19–45. It should be emphasized that the date 'May 14, 1904', printed on the first and last of these pages (*N.N.* i, 19 and 45), is not the date of composition either of the original Admiralty House print (F.P. 4932) or therefore of its developed version in *N.N.* F. presumably inserted 'May 14, 1904' for dramatic effect; it was the date of Selborne's invitation to F. to succeed Kerr as First Sea Lord.

comprehensive nature. Nucleus crews had already been introduced as part of the personnel reforms of 1903.[1] The evolution
of Fisher's demand for fast, powerful battleships and armoured
cruisers has been traced through his Mediterranean period.
How far had these ideas on design undergone further development by August 1904?

Evidence of sustained investigation of this subject by Fisher
during the year ending in July 1904 seems to be totally lacking.
The one important new idea in the print of August 1904 appears
to be that of uniform armament—unless this was already comprised by Fisher's reference to 'equal gunfire all round' in his
letter of 28 January 1902 to Arnold White. No doubt, as suggested by Professor Marder, Fisher was influenced by recently
published expressions of opinion in its favour.[2] Cuniberti's
'Ideal Battleship' of 1903 may have impressed him. However, it
has just been seen that in the Admiralty House print Fisher
advocated 10-inch guns for the battleships, not Cuniberti's
12-inch.

The process of elaboration and amendment of Fisher's August
print by his unofficial staff of experts (Captains H. B. Jackson,
J. R. Jellicoe, R. H. Bacon, and C. E. Madden; also Commander
Wilfred Henderson and the civilians W. H. Gard and A. Gracie)
took place in September and October. Selborne meantime
agreed that these 'seven brains' (as Fisher called them) were to
be appointed to the Admiralty so that they could help Fisher to
implement the reforms. By the time that the scheme was printed
(soon after Fisher's arrival at the Admiralty, in *Naval Necessities*,
volume one, printed in November), he was wobbling between
the 10-inch and the 12-inch gun.[3] During November, he reached
a decision:

To sum up, we have the choice of three main armaments:—

(1) Mixed 12-in. and 9·2-in.
(2) All 9·2-in. or 10-in.
(3) All 12-in.

Of these, unhesitatingly, all 12-in. guns is the armament for a
modern battleship.[4]

[1] F.P. 4729, 'First Progress Report' (P. 6/03), p. 65.
[2] *Anatomy*, p. 527.   [3] *N.N.* i, 43.
[4] *N.N.* i, 61. The text of *N.N.*, vol. i, and of the *Report of the Committee on Designs,
1905* is conveniently available (though without printing dates) in N.R.S. *Fisher
Papers*, vol. i, ed. P. K. Kemp.

Fisher became First Sea Lord on 20 October. Almost at once, he was involved in the Dogger Bank crisis which nearly precipitated war between Britain and Russia. This raised the question of naval distribution. Therefore, before proceeding with a narrative of Fisher's share in the crisis, it will be appropriate to clarify the ideas on redistribution with which he returned to the Admiralty on 20 October 1904.

For unofficial and secret assistance in preparing his scheme of redistribution, Fisher depended upon his capable ally Rear-Admiral Prince Louis of Battenberg who had succeeded Custance as D.N.I. in November 1902.[1] In February 1902 Fisher had recommended the Mediterranean-based scheme described in the previous chapter.[2] The scheme printed in November 1904 in the first volume of *Naval Necessities* is strikingly similar. There are to be only five fleets:

I.   The Home Fleet, with its strategic centre at Dover.
II.   The Atlantic Fleet, with its strategic centre at Gibraltar.
III. The Mediterranean Fleet, with its strategic centre at Alexandria.
IV.   The Western Fleet, with its strategic centre at the Cape.
V.   The Eastern Fleet, with its strategic centre at Singapore.

The Home Fleet is to have only eight battleships, as before; the Atlantic Fleet will have the eight battleships previously allocated to the Channel Fleet (now replaced by the Atlantic Fleet); the Mediterranean Fleet, which still has twelve battleships—a legacy of Fisher's agitation of 1901—will send some of them home 'consequent on the Atlantic Fleet having its *pied à terre* at Gibraltar.'[3]

On 10 November Battenberg, assisted by Fisher's five aforementioned naval 'brains', defined the reduction of the Mediterranean Fleet. Four of its twelve battleships, according to Battenberg's committee, should go home. The distribution of battleships (which was accepted by Fisher) would then be:

(a) Twelve in home waters.
(b) Eight in Mediterranean.
(c) Eight in detached fleet between these.[4]

Where, then, was the concentration in 'the North Sea' which historians have so often credited to Fisher's appointment as First Sea Lord?

---

[1] F.P. 1674, F. to Lady F., 9 Sept. 1904; F.P. 136, Battenberg to F., 8 Oct. 1904.
[2] See pp. 260-5 above.   [3] *N.N.* i, 215.   [4] *N.N.* ii, 463.

It is clearly necessary to revert to the subject of Fisher's attitude to 'the German menace' which was carried, in the last chapter, up to the time of his return to the Admiralty as Second Sea Lord.

Although he had devoted a good deal of thought to redistribution during his Mediterranean command, Fisher had no particular flair for strategy and he was preoccupied substantially by other interests between February 1902 and October 1904. However, in September 1902 Arnold-Forster (then Parliamentary Secretary of the Admiralty) compiled his 'Notes on a Visit to Wilhelmshaven, August 1902, and General Remarks on the German Navy and Naval Establishments'. Like previous observers, Arnold-Forster was impressed by the efficiency of the German Navy. He therefore called in question the current dispersion of British naval power between Gibraltar and the Far East; and he also doubted the superiority of British battleship-armament over German. He pointed to the need for a British east coast base to prevent German raids. Lord Walter Kerr (so recently badgered by Fisher to send more ships to the Mediterranean) would not admit any immediate need for an anti-German redisposition. Custance's views on the subject have already been quoted.[1] Fisher wrote no minutes on Arnold-Forster's 'Notes' but his interest in them is indicated in an attached letter from Arnold-Forster to Selborne, dated 13 October. The Secretary here attributes his decision to print his paper to Fisher's persuasion.[2]

There is little evidence that Fisher's interest in the German Navy resulted in any consecutive thought on the strategic implications. As in the case of the (still distant) submarine menace, he almost certainly believed that a general drive for efficiency and readiness would suffice to cope with the Germans. A letter which he wrote in August 1904 to Lord Knollys (private secretary to the King and a dependable friend of Fisher's) illustrates this approach: *'Vast changes are indispensable for fighting efficiency and for instant readiness for war. We have neither at present! And we have got to be ruthless, relentless, and remorseless in our reforms! Otherwise, we may as well pack up and hand over to the Germans! France is the one country we have got to be friends with!'*[3]

---

[1] See pp. 237–8 above.

[2] Add. MSS. 50287. The 'Notes' were printed on 18 Oct. 1902 (34 pp.).

[3] *F.G.* i, 327.

Certainly, until Fisher derived some anti-German impulses from the Dogger Bank crisis, it may be assumed that the redistribution scheme, as originally printed in November, was deemed to provide against any combination of enemies seriously envisaged up to the time of the Admiral's advent as First Sea Lord.

It now remains to give an account of his return and of his role in the Dogger Bank crisis. He spent September and the first half of October recuperating on the continent. For reasons unknown he arrived in London and took over as First Sea Lord on 20 October instead of on the 21st as he had previously intended. Because his official residence at 16, Queen Anne's Gate was not ready for occupation, he went to live at the Charing Cross Hotel. On 22 October the Russian Baltic Fleet, bound for the Far East, mistook some Hull trawlers fishing on the Dogger Bank for Japanese torpedo-boats and opened fire. For a matter of two weeks war with Russia seemed likely. This might well entail also war with Russia's ally and Britain's *entente* partner, France.

Battenberg later compiled the following account of how Fisher, though confined to his bed, seized the opportunities offered to him during the crisis:

His great scheme of Peace Organisation of the Fleet, which he had worked out at Malta, was now ready. As former Head of the Mobilizing Division I had worked at it with him . . . The scheme divided the fleet in Home waters in three main groups:—

1. Fully manned ships (the best and newest of all classes).
2. Nucleus-crew-ships (second best).
3. Reserve ships (old ships) . . .

Now to make this effective it was imperative to have more officers and men at home. These could only be procured by reducing the number of ships on foreign stations, composed of the famous class that 'could neither fight nor run away'. Fortune favoured Lord Fisher: on the day that he took his seat on the Board[1] was fought the second 'Battle of Doggerbank' between the Russian Fleet and the Hull Fishing Fleet. Arrived at Whitehall with the Influenza in him, he promptly returned to his room at the Charing Cross Hotel, went to bed and sent for me. He charged me to tell the First Lord that I was to represent him in all the troubles that now arose and gave me full instructions, that is up to the meagre information at hand. I had to attend the Cabinet meetings and conferences at the Foreign Office, etc. 'War with Russia' was the popular cry. A few days later Lord

---

[1] Actually two days after this.

Fisher dictated to me the following telegram to all C. in C.'s and S.N.O.s on foreign stations:

'War with Russia is imminent. Concentrate your fleet at Station Headquarters. Pay off immediately, all standing, the following ships (here followed the names of all the sloops and gunboats). Send home by first packet and wire date of arrival in England.'

By the time these parties arrived home we had enough officers and men for the scheme which was put into execution. It was on this brilliant scheme that the Fleet was first manned under the Test Mobilisation of July 1914,[1] and then went into the war. After the Russian imbroglio had been settled the C. in C.s, at regular intervals, sent plaintive telegrams asking when these crews of paid-off ships might be expected back again . . . No replies were ever sent . . .[2]

Although written many years after the event, this account—coming from an officer so intimately concerned—seems entirely convincing. In his August print of 1904, Fisher paid lip-service to the connexion between redistribution and strategy; but his principal aim was to eliminate useless (and costly) vessels and at the same time strengthen the home-based reserves. In any event, what advantage would have been offered by a specifically anti-German redeployment in 1904 when there was, with the Russo–Japanese War and the Anglo–Japanese Alliance, more likelihood of war with Russia, and perhaps France, than with Germany? Not only did the Russian possibility become something more in October 1904; as late as April 1905 war against Russia and France was threatened when the French in Indo-China offorded more assistance to the Russian Baltic Fleet than was agreeable to the Japanese.

On the other hand, Fisher did become personally more hostile towards Germany during the Dogger Bank crisis. 'Things look very serious', he wrote to his wife on 28 October. 'It's really the Germans behind it all.' And again (in pencil and undated): 'The German Emperor is up to mischief but we are all ready for him.[3] In fact, Germany had edged away from strict neutrality towards support of Russia at this time and the Kaiser had ordered his Navy to look out for any Japanese laying mines in the path of the Russian Baltic Fleet as it sailed for the East![4]

---

[1] Battenberg was himself First Sea Lord at that time.
[2] Kilv. MSS., envelope marked 'Chapter I', Marquess of Milford Haven (Battenberg) to 2nd Lord F., 25 Aug. 1921.
[3] Kilv. MSS., Pkt. 13.   [4] Steinberg, p. 32.

The Dogger Bank episode certainly brought Fisher's redistribution scheme under close scrutiny. On 7 November Battenberg wrote for Fisher the following memorandum:

The strength in battleships of the Home and Mediterranean Fleets now stands at 8 and 12 respectively. It is submitted that this should be reversed by transferring 4 battleships . . . from the Mediterranean to Home Fleet as soon as the present political tension is past. The reason is as follows.

Our war arrangements are primarily concerned with two combinations against us:

(a) Russia and Germany.
(b) Russia and France.

The latter was considered for some time as both the most formidable and the most probable. Events which are common knowledge make these two qualifications more applicable to case (a)—the rapid growth of the active battlefleet at Kiel being the chief cause . . . As the Kiel fleet is considerably stronger than the Toulon fleet, it follows that the Home Fleet should be considerably stronger than the Mediterranean Fleet . . .

Battenberg therefore recommended for the Home Fleet a mixture of the latest and the oldest battleships and for the Atlantic Fleet at Gibraltar '8 Majestics' as against the somewhat more modern '8 Formidables' for the Mediterranean Fleet. 'As soon as the political situation allows' the five 'China battleships' should be brought back, two of them going to the Home Fleet, and one each to the Atlantic and Mediterranean Fleets. Owing to the strengthening of the reserves effected by 'nucleus crews and two year commissions', the total numbers of fully manned battleships could be reduced from 33 to 32. The Atlantic Fleet should have joint manoeuvres with the Home Fleet as well as with the Mediterranean Fleet. The Home Fleet should 'cruise in North Sea and Scandinavian waters quite as much as in Irish Waters'.[1]

Fisher minuted: 'First Lord. This is a matter which has been carefully considered. Propose to approve.' On 9 November Selborne noted: 'I agree except that I would raise Mediterranean to ten again directly we can take the ships from China.'[2]

So this, then, may be taken as the beginning of the concentration in 'the North Sea' beloved of certain historians? Not so.

---

[1] F.P. 139 (the original paper).   [2] Ibid.

The view represented by Battenberg's memorandum of 7 November did not outlast a week. By 14 November, the situation had again been reconsidered. (In any case, it may be remarked, there was still no British base 'in the North Sea' other than Chatham; nor had the need to press ahead with Rosyth or some substitute been definitely recognized.) Now, it was decided to shift the focus of British naval power a thousand miles to the southward. This phase of Gibraltar-based strategy, which lasted for seven months without serious modification (and continued in an attenuated form at least until 1907), was thus explained by Battenberg on 14 November 1904:

The following are the reasons for which it is proposed to place the four 'King Edwards VII', ready next spring, into the Atlantic Fleet, rather than the Channel Fleet.

The Atlantic Fleet being the reinforcement of either of our main battle fleets in the north or in the south, according to where the principal enemy is located, both of these will get the benefit of specially powerful ships when they specially need them.

The Toulon Fleet will be considerably strengthened by the substitution of the three first 'Républiques' for three existing ships.

On the other hand, the large majority of the Kiel Fleet will, for some time to come, be weak in primary armament (9·4-in. v. 12-in.) ...

The reinforcing fleet would then be able to move in a body to the threatened flank at high speed, a great strategical advantage . . .[1]

But what of Fisher's own inclinations? Would he really have preferred to adhere to the principle of concentrating the best ships in the Channel, as proposed on 7 November? Fisher himself provides an answer. He notes in the margin of a print sent to Balfour in February 1905: 'The Gibraltar Fleet is the "germ" of the new scheme! We have rearranged it with our best and fastest battleships and cruisers and our best admirals . . . it is always instantly ready to turn the scale (at the highest speed of any fleet in the world) in the North Sea or the Mediterranean.'[2]

Certainly, as late as April 1905 Fisher was given solid reasons for being content with this flexible arrangement. With the Russian Baltic Fleet at the Indo-Chinese anchorage of Kamranh and Japanese tempers rising at the pro-Russian behaviour of the French, Fisher wrote to Balfour on 22 April:

The fact of the Russian Fleet sending their vessels out of the French harbour of Kamranh to search passing vessels, and utilizing that

[1] *N.N.* ii, 477–8.   [2] Add. MSS. 49710, f. 179.

harbour as they are for an indefinite time to perfect their fighting arrangements . . . seems the most flagrant and outrageous breach of neutrality possible to conceive! I suppose we have impressed all this on the French Government. Suppose the Japanese attack Roji in Kamranh Bay, as they are justified in doing. Will France fight Japan? If so, we fight France! What pickings for the German Emperor![1]

It may now pertinently be asked: how does Fisher's suggestion, late in 1904, of a preventive attack on the German Navy at Kiel, fit into the scheme of distribution described above? According to his own account, apparently contemporary, Fisher suggested such an attack to the King who replied: 'My God, Fisher, you must be mad!'[2] There can be no doubt at all that Fisher also addressed this proposition, in a convincingly serious manner, to the First Lord. On 26 December Selborne wrote to the Prime Minister, primarily to complain of Fisher's disinclination to make plans for the defence of Canada against the United States; but he continued revealingly: 'To tell you the truth this is another proof that Fisher's intellectual flaws are on the same great scale as his intellectual virtues. I told you his proposal about the German fleet at Kiel. It was no use of paradox nor said to shock. He meant it.'[3]

While he could conduct devious manoeuvres in a stealthy manner, Fisher was never much inclined to conceal his opinions. Therefore it is hardly surprising to find that he soon became widely known in Germany as the advocate of a 'Copenhagen' with Kiel as the target. The idea had already been popularized. As mentioned earlier, attacks 'à la Copenhagen' on incipient European navies had been aired in the British press in 1897–8.[4] Nor had the tolerant attitude of British newspapers to the Japanese attack on the Russian squadron at Port Arthur, before declaration of war, escaped notice in Germany. Indeed, it heightened the fears already tending to bedevil German foreign policy.[5] Fisher recorded his own views of the Port Arthur attack quite soon after the event. In a colourful letter of 20 April 1904 —designed to fire enthusiasm for submarines in the Controller, W. H. May—Fisher wrote:

It really makes me laugh to read of 'Admiral Togo's EIGHTH attack on Port Arthur'! Why! had he possessed submarines it would

[1] *F.G.* ii, 58; Monger, p. 192.   [2] *F.G.* ii, 20.
[3] Add. MSS. 49708, ff. 40–2.   [4] *Anatomy*, p. 313.
[5] Steinberg, pp. 30–1.

have been ONE attack and ONE attack only! It would have been all over with the whole Russian Fleet caught like rats in a trap! . . .

. . . How I hate pessimists! Shoot them at sight in war . . . Durnford[1] always gave me a stomach ache whenever I saw him, even a mile off! *Did he tell you?* . . . Not take the offensive? Good Lord! if our Admiral in the Mediterranean is worth his salt, he will tow his submarines at 18 knots speed from Malta to Toulon and put them into Toulon (like ferrets after rabbits!) before war is officially declared, just like the Japanese acted before the Russian Naval Officers knew that war was declared! All is fair in war! hitting in the belly or anywhere else! and the best declaration of war would be the sinking of the enemy's fleet! that's the first they ought to know of war![2]

If these were Fisher's views in the spring of 1904, it is difficult to dissociate him from an article published by Arnold White in the autumn, wherein he advocated a 'Copenhagen' to stop German naval construction. This and similar recommendations printed elsewhere in the British press led to expressions of concern from the German government.[3]

It emerges, therefore, that Fisher was almost certainly serious in suggesting a preventive attack on the German Navy. Why, then, did he agree to a Gibraltar-based distribution scheme at much the same time? Bearing in mind his above-quoted letter to the Controller on 20 April 1904, the answer is also indicated in some notes which he compiled for his successor in the Mediterranean in May 1902. While remarking on the increased strength of the Fleet, he emphasized that it was still short of cruisers and was not strong enough for 'immediate offensive action'. There was, he noted, 'no previous preparation whatever required for the first blow in a Naval war because there are enough vessels always at sea to permit this first blow to be struck without previous warning'. In other words, for the special purpose of a preventive attack, surprise was the pre-requisite rather than a redistribution of strength with its unavoidable publicity.[4]

Fisher's advocacy of an unheralded attack on Kiel illustrates his tendency to make wild judgements. While, in a sense, he 'meant it', it will be prudent to wait until his wartime conduct can be assessed before coming to a final verdict on this. The implication of the wartime evidence will be that he was capable of airing wild schemes with great force and show of conviction

---

[1] Recently Fourth Sea Lord.
[2] F.P. 4941 (printed at Ady. House, Portsmouth); mostly in *F.G.* i, 308–9.
[3] *Anatomy*, pp. 497–8.   [4] F.P. 4196, 'Notes for Successor'.

when, all the time, perhaps on a subconscious level, he doubted their practicality.

In terms of concrete achievement, there can be no doubt that the redistribution scheme enhanced British security at reduced expense.

Despite the fact that a good deal has already been published on the subject, something now has to be said about another feature of Fisher's innovations, namely the building of the *Dreadnought* and the *Invincible*.

In the case of the *Dreadnought*, much controversy has centred on the matter of timing. As long as Tirpitz was content to follow, with improvements, the best foreign designs, it certainly appears that the *Dreadnought*, by rendering obsolete the existing battle-ships in terms of which Britain held a great lead, did afford Germany an undreamt-of opportunity to draw level. However, this is to consider the matter only in the context of an Anglo–German competition. As has been shown above, Fisher set his heart on a revolutionary type of battleship when he was in the Mediterranean. As with his other reforms, he sought to raise efficiency without regard to any particular possible adversary. For the foreseeable future, doubtless, he expected Britain to build against France and Russia. In so far as the speed of construction in these two countries was markedly below that in Britain, no great danger was to be anticipated from a jump ahead. Even Custance, as he watched the early progress of Tirpitz's programme, does not seem to have stressed the danger that was to arise, not only from the technical excellence of German ship-building, but also from its comparative rapidity. One basic point fully appreciated by Fisher was, as he wrote to Selborne on 2 August 1904: 'Russia's naval decline permits us to wait a bit'—that is, before building new battleships.[1] Also, there was the economic angle which had been so prominent in Selborne's memorandum of 14 May. As Fisher observed, 'you will also see the enormous effect on next year's Estimates if, with solid ground for so doing, we mark time a little bit on new construction!'[2] Certainly, the period from October 1904 to May 1905 did bring to Britain the chance to relax in so far as she continued to build against the possible combinations named in Battenberg's memorandum of 7 November: Russia and Germany, or Russia and France. It was in January 1905 that Fisher's

[1] *F.G.* i, 321.   [2] Ibid.

Committee on Designs worked out the details of the *Dreadnought* and the *Invincible*.

Before passing on to consider some points of the designs, it may be of interest to mention that Fisher did have last-minute doubts as to the desirability of building any more battleships at all! These doubts were not occasioned by the considerations just reviewed nor do they seem to have stemmed from his recent preoccupation with submarines. In a section of his print of August 1904 (which is not reproduced in the November volume of *Naval Necessities!*) he suggests that 'fast torpedo craft' have outdated the 'battlefleet' principle and that 'battleships have no function that first class armoured cruisers cannot fulfil.'[1] However, he was apparently persuaded to abandon this extreme view between August and October.

What part, then, did Fisher play in the designing of his two revolutionary ships? With all his experience as Controller and his outstanding ability as a chairman, Fisher and his distinguished committee, which included Battenberg and all seven of the handpicked 'brains', did produce a battleship of such power that it could not be ignored by any country interested in that class of ship. However, it is something of a curiosity that Fisher does not seem to have expressed interest in what, according to Bacon, was the greatest advantage of uniform main armament. This was the ability to hit an adversary at long range by spotting salvoes of at least five shells. It is also very difficult to discover just when this method was first officially understood— even by Bacon![2] It was, of course, appreciated that, to keep outside the range of modern torpedoes, battleships would have to engage at 6,000 yards or more. The most advanced account of the connexion between uniformity of armament and range-finding seems to be in the 'First Addendum' to the Committee's report of February:

The advantage, therefore, at long range, lies with the ship which carries the greatest number of guns of the largest type; but additional advantage is gained by having a uniform armament.

A mixed armament necessitates separate control for each type; owing to a variety of causes the range passed to 12-in. guns is not the range that will suit the 9·2-in. or 6-in. guns, although the distance of

[1] F.P. 4932.
[2] Bacon, i, 251–2; *From 1900 Onward*, p. 99; *N.N.*, vol. i, and the *Report of the Committee on Designs, 1905* for a great deal of negative evidence.

the target is the same, and therefore the difficulties of control of fire increase directly with the number of types of guns in the armament.[1]

In his print of August 1904, Fisher expressed his own ideas thus:

Now—one word as to the uniform armament:—

If all the guns are of the same calibre the total amount of ammunition can be very largely reduced—there is also an immense advantage in having to provide spare articles and fittings for one type of gun instead of two or three—observe the immense advantage of interchangeability of parts. In action the carriage of one gun and the gun of another carriage being disabled, instead of disabling two units could rehabilitate one. It is a mistake also to employ valuable displacement in carrying more ammunition than will suffice for one engagement—a store-ship should be employed to replenish the ammunition like a collier does the fuel. You don't carry coal for a three year's commission![2]

In the first (November) volume of *Naval Necessities* this paragraph survives intact. It is the familiar argument for standardization, deployed at length by Fisher in his 'Gunnery' paper of early 1872 which was extensively quoted above. It typifies his constant attention to the perennial problem of limited resources. What he says is sound enough, as far as it goes; but it helps to define the limitations of his technical expertise. This paragraph may, from a different point of view, be borne in mind when examining his amphibious schemes. Fisher's argument shows that, as earlier in his career, he was unusually interested in problems of supply. If this was true up to August 1904, it is difficult to believe that, at least privately, he was unaware of the logistical implications of the amphibious projects for which he had plans prepared from 1905 to 1909. Yet these naval plans were notably weak on the logistical side.

However, while such blunders as placing the gunnery observation post abaft the funnel testify to hastiness in design, the *Dreadnought* with her ten 12-inch guns and her turbine propulsion made a profound impression once her details were released.

The *Invincible* was likewise a revolutionary ship. She, too, impelled the other naval powers to follow suit. In the case of the *Invincible* and her successors there was an important element of confusion for which Fisher must bear the chief responsibility.

---

[1] F.P. 4706, *Report of the Committee on Designs*, p. 21.   [2] F.P. 4932.

This confusion related not to the details of the design taken in isolation, but to the role for which the ship was constructed. Fisher's verdict, in a Mediterranean lecture, has already been noticed, namely that the armoured cruiser was 'a swift battleship in disguise'.[1] The same confusion has also been seen in the print of August 1904: 'battleships have no function that first class armoured cruisers cannot fulfil.'[2] Yet the same print (or rather collection of prints) comprises at the same time a conflicting principle, thus expressed by Fisher: 'All are agreed that battleships are required, and that their characteristic features, distinguishing them from armoured cruisers, are more powerful guns and more armour. The armoured cruiser somewhat foregoes these to get speed.'[3]

This conclusion accorded with the technical realities of the time and to a large extent it did prevail. Yet the confusion about the role of the armoured cruiser was never entirely eliminated. However, from the point of view of design Fisher (in August 1904) recommended 25 knots for the armoured cruiser against 20 knots for the battleship (upgraded to $25\frac{1}{2}$ knots against 21 knots by November).

In the Great War, the 'battle cruiser' proved a spectacular success in its commerce-protecting role and, as will be seen, Fisher deserves credit not only for the design of ships for this purpose but also for a major share in their operational orders at the crucial time. But how did these large cruisers come to occupy a role in the Grand Fleet not sufficiently distinguished from that of battleships? In retrospect it is clear that the armament selected at the outset for these ships would strongly influence the use made of them in a major battle. In the case of the armoured cruiser (as in that of the battleship) Fisher's sixteen guns for the main armament were soon reduced in number to avoid excessive blast, but there was a dispute over the vital question of the calibre. In August 1904 Fisher had envisaged 9·2-inch guns. Bacon (who was, of course, intimately involved in the proceedings of the Committee on Designs) subsequently wrote with regard to the *Invincible*:

The battle over the armament was a severe one; but the day was carried by the argument that the gun should be of the same calibre as that of the battleship, so that the cruisers could be used in a fleet action as a fast auxiliary squadron . . . The speed and armament

---

[1] See p. 270 above.   [2] F.P. 4932.   [3] F.P. 4932; also *N.N.* i, 36.

having been fixed, a medium armour protection only could be afforded to the battle cruisers without exceeding a reasonable tonnage.[1]

In the context of the Battle of Jutland, this 'medium armour protection' was tested with markedly unhappy results. Inadequate anti-flash arrangements are often—clearly with reason—blamed for the loss of two out of the three battle cruisers sunk. However, it is also beyond dispute that the protective armour of their decks and turrets was penetrated by German shells, whereas the German battle cruisers, having sacrificed a small margin of speed for heavier protection, came off better. (Admittedly, the subject is much complicated by the inferiority of the British armour-piercing shell at Jutland.)

But reverting to the argument in the Committee of Designs, it seems fair to attribute to the dominant Fisher the main responsibility for the conclusion reached about the armament and the role of the *Invincible*. During 1905 he reiterated the idea that there would probably be a 'fusion' of the battleship and armoured cruiser in a single design. Incidentally, it was quite true that, until an effective counter to the *Invincible* was designed abroad, 'no existing battleship could safely encounter her at the long ranges at which her superior speed would enable her to impose an action.'[2] However, this situation did not last long. The *Invincible*, completed in March 1909, could overawe existing battleships until the German dreadnoughts began to come into service towards the end of 1909!

In the Cawdor Memorandum of November 1905 the expression 'large armoured ships' comprised battleships and large cruisers alike[3] and in October 1906 the Admiralty began to classify all post-*Dreadnought* battleships and armoured cruisers indiscriminately as 'capital ships':

For the sake of simplicity we need only consider the 'capital ships' building and in contemplation (the very phrase indicates the new era, as we can no longer draw a hard and fast line between battleships and armoured cruisers). It is on the capital ship that the command of the sea depends . . . The 'Invincibles' are, as a matter of fact, perfectly

---

[1] *From 1900 Onward*, p. 101.

[2] F.P. 4709, *Report of Navy Estimates Committee*, 16 Nov. 1905, p. 14. See also F.P. 4750, 'Proposals respecting designs of the new vessels to be laid down in 1906–7' (P. 1/06), and a print headed 'Saturday, 2nd December 1905' in *N.N.*, vol. iv, at the Naval Library.

[3] *N.N.* iii, 371.

fit to be in line of battle with the battlefleet, and could more correctly be described as battleships which, thanks to their speed, can drive anything afloat off the seas . . .[1]

Another blanket term comprising both battleships and armoured cruisers was 'Dreadnoughts'. Fisher himself used it when writing to the King on 4 October 1907: 'England has 7 Dreadnoughts and 3 *"Invincibles"* (in my opinion better than dreadnoughts),—total—10 Dreadnoughts built and building, *while Germany in March last* had not begun one!'[2]

This completes the discussion of Fisher's principal innovations in the Navy. Before proceeding to deal with the impact on Admiralty policy of the first Moroccan crisis, recourse may be had to Bacon, who was Fisher's Naval Assistant from October 1904 to December 1905, for an impression of the Admiral's physical presence at this time:

> Fisher was of medium height and square of build, with very round, wide-open eyes, which fixed the gaze and compelled attention. His general expression was slightly supercilious, which, however, was constantly changing during conversation to a flickering smile, for an undercurrent of humour always pervaded his general talk . . . he listened to the thrust in controversy; then would come the sudden flash of animation, then the riposte, the flood of argument, the Biblical quotation punctuated by gesture and hammer-blows of the fist on the hand; and in the end the talk invariably ended with a smile on the face of all who had been listening to him.[3]

Bacon, who also worked close to Fisher in 1907–9 as D.N.O., afterwards wrote that the Admiral was probably 'at the zenith of his faculties in 1905–6'. However, it is not easy, on the basis of the evidence now available, to accept this whole-heartedly. It will be seen that, even during Fisher's recall period (1914–15) when he was aged 73–4 there is not much sign of a deterioration in his 'faculties'. His mental capabilities—with their usual defects—seem to have remained constant to a remarkable degree. Vitality was, after all, Fisher's most obvious characteristic. But this is not to say there was no deterioration. This will be evident more on the side of character than of intellect—overweening

---

[1] F.P. 4720, *Admiralty Policy: Replies to Criticisms* (P. 10/06), pp. 10–12. See *Records*, pp. 98–109, for a reprint of some of the document, together with F.'s italics of 1919. Even then, he evidently believed that the *Invincibles* 'could more correctly be described as battleships'.

[2] *F.G.* ii, 140.   [3] Bacon, i, 245–6.

3. Fisher as First Sea Lord

pride which tended to erode self-criticism and even, occasionally, self-control.

It was during 1905, after the Committee on Designs had completed its work, that the Navy first began to be prepared and disposed unambiguously for a possible war with Germany. The Germans, unduly apprehensive about the implications of the Anglo–French *entente*, came to the fateful decision to try to break it by pressing the French in Morocco. (According to the published terms of the *entente*, Britain promised diplomatic support for French policy in Morocco in return for similar support from France in Egypt.) The British had always been concerned about the possibility of a rival power developing a base near the western exit of the Mediterranean; and by April 1905 Lord Lansdowne, the Foreign Secretary, believed that the Germans were about to ask for a coaling station in Morocco as compensation for increasing French domination over that country. Louis Mallet, a member of the 'anti-German' group at the Foreign Office, consulted Fisher on Lansdowne's behalf to ascertain the Admiralty's view of a German demand for a port, for example Mogador. Mallet wrote privately to Sir Francis Bertie (British ambassador in Paris) about his interview with Fisher. The First Sea Lord declared: 'of course the Germans will ask for Mogador and I shall tell Lord L. that if they do we must *at least* have Tangier—of course it is all rot and it would not matter to us whether the Germans got Mogador or not but I'm going to say so all the same.' Mallet commented: 'He is a splendid chap and simply longs to have a go at Germany.'[1]

Fisher wasted no time in translating his words into action. On 22 April he wrote to Lansdowne:

> Without any question the Germans would like a port on the coast of Morocco, and without doubt whatever such a port possessed by them would be vitally detrimental to us from the naval point of view and ought to be made a *casus belli, unless we get Tangier* . . . This seems a golden opportunity for fighting the Germans in alliance with the French, so I earnestly hope you may be able to bring this about . . . We could have the German Fleet, the Kiel Canal, and Schleswig-Holstein within a fortnight.[2]

This was a somewhat bold initiative, for Fisher was otherwise occupied on that very day in writing to the Prime Minister about

---

[1] Monger, p. 189.   [2] *F.G.* ii, 55.

the danger of war with Russia and France on account of the Kamranh crisis! Balfour and Lansdowne for their part remained calm. However, the Moroccan crisis persisted. For this reason and also because of a sudden development in the Far East, the month of June saw a revolution in the basis of British naval strategy.

Captain C. L. Ottley succeeded Battenberg as D.N.I. in February 1905. On 1 May he wrote to Fisher that, some months earlier, 'nobody believed that the Baltic Fleet in its present strength would ever arrive East of Singapore.' But, he continued, 'the unexpected has happened' and a 'superior Russian Fleet is moving northward to attack Japan in the Far East'. By early June, however, the outlook had changed radically. Owing to the news of Togo's great victory at Tsushima on 28 May, Ottley now observed: 'A naval victory, crushing and decisive, such as that which has just been won in the Straits of Tsushima, must clearly exert its influence, not merely upon the immediate fortunes of the two belligerent Powers, but upon the naval policy of all other nations.'[1]

Early June also saw high tension between Britain and France on the one hand and Germany on the other. It was consequently decided that the five British battleships should now be withdrawn from the China station and the battleship strength of the Fleets in European waters should be increased as follows: Channel from 12 to 15; Atlantic from 8 to 9; Mediterranean from 8 to 9. From now onwards the distribution of the fleets became more perceptibly anti-German; but it is far from clear that, at the time, this was seen as an irreversible process. In the Cawdor Memorandum of 30 November 1905, the Admiralty stated publicly that 'the kaleidoscopic nature of international relations, as well as variations or new developments in Seapower, not only forbids any permanent allocation of numbers, but in fact points the necessity for periodic redistribution of ships between our Fleets to meet the political requirements of the moment.'[2] Even after the Algeciras Conference had begun to re-cement and strengthen the *entente*, the Admiralty argued in a 'Very Secret' document of 15 February 1906:

The Board of Admiralty, as the responsible naval advisers of the Government cannot base their plans upon the shifting sands of any temporary and unofficial international relationship. Highly as we

---

[1] *N.N.* ii, 154.   [2] *N.N.* iii, 370.

may value the *entente cordiale* we cannot but remember that similar attempts to bring together peoples whose interests have not always and through the centuries been identical, have, as a matter of history, not hitherto been uniformly successful . . . *Ententes* may vanish— battleships remain the surest pledges this country can give for the continued peace of the world.[1]

The fact remains that an anti-German redeployment had begun in June—a virtually inevitable result of Morocco and Tsushima. From then on, the policy was not reversed. A sense of smooth progression has encouraged some to draw the false conclusion that a deliberate anti-German redeployment can be traced back to 1904 and Fisher's advent as First Sea Lord. If, however, one moves forward as far as 8 November 1905, Fisher himself is to be found explaining to the Navy Estimates Committee:

Everybody could see that, owing to political circumstances, the tendency was to reduce our strength in the Mediterranean and at Gibraltar, and good reasons existed for carrying out this policy. Heads of Departments must bear in mind from this incident that at Gibraltar and Malta things were not so much needed now as formerly; the tendency being to increase the Channel Fleet and everything at home, and all this tended to economy. Four years ago there were 15 battleships in the Mediterranean Fleet and only six battleships in the Channel Fleet. Now there are 17 battleships in the Channel Fleet and only eight battleships in the Mediterranean, and that number is really unnecessarily large . . . [2]

Naturally, the effects of Tsushima are to be seen not only in policy on distribution but also in the sphere of construction. Already, addressing the same Estimates Committee on 20 July 1905, Fisher had stated that a position had been reached 'when there was no hurry for ships in any way; in this respect matters were in a very satisfactory state.'[3] What with the *Dreadnought* expected to come into service by January 1907, the naval situation seemed unusually favourable. But what of strategic planning?

When the redistribution of late 1904 was put in motion, the Channel Fleet (previously called the Home Fleet) was commanded by Sir Arthur Wilson. The Admiralty then decided to

---

[1] F.P. 4715, *The Building Programme of the British Navy*, 15 Feb. 1906 (P. 6/06), p. 9.
[2] F.P. 4709, *Report of Navy Estimates Committee*, 16 Nov. 1905 (P. 1/06), p. 43.
[3] Ibid., p. 38.

place in his hands 'the entire conduct of operations, including the plan of campaign and the disposition of the forces in home waters'.[1] This singular development testifies to the strength of Fisher's regard for Wilson, not only as a seagoing admiral, but also as a strategist. The fact that Fisher adhered to the latter opinion—that Wilson was a good strategist—until at least 1911 is a sufficient measure of his own defects in this sphere. On 24 June 1905 Fisher asked Ottley to report on the dispositions needed if Britain became involved 'in support of France'. The D.N.I. replied that the Admiralty would have little to do other than call home the Atlantic Fleet and order Wilson to commence hostilities! However, Wilson's activities would comprise commercial blockade and the Admiralty would have to consider carefully the handling of neutrals.

Wilson was duly alerted on 26 June and asked to indicate his plans. On the 27th he replied that British naval action alone would do nothing to relieve France; 'the result would depend entirely on the military operations on the French frontier and we should be bound to devote the whole military forces of the country to endeavour to create a diversion on the coast of Germany in France's favour.' He thus raised the outstanding contentious issue relating to British grand strategy in a great European war. What was the correct role of the British Army in a war against Germany where France was Britain's ally? Wilson argued:

In order to make an effective diversion we should be obliged to expose our ships in the Baltic or on the German coast in a way that would not be necessary if we were at war with Germany alone, but under present conditions, with France on our side, this is a risk that can be accepted.

The operations that it is possible to undertake against Germany are very largely dependent on the attitude to be taken by the neighbouring nations, Belgium, Holland, Denmark, Sweden, Norway, and Russia . . . Supposing all the above Powers to be neutral, the course that seems to me most worthy of consideration would be an attempt to capture the Works at the mouths of the Elbe and Weser by a combined military and naval expedition . . . As the main object would be to draw off troops from the French frontier, simultaneous attacks would have to be made at as many different points as possible . . . If Denmark were on our side, a very effective diversion might be made

<hr />

[1] *Anatomy*, p. 503.

by assisting her to recover Schleswig and Holstein, including the port of Kiel . . . it is only by putting forth the whole military strength of the Empire that we can hope to succeed.[1]

Wilson, whose ideas tended to be inflexible, adhered to this strategic approach, despite cogent arguments to the contrary, up to his term of office as First Sea Lord (1910–11) and even beyond. Under twentieth-century conditions, the amphibious projects were becoming ever less realistic, but it is interesting to note that Wilson did appreciate the scale of effort required. It was 'only by putting forth the whole military strength of the Empire' that Britain could exert material influence on the course of a great European war.

In furtherance of his amphibious schemes, Wilson pointed out the need for interservice planning. He also recommended that small vessels recently withdrawn from foreign stations should be made ready to participate (instead of being scrapped); also that old battleships should be prepared to bombard forts and that shallow-draught vessels should be earmarked for landing troops.[2]

Wilson's proposals agreed very well with Fisher's ideas about the amphibious role of the Army. Ottley supported Wilson's advocacy of joint planning and he suggested that the C.I.D. should appoint a 'Sub-Committee on Over-sea Expeditions'.[3] Fisher took up the idea at once and placed it before the Prime Minister.[4] Meanwhile, the Army had begun to consider a variety of what became known as 'continental' as opposed to 'maritime' strategy. This arose from the possibility that the Germans, in a war with France, would try to outflank the defences on the Franco–German frontier by invading Belgium. In August Sir George Clarke, now Secretary of the C.I.D., persuaded Balfour to ask the War Office to prepare a paper on the subject, including possible British support of the Belgians with two Army Corps or the equivalent.[5] The D.M.O.'s report of late September duly noted the need for Admiralty co-operation to effect speedy delivery of the troops to Belgium.[6] But what was Fisher's reaction to these developments?

---

[1] *Anatomy*, pp. 502–5.   [2] Ibid., p. 505.   [3] Ibid., pp. 506–7.
[4] Add. MSS. 49711, ff. 64–9, 'Formation of a Permanent Sub-Committee of the Committee of Imperial Defence to Consider and Elaborate Schemes of Joint Naval and Military Expeditions' (P. 7/05).
[5] Williamson, pp. 46–8.   [6] Ibid., p. 48.

At a meeting of the C.I.D. on 20 July the Prime Minister explained the need for a sub-committee 'to consider and prepare such schemes for joint naval and military operations as might be found practicable or desirable'. Fisher did his best to further the idea by suggesting that 'the Admiral and the General who would probably be selected for the chief commands of the naval and military portions of such expeditions should be associated with the Sub-Committee.' It was agreed that such a sub-committee was 'most desirable'.[1] No doubt Fisher learned by early October of the D.M.O.'s report on direct intervention in Belgium. On the 10th, the Admiral sent to Sandars a memorandum entitled 'The Elaboration of Combined Naval and Military Preparation for War', by which he hoped to entrench a maritime approach to strategy in the mind of the Prime Minister, and thus the C.I.D. He argued that the new sub-committee should adhere to the following procedure:

A digest was to be made out in the first place of the various existing schemes, stating the extent to which they had been already elaborated, and from this a short statement was to be prepared for the Prime Minister, giving a summary of such of the operations as seemed feasible against each Power or combination of Powers. In preparing this statement the main point was to be borne in mind—often emphasized by the Prime Minister himself—that under no circumstances was it contemplated that Great Britain could or would undertake single-handed a great military continental war, and that every project for offensive hostilities was to be subsidiary to the action of the Fleet, such as the occupation of isolated colonial possessions of the enemy, or the assistance of an ally by threatening descent on the hostile coast, or otherwise effecting a diversion on his behalf.

Fisher pencilled against the key passage relating to 'the assistance of an ally by threatening descent on a hostile coast': 'I don't think the P.M. or Lord Lansdowne know anything about this!'[2]

Balfour and his ailing government were hardly in a frame of mind to adjudicate between the advocates of a maritime and of a continental strategy at that time. They were not yet used to the idea that Germany was the only possible enemy of note and continued to think in the old imperial and world-wide terms. However, it seems desirable to attempt some analysis of the merits of the two schools before proceeding further with Fisher's conduct of naval affairs.

[1] Cab. 2/1, 76th meeting.   [2] Add. MSS. 49711, ff. 120–4.

Ever since the Great War, there has been a disposition on the part of some writers to criticize Britain's adoption (or acceptance?) of a continental rather than a maritime strategy against Germany. To some commentators the appeal of Britain's amphibious tradition—a favourite theme with Fisher—has proved seductive. For them, the fact that Britain suffered—in terms of her own insular history—exceptionally heavy casualties suggests that a mistaken course was chosen. Whereas in the wars against the Spanish, the Dutch, and the French, she had relied on sea power and conserved her scanty population, landing troops unexpectedly on an enemy shore where they exerted extraordinary leverage in proportion to their numbers, Britain in the Great War turned her back on her glorious past. Instead, she squandered her precious manpower, battling with continental conscripts in a quagmire stained with blood. Other writers argue that British strategy was dictated by the particular circumstances of the case. As an alternative to direct support of the French, the British Army could attempt to land somewhere on the coasts of Germany. In terms of the relevant geography, the available warlike techniques, the preparations of the enemy, the military power and efficiency of that enemy, and especially his overland transport facilities, the prospect was very discouraging. Just as Britain possessed great geographical advantages from the point of view of a distant blockade of Germany, so Germany was exceptionally well placed to defeat any expedition to her shores. In retrospect it certainly appears that—until aircraft had been developed to the stage where they could paralyse the means of overland transportation—a good railway system, together with strong military reserves and developed coastal defences, presented an obstacle which was better left alone. Modern telecommunications enhanced the advantages conferred on Germany by her short North Sea coastline. On the naval side, too, the prospects for a British amphibious attack continued to worsen. Not only did the High Seas Fleet gradually emerge as a formidable rival to the British battlefleet. Always great mining experts, the Germans in due course acquired submarines—large, effective ones.

It should not, however, be inferred that the British Army never tried to explore the maritime alternative to direct intervention in Belgium or France. At the end of August 1905 Colonel C. E. Callwell of the D.M.O.'s department struck up a correspondence with G. A. Ballard, Assistant D.N.I., about the possibility of a landing on the Baltic coast of Schleswig-Holstein. At the War Office Callwell minuted on 29 August for a departmental colleague: 'I think you should carefully consider the problem of the German Baltic coast . . . It will probably be the first thing considered by the Sub Comte of the C.I.D. when the holidays are over.' Action was taken in the first instance by Major D. Fasson who, in two pages of typescript, produced an impressive summary of the objections to the project. He covered this account with a note for one of his colleagues, Adrian Grant Duff: 'I send you a few rough notes on Fisher's invasion of Germany! I supposed in the present stage "detailed information" is not required.'

However, detailed information was in due course collected and it was conveyed by Callwell to Ballard on 3 October. Whatever the superficial attractions of a Baltic expedition, it could only be concluded from the relevant facts that such a project was impracticable.[1]

It is a remarkable fact that, from this time, Fisher tended to avoid further joint examination of the amphibious schemes. He carried this negative attitude, in the course of the next year or so, to the point almost of a naval boycott of the C.I.D. Presumably, he believed that he could personally convince the leading politicians and the King of the validity of his views; but it will be seen at length that he may have realized, perhaps not definitely admitting it to himself, that the Army's objections could not be defeated by rational argument. However, this is not to say that he did not engage in some very lively exchanges with the soldiers in the C.I.D., especially during the sessions of the Sub-Committee on Invasion of 1907-8. But this is a subject for the next chapter.

Within the Navy, too, Fisher steered into troubled waters by reviving, during 1905, the issue of interchangeability. This would have to be settled in practice when the Cadets who had joined Osborne in 1903 reached the age of 20 in 1910. The following item printed in 1905 represents one of Fisher's less

---

[1] The D.M.O.'s correspondence and materials are in W.O. 106/46 (file E2.10) and the D.N.I.'s documents are in Adm. 116/1043B. See also Williamson, pp. 48-52, and *D.S.* i, 383-6. N.W. Summerton's thesis, 'The Development of British Military Planning for a War against Germany 1904-1914', shows convincingly that the War Office examined the amphibious projects more thoroughly and realistically than did the naval planners.

accurate prophecies: 'It is absolutely safe to predict that the Naval Officer of 50 years hence will smile when he reads that his forefathers had to have an officer of Commander's rank appointed to a ship solely for charge of the main engines.'[1]

By a curious coincidence, 1955 did see the triumph of the parity of esteem implied by the common entry. Branches were abolished and Engineers once again unstitched the distinctive purple stripes which had been reinstated in 1925; but there was no one to smile at the notion of a specialist 'Chief' in charge of a ship's engines.

However, it is fair to say that, by the autumn of 1905, Fisher had carried into effect an impressive array of reforms. Sir Frederick Ponsonby, an assistant private secretary to King Edward, records: 'I asked Sir John Fisher when he did his best work, and he told me that he invariably got up at 5.30 a.m. when he was First Sea Lord and worked uninterruptedly from 6 to 9 a.m. He had a large breakfast and nothing in the middle of the day but a glass of lemonade and a biscuit.'[2]

The following communications originating from the King, then staying at Chatsworth, speak for themselves: Telegram of Thursday, 5 January 1905:

No excuse for not coming here Saturday to Monday is admissible the King considers it a command   Equerry   Please acknowledge

Note written by the King at Chatsworth on Sunday, 8 January:

Admiral Sir John Fisher is to do *no* work on *Sundays* nor go near Admiralty, nor is he to allow *any* of his subordinates to work on Sundays.

By command

Edward R[3]

Fisher appears to have reached Chatsworth (in Derbyshire) on the Sunday. The tempo of his mental activity during this brief interlude, to say nothing of his interest in political effect and public relations, declare themselves in the following telegram which he sent from Chatsworth to Walter Nicholson, his private secretary at the Admiralty, at 9 a.m. on Monday, 9 January:

Arrange for Prince Louis and Bacon to meet me at one forty on arrival at Admiralty and prepare following information for Prime

---

[1] *N.N.* ii, 208.   [2] Ponsonby, p. 328.   [3] F.P. 142-3.

Minister first numbers and types of all vessels paid off under present scheme second numbers and types of more powerful vessels substituted third numbers and types of all I think 114 new vessels commissioned with nucleus crews fourth numbers of battleships and cruisers for emergency squadron fifth numbers and types of all ineffective vessels removed from fighting strength as of no practical value sixth corresponding enormous financial future saving in not having heavy repairs of non-effective ships seventh statement of harbour accommodation for 108 battleships and cruisers now available through towing away of obsolete vessels and hence millions prospectively arranged for in making new berthing accommodation entirely obviated saving millions eighth new strategic distribution of the fleet naming the fleets and squadrons in a brief precis ninth any other effective brief graphic information suitable for Prime Minister for his proposed speech ask Prince Louis to telephone Sandars Downing St to fix Prince Louis to see Prime Minister immediately to explain all these details better than I can . . . brief statement of advantage of only one vessel of a squadron being absent from [for?] repair instead of whole squadrons being hors de combat at same time.

Sir John Fisher   Chatsworth.[1]

Amongst Fisher's reforms not yet mentioned were improvements relating to the lower deck. These will be treated in the next chapter. Now something more should be said about a sphere of activity mentioned in the telegram from Chatsworth, namely the dockyards.

It could be claimed that Fisher's enhancement of Britain's capacity for swift construction was one of his greatest achievements. Particularly in the situation created by the building of the *Dreadnought*, where the trident would quickly pass to any great naval power able to complete such ships more rapidly than Britain, celerity was an indispensable requirement. There is no sign that Fisher anticipated the severity of the shipbuilding challenge about to be mounted by Germany. Fortunately, however, he in any case aimed at rapid construction as conducive to 'a great increase of fighting efficiency'.[2] Quick building was also integral to the pursuit of 'vast economies'.[3] In a print entitled 'A Year's Work, Oct. 21, 1904—Oct. 21, 1905', the matter is summarized under the heading 'Drastic Dockyard developments': 'Rapid shipbuilding (consequently less dockyard accommodation needed in ships, basins, and docks).'[4]

[1] F.P. 144.   [2] *N.N.* i, 29.   [3] Ibid.
[4] F.P. 4854, 'Navy Reforms: A Summary' (P. 12/07), p. 54; also *N.N.* iii, 7.

Rationalization and economy provided cardinal themes:

> But see what this redistribution of the Fleet and ruthless riddance of ineffective ships and men led to.
>
> Our congested harbours and inadequate dockyards became at once more than sufficient for our needs, and 13 millions sterling in prospective or approved works (bricks and mortar) were cancelled, and in association with the policy of rapid ship-building vast economies became feasible in dockyard administration and requirements.[1]

This statement throws much light on the failure to develop a first-class naval base and dockyard on the North Sea coast of Scotland during Fisher's term of office. A dockyard at Rosyth was sanctioned in 1903 in response to public alarm about the emergent German Navy. However, Selborne indicated to Fisher in his important memorandum of 14 May 1904 that Rosyth was no longer considered an immediate necessity.[2] Apart from what has just been said about the naval dockyards, Fisher aimed also at having more ships built in private yards. The naval yards would then concentrate on repairs and a further economy could be effected by cutting the numbers of dockyard workmen. In October 1904, therefore, Fisher urged: '*Don't spend another penny on "Rosyth"!*' This elicited a protest from Selborne: 'I shall have much to say about Rosyth and Chatham. A group of considerations are omitted here altogether, strategical in respect of the German menace, war dockings and repairs at Chatham, and others.'[3] Although details are apparently unavailable, it is clear that Fisher was successful in resisting Selborne's arguments.

In connexion with Fisher's plan to reduce the dockyard personnel, it should be mentioned that Beresford took part in the early discussions at the Admiralty concerning Fisher's proposed reforms. Lord Charles was given a copy of *Naval Necessities*, volume i, so that he could indicate his reactions. He strongly queried Fisher's views on Rosyth. His eye was also caught by the First Sea Lord's declaration that reform of the dockyards 'ought to be accompanied by the disfranchisement of the Dockyard workmen, whose political interference is a great public scandal, and is utterly subversive of economy and efficiency in the Dockyards'. These sentiments fired the enthusiasm of the Earl

---

[1] F.P. 4854, p. 2.   [2] N.R.S., *F.P.* i, xx.   [3] *N.N.* i, 29.

of Selborne: 'This would be a great reform. It should apply to all public servants.' The 'aristocrat' Beresford conveyed his opinion of this anachronistic suggestion in a single word: 'Impossible.'[1]

On ship design, also, Lord Charles showed some good judgement, disliking the tendency to blur the distinction between battleships and armoured cruisers.[2]

Over a period of years Fisher persisted in restricting expenditure on Rosyth which was in most respects suited to development as a first-class base for a war with Germany. The consequences were serious. To quote Professor Marder, when the Great War began 'the base situation was shocking.' Rosyth and the secondary base at Cromarty 'were quite open to submarine attack' and the 'construction of the dockyard at Rosyth had only just begun.' As for Scapa Flow, it was 'an unprotected war anchorage with no provision for fleet repair and maintenance work', let alone anti-submarine defences.[3] A second consideration besides economy began to influence Fisher against the North Sea bases during his term of office. He came to believe that no means would be found of safeguarding the bases against penetration by submarines. In the next chapter his submarine paper of 1909 will be examined and found enlightening. As for his reference to 'that beastly bridge' across the Firth of Forth, it is hard to say whether this was more of a cover or a real objection.

Relevant to the question of Rosyth and much else is the general impression, conveyed by the mass of prints concerning the reforms of 1904–5, that Fisher's mind was then governed by purely administrative considerations. Having observed with sustained indignation, during his long naval career, countless instances of avoidable waste and costly obsolescence, he gloried in the opportunity to sweep the stables clean and concentrate expenditure on what he saw as the sinews of war. The ships were to be powerful and the crews instantly ready. He thought much less intensively about strategy and its implications. The following extract from the proceedings of the Naval Establishments Enquiry Committee, with Fisher's pencilled marginalia and underlining, conveys much of the essence of his approach to the reforms of 1904–5:

[1] F.P. 4705, p. 29.
[2] F.P. 4218.
[3] D.S. i, 426.

This very secret

Preliminary Meeting at Admiralty on
Friday, 12th May 1905.

The Committee met this day at the Admiralty, all the Heads of the various Departments of the Admiralty being present or represented at the meeting.

This verbatim report by shorthand writer of my remarks & not corrected
J.F.

Sir John Fisher said they all knew that the Committee had been formed for the purpose of investigating the whole question of the condition, organisation, and administration of the different Naval Establishments on shore. It was a corollary to what had already been done in regard to the Navy afloat. It had been arranged that every vessel that was intended to fight should have a nucleus crew on board, and that she should be fully stored and armed and in every respect ready to go out to sea instantly, the time being limited only by the time it would take to raise steam. *So far as the afloat work was concerned all these fighting vessels*

If I die will you kindly note to put this on my tomb stone!

were quite ready to go out to sea and fight a battle at a couple of hours' notice. A recent careful inspection by the First Sea Lord had elicited the fact that the vessels themselves were at the highest point of fighting and seagoing efficiency, and it was desired to bring to the same state of efficiency everything associated with the ships, that is, the building, the repairing, the storing, and the equipment generally, so that all our vessels should be built in the shortest possible time, equipped in the shortest possible time, and the stores and everything arranged in the most efficient manner possible. The first object to be attained must be efficiency at all costs. But if that efficiency could be associated with economy, so much the better. Such was the scope of the inquiry which had to be made by this Committee.[1]

Fisher's thinking about the Admiralty's directive role in war was epitomized in a note of March 1905 intended for Balfour: 'All your fighting ships must be ready to fight and fight instantly! *Our frontier is the coast of the enemy* and we've got to be there the instant or even before war is declared!'[2]

---

[1] F.P. 4743, 'Naval Establishments Enquiry Committee', p. 1 (P. 5/05). Also *N.N.* ii, 104–16.

[2] Add. MSS. 49710, ff. 186–7.

A rather similar philosophy was supposed largely to solve the problem of trade protection: 'the first duty of British fleets and squadrons will be to seek out the corresponding fleets and squadrons of the enemy with a view to bringing them to action and fighting for that which is the only really decisive factor—the command of the sea.'[1]

Selborne appears to have seen the need for rather more strategic thought and preparation than was provided by Fisher. The following comment, which he made five weeks after retiring as First Lord, also suggests that he was more conscious of the requirements of a prolonged naval effort in wartime:

Dear Sir John,

I have carefully read your memorandum of 12th May in connexion with the Naval Establishments Enquiry Committee.

Generally I cordially agree with the principles laid down and sentiments expressed. I would only add one note of warning. There are certain classes of stores which cannot be improvised on the outbreak of war nor procured from the trade, except after much lapse of time and even then not with regularity. The Elgin Commission found this to be the fact in respect of Army Stores. Much more is it true of Navy Stores? Of all such stores therefore I say let the Navy herself keep a large and over large reserve. Neither do I think that six months' supply gives enough margin of war stores generally . . .[2]

Fisher undoubtedly retained a measure of respect for Selborne. He regretted the news, at the end of February, of the First Lord's impending appointment as High Commissioner in South Africa.[3] The situation at the Admiralty also caught the attention of a former First Lord who knew Fisher well, namely Lord Goschen. On 4 March the veteran statesman wrote to Balfour:

I am wondering (with much anxiety) whom you will send to the Admiralty. The boldest plan would be to make Fisher a peer, and First Lord, not unconstitutional, but, I fully admit, a course open to many objections.

But it is equally, perhaps more objectionable to have the First Sea Lord practically a dictator, and the First Lord subordinate to him in fact . . . Besides his own intellectual equipment, perfect knowledge and powers of plausible presentation of his views, Fisher has the whole

---

[1] Adm. 116/886B, 'The Protection of Ocean Trade in War Time', mins. of Ady. meeting, 30 Apr. 1905.
[2] F.P. 177, 3 July 1905.   [3] *F.G.* ii, 52.

press at his back, and *the King is in his pocket*. I thought even Selborne's position was often made very uncomfortable.

The Navy would dislike the appointment but there is much to be said for it, especially as I don't see the strong man whom you have got to send to the Admiralty . . . you will gather from the very fact of my having put forward the idea, how anxious I am lest the position of the civilian First Lord should become intolerable to anyone who wishes to have a soul of his own under existing circumstances.[1]

On the previous day Fisher had indicated to the Prime Minister his dislike of Walter Long as a prospective First Lord—'better not to marry than have the inevitable divorce afterwards'.[2] On the 6th, however, he looked with favour on an alternative: 'Beloved Sandars! *I am overjoyed about Lord Cawdor*'.[3] Cawdor, though able, was dogged by ill health during his short term as First Lord—March to December 1905. This left Fisher virtually in sole charge at the Admiralty during the tense mid-summer period of the Moroccan crisis and Goschen expressed his anxiety on this score to the Prime Minister.[4] Selborne also intimated a degree of mistrust from Johannesburg in a letter to Balfour of 11 August:

I hear privately that Fisher, in the most lamentable absence of Cawdor, is preparing a theatrical coup for the abolition of the Coast Guard and of the Royal Naval Reserve . . . I would without hesitation part with Fisher rather than the Royal Naval Reserve . . . I know my Fisher, and unless you are very careful he will in Cawdor's absence so hocus matters that you will one day find yourself confronted with a chose jugée, unless you are very wary.[5]

What with Cawdor's absences and the death-throes of the Conservative government, December arrived without a definite decision on Fisher's future. The need for a decision arose from the fact that, on 25 January 1906, he would reach the age of 65. Unless he was specially promoted (in the absence of a normal vacancy) to Admiral of the Fleet, he would then have to retire from the post of First Sea Lord.

In November a parliamentary paper subsequently known as the Cawdor Memorandum was prepared.[6] This consisted of

---

[1] Add. MSS. 49706, ff. 306–7.   [2] *F.G.* ii, 53.
[3] Add. MSS. 49710, f. 205.
[4] Add. MSS. 49706, ff. 308–9, 14 July 1905.
[5] Add. MSS. 49708, ff. 85–7.
[6] 'A Statement on Admiralty Policy', Cd. 2791, issued on 4 Dec. 1905. Reprinted in *N.N.* iii, 365–403.

(1) a 'Memorandum on Admiralty Work and Progress' and (2) 'Notes on Some of the Principal Reforms Undertaken by the Admiralty, 1903-1905'. The main items have all been mentioned above. Unfortunately, the subject of interchangeability was included. This public revival, which did much to provide a basis for dissension in the Navy, comprised the statement that 'there will be no need for a final division into the three branches, and that specialization for a period only is necessary'. Otherwise, a section on 'Shipbuilding Policy' merits citation. It goes some way towards a definition of Fisher's brand of genius:

Before deciding on the building policy of the present year, an accurate review of our naval position as regards other Powers had to be made.

It must be remembered that however formidable foreign shipbuilding programmes may appear on paper, we can always overtake them in consequence of our resources and our power of rapid construction.

Rapid shipbuilding is of great importance, because:—

(a) The fighting vessel is sooner tested, so that improvements suggested by experience may be effected, and defects may be brought to notice in time to be avoided in succeeding vessels. Thus, it is most desirable to complete the first ship of a new class with all possible despatch.[1]

(b) It is obviously more conducive to the immediate fighting power of the fleet to push forward a limited number of vessels to completion than to spend the same money on a larger number building at a slower rate.

(c) There is the financial benefit of sooner getting interest on capital by having vessels at sea ready to fight instead of partly completed and not ready to fight, even if the number of the latter is much greater.

(d) It is economical to run all the shipbuilding machinery at its full ordinary rate of output. There is a constant gain in building more rapidly up to the point when men begin to be too closely packed to work without hindering each other, or at which excessive overtime and high rates of pay are involved.

---

[1] In fact, the following were the dates of laying down the various leading battleships of the classes started by Fisher, together with the time taken to complete them: *Dreadnought* Oct. 1905, 14 months; *Bellerophon* Dec. 1906, 26 months; *St. Vincent* Dec. 1907, 16 months; *Colossus* July 1909, 24 months. The average time taken to complete the ten battleships of these classes was just under two years. Between 1889 and 1905, the average time for completing a battleship had been 39 months in Britain, about the same in Germany, 5 years in France, and 5½ years in Russia.

(e) An immediate result of building at, say, twice the usual rate would be that only one-half as many ships would be under construction at any one time. There will be needed, therefore, for building purposes, proportionately less slip, dock, and basin accommodation.[1]

Current 'strategic requirements' were for 'an output of four large armoured ships annually', each ship to be built in two years. The Board considered that they should 'make out their programme of shipbuilding for the next year only'; 'there would be no difficulty in increasing this output' to meet intensified foreign competition.[2]

Another document emanating from Fisher's particular flair and expertise was the *Report of Navy Estimates Committee*, completed on 16 November 1905 and amounting to sixty-five pages of print. This followed, in much more detail, the precedent already set by Fisher the previous November when, despite his other preoccupations, he headed a small committee which cross-examined all departmental heads and rigorously pruned any expenditure not proved essential for 'the fighting efficiency of the Fleet and its instant readiness for war'.[3] Even the distant memory of these investigations continued to fill him with delight, as is shown by the following account falling from the machine of a hard-pressed typist to whom Fisher dictated various memoirs in 1919:

President of Committee to revise Navy Estimates. I had everybody who was responsible [for] a shilling in expenditure before me. I said to the Committee 'Gentlemen, look here, I am going to ask the questions, if anybody else wants to ask questions they must pass them up to me.

I took £10,000 at a time. 'Whichever of you is the head of the department which is responsible for that £10,000, you must have your fellows ready to come into this room.'

When I got him in front of me, I would say 'Prove to me (I knew, of course, he could not prove it) prove to *me* (not to the Committee—I was damned autocratic and damned offensive, I know) prove to me that that £10,000 administers to the fighting efficiency of the fleet and its instant readiness for war.'

There was one instance—the palings round the coast guard cottages. 'In what way do these palings, with the green paint,

---

[1] Cd. 2791.   [2] Ibid.
[3] F.P. 4709, *Report* of 16 Nov. 1905 on the Navy Estimates for 1906–7; F.P. 4736, 'Navy Estimates, 1905–6' (P. 11/04), 9 pp.

administer to the fighting efficiency of the fleet and its instant readiness for war? Now,' I said, 'look here, those palings are to keep people off the coast guard's cabbages and potatoes. I know green paint is nice to look at, nature made things green to be pleasing to the eye—but you will find no green in my eye. In future the coastguards must put up their own palings and buy their own paint.'

Then there were the glass tumblers. It was supposed to be infra dig. for anyone to have the same kind of tumbler as somebody else. So I ordered one kind of tumbler—the cheapest tumbler that could be obtained—and said, 'If they don't like it they must buy their own.'

I went through that £34,000,000. It was a herculean task . . .[1]

Thanks to these extraordinary exertions—against the indispensable background of Russian defeats—the seemingly inexorable rise in successive Navy Estimates was not only halted, but reversed. The following figures show the extent of this reversal:

1903–4	£34,457,000
1904–5	36,889,000
1905–6	33,389,000
1906–7	31,869,500

In view of his unique administrative and financial services to the Navy, not to mention the offers of outside employment rejected by him, it is understandable that Fisher should have revived the question of his remuneration as First Sea Lord. First, in March 1905 he dropped hints of further offers from private industry—'about £20,000 a year'. These brought no official response, apart from an O.M.[2] Nor did a letter to the Prime Minister, dated 26 July, have any tangible effect.[3]

On 29 October Cawdor wrote to Balfour to remind him that Fisher, as an Admiral, was due to retire on 25 January 1906:

Two things seem to me to be clear—viz.

I.   that it is desirable to continue Sir John in his present position.

II.   that it is undesirable to interfere with the rules as to age limit.

The only way to continue Sir John as 1st Sea Lord is to appoint him, by Order in Council, an Admiral of the Fleet. . . If you concur, I will approach the Chancellor of the Exchequer and the King.[4]

---

[1] F.P. 5174. See F.P. 5286 for F. dictating memoirs, etc.

[2] *F.G.* ii, 53 and n.; Lee, ii, 330. He had, incidentally, been awarded a G.C.B. in June 1902.

[3] Add. MSS. 49711, f. 59, F. to Balfour.

[4] Add. MSS. 49709, ff. 8–9.

However, the beginning of December arrived without the promotion having been effected; and on 3 December, when he was on the point of resigning as Prime Minister, Balfour reported to the First Lord an extraordinary interview which had that morning taken place between his personal secretary, W. M. Short, and the First Sea Lord. Fisher had called at 10 Downing Street when the Prime Minister—who habitually did much of his paper work in bed—was still dressing. The Admiral told Short that he had been offered a 'commercial post' at £10,000 a year and wanted to know whether Balfour thought he should take it. Fisher added that he believed he would be able to get into parliament as 'an independent member'. As such, he intended 'to "go" at the Government on Navy matters'.

> Mr. Short rather conjectured that he meant to come in as a 'free-lance'. But this is by no means so easy an operation as perhaps he thinks . . . He appears to have spoken with the utmost contempt of *all* politicians now connected with the Admiralty—from the highest even unto the lowest. It is an extraordinary situation . . . J.F. has got a story that Charlie Beresford is quite ready to take a *Radical* seat in order to obtain the opportunity of pitching into the Board of Admiralty.

How, Balfour wondered, should he reply if 'our friend' again asked for advice?[1]

Balfour resigned as Prime Minister on the next day, 4 December. Fisher's commission as an Admiral of the Fleet seems to have been held up till the last moment. Cawdor and Drury, the Second Sea Lord, signed it that day, as did the King.[2] Also, Cawdor wrote in reply to Balfour on 4 December:

> The point raised in your letter of yesterday is a very difficult one and difficult to express an opinion upon, especially as we have not got the decision as to what would happen if J.F. were to go.
> In some ways he has possibly done his work at the Admiralty—and I believe done invaluable service—but
>
> I.   What would be the effect just now if he went? Would it not be considered a victory on the part of Charlie B?
> II. Who would be put in J.F.'s place?
>
> It would need a *very* good, strong, sensible man—not necessarily a genius of the J.F. type—but still a man who would command public confidence, and who could pull the Navy together—and such a man

---

[1] Add. MSS. 49709, ff. 41-6.   [2] F.P. 188.

to succeed J.F. would be very difficult to find—but you do not ask for an answer now, and I will keep turning the matter over before we meet . . .[1]

In more than one respect, this was a perceptive appraisal. From January 1906 until his retirement in January 1910 Fisher would impart drive to naval administration and minimize 'parasites', much as before; but there would be no record of constructive reform comparable with the achievements of the first fourteen months of his term in office. Rather, the seeds of disruption, already noticed by Cawdor, would flourish. In the Selborne Memorandum of 1902 a 'lifelong community of sentiment' had been named as one of the main objects of the educational reforms. From 1906 to 1909 the service was so much riven by dissension as to resemble something of a jungle—where head-hunting was not unknown!

Conceivably, if Beresford could have brought his insubordinate tendencies under firmer control during his later career, he might have been considered as a successor to Fisher in January 1906. With his superior ability to use a staff, he would almost certainly have given the Navy the general staff which it badly needed to complete Fisher's principal reforms. However, a few months before hoisting his flag, in June 1905, as Commander-in-Chief of the attenuated Mediterranean Fleet, Beresford apparently clashed with Fisher at the Admiralty. Fisher wished him to serve on one of his committees. Beresford objected to his command of the Atlantic Fleet being foreshortened for this purpose. According to King-Hall's account:

Fisher replied: 'Well, then, you will not go to the Mediterranean', upon which the pent-up wrath of the years between the two men broke out, and Beresford said: 'You dare to threaten me, Jacky Fisher. Who are you? I only take my orders from the Board. If I have to haul my flag down on the 7th February, I will resign the Service, go down to Birmingham, get into the House and turn out both you and Selborne . . .' More words passed, the result being that Beresford had his way, but I shall be surprised if Fisher does not play some trick on him, and pay him out in some way or other.[2]

While this story lacks corroboration, it fits the known facts of the Fisher–Beresford relationship.

[1] Add. MSS. 49709, ff. 21–2, dated 5 Dec., presumably in error—see text: 'yesterday'.
[2] King-Hall, p. 326; diary for 3 Mar. 1905, recording information from Rear-Admiral C. J. Barlow.

Howbeit, 4 December 1905 saw Fisher's position consolidated by his promotion. On the same day, his last in office, Balfour compiled a balanced memorandum on the subject of Fisher's remuneration. In characteristic Balfourian terms, it assesses the First Sea Lord's achievement since October 1904:

The point raised by Sir John Fisher in the memorandum which I have just received from him is one of great interest. But as I am now holding office only until my successor be appointed, I do not feel justified in doing more than set forth the main principles which, it seems to me, will have to be considered by the Treasury before coming to a final conclusion on Sir John's appeal.

There are two quite distinct lines of argument on which he relies in support of the contention that the salary of the First Sea Lord should be increased; the first depending on general grounds, the second personal to himself. On the general grounds I do not now propose to say anything . . . The argument based on *personal* claims stands, however, somewhat outside the ordinary routine of Treasury practice, and I may permit myself of offer some observations on it.

What this part of Sir John's argument really comes to is that he should receive special consideration, *not* on account of the services rendered outside the ordinary functions of his office, but on account of the exceptional manner in which those functions have, in his particular case, been performed. Now, undoubtedly, such a claim runs counter to accepted practice. According to that practice a scale of salary is fixed for the said officer by the Treasury, and by Parliament, which is supposed to be, on the average, adequate for the services rendered by the person occupying it. If the official is *below* the average in efficiency, he is, on this system, *over*-paid: if he be *over* the average, he is *under*-paid. But the variations on either side of this line are not normally supposed to be of sufficient magnitude to create serious injustice in individual cases.

What will now have to be considered is whether, in Sir John Fisher's case, this deviation from the normal has not been so great as to give him a legitimate claim to special treatment; and whether, even if this be so, the inconvenience of departing from established rules is not so great they should not at all costs be adhered to.

For my own part, I can only say that if ever a case for running this risk existed, it exists in the case of Sir John Fisher. I have been in the closest touch with the Admiralty since he became First Sea Lord, and I have discussed with him many of the schemes which the Board of Admiralty have since carried into effect, even before he belonged to it. The policy begun by Lord Selborne, and carried on by Lord Cawdor, has been a revolutionary one; and if the revolution be beneficent (as I am confident that it is), there can be no doubt that the part played by Sir John Fisher differs not in degree only, but in kind, from that of the majority of First Sea Lords. This, of course, does not mean that the latter have fallen short of their duty; we do not want revolutions every five years. But it *does* so happen that at the very moment when the changed conditions of naval sea-power rendered administrative revolution necessary, in Sir John Fisher was found a man of genius peculiarly fitted to aid in its execution. The Admiralty claim that they have reduced expenditure—which is important—and greatly increased the fighting efficiency of the Fleet—which is still more important. I believe both claims to be well-founded; and whether the man who has enabled the Government to carry through a change so great and so useful should not receive some special treatment is a question which, I think, cannot be lightly dismissed . . . The difficulties in the way are great; they may be insuperable; but it must not be forgotten that if we, as a country, insist on paying much less than its market value for exceptional capacity, we cannot complain if we occasionally lose it at the moment when we want it most.[1]

The Conservative leaders had feared for the future of the country's armed services once Campbell-Bannerman became Prime Minister (which he did on 5 December). The crushing victory achieved by the Liberals in the general elections of January 1906 did nothing to lighten the Conservatives' sense of impending doom. However, what with Fisher's own radical proclivities, it comes as no surprise to find him claiming in his memoirs to have struck up a very friendly relationship with Campbell-Bannerman during visits to Marienbad.[2] It is certainly the case that the change of government was not to Fisher's immediate disadvantage. The new Board of Admiralty, headed by Lord Tweedmouth, soon formulated a proposal 'to apply for an Order in Council to raise the half-pay of Admiral of the Fleet Sir John Fisher, First Sea Lord of the Admiralty, to £2,000 a year as an acknowledgement to him personally of exceptional and special service, this special rate to continue to be paid to him after retirement'. The Treasury replied on 30 December 1905, readily assenting. This meant that Fisher would now receive the following emoluments: £2,000 in half-pay (instead of £1,222); a salary of £1,500 as First Sea Lord, together with a furnished house (16, Queen Anne's Gate); and £365 as Principal Naval Aide-de-Camp, which brought the total to £3,865. The Lords of the Treasury observed that 'it is not intended that this increase of half-pay should be granted to every

---

[1] Add. MSS. 49711, ff. 133–42.   [2] *Records*, p. 31.

First Sea Lord who attains during his tenure of office the rank of Admiral of the Fleet, but only that the Admiralty should have the power to recommend such increase in acknowledgement of exceptional and special service as has been rendered by Sir John Fisher.'[1]

[1] F.P. 193 (copy); see also *F.G.* ii, 66 and n.

CHAPTER 8

THE YEARS OF DISSENSION
(1906–1910)

THE issue of British grand strategy in an Anglo–French conflict with Germany came to the fore at the end of 1905. The circumstances were unusual and interesting. International tension was mounting ahead of the Algeciras Conference where the future of Morocco was due to be settled. The French sought reassurance from Sir Edward Grey, the new Foreign Secretary, that the Liberal government intended to uphold the *entente* against German pressure. On 20 December 1905 Paul Cambon, the French ambassador, received a fair degree of reassurance. Meanwhile Clarke, feeling 'derelict' without Balfour at the head of the C.I.D., was uneasy about the preparedness of the services. Hitherto, the War Office had been the main object of his criticism. But on 8 December he wrote to the late Prime Minister:

> I do not wonder that naval and military opinion often tries you by its variety and inconsequence. Few men in these two services learn to think, or to set out reasons for a policy in logical form. As their ideas are often based upon nothing more solid than crude impressions, a few searching questions may completely upset them. The Admiralty just now is much too prone to assertions which may be only rough guesses, and even when it is right it is apt to overstate a case. I often miss Prince Louis's cool view of things.[1]

On the 14th Clarke questioned Ottley about naval preparedness. The D.N.I. said he would consult Fisher and see Clarke again the next day.[2] On the 15th Clarke reported the result to Esher:

> Ottley tells me that the Admiralty studies go no further than the mobilization of the reserve fleet, and bringing up the Atlantic fleet in certain circumstances. The Naval C's in C have their war orders, which tell them what ships will go to them. Arrangements are made for mobilizing signal stations along the coast. This is practically all that has been done and it is not nearly enough. The system under

---

[1] Add. MSS. 49702, ff. 190–1.
[2] Esher Papers 10/37, Clarke to E., 14 Dec.

which the supreme direction passes wholly to Wilson, who has not only to fight, but to make all arrangements for protecting commerce if necessary, is I hold quite unsound . . .

The questions:

Whether our Channel fleet could go to the Baltic early in war— a great advantage to the French if practicable, which I doubt.

Whether a landing in Schleswig Holstein is practicable. (I think not.)

Whether a landing in Denmark could be made (I think it could) if Denmark were involved. (The position of Denmark would be very difficult if we were to operate in the Baltic.)

What proposals for joint naval action should be made to the French.

Whether we should proceed at once to lay blockade mines at the mouth of the Elbe.

The above and other questions which I suggested have not been thought out at all. The fact is that Admiralty need a G.S. quite as much as W.O. and there is nothing of the sort. Ottley promised to speak to J.F.; but there are not enough men to study these things.[1]

In the same letter, Clarke referred to questions which he had put to the War Office staff in September. As previously mentioned, he had for long supported the amphibious approach to grand strategy. However, in the particular context of a German invasion of Belgium he showed no disposition to condemn out of hand the General Staff's plans: 'The G.S. (as you will see) think that 2 Army Corps could be landed in Belgium by the 23rd day from mobilization. By this time decisive battles might have been fought on the frontier.'

The politicians were at this time much distracted by the forthcoming general elections and Clarke, though lacking constitutional powers, felt responsible for making advance preparations to meet a surprise move by Germany. He convened at the C.I.D. offices on 19 December the first of four informal meetings. On this first occasion, he was joined by Esher, Ottley, and General Sir John French, commander of the regular troops at Aldershot.[2]

Ottley's participation, obviously, was known to Fisher. Perhaps by design, the membership of the C.I.D. group was restricted to those who tended to favour an amphibious strategy. The most notable absentee was the D.M.O., Major-General

[1] Ibid., 15 Dec.
[2] For accounts of these meetings and the inception of the Anglo–French military talks, see Williamson, Ch. 3, and Monger, Ch. 9.

J. M. Grierson, who privately informed the French military attaché on 20 December that the Admiralty's Schleswig-Holstein plan was 'ridiculous'.[1]

On 19 December the group agreed that a fleet might go to the Baltic in order to threaten the German coast; and it was supposed that 100,000 British and 100,000 French troops might land there. However, it was recognized that such an expedition could not at once be launched on the outbreak of war. It therefore unavoidably followed that direct co-operation with the Belgians or the French was a possibility requiring further investigation.

Colonel Repington, the military correspondent of *The Times*, now came into the picture as an intermediary. On 5 January Clarke and Esher gave him a list of questions to pass on to Huguet (the French military attaché) and thus the French General Staff. Sooner or later Britain would have to recognize that France would be an indispensable partner in land warfare against Germany; therefore, the French reply to Clarke's questions was of fundamental importance to the evolution of British strategy. Predictably, the French General Staff wished the British troops to support the French Army as soon as possible after the outbreak of war. Naval strategy could be left to the British Admiralty. With regard to amphibious possibilities Clarke inquired: 'What is the French opinion concerning landings on the German coast? If we could send 100,000 men for such an operation and assisted France with transports, could she supply another 100,000 men, and in what time and at what ports?' To this the French replied: 'Considering the probable numerical superiority of the Germans, this kind of operation at the beginning of the campaign seems "très délicate", and should presumably be tried only in exceptional circumstances.'[2]

Meanwhile, on 6 January Clarke, Esher, Ottley, and French again met in informal conference at the C.I.D. offices. Ottley brought with him a scheme for the transport of the British troops to the continent. Even without the replies of the French General Staff (which did not reach England till the 11th) the group agreed that a landing on the German coast was 'impractical'; immediate British support could be given only in Belgium or France.[3]

---

[1] *D.D.F.*, 2nd Series, vol. viii, no. 256.
[2] Repington, i, 6–8; *D.D.F.*, 2nd Series, vol. viii, no. 389.
[3] Cab. 18/24; and see Monger, p. 246, and Williamson, pp. 71–2.

On the 9th and 10th the British government began at last to play some part in the proceedings with Grey's approval of the military exchanges. The French replies were duly received and on the 12th Clarke's group met again—this time reinforced by the D.M.O. Transportation of two Army Corps to the French Channel ports (in preference to Antwerp) was discussed. Ottley's continued participation implied Fisher's willingness to co-operate. However, Clarke prudently decided to confirm this in person.

Apart from Ottley's attendance at Clarke's meetings, Fisher had so far taken no part in the proceedings, except for holding an unofficial conversation with the French naval attaché on 2 January. Then, he expatiated on the naval strength which the British Admiralty could bring to bear but made no suggestion about co-ordinating Franco–British war plans.[1]

Clarke saw Fisher on (or about) 13 January and he reported the result to Esher:

> It was all very unsatisfactory. F is convinced that there will be no trouble, so is not greatly interested . . . He told me what he said he had not even confided to Ottley . . . This is merely that he wants our Navy to do everything, that we have ample force, that the French would be in the way and so on. I said that it would be absolutely necessary to consider French susceptibilities, which he seems to ignore. Then he said he wished the French torpedo craft and submarines to be concentrated near the Straits of Dover, as apparently they will be.
>
> He was averse to having a secret code of signals ready to give to the French, although he seemed to realize that the danger of mistakes is very great . . .
>
> Fisher then said that he would never be a party to military co-operation with the French on French territory; but I pointed out that, in this case also, we must be guided by French wishes to some extent . . . Of course the French G.S. are thinking of the moral effect upon their own troops of which they are better judges than we are.
>
> Then F said it would be a nuisance to the navy to have to guard the 'Ferry', that the navy wanted to 'get away to sea', etc. . . . His mind was still running on the Schleswig Holstein plan; but I said that, after examining the charts, that coast appeared peculiarly unfavourable to a landing and more conveniently situated for the German forces than the Baltic. I said I understood that the Admiralty thought it inadvisable to send a fleet with transports into the Baltic at the

[1] D.D.F., vol. viii, no. 308.

outset of war. He denied this and did not seem to think the difficulty too great; but I could see that he had never studied the question at all.

In any case, clearly to carry some 75 transports through either the Sound or the Belts would be a vastly more difficult and absorbing business for our Navy than to safeguard the 'Ferry'.

Finally I gathered that the idea of selecting a cache for our battle-fleet where torpedo boats and submarines would not find it, was occupying F's mind. This seemed inconsistent with much that he had said and left me marvelling. He may have intended to mystify me, though I do not think so. My strong impression remains that nothing has been *thought out* and that so far as preparedness, other than the mere mobilization of ships is concerned, the Admiralty is not at all in advance of the W.O.

I think it would be most useful if you could see Fisher tomorrow, and without hinting that I have written to you, draw him gently on these points. Unless they can be cleared up to a reasonable extent, I do not think we can proceed much further.

I am disgusted to hear that Mr. A[rthur] B[alfour] has been defeated [at Manchester].[1]

During the remaining four years of Fisher's term as First Sea Lord, the feasibility of a Baltic expedition or a landing on the German North Sea coast was never thoroughly and realistically examined at the Admiralty. At the heart of the matter was Fisher's continuing refusal to establish a naval general staff with responsibility for drawing up war plans. When Corbett revived the subject in December 1905, Fisher replied: 'I have not seen my way to dis-associate the 1st Sea Lord from the present way of doing business, but there's force in your remark (not written but implied) that an effete 1st Sea Lord would be the very devil!'[2] All the details of the Navy's real plans were to be kept, ostensibly for security reasons, in two heads—those of A. K. Wilson and Fisher!

Presumably Clarke's approach to the First Sea Lord convinced the latter that the strategy of direct support was prevailing at the C.I.D. Fisher therefore withdrew the naval representative from Clarke's group. On 18 January Ottley wrote to Clarke:

My dear Sir George,

Sir John Fisher begs me to say, in reply to your note just received, that he has spoken to Lord Tweedmouth on the question and he does

---

[1] E.P. 10/38, n.d., but *c.* 13 Jan. 1906.
[2] F.P. 191, 22 Dec. 1905 (copy).

not think it would be advisable for us to participate in any more discussions on this question, *just at present.*

In great haste, and with deep regret,

> Yours v. sincerely,
>
> C. L. Ottley.

On the same day Clarke forwarded this note to Esher and commented:

> I rather expected enclosed. It is unwise and a pity. No possible harm can arise from taking reasonable precautions . . .
>
> I know you are inclined to think that all will be well as far as the Admiralty is concerned. I wish I could share this belief . . . One brain, if supremely competent, may direct, but is necessarily quite unable to cope alone with complex questions requiring careful thought and study . . . I also dislike much the see-saw of responsibility between Fisher and Wilson, and I do not expect that the former will suddenly assume the responsibility in war, while the latter is a person full of strong idées fixes which are not all sound by any means . .
>
> I think further that if, as is possible, Grierson has been permitted to go further than is considered wise, there should be *all the less* reluctance on the part of the Admiralty to play up, because clearly, one department of state commits all.[1]

Both then, and in future years, Esher remained confident of Fisher's capacity to deal with all aspects of naval policy, including the preparation of war plans. This misconception stemmed from Esher's lack of direct knowledge of the Navy. Consequently, his considerable influence was exerted in support of Fisher's attitude. Only when Fisher's narrowly departmental approach began to constrict the general effectiveness of the C.I.D. did Esher complain of the First Sea Lord's 'Achillean attitude'. On the whole, Clarke's criticisms were very much to the point, especially with regard to the need for a responsible naval staff to prepare war plans; but he could not rally enough support to affect the position before he left the C.I.D. in 1907.

Some further light is shed on Fisher's disinclination to 'ferry' troops to France by his letter of 23 December 1905 addressed to the new First Lord:

> Enclosed the heads of what I ventured to mention to Mr. Haldane! We must pray and do our best for him to prosper and not be wrecked, as have been all his predecessors ! . . .

[1] E.P. 10/38, 18 Jan. 1906.

The Cardinal Points of Army Reform

1. Reduction of the Regular Army . . .

3. *The Garrisons of Fortresses* . . . If the Navy is not predominant, no fortress will avail us from making peace, *there and then!* because STARVATION comes in and compels it. But not to excite wrong emotions in the public mind, let it be said as a preliminary statement that NOW, owing to the

(a) unprecedented strength of our Navy at the present time,

(b) the collapse of Russia,

(c) the consequent absolute dependence upon us for its life by France,

that *now* is a time for a *pause* and a reduction in military strength, etc. . . .

Lastly, can it be defended that the Army Estimates should be 29 millions and almost the same as the Navy Estimates, when our national life depends absolutely and solely on the Navy, and the Army no use without it to save the Empire from ruin?[1]

In fact, while there was substance in Fisher's generalities about the Navy, it hardly followed that the moment of 'absolute dependence' of France on Britain called for a cut in the British Army. If the German Army invaded France, just how relevant to the immediate problem would the British Navy be? It seems clear that the Navy's claim to public money assumed more importance in Fisher's mind at that time than the problem of how to avoid a German domination of Europe.

It was certainly the case that the Liberal election victory implied reduced spending on defence. In the election campaign, cuts had been promised on the traditional grounds of economy. There had also been talk about spending on social reform together with hopes for international agreement on arms limitation. However, in January 1906 the new government approved the estimates already prepared for 1906–7, including the provision (under the Cawdor programme) for construction of four big ships. Nevertheless the Admiralty took the precaution of preparing a long document entitled *The Building Programme of the British Navy, 15 February 1906*. This print contains much interesting information—for instance a reference (on pp. 3–4) to 'Russia, certainly our most likely potential enemy in May

---

[1] *F.G.* ii, 65–6.

1905'. However, the crux is to be found towards the end (on p. 37):

If in deference to popular clamour the ship-building programme of this country were now to be reduced, it is *inevitable* that, if the 'Two Power Standard' is to be maintained, a year or two hence a very great increase upon the *present* programme will become absolutely necessary. This procedure of cutting down one year and increasing the next is contrary to all business principles, and must ultimately involve the country in far greater expense than the present organised and reasoned development . . . It may, perhaps, be contended that the foregoing argument is based upon the necessity of maintaining the 'Two Power Standard', and that, in view of present international politics, that standard should be abandoned . . . Alliances can be made and broken more easily than battleships can be constructed. Those upon whom the country has placed the responsibility for the sufficiency and efficiency of the Naval forces would betray a great and solemn trust if they placed their reliance upon anything so unstable as international relationships, [1] unless regularised and consecrated by definite treaties of alliance.[1]

Further arguments for laying down four dreadnoughts are deployed in a print of April, entitled 'The Balance of Naval Power, 1906'. A copy of this 'Secret' paper was sent to Thursfield who continued to defend Fisher against his critics.[2] However. the above-quoted statement of 15 February is more remarkable, It was to be amply vindicated by 1909. Unfortunately, the government proceeded to demand economies additional to those already achieved by Fisher. The result is indicated in 'Memorandum of a Meeting of the Sea Lords at the Admiralty on Saturday, 26th May, 1906, to consider future Shipbuilding Arrangements, etc.—held in accordance with the wishes of the First Lord, to consider and advise him as to possible reductions.'[3] The *Dreadnought* (launched in February 1906) had occasioned 'delays in foreign naval programmes'. It was therefore decided 'to drop out one of the four armoured vessels which it had been intended to lay down towards the end' of the current financial year. The explanation for the Admiralty's retreat from its well-founded argument of 15 February lies in the demands for further economies communicated by Asquith. The latter—scarcely recognizable as a 'Liberal Imperialist' while Chancellor of the

[1] F.P. 4715, 44 pp., P. 6/06, classified 'Very Secret'.
[2] N.M.M., THU/2.   [3] F.P. 4774 (P. 6/06).

Exchequer—wrote on 24 May to the unhappy Tweedmouth that 'nothing that Sir John Fisher could say would affect' his demands.[1]

Not only was one big ship dropped from the programme for 1906–7; with the Hague Conference and the possibility of arms limitation in view, the government persuaded the Admiralty to agree on 12 July 1906 to lay down only two big ships in 1907–8 —though a third was to be laid down if there was no arms agreement. There is no doubt that the responsibility for these unwise reductions must be laid on the Liberal government. What is disconcerting about Fisher's reaction is his complete abandonment of the far-sighted policy advocated in February and his switch to a phase of excessive confidence in the sufficiency of the reduced building programmes. Tweedmouth, with good cause, remained uneasy; but by September he was in receipt of hearty reassurances from Fisher, such as: 'Our present margin of superiority over Germany (*our only possible foe for years*) is so great as to render it absurd in the extreme to talk of anything endangering our naval supremacy, *even* if we stopped all ship-building altogether !!!'[2] True enough, the Germans were some two years away from mounting a serious threat to the British lead in dreadnoughts; but by 1909 a panic would occur. Fisher had too readily exchanged a far-sighted for a short-sighted policy.

Nor were the cuts in dreadnought-building sufficient to meet the government's financial requirements. During the summer Fisher was busy with a further scheme of redistribution which stimulated public criticism of his administration. Already on 29 May he was informing the First Lord that he had discussed with the Controller, the Accountant General, and the D.N.I. 'the effect of withdrawing six battleships and four armoured cruisers now in full commission and placing them in commission in reserve (that is with nucleus crews) and reducing the personnel by 2,000 men.' This would save about £¼ million in 1907–8, but 'it would not do to say that the Estimates for 1907–8 could be reduced by that amount as we have an automatic increase in

[1] Tweedmouth Papers, A 63, 24 May 1906. See also Asquith's letter of 23 May explaining the government's decision not to continue with the previous practice of financing naval works by loan bills. The effect of this decision was to make naval works a charge on the Navy Estimates, thus reducing the money available for shipbuilding, etc. H.P. Willmott's thesis, 'The Navy Estimates 1906–1909', provides much useful detail for the period covered therein.

[2] *F.G.* ii, 91.

other Votes that this saving may be required for.'[1] Meanwhile, there had been indications of discontent in the Mediterranean Fleet before the phase of enforced economies began.

As Commander-in-Chief in the Mediterranean, Beresford followed Fisher's and his own previous practice by striking up a private correspondence with the new First Lord. On 21 February 1906 he protested against the reappearance of 'interchangeability' in the Cawdor programme; but he added, reasonably enough: 'I think that nearly all the reforms with regard to Material, Distribution, etc. are admirable.'[2] On 2 March Tweedmouth wrote to Fisher that he provisionally accepted the education scheme 'as a whole'; however, he thought that 'interchangeability' needed 'special watching'. Fisher replied at once, protesting against distinctive treatment for the 'policy of interchangeability' which he considered *'so absolutely vital'*.[3] Doubtless the First Lord conveyed to Fisher the gist of Beresford's complaints as they came in. On 10 March Lord Charles was writing: 'The Service is very sore and irritated throughout, not so much upon what is done, as upon the way in which things are done.' He referred to discourtesy, such as his being put under Wilson's command for the joint manoeuvres without previous warning. Those 'little gentlemany etiquettes' which 'made the Service run smoothly' had, he averred, been 'entirely abandoned.[4]'

By April the First Sea Lord was receiving private accounts of Mediterranean discontents from Captain R. H. Bacon, lately his Naval Assistant at the Admiralty. Unbeknown to Bacon, whose career was to be blighted as a result, Fisher had copies of these letters printed.[5] Two of the four letters, having fallen into unfriendly hands, were quoted with damaging effect in April 1909. Meanwhile, on 24 April 1906 Fisher complained to Tweedmouth of Beresford's 'unprecedented conduct' in 'publicly reflecting on the conduct of the Admiralty and in discrediting the policy of the Board'.[6] This was fair comment—even if Fisher himself had established similar precedents. In September 1905 Esher had remarked to Balfour regarding Fisher: 'Two

---

[1] Tweedmouth Papers, A 95.
[2] Ibid., A 159–60.
[3] *F.G.* ii, 69 n.; Tweedmouth Papers, A 86.
[4] Tweedmouth Papers, A 161.
[5] F.P. 4762–4, all P. 4/06. Only F.P. 4764 is not in *F.G.*, vol. ii.
[6] *F.G.* ii, 79.

years ago, as C.-in-C. at Portsmouth, he snapped his fingers at the "Board of Admiralty" and urged every C.-in-C. to do likewise.'[1] Lord Tweedmouth during his term of office evidently found it difficult to decide which Admiral was more productive of unrest in the Navy, Fisher or Beresford. Rosslyn Wemyss, still a neutral observer at the time, wrote to his wife after visiting the Admiralty in April 1906: 'I thought Lord Tweedmouth a most pleasant man but he gave me the idea of being much torn between the Fisherites and the anti-Fisherites, and no wonder, considering that he can't possibly know enough of the subject himself to be able to form any sort or kind of an opinion.'[2] The remarkable upshot was that, in July, Beresford was offered the command of the Channel Fleet in succession to Wilson. On 7 August he signified his acceptance on the understanding that, like Wilson, he would hold the chief command in home waters and be responsible for 'organising the Fleet for War and immediate action'.[3] By the time Lord Charles took command of the Channel Fleet in April 1907, his position did not match his expectations.

By July 1906 the reorganization consequent on Asquithian pressures had been delineated at the Admiralty. It was proposed to place seven battleships in reserve. All the larger ships then in reserve would have nucleus crews strengthened to three-fifths of their full complement. In the Channel Fleet there would now be 14 battleships instead of 17. The Atlantic and Mediterranean Fleets would each have 6 battleships instead of 8. An Admiralty print commented that if the 7 battleships now placed in reserve had all been allocated, with full complements, to the Channel Fleet, this force with a total of 21 battleships would have been unnecessarily strong—indeed 'a menace to Germany of the grossest description'. Taking account of the nucleus-crew ships, the scheme did in fact provide an ample concentration of naval power in home waters. It is worth remarking for future reference that the Admiralty did not imagine this concentration would pass unnoticed by the Germans. Rather, it was 'suspected that the German Admiralty' would 'see that their comparative position' had 'not been improved'.[4] In meeting both immediate

---

[1] Add. MSS. 49719, f. 17, 15 Sept. 1905.   [2] Wemyss, p. 81.

[3] Bennett, p. 279; Tweedmouth Papers, A 179, Beresford to T., 30 Oct. 1906.

[4] F.P. 4720, *Admiralty Policy: Replies to Criticism, October 1906*, pp. 33–4. This compilation extends to 144 pages; P. 10/06.

strategic requirements and the government's demand for further economies, the scheme was well conceived. It did not store up trouble for the future after the manner of the cuts in projected construction of battleships.

News of the scheme leaked to the press while Fisher (during September–October) was on a continental holiday. He seems to have been surprised by the subsequent outcry. To quieten both the First Lord and the critics, the Admiral hit on the idea of 'a fresh "Home Fleet" '. Its *corps d'élite* would consist of the seven battleships about to be manned with nucleus crews together with four similarly manned armoured cruisers. Thus there would be 'a homogeneous perfectly constituted *Reserve Fleet* always in "Home Waters", working under the supreme command of one Admiral', with its main elements based on Chatham and Dover. It would provide a safeguard against German attack if the Channel Fleet was away on a cruise.[1]

On 23 January 1907 Battenberg (then Rear-Admiral commanding the second cruiser squadron at Portland) wrote to Thursfield who, of course, was an old connexion of his as well as Fisher's. Thursfield had embarked on a series of articles in *The Times* in which he was to examine recent public criticisms of the Admiralty. Battenberg evidently supposed that Thursfield might not have been fully informed about the evolution of the Home Fleet so he supplied the following enlightening details:

I have just read with interest and pleasure the first of your articles on the 'State of the Navy' . . . As you know, I am a firm believer in the genius of John Fisher. Ever since I joined him in the Mediterranean, as a senior Captain, he has honoured me with his confidence, and . . . has practically consulted me on—or rather freely submitted for my criticism—all his many schemes. Amongst the number there were a 'good few' which were not carried out . . . Now the first and so far only scheme (and this a big one in its effects) brought out by J.F. of which I had not a previous inkling, is this 'Home Fleet'. Since I have been within reach of the Admiralty this winter, and have discovered bit by bit the particulars of this grand scheme, I am more and more astounded. It is simply topsy-turveydom and opposed to all our hitherto accepted principles. (The D.N.I., who was never consulted, is altogether opposed to it—but this is only for your private ear.)[2]

---

[1] *F.G.* ii, 98–9, F. to Tweedmouth (from Italy), 11 Oct. 1906; Kerr, pp. 218–19.

[2] Ottley's dislike of the projected Home Fleet is implied in F. to Corbett, 10 Jan. 1907 (F.P. 214, copy).

'At first, no doubt, J.F. meant merely to improve the Reserve Fleet, but by degrees he has inverted the whole thing until we have now reached the stage where this Reserve Fleet of partially manned ships, is put forward as the force for striking an instant blow in war, whilst the *real* fleet, trained by A. Wilson and W. May is relegated to the second place.[1]

It is the intention of J.F. to form the Sheerness–Chatham Division of the Home Fleet of our *eight* best battleships . . .[2]

To throw dust in the eyes of the public, the sixteen ships of the Sheerness–Chatham Division . . . will have the deficiencies in their complements [over and above the nucleus crews] made up with youths and boys . . . We have in the Channel and Mediterranean full Admirals and Vice-Admirals as Seconds, in the Atlantic a Vice-Admiral, all supposed to be men who have steadily gained experience to fit them for these high commands. In the Home Fleet we have a Rear-Admiral [namely Francis Bridgeman], who has never experienced any independent command before, to command twenty-four battleships [including the more obsolete ships at Portsmouth and Devonport] and Heaven knows how many cruisers, with four junior Flag Officers!

Where is the sense of this, even the sense of proportion? But more: Bridgeman is to have a Flag Officer, a Commodore, and about 160 torpedo-craft under his orders.

Now let us see what *could* be. Germany keeps sixteen battleships *at present* in full commission, and in splendid fighting order. By permanently joining the fourteen Channel Fleet ships and the six of the Atlantic Fleet (not now required) we could make sure of always meeting this potential enemy—the only one of any consequence—with a fleet, well trained and in preponderance of five to four—not to mention more powerful units . . . The C.-in-C. of Channel Fleet (our very best or experienced Admiral of the day) would, of course, be the Admiralissimo in the Home Waters, in wartime . . .

I am very sorry to have to go against J.F. but I can't help it. If J.F. were to put his scheme before me, he would have a reply like the one I have written above . . . The feeling amongst all thinking naval men is one of consternation. May entirely agrees with me and means to tell Lord Tweedmouth. Towards the King, Prince of Wales, and others I keep silence, but I shall not rest until this whole monstrous scheme is knocked on the head, and the principles, which J.F.

[1] Prince Louis is here counting the Atlantic Fleet as part of the main battlefleet at home. May was C.-in-C. Atlantic Fleet from 1905 to 1907.

[2] A memo. of 6 Dec. 1906 written by Ottley shows the *Dreadnought* as flagship of the Chatham Division of the Home Fleet and allocates the *Lord Nelson* to that division. (F.P. 4722, *The Home Fleet* (P. 2/07) p. 26.)

lectured to us about with iteration and emphasis, at Malta, and now tramples under foot, are once more firmly established.[1]

In a letter of 24 February 1909, addressed to King-Hall, Battenberg commented on the whole episode of the Home Fleet:

. . . J.F. was determined that Beresford would not have so big and honourable a command [as Wilson had held]. I think C.B. has been badly treated, although he is not a patch on Arthur Wilson, as he himself firmly believes . . . You know how much I admire J.F. He is a truly great man, and almost all his schemes have benefited the Navy. But he has started this pernicious partisanship in the Navy—there is no denying it. Anyone who in any way opposed J.F. went under. His hatred of C.B. has led him to maintain for the past two years an organization of our Home forces which was indefensible . . .[2]

Prince Louis's views, as expressed in both the above-quoted letters, carry conviction. He had no reason to like Beresford. On 24 July 1906 he had written to Fisher: 'Beresford and Lambton and all that tribe gave out . . . that I was a damned German who had no business in the British Navy and that the Service for that reason did not trust me . . . I feel I can never forget this . . . a drop of poison in my cup of happiness of a lifetime devoted truly and wholly to our great service.'[3]

At the Beresford Inquiry of 1909 Sir Arthur Wilson, who had no ties with Lord Charles, also stated his opinion of the scheme comprising the Home Fleet. Sir Edward Grey asked whether he agreed that the organization of the home-based fleets in 1907-8 had been open to criticism but that this had been rectified in March 1909. Wilson replied: 'Yes, I think so. I did not like the change at all when I gave up the command. I thought it a very bad change. But I think the new change has put it right.'[4]

These adverse judgements strongly suggest that Fisher, irritated by Beresford's behaviour during 1906, deliberately placed him in a position which he was likely to resent. Nor do the copious related Admiralty prints succeed in justifying the new organization on its own merits.[5]

---

[1] Kerr, pp. 216-21.   [2] Ibid., pp. 225-6.   [3] F.P. 203.
[4] Cab. 16/9A, 13th meeting, 24 June 1909.
[5] F.P. 4720; F.P. 4783, 'Admiralty Minute', 23 Oct. 1906 (P. 10/06), establishing a 'Home Fleet' with its own C.-in-C. and a sliding scale for determining the strength of nucleus crews; F.P. 4722, *The Home Fleet, December 1906*, 53 pp., P. 2/07, stating that 'the Nore Division of the Home Fleet will be fully manned' and have the *Dreadnought* as flagship.

The major print on *The Home Fleet* states: 'The Home Fleet as constituted by the Admiralty Minute of October 23, 1906, is the gradual and logical development of the Redistribution of the Fleet, as arranged in October 1904.' But no evidence is adduced to substantiate this claim. Indeed, as indicated above, the reorganization of 1906 was undertaken to meet the new government's demands for further economies, and the earlier redistributions of 1904–5 were to a large extent governed by changing circumstances. Nor does the subsequent claim (of 1909 and after) that the separate Home Fleet arose from diplomatic considerations, or from 'fear of exciting the attention of the German Admiralty', seem at all convincing.[1] As remarked above, Fisher and Ottley always expected the 'German Admiralty' to assess the scheme and conclude that it was not to their advantage.[2] So why did the Admiralty not adhere to 'logical' principles by allowing Beresford to inherit Wilson's unified command? It has already been seen that, in the Mediterranean, Fisher himself had argued for concentration of strength in quiet times, rather than during a crisis, because it was less objectionable from a diplomatic viewpoint.[3] In any case, such delicacy was hardly consistent with Fisher's previous attitude towards Germany since 1904. For example, he wrote to Corbett on 28 July 1905: 'With great difficulty I've got our Channel Fleet up the Baltic and cruising in North Sea. "Our drill ground should be our battle ground." Don't repeat that phrase, but I've taken means to have it whispered in the German Emperor's ear!'[4]

On the same day Clarke wrote to Sandars deploring the choice of a period of tension for this cruise: 'Quite a large proportion of Germans really believe that we mean to strike a sudden blow at their fleet in the style of the Copenhagen performances.'[5] Fisher's talk about this possibility did reach the Kaiser's ear and the First Sea Lord never expressed regret on that account.[6]

News of the impending reorganization of the fleets reached Beresford in the Mediterranean during the autumn of 1906. He seems to have acquiesced in the pre-Home Fleet proposals. However, on 5 November he received the Admiralty Minute of 23 October which established the Home Fleet under its own

---

[1] Cf. *Memories*, p. 246 and *D.S.* i, 41–2, 73–4.
[2] F.P. 4720, pp. 33–4.
[3] See p. 244 above.
[4] *F.G.* ii, 63.
[5] Add. MSS. 49701, ff. 283–4.
[6] See *F.G.* ii, 146 and note.

Commander-in-Chief; and he wrote forthwith to Tweedmouth: 'I see that the whole of the Torpedo Flotilla are to be placed under the C in C of the Home Fleet for administrative purposes. This I think is sound and good, but I must point out that the organisation for War and the training for War must be made out under the direction of the man who is to command these vessels in War.'[1] This, of course, was in line with the arguments used by Fisher when commanding in the Mediterranean.

Beresford's return to England in January 1907 marked a rise in blood-temperatures. On the 21st Fisher wrote to George Lambert, Civil Lord of the Admiralty and a keen Fisherite:

I had three hours with Beresford yesterday, and all is settled, and the Admiralty don't give in one inch to his demands, but I had as a preliminary to agree to three things:

    I.   Lord C. Beresford is a greater man than Nelson.

    II. No one knows anything about the art of naval war except Lord C. Beresford.

    III. The Admiralty haven't done a single d——d thing right.[2]

Yet, in so far as Beresford was inclined to over-estimate his natural deserts, was it likely that he would peacefully accept the Admiralty's continuing intention to establish the Home Fleet? Having hoisted his flag in the *King Edward VII* on 16 April, he found that the duty to draw up war plans, inherited from Wilson, offered inexhaustible opportunities for worrying the Admiralty. In exploiting this situation he was capably abetted by his second-in-command who was none other than Vice-Admiral Sir Reginald Custance.[3] The previous delegation to Wilson of strategic preparation was in any event unsatisfactory; but its minimum requirement was close consultation and complete mutual trust between the First Sea Lord and the Commander-in-Chief of the Channel Fleet. The extent to which Fisher was prepared to trust Beresford in the sphere of war plans is defined by a marginal comment on a print relating to Japanese practice in 1904–5. Fisher noted: 'Impossible to tell Lord C. Beresford anything as he talks at random about the most secret matters to

---

[1] Tweedmouth Papers, A 180.

[2] *F.G.* ii, 115.

[3] Custance had latterly dedicated a spell on half-pay to attacking, under a pen-name, the policies associated with Fisher—especially the building of dreadnoughts.

any or every listener (ladies included).'[1] Therefore Beresford's seemingly innocent desire to see the plans prepared by Wilson as Commander-in-Chief led to much sparring and equivocation. Fisher would not disclose to Lord Charles the intentions locked away in his own mind, and extended this prohibition to Wilson's similar (but inflexible) plans.

It is remarkable that Fisher did not recognize that an intolerable situation had already arisen. His conviction that war was not imminent—noticed by Clarke in January 1906—was no doubt strong in the quiet conditions of 1907. In any event, he seems never to have comprehended the value of making thorough plans in peacetime. At best, his attitude towards war plans was merely tentative; he saw them as a useful educational exercise without admitting that their thorough preparation might clarify some basic strategic realities.

However, with an eye on his critics, Fisher had initiated a degree of preparation at the end of 1906. A committee was appointed under Captain G. A. Ballard (who was last noticed corresponding with Callwell about a possible landing in Schleswig-Holstein) to draw up some war plans. The work was to be done at the War College, Portsmouth.

The president of the War College, Captain E. J. W. Slade, had already written a paper entitled 'War with Germany' and dated 1 September 1906.[2] This was incorporated in the plans compiled by the Ballard committee which were printed in April–May 1907. Under the new title of 'General Remarks on War with Germany: A Preamble for Reflection and Criticism', Slade's plan comprised the second part of the whole series. It focused on a German invasion of the Netherlands or Belgium, taking little account of whether or not France was Britain's ally. The main prescription was the capture of a German island, preferably Borkum, whence the German North Sea ports could be closely blockaded. This proved a recurrent theme in naval planning, even after the beginning of the war of 1914. However, despite the fact that Slade, as well as Ottley, was associated with the work of the Ballard committee, the latter body reached markedly

---

[1] Cab. 1/7, ff. 133–5, including 'Memorandum by Captain Pakenham, CB, MVO, British Naval Attaché on the War Direction of the Japanese Navy', 17 Jan. 1908. F.'s comment is written beside P.'s statement that 'there can be no doubt that before the war began its proposed strategy was exhaustively discussed with Admiral Togo.'

[2] Adm. 116/1036 B (P. 8/06).

different conclusions. The committee, with Ballard and Hankey (the secretary) as its dominant nucleus, agreed that close blockade, with its increasing attendant dangers in the form of mines and torpedoes, should be avoided; and coastal landings were likewise deprecated. Instead, it was recommended that reliance be placed on a distant economic blockade.[1] On Fisher's instructions, doubtless, plans were also investigated for blockading Kiel, the easterly German Baltic ports, and the German North Sea ports; but the committee specifically recommended that, if attempted at all, these operations should be concerted with the French.[2]

At Fisher's request Julian Corbett, now a civilian lecturer at the War College and a friend of Slade's, wrote a scholarly introduction to the war plans.[3] The historian, like the committee, remarked on the 'great risk and disadvantage' imposed by modern developments on a system of close blockade.[4]

What, then, were Fisher's own views? No systematic account of these was ever recorded. Two violently contrasting themes certainly recurred in his mind; the offensive idea of an expedition to the Baltic and the daunting anticipation of the coming dominance of the submarine. As Clarke observed after the interview of January 1906, the latter theme tended to nullify the first. The only substantial paper relating to the war plans and attributable to Fisher himself is a typescript of ten pages. This was probably compiled in December 1908 and takes the form of a commentary on the war plans as they stood at that date.

The war plans, Fisher observes with satisfaction, now extend to 780 pages of print and manuscript. He attaches particular importance to the 'Remarks on the War Plans' written for him by Sir Arthur Wilson in May 1907. For example, he quotes with approval Wilson's opinion that during 'the period of strained relations before the war' it would be advisable to station the 'large ships' away from the North Sea where they would be safe from 'treacherous attack'. (This passage in the 'Remarks' echoes Fisher's own reference to a 'cache' during his interview with Clarke in January 1906.) Indeed, comments Fisher, 'It would be suicidal to expose the armoured units of our Fleet to a

---

[1] N.R.S., *F.P.* ii, 346–445. Some material is printed here which is not contained in the main source at the P.R.O., namely Adm. 116/1043 B, Part I.

[2] N.R.S., *F.P.* ii, 432, 436.

[3] F.P. 233, F. to Corbett (copy), 17 Mar. 1907.

[4] N.R.S., *F.P.* ii, 338.

surprise Torpedo attack by stationing them before War within
striking distance of the enemy . . . At such a time the North Sea
and East Coast should swarm with our Destroyers and Submarines backed with their supporting Cruisers.'[1]

Having thus commended Wilson's caution, Fisher endorses
his excessive audacity. Developing his theme of June 1905,
Wilson observes:

> The only way in which we could give serious assistance to France
> would be by a floating army, making raids on different parts of the
> German coast and so diverting troops from the main theatre of war . . .
> If constantly attacked with energy from different directions, even by
> comparatively small forces supported by the fleet, they will be obliged
> to draw transport, supplies, food, ammunition, and stores of all kinds,
> from sources that would otherwise be used to supply the main army . . .
> To make such a diversion effective, the raids must be carried out with
> a certain recklessness of life and yet not pushed so far as to risk being
> cut off entirely. The vessels used for their support would have to be
> freely risked, and therefore should be as far as possible of obsolete
> types . . . using our present active fleets to prevent any interference
> on the part of the seagoing fleet of the enemy.
>
> The most effective operation that could be attempted with this
> object would be:—
>
> An attack on the mouth of the Elbe, by making a direct attempt to
> run by the forts at Cuxhaven and block the canal and threaten
> Hamburg.[2]

In October 1908 an unusually critical print emanated from
the War College on the subject of 'Forcing the Defences of
Cuxhaven'.[3] The paper includes schemes for carrying out the
operation but comments:

> The fact, however, cannot be disguised that the project is one which
> can only be regarded as justifiable in the direst extremities.
>
> It is full of danger from the outset, and, as far as can be seen,
> dangers which would be productive of loss altogether incommensurate
> with the advantages likely to accrue.

By the end of 1914 Fisher, confronted with the stark realities
of war, would adopt a similar view of such risky propositions.

---

[1] Adm. 116/1043 B, Part I. F.'s typescript has not been published. The original
MS. of Wilson's 'Remarks' is in F.P. 4231. The printed version (of 5 June 1907)
judiciously omits a section implying that it was not clear to Wilson where the
C.-in-C.'s responsibility began and ended. This printed version is in N.R.S.,
F.P. ii, 454–64.

[2] N.R.S., F.P. ii, 459–60.

[3] P. 5.10.08, 13 pp.—Adm. 116/1043 B, Part I.

However, in his commentary of December 1908 his approval of Wilson's ideas is unambiguous: 'The use of our Army is touched upon with a master hand by Sir A. Wilson . . . He presumes there the French alliance. In this connection it is most instructive to notice that the French frontier is one vast fortress whilst the Germans put their whole faith in their Field Armies, that is, in the Offensive!'

But even amid such peacetime fantasies, it is scarcely conceivable that every feature of Wilson's offensive proposals appealed to Fisher—for example, the vision of the old battleships of the 'River Squadron' bursting through the minefields, thanks to their 'cow-catchers', forcing the Elbe, and bearing down (at eight knots) on the astonished German battlefleet to wreak destruction with ram and torpedo![1] In 1904, Fisher had described the ram as 'absolutely useless in war, and a temptation to do wrong in a fight'![2]

Again, when one passes in review his earlier experience of opposed landings and his promotion of amphibious exercises up to the time of his final command at Portsmouth, it is difficult to believe that Fisher's pre-war advocacy of coastal landings was completely genuine. During 1907–8 plans were produced at the War College for these coastal projects with scant regard for logistical considerations; yet who was more likely to take an interest in this aspect of the plans than Fisher? Indeed, while continuing to demand 'an Army to *attack*',[3] he also began to manifest a negative attitude towards any kind of major British military role in Europe. A letter which he wrote to the King from the southern Tyrol on 4 October 1907 includes the following statement:

our intervention in Continental struggle by regular land warfare is impracticable, and combined naval and military expeditions must be directed by us against the outlying possessions of the enemy, or, in the splendid words of Sir E. Grey, 'The British Army is a projectile to be fired by the Navy.' The foundation of our policy is that the communications of the Empire must be kept open by a *predominant Fleet*.[4]

A similar attitude is implicit in his remark to Esher of 8 May 1908: 'The Army too big for a little war, too little for a big war!'[5]

---

[1] N.R.S., *F.P.* ii, 460–1. [2] *N.N.* i, 40.
[3] *F.G.* ii, 201, F. to E. Goulding, Nov. 1908. [4] *F.G.* ii, 143.
[5] E.P. 10/42; also *F.G.* ii, 176—but the date is 8 May, not the 5th.

It is therefore quite possible that a strand of the First Sea
Lord's real thinking is represented by the cautious but realistic
plans preferred by the Ballard committee. Hankey has described
it as working under Fisher's 'own personal supervision'; and
elsewhere he wrote: 'We worked under Fisher's immediate
inspiration, who saw Ballard once or twice a week in London,
while I kept in touch with Ottley.'[1] After four months of study,
they concluded that the most practicable way to bring pressure
to bear on Germany was to impose a distant economic blockade.
The blockading cruisers, remote from the enemy's torpedoes
and minefields, would seal off the entrances to the North Sea. As
for landings on the German coast, the committee firmly stated:
'we have no military force of sufficient strength to follow up the
action of our fleet by conducting operations on shore.'[2] Fisher
adopts a somewhat similar stance in part of his commentary of
December 1908 where he states that

we are prepared to deal effectively with the 942 German mercantile
vessels that cover the ocean. The one great drawback is that if France
is our ally Germany may get her compensation on land for this
slaughter of her commerce. So it is 'splendid isolation' that England
wants. The geographical position of Germany immensely favours us
in a maritime war. The British Isles form a huge breakwater 600 miles
long barring the ingress and egress of German vessels from the ocean
—Dover rendered impassable by the Destroyers and Submarines,
and the Northern passage from the North Sea to the Atlantic can be
as completely barred . . .[3]

Finally, it will be convenient to clarify here the extent to which
close blockade survived in the war plans printed in the spring of
1907. Captain Slade advocated the capture of a German island,
preferably Borkum, as an advanced base for the purpose of close
blockade of the German North Sea ports. Wilson, in his 'Remarks', provided a variant of this scheme. Like Slade, he wanted
Borkum to be captured 'immediately on the outbreak of war'.
However, assuming war between Britain and Germany alone,
he recommended a close observational blockade by destroyers
only; and these were to retire at night. In his commentary of
December 1908, Fisher approved of this modification.[4]

The various plans, including Wilson's 'Remarks', were in
print by June 1907 and were handed to Beresford—but without

---

[1] Hankey, i, 39.   [2] N.R.S., *F.P.* ii, 364–5.   [3] Adm. 116/1043 B, Part I.
[4] N.R.S., *F.P.* ii, 349–50, 455–6; Adm. 116/1043 B, Part I.

a commentary by Fisher. Indeed, the latter blanketed the conflict between one plan and another by having the following advice printed on the cover of Slade's contribution (which followed Corbett's introduction): 'The opinions and plans herein (to which others will be added from time to time) are not in any way to be considered as those definitely adopted, except where that is expressly stated, but are valuable and instructive because illustrative of the variety of considerations governing the formation of War Plans.'[1]

Thus the Admiralty did not produce—or possess—a settled, detailed plan. Beresford, lacking even the inadequate staff available at the Admiralty, was required to furnish for scrutiny yet another (necessarily inadequate) plan. Beresford responded by pointing out that he wished to see the plan formulated in earnest by Wilson when he was in command rather than his current recommendations. Presumably in the hope of shaking Fisher's strong position at court, he had already written on 21 May to Lord Knollys (who was still closely linked with Fisher):

I am most distressed and alarmed at the complete absence of organisation and preparation for war in the Fleet. It is a danger to the State, and if Germany attacked us suddenly, she would inflict terrible disasters on us, and she might win. My predecessor had sixty-seven ships, although I can find no plan as to what they had to do: I have only twenty-one—at this moment thirteen. The Home Fleet is the greatest fraud ever perpetrated on the public . . . As far as war preparation goes this is chaos and pandemonium. I am doing the best I can to help Authority to get things right . . .[2]

However, the numerical strength, state of training, and mobilization arrangements of the British fleet, together with the immaturity of the German Navy, did make an attack very unlikely in 1907. Fisher, incensed by Beresford's language 'in an official conversation' which included such remarks as 'the Empire is in jeopardy', as well as the claim of Captain Sturdee (Lord Charles's Chief of Staff) that he was 'living over a live mine', bitterly complained of such criticism in a memorandum on 'War Arrangements' which was prepared for Tweedmouth in June:

The truth is that such language on the part of Lord Charles Beresford and Captain Sturdee, besides being insubordinate, is perfectly

---

[1] Adm. 116/1043 B, Part I. (F.P. 4829 comprises the 'War Plans' but not Wilson's 'Remarks'.)

[2] Bennett, pp. 286–7.

preposterous. . . Our superiority over Germany is so overwhelming, and the superiority of our personnel and of our gunnery practice is so great, that the Germans know it would be madness for them to provoke a war . . . One third of the crew in every German man-of-war are newly entered raw recruits . . .

. . . the records have been searched in vain for any communication from Sir A. K. Wilson . . . calling in question the wisdom of Admiralty policy or questioning the War Orders given to him [in June 1905], but within a month of Lord Charles Beresford assuming his command, we have received a mass of insubordinate letters.

Sir A. Wilson is an officer literally *nulli secundus* in his aptitude for the command of a fleet and his genius for war . . . But what are all these letters from Lord Charles Beresford except a distinct reflection on Sir A. Wilson? What of the statement that he (Sir A. Wilson) 'had turned over the Channel Fleet absolutely unprepared for war'? . . .

Fisher therefore proposed that 'a carefully worded letter' should be sent to Beresford explaining why war was improbable. He continued:

Secondly, it seems advisable that a revised set of War Orders for the Channel Fleet should be issued to Lord C. Beresford with the object of disabusing him of the idea that now possesses him that his is the sole responsibility for the conduct of a naval war . . .

It is also imperative that Lord C. Beresford should be distinctly informed that the British Admiralty has no more intention of abdicating its functions than the Japanese Admiralty had. . . in dictating to Admiral Togo the various stages of the Japanese campaign against Russia . . .

Having laid further stress on Britain's naval strength, Fisher remarked:

It is as well to reiterate that the Home Fleet is still in process of development, and as has been repeatedly stated, will not attain its full development until May 1908, if then . . . The Channel and Atlantic Fleets are on another and entirely different basis. They are commissioned definitely for two years' service, and could be sent tomorrow on distant and prolonged service, involving indefinite absence from home . . .[1]

The First Lord replied on 8 June. He did not wish to place Fisher's complaint—which included an account of Lord Hood's

---

[1] N.R.S., *F.P.* ii, 464–8 (F.P. 4836, P. 6/07).

dismissal in 1795—before the Board in its 'present form'.[1] Tweedmouth stated that his aim was to consult and conciliate informed opinion in the service. He readily agreed that objection could be taken to Beresford's methods and conduct; but he pointed out that there was another side to the picture.

I know him to be ambitious, self-advertising and gassy in his talk, but we all knew those bad qualities of his, and no one better than you, when you very wisely recommended his and Sir Reginald Custance's appointments . . . Lord Charles has especially a large share of the good qualities. He is cheerful, active, zealous in the Service, and his power of attracting and enlisting the sympathies, abilities and affection of officers and men alike who are placed under him is remarkable.

The First Lord wrote in conclusion:

I am the last person in the world to abrogate one iota of the supremacy of the Board of Admiralty, but I do think we sometimes are inclined to consider our own views to be infallible and are not ready enough to give consideration to the views of others who may disagree with us but who give us ideas and information which can be turned to great use.[2]

While it may have been unfortunate from the point of view of service discipline, Tweedmouth's reluctance to take decisive action against Beresford can certainly be understood. The depth of Fisher's resentment of Tweedmouth's attitude is suggested by a remark dictated in 1919 when Fisher was assembling his memoirs: 'Tweedmouth, by a divine help, became a lunatic, and no one knew it but myself but I knew he was going to become a maniac.'[3] On the one hand, the First Lord might well have questioned whether the Channel and Atlantic Fleets should be earmarked (as indicated in the 'War Arrangements' quoted above) for 'distant and prolonged service'. He might have eased the Fisher–Beresford antagonism on a basis of placing the Home Fleet more directly under Lord Charles. On the other hand, Tweedmouth might have followed up Fisher's hint that full strategic control should be restored to the Admiralty. But the First Lord took neither of these courses. Instead, on 5 July he

---

[1] F.P. 4836 comprises three major documents: 'War Arrangements', 'The Home Fleet', and 'Memorandum on the Relations of the Commander-in-Chief Channel Fleet and the Board of Admiralty'. There are also four appendices (one being about Hood). In all, there are 30 pp. of print (P. 6/07).

[2] *F.G.* ii, 125–6.   [3] F.P. 5174.

held a tripartite conference at the Admiralty to seek harmony through discussion. Judging by the minutes, Beresford was out-argued by Fisher—as was indeed to be expected. While the basic issues represented by the Home Fleet and the preparation of war plans remained unsettled, Beresford was mollified for the moment by the addition of two armoured cruisers and twenty-four destroyers to the Channel Fleet. Beresford's most positive contribution to clarification of a probable plan of campaign was not very impressive. He declared: 'I think Wilson's is a splendid plan, though I do not agree with him about sending the destroyers over. I get there with everything you give me.'

Delighted, no doubt, with their value as propaganda, Fisher lost no time in having the minutes of the conference printed. On 8 July a copy, extending to twenty pages of print, was dispatched to Balfour, accompanied by the First Sea Lord's jubilant com-mentary. The printed enclosures included a conciliatory letter of 6 July from Fisher to Beresford, together with the above-quoted 'War Arrangements', and the latest print about the Home Fleet.[1]

In the paper on 'War Arrangements', Fisher indicated that a plan should be prepared for 'each and every eventuality'. Indeed there is no reason to doubt that he had considered which features of the existing plans he would adopt in various circum-stances. Yet the possibility of confusion in the event of war seems only too evident. Thus, on 23 January 1908 he stated to Tweed-mouth that he was 'at absolute variance' with Wilson's 'cardinal feature of "Sweeps" '. (In his 'Remarks', Wilson had suggested 'large sweeps of the North Sea with the whole available force at uncertain intervals'—and this did in the event form part of British strategy in the Great War.) Again, in the same letter to Tweedmouth, Fisher described Wilson as being 'dead against the Battle Fleet being anywhere near the North Sea, whilst Lord C. Beresford is as strongly for it'; and he commented enig-matically: 'In this case the Admiralty view is opposed to both of them.'[2]

It has to be remembered that, since 1906, more in the way of naval planning had been undertaken than ever before in time of peace. Nevertheless, it is equally clear that without the estab-lishment of a responsible planning department at the Admiralty,

---

[1] Add. MSS. 49711, ff. 232–64. As indicated above, both 'War Arrangements' and 'The Home Fleet' were P. 6/07. The other enclosures were P. 7/07.

[2] F.G. ii, 155–6.

unreality and inconsistency would persist. After Fisher's retirement in January 1910, the position did not improve. As a result of the Agadir crisis, the need for a naval general staff was exposed and began to be seriously investigated. Of particular interest for an understanding of Fisher's arrangements and their defects is a memorandum written in October 1911 by Ballard. (This was the Captain G. A. Ballard who headed Fisher's committee of December 1906 to April 1907.) Ballard wrote the memorandum for Ottley who was then Secretary of the C.I.D.; and Ottley passed it on to Churchill who had become First Lord of the Admiralty in October 1911. Ballard explained that, in 1906–7, 'a series of outline plans for war with Germany were drawn up by a very small committee of officers chiefly serving outside the Admiralty altogether, none of whom had received anything approaching to a sufficient training in the subject.' These plans were duly issued 'and were freely criticized by some of the officers whose duty it would have been to carry them out in war, but whose alternative suggestions were based upon no better opportunities for studying the subject, and lacked any appearance of a better understanding of the situation'. The resulting conflict of opinions led, in Ballard's opinion, 'to indecision and chaos that would have been disastrous in war'. This 'state of affairs was exposed' by the C.I.D. in August 1911. However, up to the time of Ballard's writing (October 1911) nothing definite had been done 'to remedy the primary and only vital defect in the system which produced such results, viz.:— an entire lack of training of the officers who are called upon to do the work'. He urged that the planning department should be given a recognized status. Working under the First Sea Lord, it should have charge of all dispositions and movements. The only possible source of opposition to such a reform was the civilian 'M' branch.[1]

It may here be added that a strengthening of Admiralty staff on its technical side might have corrected some of the shortcomings in matériel exposed during the Great War.[2] Much has already been published about these shortcomings. The evident sinkability of the British as compared with the German battle cruisers is a leading example. The three *Invincibles* were the first ships of this type; but by 1908, when the *Indefatigable* was

---

[1] Cab. 17/8, memo. by Capt. Ballard, typed copy, 14 pp.

[2] Jellicoe's book *The Grand Fleet, 1914–1916* is useful in this connexion; also, of course, the five vols. of *From the Dreadnought to Scapa Flow*.

designed, it was known that the Germans were constructing a very substantial equivalent. Yet the Admiralty chose to build a ship with similar light protection to that previously given to the *Invincibles*. This decision must be attributed, at least in large part, to Fisher's persistent preference for speed over armour; yet he continued to envisage a species of battleship role for these large cruisers. At the Battle of Jutland the *Indefatigable* was sunk by the *Von der Tann*, the very ship on which the British battlecruiser should have been an improvement. (The *Von der Tann* was ordered in 1907.) As previously mentioned, interpretation of the sinkings at Jutland is bedevilled by the comparatively low efficiency of British shells. While it is not possible to prove the point, it seems a fair presumption that a stronger technical staff at the Admiralty might, for example, have dealt more effectively with the matter of the shells. As regards the design of the *Indefatigable*, Fisher's personal enthusiasm is beyond doubt. On 9 September 1908 he wrote to Esher: 'By the way, I've got Sir Philip Watts into a new *Indomitable* that will make your mouth water when you see it! (and the Germans gnash their teeth!).'[1]

Of course, the wartime revelation of such shortcomings does not justify the common criticism that Fisher was excessively interested in matériel. The Germans provided formidable competition in this sphere and, from the British viewpoint, Fisher's impulsion was badly needed on that account.

However, before leaving the technical aspect of Fisher's activity as First Sea Lord, it will be convenient to bring up to date his connexion with British mining. During his time as D.N.O. attempts were made in the *Vernon* to develop an independent mine. The result was the over-sensitive 'electromechanical' or E.M. mine, equipped with Ottley's 'automatic sinker' for laying the mine at a predetermined depth. However, mines and torpedoes were A. K. Wilson's special concern at that time. In February 1895, when Fisher was Controller, the Admiralty decided 'not to adopt blockade mines as a form of naval warfare' and stopped the experiments in the *Vernon*. In so far as such mines would discourage an enemy's fleet from leaving port, they were to be deprecated.[2] In 1900, as Commander-in-Chief in the Mediterranean, Fisher pressed for the provision of independent mines and, as Second Sea Lord, he backed this up with

---

[1] *F.G.* ii 195. See Parkes, pp. 513–16, on these battle cruisers.
[2] Cowie, pp. 28–30; *N.N.* ii, 177 (N.R.S., *F.P.* ii, 97).

a memorandum of 1902. He was then mainly interested in the idea of dropping mines in the path of an approaching enemy fleet; but he referred to their other offensive and defensive uses. He also pointed out the need for fast minelayers. But experimental work in the *Vernon* was again discontinued in 1903.[1]

Then, extending into Fisher's term as First Sea Lord, came the Russo-Japanese War. Not only did independent mines sink many ships on both sides—markedly more than did the torpedo —but a mine-expert in the person of Ottley became D.N.I. in February 1905. Thus, a fresh appraisal was undertaken of mines in relation to the Royal Navy. Meanwhile (as previously noticed) Bacon had, in 1903, argued that the submarine had rendered obsolete the permanent fields of observation mines which, under the control of the Royal Engineers, had for more than thirty years afforded protection to British ports. By 1905, these mines (having been transferred to the Navy) were being progressively removed.[2]

In May 1905 a committee assembled on Fisher's instructions to consider 'the number of Automatic Submarine Mines required to be held in readiness by the Navy'. Ottley was the chairman; Bacon was a member of the committee. The provision of 10,000 mines was recommended, of which 3,000 were designated for use against the Germans in the North Sea. In war the 3,000 were to be laid about 10 miles off the mouths of the Elbe, Weser, and Jahde. For reasons of economy the committee did not advocate provision of 'permanent vessels for laying mines'.[3] Subsequently orders were placed for 1,000 mines of the 'naval spherical' type. By the beginning of 1906 it was still intended to accumulate 10,000 independent mines. It was then also decided to convert the old light cruiser *Iphigenia* into a minelayer. Altogether, seven such ships were converted. The Great War began before any nation had designed and built a ship specifically for minelaying.

By 1914, Britain had experimented with foreign types of mine fitted with Hertz horns, but none of these designs had been adopted. There were about 4,000 spherical mines in stock. Not only were these numbers deficient. The efficiency of the mines was low. In April 1915 Fisher was expressing a wish 'to be

[1] Cowie, p. 31; F.P. 4703, *Remarks on Tactical Exercises, etc.*, P. 6.12.02 (reprinted in *N.N.* ii, 186–9).

[2] Cab. 2/1/115 and 2/1/122, 60th and 64th meetings of C.I.D., 2 Dec. 1904 and 1 Mar. 1905.

[3] Cowie, pp. 31–5; *N.N.* ii, 160–7; Sueter, pp. 287–8.

"even" with the principal culprits'. Evidently he saw no compelling reason to blame himself! It was indeed true that in April 1905 he had regarded an abundance of 'offensive' mines as 'an imperative immediate strategic necessity'.[1]

However, by January 1908 the First Sea Lord had adopted a different view. The first minesweepers were then being equipped and, in consequence, countermining had been abandoned. At a C.I.D. sub-committee, the 'invasionists' of the day suggested that the Germans might 'paralyse' the Navy by mining the Straits of Dover. Fisher retorted that the mines could easily be cleared but he added that he would not explain the relevant technique. This would be to 'throw away one of the deepest secrets' possessed by his service.[2] In June 1908 instructions were issued to Beresford which reflected a similar low opinion of the efficacy of mining: 'it appears that channels obstructed by mines can be readily cleared, and will thus in themselves present no serious obstacle to the movements of a Fleet.'[3] Nor does Fisher seem to have rated mining more highly after his retirement from the Admiralty. In May 1911 he wrote: 'I have had a dear letter from Sir George Murray, who spontaneously writes to me that the Admiralty is going strong, and all is well, except for an extraordinary desire to revert to submarine mines, which fills him with astonishment, but they were exposed so mercilessly, only 5 years ago, as d—d folly, that I told Murray in reply he need not fear.'[4] While it may be fairly concluded that Fisher was himself a good deal to blame for the parlous state of British mining in 1914, the following comment made by Jellicoe in 1917 (when he was himself First Sea Lord) may be noted in partial mitigation: 'As regards mines, our deficiencies are due to a certain extent to the deliberate abandonment of defensive mining by Lord Fisher, but far more to the continual cutting down of the Estimates for the provision of offensive mines which was in progress to my certain knowledge for the four or five years before war broke out.'[5]

---

[1] Cowie, pp. 35–7; F.P. 4751, 'Report on Fleet Auxiliaries' (P. 1/06), pp. 28–9; F.G. iii, 199; Add. MSS. 49710, f. 246, F. to Balfour, Apr. 1905.

[2] Cab. 16/3, proceedings of sub-committee on invasion, 27 Jan. 1908.

[3] Adm. 116/1090, Torpedo and Submarine Manoeuvres, 1908.

[4] F.G. ii, 372.

[5] Adm. 116/1430, 'Report of Sir Sothern Holland's Committee: Remarks of CNS', 17 Oct. 1917. Jellicoe was at the Ady. as D.N.O., 1905–7, as Controller, 1908–10, and as Second Sea Lord, 1912–14.

While Fisher's influence on technical developments may not have been uniformly beneficial, there was another sphere in which he continued to exert an influence both enlightened and progressive. In the last resort, the morale of the lower deck would be decisive for the Navy's performance in a long war. Fisher, of course, was not unique in recognizing this, but his modernity and sociability are seen to particular advantage in this regard. Since the turn of the century, discontent had grown among the ratings in respect of their living conditions, pay, and chances of promotion from the lower deck. In a letter to Selborne of 5 August 1902 Fisher had demonstrated his insight into these matters:

There has been a vast change in the bluejacket of late years, which our older officers have failed, I fear, fully to recognize. They are far more discriminating and far more susceptible to want of fairness and far more critical of the qualities of those above them than they used to be, and, consequently, they are far more sensitive to the whip and spur of discipline than they were, and . . . I personally am convinced that for these reasons you can nowadays maintain discipline more easily . . .[1]

In 1903, while Fisher was Second Sea Lord, a hundred senior Warrant Officers were promoted to Lieutenant in the executive, engineer, and carpenter branches; and the pensions of Chief Petty Officers were improved. Despite the prevailing emphasis on economy, further improvements were made after Fisher became First Sea Lord. In the Cawdor Memorandum of 1905 it was announced that provision allowances would be paid to men on leave. At the same time an outstanding grievance was removed. Instead of retaining part of a rating's allotment to his dependants as a security against his deserting or dying on foreign service, the authorities thenceforward paid the whole amount. Provision was also made for promotion of Stokers to warrant rank (in addition to the avenue by way of Mechanician dating from December 1902).

The First Sea Lord's understanding and flexibility may also be seen in connexion with the disturbances amongst stokers under training at Portsmouth barracks in November 1906. He sent a telegram in cypher to the King at Sandringham saying that the press had exaggerated the incident. He continued: 'The men concerned are young Stokers who have recently joined the

[1] F.G. i, 257.

Navy and are unaccustomed to discipline but it is of course possible that want of judgement has been shewn. If so it will be elicited by Court of Enquiry and will be promptly dealt with.'[1] Whereas Beresford, on receiving the news of the incident at sea, wrote to the First Lord in purely condemnatory terms about 'such a disgrace', the court of inquiry found that Fisher's suspicion of mishandling was justified.[2]

During Fisher's term as First Sea Lord the rates of pay were not raised, as such. However, the reform both of the system of victualling and of the naval canteens, carried out in 1907, represented an improvement in the rating's standard of life which was no less valuable for being overdue. Lionel Yexley calculated that the reform was worth about 7d. a day in relation to the Able Seaman's substantive pay of 1s. 8d. a day. This was therefore a change of some magnitude. Yexley, an ex-Able Seaman who had started a monthly paper called *The Fleet* for the lower deck in 1905, became devoted to Fisher. The latter made himself accessible to Yexley who was convinced that, without the First Sea Lord's consequent personal intervention, the victualling reform of 1907 would not have been effected. Thanks to Fisher, the Login Committee was appointed and 'made a clean sweep of a system that had been in vogue since 1799'.[3]

Finally, Fisher's approach to the problem of naval discipline may be discerned in the Admiralty's moderation of punishments from 1907 and in the announcement of October 1909 that detention quarters would be built at the three main naval ports. The practice of sending naval offenders to civilian prisons would cease. The said offenders would wear naval uniform and do physical training and service drill in place of shot-drill and picking oakum. The object was to provide punishments that were 'deterrent' but 'not degrading'.[4]

Unfortunately, from the autumn of 1907 onwards Fisher was increasingly distracted from constructive work by the activities of Beresford and his real or imagined associates. In the sphere of national strategy, there were new opportunities for interservice

---

[1] Tweedmouth Papers, A 107, 6 Nov. 1906.

[2] Ibid., A 181, 7 Nov.; Adm. 116/1022, Portsmouth R.N. Barracks—Disturbances Nov. 1906.

[3] Yexley, *Our Fighting Sea Men*, pp. 217, 224; *The Fleet*, Oct. 1930. I am indebted to Cdr. H. Pursey for help with this item.

[4] Yexley, op. cit., pp. 274, 277–9.

consultation and agreement. These stemmed from the friendship of Major-General J. S. Ewart, D.M.O. since October 1906, and Captain Slade, whom Fisher moved from the War College to succeed Ottley as D.N.I. Ottley, to Fisher's satisfaction, succeeded Sir George Clarke as Secretary of the C.I.D. on 24 August 1907. Clarke, having been reduced to impotence at the C.I.D. by the service departments, was glad to accept the governorship of Bombay—such an appointment having for long been a goal of his ambition.

However, in August 1907 there were two developments which disturbed Fisher. Ewart conveyed to the French some details of the British force which would support the French Army in the event of the British government deciding to intervene against Germany. There would be one cavalry division and 50,000 horses, four infantry divisions, and some 300 guns. They could all be deployed in France by the nineteenth day of British mobilization.[1] Very soon after this, the question of invasion again came to a head. Curiously, Fisher's anxiety about this latter development seems to have exceeded his qualms about the former. For example, having been informed unofficially about Ewart's scheme he allowed D.N.I. to co-operate in preparing plans for transporting the British expeditionary force (B.E.F.) to France. (Admittedly, little effective work was done in this respect before 1911.)[2] But Fisher reacted much more violently against the revived invasionist party, apparently failing to see clearly that their defeat would strengthen the hand of the General Staff in advocating a 'continental' strategy. He presumably saw a home defence army as more objectionable than a B.E.F. because it more directly usurped the proper functions of the Navy and consequently represented a greater threat to future naval estimates.

The invasion question had been raised on this occasion by Field-Marshal Lord Roberts, Repington, and others. They argued—plausibly enough—that whereas the C.I.D. inquiry of 1903 had assumed France to be the invader, a fresh inquiry was now required on the basis of a possible invasion by Germany. Balfour[3] and Clarke having suggested action by the C.I.D.,

---

[1] Williamson, p. 113; Summerton (thesis), pp. 190–1.

[2] B.D. vii, 627–8 (No. 639), memo. by Nicholson, 6 Nov. 1911. Summerton's thesis supplies more information to the same effect.

[3] Balfour, in opposition, retained some links with the C.I.D.

Fisher wrote angrily to Tweedmouth on 17 August that a refutation was 'being elaborated' by the Admiralty. 'The defence of the country against oversea attack is in the hands of the Admiralty, and I strongly deprecate the suggestion of a Sub-Committee of the C.I.D. being appointed to investigate it.'[1]

The Admiralty memorandum on 'Invasion and Raids' extends to fifty-five pages of print and comprises a lengthy paper by Slade and a shorter one, of five pages and dated 22 August 1907, by the First Sea Lord. Fisher dwells on the ignorance of the invasionists and the Admiralty's exclusive responsibility for preventing invasion. He stresses the extent of naval preparation, making particular mention of 'a permanent flotilla of our latest type of submarines, with their parent ship, stationed at Harwich' and currently exercising off the east coast. (In fact, as mentioned in the last chapter, these submarines were still too small to be very effective.) Fisher also dilates on the strength of the Home Fleet. By the summer of 1908, he argues, it will be more than a match for the whole German battlefleet. He then expounds his present views on British amphibious capabilities, apparently hoping to defeat at a single blow the arguments both of the invasionists and of the continentalists of the General Staff.

No, the fact is, and we know it has been thoroughly appreciated by the German Admiralty, that the creation of the British Home Fleet precludes the idea formerly existent in some sanguine German minds of the possibility of a raid or invasion. Not only so, but we have evidence of the Home Fleet bringing home to the Germans the likelihood of a successful British attack on their coasts and harbours, for an important Commission of naval and military German experts has recently been visiting Cuxhaven and Borkum and the coast in the vicinity in order to elaborate a system of defence which will involve a very large financial outlay.

With the British Fleet at its present strength and as at present distributed and with its present fighting efficiency, a German invasion or raid can be only a dream! This is not saying that the military forces are unnecessary or that they should not be organized and exercised. A force of 70,000 British troops, complete in all arms, is a weapon essentially necessary to give effect to the activity of the Fleet, 'a projectile to be fired by the Navy', as Sir E. Grey said.

Such a military force, organized to be embarked at a few hours' notice, and to be capable of being assembled within a few days at a secret rendez-vous in the North Sea, and always shifting its position,

[1] Add. MSS. 41231, f. 163, F. to Tweedmouth, 17 Aug. 1907 (copy sent to Campbell-Bannerman on T.'s instructions).

as would be easy and essential, would constitute such a menace to Germany as would probably occupy a very considerable portion of the German army in providing for the unknown point of landing of this British raiding force.[1]

Esher was 'furious' at Fisher's obstruction. 'I have written to Campbell-Bannerman and Haldane', he wrote to his son on 23 August, 'and this morning I hear that Campbell-Bannerman decided to overrule the Admiralty.'[2]

Fisher went to Carlsbad for his summer holiday but his anxieties concerning the inquiry continued to mount. He was particularly disquieted to learn that General Nicholson, now Quartermaster-General, was to be a member of the C.I.D. sub-committee, and on 16 September the Admiral wrote to Esher to find out 'why that double dealing arch-fiend Nicholson is hauled into it'.[3] On the 18th he wrote to Ottley (now installed as Secretary of the C.I.D.):

We are going to have a big job over the re-raised invasion bogey but I daresay we shall flatten out Repington & Co. . . . I am trying to get out of Esher, but in vain, why Sir W. Nicholson has been imported into this question. You know how villainously he fought against the Admiralty over this invasion question and insulted Battenberg and told B. his (Nicholson's) day would yet come to conquer. It's quite likely that he may be in collusion with Repington while outwardly the impartial enquirer into the supposed new state of things. Beresford is also in the business with Repington & Co.—no doubt you saw Repington's veiled allusion to the desirability of Beresford being Admiralissimo.[4]

Fisher, very much on the defensive against the allied Beres-fordians and invasionists, tended in the coming months to over-state the soundness of the Navy's comparative position.[5] Although he had probably received a letter of 1 October from Esher, warning him against overconfidence, Fisher wrote to the King from the Tyrol on 4 October:

In March this year *it is an absolute fact* that Germany had not laid down a single Dreadnought, nor had she commenced building a single

---

[1] Cab. 1/7/740, P. 9.10.07, pp. 15–19. There is also a version of 57 pp., P. 4.11.07, in F.P. 4961 (and elsewhere).

[2] Esher, ii, 247.   [3] Esher Papers 10/42.

[4] F.P. 256 (copy). Unfortunately Ottley's papers are apparently no longer extant.

[5] See Roberts Papers (National Army Museum), 7101–23, 62 for ample evidence of collusion between Beresford and Repington. Moon's thesis is again useful here.

ship for 18 months (*Germany has been paralysed by the Dreadnought!*) The more the German Admiralty looked into her qualities, the more convinced they became that they must follow suit . . . their existing Battle Fleet was utterly useless *because utterly wanting in gun power!* . . . it meant spending 12½ millions sterling on widening and deepening the Kiel Canal . . .

England had 7 Dreadnoughts and 3 'Invincibles' (in my opinion better than Dreadnoughts), total—10 Dreadnoughts built and building, *while Germany in March last had not begun one!* even if in May last a German Dreadnought had been commenced! . . .

But there is one more private piece of information for Your Majesty alone. Admiral Tirpitz (the German Minister of Marine) has privately stated in a secret paper that the English Navy is *now* four times stronger than the German Navy! . . . But we don't want to parade all this, because if so we shall have parliamentary trouble. Sir John Brunner, M.P., and 150 Members of the House of Commons who are Sir Henry Campbell-Bannerman's warmest supporters and have been his steadfast friends in adversity have sent him quite recently one of the best papers I have read, convincingly showing that we don't have to lay down any new ships at all—*we are so strong*. It is quite true! . . .[1]

In fact, this appraisal was already invalid. On the previous day, 3 October, the British naval attaché was reporting from Berlin indications in the press of acceleration in the future rate of German shipbuilding.[2] By 7 November, Tweedmouth was intimating to the cabinet the implications of the German intention to replace battleships after twenty instead of twenty-five years.[3] However, it seems that Fisher saw no cause for real concern in this development.

A Beresfordian demand for an inquiry into Admiralty policy was reinforced at this time by the founding of the Imperial Maritime League. On 9 November the First Sea Lord was guest of honour at the Lord Mayor's banquet. Fisher (who had returned to England only a fortnight earlier) decided to improve the occasion by counterattacking his various critics and enemies on the ground of overwhelming British naval superiority. The speech was ill-timed and ill-judged. It weakened the Admiralty's bargaining position just as a struggle was developing with the government over the estimates for 1908–9—a struggle which was

---

[1] *F.G.* ii, 139–41.   [2] *D.S.* i, 135.
[3] Cab. 37/89/87, 'Naval Establishment at Rosyth—Postscript'. Mr. H. P. Willmott kindly drew my attention to this reference.

assuming particular importance in the light of the proposed amendment to the German Navy Law. Fisher's pronouncements made even Arnold White 'shudder' at the prospect of future recriminations.[1] However, the speech was well received on the occasion of its delivery:

> As to the strength, the efficiency, and the sufficiency of the Navy, I am able to give you indisputable proofs . . . And that large Fleet is *nulli secundus*, as they say, whether it is ships or officers or men. (Cheers.) Now, I turn to the other point, the gunnery of the Fleet. The gunnery efficiency of the Fleet has surpassed all records—it is unparalleled . . . (Cheers.) You must hit first, you must hit hard, and you must keep on hitting. (Cheers.) If these are the fruits, I don't think there is much wrong with the government of the Navy. (Cheers.) . . . our object has been the fighting efficiency of the Fleet and its instant readiness for war; and we have got it. (Cheers.) And I say it because no one can have a fuller knowledge than myself about it, and I speak with the fullest sense of responsibility. (Cheers.) So I turn to all of you and I turn to my countrymen and I say—Sleep quiet in your beds (laughter and cheers), and do not be disturbed by these bogeys—invasion and otherwise—which are being periodically resuscitated by all sorts of leagues. (Laughter.) . . .[2]

During the early moves in connexion with the Navy Estimates, Fisher seems to have been preoccupied with the onset of the invasion inquiry. Esher thus recorded the first meeting of the sub-committee on 27 November:

> The Defence Committee began the enquiry into 'Invasion' to-day. Lord Roberts' peroration, delivered with rhetorical emotion, was very well done. Repington put his case admirably, and the mass of information, and carefully compiled detail, were most impressive.
>
> Fisher was full of suppressed wrath. I said to him that he was fond of quoting Mahan's famous passage about Nelson's storm-tossed ships . . . and it should remind him that the C.I.D., upon which he wished he had never looked, stood between him and a Royal Commission to enquire into the state of the Navy.[3]

Fisher was himself a member of the sub-committee. Presentation of the Admiralty's views was left to Slade who received much unobtrusive assistance from Corbett. Both Slade and Corbett were proponents of an amphibious strategy and their influence

---

[1] *F.G.* ii, 150n.
[2] F.P. 4852, 'The Guildhall Banquet', P. 11/07; also *Records*, pp. 83–5.
[3] E.P. 2/10 (unedited version).

may be seen in Fisher's memorandum of 22 August, quoted above, especially where he dwells on the distracting effect of a British seaborne force in the North Sea. Slade and Corbett were encouraged by Ewart's readiness, as D.M.O., to examine a wide range of options. They were prepared to concede from the beginning of the invasion inquiry that the Army had a legitimate part to play in home defence. At the same time they hoped that naval concession of this basic point might conduce to military co-operation with their amphibious ideas. Indeed Ewart, on his own initiative, had begun by August 1907 to look into the question of Denmark and British entry into the Baltic in a German war; and at the end of October he had privately sent to Slade a paper on the subject. Slade was asked whether the Navy planned to use the Belts. If so, would military assistance be required and on what scale? The records of the subsequent investigations, extending well into 1908, show that—contrary to what has sometimes been asserted—the 'Baltic scheme' did receive close attention before the Great War. It also emerges that the D.M.O.'s department took a more realistic view of the problem than did Fisher's ill-organized planners.[1]

However, before proceeding further with the invasion inquiry and Fisher's relations with the Army, it will be convenient to deal with his concurrent role in the affair of the Navy Estimates for 1908. The proposed amendment to the German Navy Law was published on 18 November 1907. The Germans would lay down four instead of three dreadnoughts each year during the period 1908–9 to 1911–12.[2]

The British programme for 1908–9 had been provisionally agreed in meetings held at the Admiralty under Fisher's chairmanship in June 1907. Because of Britain's lead in dreadnought battleships, only one of these was to be laid down in 1908–9; this would complete a class of four ships, making eight dreadnought battleships in all. There were also to be two armoured cruisers. Although it was proposed to arm them with 9·2-inch guns, they were intended for 'pressing home a reconnaissance' as well as for the protection of commerce. 'There was also',

---

[1] W.O. 106/46 (files E2.14–16); Adm. 116/1043 B, Part I for N.I.D.'s copy of paper on a military expedition to Zealand, P. 30.6.08; N.M.M. Slade Papers, including diary for 1908; diaries of Ewart and Corbett. Summerton's thesis provides an excellent account of the bi-service investigations into the Baltic question, 1907–8.

[2] D.S. i, 135–6.

according to the relevant print, 'a strong consensus of opinion that a type of *unarmoured* vessel was also urgently necessary to act as parent-vessels to the large and increasingly numerous flotillas of our Destroyers when operating on an enemy's coast, as well as to meet the vessels of the same type now being built by foreign nations (more particularly by Germany).' Jellicoe, then D.N.O., described these cruisers as forming 'an inshore watching squadron' with the destroyers 'off an enemy's port'—thus confirming that close blockade remained official policy. It was therefore decided to include '5 improved "Boadicias" ' to meet such needs. This decision signified abandonment of Fisher's proscription of light cruisers which had continued in effect since 1904. These five light cruisers would cost a total of £2 million compared with £1,800,000 for the battleship and £2,200,000 for the two armoured cruisers. Otherwise there would be twelve new destroyers 'with superior endurance and sea-keeping qualities to the most recent German Destroyer'. In fact, these destroyers (of the 'Beagle' class) were to prove both slow and under-gunned compared with their German contemporaries. Fisher's preceding class of 'Tribals' (1905–8) was weakly armed and lacked the endurance required for operations in the North Sea. Consequently the destroyer position remained unsatisfactory for some years after 1908. The programme of 1908–9 was to be completed by allocating £500,000 to submarines; 'and it was agreed that the precise numbers and types to be provided should be determined later by the results obtained with the latest type of the D class.' The *D*.1 did not come into service till 1909. She was the first British 'overseas' submarine—diesel-driven, like her successors. The Germans meantime were already developing a similar class of vessel.[1]

In the light of the German Navy Law amendment, the British programme was barely adequate; yet even this programme was in jeopardy from November 1907 to February 1908. Initially, it was the junior Sea Lords who chiefly resisted the government's pressure for reductions—stemming from the need to provide for old-age pensions from January 1909 onwards. Fisher, however, was at first prepared to comply with the cabinet's wishes.

During November 1907 the Navy Estimates Committee at the Admiralty discovered that the 1907 figure of £31,419,500 would

---

[1] F.P. 4724, *Navy Estimates Committee, November 1907*, P. 2/08, pp. 12–19; March, p. 85; T. D. Manning, pp. 51, 54; Jameson, pp. 96–100.

have to be increased by upwards of two millions, instead of one million (previously expected). The increase was due to the higher price and consumption of coal, the exhaustion of 'redundant' stores, new apparatus for cooling cordite in the magazines, and 'the great increase in the estimate for repairs'. On 21 November Tweedmouth communicated this 'bomb' to Asquith.[1] The Chancellor at once replied: 'I need hardly tell you that I cannot and will not be responsible for submitting such estimates to the House of Commons.'[2] Tweedmouth agreed to seek reductions 'consistent with efficiency' and 'without materially interfering with the progress of the shipbuilding programme'. He pointed out that the construction vote was the lowest for several years.[3] Fisher duly drafted a memorandum which the First Lord circulated to the Controller (Rear-Admiral Sir Henry Jackson) and the Financial Secretary. This indicated various savings, such as deferred payments for armour plating and cuts in stores, which he thought 'might safely be accepted'. The sequel was thus recorded by the First Lord's private secretary, V. W. Baddeley:[4] 'N.B. This memo. was drafted by Sir J. Fisher and was circulated, but was then withdrawn at the request of the other Sea Lords.   V.W.B.'[5]

The cabinet met on 26 November and refused to accept the unreduced estimates. Campbell-Bannerman directed Tweedmouth to see that they were 'completely revised' and specifically requested omission of the proposed battleship.[6] On 29 November Baddeley addressed the following minute to the Controller:

The First Lord's proposals (as recommended by the Estimates Committee at which you were present) were not accepted by the Cabinet on Tuesday [26th], and he was instructed to go further into the question with the assistance of Sir E. Grey and Mr. Runciman . . . with a view to the production of a revised estimate, not to exceed last year's total, by the time the Cabinet reassembles in January.

Sir J. Fisher has indicated means by which further reductions, if insisted upon, can be brought about. These are:—

---

[1] Tweedmouth Papers, J 1.
[2] Ibid., J 2, 21 Nov.
[3] Ibid., J 4, 22 Nov.; J 6, memo. for 1st Sea Lord *et al.*, 23 Nov.
[4] Successful in his career as a civil servant, he subsequently wrote the *D.N.B.* articles on Fisher and other naval figures.
[5] Ibid., J 5, n.d.   [6] Ibid., J 8.

Vote 8 (a) Postpone *Vanguard* till March.[1]

(b) Alter new programme to $\begin{cases} 1 & \text{armoured cruiser} \\ 10 & \text{Boadicias} \end{cases}$

instead of $\begin{cases} 1 & \text{battleship} \\ 2 & \text{armoured cruisers} \\ 5 & \text{Boadicias} \end{cases}$

(c) Stop repairs of more obsolescent ships.

(d) Delay payments for contracts on existing shipbuilding programmes . . .[2]

Once again—and on this occasion even more importantly—it was the junior Sea Lords, namely Vice-Admiral Sir William May, Rear-Admiral Sir Henry Jackson, and Rear-Admiral A. L. Winsloe, who stepped into the breach. Rejecting the proposed cuts, they drew up a 'Memorandum by the Sea Lords for the Information of the First Lord'. At the top of the typed copy Fisher wrote: 'Signed by the 4 Sea Lords and given to the First Lord on Dec. 3rd 1907'. May (who kept the paper) added in blue pencil: 'This was the result of the Memo. by the three Sea Lords. Fisher decided to support us—the question of resignation was too much for him.'[3]

Before examining the text of the memorandum, it is appropriate to ask why the First Sea Lord was reluctant to sign it. The answer comes readily to hand. On 25 November he observed to Lord Cawdor: 'Beresford and all the malcontents are now coalescing to have a Parliamentary enquiry or a Royal Commission on Admiralty policy and administration.'[4] Looking at British naval strength from this point of view, he wrote to Balfour on 29 November:

The worst of an enquiry would be that it would show the Navy to be so strong that an enormous reduction in shipbuilding could not be resisted. In March 1910 we shall have *actually at sea* 7 *Dreadnoughts* and 3 *Invincibles* (which are as good as Dreadnoughts) and not one

---

[1] This was the third battleship of the 1907 programme, her construction being contingent on the failure of the Hague Conference to achieve arms limitation. In the event, she was laid down on 2 April 1908.

[2] Ibid., J 9.

[3] N.M.M., May Papers, MAY/9. I am grateful to Dr. John E. Moore for mentioning this document to me. See also Richmond's article on May in the *D.N.B.*

[4] *F.G.* ii, 151.

single Foreign Dreadnought will then be ready. 4 German Dreadnoughts and one German Invincible will be ready at *the end* of 1910.
No French ones till later.[1]

It is clear that the mounting pressure of Beresfordian criticism,
coupled with the invasion inquiry, hardened Fisher's tendency
to overstate British strength. But his assessment was to prove
seriously wide of the mark. The Germans did better than he
predicted; the first two battleships were completed by the
autumn of 1909 and two more by the spring of 1910. Fortunately,
however, he gave way to the junior Sea Lords, led by May, and
signed the following memorandum which helped to save the
Admiralty's face when, a year later, a naval panic duly
developed:

The publication in the last few days of the official programme of
German shipbuilding makes it clear that we have got to face largely
increased Naval Estimates in order to preserve our naval supremacy,
and it seems an imperative necessity that we should adhere to what
really may be characterised as a very modest shipbuilding programme for next year (1908–1909), viz.:—

    1   battleship,
    1   armoured cruiser,
    6   'Boadicias',
  16   destroyers,
    and 500,000 l. for submarines.

Although it is quite true that our preponderance in battleships at
the present moment might justify the omission of the solitary battleship proposed, yet with the full knowledge and absolute certainty
(now afforded by the German programme just issued) of having to
commence a large battleship programme in 1909–10, it would be
most unbusinesslike, and indeed disastrous, to close down the armour
plate industry of this country by the entire cessation of battleship
building. It would be similarly disastrous to abruptly stop the manufacture of heavy gun mountings, which the omission of the battleship
would also involve. In fact it would really be the right course, to help
the Estimates of 1909–1910, to lay down two battleships next year
(1908–1909). If the Germans maintain their programme (and there
is no reason to doubt it) we should be forced to a programme of five
battleships a year in 1910, and perhaps in 1909—this will depend on
the rapidity of their shipbuilding . . .

The 'Boadicias' and destroyers are urgently required. A large
number of our destroyers are reaching their age limit and must be

---

[1] Add. MSS. 49712, ff. 22–3.

replaced, and the 'Boadicias' are imperatively needed to replace the older cruisers, which are now entirely lacking, from age, in the primary requisite of speed . . .

The Estimates for 1908-1909 have been very carefully prepared, and it is not considered possible to effect further reduction, and the increase of rather more than $1\frac{1}{4}$ million over the Estimates of last year cannot be looked upon but as most moderate . . .

As before mentioned, comparing the relative strength of the battleships of France and Germany, our present position is a sound one, but in 1909 we may be forced to a programme of five battleships a year, and in view of that likelihood it is inadmissible to have a less programme than that carefully discussed and decided upon by the Board of Admiralty . . .

(Signed)   J. A. FISHER.
W. H. MAY.
H. B. JACKSON.

Admiralty,   A. L. WINSLOE.
December 3, 1907.[1]

As late as 20 December Fisher doubted that there was real cause for concern, though he was beginning to agree that a big programme might be needed by 1909. He wrote to Tweedmouth: 'May and Winsloe are very much exercised over the German Programme. May has been to see me again tonight. I think he has got "Hysteria Germanicus" as Lord Eversley would say! No doubt if the Germans stick to their programme we shall have to go in heavy for Battleship building in 1909-10.'[2]

In February 1908 the cabinet forced the Admiralty to accept an increase in the estimates of only £900,000 instead of the £$1\frac{1}{4}$ million stipulated in the memorandum of 3 December. Fisher had been threatened by 'Loulou' Harcourt (First Commissioner of Works) with replacement by Beresford but had refused to make any concession at that time.[3] Even if the enforced economies slowed down current building, the projected programme for 1908—barely adequate as it was—did survive substantially intact. The armoured cruiser, the ill-fated *Indefatigable*,

---

[1] F.P. 4242. This printed version, entitled 'Report to the First Lord, on the Navy Estimates 1908-1909, by the Sea Lords', embodies the text of the memo, in N.M.M., MAY/9. It was printed as a cabinet paper, 20 Jan. 1908.

[2] Tweedmouth Papers, B 147A, 20 Dec. 1907.

[3] Esher, ii, 280-4 is the standard source. However, Gollin, pp. 44-5, prints a letter of 7 Feb. from F. to J.L. Garvin which casts some doubt on the assertion that Beresford was prepared to accept Navy Estimates of £30,000,000. (The final figure for 1908-9 was £32,319,500.)

was finally given 12-inch instead of 9·2-inch guns. Otherwise the programme conformed with the Sea Lords' memorandum of 3 December.[1]

Meanwhile, at the second meeting of the invasion sub-committee on 12 December, the naval case had been aired. This was based on a 'Memorandum by the Director of Naval Intelligence on Invasion in Reply to the Memoranda Presented by Lord Roberts and Colonel Repington'.[2] On finding that Slade and Corbett were accepting the need for a small home defence army, Fisher had objected; but he gave way to Slade's insistence that this part of the memorandum should stand.[3] The statement emphasizes the hazards of a German transit in the face of British naval opposition but declares that the Navy does not see 'resistance to invasion as a purely naval problem'. The 'home army' should be strong enough to make an invader bring at least 70,000 troops with him. This will ensure preparatory activity on a scale bound to be reported by British intelligence. The Navy regards invasion 'essentially as a problem of combined strategy, and desires nothing so much as a thorough and reasoned understanding between the two services as to their respective functions in that behalf.'[4]

Despite his reservations, Fisher was pleased with the reception given to the memorandum. On 23 December he sent Balfour a copy of 'the "Magnum Opus" ' which had ' "*swept the Board*" on Defence Committee'.[5]

Meanwhile Beresford, insistent on the shortage of small cruisers and of destroyers serviceable in the North Sea, wished to give evidence before the invasion sub-committee or before a special committee of the cabinet. Fisher was much occupied in warding off these threats to his position.[6] Slade's diary[7] illuminates some of the anxieties besetting the First Sea Lord during the first two months of 1908:

[1] F.P. 4242, typescript headed 'Vote 8'. H. P. Willmott's thesis was very useful for the affair of the 1908 estimates, taken as a whole.

[2] Cab. 16/3 B, Appendix XVI. This emanated from 'Memorandum on Invasion, in Reply, etc.', similar text, P. 4.12.07 (F.P. 4965).

[3] Corbett's diary, introductory notes relating to 1907. (The first daily entry is for 10 Mar. 1908.)

[4] Cab. 16/3 B.   [5] Add. MSS. 49712, ff. 23–4.

[6] Esher, ii, 262; Roberts Papers, 7101–23, 62, Beresford to Repington, 17 Nov. 1907; Tweedmouth Papers, B 27, F. to T., 16 Jan. 1908; Add. MSS. 49713, ff. 177–84, Beresford to Balfour, 7 Mar. 1908.

[7] N.M.M., Slade Papers.

7 Jan. 1908   There is no doubt that Sir J. is in a most nervous state as regards Lord C. and what he may do.

17 Jan. 1908   It appears as if there is to be a regular attack on Sir John when Parliament meets.

24 Jan. 1908   The nearer that the meeting of the Invasion Committee gets the more nervous Sir J. seems to get.

4 Feb. 1908   Sir J. was quite pleased with the course of things [at the invasion inquiry] today and said he felt much more satisfied.

7 Feb. 1908   Sir J. sent for me to his house and talked about the Invasion paper. He is anxious about it and says that Haldane is behaving in the most unprincipled way. Lloyd George apparently told Sir J. that H. had got hold of the Prime Minister and had impressed him with the idea that the Admiralty had been asking for a big Territorial Army. Sir J. says that there are wheels within wheels and that there is a strong party in the Cabinet who want to eject Lord T[weedmouth] . . .

15 Feb. 1908   Sir John is very nervous again about the Invasion Committee. He wants to lay down figures and details and I want to keep the thing on broad principles. I had a long talk with Ewart about it and he and I are quite agreed. I hope he will be able to calm Nicholson down and prevent his raising questions which no one can answer. Sir John has no idea how he confuses the issues when he launches out on one of his digressions.

25 Feb. 1908   Sir J. is still very jumpy over the estimates. He has spent a large part of the day prompting Mr. Robertson as to what he is to say.[1]

5 Mar. 1908   Robertson was quite unequal to the debate in the House on the Estimates. He could not hold a candle to Lee and Balfour.[2]

Although closely pressed by his enemies, Fisher did not lack defenders. The King supported him consistently; and on 6 February Esher published in *The Times* a vigorous rebuttal of the Imperial Maritime League which aimed to remove Fisher

---

[1] Edmund Robertson, Parliamentary Secretary of the Admiralty, and spokesman in the Commons, had been a keen 'economist'; but he accepted that it was essential to defend the 1908 estimates.

[2] The Conservatives tried to force the government to admit that it had made last-minute cuts to placate its radical supporters.

from his post. Esher's final paragraph provoked a letter from the Kaiser to Lord Tweedmouth; and in April Tweedmouth was removed from the Admiralty on the ground of his indiscreet handling of the matter. Esher's letter ended as follows: 'There is not a man in Germany from the Emperor downwards who would not welcome the fall of Sir John Fisher. And for this reason only, apart from all the others, I must beg to decline your invitation to join the Council of the Maritime League.'[1]

In the sphere of the press, J. L. Garvin had emerged as Fisher's most valuable ally. The First Sea Lord had plied the journalist with Admiralty prints, some of them 'Secret', since 1905; but the connexion developed further when Garvin became editor of *the Observer* at the end of January 1908.[2] This furtive association took up much of Fisher's time and energy. Admittedly, he was in an increasingly tight corner. Even the sympathetic Sir Edward Grey told him that 'it was represented to him that Beresford had the whole Navy.'[3] While it would have been truer to say that the service was riven in twain, Beresford certainly had most of London society on his side. His rancour against Fisher was nurtured by Lady Charles—a 'poisonous woman' according to the First Sea Lord.[4]

Slade, who was anxious to improve relations between Fisher and Beresford, was asked by the latter to see him at Claridges Hotel where he was ill in bed. Lord Charles wished to 'discuss the plan of campaign'—against the Germans, presumably! With difficulty Slade obtained Fisher's permission. In the sitting-room he encountered Lady Charles. 'She is a terrible looking woman', Slade noted, 'very stout, very much got up, rouged apparently, with fair hair and a sort of turban which she apparently always wears.' Subsequently the D.N.I. agreed with Fisher that it was impossible to attain a permanent understanding with Beresford. Lord Charles would profess satisfaction at a meeting but afterwards he would succumb to 'the influence of Lady C and Custance'. However, Slade soon came to the general conclusion that there was little to choose between Fisher and Beresford; 'as long as they are in their respective positions they will fight each other', he noted pessimistically.[5]

---

[1] F.P. 278 is a copy of Esher's actual reply to the League dated 22 Jan. 1908. Excisions were made before publication in *The Times*.
[2] Gollin, pp. 35–92.   [3] *F.G.* ii, 161.   [4] Ibid., p. 151.
[5] N.M.M., Slade Papers, diary, 6, 7, 21 Jan. 1908.

Fisher's opponents often charged him with being vindictive. While Professor Marder is probably correct in believing that 'his bark was generally more dangerous than his bite', the Admiral became ever more prompt to designate new enemies as his feud with Beresford approached its climax. In 1928 Bacon, having undertaken to write Fisher's biography, consulted Sir Walter Nicholson who had been the First Sea Lord's private secretary from 1904 to 1910. Nicholson replied that he did not think Fisher indulged in 'deliberate persecution' but he did believe that 'he went a good deal further than an honest adverse opinion of capacity would justify in keeping Beresford & Co.'s friends (or suspected friends) away from the jobs which would naturally have fallen to them.'[1] This tendency was certainly evident to Slade early in 1908. For example, Captain M. E. Browning, who had hoped to engineer a *détente* on relieving Sturdee as Beresford's Chief of Staff, was quickly dubbed 'a traitor' by the First Sea Lord—'most unjustly', thought the D.N.I.[2] A few days later, on 13 January, a dispute arose about an appointment for G. G. Aston—subsequently Colonel-Commandant of the Royal Marine Artillery, 1914–17. Fisher 'would not listen' to arguments in Aston's favour. Slade commented: 'He is another traitor because he signed a minority report on the Marine Training Committee. [Fisher] said he had had enough of magnanimous actions and he was going to keep his enemies under in future. All the good men who used to be Sir J.'s men in the past are now with very few exceptions styled Traitors.'[3]

Although he seems never to have been definitely excluded from the 'Fishpond', Commander H. W. Richmond became markedly critical of Fisher at about this time. In December 1906 he had returned to the Admiralty as the First Sea Lord's Naval Assistant. By April 1907 he was describing 'the Admiralty organization for War' as 'beneath contempt' but he still thought that Fisher was 'a genius' and the best hope for those who wanted a general staff at the Admiralty. He wrote in his journal: 'If we let him go without having introduced it we may whistle for a generation for another man strong enough and cunning enough to contend with the tremendous Civil Service power which has to be got out of the way.' He noted that Ottley, then still D.N.I.,

---

[1] Kilv. MSS., Pkt. 38, 8 Oct. 1928.
[2] Slade's diary, 9 Jan. 1908.   [3] Ibid., 13 Jan.

was 'very keen on the formation of a G.S.'[1] However, by the time he went to sea in the spring of 1909 as May's Flag-Captain in the *Dreadnought*, Richmond had abandoned this hope: 'The Admiralty plans are to my mind the vaguest amateur stuff I have ever seen . . . The worst of it all is that I do not see who is going to carry through a reorganization. Fisher, supreme in his contempt for history and distrustful of all other men, will neither seek nor accept counsel.'[2]

In fact, the pressures of late 1907 did induce Fisher to discuss strategy and war plans to a greater extent than before. He set up a Strategy Committee with Slade as a regular member. Others, such as Captain R. S. Lowry, the president of the War College, attended on an *ad hoc* basis.[3] Slade commented, after leaving the Admiralty early in 1909, that the committee lacked full information on the policy of the Board and that this resulted 'in purely academic plans being produced'.[4] However, during much of 1908 he took an over-optimistic view of the state of the naval war plans and thought that there was no urgency about forming a general staff with 'executive functions'.[5] Corbett seems to have agreed with him at the time.[6] The historian may have encouraged the eighteenth-century tendency of Slade's strategic thought. The D.N.I.'s sustained interest in operations on the German North Sea coast is indicated in various diary-entries, such as:

1 Feb. 1908   'Strategy Committee. Noon. Had a most interesting discussion. Sir J. agreed that the best form of defence would be to send an army to sea. It would paralyse all German initiative and would tie up a large portion of their forces to the sea coast.

22 Feb. 1908   We . . . went on to discuss the blocking of the Elbe. [Capts. O. de B.] Brock and [A. G. H.] Moore were against it, but I think we came to the conclusion that it should be done if possible.

Meanwhile, at a meeting of the invasion committee on 20 February, Fisher and Slade had contrived to score a debating success against General Nicholson in connexion with the Navy's desire for 'a sea-going Army'. Slade contended that the mere

---

[1] N.M.M., RIC/1/7, Apr. 1907.
[2] Marder, *Portrait of an Admiral*, pp. 48–9.
[3] Slade's diary, 17 Jan. and 1 Feb. 1908; F.P. 395, W. Nicholson to McKenna 28 June 1909.
[4] Cab. 16/9 B, Slade to Asquith, 8 May 1909.
[5] Slade's diary, 28 Mar. 1908.   [6] Corbett's diary, 26 Mar.

threat posed by a British amphibious force of some 60,000 troops would deter the Germans from embarking to invade Britain. Fisher declared: 'I put it on higher ground than that. The success of the Navy cannot be carried to its proper conclusion unless you have got a military force able to land and take advantage of it.' Instead of emphasizing the strength of the Germans' defensive position, Nicholson contended that Britain had no 'monopoly of amphibiousness' and that the Germans were also 'trying to be amphibious'. This argument was easily destroyed by reference to British naval superiority, and Fisher agreeably remarked to the discomforted General: 'I think that has been a boomerang for you.'[1]

However, an appearance of inter-service amity, carefully fostered by Slade, was usually maintained at the meetings, despite Fisher's interventions—the liveliest of which were excluded from the official minutes. Slade recorded:

26 Mar. 1908   Sir J. who had a bad cold was very much inclined to interfere, but he did not go very much off the line.

2 Apr. 1908   Sir J. said a great deal about submarines . . . no enemy's ships reaching coasts, etc., etc. Very wild statements. I afterwards spoke to him about it and he promised to have it all expunged.

29 May 1908   Mr. Balfour made a most excellent speech . . . Unfortunately the General Staff had prepared a Memorandum which they wanted to get off and Sir W. Nicholson [now C.I.G.S.] therefore read. There was nothing in it that was really objectionable but they did refer to the Army setting the Navy free, etc. This raised Sir J. and at the end he quite lost his temper and shouted out that he did not agree with a word that had been said . . . McKenna [Tweedmouth's successor as First Lord] chimed in like a little dog who barks when the big dog barks.

In any case, the committee was by then ready to settle for a home defence army of 70,000.[2]

By March 1908 the Conservatives were pressing the government in the Commons on the subject of the building programme. On the 9th Balfour asked whether British and German adherence to existing programmes would not produce a German lead in capital ships by the autumn of 1911. The next day Fisher sent

[1] Cab. 16/3 A, pp. 158–161.   [2] Cab. 3/2/1/44 A, report, 22 Oct. 1908.

Slade to Asquith who was deputizing for the ailing Campbell-Bannerman. Asquith had been presiding at the invasion inquiry and, now that he was also acting as Prime Minister, he showed more interest in the Navy. He 'closely' questioned the D.N.I. and 'very soon got hold of all the vital points'. Slade noted: 'I explained that since Germany built in 30 months and we built in 24 we could only start 6 months behind Germany, whereas we generally started 8 to 9 months behind her. There were thus 2 or 3 months in each year when Germany was ahead of us by one year's programme.' Later in the day, Asquith 'made a very good little speech' in the Commons, saying that Britain would arrange her shipbuilding so as to ensure superiority in 1911. He also reaffirmed the Two-Power Standard and repeated a British offer regularly to exchange information about construction. The Germans, however, continued to show no interest in this suggestion.[1]

At first, Fisher seems to have regarded Tweedmouth's removal in April as a threat to his own position; nor was McKenna's record as a naval 'economist' reassuring. However, when agreeing to McKenna's appointment the King stipulated that Fisher should remain as First Sea Lord. Asquith seems to have had no idea of forcing a change.[2] Having been 'fascinated' during a preliminary session with Fisher on 19 April, McKenna was fully in harness by early May. According to Slade he was a 'youngish man with a bald head covered with brown down as if he was using a hair restorer'—'pleasant in manner, sharp and quick'. Fisher, intent on saturating McKenna with his ideas, was virtually inaccessible for some days. He concentrated on the building programme for 1909–10. On 6 May Slade heard that this was to include four battleships. 'Not enough', he commented, 'by at least 1 and really by 2. It was a supreme bit of folly not to have laid down 2 this year.'[3]

But Fisher was delighted with his educative achievements. On 8 May he wrote to Esher:

My beloved E.,

Burn this when read. Yesterday with all Sea Lords present McKenna formally agreed to FOUR Dreadnoughts, AND IF NECESSARY SIX Dreadnoughts, next year (perhaps the greatest triumph ever

---

[1] Slade's diary, 11 Feb., 10 Mar. 1908; *D.S.* i, 139–40.
[2] *F.G.* ii, 172 and n. (F.P. 305).
[3] *F.G.* ii, 175; Slade's diary, 4–6 May 1908.

known!) . . . He (McKenna) funks Lloyd George [now Chancellor of the Exchequer] . . . this is what I suggest to you to impress on Lloyd George. *Let there be no mistake about two keels to one in Dreadnoughts!* . . .

I wonder if this is all clear to you that McKenna is going to give us the *numbers* for next year all right, but is wobbling over the money provision to the detriment of the year after. Shove in again the great fact the Navy and Army Estimates not far different in magnitude, and yet the Army can't fight Bulgaria and the Navy can take on the lot. 'Ut veniant omnes!!!' The Army too big for a little war, too little for a big war! You might tell Lloyd George he can rely on my parsimony, but he should give McKenna the tip that he is going for 4 or 5 millions on the Army Estimates (not all at once, of course) to give it to Navy. Don't let Lloyd George go at the King like a bull at a gate. Francis [Knollys] must pave the way, and then let the Celtic eloquence come in! . . .

Yours,
J.F.[1]

Fisher was scarcely less interested in McKenna's attitude towards Beresford. Perhaps the least agreeable episode of the whole Fisher–Beresford feud was the Levée incident of 11 May when Beresford turned his back on Fisher's outstretched hand. Slade's diary throws light on the immediate background to this notorious event:

11 Apr. 1908   An easy day as Sir J. went off to Portsmouth. He has taken a request of Lord Charles to be supplied with the publications issued by the War College very much en grippe. He has taken up the attitude that nothing should be sent to him without the sanction and authority of the Admiralty. It is an impossible attitude to take up, but he is so bitter against Lord C. that anything he does or says is wrong.

24 Apr. 1908   There is a lot of friction going on again between Lord C. and Sir J. The former asked for a mining vessel and submarines but he has only had a rude reply. What the result will be is only to be conjectured, but he will not sit down under the rebuff. Now Sir J. is frightened at what he has done and is wanting orders made out so that there shall be no chance of Lord C. saying that he does not intend to use the mining ships that are going to be sent to him for the manoeuvres. Sir J. is not well and looks very old and worn today.

[1] *F.G.* ii, 175–6; but the date appears to be 8, not 5 May (E.P. 10/42).

Beresford duly complained about the refusal of minelayers and submarines in a letter of 5 June to McKenna; and—not surprisingly—the matter was submitted to the C.I.D. inquiry into Admiralty policy in 1909.[1] However, the Levée incident had already occurred before Beresford wrote his letter. Slade was an eye-witness:

'Went to the Levée on duty as A.D.C. for the first time . . . Sir J. met me at the door and said in a cheery tone that he had altered the whole scheme of the manoeuvres. He spent his time before the King came in trying to persuade various members of the Cabinet to accept his views about Canada [that Britain should have nothing to do with defending her against the United States].

A very unpleasant occurrence happened between Sir J. and Lord C. The former was standing against the wall talking to Winston Churchill and Lloyd George when Lord C. passed after having made his bow. He shook hands with Lloyd George and Winston Churchill but when Sir J. put out his hand he turned his back on him. He behaves just like a naughty schoolboy.[2]

The feud was now becoming intolerable. For some time Fisher had been blaming the weakness of the cabinet for the lack of action against Beresford, but it was clear enough that Lord Charles was not wholly responsible for the rift. Haldane, in particular, was in any case unhappy about the lack of interservice co-operation for which he blamed Fisher and Nicholson.[3] However, some important changes were now made with regard to the Commander-in-Chief's responsibilities. These were precipitated by Beresford's latter to McKenna of 5 June which by no means confined itself to the Admiralty's refusal of minelayers and submarines. Lord Charles levelled a number of charges against the Admiralty which he—or Custance—summarized as follows:

(1) The allocation of the fleets in home waters.

(2) The constitution of the Home Fleet.

(3) The absence of any definite plan of campaign made out between the central authority—who must be responsible—and the Commander-in-Chief afloat.

(4) The shortage of small cruisers.

[1] Cab. 16/9A, p. 188; 16/9B, pp. 44–8.
[2] Slade's diary, 11 May 1908.
[3] Corbett's diary, 19 June.

(5) The shortage of destroyers suitable for extended offensive operations in the North Sea.

(6) The absence of any properly-defended strategical port on the North Sea coast suitable as a naval base.[1]

A few days earlier Sir William May, who in any case believed that the fleets in home waters should be united under one Commander-in-Chief, had impressed on McKenna that it had been a great mistake to hand over to Wilson control of strategical dispositions. He argued (in Slade's words) that the Admiralty 'must now recover their position and have it clearly understood that the direction of the war must come from here and not from sea'. On 22 June the D.N.I. noted: 'Sir J. has at last decided to alter the war orders of the various Fleets—taking back the responsibility for all movements to the Admiralty.' Fisher worked out the details of the war orders with Slade. 'I think they will do now,' wrote the latter, 'at any rate until his new distribution of the Fleet comes about.'[2] Fisher himself drafted the official letter of 1 July, covering the new war orders, and the key passages were repeated verbatim in McKenna's reply of 1 July to Beresford's letter of 5 June. The official letter stated that the Admiralty alone was responsible for 'all matters of policy' such as shipbuilding, 'the strategic distribution of the fleet in war', and 'the general plan of operations to be followed on its outbreak'. The letter ended with an expression of Fisher's attitude to war plans:

In conclusion, I am to make clear that, while their Lordships will always ensure a largely preponderant force being in the neighbourhood of the North Sea, the exact disposition and plan of action must depend upon the attendant conditions and political and other circumstances of the moment. Nevertheless it is of great importance that every probability should be thought out and provided against, and accordingly no one single plan of action, however perfected, can be accepted as final.

McKenna, for his part, concluded by warning Beresford that his poor relations with the First Sea Lord threatened 'the success of Admiralty Administration and the efficiency of the Fleet'.[3]

Enclosed with the Admiralty's letter to Beresford of 1 July were the new war orders. At the commencement of hostilities

---

[1] Cab. 16/9B.   [2] Slade's diary, 2, 22, 23 June 1908.
[3] F.P. 317 and 318 (with a note in F.'s hand) are copies.

he would have command of the Channel and Atlantic Fleets. (The Home Fleet was apparently to be held in reserve.

The following are the main features of the operations for which the Commander-in-Chief in the North Sea is responsible:

1. The principal object is to bring the main German fleet to decisive action, and all other operations are subsidiary to this end.

2. The Commander-in-Chief will direct the movements of the 1st Cruiser Squadron and Destroyer Flotillas off the German coast.

3. He is to establish a cordon of cruisers from the Skaw to Norway.

The extent to which close blockade survived in the war orders is probably attributable to Slade rather than Fisher. (See pp. 366-70 above.) The 'North Sea Battle Fleet' was to retire at night to a position 'not less than 170 miles from the nearest point on the German coast, where a destroyer base' was to be 'established'. At night, the British destroyers (six plus a scout off the Elbe and a similar force off the Jahde) would continue to 'patrol off their respective rivers, and the cruisers would steam away from the coast, returning in time to support the destroyers at daybreak, when they are most likely to be attacked by enemy cruisers'. During the day, 'a couple of destroyers off each river mouth as a watch will be sufficient.' A 'squadron of armoured cruisers' was to keep 'out of torpedo range beyond the small cruisers.'[1]

Fisher's projected redistribution of the fleets would eliminate at a blow both Beresford's command and a fundamental cause of his antagonism towards the Admiralty. By July the feud— complicated by the second of two incidents between Lord Charles and Sir Percy Scott—was receiving much attention in the press. While *The Times* demanded that Beresford be brought more effectively under naval discipline, there was no lack of calls for Fisher's dismissal. Quite a popular alternative was the dismissal of both! Thus, when McKenna placed before the cabinet the scheme of redistribution, based on the absorption of the Channel into the Home Fleet early in 1909 and the consequent fore-shortening of Beresford's expected three years in command, there was some ministerial resistance. In December 1908 Mc-Kenna finally prevailed. When, in March 1909, the reorganiza-tion took place, Beresford had to haul down his flag and come ashore. Sir William May became Commander-in-Chief of the

[1] Adm. 116/1043 B, Part I.

new Home Fleet. At last, the chances of confusion in wartime had been much reduced.

An intriguing feature of Fisher's strategic thinking in the second half of 1908 was his preoccupation with the United States. On 30 August he commended to Arnold White 'THE FEDERATION OF ALL WHO SPEAK THE ENGLISH TONGUE' which he dignified as 'that great and impending bulwark against both the Yellow man *and the Slav*'. (This last sentiment might have surprised the Grand Duchess Olga, Fisher's dancing partner at Reval the previous June, who had been much taken with his 'frolic and jollity' during King Edward's visit!) However, if only in the context of maintaining the Two-Power Standard, Fisher spent a surprising amount of time discussing plans for war against Germany combined with the United States. In July he was proposing to station the Home Fleet on the Irish coast to attack the Americans as they came across. Slade deemed this plan 'the most hopelessly puerile thing that he could possibly bring out'. In November (at a meeting on the Two-Power Standard) Fisher advocated 'a fleet in Lough Swilly ready to meet the American Fleet if it came over'. Slade commented: 'What was going to bring it over he did not specify.' However, the possibility of war with the United States was not taken very seriously, in so far as it was agreed that the Two-Power Standard 'must be left in a nebulous state' unless the Prime Minister was 'forced to define it'.[1] Nevertheless, in his commentary on war plans of December 1908 (see pp. 367–70 above) Fisher returned to the subject of the United States. Assuming a unified Home Fleet, he observed:

If the United States combine with Germany, yet for the first ten days it is Germany alone we have to deal with, as we should not send our Fleet across the Atlantic. We should await the United States Fleet after their journey of 3,000 miles, and we must greatly hope that the advent of the United States Fleet would induce the German Fleet to emerge from their Port to effect the desired junction. Neither the German nor the United States Fleet alone stand a chance against ours, and not much chance even if united, especially remembering the inevitable difficulties and dangers of co-operation of two Fleets of different nationalities (e.g. Trafalgar). One might almost wish the United States would join Germany.[2]

[1] Slade's diary, 22 July, 16 Nov. 1908.
[2] Adm. 116/1043 B, Part I. In the same file, see also 'War Plan, W.4: England v. Germany and the United States', 8 Dec. 1908 (P. 11.12.08).

All this makes strange reading in so far as there was real international tension that autumn which was in no way connected with the United States. A sharp Franco–German clash over an incident in Casablanca coincided with a prolonged crisis arising from the Austrian annexation of Bosnia-Herzegovina.[1] The state of inter-service preparedness is illuminated by Slade's diary entry for 6 November:

> The situation is not improving and the politicians are getting nervous. I have been asked for information which shows that they consider the situation critical.
>
> I got Ewart to come down to my room and we talked the position over and came to the conclusion that we must be ready with some scheme. We are accordingly going to meet tomorrow and draw up a more or less detailed plan.

It so happened that, before the Casablanca crisis came to a head, Ottley had persuaded Asquith to appoint a new C.I.D. sub-committee so that British grand strategy in a European war might at last receive high-level consideration. The main outcome was that the General Staff's plan for direct support of the French left flank emerged as the only practicable option. This sub-committee on the 'Military Needs of the Empire', as affected by the continent, met on 3 and 17 December 1908 and on 23 March 1909. Its report was dated 24 July 1909.[2]

Fisher's role in this investigation has presented a historical problem. Bacon saw fit to publish a document relating to one of the meetings of the sub-committee which recounts 'an impassioned diatribe' delivered by Fisher 'against the War Office and all its ways, including conceit, waste of money, and ignorance of war'. This is supposed to have followed his declaration that the proper course was to land the British Army on 'a stretch of ten miles of hard sand on the Pomeranian coast which is only ninety miles from Berlin' and that direct support of the French 'would be an act of suicidal idiocy'.[3] To judge by his correspondence and memoirs, all this represents some favourite themes in Fisher's private talk, but it is most unlikely that he treated the 'Needs of the Empire' committee to so uninhibited an exposition. First of all, Bacon's document is studded with inaccuracies. This may be seen by setting it alongside any reliable account of these

---

[1] Williamson, p. 132, etc.
[2] Cab. 16/5.
[3] Bacon, ii, 182–3. See also *D.S.* i, 388n.

matters.[1] Moreover, in letters of 17 January and 15 March 1909 Fisher assured Esher, who had also been at the first two meetings, that he would never disclose his amphibious plans to the C.I.D. As his reason for this concealment—which prevented the committee from fully considering the naval alternatives to direct support—he pointed to the security risks.[2]

In fact, there are indications that Fisher had reached the point of doubting whether the amphibious schemes could be convincingly defended against the criticisms accumulated by the D.M.O.'s department. For the benefit of the sub-committee, the General Staff embodied its views in a memorandum of 27 November 1908. This cogent document developed the arguments already indicated above (see pp. 333–4) against the Baltic scheme and concluded that the only feasible option was to afford direct support to the French Army.[3] On 28 November Slade noted: 'Sir J. wanted to see me about the meeting on Thursday on the subject of the Military Needs of the Empire. His view is that we had better not say anything at all about it.' Fisher was presumably referring to the various amphibious schemes, and to the Baltic scheme in particular. In the immediate background were the joint studies of the Baltic problem to which reference has been made. By the end of 1908, Ewart's department had revealed the weakness of the naval proposals for occupying Zealand prepared by the War College for the N.I.D.[4] The D.M.O. took no initiative to terminate the investigation, but in October one of Slade's assistants, Captain O. de B. Brock, saw the relevant War Office file; and in a letter to Colonel Gleichen he admitted that the War College scheme was 'a mass of verbiage'.[5] Meanwhile the assumption that the Navy would co-operate in dispatching the B.E.F. to France began to appear in War College plans in August and September.[6] It looks as if Slade, at least, was convinced of the need for an expeditionary

---

[1] See, for example, Williamson's admirable monograph.

[2] *F.G.* ii, 220, 232.

[3] Cab. 16/5, Appendix IV.

[4] The culminating naval memo. was 'Military Expedition to Zealand in support of the Danes against German invasion', N.I.D., P. 30.6.08 (W.O. 106/47/E2.16 and Adm. 116/1043 B, Part I).

[5] W.O. 106/47/E2.16, 19 Oct. 1908.

[6] Adm. 116/1043 B, Part I, 'War Plan: England and France v. Germany, W.3', Part I, P. 28 Sept. 1908, and Part II, P. 19 Aug. 1908. Both parts of the plan provide for operations on the German coast; Part I aims at the seizure of an off-shore island and close blockade.

force of four infantry divisions and one of cavalry, as proposed by Ewart.[1] (Such a plan would leave the possibility of using one or two infantry divisions for coastal operations.) Moreover, when the Prime Minister asked at the meeting of 3 December 'whether the Admiralty were prepared to guarantee the safe transport of the troops in the manner detailed by General Ewart', the First Lord 'said that the Admiralty could give this guarantee'.[2]

However, it seems clear that Fisher did perpetrate some kind of scene on 3 December, even if it did not reach the proportions indicated by Bacon's document. Fisher himself did not use the paper when compiling his memoirs. Instead he tried in February 1918 to glean some account of the affair from the C.I.D. records.[3] There was, however, no trace of it in the official minutes. Finally, in April 1919, Esher appears to have produced some notes concerning what Fisher described as this 'furious meeting on December 3, 1908'.[4] In any case the following account compiled by Fisher himself seems, despite some evident inaccuracies, to deserve quotation:

There was what was called a Plenary Meeting of the Committee of Imperial Defence—long, long before the War . . .

It was curious that Mr. Asquith as Prime Minister sitting at the head of the table with his back to the light had me exactly opposite him at the other end of the table . . . Our military colleagues with white wands and splendiferous maps pointed out to their enthralled listeners the disposition for war on the French frontier and seemingly all were swept off their legs! I suppose I looked glum. The Prime Minister said, 'Sir John, we've not heard you say anything.' I said 'No! it's purely a military matter!' 'But you've something on your mind,' said he; 'say it.' I steadfastly looked at the Field Marshal and his wand and said, 'If I were the German Emperor I should tell my millions to '*Fight neither with small nor great* but fight only with the 160,000 English and decimate them and massacre them" '; and indeed Mons came near to it . . .

The Prime Minister adjourned the meeting without a conclusion, and as I walked away with Esher I asked him unanswered if we weren't all d——d fools?[5]

---

[1] Slade's diary, 3 Dec. and especially 11 Nov. 1908.
[2] Cab. 16/5.   [3] *F.G.* iii, 511–12.   [4] *F.G.* iii, 579.
[5] F.P. 5101, pp. 26–7. In fact, it was not a plenary meeting but a strong sub-committee; Nicholson was not promoted to Field-Marshal till 1911; and Ewart's B.E.F. numbered less than 110,000 men.

Even Fisher deemed it adequate to entitle this account 'A Dramatic Incident'; and Slade, the faithful chronicler of the Admiral's outbursts before the invasion committee, confined himself to a single remark: 'We had a very interesting discourse on the probable French dispositions from Ewart.'[1]

According to the minutes, the final exchange on 3 December consisted of Asquith's question whether 'the Admiralty wished for any troops to be placed at their disposal in connection with the naval war plans' and Fisher's reply that 'no soldiers were required as it took time for them to mobilize, and naval measures would have to be taken without delay.'[2] The only alternative to Ewart's plan offered by the Navy—this at the second meeting—was reliance on an economic blockade of Germany.[3]

At the third meeting, on 23 March 1909, Fisher made it clear that he did not wish to contest the General Staff's assessment of the Baltic question. He accepted that the Germans would occupy Zealand and Fünen in time to deny the Belts to the British. As a possible solution, he suggested an arrangement with Sweden whereby she should deepen the Sound, thus leaving a neutral channel open to British battleships. The committee, however, concluded that the Danes would probably fail to impede a German invasion and that the 'closing of the Baltic to ships of the largest type' was a likely consequence. Therefore the committee, while recognizing that an economic blockade by the Navy did constitute a strategic option, saw the General Staff's plan as the obvious way of giving timely assistance to the French. It reported that 'in the event of an attack on France by Germany, the expediency of sending a military force abroad, or of relying on naval means only, is a matter of policy which can only be determined when the occasion arises by the Government of the day.'[4]

Superficially, therefore, Fisher was justified in considering that no choice had been made between the alternative strategies discussed by the sub-committee. On the other hand this strong committee, with the Prime Minister at its head, decided that 'in the initial stages of a war between France and Germany, in which the Government have decided to assist France, the plan to which preference is given by the General Staff is a valuable one, and the

---

[1] Ibid.; Slade's diary, 3 Dec. 1908.   [2] Cab. 16/5.
[3] Ibid., 17 Dec. 1908; also Appendix V.
[4] Ibid., proceedings of 23 Mar. and report of 24 July 1909.

General Staff should accordingly work out all the necessary details.'[1] Consequently, after Fisher's retirement, Asquith and Haldane were disturbed by the revelation, at a C.I.D. meeting of 23 August 1911, that the Navy was not fully co-operating with the General Staff on this matter. In the upshot Churchill displaced McKenna as First Lord and wasted little time in removing Sir Arthur Wilson, who had been following Fisherite policies, from the post of First Sea Lord.

By the time that he signed the sub-committee's report on 24 July 1909, Fisher's sands at the Admiralty were running out. He had seriously considered retiring the previous autumn, being uncertain of his relations with McKenna who had thus far failed to get rid of Beresford. On 2 November 1908 Esher wrote in his journal:

> Jackie . . . asks me to think over the proposition that he should retire next November with a Peerage (which has been promised) and that he should inform McKenna of his intention before long. It is the wiser course. He would lose £3,000 p.a., but he would be left with £2,000 p.a.—enough for him and his wife. He would avoid in this way an inevitable fall![2]

However, Fisher soon decided not to write to McKenna. 'The fact is' Esher noted on the 9th, 'he cannot bring himself to say Goodbye to the Admiralty, even a year hence.'[3] In December Beresford was officially informed that he was to come ashore on 24 March and Fisher's position seemed stronger.

But in December 1908, against the background of the persisting Bosnian crisis, a major scare arose in connexion with the rumoured acceleration of the German building programme. The naval crisis has been covered in detail by Professor Marder.[4] Here, the main consequence to note is the harsh criticism of Fisher in the press from March 1909 onwards. In fact, it now seems that the Germans had no intention of accelerating their programme.[5] But, as has already been indicated, the British programme for 1908–9 was too small, coming after the cuts already made in the Cawdor programme. Even a rumour of acceleration now spelt danger. So there was at least some justification for the view of the *Daily Express* on 20 March 1909 that Fisher was 'responsible for the starving of the Navy during the

---

[1] Ibid., report.   [2] E.P. 2/11.
[3] Ibid.   [4] *D.S.* i, 151–86.
[5] Information from Dr. Jonathan Steinberg.

last three years . . . If he had threatened resignation when an unsatisfactory programme was being prepared he would have forced the hands of the economaniacs. Moreover, his notorious "sleep safely in your beds" speech was a direct justification of Radical policy.'[1] Writing that day to Davidson (an assistant private secretary to the King) Fisher defended himself by referring to the memorandum of 3 December 1907. (See pp. 389–91 above.) The King was 'much annoyed' that Fisher had not drawn his attention to the document at the material time.[2] Of course, the reason for this omission was that the First Sea Lord did not then whole-heartedly accept the need for such a statement.

However, there is no doubt about the vigour with which Fisher supported McKenna's fight for the big dreadnought programme of 1909–10. On 15 March, for instance, as the struggle was coming to an end, J. S. Sandars noted for Balfour: 'Esher does not deny that all our trouble has arisen from the reduced programmes of '07–'08 and '08–'09; but the damage being now realized FISHER has fought his battle with the Govt. *well*—he has not conceded a point.'[3]

Fisher's inclination to be something of a radical in politics has already been noticed. He had maintained a close relationship with Lloyd George and Churchill, the leading radicals and naval 'economists' in the cabinet, through the summer of 1908. Slade noted on 25 July:

> It appears according to [Fisher] that the Cabinet is about equally divided, Lloyd George and Churchill standing for a general reduction all round so as to get money for old age pensions; Asquith, Grey and Haldane standing for keeping up our strength . . . I cannot quite understand what part Sir J. is playing. I rather think he looks on Lloyd George as the coming man, and is inclined to play his games, but at the same time he does not want to break with the others.[4]

On 14 August 1908 Churchill acknowledged Fisher's congratulations on his engagement. 'Isn't it wonderful', wrote Churchill; and Fisher noted: 'I was perhaps the first to be told.'[5] Nevertheless, Fisher was already strengthening McKenna's resolve to lay down six rather than four dreadnoughts in 1909–10.[6] As for McKenna, he conducted the naval case in the

---

[1] *D.S.* i, 186.
[2] Ibid., p. 187; Lee, ii, 680–1.
[3] Add. MSS. 49719, f. 78.
[4] Slade's diary.
[5] F.P. 330.
[6] *F.G.* ii, 185, F. to McKenna, 28 July 1908.

cabinet with ability and great pertinacity. It seems to have been he, rather than Fisher, who was first convinced of the need for eight rather than six new dreadnoughts in the programme of 1909–10.[1]

Finally the cabinet agreed that four dreadnoughts would be laid down in 1909 and four others would be added by 1 April 1910 if they were found necessary to ensure British naval supremacy. The short-sightedness of the cuts in the Cawdor programme was brought home by the reported inclusion of dreadnoughts in Austrian and Italian programmes; and, on 26 July 1909, the government announced that the four contingent ships would be laid down before the end of 1909–10, without prejudice to the programme for 1910–11. However, the sudden decline in Britain's naval position had been signified in May 1909 when Asquith conveyed to the Commons the impression—in fact well founded—that Britain had abandoned the Two-Power Standard.[2]

By the summer it was known, at least, that the suspected German acceleration had not been translated into output; and in June Fisher was revelling in a display of British naval power at Spithead for the edification of the Imperial Press delegates. His conduct did not endear him to all his naval acquaintances! Richmond unburdened himself to his journal. An extract will suffice:

> Fisher must have the Press men to himself: *he* must be the centre of the show: *he* must get his réclame. It was disgusting. There he was right in his element in the middle of this mob of people none of whom knew anything about the Navy, telling them this, telling them that . . . Where the degradation comes in is in the 1st Sea Lord so lowering himself as to think it necessary that he alone should be the one and only star in the firmament: that his colleagues are nothing . . . Even Sir William [May, the Commander-in-Chief], who is usually very guarded about what he says, let himself go on this occasion and expressed his distaste of the whole matter.[3]

But it was possible to take a different view of these activities. 'Wasn't it glorious?' wrote Esher to the First Sea Lord on 14 June. 'There is no doubt that you did a great stroke with that show and it was a coup not only for the Empire but for you.'[4]

---

[1] McKenna MSS., 3/4/23, F. to McKenna, 22 Dec. 1908. See Willmott's thesis for much detail on the affair of the 1909 estimates.

[2] *D.S.* i, 170–1, 182–5.   [3] N.M.M., RIC/1/8, 22 June 1909.   [4] F.P. 393.

Early in 1909 Fisher parted company with Slade who had been promoted to Rear-Admiral on 5 November 1908 after eight years and ten months as a Captain. 'This establishes a record which it will be hard to beat', the D.N.I. noted that day.[1] But mixed considerations had produced this happy event. On 4 January 1909 Ewart wrote:

I am very sorry to hear that Rear Admiral Slade is leaving the Naval Intelligence Dept to take up command of the East Indies station. We shall miss him very much for whilst he has been DNI the two Intelligence Departments have worked most harmoniously. I can't help thinking—and I know Slade thinks it—that old Fisher is deliberately getting rid of him. Slade has shown himself to be a strong man, no tool, and he has been perhaps too friendly to the Military.[2]

On 2 March Slade paid a farewell visit to the Admiralty. McKenna was 'very optimistic and cocksure'.

Saw Sir J. also who was very slimy and soapy—said that if I wanted any job done I was to write and ask him . . . May said he did not think Sir J. would stay very much longer and that he did not want to step into his shoes. He was quite emphatic on this front, and said that now or at any other time he did not want to be 1st Sea Lord.[3]

Indeed, this came near the crux of the matter. While naval affairs had not gone uniformly well since 1906, who was fit to replace Fisher? When he did finally retire in January 1910, the Navy turned to Wilson who was extremely obstinate, utterly opposed to a naval general staff, and even less realistic than Fisher in his strategic ideas. Wilson had retired as a much respected Admiral of the Fleet in 1907! Yet there was no suitable younger man apart from Battenberg—and despite relatively quick advancement he had reached only the rank of Vice-Admiral by 1910 at the age of fifty-six. He appears to have been past his best by the time he replaced the unimpressive Bridgeman as First Sea Lord in 1912.

Fisher had for long been fully aware of the need for younger admirals and it is one of the marks of his superiority that other leading officers deplored his efforts to improve matters in this respect. For instance Sir Gerard Noel—recently promoted to

---

[1] Slade's diary.
[2] Ewart's diary. The theses of Summerton and d'Ombrain led me to this item, kindly supplied by Mr. Hector Munro, M.P.
[3] Slade's diary.

Admiral of the Fleet—sent to McKenna a lengthy catalogue of unimpressive complaints dated 12 February 1909.[1] *Inter alia,* Noel lamented: 'One of the most harmful things that has happened of late is the rapid flow of promotion to the rank of Rear-Admiral, due to so many Admirals being allowed (if not persuaded) to retire.' McKenna replied with a single sentence: 'Many thanks for your letter which I shall study with care.'[2] Such brevity implies a just estimate of the value of Noel's advice, extending to five closely typed pages.

Through force of personality, eloquence, vitality, intelligence, knowledge, and cunning Fisher seemed to tower above any possible candidates for his post; yet the pressures for his removal were gathering irresistible strength. The conservative press was not alone in holding him at least partly responsible for the recent dreadnought scare, and the Beresfordians were in full cry. 'Charlie B' himself, having duly hauled down his flag at Portsmouth on 24 March 1909, made a triumphal progress to London where he mobilized support for a conclusive assault on the Fisher regime. At much the same time two of Bacon's letters from the Mediterranean, imprudently printed by Fisher in 1906, fell into the distinctly unfriendly hands of Sir George Armstrong who fully exploited the theme that Bacon had been sent out by Fisher as a spy.[3] Even before this development, the hatred of Fisher in some naval circles had approached the level of fanaticism. For example, on 7 December 1908 old Sir Frederick Richards —once so appreciative of Fisher—had written to Noel expressing his 'sense of relief' at the latter's promotion to Admiral of the Fleet and adding: 'Sincere congratulations and may you be on the spot with the other good and true men when the time comes for the application of the surgical knife for the removal of the cancer which is eating into the heart of the Navy.'[4]

Armstrong's revelations turned the one-friendly Prince of Wales finally against Fisher.[5] Indeed, the charge of espionage seems to have been widely accepted in the Navy.

Meanwhile, Beresford sent to the Prime Minister a letter, of 2 April 1909, which argued in some detail that the Navy had not been properly organized for war since 1907. Moreover, he

[1] See Bonar Law Papers 27/1/29 for a copy of this memo.
[2] N.M.M., NOE/5, 13 Feb. 1909.
[3] *D.S.* i, 190.   [4] N.M.M., NOE/5.
[5] *D.S.* i, 191–2; see also E.P. 2/12 (journal) 10 and 14 Apr. 1909.

alleged that the recent scheme of redistribution had not eliminated the weaknesses of the arrangement forced on him in 1907.
He also complained that he had never received from the Admiralty a strategical plan which could be put into effect.[1] Asquith
accepted the need for an inquiry. He decided to appoint a sub-
committee of the C.I.D. for this purpose.[2] The First Sea Lord
fumed about 'treachery' and dubbed the cabinet 'a pack of
cowards'.[3]

The sub-committee was composed of Asquith, Lord Crewe,
Lord Morley, Grey, and Haldane. It heard evidence on fifteen
days, the first being 27 April and the last 13 July. Haldane wrote
of the first meeting that it was 'dramatic—Beresford and Fisher
in deadly fight before us'.[4] However, Fisher played no active
part in the proceedings. The Admiralty's case was conducted,
with marked ability, by McKenna.

Evidence was heard successively from Beresford, McKenna,
Custance, Captains H. H. Campbell and A. R. Hulbert of the
N.I.D., Sir Arthur Wilson, Beresford (a second time), and
Bridgeman. Beresford devoted too much of his effort to the
exposition of past grievances. As far as the organization and
distribution of ships in home waters were concerned, the
termination of his own command did coincide with basic
rectification. However, he succeeded in getting his grievances
acknowledged in the published report, although McKenna
managed to entrench the conclusion that the arrangements of
1907–9 were part of a well-planned evolution, partly governed
by diplomatic considerations.[5] In the report, it was stated that

while the Committee are of opinion that the Admiralty would have
been better advised in adhering throughout to the principle of placing
the chief command in Home waters in the hands of a single officer,
they think that the exceptional difficulties which confronted the
Board during this transitional stage in the evolution of the Home
Fleet justified the dispositions made.

---

[1] Cab. 16/9, 'Report and Proceedings of a Sub-Committee of the Committee
of Imperial Defence appointed to inquire into certain questions of Naval Policy
raised by Lord Charles Beresford'. The letter is also in the published report
(C. 256).

[2] Ibid.

[3] *F.G.* ii, 245, 249.

[4] Haldane Papers 5981, ff. 173–4, H. to his mother, 28 Apr. 1909. For accounts
of the inquiry from differing standpoints, see *D.S.* i, 192–200 and Bennett,
pp. 302–6.

[5] See pp 363–4 above for indications to the contrary.

The committee also believed 'that no danger to the country resulted from these dispositions'.

The second group of criticisms concerned the shortage of cruisers and destroyers. Beresford explained quite effectively that there were not enough destroyers suitable for extended operations in the North Sea. The report stated that 'expert opinion' was 'sharply divided' on this subject. (Actually, the Admiralty was making renewed efforts to repair the deficiency. Following the sixteen destroyers of the 1908 programme, mentioned above, were twenty of the improved 'Acorn' or 'H' class, ordered in 1909.) With regard to light cruisers, Beresford reiterated the charge levelled earlier by Sir William White that useful vessels had been scrapped before replacements could be provided.[1]

It was true enough that Fisher had stopped the construction of light cruisers between 1904 and 1907—a fact not admitted to the committee. However, the Admiralty was now laying down six a year against Germany's two. The committee concluded that provision for the protection of trade was adequate.

Thirdly, Beresford attacked the Admiralty on its weakest ground, that of war plans. The committee reported:

In connection with the question of War Plans it should be mentioned that Lord Charles Beresford attributed many of the Admiralty's alleged shortcomings to the absence of a proper strategical department. The First Lord of the Admiralty furnished the Committee with a résumé of the steps which have been recently taken to develop a War Staff at the Admiralty, and indicated further advances in this direction which are in contemplation.

This apparent conversion of the Admiralty was scarcely due to the merits of Beresford's exposition of the need for such a body. He provided no systematic analysis of the requirement for a War Staff; and the training of staff officers did not enter into his picture. Nor did he receive enlightened support from Custance who argued—much as Fisher or Wilson might have done—that 'plans prepared by a Committee are not only useless, but dangerous' and that the plan 'must be in the head of the officer

---

[1] Under the *nom de plume* of 'Civis', White published several of his critical articles in a small book, *The State of the Navy in 1907: a Plea for Inquiry*. However, with regard to the scrapping White was mainly concerned to show that the public had been misled. Of 155 vessels struck off the list by a 'courageous stroke of the pen', 65 of the more useful had been surreptitiously restored to it!

who will conduct the war'![1] The crucial point was that Beresford was preaching largely to the converted. By March 1909 Haldane had made up his mind, according to Esher, that the Admiralty 'will do no good until they have reorganized and got a General Staff'.[2] Incidentally, this should not be taken to mean that Haldane had formed a low estimate of Fisher's abilities as a First Sea Lord taken in the round. He was to prove the contrary in October 1914.[3] But on the subject of a naval general staff Haldane enlisted the help of Esher who left a memorandum about it with Asquith on 26 April—the day before the inquiry opened.[4] Esher had also been discussing the matter with McKenna and Fisher.[5] Not long after, Beresford's representations at the inquiry led Asquith to send a telegram to Slade. In response, Slade wrote from Bombay that he (now) believed the Naval Intelligence Department should be strengthened and that its head should be a member of the Board of Admiralty.[6]

The hearing of evidence terminated on 13 July. On 12 August the report was issued as a parliamentary paper. Between these two dates Hankey intervened with regard to the naval staff question. Since January 1908 he had been an assistant secretary at the C.I.D. At least in part he owed his appointment to Fisher. In November 1908 he transmitted to Fisher a paper on the establishment of a general staff at the Admiralty.[7] In connexion with his influence on the report of the Beresford inquiry, he has left the following account:

After a meeting at which the sub-committee had discussed the general lines of their report without the presence of any representative of the Admiralty or of Beresford, I took upon myself, without authority from anyone except Ottley, to go to McKenna and tell him that my personal impression was that the sub-committee would report favourably to the Admiralty provided that they would come forward with a scheme for the creation of a General Staff. McKenna passed me on at once, with his blessing, to Fisher, whom I found in bed with an attack of influenza in his house at Queen Anne's Gate. I felt rather a brute in raising the subject at all. One of Fisher's obsessions was an entirely erroneous belief that Haldane was his relentless and vindictive enemy. He would *not* have a General Staff imposed by Haldane, and he would *not* have an army organization forced on the Navy.[8]

[1] Cab. 16/9A, 11th meeting, 8 June.   [2] Esher, ii, 374.
[3] Gilbert, p. 144.   [4] E.P. 2/12 journal, 26 Apr.
[5] Ibid., 25 Apr.
[6] Cab. 16/9B, Slade to Asquith, 8 May 1909. See also p. 396 above.
[7] Roskill, i, 99.   [8] Hankey, i, 73–4.

Fisher finally agreed to make a gesture based on Hankey's ideas—much emasculated, in the event. In October the establishment of a Navy War Council was announced—'the most absurd bit of humbug that has been produced for a long time', thought Richmond.[1] However the concession—such as it was—allowed the Admiralty to escape with more dignity than it might have done in terms of the published report. The 'General Conclusion' was worded as follows:

In the opinion of the Committee, the investigation has shown that during the time in question no danger to the country resulted from the Admiralty's arrangements for war, whether considered from the standpoint of the organization and distribution of the fleets, the number of ships, or the preparation of War Plans.

They feel bound to add that arrangements quite defensible in themselves, though not ideally perfect, were in practice hampered through the absence of cordial relations between the Board of Admiralty and the Commander-in-Chief of the Channel Fleet. The Board of Admiralty do not appear to have taken Lord Charles Beresford into their confidence as to the reasons for dispositions to which he took exception; and Lord Charles Beresford, on the other hand, appears to have failed to appreciate and carry out the spirit of the instructions of the Board, and to recognize their paramount authority.

The Committee have been impressed with the differences of opinion amongst officers of high rank and professional attainments regarding important principles of naval strategy and tactics, and they look forward with much confidence to the further development of a Naval War Staff, from which the Naval members of the Board and Flag Officers and their staffs at sea may be expected to derive common benefit.

When the report was published on 12 August Fisher was on holiday in the South Tyrol. He derived less pleasure from reading it than did Beresford. On 28 August he wrote to Esher: 'You use the words I used in describing the Beresford Report to McKenna—that "*5 Cowards signed it!*" '[2] Haldane, as reported by Esher, thought the document was 'a model of ingenuity'.[3] This, indeed, it was! Fisher and his friends resented the absence of specific appreciation of his work for the Navy. Presumably,

---

[1] Marder, *Portrait*, p. 62.
[2] *F.G.* ii, 261.
[3] Add. MSS. 49719, f. 98, Esher to Sandars, 24 Aug. 1909.

if the committee considered the point, it was felt that such a gesture would entail a general distribution of compliments.

In effect, the report ensured that Fisher would shortly retire with appropriate acknowledgement of his services as First Sea Lord.

One of the most important complaints made by Beresford in his letter to McKenna of 5 June 1908 concerned the lack of a properly developed base on the North Sea coast. This, however, did not fall naturally within the scope of the inquiry. Indeed the onset of the inquiry seems to have interrupted a discussion of the subject at the Admiralty. This arose in April 1909 between Fisher and Jellicoe who (as a Rear-Admiral) had returned to the Admiralty as Third Sea Lord and Controller in October 1908. Jellicoe was anxious to hasten the development of Rosyth. Fisher, however, had willingly co-operated with the government in minimizing expenditure on this project.[1] As has already been explained (pp. 337–8), Fisher's attitude was influenced by his vision of the coming dominance of the submarine in the North Sea. In April 1909 he produced a paper entitled 'The Submarine Question' which contains a not-untypical mixture of insight and questionable judgement:

. . . Our latest submarines, as a result of the embodiment of our own ideas and improvements over 5 years, are now 5 times the displacement of [the] 'Holland' and hardly recognisable even as a development.[2]

To the completion of this latest type of submarine is due the following two conclusions, which have forced themselves to the front during the last year:—

(1) The latest type of submarine has the power of remaining autonomous for two months or more, a characteristic that does not apply to any other type of war vessel from destroyer to battleship, on account of the necessity for renewal of their fuel, etc., etc.

(2) No practicable means at present exist or appear to be feasible for effecting the destruction of the latest type of submarine, or of being even warned of her approach, since she requires no attendant surface vessels to assist her, that may betray her presence.

---

[1] *F.G.* ii, 496; Lloyd George Papers B 1/3/2, F. to L.G., 17 Dec. 1907.
[2] This came close to admitting that production of coastal submarines in large numbers had been a mistake.

The question arises, what should be done in view of these two definite facts? Three conclusions offer themselves:—

(1) Continuous effort must be directed towards elaborating a 'submarine destroyer', just as the advent of the Torpedo Boat produced the entirely British antidote, the 'Torpedo Boat Destroyer'.

(2) The submarine of the latest type is bound in time to supplant the present Torpedo Boat Destroyer in so far as the latter's functions as a torpedo vessel are concerned, for the reason that the submarine's fighting capability by night is becoming in excess of that of a destroyer, whilst she retains her capacity for day fighting unimpaired.

(3) It is inevitable that when the Germans fully realise the capability of this type of submarine—they probably do not do so yet, on account of having had small experience with them at sea (they have but 3 to our 60)—the North Sea and all its ports will be rendered uninhabitable by our big ships—until we have cleaned out their submarines.

The first practical necessity that arises from a consideration of the above facts is that—in view of the Germans having, this year, for the first time, devoted a large sum of money ($\frac{1}{2}$ a million) to the construction of modern submarines—this country must produce more than the six a year which our present vote provides.

The Head of the submarine branch of our Service [Captain S. S. Hall] has been enabled, unknown, to go on board and study the latest development of the German submarine (a reason why this paper of which no copy exists, should be kept secret). He has satisfied himself that the Germans possess a class of vessel which though not yet equal to ours, is equally capable of development and of maintaining itself at sea, unaided, for long periods . . .

To sum up:

The arguments in this brief record in no way attempt to lessen the influence and necessity of big armoured ships—the latter will after all govern the final conflict for command of the sea on the ocean lines of communication.

They do however point to a complete approaching revolution in the type of our war with *any* power, particularly with any European power on account of the narrow waters of the North Sea and Baltic, English Channel and Mediterranean being denied to large ships of war until the submarine is cleared out.

———

A collateral issue which flows from all this is the absolute death blow to fears of Invasion.[1]

[1] F.P. 4238.

On 18 April Jellicoe commented: 'I entirely agree in the conclusions that we must spend more money on submarines, and that we must devise something in the shape of a submarine destroyer. The sooner we get an air ship the better since we may find the solution here, for day work at any rate.'[1]

It was indeed a mark of Fisher's inexhaustible interest in new technical developments that he, with Bacon, had taken up in 1908 the idea that the Navy should acquire a large airship for experimental purposes and especially with a view to reconnaissance.[2] But Jellicoe saw cause for concern in some of the implications of Fisher's paper:

My fear is that this submarine question may be made an excuse to avoid spending—what appears to me essential money—on dock accommodation on the East Coast. I feel that our present situation in this matter is one of the utmost gravity and open to much criticism, and I hope you will agree with me that nothing that can occur in the next 8–10 years should lead us to abandon the provision of necessary docks on this coast. Even if Germany spends a million a year on submarines, it will be 8 years before the submarine menace in the North Sea is really bad, and I don't imagine we shall wait eight years for the war.

He added that destroyers would still be needed as long as other nations possessed them. Submarines could not catch them.[3]

Fisher's reaction to Jellicoe's letter is indicated in the margin of a copy. He agreed with the argument that east coast docks should be provided; also that destroyers would be needed. It thus remained true that he could accept criticism—if he had invited it! However, he dissented from Jellicoe's view that, at some stage of the war, 'our own Battle Fleet will be forced into the North Sea to endeavour to bring the German Fleet to action.'[4]

Fisher seems ultimately to have settled for the idea of a refuelling base at Cromarty but his conversion to the principle of an east coast dock proved ephemeral.[5] In any case, his time at the Admiralty was drawing to a close.

In October 1909 his retirement was arranged. On the 26th Asquith intimated that he would be raised to the peerage on the King's birthday, 9 November. The Prime Minister continued: 'I desire, at the same time, to express to you the sincere and

---

[1] F.P. 382.   [2] *F.G.* ii, 186; Higham, pp. 5, 6, 10, 36–9, 72–3.
[3] F.P. 382.   [4] F.P. 413.   [5] *F.G.* ii, 475–6.

grateful acknowledgements of His Majesty's Government for the great work—unique in our time—which you have accomplished in developing and strengthening the Navy, and assuring the maritime supremacy of Great Britain.'[1]

This was a just appreciation, though it applied perhaps more appropriately to services rendered during the score of years before 1906—especially 1899 to 1905—than it did to the four years leading up to the Admiral's retirement. There is some substance in the claim that the major reforms of 1904-5, which entailed the elimination or attenuation of overseas commands, were certain to breed antagonism to the prime mover; but it is equally clear that Fisher must bear a large share of responsibility for the bitter dissension of the years 1907-9. Nor were there any great constructive reforms to set alongside those of 1904-5. Instead, the crowning innovation of a general staff was deliberately withheld from the Navy because Fisher did not recognize, or comprehend, his own limitations. The same defect goes far to account for the lack of co-ordination between the Admiralty and the War Office. On the credit side, however, the dreadnought programme of 1909-10 did restore the unwise cuts of the previous three years; the problem of the lower deck was handled in an enlightened manner; gunnery was improved, thanks largely to Fisher's appointment of Percy Scott as Inspector of Target Practice (1905-7)—though Scott's directors were not adopted while Fisher was First Sea Lord; officers were promoted to flag rank at an earlier age; minesweeping began; and 13·5-inch guns were adopted in time for mounting in most of the dreadnoughts of 1909-10.

With regard to the adoption of a general staff, Fisher had certainly led Selborne to believe that he intended to take positive action in the matter. When Churchill replaced McKenna as First Lord in 1911, he received a letter from Selborne on the subject:

I think I know one of the special tasks you have in hand. I bequeathed that task as an urgent legacy to Fisher nearly seven years ago and gave him all the material for its fulfilment. To my surprise and disgust on my return from South Africa [in 1910] I found he had done nothing; I say 'surprise' because I thought it would have been a job after his own heart, but obviously I was wrong.

Prince Louis is just the man to help you.[2]

---

[1] *F.G.* ii, 273 (F.P. 421).
[2] R. Churchill, ii, comp. ii, 1347, 29 Nov. 1911.

However, Fisher's term of office taken as a whole does possess a unique quality which has probably not yet been fully conveyed. An explanation is needed, over and above the record of his administration from 1906 to 1910, to account for the conviction of Haldane in October 1914 and of Selborne in May 1915 that, even then, despite his age and known defects, Fisher was the best person available for the post of First Sea Lord. Likewise the extent to which Fisher continued to fascinate Winston Churchill, despite the Dardanelles episode, remains a source of astonishment. There was obviously a potent factor present which tends to escape the documentary record. This was what was sometimes called Fisher's 'demonic' quality—best captured by the journalists. For instance, the enthralled Harold Begbie wrote towards the end of Fisher's life:

No man I have met ever gave me so authentic a feeling of originality as this dare-devil of genius, this pirate of public life, who more than any other Englishman saved British democracy from a Prussian domination.

It is possible to regard him as a very simple soul mastered by one tremendous purpose and by that purpose exalted to a most valid greatness . . . He was asked on one occasion if he had been a little unscrupulous in getting his way at the Admiralty. He replied that if his own brother had got in front of him when he was trying to do something for England he would have knocked that brother down and walked over his body. Here is a man, let us be quite certain, of a most unusual force, a man conscious in himself of powers greater than the kindest could discern in his contemporaries, a man possessed by a daemon of inspiration. Fortunately for England this daemon drove him in one single direction: he sought the safety, honour, and glory of Great Britain . . .[1]

Although writing from a more critical standpoint, the naval journalist and inventor A. H. Pollen registered Fisher's 'demonic' characteristics in an even more striking manner:

We have, then, to take certain factors as being dominant in Fisher's mental composition. First, there was a passionate devotion to, and affection for, the Service . . . Next, there was an eager expectancy that welcomed every new marvel that advancing science gave to manufacture . . . It was an expectancy quickened by an imagination that more than once amounted almost to prophetic vision. His religious practice both fortified his natural leaning to believe on

---

[1] Edward Harold Begbie, *The Mirrors of Downing Street: Some Political Reflections*, London, 9th ed., 1920, pp. 39-40.

impulse, and with a faith that could move mountains, and trained him in a certain aphoristic method of expression which is the mark of those who hold dogmas as realities which, whether consonant with reason or not, are not tested, as they can neither be proved, nor explained, by reasoning alone . . . He was a man not of mind but of vision and of will. His track is marked not by thought but by action . . . As was said of Luther, he had an extraordinary power of imagination and of word . . . He was, in short, a daimonic creature. His policy is not a philosophy or a doctrine, but the overflow of himself . . . It seems hardly an exaggeration to say that he in a large measure paralysed the intelligences of those with whom he worked: sometimes indeed paralysed his own . . .[1]

Even level-headed officers like Battenberg and Hankey formed an impression of Fisher's 'genius' which may in part be attributed to the extraordinary characteristics indicated by Pollen. For example, Hankey went so far as to write in his memoirs that the lack of a Naval Staff at the Admiralty in 1909 'did not matter much, so long as the strategical side was directed by a genius like Fisher, who supplied the need himself, with the personal assistance of men of the calibre of Ottley', together with various '*ad hoc* committees'.[2] Yet it has been shown above that Fisher's own strategic ideas, though flexible and imaginative, were also erratic, inconsistent, and often based on hunches rather than on thorough examination of the ascertainable facts. Indeed, it is usually difficult to discover what his settled strategic views were at any given date. Fisher, almost as much as any First Sea Lord of the period leading up to the Great War, needed the fact-finding capacity and corrective influence of a fully fledged Naval Staff.

Having been duly raised to the peerage on 9 November, the first Baron Fisher of Kilverstone reluctantly retired from the Admiralty on 25 January 1910—his sixty-ninth birthday. In terms of self-discipline he had somewhat deteriorated since passing the age of sixty-five; but his 'demonic' qualities, charged by exceptional energy, became even more marked—as may be gathered from inspection of the mounting torrent of his published correspondence. If Churchill could write to him in May 1916 that 'destiny' had not done with him yet, it certainly had not finished with him in January 1910!

---

[1] *Naval Review* (1930), pp. 161–2. This forms part of a review article on Bacon's recently published biography of F.

[2] Hankey, i, 73.

CHAPTER 9

FISHER AND CHURCHILL
(1910–1915)

WHEN Fisher retired to his son's home at Kilverstone in 1910 he took pleasure in the beauty of the natural surroundings but did not easily accept the atmosphere of peace. His wife, who accompanied him, would clearly have welcomed an end to bitterness and strife. Corbett has left a record of a visit to Fisher at Queen Anne's Gate shortly before his retirement: 'In drawing room afterwards saw Lady Fisher—a charming woman—who is apparently devoted to him and sincerely believes in his disinterestedness, as I do on the whole. She said they had never cared for the rewards and she could not understand Beresford's personal animosity.'[1]

However, despite his sustained church-going and his wife's hopes for an end to personal contention, Fisher's mood on leaving the Admiralty was not very conciliatory. To mark the day of Fisher's retirement Vice-Admiral Egerton (last noticed on the defensive against Fisher in 1903) wrote the following letter (dated 25 January 1910) from the Cape of Good Hope:

Dear Lord Fisher,

As you are now leaving the Admiralty I feel that the strings are loosened to a certain extent and that I may write to you in a more private way than I could before, and I should now like to express my gratitude for the many kindnesses and hospitality my wife and I have received from you and Lady Fisher in days gone by dating from the 'Northampton' in 1879, and though my actions at a later period have not met with your approval, yet I am indebted to a large extent to your forgiveness in being in the command I now hold, and therefore venture to send this letter in the hope that you will receive it in the spirit it is written, and accept my congratulations on the honours bestowed upon you and my best wishes, in which my wife joins me, that you and Lady Fisher may live many years to enjoy them.

Yours sincerely,
G. le C. Egerton.[2]

---

[1] Corbett's diary, 15 Nov. 1909.   [2] F.P. 460.

At the time of the Beresford inquiry Esher described Fisher as 'a fine courageous fighter'.[1] In Fisher's mind, Egerton was associated with the supply of information to Beresford on that occasion, and he pencilled at the head of Egerton's letter (which also received emphatic treatment from a red pencil): 'Admiral Egerton Judas Iscariot. He sold me to Beresford for 30 pieces of silver. In reply to this letter I told him to hang himself.'[2]

During the year 1910, Fisher's reputation was steadily enhanced by the inadequacy of his successor, Sir Arthur Wilson. This was scarcely anticipated by Fisher. In November 1909 he deemed Wilson's selection 'a master stroke and a dramatic stroke'; and in June 1910 he still thought him 'unassailable' and 'doing splendidly'.[3] Possibly with Fisher's encouragement, Wilson made it clear from the outset that he had no interest in Esher's attempts to strengthen the co-ordinating role of the C.I.D.[4] Nor did he take any steps to develop a Naval Staff. Indeed, Pollen's apprehensions, as communicated to Slade just before Wilson's arrival at the Admiralty, proved well founded:

Some troubles of a painful and rather degrading kind his advent will undoubtedly silence. It will, however, I think, be a surprise to those who objected most to the Fisher regime, on the ground of the First Sea Lord's autocracy, to discover that they have really exchanged King Log for King Stork. With all Fisher's remarkable qualities, I do not think that he ever had that total disregard for the opinion of other people which is the true mark of the autocrat. As far as I know Sir Arthur Wilson, he possesses this disregard to an absolutely unparalleled degree . . . I do not believe that Wilson has any capacity for compromise in matters of principle.[5]

By September, even Haldane was deploring the change at the Admiralty—'closed to all new ideas and new developments'.[6]

Meanwhile, late at night on Friday, 6 May, Fisher's staunch defender King Edward VII breathed his last. In response to a telegram from Queen Alexandra on the 9th, Fisher went up to Buckingham Palace where (as Lady Fisher noted afterwards)

He walked into a room where our dear Queen stood alone with her dead husband. It was a most trying moment for both of them . . .

[1] Esher Papers 2/12, 14 May 1909.
[2] F.P. 460. See also F.G. ii, 254n.
[3] F.P. 437, F. to Corbett, 19 Nov. 1909; F.G. ii, 300.
[4] Add. MSS. 49719, Esher to Balfour, 24, 31 Dec. 1909.
[5] N.M.M., Slade Papers, 24 Jan. 1910.
[6] Esher, iii, 25.

Jack kissed her hand but she kept holding his hand and with deep emotion speaking of him and his love for Jack . . .

I am proud to think my husband never made use of the influence he had with him for his own advantage. All his thought was what was good for the Country and for the Navy he has loved and served so faithfully. And the King knew it and valued him accordingly.[1]

Already on the 7th Fisher had written a letter of sympathy to the new King who replied in appreciative terms on the 26th.[2] But Fisher, although he did not entirely give up the attempt, failed to match Esher's suave transition from the old Court to the new. In April 1911 Esher was able to write to Fisher from Windsor: 'We have been here a fortnight. It is as quiet as a vicarage. Very domestic and peaceful. A great contrast. Necessarily I have seen a great deal of the King . . . He is assiduous and conscientious . . . But, of course, he lacks, and always will, his Father's magnetism . . .'[3] Fisher, for his part, soon tended to snipe at both monarch and monarchy. 'Kings like herrings are cheap today', he informed Arnold White on 22 October 1910.[4]

During the year Fisher remained closely in touch with naval affairs. He was even more friendly than before with McKenna and wrote a remarkable number of exuberant letters to the First Lord's youthful wife. Letters to other friends were ever more extravagantly expressed. By December 1910, Mrs. McKenna was being addressed as 'My forlorn and devoted Pamela!' and regaled with all manner of information and gossip:

Napoleon B. [Haldane] is restless to get out of the War Office— said to be hankering again for the Admiralty . . . Sir W. May is working the backstairs leading to the royal apartments to ensure himself succeeding ' "ard" art' [Wilson], and I think if I were Reggie [McKenna] I should almost be inclined to . . . sell May as he so richly deserves . . . I can fancy the loss that Jellicoe is, but we have to remember that where he now is [having moved from being Third Sea Lord to command the Atlantic Fleet, now based at Dover] he practically will command the Fleet in war . . . That pestilent cad, Sir William White, is, I fancy, providing Winston with ammunition against the Navy Estimates . . . Garvin . . . is being got hold of by the Duchesses a bit about Beresford,[5] but it's only hearsay. He writes to me as truly as ever.[6]

[1] Kilv. MSS., Lady F.'s notebook.   [2] F.P. 485.
[3] F.P. 522, 24 Apr. 1911.   [4] *F.G.* ii, 342.
[5] Lord Charles hoped to be made an Admiral of the Fleet.
[6] *F.G.* ii, 344–5.

This particular letter terminated: 'Always your affectionately, Jacky'. But usually, whoever was the recipient, he signed himself simply 'F.'—after a sign-off phrase such as 'Yours till Hell freezes'.

Apart from his interest in Jellicoe's future as a Commander-in-Chief, Fisher took up the sterile cause of diesel engines in battleships. In August 1910 he wrote to McKenna: 'The *Lion*[1] as superior to the *Dreadnought* as the *Dreadnought* to all before her, and your coming "Motor Battleship" as superior to the *Lion* as the *Lion* to the *Dreadnought!*' In the same letter, he touched on a subject which he had been pursuing with true insight since 1906 —perhaps even earlier: 'This democratic country won't stand an aristocratic Navy! Ninety per cent AT LEAST of the officers from the Upper Ten! (as they may be called!) . . . It would be a great coup if you got that through: State-paid education and a sufficiency of pay to live on.'[2]

Fisher's earliest official paper on this subject is 'State Education in the Navy', headed 'Strictly Private and Secret' and printed with special security precautions in March 1906. (The version published in *Records*, pp. 160–2, is an abridgement of the print of 1906 and the claim that it 'was prepared in 1902' is unacceptable.) The paper is truly expressive of Fisher's radicalism and a forerunner of twentieth-century meritocracy. It estimates that a parent will need £1,000 to see a son through Osborne and Dartmouth till he becomes a self-supporting Lieutenant.

In other words, the officers of the Navy will be drawn exclusively from the well-to-do classes, or, as some critics will put it, from the aristocratic classes . . . under the old system many engineer cadets were of quite humble extraction, but even this outlet or safety valve for democratic sentiment is now finally closed . . . The democratic sentiment will gradually acquire such force that it will wreck the present system in the long run if it is not given an outlet . . . there are not more than 1,500,000 people in all from whom officers for the Navy can be taken . . . The remainder of the population is 41,500,000, and of these no single one can ever hope to become an officer in the Navy! . . .

Nor is it the money barrier alone which excludes them. An exclusive system of nomination is distasteful, if not alien, to the democratic sentiment . . .[3]

---

[1] The latest armoured cruiser.
[2] *F.G.* ii, 337, 22 Aug. 1910.
[3] F.P. 4754, proof, P. 3/06.

The body of the paper was probably written by Thursfield.[1] But the following 'Conclusion' (excluded from subsequent prints on the same subject) is so characteristic of 'Radical Jack', and so symptomatic of the bitterness which developed between Fisher and the Beresfordians that it deserves reproduction here:

There will be immense opposition; there always is! Bows and Arrows died hard in the Navy, so did masts and sails; water-tube boilers were going to boil our stokers! To do away with the special navigating class of officers was to ruin the Navy, yet it has reduced wrecks and groundings of ships 30 per cent, and a vessel can go to sea now even if the usual Navigating Officer is sick! Salt beef has gone, and the Service is going to the devil! snuff-boxes were made out of it. Boarding pikes have only just left us. Greek is dead, but, alas, Latin still lives! as the shore-going schoolmasters apparently can't teach anything else, and we must have *some* test for boys entering the Navy; but they learn it no more after entry, which gives Lord Goschen sleepless nights!

The opposition was simply prodigious to Lord Kelvin's compass and sounding machine, perhaps the two greatest because the most life-saving of human inventions. A distinguished Admiral, when First Sea Lord, objected to torpedoes because there were none when he came to sea, and to midshipmen having baths, because he never washed! Yes! the Bow and Arrow party are still with us, and we are 'a retrograde Admiralty'![2] They can't bear the 'Dreadnought'— she is too fast!—and they hate big guns. They'll hate Heaven, probably, because there's no more sea there, and they won't like all the harps playing the same tune. Fancy! Complete interchangeability! Admiral Lambton and a Lieutenant (E) exchanging harps! It will be Hell!

But this new scheme will be much more Hell to the 'Bow and Arrow' party than is Interchangeability, and the making of every Naval officer into an Engineer. Public opinion is the only force able to effect this reform. This is a free country, where everyone can do as he likes, and, if he doesn't he is made to! This is a case![3]

Fisher pressed frequently for this reform, both before and (even more) after 1910, aiming to influence the leading journalists as well as the First Lord of the day. But it was not till a second world war had jolted opinion that fees were abolished at Dartmouth.[4]

---

[1] *Records*, p. 160. F. was in close touch with Thursfield in Mar. 1906.

[2] An allusion to an article in *Blackwood's Magazine*, June 1905.

[3] F.P. 4754, proof, p. 3/06.

[4] *D.S.* i, 32.

Fisher's recommendation of Jellicoe was more readily accepted.[1] On 23 October 1910 the former wrote to Balfour who, as Leader of the Opposition, had lost none of his former interest in defence:

My absorbing thought for six years has been the one point you mention. To push young men to the high commands who will think in submarines and 13½-inch guns. Such a one—the first fruits of ceaseless importunity—goes as Commander-in-Chief of the Atlantic Fleet next month—Sir John Jellicoe. Phenomenally young and junior. He will be Nelson at Cape St. Vincent until he becomes 'Boss' at Trafalgar when Armageddon comes along in 1915 or thereabouts—not sooner! Others follow in his footsteps.[2]

In the event of Armageddon, he did not envisage an inactive role for himself. Indeed, his protégé Hankey, who despite his youth was already aspiring to succeed Ottley at the C.I.D., encouraged Fisher in the belief that he would be recalled to direct naval policy in war. On 25 January 1911, Fisher's seventieth birthday, it was announced that he had retired as an Admiral of the Fleet on the active list. Hankey commented on the 26th: 'If there were a war you would not remain long in retirement for your country would at once call upon you—like Cincinnatus—to come up to Town and run the war. This is the main reason for your continuing to be a member of the Defence Committee.'[3]

Fisher saw no reason to disagree with this assessment. He replied from Kilverstone on 29 January:

My beloved Hankey,

. . . McKenna came straight here from Windsor Castle to spend my birthday with me and we talked of you . . . In that period [of the next four years] I think it is decided I return to Admty at Whitehall if war (you must burn this) . . . McK. thinks you will succeed Ottley if we work things right. A great effort has been made with the Prime Minister to supplant Ottley by Slade but it has utterly collapsed. The P.M. just laughed at the King! but doesn't it show how the atmosphere is that of Rehoboam and his young men! . . . The Old Guard round the King (Knollys, Frederick Ponsonby, etc.) are staunch to me to a man . . . *But every single one else in cabal against me* and would give worlds to get me discarded from C.I.D. . . . *In one year from now I will come out in the open* . . .[4]

[1] *F.G.* ii, 345, 348–9.   [2] *F.G.* iii, 32–3.
[3] Roskill, i, 109–10 (F.P. 516.)   [4] Hankey Papers.

In May 1912 Wilson would reach the age of seventy. Up to the time of McKenna's removal from the Admiralty in October 1911, Fisher entertained 'great hopes of succeeding Wilson as First Sea Lord in the Spring' of 1912—at the age of 71 ![1]

In February 1911 Fisher and his wife went to the continent for an extended stay. Until the spring they were in Italy and the Admiral started to draft his memoirs. They moved on to Bad Nauheim and, in August, to Lucerne. By then, the Agadir crisis was in progress. The previous month, Lloyd George had delivered his famous Mansion House speech. Sir Arthur Wilson, convinced that there would be no war, went to Scotland for a weekend's shooting. It was found, while he was away, that no one at the Admiralty could produce the Navy's war plan. The plan was in fact situated where Fisher thought it should be—in Wilson's head. Just in time for McKenna to receive his message before the critical C.I.D. meeting of 23 August, Fisher wrote to the First Lord warning him (clearly not for the first time) against the General Staff's plan of continental intervention.

REST ASSURED that if the Government land a single British soldier in France (or even entertain any plans for it), there will be an upheaval in England that will cast them out of office! . . . The whole single object is compulsory service and an increase of the Army Estimates and military influence. I much fear the Prime Minister may be 'nobbled' by 'Napoleon B.'[2]

Wilson, for his part, was in any case ready to take a line more openly independent of the War Office than Fisher had done before the sub-committee of 1908–9, but Fisher's letter may well have had some influence on McKenna's conduct at the C.I.D.[3] The First Lord lost no time in stating that the Navy could not co-operate in transporting the B.E.F. on the outbreak as 'the Transport Department especially would be fully occupied in taking up Fleet Auxiliaries.' He ended (more plausibly) by opposing the D.M.O.'s plan to send all six regular divisions to France. The threat of a German invasion was now the Admiralty's best weapon against the War Office! However Churchill, whose natural interest in defence had been thoroughly aroused

---

[1] Add. MSS. 49719, 'Mem. of a Conversation with Lord Esher' by Sandars, Nov. 1911.
[2] F.G. ii, 380, 20 Aug. 1911.
[3] See also Roskill, i, 101–2, for Hankey's role.

during the crisis, did not fail to point out that the Navy had always claimed that invasions and raids were impossible.

By contrast with the precise and masterful Henry Wilson (who had succeeded Ewart as D.M.O. in 1910) Sir Arthur Wilson made a poor impression on the committee. In outline, he revealed the war plans which had been denied to Beresford and safeguarded in his own head—and Fisher's. Landings would be made on the Frisian islands and on the German North Sea coast; destroyers would maintain as close a blockade of the German ports as they could. Nicholson commented that the amphibious schemes might have been valuable about a hundred years earlier 'when land communications were indifferent'. Now, however, when these communications were 'excellent' he was sure they were 'doomed to failure'. Nothing daunted, A. K. Wilson, having disposed of the German battlefleet, made his way into the Baltic. He also proposed that one of the six regular divisions should co-operate in the capture of Heligoland—a suggestion which Nicholson angrily rejected as 'madness'.[1]

As a result of this meeting, Haldane pressed urgently for changes at the Admiralty. The Navy seemed unable to comprehend the objections of the War Office to the projected amphibious operations. With regard to the transportation of the B.E.F., also, full co-operation was essential. By late September Churchill had joined Haldane in demanding the establishment of a Naval War Staff. Asquith, while disliking the prospect of continental involvement, considered Sir Arthur Wilson's alternative unworthy of serious consideration. In consequence, Churchill became First Lord on 25 October 1911 and McKenna went to the Home Office in his stead.[2]

Fisher, in Lucerne, was aghast to hear that Wilson had revealed his intentions to the C.I.D. On 29 August he wrote to Hankey:

I am so astounded at A.K.W. divulging one little iota of his plans! He swore to me he never would—and if you remember he very fully satisfied Asquith at the Beresford Enquiry in saying that only he (AKW) and I really knew our War Plans[3] and this smashed Beresford in Asquith's mind (so I was given to understand!) as Asquith saw the folly of anyone but myself and A.K.W. knowing; and that he (Asquith) brooded over it was apparent by his saying to me a year

---

[1] Cab. 2/2/2; Williamson, pp. 182–94, for a balanced summary.
[2] Williamson, pp. 192–6.   [3] 1905–8.

afterwards referring to Beresford: 'Of course I understand you never would have been such a fool as to divulge what was so secret to anyone.' So I am really upset at A.K.W. having been thus drawn as it will be made use of hereafter as a precedent when perhaps I again appear on the scene next July.[1]

This indicates the extent to which Fisher had agreed with Wilson's plans. Further confirmation is provided by the former's letter of 10 November to Arnold White:

> There's a d——d pernicious report being spread that A. K. Wilson had no war plan and that the English Fleet was not ready! To throw rotten eggs at the man who undoubtedly will be our Admiralissimo for the next 5 years certain is simply damnable! . . . his dispositions of the Fleet were all studied and perfect. As I believe I am the only one he ever trusted with his plans, I can speak.[2]

Fisher's own ideas about war plans had evolved to an extent since 1908, mainly on account of the development of large submarines. His submarine paper of 1909, together with some of his subsequent exchange with Jellicoe, was given in the last chapter; but he did not progress far in working out the strategic implications before 1913. On 10 January 1911 he wrote to Jellicoe: 'hardly anyone but yourself . . . clearly realizes the immense alteration in both tactics and strategy which the development of the submarine now causes. I am quite sure A. K. Wilson don't realize it, from our conversation together when he was last at Kilverstone.'[3]

Despite frequent protestations that he would not 'get between the limelight and A.K.W.', Fisher was in secret conclave with Churchill in England just three days after the latter became First Lord of the Admiralty! The strange brand of infatuation which persisted between Fisher and Churchill had originated at Biarritz in April 1907. Fisher then 'fell desperately in love' with Churchill; and in 1908, though Churchill was emerging as a naval 'economist', Fisher was (as noted above) 'perhaps the first to be told' of the young minister's engagement to Clementine Hozier. After the 'separation' engendered by their conflict over the 1909 estimates, Churchill assured Fisher of his 'unaltered feelings' (to quote Fisher). On Esher's advice, Fisher in March 1910 reopened communication with Churchill and received 'by return of post a most affectionate letter'.[4] Despite his opposition

---

[1] Hankey Papers. [2] *F.G.* ii, 414–15.
[3] Ibid., p. 349. [4] *F.G.* ii, 226, 313, 396, 401.

to the 1909 estimates, Churchill always accepted the principle of British naval supremacy and shared Fisher's view of the subordinate role of the Army; but the Agadir crisis had greatly strengthened his interest in the projected B.E.F.

On 25 October 1911, Churchill's first day at the Admiralty, Fisher in Lucerne was busy with detailed recommendations for the new First Lord: Battenberg to succeed Wilson as First Sea Lord ('he will just "*roll up*" all Admiralty opponents in the Committee of Imperial Defence'); Sir George Egerton to be replaced as Second Sea Lord; Jellicoe to become second-in-command of the Home Fleet ready to emerge as 'THE FUTURE NELSON'; Ballard '*at once*' to succeed Bethell as D.N.I.; etc., etc.[1] Despite his preoccupations, Churchill for his part had Fisher in mind on 25 October. Before leaving the Home Office that morning to go to the Admiralty he wrote:

My dear Lord Fisher,

I want to see you very much. When am I to have that pleasure? You have but to indicate your convenience & I will await you at the Admiralty.

Yours vy sincerely,

Winston S. Churchill.[2]

Despite qualms about loyalty to McKenna (who much resented his removal from the Admiralty) Fisher was writing to his son from Reigate Priory by 28 October:

Mr. & Mrs. McKenna met me at Charing Cross and Winston Churchill was there . . . I spent 3 hours with the McKennas, fearfully cut up at leaving the Admiralty and then I motored down here with Winston Churchill where half the Cabinet are now staying and it's 1.30 p.m., but if I don't write now I shall have no time tomorrow . . . I think Winston Churchill will do all I've suggested to him. He's very affectionate and cordial . . .[3]

It should doubtless be remarked that such attention to the talk and views of another was hardly characteristic of Churchill. His preferred form of conversation was a monologue delivered by himself! But Fisher, like Lloyd George, could be certain of a hearing. Churchill long remembered his original meetings with Fisher at Biarritz.

[1] *F.G.* ii, 397–400. To avoid notice, the two letters involved were sent t Churchill by way of the Liberal journalist J. A. Spender.

[2] R. Churchill, ii, 396 (F.P. 534).   [3] Kilv. MSS., Pkt. 4.

We talked all day long and far into the nights. He told me wonderful stories of the Navy and of his plans—all about Dreadnoughts, all about submarines, all about the new education scheme for every branch of the Navy, all about big guns, and splendid Admirals and foolish miserable ones, and Nelson and the Bible, and finally the island of Borkum. I remembered it all. I reflected on it often. I even remembered the island of Borkum when my teacher had ceased to think so much of it.[1]

Likewise at Reigate, when Churchill discussed his intentions —notably to establish a War Staff and to perfect transport arrangements for the B.E.F.—Fisher 'passed into a state of vehement eruption'. The Admiral (according to notes which he gave to Churchill at Reigate) developed the theme that '100,000 soldiers embarked in Transports' would divert 'one million German soldiers' from the Vosges. However, he does not seem to have offered prolonged opposition to the principle of direct support of the French. Moreover, he accepted the innovation of a Naval War Staff. Indeed, in a letter of the 26th from Lucerne he had already offered himself as its chief![2] Churchill records how Fisher re-established his spell:

I plied him with questions, and he poured out his ideas. It was always a joy to me to talk to him on these great matters, but most of all was he stimulating in all that related to the design of ships. He also talked brilliantly about Admirals, but here one had to make a heavy discount on account of the feuds. My intention was to hold the balance even, and while adopting in the main the Fisher policy, to insist upon an absolute cessation of the vendetta . . . I began our conversations with no thought of Fisher's recall. But by the Sunday night [29 October] the power of the man was deeply borne in upon me, and I had almost made up by mind to do what I did three years later, and place him again at the head of the Naval Service . . . All the way up to London the next morning I was on the brink of saying 'Come and help me' . . .

But Churchill was deterred by the thought of renewed dissension and by anxiety about 'the poise of the mind at 71'. Asquith, too, was against Fisher's restoration at that time.[3]

Having returned to Lucerne, Fisher wrote to Hankey on 3 November. In excited accents he recounted some of his recent outpourings to Churchill:

---

[1] W. Churchill, i, 73.   [2] R.C. ii, comp. ii, 1300–3.
[3] W. Churchill, i, 77–8.

I had an 'all night sitting' with Winston and converted him. These new class 'E' submarines with 4 inch quickfiring guns, 4,000 miles radius of action, 5 torpedo tubes and absolutely *self-sustaining* and *more weatherly* than the Mauretania and fitted with wireless and that only a stone wall can prevent going into any harbour will revolutionize naval warfare and make the United States eager for our friendship when Germany eventually goes for Brazil because of her overflowing population![1]

Exaggerating the implications of these submarines, Fisher impressed on Churchill that the days of the destroyer were numbered and that he saw no use for 'any of the intermediate types of vessels' in the longer run.[2] Yet in *The Grand Fleet* Jellicoe was later to acknowledge Churchill's efforts to meet 'the crying need' for light cruisers. The First Lord likewise rejected Fisher's angry condemnation of a secondary armament in battleships. In fact, during the next three years, Churchill exercised rather more discretion in sifting Fisher's imaginative but erratic advice than one may readily glean from *The World Crisis*. It must be remembered that this impressive work was written by Churchill largely for his own justification, not many years after he and Fisher decided to stand or fall together in testifying before the Dardanelles Commission of 1916. In his book Churchill understandably gave maximum weight to the considerations which led him to restore Fisher as First Sea Lord in wartime at the age of seventy-three.

Important steps taken by Churchill, at least partly in response to Fisher's advice, included the appointment of Jellicoe as second-in-command of the Home Fleet with a view to his commanding the main fleet in war. Fisher's predictions about the date of 'Armageddon' tended by this time to cluster near the mark, one of the happiest being addressed to Mrs. McKenna on 5 December 1911 (though the adduced reasons proved largely irrelevant):

My dear Angel,
    . . . Now I will give you the whole effect of what has happened in one word!
'JELLICOE!'
I say 'Nunc dimittis'! For in two years he will be Commander-in-Chief of the Home Fleet . . . The Battle of Armageddon comes along

---

[1] Hankey Papers.
[2] Ibid.; R.C. ii, comp. ii, 1302.

in September 1914. That date suits the Germans, if ever they are going to fight. Both their Army and Fleet then mobilized, and the Kiel Canal finished, and their new building complete . . .[1]

Churchill was fortified also in his speedy adoption of 15-inch guns by Fisher's ecstatic encouragement. The Admiral attached great importance to the progressive increase in the weight of shell: 12-inch 850 lb.; 13·5-inch 1,400 lb.; 15-inch 1,920 lb. He wrote to the First Lord on 10 November: 'I've been looking up what the 15 inch gun will do! It will "stagger humanity"! Just glorious!'[2] With Fisher's 'violent' support, Churchill took the risk of ordering the 'whole outfit' of guns. Presumably, the *Queen Elizabeth* would not otherwise have been ready for service in January 1915.[3]

From Saturday, 18 November, till the following Monday, Fisher was again in England for secret conversations with the First Lord—this time aboard the Admiralty yacht *Enchantress* at Plymouth. On the last day the Admiral wrote to his staunch friend George Lambert (Civil Lord of the Admiralty, 1905–15): 'A hasty line to say how sorry I was not to have a chance to talk with you, but Winston (as you saw) monopolised me and more so after you went! I look forward with delight to your coming to Kilverstone with your dear wife, I hope next August, as I think I will be there then.'[4]

Fisher's influence was particularly valuable in connexion with the lower deck. Churchill, recently a leading social reformer, was receptive to Fisher's championship of the ratings—even if his interest in the subject seems to have receded by the time he wrote *The World Crisis*. Since 1910 discontent on the lower deck had been accompanied by much labour trouble in the country. It may well have been this combination of pressures which produced finance unavailable to the Fisher regime. The pay of seamen and Petty Officers was an important issue, but Fisher was even more interested in furthering the earlier promotion of ratings and marines to commissioned rank. Churchill effected improvements in both respects in 1912. He also seems to have sympathized with Fisher's continued pleas for the free education of Cadets but did not get further than the provision of a number

[1] *F.G.* ii, 419.
[2] R.C. ii, comp. ii, 1329.
[3] W. Churchill, i, 123.
[4] F.P. 545 (copy), 20 Nov. 1911.

of scholarships. Amelioration of punishments and disciplinary procedure also doubtless owed something to Fisher.[1]

However, it was still the technical aspect of naval policy that excited the Admiral's most passionate enthusiasm. Even before Churchill became First Lord, Fisher was becoming obsessed by the idea of converting the Navy entirely to oil fuel, not least because he envisaged the diesel engine as the marine engine of the immediate future. This engine was already proving itself in submarines and other small vessels by 1908; but in due course it was found unsuitable for any ship, from destroyer upwards, requiring high power. Meantime Fisher was insistent on exclusive oil-firing (as distinct from the earlier technique of oil-spraying) for the turbine propulsion of the new 15-inch gun battleships—the 'Fast Division'. At considerable expense, oil-firing did in the event permit these majestic ships to steam at 24 knots. In power, speed, and protection, they comprised a true elite. 'The first desideratum of all is *Speed!*' emphasized Fisher when designs were being considered in December 1911.[2]

Relations between Fisher and Churchill were inherently unstable, though the instability lay more on the side of the 'wild and volatile' Fisher (to quote Sir Francis Hopwood).[3] In February 1912 Fisher wrote of Churchill that 'so far every step he contemplates is good, *and he is brave, which is everything!*'[4] But Churchill declined to be shackled by Fisher's old animosities in the matter of appointments and April found the Admiral writing from Naples (where he and his wife had been since December): 'I regret that in regard to what you say and what you have done in the appointments of Sir Hedworth Meux [formerly Lambton], Sir Berkeley Milne, and Sir Reginald Custance, I fear this must be my last communication with you in any matter at all.' He asserted that Churchill had 'betrayed the Navy'.[5] Fisher was to feel justified in his low opinion of Milne when the *Goeben* and *Breslau* escaped to Turkey in August 1914; but the other two appointments were harmless enough. Fisher's attitude might have been taken as a warning by Churchill. Instead, he was to

---

[1] R.C. ii, comp. ii, 1302, 1325, ibid., comp. iii, 1527, 1932; *F.G.* ii, 402, 441. See F.P. for F.'s correspondence with Yexley (1909–19), and especially F.P. 2156, F. to Y., 19 Oct. 1911 (copy) on promotion, and 2189, 4 June 1912, et seq., on pay.

[2] R.C. ii, comp. ii, 1351–2.

[3] Ibid., p. 1928. The future 1st Baron Southborough had recently been appointed an additional Civil Lord of the Ady.

[4] *F.G.* ii, 430.   [5] Ibid., pp. 450–2.

insist on furnishing the old Admiral with sufficient power to bring his own career as First Lord to an abrupt and traumatic conclusion.

Destiny in the shape of the insatiable Churchill had not done with Fisher, though Fisher had written 'Adieu'. From Naples the Admiral wrote to Esher on 29 April 1912:

Winston writes to me most effusively, but it's no good—

'Facta non verba'

He 'pump-ships' down my back, but it's no use! Some people can't resist hot water down their backs . . . And he sends me the innermost secrets of war to criticize. Nevertheless, he has sold his Country for a mess of pottage, SO I'VE DONE WITH HIM! . . . *The mischief is done!* Milne, an utterly useless Commander . . . is now Senior Admiral afloat, and Hedworth Lambton's appointment to Portsmouth renders him eligible to be First Sea Lord . . . The Providence of God may take both Milne and Lambton into another world any day! *I believe in Providence!* Nearly all my enemies have gone to Hell![1]

Churchill, however, was quite determined to resume close touch with Fisher. Personal fascination apart, the decision to build the oil-fired 'Queen Elizabeths' had urgently raised a major problem. If these great battleships were to burn oil only, it followed that a similar technique would be applied to new vessels generally. Thus the source and security of the oil supply became a prime issue of naval policy. Churchill intended to have the subject investigated by a royal commission. Fisher meanwhile was insisting that Churchill had 'succumbed to Court influence *where McKenna would not*'.[2] But in May the intrepid First Lord boarded the Admiralty yacht, with the Prime Minister and his daughter Violet in train, and sailed for Naples. Prince Louis of Battenberg, now Second Sea Lord, was also on board. He had narrowly missed being made First Sea Lord in December 1911 but his German origins were permitted to tell against him on that occasion. Rear-Admiral David Beatty, Churchill's Naval Secretary, wrote to his wife from Naples on 24 May:

We arrived here from Elba this morning . . . That old rascal Fisher arrived on board directly we got here looking very well and young, never stopped talking, and has been closeted with Winston

---

[1] Ibid., pp. 458–9.   [2] Ibid., p. 460.

ever since . . . Do not mention in conversation to anyone that Fisher is in close confidence with Winston. It would be most injurious to the Service, if it ever got out, and the Navy would hate it . . . Prince Louis hates it and keeps out of the way as much as possible.[1]

By the time that the *Enchantress* sailed on the 26th it seemed that Fisher had agreed to be chairman of the royal commission. Soon afterwards he changed his mind. On 11 June Churchill addressed to him the following unforgettable communication:

My dear Fisher,

We are too good friends (I hope) & the matters wh we are concerned are too serious (I'm sure) for anything but plain language.

The liquid fuel problem has got to be solved . . . No one else can do it so well. Perhaps no one else can do it at all . . . But this means that you will have to give yr life & strength, & I don't know what I have to give in exchange or return. You have got to find the oil: to show how it can be stored cheaply: how it can be purchased regularly & cheaply in peace, and with absolute certainty in war. Then by all means develop its application in the best possible way to existing and prospective ships. But on the other hand yr R. Commission will be advisory & not executive . . . Its report must be secret. . .

I recognise it is little enough I can offer you. But yr gifts, your force, yr hopes, belong to the Navy, with or without return; ; as yr most sincere admirer, & as the head of the naval service, I claim them now—knowing full well you will not grudge them. You need a plough to draw. Yr propellors are racing in the air.

Yrs ever in warm regard

W   [2]

This appeal was not resisted. On 19 June Fisher returned to England.

Although his private income (including Lady Fisher's but of course excluding his £2,000 a year in half-pay) amounted to little more than £300, the Admiral sold his Shell oil shares at 'great prospective loss' as soon as the terms of his appointment were agreed.[3] Clearly, his interest in the possibilities of the internal combustion engine went far to induce him to undertake the chairmanship. While Churchill was primarily concerned to

---

[1] Chalmers, p. 114. See also Bonham-Carter, pp. 253–4, for an entertaining account.

[2] R.C. ii, comp. iii, 1929. The original appears to be no longer extant, but much of it was copied by Lady F. (Kilv. MSS., Pkt. 3).

[3] *F.G.* ii, 331, 337; R.C. ii, comp. iii, 1939.

ensure a supply of oil, the name of Fisher's body, the 'Royal Commission on Fuel and Engines', expresses the compromise reached.

In the role of chairman Fisher displayed his usual verve and ability. When the initial report was signed on 27 November 1912 the other members of the commission were George Lambert, Civil Lord of the Admiralty, Sir Boverton Redwood, government adviser on petroleum, Sir Philip Watts, F.R.S., latterly Director of Naval Construction, Engineer Vice-Admiral Sir Henry Oram, F.R.S., Vice-Admiral Sir John Jellicoe (who was about to become Second Sea Lord), Sir William Matthews, past President of the Institution of Engineers, Sir Thomas Holland, F.R.S., Professor of Geology at Manchester University, Sir Edward Thorpe, F.R.S., late Principal of the Government Laboratory, Alexander Gracie and Alfred Yarrow, the shipbuilders, and Dr. George T. Beilby, F.R.S., Chairman of the Glasgow and West of Scotland Technical College.

The report of 27 November, classified 'Secret', states that oil-firing produces higher speed than coal or coal and oil; increased radius of action; speedier and easier refuelling; 'a reduction in the stokehold personnel of some 55 per cent'; quicker initial production of steam; greater efficiency of operation; and a saving in the cost of construction. 'The reduction of first cost in the vessel herself, and the saving in cost of upkeep because of her smaller crew and of the lessened cost of repairs for the smaller vessel, constitute overwhelming advantages in favour of oil fuel.' For storage, steel tanks should be used. 'The important evidence given as regards various oil-producing areas indicates that large supplies of oil fuel of satisfactory quality can under existing circumstances be obtained.' Deposits of bituminous shale in Scotland do not so far offer a commercially viable source of supply at home. Therefore, the question of storage is of cardinal importance.

The rate of progress in the provision of storage must, of course, be proportionate to the increase in number and power of the oil-using vessels in the Fleet, and we hold the decided opinion that the stock of oil-fuel should never be allowed to fall below at least four years' current peace consumption.

Every acceleration in the accumulation of this reserve will directly increase the security of the nation against war risks, price combinations and fluctuations of supplies.

Indeed, tank capacity 'should be at least 30 per cent in excess of the above specified minimum'.[1]

For Fisher, the most absorbing issue involved in this initial phase of the commission's work was the applicability of diesel propulsion to battleships. At this stage, he was more concerned with eliminating smoke and identifiable funnels than with economy, though the question of endurance also loomed large. On 20 September 1912 he wrote to Esher:

> The imagination can't picture that '*a greater than the Dreadnought is here!*' Imagine a silhouette presenting a target 33 per cent less than any living or projected battleship! No funnels—no masts—no smoke —she carries over 5,000 tons of oil, enough to take her round the world without refuelling! . . . Ten motor boats carried on board in an armoured pit in the middle of her, where funnels and boilers used to be. Two of these motor boats are over 60 feet long and go *45 knots!* and carry 21-inch torpedoes that go 5 miles! *Imagine these let loose in a sea fight!* Imagine projectiles over a ton weight! . . .[2]

But a crucial factor in the attainment of high speed was the turbine. Fisher therefore pressed Sir Charles Parsons 'to associate the turbine with the principle of internal combustion propulsion'.[3] On 21 November Parsons gave evidence to the commission. Fisher's introductory remarks, including reference to his long connexion with Parsons, are of interest:

> I think I ought to give you an exposé of the position before we ask you any questions. I feel the more led to this because if anybody has reason to be grateful to you, I have personally, in regard to the past history of the Admiralty in reference to the turbine and the Dread-nought . . . I well remember, I should like to tell those present, Sir Charles coming and sitting on the sofa in my room, as Controller of the Navy, when we developed this new design to him [doubtless referring to the first turbine destroyers], and told him of the plunge we were going to make. At that time I really believe the majority of engineers looked upon the turbine as a wonderful piece of ingenuity but as a practical impossibility . . . We have arrived now at this position—and I appeal to my friend on the left, Sir John Jellicoe, as to its truth—that the whole Navy is absolutely enthusiastic over the turbine . . . I say this before Sir Charles, because it looks a sort of ungracious and unthankful thing to ask him to come to this table and

---

[1] F.P. 4488, *Royal Commission on Fuel and Engines*—a large bound volume— includes the above-quoted 'First Report' of 27 Nov. 1912 and the two subsequent reports of 27 Feb. 1913 and 10 Feb. 1914. ('Secret'.)

[2] *F.G.* ii, 479.   [3] Ibid., p. 481.

ask him to commit hari-kari and ask him to advise us upon the introduction of the oil engine . . .

Fisher went on to describe the 'oil engine' as essential by virtue of endurance, the saving of personnel, and economy. Parsons, however, expounded the technical objections against large diesel units. As for diesel-driven turbines, he stated: 'I do not think the internal combustion turbine will ever come in. The internal combustion turbine is an absolute impossibility.'[1]

Fisher's continuing hope that diesel propulsion might yet be developed for large warships is reflected in the commission's second and third reports, dated 27 February 1913 and 10 February 1914. Even in the third (and final) report the commissioners expressed the belief 'that the perfected oil engine will be the future source of power of fighting ships, because the radius of action of the fleet will thus be so greatly increased, its fighting efficiency so largely added to, and its instant readiness for action provided'. More generally, they stated that the validity of their first report had been confirmed by their subsequent inquiries. Once more, they emphasized the importance of storage and reserves.[2]

Unofficially, Fisher had meanwhile continued to advocate diesel engines for warships in general. For instance, he wrote to Churchill on 31 March 1913:

I said to Oram the other day before the Commission. How many hours is prudent to warm up the engines before going full speed? He said about 8 hours but it could be less. With the oil engines you start full speed ahead at once—see the fighting advantages!! and yet there are bloody fools who like Canute want to stem the tide of internal combustion![3]

However, by this date the submarine, in particular, was once again occupying the Admiral's thoughts; and the result was the most dramatic and remarkable of all the papers which he ever produced, 'The Oil Engine and the Submarine'.

From the Reigate meeting onwards Fisher had pressed Churchill to build more submarines because he continued to see in them the key to domination of the North Sea. At the oil commission, on 11 December 1912 and subsequently, he heard

---

[1] F.P. 4488, first report, with proceedings, 24 Sept. 1912–14 Jan. 1913, pp. 386–403. See also Appleyard, pp. 141–2, 175–81.
[2] F.P. 4488.   [3] R.C. ii. comp. iii, 1938. See also *F.G.* ii, 488.

evidence about German companies producing diesel engines for
the German and other navies. Moreover, in 1913 the first four
diesel-driven U-boats—essentially overseas submarines—came
into service.

When Fisher came back to England from Naples in June 1912,
he found the First Lord preoccupied with proposals to redistri-
bute British naval strength in response to Tirpitz's new Navy
Law (passed by the Reichstag in May 1912). He wrote a memorandum for Churchill, agreeing with his plan to withdraw all the
(pre-Dreadnought) battleships from Malta. 'It is futile', the
Admiral remarked, 'to be strong in the subsidiary theatre of war
and not overwhelmingly supreme in the decisive theatre.' He
also argued that the 'immense development of the submarine
precludes the presence of heavy ships of war or the passage of
trade through the Mediterranean Sea.' British submarines could
prevent the capture of Malta, just as enemy submarines could
sever the Mediterranean trade routes.

If it be observed that Christian nations (though pretty bad) would
be shocked by the murder of defenceless trading vessels carrying our
food from the Black Sea, would anyone hesitate to send to perdition
some two thousand soldiers packed in a transport trying to invade
England, as compared with only the dozen men forming the crew of
the grain ship?
The essence of war is violence and moderation in war is imbecility! Nor
would it be waste of torpedoes to use them to sink these valuable
cargoes of grain and merchandise. A line of submarines and destroyers
across the [Strait] of Gibraltar or the Malta Channel or other narrow
spaces need only sink a few ships to stop the trade effectually.[1]

On 4 July 1912 Fisher attended a plenary meeting of the
C.I.D. at which the proposed withdrawal of large ships from the
Mediterranean was discussed. Towards the end of the proceedings Churchill referred to the effect of 'torpedo craft and
submarines' in deterring an invasion of Malta; and Fisher
opened his account by asserting that 'the danger to transports
from submarine and torpedo attack was so serious that any idea
of invasion anywhere in face of them was out of the question.' In
answer to Asquith, he also stated that he 'had absolute confidence
in the power of the submarine' against heavy warships; if Britain

---

[1] *F.G.* ii, 468-9 (F.P. 4281, copy). This memo. of 24 June 1912, entitled 'Battleships and Trade in the Mediterranean', seems to have been locked away by
Churchill.

provided 'adequate flotillas of submarines and destroyers at Malta, Gibraltar, and Alexandria no battleship could move in the Mediterranean'. Nor did he expect trade to pass through the Mediterranean in wartime. The implications of this statement for British trade in general were not discussed because McKenna, still focusing on the subject of submarines versus battleships, observed that 'if this estimate of the power of the submarine was correct the North Sea was equally unsuitable for battleships.' 'LORD FISHER said that our battle fleet would not be in the North Sea. It would be off the North Coast of Scotland or outside the Straits of Dover. If the German Fleet came out it would be attacked by submarines and destroyers, if it came out far enough it would then have to fight our battle fleet.' This elicited no response from the First and Second Sea Lords of the day, Bridgeman and Battenberg. Perhaps they had already fallen into the habit of waiting for the First Lord to speak on the fundamentals of naval strategy! Shortly afterwards Churchill duly observed that 'the Board of Admiralty did not entirely accept Lord Fisher's views on submarines'![1]

Evidently Fisher's ideas on strategy in the North Sea still resembled those adumbrated in his commentary on war plans of December 1908 and his submarine paper of April 1909. Yet he still had not carried his views to their logical conclusion, namely that a close blockade of the German North Sea ports and a landing on the German coast were alike impracticable. However the Admiralty, though taking a more moderate view of the submarine menace than Fisher, had decided by the summer of 1912 to abandon close blockade. Orders were issued for an 'observational blockade' whereby a line of cruisers and destroyers would patrol between south-west Norway and the middle of the North Sea. It was accepted that cruisers and destroyers patrolling near the German coast could be overwhelmed in detail by sudden enemy attacks. Extension of similar reasoning to observational blockade led to its eleventh-hour replacement by distant blockade in July 1914.[2]

In sum, therefore, Fisher's long-standing preoccupation with submarines had, up to 1913, done little to improve the Navy's war plans. Ironically, the very slowness of the evolution towards realistic plans produced a valuable strategic surprise, because the Germans entered the war firmly believing that the British

[1] Cab. 2/2/3.   [2] D.S. i, 371–2.

would play into their hands by immediately launching a rash naval offensive.[1] However, in 1913 Fisher still had a unique contribution to make to British thinking about submarines.

By March 1913 the second report of the oil commission had been completed and Fisher was brooding on the problem of ensuring the country's supplies of food and oil. He envisaged a 'series of tubes' as the 'simple remedy'—'a score of them (say) between Dover and Calais' would make it more difficult for German raiders to interfere with British imports.[2] At much the same time he was 'preparing an upheaval' for the First Lord on submarines as *the coming force*.[3] The form taken by this 'upheaval' owed a good deal to Fisher's acquisition, in April, of Captain S. S. Hall as one of the secretaries of the oil commission. As Inspecting Captain of Submarines (1906–10), and thereafter, he supplied Fisher with information about submarines. His views are reflected in the title of a paper which he sent to Fisher in August 1909: 'The Question of the Submarine Menace'.[4]

At the beginning of March 1912 Hankey had succeeded Ottley as Secretary of the C.I.D. Fisher had been among his backers, describing him as 'Napoleonic and Cromwellian'— rather as he dubbed Jellicoe 'Nelson'. On 13 April 1913 Fisher wrote to Hankey that he was again, after a long interval, discussing the submarine question with Balfour (who had ceded the Conservative leadership to Bonar Law in 1911). Hall, remarked the Admiral, 'could give a lovely lecture to Balfour at any time he wished'.[5] Fisher's own interest in the subject was further stimulated by the C.I.D.'s third investigation of the invasion problem—Balfour and Esher being members of the sub-committee. Not only did Fisher believe that British submarines had made invasion impossible; he also glimpsed salvation in the unlikely form of the German U-boats because they might discourage the transportation to France of the B.E.F.! The caution marking the Admiral's strategic attitudes after his recall in 1914 was establishing itself in 1913, though his Pomeranian fantasy lived on, at least as a talking-point. On 25 April 1912 he had written to Esher: 'I fully agree with you

[1] *D.S.* ii, 44–5; Bell, p. 200.
[2] F.P. 4497, 'Our Food and Oil in War', P. 3/13. See also R.C. ii, comp. iii, 1936, F. to Churchill, 10 Mar. 1913.
[3] Ibid., p. 1937.
[4] F.P. 413, enclosure with Hall to F., 3 Aug. 1909.
[5] Hankey Papers.

that the schemes of the General Staff of the Army are grotesque.'
Yet in the same letter he extolled the attractions of a landing '90
miles from Berlin on that 14 miles of sandy beach'.[1] By 1913, however, he was reverting to the idea of eliminating the British Army
altogether; whereas Esher, having advocated 'a really supreme
navy—and no army' in July 1912, sided with the invasionists at
the C.I.D. in 1913 in order to defeat Henry Wilson's plan to
send all six regular divisions to France on the outbreak of war.[2]

Fisher was busy with the preparation and refinement of his
submarine paper from May 1913 till his departure from the oil
commission's offices in February 1914. During that time he had
at his disposal a staff including Captain Philip Dumas (British
Naval Attaché at Berlin, 1906–8), Captain S. S. Hall, and
Engineer Lieutenant C. J. Hawkes—to say nothing of printing
facilities which were enthusiastically utilized. The first and
second editions of the paper, produced in May and June, were
sent to Balfour, Hankey, Jellicoe, and Lord Sydenham (Fisher's
old friend Sir George Clarke!).[3] The third edition, of November,
included 'answers to all suggestions and corrections by Mr.
Balfour, Lord Sydenham and Sir John Jellicoe'.[4] Then Corbett's
editorial help was enlisted.[5] Lastly, Esher offered some comments.[6] Meantime editions were printed in November and
December; and finally in January and February 1914.

The original version of 15 May 1913 (sent to Balfour and
Hankey) had no title. It began: 'No means exist of preventing
an enemy's submarines from coming out of their harbours and
cruising more or less at will, short of mining and blocking operations on a very large scale.' After thus stressing the potential
importance of mines (!) the paper explained that 'a close invest-
ment' of the British North Sea ports by German submarines
would be five times as difficult as a similar blockade of the
German exits by British boats. From this point of view, the
Germans lacked the requisite number of boats.

Unless the Germans take their larger submarines with their battlefleet to assist in a fleet action as they are suspected of intending to do

[1] *F.G.* ii, 454–5.
[2] F.P. 584, E. to F., 13 July 1912; Williamson, p. 309.
[3] F.P. 694, 704, and 706; Hankey Papers, F. to H., 16 May, 5, 19 June, 19 Dec.
1913; *F.G.* ii, 486–7.
[4] F.P. 748a, Dumas to F., 25 Nov. 1913.
[5] F.P. 752, Corbett to F., 30 Nov. 1913, etc.; *F.G.* ii, 494–5.
[6] F.P. 761, E. to F., 23 Dec. 1913.

with their destroyers, the only other forecast that can be made of the manner in which they intend to use their submarines is that they will endeavour to menace our southern and western coasts and possibly commerce . . . As submarines grow and become able to keep the sea for longer periods it will become impossible to say where they may *not* be met . . . the risk . . . will be greatest in enclosed waters such as North Sea, Mediterranean, etc. IT WILL BECOME INCREASINGLY DIFFICULT FOR ANY OR EITHER POWER TO OBTAIN THE COMMAND OF SUCH SEAS AS THESE, IN THE ACCEPTED SENSE OF THE TERM, IT WILL RENDER THE DESPATCH OF EXPEDITIONARY FORCES ACROSS THEM A MORE AND MORE HAZARDOUS BUSINESS THAN EVER IT HAS BEEN BEFORE, AND THIS APPLIES EQUALLY TO THE INVASION OF ENGLAND OR TO THE DESPATCH OF OUR EXPEDITIONARY FORCE OVERSEA.

CONSIDERING THE SAFETY OF ENGLAND IT WOULD THEREFORE APPEAR THAT THE DEVELOPMENT OF THE SUBMARINE (PROVIDED WE KEEP AN EQUAL OR LARGER NUMBER THAN PROSPECTIVE ENEMIES) WILL RESULT IN INCREASED SAFETY.[1]

On 17 May, probably, Hall gave Fisher a note wherein he predicted the 'extermination of surface war vessels by submarines of 2,000 tons'.[2] From Hawkes the Admiral received details of submarines then under construction, including an overseas type of 1694 tons being built by Vickers.[3] Fisher summed up his ideas on a small sheet of paper, with liberal underlining in red:

*The Submarine of 1,700 tons displacement is now
the dominant factor of Naval War.*

NO ONE HAS DISCOVERED HOW TO DESTROY A SUBMARINE!

A SUBMARINE WILL KEEP THE SEA LONGER THAN A DREADNOUGHT!

No Invasion or Raid is possible.

No Expeditionary Force can leave these shores.

So don't worry about Conscription or Territorials.

But German submarines will blockade our commercial Ports so you had best agree to Channel Tunnel and Private Property at Sea immune.[4]

---

[1] Hankey Papers, typescript, 4 pp., covered by F. to *H.*, 16 May 1913.
[2] F.P. 4287, with a cutting of 17 May attached.   [3] F.P. 690, 17 May.
[4] F.P. 4284, n.d.—but F.'s substitution of '1,700 tons' for '1,500' tons' in the heading is indicative.

On 20 May Balfour acknowledged the Admiral's paper of the 15th. He was—as formerly—inclined to believe that Britain was not likely to benefit from the development of the submarine. Neutralization of neighbouring waters meant a worsening of Britain's relative position.

If there was any chance of such an extreme hypothesis being realized, we should not only be useless allies to any friendly power on the Continent, but we should have the utmost difficulty in keeping ourselves alive.

Should we not, among other things, have to reconsider our views about the capture or rather the destruction (for a submarine could not capture) of private property at sea?[1]

From that time onwards the paper was steadily improved by what resembled one of Fisher's *ad hoc* committees. Balfour was, of course, correct in describing complete neutralization as 'an extreme hypothesis'. But above all his letter prompted Fisher to develop his most significant point, namely that attacks by U-boats on commerce were to be expected.

In June a second version, considerably altered and expanded, was produced under the title of 'The Oil Engine and the Submarine'. It extends to eight large pages of print. The format is very dramatic—more so than that of the later editions quoted in *Records* and *The Jellicoe Papers*.[2] The style is substantially Fisher's own.

The Admiral at last declares against any form of blockade of the German coast by British surface vessels.

Three years ago even the distance at which it was considered to be *dangerous* for a vessel to remain off an enemy's base was found *as a result of a trial* to be 300 miles (report of trial is attached). If this distance be divided by six it may fairly be said that a blockade as loose as 50 miles is impossible without a gradual but certain loss of the surface ships employed in the blockade if hostile submarines are present.

But this does not mean that the British cannot blockade the German coast at all. Indeed, 'English blockade of the German outlets is vitally essential.' 'Yes, the larger submarines are the only type of vessel capable of maintaining any form of blockade,

---

[1] *F.G.* ii, 485–6 (F.P. 691).
[2] F.P. 4290 comprises proofs, with corrections and additions by F. (P. 6/13). Cf. *Records*, pp. 181–5 and N.R.S. *Jellicoe Papers*, i, 31–6.

they have sea-keeping qualities far in advance of any surface vessel, and by reason of their internal combustion engines they can remain on their beat ready for full speed without any expenditure of fuel.'

The older and smaller types (he continues to assert) 'do not become obsolete'. They are ever ready to counter an enemy raid; they can start their engines at once 'from "cold" like a taxi-cab'. Acting 'in conjunction with the destroyers and torpedo boats of the patrol flotillas, they form a most valuable second line of defence, and the most bigoted conscriptionist will allow that they would be a formidable hornet's nest' for an invading or raiding enemy.

There follows a section on 'The Enemy's Submarines' which develops in more detail the points made in the original paper of 15 May. The dubious theme that 'the development of the submarine'—given numerical superiority—will afford Britain 'increased safety' is maintained. Against this item Jellicoe (who returned his copy on 30 June) wrote: 'Concur'.[1]

But the most striking product of Fisher's collaboration with Balfour is undoubtedly the section on 'Submarines and Commerce'. This section begins even more alarmingly than the version which subsequently came as a shock to Churchill and Asquith: 'The suggestion that Germany, by stationing submarines off our principal commercial ports, may occasion greater damage than we can effect by means of our whole sea power is perhaps open to argument.' The general purport, however, resembles that of the later versions:

If Germany fights in alliance with Austria and Italy against Britain, France, and Russia, she will find herself commercially 'in a very tight place indeed'. Britain's position—submarines excluded—'is reasonably secure'. But 'when it is realised that the enemy's submarines may be met off all our own commercial ports' there will be an impact 'on freight and insurance rates'.

It cannot now be long before this fact will become generally known to the public, and it is desirable to consider fully the question of diverting our commerce to our far western ports in war time, and of developing the port and railway facilities of such harbours as Plymouth, Falmouth, Bristol Channel ports, Fishguard, Holyhead, etc. . . .

Again it will be impossible for submarines to deal with merchant ships in accordance with international law. Is it presumed that they

---

[1] F.P. 706.

will disregard this and sink any vessel heading for an English commercial port?

Then comes the crux:

It must be admitted that this submarine menace is rather a desperate business for British commerce, for no means can be suggested at present of meeting it except by reprisals. All that would be known would be that a certain steamer did not arrive or that some of her boats [had been] picked up with a few survivors to tell the tale.

It would be an altogether barbarous method of warfare, but if it is done by the Germans, the only thing would be to make reprisals. Many of these reprisals suggest themselves which might cause the sinking of our merchantmen by German submarines to be stopped.

One is inclined to think in this light the arming of our English merchantmen is unfortunate, for it gives the German submarine an excellent excuse (if she wishes one) for sinking her, namely, that of self-defence against the gun of the merchant steamer.

Jellicoe noted in the margin: 'I cannot conceive that submarines will sink merchant ships without warning.' Elsewhere he remarked, with reference to Fisher's wish to substitute twenty large submarines for a dreadnought: 'But I would not cease building Dreadnoughts.'[1]

Lord Sydenham had been 'very "stand off" ' on first meeting Fisher again early in June; but the Admiral thawed him out and he duly received a copy of 'The Oil Engine and the Submarine'.[2] He wrote to Fisher about it on 24 June and, at greater length, on the 28th. He agreed that the arming of merchantmen was asking for trouble. Having formerly attracted Fisher's wrath by his opposition to the building of dreadnoughts, he took the opportunity of remarking that the submarine paper supplied 'the most destructive argument against large battleships' that he had yet seen! With regard to invasion, he thought that this could easily be prevented by surface vessels unassisted by submarines. Quoting from the paper, he agreed that submarines would be 'a constant and harassing menace' in the North Sea, but he believed that an admiral with 'something big in view' would 'carry through his task without much loss'. On the cardinal point he wrote:

'Submarines and Commerce' (p. 6). I cannot believe that submarines will sink unarmed ships and I do not see how they can easily

---

[1] F.P. 4290, nos. 1-4. No. 3 has Jellicoe's marginalia.
[2] Hankey Papers, F. to H., 5 June 1913.

convoy them into port. In more barbarous days, unarmed ships were not summarily sunk, and modern sentiment could not stand such proceedings. On the other hand an armed tramp would be fair game for his torpedo.

Finally, Sydenham suggested lines of approach to the destruction of submarines:

An aeroplane sights a submarine on the surface. It can be over it before submergence is complete. If it can skim low enough to drop a high explosive charge over the submarine, the latter is doomed. If located with sufficient accuracy the submarine's course under water can be followed. An accurately dropped high-explosive with delayed fuze would end the career of the submarine.

However, these valuable remarks were not sufficiently represented in the revised version of the paper printed in November.[1]

In August, Fisher took what proved to be his last holiday in Marienbad. Meanwhile Churchill's curiosity about Fisher's promised 'upheaval' had been fully aroused. Having wrested from Commodore Roger Keyes (in charge of submarines) a copy of the final (unsensational) section of the June print, the First Lord wrote to the Admiral on 30 August:

But surely this is the very letter or paper about which you spoke to me some time ago, and which you said you were going to show me? . . .

When am I going to have the pleasure of taking you for a cruise? I shall be afloat for the whole of the next two months, and it would be delightful to have a few good long days talk.[2]

Fisher, however, declined to go aboard the *Enchantress* either then, or in response to further invitations in November. Writing on 5 September, he explained to Jellicoe: 'I don't care about being mixed up with the job lot he gets on board with him, such as Custance & Co., and also he's playing up to certain people who don't have my sympathies at all, never have, and never will!'[3]

By November the paper was virtually ready to be given to the First Lord. Fisher, however, wanting it to be shaped into 'a work of art', sent a proof to Corbett on the 29th. The next day Corbett thus expressed his immediate reaction: 'It makes me feel as if I had a flash of lightening by the tail.'

[1] F.P. 704 and 705, Sydenham to F., 24 and 28 June 1913; F.P. 4293, no. 1, P. 11/13.
[2] F.P. 720.   [3] *F.G.* ii, 492; R.C. ii, comp. iii, 1799.

Corbett's amendments were more than merely verbal. He criticized the suggestion that Britain should reconsider her views on the capture of private property at sea. 'You show', he wrote, 'that given all you anticipate from the submarine, we by the advantage of our geographical position can entirely stop German oversea trade while she will have difficulty in making any *effective* impression on ours.' Like Sydenham, he saw aircraft as a possible antidote to submarines. Finally, aligning himself with Jellicoe (and to an extent with Sydenham), he did not think that submarines 'would incur the odium of sinking merchant ships out of hand'.[1]

Fisher did not give way on this last point; and his view (to which Balfour and Esher also subscribed) proved devastatingly correct. But he deferred to Corbett by adding a note on 'capture at sea'. This, he wrote, should be retained on account of Britain's geographical position, the uncertainty concerning the effect of aircraft, the limited range of vision from a submarine's deck, the consequent inducement for it to attack trade as this converged on a port, and the increased possibility of counterattack by aircraft in such an area. He also doubted whether 'powerful neutrals' would recognize 'blockade by submarines only'.[2]

As a further improvement, food and oil were designated as the chief prey of the marauding U-boat. Fisher had, in early November, imported the Channel Tunnel into the paper as a partial solution, but he had excised it by the end of the month as liable to assist the transportation of the B.E.F.![3] So when, on 6 December, the long-awaited paper was sent to Churchill, the development of the west-coast ports stood as the main remedy.

The paper certainly produced an effect on those who read it at the Admiralty. Unfortunately this tended to take the form of paralysis rather than desire for action. In the seven remaining months of peace, the search for an antidote to the submarine should have been stimulated; but the Navy of 1914 hoped that high speed, zig-zagging, and large destroyer screens would meet the case. Indeed, as far as warships were concerned, these measures were quite effective. It was in defence of commerce that devices for detecting and destroying submerged submarines would be desperately needed.

[1] F.P. 752.
[2] F.P. 4293, nos. 5 and 6, P. 12/13, 16 pp.
[3] F.P. 4293, no. 5; *F.G.* ii, 495.

Churchill acknowledged receipt of Fisher's 'epoch making Memo about Submarines' on 12 December and promised to communicate further when he had 'thoroughly digested it'.[1] On 1 January 1914 he wrote:

I have read and re-read with the closest attention the brilliant and most valuable paper on Submarines which you have drawn up for the Admiralty, and I have requested my naval colleagues to study it forthwith.

There are a few points on which I am not convinced. Of these the greatest is the question of the use of submarines to sink merchant vessels. I do not believe this would ever be done by a civilised Power. If there were a nation vile enough to adopt systematically such methods, it would be justifiable, and indeed necessary, to employ the extreme resources of science against them: to spread pestilence, poison the water supply of great cities, and, if convenient, proceed by the assassination of individuals. These are frankly unthinkable propositions and the excellence of your paper is, to some extent, marred by the prominence assigned to them.[2]

Like you, I am disquieted about our submarine development and it is clear that in the near future we must make an effort on a greatly increased scale to counter the enormous programmes in which Germany has been indulging for the last 6 years . . .[3]

One development at least partly attributable to the paper will soon be noticed. On Fisher's return to the Admiralty, Churchill urgently charged him with the provision of more submarines. Also, once the Germans moved, late in 1914, towards a policy of unrestricted attacks by U-boats on commerce, this seemed an impressive confirmation of Fisher's genius and foresight. Clearly, his originality lay in what Churchill had reproved, his capacity to think the unthinkable. As he had revealed in the lobbies at the Hague conference of 1899, he accepted the prospect of total war; and as he had shown in his submarine paper of 1913, he was prepared to react to unrestricted sinkings by taking reprisals against captured U-boat crews or other enemy nationals. During the early part of the war he was to urge similar measures in reply to Zeppelin raids on British towns.

The effect of the submarine paper on Jellicoe was also important. It accentuated his caution when commanding the Grand Fleet during the war, and his success in avoiding losses

[1] F.P. 759.
[2] This last sentence was heavily underscored by F.
[3] F.P. 763.

to torpedoes fired by U-boats owed something to the impact of Fisher's views. Meanwhile, after receiving Fisher's print of December 1913, Jellicoe wrote to Churchill reinforcing Fisher's argument that Britain should build large numbers of submarines.[1]

At the Admiralty, the paper failed to convince Battenberg (First Sea Lord since December 1912) of the likelihood of unrestricted attacks on commerce. He wrote to the First Lord that the paper was 'marred by this suggestion'.[2] Commodore Keyes likewise found the idea 'impossible and unthinkable'.[3]

Dissatisfied with the Admiralty's reaction Fisher, on 8 May 1914, sent the paper to the Prime Minister. 'IT IS REALLY MOMENTOUS!' he assured Asquith in his covering letter. He reiterated his usual complaint about the Germans having more submarines than the British—a misleading line of thought in view of Britain's superior surface fleet. (German commerce could best be throttled by British surface vessels. More British submarines would not do much to counteract the U-boats.) Fisher, however, commented further:

I have said all this to Winston till I am sick! (and made him sick too I fear!) Myself I should drop a Dreadnought secretly and go in for 20 submarines instead.

There are a lot of idiots who lecture at the Naval War College and write in the papers that Tirpitz won't use his submarines to sink merchant ships! The civilized world they say would execrate him!

Skobeleff exterminated the Turcomans (man, woman and child!) Was he recalled? Was Russia banned? General Nogi had no prisoners in Manchuria till some European busybody asked where they were! The Mexican Generals murder ad lib.!

The Essence of War is violence and moderation in War is imbecility!

'La raison du plus fort est toujours la meilleure.'

The enclosed copy of the submarine paper is unsullied by any mark or comment. Even in the ordinary way, problems of defence held little natural appeal for the highly civilized Asquith. Fisher's brutal communication failed to galvanize the Prime Minister into remedial activity, though the Admiral at least was able to report to Jellicoe, on 25 May, that he had inflicted a degree of trauma: 'The Prime Minister has asked me to dine with him, but I've declined. I let fly at him about submarines,

[1] *F.G.* ii, 497. [2] W. Churchill, ii, 280. [3] Keyes, i, 53.

and he is evidently *greatly moved! but he entreated me to say nothing! Burn this!*[1]

From January to April 1914 Fisher seems to have kept clear of Churchill. The First Lord was disconsolate. On 1 January he wrote to Fisher: 'Contact with you is like breathing ozone to me.' By 24 February his official private secretary was intimating: 'Winston is quite cross with you for not coming to see him. He says he wants to talk to you badly about many things.'[2] However, meetings were more frequent from May onwards, partly because the oil commission had disbanded late in February. The following tribute, signed by the distinguished membership of the commission, indicates that Fisher's age had not detracted from his performance as chairman:

We, the undersigned, members of the Royal Commission on Fuel and Engines, desire to place on record at this, the final meeting of the Commission, our deep sense of the dignity, conspicuous ability, and impartiality with which you have presided over the sittings of the Commission and conducted the proceedings, as well as the national value of the services which you have rendered in facilitating the discharge of the responsible duties entrusted to the Commission by His Majesty the King.[3]

It was but a few months later that Churchill was 'narrowly' watching the seventy-three-year-old Admiral with a view to his recall, and it is hardly surprising that he then found no reason to doubt 'his physical strength and mental alertness'.[4]

In July 1914—a quiet month on the eve of war—Fisher was staying with Churchill aboard the *Enchantress* at Portsmouth. The First Lord arranged for the Admiral to go over to Fort Blockhouse so that he could see Keyes and the latest submarine. Keyes has left an amusing and entirely credible account of Fisher's visitation. The Admiral was convinced that Keyes was largely to blame for Britain's inferiority to Germany in submarines. (Keyes had succeeded S. S. Hall as Inspecting Captain of Submarines in 1910 and was elevated to Commodore in charge of the submarine service in 1912.) Fisher arrived at Fort Blockhouse 'in a very aggressive mood' and asked why Britain had built so few boats. Keyes remarked that it was he, Fisher, who

[1] Asquith MSS., 25, ff. 186–8 (for F. to A., 8 May) and ff. 192–9 (for 'The Oil Engine and the Submarine'); *F.G.* ii, 507.
[2] F.P. 763 and 790.   [3] F.P. 794, 10 Feb. 1914.
[4] W. Churchill, i, 401–2.

had adopted the policy of building large numbers of ineffective coastal submarines to replace defensive minefields. The Admiral said that this did not answer his question; nor was his temper improved by the supplementary response. This was to the effect that Fisher himself had given Vickers their monopolistic position. In consequence, they had geared themselves to build small submarines of limited prospective value, while preventing other firms from building submarines to improved Admiralty designs. Otherwise, there was only the limited capacity of Chatham Dockyard available. Fisher spat out the words 'Very interesting!' and forthwith departed. When, some three months later, Keyes learnt of Fisher's restoration as First Sea Lord, he was patriotic enough to welcome it on the grounds that Fisher would 'make war'; but he fully expected to be bracketed with the enemy![1]

When Britain went to war on 4 August, the Grand Fleet was already on station. Earlier in the day Sir John Jellicoe had assumed command and proceeded to sea from Scapa Flow. The strategy of distant blockade began to exert its slow but inexorable pressure on Germany. While the German High Seas Fleet awaited, hopefully but in vain, a British attempt to establish a close blockade, the B.E.F. crossed to France unhindered. But these silent successes did not gratify a public impatient for a great victory at sea.

Churchill, for his part, had accepted with marked reluctance the defensive posture of the British fleets. In 1913 he had instructed Rear-Admiral Lewis Bayly to examine further the offensive possibilities associated, from 1905 onwards, with A. K. Wilson, Slade, and Fisher. In July 1913 Ballard, now Director of Operations, condemned as unacceptable gambles the schemes submitted by Bayly for the capture of an advanced base— Borkum, Sylt, or Heligoland. On the eve of war Churchill resurrected these proposals and on 31 July 1914 he sent them to the Prime Minister. Major-General Henry Wilson promised to investigate the matter personally from the Army's point of view; but, war having supervened, he asked Major Hereward Wake to examine the amphibious possibilities indicated by the First Lord. Wake reported, inter alia:

There are certain points having an important bearing on this class of operation to which I venture to draw attention.

[1] Keyes, i, 53–5, 133; Jameson, pp. 102–7.

It is true that the Japanese occupied an oversea base for torpedo craft in hostile country with success. But they were able to choose islands with few inhabitants and cut off from the mainland . . . These conditions are probably all impossible of fulfilment in the case of the places selected for report by the First Lord.

The instances given in his report by Admiral Bayly belong to the 18th century and were carried out under entirely different conditions to those which now exist. To mention a few factors only, steam, telegraph and telephone, torpedoes, mines, and very long range guns, did not exist, nor were trained armies in large numbers at hand . . .

In the case of the places selected, information on vital points does not appear to exist . . .

The question for consideration is whether the advantages to be gained are commensurate with the risks incurred. In the particular places examined this does not appear to be the case; but it is possible that a wider survey might reveal the existence of other spots to which these objections do not apply with so much force.

The failure of such an undertaking would undoubtedly involve worse results than the mere loss of the men, guns, ships and stores engaged. There ought to be a reasonable chance of success, not only in the preliminary operation of establishing the base, but in the power to maintain it for any useful period.[1]

What with this criticism and the manifold distractions of the first three months of war, Churchill did not revert in earnest to the theme of an advanced base until December. The problem of Fisher's wartime attitude to these amphibious projects, linked with his own Baltic theme, may now be tentatively broached. With Wake's remarks in mind, three of Fisher's letters of January 1915 may at once be quoted:

4 Jan. 1915   (to Churchill): I agree that Borkum offers great possibilities, but it's a purely military question whether it can be held.

11 Jan. 1915   (to Jellicoe): You say golden words when you protest *'against taking risks for which there is no compensating advantage'*.

18 Jan. 1915   (to Churchill): I have no wish whatever to cold-douche any projects for our being troublesome to the enemy . . . But I desire to emphasize the necessity of sticking to the enemy's vitals![2]

---

[1] Adm. 137/452, 'Seizure of Advanced Base'. Wake's report was sent to the Ady. by Callwell (Wilson's successor as D.M.O.) on 11 Aug. 1914.

[2] *F.G.* iii, 122, 127, 132.

Here, it will suffice merely to sow some seeds of doubt. What were Fisher's strategic intentions when he returned to the Admiralty? Was his great 'Armada' not intended from the outset for the hazards of the Baltic, as he and Churchill subsequently testified? Did he change his mind about the expedition? If so, when and why?

During August, September, and October 1914 Fisher 'constantly' visited Churchill at the Admiralty.[1] Despite the chancy success in the Heligoland Bight on 28 August, there was on balance not much to offer the public during these months. The *Goeben* escaped to Turkey and Sir Berkeley Milne earned Fisher's probably excessive condemnation.[2] The defensive posture of the High Seas Fleet deprived Jellicoe of any chance to fight a major battle. On 22 September the *Cressy* and two other old armoured cruisers were sunk by a U-boat in the North Sea with heavy loss of life. This confirmed Fisher in his pre-war view that large ships should normally be kept out of the North Sea because of the submarine menace.[3] Meanwhile Churchill was waxing impatient with what he regarded as lack of enterprise on the part of Battenberg and the War Staff. For the control of naval operations he had established a War Staff Group consisting of himself, Battenberg, Vice-Admiral Sir Frederick Hamilton (Second Sea Lord), Vice-Admiral Sir Doveton Sturdee (Chief of the War Staff), and William Graham Greene (Secretary of the Admiralty). Prince Louis, depressed by attacks in the press on his German birth, was unwell. Churchill yearned for the dynamism of Fisher. On 19 October Lord Haldane offered the suggestion that he should restore Fisher as First Sea Lord—and that he should bring back A. K. Wilson as well![4] On the 20th, Churchill secured Asquith's approval.[5] Subsequently, Fisher stated that King George blocked his appointment for ten days.[6]

What qualities were requisite in a First Sea Lord at that time? In view of the geographical and other strategic conditions, patience was a prime virtue—as Fisher himself was to stress in an important memorandum of 25 January 1915. As many senior officers recognized, a strong man was needed—someone who

---

[1] Cab. 19/33, Dard. Comm., p. 190.
[2] N.R.S. *The Mediterranean 1912–14*, p. 242.
[3] *F.G.* iii, 61; see also his letter to Jellicoe of 28 Oct. 1914 (Ibid., p. 64).
[4] Gilbert, p. 144.
[5] Ibid., p. 147.
[6] Cab. 19/33, Dard. Comm., F.'s evidence, p. 190; *F.G.* iii, 65n.

could withstand Churchill when bent on an unsound project. In view of the First Lord's determination to restore Fisher, on the assumption that he, Churchill, could control the Admiral, it is paradoxical that Fisher alone seemed to interested observers to be capable of controlling Churchill! Indeed, he did ultimately succeed in terminating Churchill's activities at the Admiralty altogether—and then destroyed his own position as an immediate sequel. If Fisher had better understood the need for a naval general staff, no doubt he could have reorganized Churchill's still-advisory Naval War Staff and placed it under his immediate leadership. Then he should have been able to moderate Churchill's eager pursuit of unsound projects without destroying his partnership with the First Lord, unique in the annals of the Admiralty. As it was, he resorted to various forms of sabotage in order to brake the progress of the man who had so pertinaciously insisted on recalling him to office.

The King based his objections on enduring distrust of Fisher in the Navy and on the Admiral's age. Fisher's opinions were constantly changing now, according to the King's information.[1] In fact, there had been little change in Fisher from the last point of view. Rigidity, like A. K. Wilson's, had never been one of his characteristics. Distrust did persist amongst some of the senior officers, such as Rosslyn Wemyss, but it was not an important factor in 1914. But Fisher's age—seventy-three, not seventy-four as the King and others thought—was indeed a material objection, notwithstanding indications to the contrary.

On 30 October Churchill seized a green pencil and wrote to Fisher: 'The King wishes to see you, after 11.30 this morning or before 5.30 this afternoon as most convenient.' And on the back of the sheet of note-paper he added:

> 'Your
>> "Troubles"
>>> Tell me them
>>>> please.'

Fisher wrote below the first message:

O let not the foot of pride come against me!   Psalm 36, Verse 11. Lord, let me not be highminded: let me have no proud looks! Let

---

[1] Nicolson, pp. 250–1.

me refrain my soul and keep it low like as a child that is weaned from his mother. Yea, let my soul be even as a weaned child!

Psalm 131.[1]

It certainly appears that Fisher and Churchill were agreed on the ultimate desirability of an expedition to the Baltic, though the contemporary evidence is not very precise or reliable. Indeed, a historiographical problem must now be unravelled. The difficulty stems mainly from the fact that, in August and September 1916, the two men—having resumed their friendship after the débâcle of May 1915—proceeded to concert their evidence for the Dardanelles Commission.[2] On 16 August 1916 Fisher wrote to Churchill: 'I think YOU made an excellent point of enlarging on the Armada of 593 vessels and my reluctance to leave that task unfinished.'[3] Garvin was recruited by Fisher as an adviser and he worked with Churchill as well.[4] The following paper kept by Fisher may probably be attributed to the journalist:

I must think that the Admiral's case would be more strongly constructed upon a different basis altogether . . . We begin with two fundamental principles, different but not at first conflicting.

(a) Lord Fisher's mind at the Admiralty was already [by the beginning of 1915] concentrated upon the Baltic project and the vast scheme of new construction required for the successful achievement of that great design. But that design could only come into play after a certain period.

(b) The Russian need [for help found Fisher and Churchill at first united but then increasingly divided over the Dardanelles project].

. . . Conviction then on Lord Fisher's part that at any cost he must free himself from further responsibility for the Dardanelles enterprise, because its demands on naval resources had now reached the point where it jeopardised what Lord Fisher thought a far greater thing—the Baltic project. This had been the real focus of Lord Fisher's purposes at the Admiralty, and the standpoints of the First Lord and the First Sea Lord, which had been by no means incompatible at the outset, had gradually diverged until they had become totally irreconcilable . . .[5]

[1] F.P. 829.
[2] F.P. 1257, 1260, 1267, 1272, all Churchill to F., Aug.–Sept. 1916. Gilbert, pp. 802–8, extensively quotes these and other relevant documents.
[3] Gilbert, p. 803.
[4] Ibid., p. 808.
[5] F.P. 4417, unsigned typescript.

Fisher then set to work and redrafted his case in conformity with this rationalization.[1] Still closely in touch with Churchill, Fisher gave evidence along these lines before the Dardanelles Commission on 11 October 1916.[2] All this needs to be borne in mind when using *The World Crisis* and Fisher's memoirs as sources for dealing with the history of the 'Baltic project'. Indeed, it is significant that Fisher does not seem to have adopted 'The Baltic Project' as the title for his paper on this subject until September 1916.[3]

If read against the foregoing background, Churchill's account in *The World Crisis*[4] will be seen to avoid specifying the connexion (if there was one) between Fisher's arrival at the Admiralty, the programme of construction, and the Baltic idea. Indeed, the commonly accepted account that, on 3 November 1914, Fisher held a conference at the Admiralty and arranged that day for some 600 vessels to be built, is derived from the doctored evidence given to the Dardanelles Commission. The conference was in fact mainly concerned with the provision of submarines. Otherwise Fisher decreed that all 'red-tape methods—very proper in time of peace—were now to be abandoned.' But before the wording of the minute was changed, the only reference to provision of vessels other than submarines was: 'Arrangements would be made in due course to obtain additional vessels of other types in a similar manner.'[5]

In September 1916 significant alterations were made to Fisher's original copy of the minute of the conference. These give the impression that all the construction orders placed in fact over a period extending from November 1914 to May 1915 were initiated on a single day, 3 November 1914; also that all these vessels were specifically intended for 'the Baltic and North Sea'.

[1] Compare the earlier with the later materials, especially the 'Preamble: Précis of Lord Fisher's Case' (Adm. 116/3454, P. 9/16, 2pp.) with the prints of 10/16 (ibid.). The evolution of F.'s case may be traced in detail in F.P. 4413–36, 4904, 4911–13.

[2] Cab. 19/33.

[3] F.P. 4427, P. 9/16. Till then, the title of the paper was 'On the possibility of using our Command of the Sea to influence more drastically the Military Situation on the Continent.' See Corbett's original draft of 19 Dec. 1914 (F.P. 874) and the print of Feb. 1915 (F.P. 4343). The text, with F.'s italics, is in *Records*, pp. 217–22.

[4] Vol. ii, p. 39.

[5] F.P. 4424, typescript dated 3 Nov. 1914 and stating 'The First Sea Lord presided at a Conference this day at the Admiralty.' This minute of the conference is interleaved in an early draft of F.'s case for the Dard. Comm., Aug. or Sept. 1916. See also F. to Jellicoe, 19 Nov. 1914 (*F.G.* iii, 76).

Indeed, for the minute was substituted a short paper entitled 'Statement of New Shipbuilding Inaugurated by Lord Fisher'. This paper embodies the following changes to the text of the minute:

(1) Addition at the head of the paper:

Note. The following memoranda [including a list of 612 vessels ordered] are inserted as vital to the explanation of Lord Fisher's reluctance to resign on the Dardanelles question. It will be seen that Mr. Churchill had given him sole charge of the creation of this armada of new ships, *intended for great projects in the Baltic and North Sea.*

(2) Deletion of the first sentence of the minute:

The First Sea Lord explained that the Conference had been summoned primarily with the object of expediting the delivery of twenty Submarines which were to be at once commenced.

Substitution of:

Lord Fisher explained to those present that this Conference had been summoned with the approval of Mr. Churchill, primarily with the object of expediting the delivery of 20 submarines which were to be at once commenced, but in the second place a big further programme *for a special purpose* had been decided on.

(3) Addition at the end:

Note. After this, a meeting of all the shipbuilding firms of the United Kingdom took place at the Admiralty under the presidency of Lord Fisher, and the programme was parcelled out there and then.[1]

In Fisher's published memoirs, the transformation is complete. The final '*Note*' now ends with the words 'the programme mentioned above in italics was parcelled out there and then.' Next, the 'Building Programme' of 612 assorted vessels is given and specifically ascribed to the 'Meeting on November 3rd, 1914'.[2]

The fact of the matter is that only the twenty submarines were 'parcelled out there and then'. The piecemeal evolution of Fisher's building programme will be traced as this narrative proceeds. It will be seen that many of the ships were intended primarily for Jellicoe and the Grand Fleet and not especially for the Baltic or Churchill's coastal projects in the North Sea.

[1] F.P. 4427, P. 9/16, p. 10, compared with the typed minute in F.P. 4424.
[2] *Memories*, p. 88.

Fisher's subsequent reputation has suffered from his decision to overstate, before the Dardanelles Commission, the extent to which his conduct as First Sea Lord was actuated by 'the Baltic plan'.[1] In *Memories* he reinforced the overstatement.[2] Finally, it is worthy of remark that Corbett did not give the Baltic paper to Fisher 'in the early autumn of 1914', as stated in *Records* (p. 217). This dating also derives from the preparation of materials for the Dardanelles Commission.[3] Corbett's handwritten draft was sent to Fisher on 19 December 1914—a matter of seven weeks after the latter's recall on 30 October. Before that, the First Sea Lord does not seem to have possessed a Baltic plan on paper. (See also pp. 472–3 below.)

Churchill's evidence for the Dardanelles Commission, like his account in *The World Crisis*, avoids definite misrepresentation. Fisher's opposition to the naval attack on the Dardanelles is not ascribed to the Baltic project; nor is the Baltic paper given a date. Indeed, Churchill does not mention the paper in his evidence to the commission. In his book, he is content to refer to Fisher's support for the Baltic idea, including the use of Russian troops, which the First Lord had himself suggested in August 1914. However, he leaves the reader free to accept Fisher's version. He simply writes of the Baltic scheme: 'In a weighty memorandum, which has since been published, he stated his case with sure insight. It was undoubtedly the prime goal of a naval offensive.'[4]

After Fisher's death in 1920 and his own publication of *The World Crisis* in 1923, Churchill was given cause to reconsider his wartime relationship with Fisher and thus the Admiral's connexion with 'the Baltic plan'. It was not until 1927 that Churchill discovered how far Fisher had gone in attacking his position, both at the Admiralty and in the cabinet, in May 1915.[5] Then, in 1929, Bacon's biography of Fisher was published and Churchill was much nettled by the author's criticisms of himself. He therefore published a revised account of his dealings with Fisher. This first appeared in *Nash's Magazine* in April 1930 and it was subsequently included in *Great Contemporaries*. This account is of

---

[1] For his evidence to this effect, see Cab. 19/33, pp. 191, 197–9, 204–5, 208.
[2] pp. 65, 68, 73, 86–8. A relevant para. on p. 55 avoids inaccuracy.
[3] F.P. 4427, P. 9/16.
[4] W. Churchill, ii, 39. His evidence to the Dard. Comm. is in Cab. 19/33. (F.P. contain copies of most of the proceedings of the Dard. Comm., up to the first report.)
[5] Asquith, ii, 92–3.

great importance for a true assessment of Fisher's wartime role at the Admiralty. Churchill writes:

My bringing Fisher back to the Admiralty in 1914 was one of the most hazardous steps I have ever had to take in my official duty. Certainly, so far as I was personally concerned, it was the most disastrous. Yet looking back to those tragic years I cannot feel that if I had to repeat the decision with the knowledge I had at that time, I should act differently. Fisher brought to the Admiralty an immense wave of enthusiasm for the construction of warships. His genius was mainly that of a constructor, organiser and energiser . . . To build warships of every kind, as many as possible and as fast as possible, was the message, and in my judgement the sole message, which he carried to the Admiralty in the shades of that grim critical winter of 1914. I, concerned with the war in general and with the need of making British naval supremacy play its full part in the struggle, was delighted to find in my chief naval colleague an impetus intense in its force but mainly confined to the material sphere. I therefore gave him the freest possible hand and aided him to the best of my ability . . .

His biographer is at pains to prove him an audacious naval strategist and war leader. We are reminded that he had a wonderful plan for forcing an entry into the Baltic with the British fleet, for securing command of that sea, cutting Germany from the Scandinavian supplies, and liberating Russian armies for an amphibious descent upon Berlin. It is quite true that Lord Fisher frequently talked and wrote about this design, and that we together authorised the building of a number of steel-protected flat-bottomed boats for landing troops under fire. I do not however believe that at any moment he had framed a definite or coherent plan of action. Still less do I believe that he had the resolution which, after the long and comparatively easy stages of preparation were completed, would inevitably have been required. He was very old. In all matters where naval fighting was concerned he was more than usually cautious. He could not bear the idea of risking ships in battle. He settled down upon a doctrine widely inculcated among our senior naval officers, that the Navy's task was to keep open our own communications, blockade those of the enemy, and to wait for the Armies to do their proper job. Again and again, orally and in writing, I confronted him with the issue 'Before you can enter the Baltic you must first block up the Elbe. How are you going to do this? Are you ready to take the islands and fight the fleet action necessary to block the Elbe? Can you divide the fleet and enter the Baltic with a part while the Germans are free to sally out with their whole strength from either end of the Kiel Canal?' Deep and sometimes fiercely intimate as was our association, courageous as he was in thought, brutally candid as he was in discussion, he never would face this pretty obvious question. I must record my conviction that he never seriously intended to dare the prolonged and awful hazards of the Baltic operation, but that he talked vaguely and impressively upon this project, which was in any case remote, with a view to staving off demands which he knew I should make upon him (which indeed all the allied Governments including markedly President Wilson and the United States made upon their Admiralties), to use the naval forces more directly in the main shock of war.[1]

For the most part, this account is convincing. It strips away the camouflage manufactured in 1916 and after. Paradoxically, it does more to rehabilitate than to denigrate Fisher's reputation as a strategist. If the Admiral wished to rely on distant blockade until a fleet action could be fought on favourable terms or until a good opportunity developed for a combined operation, it would be difficult to quarrel with his policy. If 'the Baltic plan' was little more than a talking-point, useful for warding off Churchill's most dangerous and unpromising projects, this should redound to Fisher's credit!

On 31 October 1914 Churchill marked the occasion of Fisher's return to the Admiralty by asking him 'to obtain 20 submarines additional to those now ordered in the shortest possible time'. He added: 'Let me also have your proposals for accelerating to the utmost those now in hand.'[2] As related above, Fisher placed orders for the twenty submarines on 3 November and at the conference he issued a memorandum about means of expediting construction.[3] That same day, by 'a wonderful coup', an order was placed with Charles M. Schwab of the Bethlehem Steel Corporation in America 'for very rapid delivery' of twenty more submarines, together with 'small craft and guns and ammunition'.[4] The course of events in the North Sea since August had done nothing to cause Fisher to change his mind about the importance of submarines but there is no evidence that he was linking them with the Baltic idea.

Churchill, however, was already interested in monitors. On learning that Schwab had available four turrets with two 14-inch guns to each, the First Lord suggested to Fisher that monitors should be built to receive them. 'The Admiral was delighted with the plan, and in a few hours he was closeted with his constructors

---

[1] W. Churchill, *Great Contemporaries*, 'Lord Fisher and his Biographer' (Reprint Society, 1941), pp. 300–2.
[2] Adm. 1/8402 (file 419).   [3] F.P. 4305; also *Memories*, pp. 88–90.
[4] *F.G.* iii, 66, F. to Jellicoe, 3 Nov. 1914.

designing the vessels.' It seems quite likely that Fisher visualized these slow, tubby monsters blasting north Germany with their mighty guns as swarms of Russian soldiers debouched from boats onto a stretch of Pomeranian sand; but direct evidence is lacking. Churchill, for his part, intended to use the monitors in the North Sea—on the coasts of Belgium or Germany.[1] In a minute written for Fisher's information on 11 December, the First Lord referred—appropriately enough—to 'heavy inshore work'. He continued:

> We require now to make ships which can be built in 6 or 7 months at the outside, and which can certainly go close in shore and attack the German Fleet in its harbours. These are special vessels built for a definite war operation, and we must look to them in default of a general action for giving us the power of forcing a naval decision at the latest in the autumn of 1915 . . . The root principle is to build vessels to be ready in June capable of going in to fetch them.'[2]

Meanwhile, Fisher's attention had been much concentrated on submarines during his first weeks in office. He lost no time in bringing Captain S. S. Hall to the Admiralty from service in the North Sea in order to make him Commodore (S) instead of Keyes.[3] However, it was not until February that he succeeded, because Churchill resisted the removal of the gallant officer in question. On 3 February Fisher confided to Jellicoe: 'What I really cared about is getting rid of Keyes *who is no good at all for Submarines* but he is a special pet of the First Lord—why I don't know! he has made a mess of the Submarines in the last 3 years but of course he knew nothing about it.'[4] In the interim Hall was employed as hastener of submarine construction. Fisher's recall had transformed Hall's position in the service, as indicated by a letter he wrote to the Admiral some months before the war:

> Keyes quite openly tells me that (if he is asked) he will oppose my relieving him
>
> (1) because they will not make me a Commodore
> (2) because there is strong opposition to me in several quarters because I am a protegee [*sic*] of yours![5]

Keyes has left an account of the conference of 3 November 1914 which confirms the impression that it was almost entirely

---

[1] W. Churchill, i, 457–9. See also his memo. of May 1915 on the state of the Navy in ibid. ii, 527.

[2] F.P. 865.

[3] Keyes, i, 130–3.

[4] Add. MSS. 49006, ff. 134–5.

[5] F.P. 758, 11 Dec. 1913.

concerned with submarines.[1] Fisher's attitude to the Commodore (S) was openly hostile. Later in the day, Keyes furnished suggestions for implementing the programme, such as substituting 'repeat "E" boats for "G" boats recently ordered' in the interests of celerity. He enclosed a separate paper explaining in detail his difficulties over submarine-building during the past three years. Marginal scoring on this print suggests contempt—presumably Fisher's.[2]

The submarine programme raised the Admiral to a peak of enthusiasm. In a memorandum of 5 November he wrote:

The situation was explained at the Conference on November 3rd . . . The first boats ought to be completed ready for trials in eight months, and the whole in eleven months. At least these dates must be strenuously worked for. To enable this to be done, engines for 25 boats will be commenced. The extra five will feed the 20 if defective parts are developed . . .

As *TIME* must be the primary consideration, cost will of course be higher than with peace procedure . . .

Preliminary steps have already been taken respecting batteries, main motors, periscopes, torpedo tubes and similar parts, so that these will all be ordered within a fortnight, unless there are very special reasons, which I will personally examine at once the moment a hitch occurs.

If building 'E' type hulls, instead of 'G', will reduce time of construction by ever so short a period, this will be done . . .

The Second Sea Lord is taking steps for the training of the personnel required for these new boats.

Heads of Departments not to write minutes, but to come to me at once personally if difficulties are met with, however trivial—so that there may be no excuse whatever hereafter for delay . . .[3]

By 10 November six firms had stated that they could build two boats as quickly as they could build one and the Controller (Rear-Admiral Sir Frederick Tudor) proposed to order the extra six. The same day Churchill minuted:

Approved.

This is additional to the 8 extra ordered 6 weeks ago.

26 + 8 = 34, + the normal programme of 1914–15 (10) [corrected to read (9)] + 20 U.S.A. = 64.

(Please check figures.)

[1] Keyes, i, 130.
[2] Adm. 137/2067, f. 672 et seq.; Keyes, i, 130–1.
[3] Adm. 1/8402 (file 419).

The corrected total number of submarines on order turned out to be 63.[1]

Fisher was writing to Jellicoe almost daily. On the 19th he conveyed the extent to which submarines had thus far absorbed his efforts:

Don't worry about the submarines. We have 95 now on order. Half a loaf is better than no bread! To-day I begin the destroyer campaign—not that I much believe in them. It's d——d little they have done so far. Their guns *never* hit anything. They can't ram a submarine. Three German submarines have been rammed ineffectively by destroyers. The destroyers more damaged than the submarines.[2]

However, Jellicoe soon afterwards impressed on the First Sea Lord the general usefulness of destroyers in the struggle with the U-boats:

Your submarine paper when President of the Oil Fuel Commission must be interesting reading now. It has all come true, even to the sinking of merchant ships, in which no one believed at all. I remember Prince Louis saying it was unthinkable. I hope we are building every TBD that the country can produce. They are *the* great antidote. All SM officers, our own and the German, dread them.[3]

It seems clear that the destroyers ordered by Fisher were mainly intended for service in the North Sea. The Baltic scheme did not directly affect the issue. Despite Fisher's doubts about the future usefulness of the destroyers, their construction proceeded rapidly. Orders were placed, mainly for the Admiralty 'M' class design (about 900 tons), as follows: 10 in early November, 22 at the end of the month, 18 in February, and 22 in May. (The ordering of this final batch was initiated before Fisher left the Admiralty on 15 May.) The time taken to complete these 72 vessels varied widely. Launchings began in August 1915 and finished in January 1917. Two of the May order were apparently not built at all. In addition to these destroyers, two flotilla leaders (repeat 'Kempenfelts' of about 1,650 tons) were ordered in May.[4]

In December, construction of monitors began in earnest. According to Churchill, he and Fisher 'embarked in the closest agreement on a very large policy of monitor building'.[5] However,

---

[1] Ibid.   [2] *F.G.* iii, 76.
[3] Ibid., pp. 87–8, 5 Dec. 1914.
[4] March, pp. 174–80; Adm. 1/8421 (file 139).
[5] W. Churchill, ii, 527.

in view of his general caution, it is probable that the Admiral was by then linking the monitors with the Baltic project as a counterweight to Churchill's revived desire to attack the German coast. Oliver became Chief of Staff and an Acting Vice-Admiral on 5 November, and he for long remembered the arguments about strategy at the daily meetings of the War Staff Group. (This body was reconstituted after Fisher's return as First Sea Lord and now included the seventy-two-year-old A. K. Wilson.) Regarding the months of November and, more particularly, December, Admiral of the Fleet Sir Henry Oliver long afterwards wrote:

> Fisher, Wilson, Graham Greene (Secretary) and I and others discussed future possible and impossible operations. Churchill wanted to land troops at Borkum Island and capture it. Emden was to be captured at the same time—both impossible to hold if captured as we had not the land forces. Fisher wanted to send the Grand Fleet into the Baltic and convey a Russian Army from Petrograd to land and take Berlin. How the fleet would pass the Great Belt in single line ahead with the German battle fleet deployed and crossing the T did not interest him, or how the fleet could be supplied in the Baltic.
>
> Wilson wanted to bombard Heligoland with the old pre-Dreadnought battleships and land and capture it . . . I hated all these projects but had to be careful what I said. The saving clause was that two of the three were always violently opposed to the plan of the third under discussion. I was glad when the Dardanelles project came along as it took the old battleships out of the North Sea Picture.[1]

The hypothesis that Fisher was using the Baltic idea as a talking-point rather than a practical proposition is supported by his cautious attitude to the conduct of operations in general. As Churchill was eventually to remark in his essay of 1930 (see pp. 463–4 above), this caution was well masked by a great deal of violent talk. In fact, there was only one considerable strategic risk taken by the Admiralty on Fisher's initiative. This was the sudden, and as it proved most timely, dispatch of the battle cruisers *Invincible* and *Inflexible* to the Falkland Islands. Over Jellicoe's protests, Beatty's Battle Cruiser Squadron was further depleted when the *Princess Royal* was sent to the West Indies.

On 4 November (the day following the conference on the submarine programme) news was received of the annihilation

[1] W. James, pp. 137–8.

of Rear-Admiral Cradock's weak squadron by Spee's powerful cruisers at the Battle of Coronel. Churchill and Fisher agreed on Spee's probable future movements and thus on the dispatch of a force to the Falklands. It was Fisher who wanted to send two of Jellicoe's battle cruisers rather than one. Jellicoe was consequently ordered to detach the ships at once to Devonport. They arrived there on Sunday the 8th. The dockyard authorities asked to continue working on the ships until Friday the 13th. Fisher's reply of 9 November was crucial. As he wrote to Beatty on 11 December in reply to a congratulatory telegram: 'The answer went "SAIL WEDNESDAY", and we added a postscript they might embark the dockyard if they liked. AND THEY LEFT!'[1] The battle cruisers were just in time to catch and overwhelm Spee. The threat of commerce-raiding by powerful squadrons of German cruisers was definitively removed. To that limited but material extent, Fisher's pre-war construction of battle cruisers to the exclusion of light cruisers received its justification. In 1928 Bacon wrote to Captain Thomas Crease, Fisher's Naval Assistant from the time of his recall, about the sending of the vital telegram on 9 November. Crease was definite and emphatic that Fisher personally had sent it.[2] Indeed, Churchill handsomely acknowledged Fisher's leading role in the affair as soon as the news of Sturdee's victory was received on 10 December:

My dear,

This was your show and your luck . . . Your *flair* was quite true. Let us have some more victories together and confound all our foes abroad—and (don't forget)—at home . . .[3]

As the First Lord well knew, Fisher was unlikely to forget his enemies at home! From the outset he had exerted himself to displace the Chief of Staff, Vice-Admiral Sturdee—tainted by his former connexion with Beresford and placed in a ridiculous light for his views on submarines, as reported to Fisher by Hall shortly before the war.[4] After the Battle of the Falklands, the Admiralty treated Sturdee with scant generosity. Admittedly, the latter's pomposity and conceit did not necessarily endear him to other officers.[5] But the spectacle of Fisher revelling in the congratulations showered upon him, while busily denigrating

---

[1] *F.G.* iii, 92.　　[2] Kilv. MSS., Pkt. 38, 23 Oct. 1928.
[3] *F.G.* iii, 91.　　[4] F.P. 803, 26 Apr. 1914.
[5] *D.S.* ii, 92–3; information from Admiral Sir William James.

Sturdee's contribution and decimating his recommendations for honours, does not command whole-hearted admiration.

The memory of old times also affected the First Sea Lord's attitude towards Rear-Admiral Leveson, the Director of Operations, as Oliver recounts:

> Fisher had a hatred of the D.O.D. R.A. Leveson, and when Fisher was yarning in my Office, as he often did, and Leveson came in, as soon as he went out Fisher would say he was a 'traitor'. I asked him once what he had against Leveson and he said he could not remember but he knew he had something. Fisher was so set against Leveson that I went to Churchill and told him and asked that he might get a command at sea and Churchill sent him to the 2nd Battle Cruiser Squadron.[1]

It is unlikely, in fact, that Fisher could not recollect the causative link! This was Leveson's pre-war appointment as Flag-Captain to Sir William May. It will be remembered that May had disagreed with Fisher on important points of Admiralty policy between late 1907 and early 1909; and, as far as Fisher was concerned, May was relegated from being 'the proper man' to replace Beresford (February 1907) to the category of 'sneak' (December 1910) for 'working the backstairs leading to the royal apartments.'[2] On 22 December 1914 Captain H. W. Richmond, who was now Assistant D.O.D., commented in his journal:

> Fisher, unfortunately, at this supreme juncture, seems more busy in getting at his enemies than at those of his country. He is after 'Sir Berkeley Goeben' [i.e. Milne], as he calls him, at this moment, and also Sturdee. Leveson he has got rid of, and [Captain Thomas] Jackson takes his place. It is rather pitiable to see this curious passion of his so ruling even at this time.[3]

Meanwhile the cautious tendency of Fisher's strategic approach had gathered strength since the detachment of the battle cruisers early in November. The close relations between Fisher and Jellicoe go far to explain the former's attitude.

Soon after resuming the mantle of First Sea Lord, Fisher wrote to Jellicoe: 'I'm sure you'll AT ONCE telegraph to me personally in cypher if you *want anything or wish anything altered*

---

[1] N.M.M., Oliver Papers, 'Recollections for Rear-Admiral R. D. Oliver', p. 119.

[2] *F.G.* ii, 118 and 344.   [3] Marder, *Portrait*, p. 133.

or doubt the wisdom of any orders you get!'[1] He quickly formed the habit of writing almost every day to his former protégé, often addressing him as 'My beloved Jellicoe'. The Commander-in-Chief was much upset by the detachment of the *Princess Royal* soon after that of the *Inflexible* and *Invincible*, and he wrote to Fisher on 10 November: 'I trust that the decision to send another battle cruiser away from the Grand Fleet will be reconsidered.'[2] Indeed, Professor Marder calculates that, taking account of the loss of the modern battleship *Audacious* to a mine, and also various breakdowns and unavoidable refits, the detachment of the three battle cruisers in the first half of November afforded the High Seas Fleet its best opportunity of the whole war in terms of relative strength.[3] Beatty reinforced Jellicoe's arguments. On 15 November he wrote to Fisher: 'I am sure that no one realizes more clearly than you do that the main object of all strategy is to muster overwhelming strength in the decisive area, and the decisive area is the North Sea.' Fisher's marginalia denote scepticism about the validity of the fuss generated in the Grand Fleet. However, he was extremely solicitous when writing to Jellicoe on the 16th.[4] There is no reason to think that he disagreed with Beatty's expression of principle. He continued his intimate correspondence with Jellicoe (and with Beatty). The invasion scare of November also focused attention on the North Sea. By the later part of December, Fisher's agreement with Jellicoe's strategic views had become emphatic. On the 26th he wrote to the Commander-in-Chief: 'I am in accord with you as to bearing in mind ALWAYS *the big thing* of the War! which is to keep our Big Fleet in big preponderance, intact and ever ready to cope with the German Big Fleet!'[5] On the same day he urged this principle on Churchill, writing that 'it seems imperative to refix in our minds the one pervading governing condition of the present war at sea, which is to keep a big preponderance of sea force ever ready to cope with the Big German Fleet at its "SELECTED" moment and our "AVERAGE" moment (to use classic words!).'[6]

These views conformed with one category of Fisher's pre-war

---

[1] Add. MSS. 49006, ff. 41–2 [7 Nov. 1914].

[2] *F.G.* iii, 67. See also N.R.S. *Jellicoe Papers*, i, 79–93, for J.'s protests and representations.

[3] *D.S.* ii, 43–4.   [4] *F.G.* iii, 72–3.   [5] Ibid., p. 111.

[6] F.P. 887 is a holo. draft by F., misdated 26 Nov. 1914. The text is in *F.G.* iii, 112–13.

pronouncements; but they were a far cry from the reckless offensive projects aired by him in talk and private correspondence, including the daily sessions of the War Staff Group. He had intervened boldly to achieve the destruction of Admiral Spee. Some risk had been taken—no doubt correctly—over the strength of the Grand Fleet. But between the detachment of the battle cruisers in early November and the victory of 8 December, Churchill's desire for a naval offensive in the North Sea, together with the invasion scare, reinforced Fisher's underlying affinity with Jellicoe's cautious views. Superficially, Fisher was at one with the First Lord in wanting an offensive. It was rather as if, having been restored to the Admiralty by Churchill, he could not bring himself to admit to the latter that the grim realities of the war had to be taken seriously and that he saw no alternative to a policy of conserving the Grand Fleet against a possible day of battle. He backed Churchill's Borkum scheme at the War Council on 1 December and on 7 January, saying at the former meeting that it was important to adopt an offensive stance. 'The present defensive attitude of our fleet [Fisher maintained] was bad for its *moral*, and did not really protect it from the attacks of submarines.' But it was Churchill who presented the details of the project on both occasions.[1] In *The World Crisis* Churchill commented on Fisher's attitude to the scheme:

He spoke a great deal about Borkum, its importance and its difficulties; but he did not give that strong professional impulsion to the staffs necessary to secure the thorough exploration of the plan. Instead, he talked in general terms about making the North Sea impassable by sowing mines broadcast and thus preventing the Germans from entering it while the main strength of the British Fleet was concentrated in the Baltic.[2]

In fact, the pre-war neglect of mines (stemming in part from Fisher himself) rendered this project even less practicable than it might otherwise have been. The nearest thing to a serious investigation of this version of the Baltic scheme arose, probably, from a conversation between Fisher and Corbett over lunch in the First Sea Lord's quarters at the Admiralty in mid-December.[3] On the 19th Corbett sent Fisher the 'Baltic paper' in manuscript. In a covering letter he wrote:

[1] Cab. 42/1.
[2] W. Churchill, ii, 41–2.
[3] Corbett's diary, 14 Dec. 1914.

In the enclosed memo. I have endeavoured to state your case for the Baltic as well as I can—setting out such objections as occurred to me and meeting them—to show the difficulties had been considered.

There is one—unfortunately rather obvious—objection which I have not mentioned because I don't see how to meet it. It is this— if it is possible for us to make the North Sea untenable with mines, is it not even more possible for the Germans to play the same game in the Baltic? Perhaps you can see a way of meeting this—it is sure to be taken by those who have no stomach for your plan.

I am not at all satisfied with what I have done, and if you see anything I can add or alter—out of your better knowledge—it will be a great pleasure to try again . . . I have not had the memo. typed as there is no one I feel I ought to confide it to.[1]

It is significant that Fisher never asked for a revision of the paper.

During the arguments of the War Group about the form of a possible naval offensive—Borkum, Heligoland, or the Baltic— there was another project mooted in December which enlisted Fisher's more genuine interest. This was the proposal that Sir John French's army should advance up the Belgian coast to Zeebrugge—a potential base for U-boats—supported by the guns of the Channel Fleet. (This fleet, comprising the older pre-Dreadnoughts, normally guarded the Straits of Dover.) On 9 and 11 December Fisher declared to Jellicoe and Beatty his enthusiasm for this scheme. 'Our coast bombardments are futile now,' he wrote to Jellicoe, 'as no military advantage taken of them! 10,000 British soldiers at Zeebrugge after the bombard-ment would have turned the German flank.'[2]

The bombardment of Yarmouth by Hipper's battle cruisers, and especially the inconclusive sparring of the main British and German fleets at the time of the Scarborough raid of 16 Decem-ber, intensified Fisher's concentration on the needs of the Grand Fleet. The reports of Jellicoe and Beatty led Fisher to revive the suggestion, which (according to *The World Crisis*) he had made on his return to the Admiralty, to convert the battleships *Renown* and *Repulse* into battle cruisers. Little work had actually been done on the ships. Even in December 1914, it remained Admiralty policy not to lay down any ships which could not be completed by the end of 1915. When reviving his proposal, Fisher seems to

---

[1] F.P. 874. The text of the memo. is in *Records*, pp. 217–22.
[2] *F.G.* iii, 90 and 92.

have wanted new battle cruisers of very high speed for one purpose only—to catch the fastest German battle cruisers. Of course,
his usual predilection for big, fast ships had been strengthened
by the Falklands victory.[1] Although Fisher was airing the Baltic
scheme at the Admiralty,[2] it does not seem at first to have been
linked with the battle-cruiser suggestion. On 21 December
Fisher wrote to the First Lord: 'I fear you have missed my point
about the 32-knot "Rhadamanthus"! (So quickly built and
cheap!) The only vessel than can "*catch*", not "keep up with"—
she has to catch!!!!!!—the German battle cruiser *Lützow*, of
28 knots, is the English *Tiger*, of 29 knots . . . We have got to
have 3 "Rhadamanthi"! . . .'[3] And on the 22nd he wrote to
Jellicoe: 'Your letter about the raid was quite excellent and very
clear. "*Battle cruisers and more battle cruisers*" is the watchword! . . .
That way lies the path to glory. Cumbersome battleships are
rotten. Slow men and slow ships mean failure . . .'[4]

Then the battle-cruiser and Baltic ideas converged. On 23
December Fisher declaimed to Jellicoe: 'SPEED IS EVERY-
THING!' But elsewhere in the same letter he referred to the
completion in March of eight monitors with 14-inch guns 'and
drawing only 9 feet of water'.[5] On the 25th, he reiterated to the
First Lord: 'It is entirely a question of speed.'[6] On the 27th he
turned to the draught of the battle cruisers, informing the
Controller that it was 'VITALLY IMPERATIVE FOR
STRATEGIC REASONS to keep the *deep draught UNDER* 26
FEET!' Churchill approved the proposal on the 28th.[7] However,
even Fisher did not expect the ships to be completed before
April 1916.[8]

Churchill was increasingly frustrated by the strategic outlook
in December. Fisher kept on talking about the combined operation at Zeebrugge (which Churchill also wanted but could not
get approved in the War Council) and about the Baltic idea. As
Oliver observed (see p. 468 above), this tended to nullify
Churchill's Borkum project, though the First Lord deemed
capture of this island an indispensable preliminary to a Baltic
expedition and was puzzled that Fisher did not whole-heartedly
accept this.[9] There are also distinct signs of Fisher being irritated

---

[1] *D.S.* ii, 95.   [2] *F.G.* iii, 107, Churchill to F., 22 Dec. 1914.
[3] Ibid., p. 104.   [4] Ibid., p. 106.   [5] Ibid., p. 108.
[6] Ibid., p. 110.   [7] Ibid., p. 114.   [8] Ibid.
[9] Ibid., p. 107, Churchill to F., 22 Dec. 1914.

with Churchill round about 20 December.[1] Partly, doubtless, as a substitute for the perilous Borkum scheme, Fisher began in late December to press for a much more offensive mining policy.[2] But even more obviously he assumed the point of view communicated by Jellicoe, namely that aggressive mining of the Heligoland Bight was the best available means of hampering the German fleet and forcing it to disclose, by sweeping the mines, its intention to emerge. Churchill consistently opposed this 'blockade mining'—and 'ambush mining' also. The enemy, he argued, could always remove the blockade mines; moreover, these mines would hinder any British offensive schemes, such as the capture of Borkum, which in his opinion offered the best means of winning the war in 1915.[3]

Fisher's preoccupation with the strength of the Grand Fleet became more evident towards the end of December. Intent on avoiding losses, especially to U-boats, he wrote to Jellicoe on the 26th: '*In my decided opinion your Fleet and no big ship of your Fleet should EVER be in the North Sea. NEVER.*' He expressed continuing concern over the loss of personnel in the earlier sinkings of the three 'Cressy' class cruisers, and writing on the same day to Churchill stressed the same theme—'with the *Hawke* sent to the bottom off Peterhead, together with an immense number of irreplaceable invaluable officers and men—with the holocaust of the three cruisers losing more officers and men than in all Lord Nelson's battles put together'.[4] The essential point is that the First Sea Lord was forcefully opposing a policy of risking big losses of personnel in activities which could be avoided or reduced. The Grand Fleet would, in his view, be ultimately weakened by such losses, even if the ships in question did not belong to the main battlefleet. He had adopted this viewpoint before the Dardanelles project came to the fore.

Fisher was now looking for small vessels to take over much of the patrolling and escorting in the North Sea.[5] Oliver, in a minute of 30 December, submitted a proposal to build twelve fleet minesweepers, capable of acting against submarines and of replacing destroyers as escorts. He suggested that they be called sloops. These vessels were also to be of shallow draught, with

[1] Ibid., p. 99, F. to Jellicoe, 20 Dec.; F.P. 879, Churchill to F., 21 Dec.
[2] F.P. 4325, memo. of 31 Dec. 1914; *F.G.* iii, 104, F. to Churchill, 21 Dec., and 122–3, memo. of 4 Jan. 1915.
[3] *F.G.* iii, 105, 128, W. Churchill, i, 519–21.
[4] *F.G.* iii, 111–13.   [5] Ibid., pp. 113, 115.

room for 600 troops on deck, and were to 'have as good gun-power as German destroyers'. On 6 January Churchill directed that the number of sloops to be built should be increased to twenty-four.[1] The extent of Fisher's concern for the Grand Fleet is reflected in Oliver's latter-day comment on the distribution of the original sloops: 'Jellicoe got the first 12 to my disgust. I wanted them for the Channel and Irish Channel where sub-marines were busy.'[2]

Jellicoe certainly appreciated the value of these vessels, Referring to a discussion he had held with the Prime Minister, he wrote on 18 July 1915 to Fisher's successor: 'I told him we wanted *at once* 65 more sloops laid down. I certainly want 30 more up here.'[3]

On 31 December 1914 a proposal to order forty-two more submarines was placed before Churchill. He sensibly minuted on 7 January:

> We have 77 subs. in comn. & 75 building. This is a proposal to build 42 more. I do not see any relation between this & our tactical requirements . . . To issue new orders is not to get new work done, but only to produce a paper effect, at the expense of existing contracts. It is much more important to concentrate energy and attention upon the rapid & punctual delivery of the immense programme now under construction than to enlarge it . . .[4]

The First Sea Lord had backed the proposal but Churchill's remarks seem to have imbued him with a better sense of propor-tion regarding submarine construction. In any case by 7 January Fisher was embroiled in the Zeppelin question and the Dardan-elles operation had been mooted.

By the beginning of January 1915, the impasse on the western front and the general lack of movement in the war had induced a widespread feeling of frustration. The Russian request for a diversion to relieve Turkish pressure in the Caucasus acted as a solvent. Fisher was still prepared to welcome a combined opera-tion at Zeebrugge or elsewhere—under favourable conditions. As early as September 1914 Churchill had suggested a combined attack on the Dardanelles by Greek, or other, troops and British warships; and again at the War Council of 25 November he had raised the idea with Fisher's 'hearty concurrence'. Indeed, according to Hankey's minutes, the First Sea Lord 'asked

---

[1] Adm. 1/8407 (file 492).   [2] W. James, p. 140.
[3] N.R.S., *J.P.* i, 173.   [4] F.P. 891.

whether Greece might not perhaps undertake an attack on Gallipoli on behalf of the Allies'—an interesting example of his freedom to speak in the War Council on the general conduct of the war.[1] Moreover, Fisher then began to send horse-boats to Alexandria in anticipation of a combined attack on the Dardanelles.[2] Therefore there is nothing surprising in the welcome which the Admiral gave to the suggestion of such an attack following the Russian appeal of 2 January. On the 3rd he wrote to Churchill:

> . . . I CONSIDER THE ATTACK ON TURKEY HOLDS THE FIELD! But ONLY if it's IMMEDIATE. However, it won't be! Our Aulic Council will adjourn till the following Thursday fortnight! . . . We shall decide on a futile bombardment of the Dardanelles, which wears out the irreplaceable guns of the *Indefatigable* . . . What good resulted from the last bombardment [on 3 November]? Did it move a single Turk from the Caucasus? . . .

He went on to suggest details of the composition of the military force; also 'previous feints before they arrive with troops now in Egypt against Haifa and Alexandretta, the latter to be a REAL occupation'. The Greeks, Bulgarians, Russians, Serbs, and Roumanians were all to be involved. Light-heartedly Fisher added the fateful suggestion: 'Sturdee forces the Dardanelles at the same time with the "Majestic" class and "Canopus" class! God bless him!'[3]

On the following day, 4 January, Fisher offered his resignation as First Sea Lord.[4] This move was in no way connected with the Dardanelles. London was threatened with Zeppelin attacks and Churchill had previously (in September) accepted the Admiralty's responsibility for the aerial defence of the country. A lengthy report on the subject was completed for Fisher on 2 January.[5] Asquith wrote in his diary on the 5th: 'Old Fisher seriously proposed, by way of reprisals for the Zeppelin raids, to shoot all the German prisoners here, and when Winston refused to embrace this statesmanlike suggestion sent in a formal resignation of his office. I imagine that by this time he has reconsidered it.'[6]

---

[1] W. Churchill, ii, 47; Cab. 42/1. [2] W. Churchill, ii, 48.
[3] *F.G.* iii, 117–18. [4] Ibid., p. 124.
[5] F.P. 897, 'Report on the present position as regards possible Zeppelin attack on London', by Commodore M. F. Sueter, 2 Jan. 1915 (typescript, 9pp.).
[6] Asquith, ii, 54.

However, Fisher was still much preoccupied by this problem at the War Council of 7 January and seems to have again offered to resign soon after the meeting.[1] This distraction helps to explain his lack of attention to Churchill's parallel exploration of the possibility of forcing the Dardanelles with old battleships. For instance, he surprisingly agreed to Churchill's telegram of 3 January to Carden in the Mediterranean, asking whether he thought the Dardanelles could be forced by ships alone.[2]

Further to Fisher's belief in the efficacy of reprisals it will be recalled that, in his submarine paper of 1913, he suggested such action to discourage unrestricted attacks by U-boats on commerce. In April 1915 it came to the notice of the King that the Admiralty was proposing to mete out 'differential treatment' to captured U-boat personnel. This apparently meant that life in prison was to be made unusually disagreeable for them. Being much concerned that Britain should maintain 'generous and magnanimous consideration of our prisoners of war', the King immediately impressed on the Prime Minister his disapproval of the Admiralty's policy. However, this policy was not revoked until after Churchill and Fisher had left the Admiralty—by which time the Germans were retaliating in kind.[3]

In the middle of the Zeppelin affair, Churchill found it necessary to seek agreement with Fisher on a number of points. Writing on 4 January, he wished to confirm that Borkum was 'the key to all Northern possibilities', that a division of infantry should be earmarked for its capture, and that the 'heavy ships and flotillas' should be conserved and rested for the associated naval offensive. By contrast he was cautious about 'the Turkish places'. Using an argument suggestive of Fisher's ultimate attitude to the Dardanelles he remarked: 'Germany is the foe, and it is bad war to seek cheaper victories and easier antagonists.'[4]

Replying on the same day (4 January), Fisher settled for the basic position towards which he had been gravitating for some time. He said that it seemed necessary to state what British naval policy was:

---

[1] F.G. iii, 124n.
[2] W. Churchill, ii, 97.
[3] Nicolson, pp. 255, 272–3. With F.'s papers is an undated note in his hand: 'What to do with the *German Submarine Crews!*

> 'Thou shalt not kill, but need'st not strive
> Officiously to keep alive!' (F.P. 5102.)

[4] F.G. iii, 121.

In the first place, that policy is to conserve our naval superiority over the Germans and in no wise jeopardize it by minor operations whose cumulative effect is to wear out our vessels and incur losses in ships and men. We can't afford any more losses or any further deterioration except for absolutely imperative operations.

He accepted the idea of preparing for a 'landing expedition on the North Sea coast'—and he adhered to it at the War Council of 7 January; but he evinced little real enthusiasm. 'I agree', he wrote, 'that Borkum offers great possibilities, but it's a purely military question whether it can be held.' He whole-heartedly agreed with the proposal to conserve and rest the fleet for the projected offensive. Then he remarked: 'I also attach the Baltic paper.' This, of course, was Corbett's memorandum of 19 December.[1] Finally, however, he urged the 'overwhelming' advantages to be derived from Hankey's plan for a combined operation to open the Dardanelles. Up to this point, then, Fisher was more in favour of the Dardanelles project than was Churchill —provided always that it was a combined operation.[2]

As has been noticed above, Churchill spent the next few days investigating the idea of old battleships, without troops, forcing their way through the Dardanelles. Of course, Churchill himself would have preferred a combined operation but it appeared that troops would not be made available. A curious item, which may have strengthened the First Lord's interest in attacking with ships only, was a paper written for him at this time by Vice-Admiral Sir Lewis Bayly, Commander-in-Chief of the Channel Fleet, and prolific author of the wild amphibious plans of 1913. His proposal to force the Dardanelles was forwarded from the *Lord Nelson* at Portland on 8 January and was read by the First Lord the next day. Bayly proposed to attack with the 5th Battle Squadron (*Lord Nelson*, etc.) and rush 'as fast past, and as close to, the forts as is possible; to enter the Dardanelles just before dawn'. Currently described by Fisher as 'a pig-headed officer', Bayly was about to be placed on half-pay by the Admiralty for

---

[1] F.P. 4338 is a typescript copy which F. subsequently used to provide an appendix to his memo. of 25 Jan. (See p. 482 below.) The two papers were printed for the first time in Feb. 1915. F.P. 4343 comprises the original proof (P. 2/15) from which 50 revises were printed (also P. 2/15). F. was later confused about this, believing he had sent the complete print, including the Baltic paper, to the Prime Minister and to Jellicoe on 25 and 29 Jan. respectively. See *F.G.* iii, 150, 344, 379.

[2] *F.G.* iii, 121–2, 4 Jan. 1915.

failing to take normal precautions against submarines and losing the old battleship *Formidable* with most of her crew.[1]

Unsettled by the Zeppelin affair and out of sympathy with Churchill's offensive intentions in the North Sea, Fisher may well have been taken by surprise when a naval attack on the Dardanelles was quite suddenly, at the end of a rather dismal meeting, approved in principle by the War Council of 13 January.[2] For him, the main item of interest on the agenda had been further discussion of the proposed combined operation on the Belgian coast.[3] The extent to which he anticipated any bold decision by the War Council is indicated by the following, written on the day before the meeting:

> *In everything we are confronted by some political expediency! and my patience is pretty near exhausted!* 'PROCRASTINATION', 'VACIL-LATION', 'INDECISION' are the watchwords of the War Council and all it directs! *I really don't think I can stand it!* I presume either A.K.W. or Sturdee would be First Sea Lord. *I think either would be considered a master-stroke by the politicals!*[4]

The indications are that Fisher did not take very seriously Churchill's earlier investigation of the naval possibilities at the Dardanelles. Already in the habit of approving preparation for improbable schemes in the North Sea, he may well have been temporizing, at first, with regard to the Dardanelles. By contrast, when the Zeebrugge question was discussed about half-way through the War Council meeting, he firmly 'demurred to any attempt to attack Zeebrugge without the co-operation of the army along the coast'.[5] Meanwhile on the 12th, the day before the War Council, he apparently agreed that, what with a fairly detailed proposal from Carden on the 11th and some encourage-ment (confined to narrow tactical aspects) from Admiral Sir Henry Jackson (employed on special duties at the Admiralty), preparations for a naval attack on the Dardanelles should go ahead.[6] For instance Fisher either promoted, or at least actively co-operated with, the idea that the *Queen Elizabeth* could fire at

[1] Adm. 137/1089, ff. 25–31; *F.G.* iii, 120.

[2] Hankey, i, 265–7.

[3] *F.G.* iii, 129, F. to Jellicoe, 12 Jan. 1915.

[4] Ibid., 128–9.

[5] Cab. 42/1, 13 Jan. 1915, p. 7.

[6] F.P. 4906 and 4910 comprise the 'General Orders and Reports' and the 'Admiralty Telegrams' for the 'Naval Operations in the Dardanelles', printed for the Dard. Comm. in Sept. 1916.

the Dardanelles forts as part of her gunnery trials.[1] Churchill, for his part, was much encouraged by this suggestion. The splendid new battleship, with her 15-inch guns, could easily outrange the Turkish forts—otherwise Fisher would certainly not have entertained the suggestion. In a general way, too, the First Lord was swayed by the argument that modern, low-trajectory naval guns would be a great advantage against the high parapets and exposed guns of the Dardanelles forts, and therefore capable of overturning the apparent lessons of the past regarding ships versus forts.[2]

Fisher seems never to have directly challenged the project on the level of technical feasibility either in the discussions of the War Group or of the War Council. A. K. Wilson, a neutral witness (who had attended War Council meetings), testified before the Dardanelles Commission in 1916: 'I do not think he ever expressed an opinion against the practicality; but, like everybody else, he had certain doubts. We all had doubts, because there were so many uncertain factors.'[3]

Elsewhere in his evidence, Wilson stated that he was not much in favour of the project because it interfered with the schemes he was preparing for 'the Belgian coast, and the coast of Germany, and so on'. Asked whether he personally thought the Dardanelles operation should go ahead or not, he replied: 'If I had been First Sea Lord it would not have gone on.' With reference to the crucial War Council meeting of 28 January at which Fisher failed to declare his opposition to the project, Wilson was asked: 'Had you been in the position of the present First Sea Lord and the Minister at that Council had taken up a policy with which you did not agree you would have felt called upon to say anything adverse to him?' Wilson responded: 'Most certainly, I should.' 'At the Council?' 'Certainly.' Finally, while he thought that Churchill, at the War Council of the 28th, 'rather passed over' those segments of Admiralty opinion unfavourable to the Dardanelles, he did not think that Fisher had been overruled. He thought that Fisher 'had come in'.[4]

A member of the War Group who testified on the gunnery issue was Oliver. He was impressed—as they all were to some

---

[1] N.M.M., Oliver Papers, F. to O., 12 Jan. 1915.
[2] W. Churchill, ii, 103–9.
[3] Cab. 19/33, p. 275; and see p. 170 above.
[4] Ibid., pp. 139, 140, 275–6.

extent—by the possible effect of modern projectiles on forts.[1]
But he did not mention that, as noticed above, he tended to
support the Dardanelles operation because it would keep the old
battleships away from unsound projects in the North Sea.

However, there is no doubt at all that, between 13 and 28
January, Fisher became adverse to the Dardanelles project on
strategic grounds. On the 19th he complained to Jellicoe (who
was anxious for him to remain at the Admiralty to 'check Mr.
Churchill's dangerous assumption of executive authority') :[2]

And now the Cabinet have decided on taking the Dardanelles
solely with the Navy, using 15 battleships and 32 other vessels, and
keeping out there three battle cruisers and a flotilla of destroyers—
all urgently required at the decisive theatre at home! There is only one way
out, and that is to resign! But you say *'no'*, which simply means that
I am a consenting party to what I absolutely disapprove. *I don't agree
with one single step taken*, so it is fearfully against the grain that I remain
on in deference to your wishes. *The way the War is conducted both ashore
and afloat is chaotic! We have a new plan every week!*[3]

All this can have done little to reassure Jellicoe whose anxiety
was affecting his health. Fisher renewed his complaints on
21 January, assuring Jellicoe that the Dardanelles would be 'a
serious interference' with their 'imperative needs in Home
waters'. He claimed that he had 'fought against it "tooth and
nail" '. After dwelling on the needs of the Grand Fleet, he added:
'I just abominate the Dardanelles operation, unless a great
change is made and it is settled to be made a military operation,
with 200,000 men in conjunction with the Fleet. I believe that
Kitchener is coming now to this sane view of the matter.'[4]

With much help from Hankey and Corbett,[5] Fisher now proceeded to mobilize his views in a 'Memorandum by the First
Sea Lord on the Position of the British Fleet and its Policy of
Steady Pressure', dated 25 January.[6] In retrospect, Churchill
seems to have thought that the memorandum represented a

---

[1] Ibid., p. 133.   [2] Jellicoe, 'A Reply to Criticism', *D.S.* ii, 272.
[3] *F.G.* iii, 133.   [4] Ibid., pp. 141–2.
[5] Hankey, i, 269; Corbett's diary, 25 Jan. 1915.
[6] See pp. 457, 479 n. 1 above. F.P. 4336 is the typed copy from which the original
printings were made in Feb. 1915 (with the Baltic paper as an appendix—also an
original printing). F.P. 4337 is one of several typed copies, marked 'Very Secret',
and signed by F.—ready for circulation to selected politicians. These typescripts
(F.P. 4336–7) consist of the memo. of 25 Jan. 1915 only. The text is almost completely reproduced in *The World Crisis*, ii, 154–7.

sudden change of view on Fisher's part.[1] But this was not the case. The paper is essentially a development of the views which Fisher had communicated to the First Lord on 4 January. (See pp. 478-9 above.)

The memorandum argues that, in view of discussion by the War Council of various coastal projects, including action by the Navy alone, a 'statement of principle appears a fundamental necessity to any decision in regard to naval action against coast fortifications'. From a maritime point of view, Germany has been kept on the defensive for a matter of six months. This has cost her all her overseas trade and subjected her to great pressures. Consequently the Germans 'only await a favourable moment to pass from the defensive to the offensive'. They seek to 'scatter' British naval strength through attacks on trade; also to reduce Britain's 'main strength by submarines and mines'. This resembles the kind of situation often experienced by Britain during the French wars. 'Our reply today must be the same as our reply was then, namely, to be content to remain in possession of our command of the sea, husbanding our strength until the gradual pressure of sea power compels the enemy's fleet to make an effort to attack us at a disadvantage.' Therefore, to risk warships in bombarding fortified places without military co-operation is to play into Germany's hands. 'The sole justification of coastal bombardments and attacks by the Fleet on fortified places, such as the contemplated prolonged bombardment of the Dardanelles forts by our fleet, is to force a decision at sea, and so far and no further can they be justified.' In view of the 'great strength and splendid gunnery efficiency' of the High Seas Fleet, what is required is the patient conservation of the British fleet. Meanwhile the economic blockade of the North Sea should be made more stringent.

Otherwise, the memorandum does refer to offensive possibilities. Towards the beginning there is a reference to the effect of 'destruction of the High Sea Fleet'; this might expose the German Baltic coast to a Russian invasion. (When printing the memorandum in February, Fisher decided to append Corbett's Baltic paper as an elaboration of this item.)[2] Elsewhere, the paper declares Fisher's continuing desire for 'military co-operation with the Navy in such operations as the attack of Zeebrugge

---

[1] W. Churchill, ii, 149.
[2] F.P. 4343 includes F.'s manuscript insertion to this effect.

or the forcing of the Dardanelles, which might bring out the German and Turkish fleets respectively'.

Finally, however: 'Being already in possession of all that a powerful fleet can give a country, we should continue quietly to enjoy the advantage without dissipating our strength in operations that cannot improve the position.'

Having produced this sound and sensible statement of his position, why did Fisher not adhere to it at the fateful meeting of the War Council on 28 January?

On the 25th he sent a copy of the memorandum to Churchill, saying that he did not wish 'to continue a useless resistance in the War Council to plans' with which he could not agree.[1] He therefore asked that the memorandum be printed and circulated to the members of the Council. Replying on the 26th Churchill emphasized the apparent overwhelming superiority of the British Navy. His own paper was printed and circulated to members of the War Council.[2] It is an extraordinary fact that Fisher's memorandum was denied similar treatment. Asquith was in favour of the Dardanelles venture, and when Churchill showed him Fisher's paper and his own reply, the Prime Minister evidently agreed with Churchill to suppress the 'Memorandum by the First Sea Lord'.[3] Early on 28 January Fisher wrote to Asquith confirming—as he had intimated on the 27th—that he did not intend to go to the War Council that morning. He continued:

I am not in accord with the First Lord and do not think it would be seemly to say so before the Council. His reply to my memorandum does not meet my case. I say that the Zeebrugge and Dardanelles bombardments can only be justified on naval grounds by military co-operation, which would compensate for the loss in ships and irreplaceable officers and men. As purely naval operations they are unjustifiable, as they both drain our naval margin—not too large in view of collisions, such as *Conqueror* and *Monarch*, mines and submarines, such as *Audacious* and *Formidable*, and other previous great losses, and fools as admirals, such as Bayly . . . I am very reluctant to leave the First Lord. I have a great personal affection and admiration for him, but I see no possibility of a union of ideas . . .[4]

[1] W. Churchill, ii, 154.
[2] Ibid., pp. 154, 159–62; Gilbert, p. 264.
[3] F.P. 920, Churchill to F., 26 Jan. 1915.
[4] *F.G.* iii, 147–8.

It was probably in order to placate the Admiral that Churchill at this time approved the first two (out of three) of the former's proposed (freak) light battle cruisers. That they were 'chiefly' intended to enter the Baltic 'through the international highway of the Sound' was emphasized by Fisher's requirement of 'shallow draught'.[1] Clearly, Fisher continued to talk a great deal about the Baltic project; and this goes far to explain the Prime Minister's remarkable lack of attention to the First Sea Lord's memorandum of 25 January and to his letter of the 28th.

Asquith summoned Churchill and Fisher to see him at 10 Downing Street at 11.10 a.m. on the 28th—twenty minutes before the meeting of the War Council was due to begin.[2] Fisher briefly restated his view that, without military co-operation, neither the bombardment of Zeebrugge nor that of the Dardanelles could be justified. Before the Dardanelles Commissioners, Asquith thus recounted his interpretation of Fisher's attitude to the Dardanelles project:

As I understand, because I had frequent conversations with him, Lord Fisher's objection to the Dardanelles operations was not so much a technical objection upon naval grounds. It is quite true that, I think throughout, he thought the best chance of success for such an operation would have been a combined operation in which both the land and sea forces were engaged; but Lord Fisher's main objection, at least the one he always impressed on me, was not based in any degree upon the technical or naval merits or demerits of the Dardanelles operations, but upon the fact that he preferred another objective. Lord Fisher's eyes were always upon the Baltic, and he regarded with great suspicion, more than suspicion, great dislike, anything which would diminish the opportunities or impair the force of his projected Baltic operation.[3]

This statement was supposed, *inter alia*, to clarify what had transpired at the interview of 28 January. However, it is noticeable that the Prime Minister avoided saying that Fisher on that occasion gave the Baltic scheme as the ground of his objection to the Dardanelles operation. The evidence of Churchill and of Fisher himself likewise avoided such an account of the First Sea

---

[1] *F.G.* iii, 145, 150, F. to Churchill, 25 Jan., and F. to Jellicoe, 29 Jan. 1915. See Parkes, pp. 618–24, for the original details and subsequent transformations of the 'three extraordinary vessels' *Courageous*, *Glorious*, and *Furious*. They were laid down in Mar., May, and June 1915.

[2] *F.G.* iii, 149.   [3] Cab. 19/33, 18th day.

Lord's objection—though *The World Crisis* afterwards stated that Fisher 'indicated his preference for a great operation in the Baltic or for a general advance of the Army along the Belgian coast with strong naval support'.[1] Asquith was asked about Fisher's memorandum of 25 January. He agreed that Fisher sent him a copy but saw fit to comment that 'it was really a plea for the Baltic.'[2] This interpretation would have been difficult to sustain before Fisher decided to annex the Baltic paper to the memorandum, for printing, in February 1915. But justifiably or not, Asquith seems to have assumed during the interview of 28 January that the Baltic project underlay Fisher's opposition to the Dardanelles. As Churchill wished to bombard both Zeebrugge and the Dardanelles and Fisher wished to bombard neither, Asquith terminated the interview by ruling 'semi-seriously' that the Zeebrugge operation was off and the Dardanelles was on![3] The three men then went straight to the room where the rest of the War Council had assembled.

At the Council, the morning session covered a number of subjects, one of the lesser items being the German raider *Königsberg* which was under siege in the Rufiji River. In his recollections, Oliver awards to Fisher the credit for eliminating this problem by having two monitors towed out to the scene.[4] Towards the end of the session the subject of the Dardanelles was reached. Churchill stated that the Russians and the French were in favour of the naval attack, and that the latter had promised co-operation. 'Preparations were in hand for commencing about the middle of February. He asked if the War Council attached importance to this operation, which undoubtedly involved some risks?' Hankey's record continues:

LORD FISHER said that he had understood that this question would not be raised today. The Prime Minister was well aware of his own views in regard to it.

THE PRIME MINISTER said that, in view of the steps which had already been taken, the question could not well be left in abeyance.[5]

Fisher thereupon rose from the table. He was heading for the room of the Prime Minister's private secretary to intimate his resignation when he was intercepted by Lord Kitchener. In a

---

[1] W. Churchill, ii, 162.   [2] Cab. 19/33, 18th day.   [3] Ibid.
[4] W. James, p. 147.   [5] Cab. 42/1.

muttered conversation which escaped universal notice, Kitchener urged on Fisher that he was 'the only dissentient'.[1] Fisher returned to his place. Neither the First Lord nor the Prime Minister invited him to express his opinion; nor did he offer it. He allowed members of the Council to dwell on the advantages of success without drawing their attention to the risks and consequences of failure.

However, Fisher's ineffective manifestations of dissent had not escaped the eye of the First Lord. After lunch Churchill had Fisher in his room at the Admiralty. The latter's pre-war experience was reversed. The First Sea Lord was saturated to the point of signifying agreement by the arguments of the First Lord! Consequently at 6 p.m. Churchill was able to stage a triumphant reappearance at the War Council. As he afterwards stated in evidence:

We then repaired to the afternoon War Council meeting, Admiral Oliver, the Chief of the Staff, coming with us, and I announced finally on behalf of the Admiralty and with the agreement of Lord Fisher that we had decided to undertake the task with which the War Council had charged us so urgently.

This I take as the point of final decision. After it, I never looked back. We had left the region of discussion and consultation, of balancings and misgivings. The matter had passed into the domain of action.[2]

In the past Fisher had not always maintained his views under pressure, even where they were based on earnest consideration of a major aspect of policy. His surprising reversal of opinion over the enforced economies of May 1906 will be remembered; also his vacillations of December 1907 regarding the programme of construction for 1908. In 1916 he realized that he would have to justify before the Dardanelles Commissioners his failure to speak out on 28 January 1915. After a seesawing discussion with his confidants, he finally decided to assert that he and Wilson attended the War Council as technical advisers only, and that it would have been improper for him to express opposition to his departmental head in that context.[3] The Commissioners, with

---

[1] Cab. 19/33, F.'s evidence, p. 197.

[2] Dard. Comm., First Report, p. 28 (cd. 8490).

[3] F.P. 4417 is a typescript wherein the writer develops the theme that a 'complete plea of non-responsibility is simple, but very difficult to sustain'. See also Adm. 116/3454, F.'s papers concerning his resignation; F.P. 4423, etc.; Cab. 19/33, F.'s evidence, pp. 192, 200.

three exceptions, agreed in rejecting this argument. In any case, it seems unlikely that Fisher was much swayed by this consideration at the time. Indications to the contrary will be noticed shortly. Likewise Hankey, who understood both Fisher's views and his position in the War Council, wrote on 21 January 1915 to Balfour (who was a member of the War Council): 'Fisher, I find, frequently disagrees with statements made by the First Lord at our War Council. I wish he would speak up.'[1] Asquith, for his part, stated to the Commissioners that he had expected 'any of the experts there, if they entertained a strong personal view on their own expert authority, to express it'.[2] He was never given reason to suspect that the First Sea Lord took a different view. 'Lord Fisher was a person who was in the habit of giving his opinions very freely.'[3] Indeed, six days after the meetings of 28 January Fisher was writing to Beatty: 'We want brave men! ANY BLOODY FOOL CAN OBEY ORDERS!'; and he was wont to extol Nelson's 'great gift of Insubordination'.[4]

What emerges more strongly is that Fisher, despite his knowledge and volubility, may well have felt by the afternoon of 28 January that he could not argue his case effectively against Churchill at the War Council. Just a few days earlier he had been complaining to Hankey regarding Churchill: 'He out-argues me.'[5] Nor was his failure on the 28th to make any impression on Asquith calculated to fortify his self-confidence. At this point Fisher's age was probably—at last—beginning to impose itself; on 25 January he had turned seventy-four. He had, since his recall, been subjected to great and increasing strains, though he had maintained a routine which would have tested a young man, beginning his day's work at 4 or 5 a.m. and going to bed soon after 8 p.m. (This routine may have fostered misunderstanding between him and Churchill who preferred to work late into the night.) Fisher's loss of buoyancy—which was far from permanent—was balefully noted by Richmond on 19 January: 'In reality he does nothing. He goes home and sleeps in the afternoon. He is old and worn-out and nervous. It is ill to have the destinies of an empire in the hands of a failing old man, anxious for popularity, afraid of any local mishap which may be put down to his dispositions. It is sad.'[6]

---

[1] Add. MSS. 49703, f. 152.
[3] Ibid.
[5] Hankey, i, 269.
[2] Cab. 19/33, 18th day.
[4] F.G. iii, 152; Memories, p. 38.
[6] Marder, Portrait, pp. 137–8.

Another version of Fisher's subsequent plea of non-responsibility in the War Council may now be quoted: 'My opinion being known to Mr. Churchill in what I regarded as the proper constitutional way, I preferred thereafter to remain silent.'[1] This statement is not convincing, for how can it be reconciled with the fact that, on the day after the meetings of 28 January, he privately sent copies of the memorandum of the 25th to Balfour and Lloyd George? And how did his concern for 'the proper constitutional way' permit him two days later to send a copy of the same paper to Andrew Bonar Law, the Leader of the Opposition? Law was not a member of the War Council nor was he a political friend of the First Lord of the Admiralty.[2] In each case Fisher requested return of the memorandum but only Lloyd George complied. The Chancellor's covering note was very much to the point:

It is a very impressive—but distinctly disquieting—document. I wish I could disagree with it but find myself unable to do so. These views ought to be brought to the attention of the War Council.

We poor ignorant civilians must necessarily depend in these matters on the guidance of experts like yourself.[3]

But the letter to Bonar Law provides the choicest example of Fisher's constitutional rectitude. The Admiral wrote to the Conservative leader: 'I take this opportunity of enclosing for your private eye a paper I submitted to the Prime Minister but as he has decided not to circulate it to the War Council I must ask you not to quote it in any way. Why he has suppressed it is beyond my comprehension . . .'[4]

A combination of strain, near-exhaustion, natural deviousness, and temporary loss of self-confidence brought about Fisher's surrender to Churchill and Asquith on 28 January. Asquith later testified that, having once accepted the Dardanelles idea, Fisher 'threw himself most whole-heartedly into the plan' and that 'no one ever worked harder or more loyally';[5] but there can be no doubt that the Admiral's agreement was more apparent than real. When Fisher, after sharing responsibility for all the naval activities at the Dardanelles, informed the War Council of 14 May 'that he had been no party to the Dardanelles operations',

---

[1] F.P. 4436, 'Summary for the Chairman of Lord Fisher's Evidence', P. 10/16 (and *Memories*, pp. 71–3); Cab. 19/33, p. 192.
[2] Add. MSS. 49712, ff. 136–42, F. to Balfour, 29 Jan. 1915; F.P. 928, Lloyd George to F., 30 Jan.; Bonar Law Papers 36/2/57, F. to Law, 31 Jan.
[3] F.P. 928.   [4] Bonar Law Papers.   [5] Cab. 19/33, 18th day.

the First Lord and others seem to have been much astonished. According to Churchill, 'This remarkable interruption was received in silence.'[1]

Fisher admitted to the Dardanelles Commission that he was 'in a way' in favour of the naval attack. This was partly for the reason adduced by Kitchener at the War Council on 13 and 28 January that (in Fisher's words) 'you could cut your loss at any moment.' However, 'once you landed men, it became another business altogether.'[2] Undoubtedly the First Sea Lord passed through moods of hope and even optimism regarding the naval attack; but once de Robeck had in March confessed his failure to penetrate the Dardanelles, Fisher behaved as the guardian of the Grand Fleet at the expense of further operations at the Dardanelles. Oliver (who had, of course, supported the naval attack) later recollected:

> Fisher was against the Dardanelles expedition in the War Cabinet, but when it was decided, he should have co-operated in the Admiralty to further the work, but he was luke warm when he did not actively oppose measures . . .
>
> It was a very difficult matter to get ships or anything for the Dardanelles; the First Lord was keen to make a good show of it but Fisher adopted a line of passive resistance blocking everything he could, and Churchill and he were always arguing with each other, mostly by means of memos. Fisher was helped by Jellicoe's complaints about the weakness of the Grand Fleet . . .[3]

To judge by results in the sphere of construction, Fisher's energy remained at a respectably high level during his final months in office. According to Oliver, Churchill would approve new items 'to put the old man in a good temper'.[4] In February a conference at the Admiralty was followed by the placing of orders with twenty-six firms for a total of 152 large barges. These were each to carry 500 troops, to have diesel engines, and to be protected with steel shields for landings under fire. Sixty smaller barges were ordered at the same time. Fisher's covering minute, seen by Churchill on 20 February, earmarks the barges for 'Home Expeditions'.[5]

[1] Cab. 42/2, Hankey's record; W. Churchill, ii, 351.
[2] Cab. 19/33, p. 196.
[3] N.M.M., Oliver Papers, 'Recollections', pp. 148 and 151.
[4] W. James, p. 140.
[5] F.P. 944; W. Churchill, i, 458–9.

Immediately after his return to the Admiralty, Fisher had registered his continuing interest in the development of air power.[1] On 25 February he intervened in negotiations which had been dragging on, at least since July 1914, between the Admiralty and Airships Ltd. about the provision of 'a small dirigible balloon'—as distinct from the rigid type of airship unfortunately discouraged by Churchill.[2] Possessing superior endurance to seaplanes or other aeroplanes, these submarine scout airships (or 'blimps') proved very useful for anti-submarine patrols in narrow waters and near the British coasts. By 22 March Fisher was able to write to Jellicoe: 'The first of our squadron of light anti-submarine airships for work between Calais and Dover was completed day before yesterday in 18 DAYS FROM STARTING WORK! and has done over 40 miles an hour on her trial trip!' Three weeks earlier he had already informed the Commander-in-Chief: 'You shall have the second one. We shall build 50 to start with!'[3]

On 15 March—just after offering to take command of the forthcoming major attempt to force the Dardanelles—Fisher wrote to Jellicoe: 'How interesting your suggesting to me getting less costly vessels to take the place of destroyers in hunting submarines and doing convoy work, as 48 hours before your letter we had ordered a hundred "glorified whalers" of 15 knots speed, with a gun and searchlight and crew of 20 men, to be built in six weeks, I hope.'[4]

Fisher's hopes of success at the Dardanelles rose and fell with Kitchener's fluctuating intentions to send troops to Gallipoli. On 18 March the main naval attack failed. For a day or two Fisher exuberantly shared Churchill's confidence that a speedy renewal would succeed.[5] However, troops were now belatedly offered. When de Robeck requested acceptance in lieu of another naval attack, Fisher supported him—delighted that a combined operation was after all to be undertaken.[6] Then he began to reflect on the consequences of landing troops at that stage of the proceedings.

On 27 March Fisher addressed to the First Lord a substantial memorandum firmly based on the predominant importance of the Grand Fleet. He asked that a clear indication be obtained from the War Office that General Hamilton's proposed landing

---

[1] D.S. ii, 97.   [2] F.P. 946.   [3] F.G. iii, 161, 163n.
[4] Ibid., p. 164.   [5] Gilbert, pp. 357–60.   [6] W. Churchill, ii, 234.

stood a good chance of success. Indeed, considering the total loss of surprise, no question could have been more appropriate. In Fisher's view, further diversions of naval strength to the Dardanelles could be justified only by such a reassurance. He was particularly bothered at the time by signs that the Germans might be about to occupy Holland and launch a concurrent naval offensive.[1] In connexion with the Dutch danger, he referred on 29 March to '750,000 German troops unoccupied', after having located half a million in Schleswig-Holstein eight days earlier.[2] In Fisher's mind, the Baltic project must have seemed very remote. Even before the war, he had accepted the argument that a German invasion of Denmark would prevent British entry into the Baltic via the Belts. (See p. 407 above.)

Churchill, for his part, was irritated at the Admiral's failure to live up to his commitment of 28 January—flamboyantly endorsed in mid-March. The First Lord wanted the landing to proceed; and no doubt there was, in principle, some slender chance of success. In actuality, of course, this second gamble at the Dardanelles was to entail a much more costly reverse than had the first.

During his brief period of recall to the Admiralty, Fisher proved a sounder strategist than might have been expected from his pre-war record. Where he must be faulted is in his persistent contempt for the Naval War Staff which he might have re-organized with a view to governing the operational proposals of the First Lord—an amateur in naval affairs, for all his admirable courage and ingenuity. But to Fisher the Naval Staff was a collection of 'small fry'.[3] 'I was not going to play the fool with all these chaps below me', he told the Dardanelles Commissioners.[4] A. K. Wilson maintained a similar attitude. He informed the said Commissioners: 'No one had more experience than Lord Fisher and myself in the whole Service.'[5]

Yet it had not taken Fisher very long to discover that Churchill's full exercise of his constitutional powers posed a problem. Already on 20 December he was writing to Jellicoe: 'Winston has so monopolized all initiative in the Admiralty and fires off such a multitude of purely departmental memos (*his power of*

---

[1] *F.G.* iii, 171–4; also 174–80.
[2] Ibid., p. 177; Add. MSS. 49006, f. 175, F. to Jellicoe, 21 Mar. 1915.
[3] *F.G.* iii, 128, 12 Jan. 1915.   [4] Cab. 19/33, p. 199.
[5] Ibid., p. 275.

work is absolutely amazing!) that my colleagues are no longer "*superintending Lords*", but only "*the First Lord's Registry*"*!*[1] Although long since pushed out into the cold by Churchill's formation of the War Staff Group, the Junior Sea Lords offered Fisher a chance to redress the balance at the Admiralty when they wrote to him on 8 April, requesting reassurance on 'certain points connected with the conduct of the war'. Within the control of national policy determined by the cabinet, they affirmed that the final word on 'larger strategy' should rest with 'the *First Sea Lord*'.[2] By this assurance of support Fisher was offered a means of inducing Churchill to modify the machinery of strategical control. Unfortunately he was basically as contemptuous of his 'colleagues' as he was of the Naval War Staff, though on this occasion he had the good sense to write a detailed reply; but he did not refer to the crucial matter of his working relationship with the First Lord.[3] Instead of seeking a constructive solution to his difficult problem, he preferred reliance on a crude weapon. As he had intimated to Jellicoe on 28 March, he would 'keep ready to resign at any moment'.[4]

In the immediate background to the Junior Sea Lords' memorandum was a crisis in Fisher's relations with Churchill. From 2 April he began to warn the First Lord that reinforcement of the naval force at the Dardanelles had now reached a limit which should not be overstepped.[5] As Churchill was firmly resolved that the combined operation at the Dardanelles should go ahead with full support from the Admiralty, Fisher had left himself with a single drastic remedy—resignation.

Meanwhile, up to the end of his time at the Admiralty, Fisher pressed ahead in the field of construction. In March negotiations began for the supply of anti-submarine motor launches from the United States. After Fisher's departure, 550 of them were ordered.[6]

An idea of Fisher's total achievement as a wartime provider of vessels is conveyed by a 'List of Ships Ordered since 30th October 1914', which is marked 'Secret', dated 23 April 1915,

[1] *F.G.* iii, 99.
[2] Ibid., p. 188.
[3] Ibid., pp. 190–1.
[4] Ibid., p. 175.
[5] Ibid., p. 183.
[6] F.P. 1416, S. S. Hall to F., 12 June 1918, enclosing 'History and Employment of 550 Motor Launches Obtained from America'.

and annotated in his own hand. The following is the list with
Fisher's contemporary comments given in square brackets:

5 Battleships.   'ROYAL SOVEREIGNS'.
                          Altered to oil fuel, and improved armament.

5 Light Battle Cruisers.   [These 5 ships will be fighting
      'RENOWN'   within 14 months of being
      'REPULSE'   ordered. New ships of 33 knots
      'COURAGEOUS'   speed and only 21 feet draught
      'GLORIOUS'   of water. The Queen Elizabeth
      'FURIOUS'   draws 35 feet. Armed with
                             15 inch guns.]

2 Light Cruisers.   'CENTAUR' and   [3,000 tons each]
                  'CONCORD'

[All these will be fighting this summer:]

5 Flotilla Leaders.   [1,500 tons each]

56 Destroyers.

65 Submarines H . . . 20
                E . . . 35
                J . . . 6
                K . . . 4

14 Monitors 12-inch and above.
14   ,,   9·2-inch.
5   ,,   6-inch.   [Oil Engines]
12   ,,   River.

2 Coast Defence Ships.   'GORGON' and   (Norwegian:
                       'GLATTON'.   purchased.)

24 Single Screw Sloops.   [1,100 tons each—24 knots]

19 Whalers.   [about 500 tons each]

24 Patrol Boats   [22 knots speed. Seakeeping.]
      (Submarine Type).

50 Motor Launches.   [20 tons]

200 Large Barges.   [to hold 500 men each or horses
                   (oil engines)]

60 Small Barges.   [to hold 250 men (oil engines)]
                         [569][1]

[1] F.P. 4364, typescript, with subsequent alterations and additions by F. The
total of 569 excludes the 5 'Royal Sovereigns'. These were designed to burn coal,
because of uncertainty about the supply of oil in wartime, and were laid down in
1913–14. F. lost no time in ordering the change to oil.

Of course, the attempt to have ships quickly constructed on this scale involved a degree of precipitation at the design stage which, though congenial to Fisher, did not always produce happy results. Oliver afterwards remembered some of the tribulations of the Director of Naval Construction: 'The D.N.C. Tennyson d'Eyncourt was anxious to have a week more on the design to try a model [of a monitor] in the tank and to get data for the horse power required to get the speed. Fisher would not let him have the week and the result was that the first batch of Monitors could only steam 6 knots and often had to be towed.'[1]

But there can be no doubt that Fisher's provision of destroyers, escorts, and other anti-submarine vessels did constitute a remarkable contribution, fully appreciated during the great U-boat crisis of 1917. Yet direct involvement in such work was hardly part of the First Sea Lord's proper role if set against the reorganization of the Admiralty—at last spreading responsibility to the Naval Staff—which was achieved in 1918 by Geddes and Wemyss. Fisher's activities ranged from the sphere of operational policy to such expressions of the First Lord's ingenuity as the production of a tank with naval funds.[2]

Notwithstanding Richmond's aspersions of January 1915, Fisher certainly retained the confidence of Jellicoe and Beatty right up to the time of his resignation. There is no mistaking the sincerity of the following communication from Beatty dated Wednesday [19 May]:

The Commander-in-Chief told me this morning that you had resigned.

I cannot believe that—it is impossible that—the Government will accept it. It would be a worse calamity than a defeat at sea. If it is of any value to you to know it, the Fleet is numbed with the thought of the possibility. Please God it is *not* possible . . .[3]

Indeed, it is difficult to find any informed quarter in which there was not a desire for Fisher's continuance. Despite the bickering over the Dardanelles, Churchill still wanted him; despite his over-frequent offers to resign, so did Asquith.

However, by 11 May Fisher was near the end of his patience with Churchill and the Dardanelles. The First Lord unyieldingly

---

[1] N.M.M., Oliver Papers, 'Recollections', p. 136. Compare March, p. 85, for
  rushing the design of the 'Tribal' class destroyers in Nov. 1904.
[2] W. Churchill, ii, 77.
[3] F.P. 1029. *F.G.* iii, 247 has text (date unspecified).

declared: 'We are now committed to one of the greatest amphibious enterprises of history. You are absolutely committed.'[1] But the landings of 25 April had achieved no decisive success and, from Fisher's point of view, the Dardanelles had become a bottomless pit threatening to swallow up men and ships to little useful purpose. On the 13 May he wrote to Asquith:

> I desire to convey to you that I honestly feel I cannot remain where I am much longer as there is an inevitable and never-ceasing drain *daily (almost hourly)* of our resources in the decisive theatre of the War. But that is not the worst—instead of the whole of the Admiralty being concentrated on the daily increasing submarine menace in Home Waters, we are all diverted to the Dardanelles, and the unceasing activities of the First Lord, both by day and night, are engaged in ceaseless *prodding* of everyone in every department afloat and ashore in the interests of the Dardanelles Fleet . . .[2]

On Friday, 14 May, there was a meeting of the War Council. An interservice quarrel arose over Fisher's intention, in view of the increasing U-boat danger in the Mediterranean, to order the *Queen Elizabeth* back home. Fisher was highly excited; moreover he mistrusted Churchill's attempts to reassure Kitchener, inferring that a new diversion of naval resources would follow. That evening Churchill and Fisher agreed on some reinforcements for the Dardanelles and they parted amicably. In his usual way, Fisher went to bed early. When he resumed work in the small hours of Saturday the 15th, he found that Churchill had meantime decided to propose some additions, including two 'E' class submarines, to the agreed reinforcement for the Dardanelles. Fisher concluded that the First Lord was insatiable. He therefore addressed to Churchill a letter of resignation and sent a copy to the Prime Minister.[3] There is no sign that he envisaged, at that moment, any particular chain of political repercussions; nor was he bothered by the elementary consideration of handing over his post to a successor. He merely wrote: 'I am off to Scotland at once, so as to avoid all questionings.'[4]

However, he was still in Whitehall later that morning. He went to the Treasury to inform Lloyd George of his resignation. While he evidently conveyed no hint of nervous collapse, he rejected the Chancellor's suggestion that he should remain at the Admiralty till Monday the 17th so that he could explain his case

[1] *F.G.* iii, 219.
[2] Ibid., p. 221.
[3] Ibid., p. 228; Asquith MSS., 27, ff. 145–7.
[4] *F.G.* iii, 228.

to an emergency session of the War Council.[1] Lloyd George in turn visited Asquith. Somewhat belatedly, the Prime Minister began to take Fisher's stand seriously. He wrote to Fisher: 'In the King's name, I order you at once to return to your post.' Seeing that Fisher was not to be found at the Admiralty, the note produced no immediate effect! However, the Admiral was at length discovered at the Charing Cross Hotel and in the afternoon he paid a visit to 10 Downing Street, where the Asquiths were fretting at the dislocation of their weekend in the country. Fisher was apparently quite genial and relaxed; nevertheless, he declined to resume the duties of First Sea Lord.[2] He spent the evening at the Athenaeum Club—'to escape from Winston'.[3]

These unconventional but superficially good-tempered transactions cloaked the fact that the government in general and the First Lord in particular were already sitting on a time-bomb thoughtfully provided by Fisher. The Admiral came across an announcement of his being received in audience by the King—cut, doubtless, from a newspaper dating from his recall to the Admiralty. He dropped it into an envelope and, in his unmistakable handwriting, addressed it to Bonar Law.[4] Churchill meantime was under the illusion that he could, if necessary, replace Fisher during the weekend and face the Commons on the Monday with a reconstituted Board of Admiralty. On Saturday, 15 May, he addressed an appeal to Fisher:

I do not understand what is the specific cause which has led you to resign. If I did, I might cure it . . . Our personal friendship is and I trust will remain unimpaired . . .

In every way I have tried to work in the closest sympathy with you. The men you wanted in the places you wanted them, the ships you designed, every proposal you have formally made for naval action, I have agreed to . . .

In order to bring you back to the Admiralty I took my political life in my hands with the King and the Prime Minister, as you know well. You then promised to stand by me and see me through. If you now go at this bad moment and thereby let loose upon me the spite and malice of those who are your enemies even more than they are mine, it will be a melancholy ending to our six months of successful war and administration . . .[5]

---

[1] Lloyd George, i, 225.   [2] Bonham-Carter, p. 389.
[3] Hankey, i, 315.   [4] Blake, p. 243.
[5] *F.G.* iii, 229.

Fisher replied the next day:

You *must* remember my extreme reluctance in the Prime Minister's room in January to accept his decision in regard to the Dardanelles...
YOU ARE BENT ON FORCING THE DARDANELLES AND NOTHING WILL TURN YOU FROM IT—*NOTHING*. I know you so well! . . .
You will remain. I SHALL GO . . .[1]

In fact, the Admiral was chiefly concerned that Churchill should remain for the shortest time possible! On Monday the 17th he wrote to Bonar Law:

In reply to your letter, after repeated refusals by him I have written to the P.M. this morning to say that now my *definite decision* is I am absolutely unable to remain with W.C. (HE'S A REAL DANGER!) *But he is going to be kept* (so I go! at once, TODAY) . . . I regret to say your *A.J.B.* has been backing W.C. ALL THROUGH and I have refused to have anything to do with him (A.J.B.) in consequence! . . .
Don't be cajoled *privately* by the P.M. to keep silence. The danger is imminent and VITAL. I don't want to stay, but W.C. MUST go at all costs! *AT ONCE* . . . you must be most prudent and not give me away, but I feel bound to tell you as Leader of the Opposition, because *a very great national disaster is very near us in the Dardanelles!* against which I have vainly protested and did resign long ago, but Kitchener persuaded me to stop. *I was a d——d fool to do so!* . . .
W.C. is a bigger danger than the Germans by a long way in what is just now imminent in the Dardanelles. *Concentrate on the Dardanelles! . . .*[2]

By the time that Law received this letter, he had already taken political action and Asquith had agreed to form a coalition. Churchill's fate was sealed.[3] But Fisher's reference to Balfour was yet to prove significant. He never forgave 'A.J.B.' for his persuasive support of the Dardanelles enterprise, especially on 28 January 1915.[4]

On the Sunday (16 May) there had been much coming and going. Churchill sent a further appeal to Fisher. McKenna urged the Admiral to furnish the Prime Minister with more precise reasons for his resignation.[5] But what seems to have excited Fisher's resentment was a move that really operated a good deal in his favour, namely a memorandum from the Junior Sea Lords addressed jointly to the First Lord and himself. Fisher was much

[1] Ibid., p. 231.   [2] Ibid., pp. 237–8 (Bonar Law Papers 37/2/34).
[3] Blake, pp. 243–5.   [4] *F.G.* iii, 174, 594, 615.   [5] Ibid., pp. 232–4.

irritated to find that, in view of the national emergency, they not only declined to resign themselves but also sought to avert his own resignation. But he should have noted with satisfaction that they deemed 'the present method of directing the distribution of the Fleet' to be 'open to very grave objection'; also that, in pursuit of rectification, they sent a copy of their memorandum to the Prime Minister. This obviously lent much force to Bonar Law's demand of the following day for Churchill's removal and at the same time improved Fisher's own prospects.[1]

Sharing, perhaps, the Sea Lords' impression that Italy's decision to join the Allies might be in the balance, A. K. Wilson wrote a characteristic note to Fisher on same day, 16 May:

Dear Fisher,

You really must not resign under present conditions. It would mean a great national disaster and you have no right to consider your private feelings in the matter while the interests of the country are so much at stake as they are now. Do change your mind and see the thing out.

Believe me

Yours ty

A. K. Wilson[2]

However, to judge by Fisher's subsequent conduct, a good deal more influence was exerted by the following message from Esher, likewise dated 16 May. The Admiral's old confidant wrote:

My dear dear Jackie,

You will never *permanently* patch up these quarrels. The only thing to be done is to revive the office of Lord High Admiral and take it yourself. Otherwise we are beaten at sea; and unless Lord K takes the war into his own hands, ditto on land.

Yours ever

E.[3]

---

[1] Ibid., pp. 234–5, 238–9. F.P. 1007 is F.'s (original) copy of the memo. endorsed by Hamilton: 'We have sent a copy of this to the Prime Minister. 'See also Asquith, ii, 91–2.

[2] F.P. 1009.

[3] F.P. 1008. Since the beginning of the war, Esher had been in France on a confidential mission. On 17 May F. mentioned in a letter to Asquith: 'Lord Esher called here this morning unexpectedly (I did not know he was in London) and told me it was common knowledge that I had left the Admiralty, and that he knew it yesterday.' (Asquith MSS., 27.)

No advice could have been more harmful to Fisher's true interest or less appropriate to the Admiralty's needs in the context of large-scale modern warfare.

On Monday the 17th Fisher complained to Crease, his Naval Assistant, of the 'EXCEEDINGLY BAD ADVICE' he had received from Wilson and the Sea Lords.[1] Moreover, Wilson had by now assented to Churchill's desperate suggestion that he should take over as First Sea Lord. On Fisher's instructions, Crease wrote to Jellicoe about his master's resignation: 'Lord Fisher will write to you when he is less pressed and has settled down. He is absolutely broken—but full of courage and determination. Of course it will kill him in a few months.'[2]

However, by the afternoon of the 17th Fisher had still not been replaced. There were indications that the High Seas Fleet might be coming out. Fisher now forfeited the sympathy of the Sea Lords by refusing to go on duty. While his diagnosis of a false alarm was justified by the event, the adverse reaction of the Sea Lords fundamentally weakened his position.[3]

Nevertheless, a further development of 17 May gave the Admiral reason to conclude that his position was strong—so strong that he could ignore the Sea Lords and deal with them later. After agreeing to a coalition, Asquith wrote to Fisher later in the day: 'I feel bound to tell you for your own information only that a considerable reconstruction of the Government is in contemplation, and in the public interest I trust that you will neither say nor do anything for a day or two.'[4] Unfortunately, Fisher was by now inclined to say a great deal!

During the day Arthur Balfour had emerged as the First Lord designate. Taking account of their long association and Fisher's previous high opinion of Balfour's capacity in the sphere of defence, the Admiral might have been expected to welcome this selection. But he had latterly chosen to place Balfour in the ranks of his enemies, much as he had done with Haldane before the war. Brooding on the fatal events of 28 January, he made no allowance for Balfour's lack of professional information about the naval implications of the Dardanelles proposal—a lack which he had done nothing to repair in time.[5]

---

[1] *F.G.* iii, 239.   [2] Add. MSS. 49007, f. 48.
[3] *D.S.* ii, 282–3.   [4] *F.G.* iii, 239.
[5] As mentioned above, F. sent Balfour a copy of his memo. of 25 Jan., but not until the 29th (Add. MSS. 49712, ff. 136–42).

On Tuesday, 18 May, Fisher paid a visit to Hankey who wrote in his diary:

Fisher was at the office when I arrived. He says that forty per cent to sixty per cent of his energy has to be devoted to managing his First Lord, and he wants this for the Germans; so he wants to be First Lord. I pointed out to him how troublesome all the deputations . . . would be. 'Oh, I know all about receiving deputations', he said, 'the first rule is to put them in a draught.' He then kept on telling me humorous stories for about twenty minutes, till the tears came into my eyes with laughing.[1]

Fisher's train of thought reflects the advice offered by Esher—who repeated the dose later in the week.[2] When account is taken of the fact that Esher sought out the Admiral in person on Monday the 17th, his influence on Fisher assumes considerable importance.[3]

Fisher now proceeded to develop these grandiose ideas by drafting a memorandum for the Prime Minister:

If the following six conditions are agreed to, I can guarantee the successful termination of the War and the total abolition of the sub-marine menace . . .

1. That Mr. Winston Churchill is not in the Cabinet to be always circumventing me, nor will I serve under Mr. Balfour.[4]
2. That Sir A. K. Wilson leaves the Admiralty and the Com-mittee of Imperial Defence and the War Council, as my time will be occupied in resisting the bombardment of Heligoland and other wild projects . . .
3. That there shall be an entirely new Board of Admiralty . . .
4. That I shall have complete professional charge of the war at sea, together with the absolute disposition of the Fleet and the appointment of all officers of all ranks whatsoever, and abso-lutely untrammelled sole command of all the sea forces whatever.
5. That the First Lord of the Admiralty should be absolutely restricted to policy and parliamentary procedure . . .

---

[1] Hankey, i, 316.
[2] F.P. 1025 20 May 1915: 'There is only one solution.

Operations { Lord Fisher. / Lord K. / To be hanged in they fail. / To be crowned with bays if they succeed . . . Stick to this.'
[3] See p. 499 n. 3 above; also Esher, iii, 237.
[4] The draft indicates that the reference to Balfour was an addition.

6. That I should have the sole absolute authority of all dockyard work whatsoever, and complete control of the whole of the Civil establishments of the Navy.

The 60 per cent of my time and energy which I have exhausted on 9 First Lords in the past I wish in the future to devote to the successful prosecution of the War. That is my sole reason for the six conditions. These six conditions must be published verbatim so that the Fleet may know my position.[1]

Fisher appended a list of proposed naval appointments, including a new—and appropriately weak—team of Junior Sea Lords.

The Admiral's next step was to show his handiwork to Hankey who duly recorded on Wednesday, 19 May:

This morning Fisher arrived early at office with a most preposterous letter of 'terms' on which he would return, e.g. Churchill not to be a member of the Cabinet; Balfour not to be First Lord . . . He showed me his list of appointments—clearly he would indulge in 'head hunting'. I remonstrated and told him his terms were impossible, and no self-respecting Minister would look at them. I saw him again in the evening and persuaded him to abate his terms—but it was too late, they had been sent to the Prime Minister and greatly incensed him . . . I made up my mind that, whatever happened, he could not go back to the Admiralty.[2]

Though Fisher's sanity was doubted at the time by some of those most closely involved in the affair, this was scarcely justified in a general sense. His demands, taken together, denote exceptionally bad judgement, but they evolved from his circumstances in a manner which can hardly be described as irrational. He suffered a collapse not of reason but of self-criticism. With Esher's assistance, the 'foot of pride' had triumphed! As Hankey reported to Corbett, 'Jackie had got megalomania and done for himself.'[3]

The fatal effects of the memorandum of the 19th were reinforced by a letter from Churchill to Asquith on the following day. He wrote that the Sea Lords 'take a serious view of Lord Fisher's desertion of his post in time of war for what has now amounted to six days, during which serious operations have been in progress'. At the same time he communicated the well-founded apprehension of the Sea Lords that in the event of

---

[1] F.P. 1021 is F.'s draft. The text is in *F.G.* iii, 241–2.
[2] Hankey, i, 316.
[3] Corbett's diary, 22 May 1915.

Fisher's return, 'their functions' would be 'made very difficult'.[1] Indeed, they were earmarked for the block!

This charge of 'desertion' certainly made an impression on King George V. At Balmoral in August 1921 the King held forth on

the extraordinary actions of Lord Fisher in May 1915, when, after having handed in his resignation as First Sea Lord, he had virtually disappeared. The King let himself go on the duties of a naval officer and particularly of the First Sea Lord, and said, 'If I had been in London when Fisher was found I should have told him that he should have been hanged at the yardarm for desertion of his post in the face of the enemy. It really was a most scandalous thing which ought to be punished with dismissal from the service with degredation.' In fact the King got so angry that he became quite red in the face at the recollection of Fisher's actions.[2]

Meanwhile, on the 19th, Fisher had attempted to convey to Bonar Law the reasons for his hostility to Balfour:

It is impossible to explain by letter the chicanery in progress! To me it is absolutely incomprehensible that Winston having left the Cabinet should have been brought back into it by A.J.B. Except that A.J.B. has been hypnotized by Winston over the Dardanelles and now feels he ought to prevent his ruin . . . I am sure you will understand that my position would have been both intolerable and impossible with Winston in the Cabinet circumventing me and in such close intimacy as he is with A.J.B. he would be practically his adviser instead of me.[3]

Balfour, for his part, would probably have been quite ready to work with Fisher, had it not been for these recent attacks. Selborne wrote to Balfour on the 19th: 'I am very firmly convinced that you cannot improve upon Fisher for First Sea Lord.' He supplemented this with a card later in the day. He had just heard that Fisher had written 'an indefensible letter' to the Prime Minister that morning 'and that Asquith practically sacked him there and then'. But Fisher's friends had 'urged him to apologise and withdraw'. He hoped that Fisher would not be henceforth excluded because he was 'the best available'.[4]

---

[1] Asquith MSS., 14, 20 May 1915.
[2] R. R. James, *Memoirs of a Conservative: J. C. C. Davidson's Memoirs and Personal Papers, 1910–1937*, London, 1969, p. 108.
[3] Bonar Law Papers 50/3/1.
[4] Add. MSS. 49708, ff. 243–4, 248–9.

On the 20th Balfour replied:

I am afraid that Jacky is a little mad. He has been using, I hear, the most violent language about me, whom I believe at one time he used to 'butter up to the skies'. I am not sure that even if Asquith consented to his remaining at the Admiralty, he (Fisher) would consent to serve under me. There would be no use our attempting to work together unless he really was prepared to go cordially with me.[1]

By 20 May, then, Fisher's position had collapsed. Hearing on the 21st that the Admiral was now 'intriguing with journalists', Hankey determined to get him out of London. On Saturday, 22 May, Hankey recorded:

In the morning I saw Balfour for a short time, but spent most of the morning in getting pressure put upon Fisher from various quarters to go right away to Scotland, away from journalistic influences, as he may do himself and the nation great harm by an indiscretion in his present excited state. I saw him, and took the line that he ought to adopt the role of the 'strong, silent man', injured, but still keeping silent. I reminded him that he had given this advice to Kitchener with excellent results, and told him it was his one chance of getting back to the Admiralty.[2]

Hankey undertook to obtain from Asquith the First Sea Lord's official release. When Fisher was already on an afternoon train, bound for the Duke of Hamilton's estate in Lanarkshire, the Prime Minister—in a thoroughly bad temper—acceded to Hankey's request. Fisher received a telegram to this effect at Crewe. That evening Asquith ended an active connexion with the Navy dating from 1854 by writing in the following terms:

Dear Lord Fisher,

I am commanded by the King to accept your tendered resignation of the Office of First Sea Lord of the Admiralty.

Yours faithfully,
H. H. Asquith.[3]

But Fisher's contribution to the national war effort looked different from the Grand Fleet. On 29 May Jellicoe wrote:

[1] Add. MSS. 49708, ff. 249–50.
[2] Hankey, i, 317–18.
[3] *F.G.* iii, 247 (F.P. 1033, 22 May 1915).

My dear Lord Fisher,

It is difficult to write when one feels so deeply. I waited first until the question was definitely decided and then did not know what to say, but feel that I must write now.

We owe you a debt of gratitude for having saved the Navy from a continuance in office of Mr. Churchill, and I hope that never again will any politician be allowed to usurp the functions that he took upon himself to exercise. The same thing will not occur in Mr. Balfour's case . . .

I have seen Mr. Balfour and had a long interview. He seems sound but after the Dardanelles business I mistrust everyone who in any way supported the early policy of that monument. I am glad to see that in the leading article of the Times of the 27th, your work at the Admiralty is recognised. History will show that your six months of office there revolutionised the situation and laid the foundations of the new Navy with which the war will be fought out: only your energy and foresight could have done it. The whole Navy knows it—even your enemies admit it loudest—and I trust that you will find consolation in the fact. For myself you are the one man in the Empire.

Yours always devotedly

J. R. Jellicoe[1]

Meanwhile the coalition government entered office on 25 May. Balfour was First Lord. Sir Henry Jackson became First Sea Lord. Churchill lingered on disconsolately as Chancellor of the Duchy of Lancaster. Finally, in November, he decided to go and serve as an officer on the western front.

[1] F.P. 1041.

CHAPTER 10

EPILOGUE (1915–1920)

HAVING excluded himself from office as First Sea Lord, Fisher endlessly fretted after a method of return. Possibly in the hope of keeping him out of mischief, Balfour suggested on 26 June that he might like to be 'Chairman to the new Inventions Committee' and thereby do 'a great public service'. The Board of Invention and Research proved a frustrating sphere of activity. This was at least partly due to fear at the Admiralty that Fisher would somehow use his position at the B.I.R. to clamber back into power and lop the heads of those suspected of keeping him out. By October 1916, the B.I.R. was known in some service quarters as 'the Board of Intrigue and Revenge'![1] The Board, supposed to encourage and organize scientific effort for the benefit of the naval service, was assisted on a voluntary basis by such men as the physicist Sir Joseph Thomson, the propulsion expert Sir Charles Parsons, the physicist W. H. Bragg, and the chemist Sir George Beilby. The offices were in Cockspur Street. After Fisher had complained loudly and often about the lack of interest shown by the Admiralty in the work of the Board, Sir Eric Geddes (First Lord from July 1917) appointed a committee of three headed by Sir Sothern Holland to investigate. The conclusions were:

(a) That men of the greatest scientific knowledge are not being used to the fullest extent and are being wasted on committee work.
(b) That B.I.R. does not work in sufficiently close touch with the Admiralty, and *vice versa*.
(c) That the scientists are not in amongst the problems they work on.
(d) That the present constitution of the B.I.R. does not admit of the individual driving and co-ordinating power which is so essential to all executive undertakings.
(e) That the multiplication of experimental establishments by the Admiralty must lead to dissipation of forces and to confusion.

---

[1] De Robeck Papers, 4/78, Cdr. J. R. Middleton to Keyes, 26 Oct. 1916 on B.I.R. notepaper: pencilled note by Keyes for de R.

The Committee therefore recommended:

(a) The abolition of the Board of Inventions and Research.

(b) The appointment of a Director of Research and Experiments at the Admiralty, responsible for the direction of all researches, inventions, and experiments under the Third Sea Lord . . .[1]

It was found that the B.I.R.'s main effort had been directed to 'the provision of means of location and destruction of submarines'. The result thus far had been the production of 'a fairly satisfactory hydrophone' and 'a magnetic destructor mine'. But by far the most interesting development associated with the work of the B.I.R. was the invention of ASDIC, now called sonar. The importance of the 'supersonic' work is barely glimpsed in the Sothern Holland report.[2]

The Sothern Holland report was not implemented in its entirety. Charles H. Merz was appointed Director of Experiments and Research (unpaid!) and had an office at the Admiralty from 18 January 1918. But it was decided to keep the B.I.R. in existence after all. It remained outside the Admiralty building, but Merz was a member of both organizations. This provided a better working arrangement; it continued till the end of December 1918. It is quite unclear whether or not Fisher appreciated the special importance of the work on echo-detection of submarines which first began to show fruit, under his aegis, in 1917. He certainly gave Merz the benefit of his views on the running of the war and the idiocy of the authorities in failing to utilize fully the genius and second sight of Admiral of the Fleet Lord Fisher of Kilverstone! As the latter wrote to his faithful adherent, George Lambert, on 8 March 1918:

Merz interviewed me yesterday before the meeting of the Magi at Victory House, and I gave it to him hot as to the past and present conduct of the War, but didn't quite finish, as Sir J. J. Thomson and the other great people came in, so I wrote Merz enclosed letter as very possibly he may be a missionary, for he seemed very greatly impressed and petrified (he was quite dumb all the rest of the meeting!).[3]

The conclusions drawn by Merz from his interview with Fisher can only be surmised; but a letter which he wrote to

---

[1] Adm. 116/1430, Sothern Holland Report, 21 Sept. 1917.

[2] Ibid., p. 13. 'ASDIC' comprises the initial letters of the 'Allied Submarine Detection Investigation Committee'.

[3] F.G. iii, 521.

Geddes on 26 November 1918 gives an interesting impression of the nature of the work accomplished by the B.I.R.:

When I came here at the beginning of this year I felt—and I think everyone felt—that there was no final and satisfactory antidote to the submarine; all lines had to be followed and this has been done. The year's work has, however, in my opinion, resulted in determining the correct method of attack, and if the war had continued this would certainly have had its effect during the next twelve months. It follows that had the problem been tackled three years before that a very large part of the shipping sunk would have been saved.

This one instance is sufficient proof I think of the absolute necessity of continuing the close association of the Naval Officer and the Scientist, which you were really the first to arrange for . . . there is—as I point out in the memorandum enclosed—ample reason for pushing the echo method of detection to the limit . . .[1]

As far as the present writer is aware, no published account is available of the original development of ASDIC, making it clear, for example, what part was played by the French or who was the leader of the British scientific team. Therefore the following extracts are given from a 'Report on the Position of Experiment and Research for the Navy' dated 31 December 1918 (the last day of Fisher's association with the B.I.R.). In this report Professor Bragg writes generally of 'echo' methods:

. . . a beam of sound of a special kind may be emitted under water from the new 'Asdic' transmitter in a form as concentrated as that of the searchlight and falling on objects underwater which may give rise to reflected or scattered sound by which the presence and position of the objects can be found. The sound is special in that the wave length is extremely short and the sound cannot be directly detected by the ear . . .[2]

Dr. R. W. Boyle deals with the history of the project:

The idea of using ultrasonic waves for signalling and locating purposes dates back to the 'Titanic' disaster . . . but no successful attempts to solve the problem were made before the war. When the war broke out the idea was revived in Paris by M. Chilowski, who brought it to the notice of Prof. Paul Langevin, with the result that Langevin and Chilowski began work on the subject in March 1915 . . .

The Admiralty B.I.R. took up this work in England in August 1916, and assigned the writer to take charge of the experiments. In

[1] Naval Library, black folder containing copies of B.I.R. materials (Crease Papers), Merz to Geddes, 26 Nov. 1918.
[2] Adm. 116/1430, report, p. 10.

the course of time many methods were tried, attention always being directed so that the work should not be duplicated . . .

Of all the methods tried by the French, ourselves, and later by the Americans, the most successful up to the present is the method of the piezo-electric property of quartz . . . Langevin was the first to try a plate of quartz as a receiver; it acted well on the first experiment . . .

We have detected a submarine lying on the bottom at horizontal distances of 400 to 700 yards, depth of water being 25 or 27 fathoms, and have given her approximate bearings.[1]

While it can scarcely be claimed that Fisher made any scientific contribution to the development of ASDIC, it cannot be denied that he presided over the organization which, under difficult conditions, accomplished a good deal in that direction. It may therefore be said that Fisher's association with the Navy began under sail in 1854 and ended with the insistent pinging of the ASDIC in 1918. His experience encompassed, at its outset, the leisurely spirit of the eighteenth century and, at its end, the feverish quest for survival by scientific technique typical of the twentieth century. Such was Fisher of Kilverstone.

Miraculously, Fisher's connexion with Churchill revived before very long, as indicated in the previous chapter. Indeed, as far as Churchill was concerned his affection for Fisher scarcely even ebbed. As soon after the débâcle as 9 June 1915 one finds Hankey writing to Fisher: 'I had a long letter from Winston the other day. In the course of it he spoke very nicely of you, and regretfully of the days when you worked well together. My impression is that one of these days he would like to make it up.'[2]

This was by no means an overstatement of the case. Fisher must have been astonished at Churchill's lack of information on the reasons for his own removal from the Admiralty! Admittedly, in his valedictory speech to the House of Commons on 15 November 1915, Churchill comprised Fisher in his catalogue of misfortune: 'I am not going to embark upon any reproaches this afternoon, but I must say I did not receive from the First Sea Lord either the clear guidance before the event or the firm support after which I was entitled to expect.'[3] This had a certain kind of plausibility. How clear should the guidance have been? No doubt proper use of the Naval Staff by Fisher would have further developed the argument deployed in the memorandum of 25 January. All one can say, otherwise, is that Churchill

---

[1] Ibid., pp. 17-18.   [2] F.P. 1049.   [3] *Hansard*, 5th Series, lxxv, 1514.

showed no inclination to benefit by such 'guidance' as he did receive from his First Sea Lord and that he thoroughly deserved the personal consequences of his ill-based self-confidence. On the other hand, with regard to 'firm support after', Churchill had a better case.

But this moment of recrimination faded into the background. In March 1916 Churchill was back in England on leave when he decided to speak in the debate on the Navy Estimates. Garvin of the *Observer* and C. P. Scott of the *Manchester Guardian* had been compaigning for Fisher's return to the Admiralty and the upshot—to the horror of Churchill's wife—was that Fisher was invited to a reconciliatory lunch at the Churchills' home in Cromwell Road. Churchill proposed to attack Balfour's record as First Lord and to cap this by demanding the recall of Lord Fisher to the Admiralty! Not surprisingly, Fisher reacted ecstatically to this incredible development.[1]

The speech was duly delivered on 7 March 1916. The attack on the passivity of the Balfour regime seems to have passed off moderately well. But as Churchill then proceeded to work round, by way of an account of his 'remarkable' partnership with Fisher, to what was intended to be a dramatic demand for the latter's restoration, the incredulity of the House was deep and genuine. It must be remembered that there were many members listening to this speech who knew approximately the contents of the ultimatum which Fisher had delivered to Asquith in May 1915, and that Churchill may have been unique among the leading politicians in his ignorance of it.[2]

Balfour was not pleased by Churchill's criticisms and, on 8 March, he took full advantage of the wide-open opportunities for counter-attack offered by Churchill's cry for Fisher's return. Churchill writhed under the flail of Balfour's wit and invective.

On the morning of the 8th Fisher, partly through journalistic belief in his Messianic qualities and partly because of genuine concern (on the part of Hankey, Jellicoe, and others) about the slowness of ship-construction, was given a chance to address the War Committee, the successor of the War Council. According

[1] Gilbert, pp. 708–11.
[2] On 23 June 1915 Crease wrote to Fisher: 'There is no doubt that Mr. Asquith and his clique have made great play with the letter you wrote to him laying down terms and conditions. Everyone more or less seems to know the contents at all events. I have no doubt it was this which caused the Tory members of the Cabinet to go back on you.' (F.P. 1060.)

4. A Placard evocative of Fisher's time at the Board of Invention. It incorporates a photograph of Epstein's bust of the Admiral, completed in 1916

to the minutes, 'Lord Fisher expressed great concern at the shortage of light cruisers and destroyers' and his remarks led the War Committee to approve in principle 'the formation of a Joint Interdepartmental Committee' to 'secure concerted action'.[1] Otherwise, however, he seems to have made an indifferent impression. Asquith afterwards told C. P. Scott that Fisher was 'a constructor, very fertile and ingenious', but 'not a strategist'. He had 'what the Americans call "hustle" '—but so did others.[2]

This episode marked the end of Fisher's serious hopes of a second recall.

Otherwise, during these last years, he continued for a time his close relationship with Jellicoe. The latter's continuing habit of confiding to Fisher his complaints and anxieties was a constant irritation to the Balfour regime. 'Nothing short of ill-health can justify or explain Jellicoe's folly in writing such letters to such a quarter', Hopwood (the Additional Civil Lord) wrote to Balfour.[3] But Jellicoe's appointment as First Sea Lord on 29 November 1916 was a decisive check to Fisher's aspirations. Early in 1917 Fisher offered himself to Jellicoe as Third Sea Lord and Controller, claiming that he could master the great U-boat crisis; but Jellicoe, after a fortnight's consideration, refused. The essence of his reply, dated 13 February 1917, was: 'There are only two posts which, in my opinion, you could hold here—those of First Lord or First Sea Lord. In any other position, I cannot help feeling that difficulties are bound to arise.'[4] Fisher was extremely bitter about this. On 16 July 1917 he wrote as follows to Jellicoe but seems, mercifully, not to have sent the letter:

My dear Jellicoe,

It is a strange irony of Fate that you should be the one I selected in 1906 to be Admiralissimo when I predicted at that time that the war with Germany would break out in August 1914 . . . and yet you should be the one to twice ruin my hopes of winning the war.

1st by giving up the Command of the Grand Fleet in November 1916 to be First Sea Lord.

2nd by refusing to let me join you as Controller of the Navy on January 31st 1917.

In the first instance you left the appointment for which you were specially fitted on the grounds that you alone could deal with the German Submarine Menace.

[1] Cab. 42/10, 8 Mar. 1916.   [2] Hammond, p. 195–6.
[3] Add. MSS. 49715, f. 80, 1 Feb. 1916.   [4] F.G. iii, 428.

In the second instance you refused me as Controller and instead accepted a Railway Engineer [Geddes, in May 1917], concurred in making him into a Vice-Admiral with precisely the powers you refused me.

And now where are you?

Yours

Fisher.[1]

In fact, the answer was: a good deal further ahead. Accompanying Geddes's appointment was a reorganization of the staff system, allowing a measure of escape from over-centralization—from a system which was (to quote Professor Marder) 'a survival from the Fisher–A. K. Wilson era of the monolithic "great man" who alone held all the secrets and gave all the orders—a system that was utterly unsuited to the growing complexity of warfare'.[2] Fisher scarcely corresponded with Jellicoe again after February 1917. The latter was replaced by Wemyss as First Sea Lord in December 1917;[3] but this possible sign of grace was eclipsed, in Fisher's eyes, by Jellicoe's publication in the spring of 1919 of his book *The Grand Fleet 1914–1916: its Creation, Development and Work*. The fact that it was rather more than fair to Fisher—for example in its complimentary reference to wartime justification of his conception of the battle cruiser—did not redeem the book in Fisher's eyes. He was annoyed by its implied attribution to him, at least in part, of responsibility for the shortage of light cruisers and destroyers at the outbreak of war, neglect of mines, and failure to provide anti-submarine defences for the east coast bases. 'But what a sad thing for our naval prestige in this war is all this *"fouling of our own nest"!*' Fisher declared to Lambert. 'Really Jellicoe ought to be shot!'[4]

Fisher had lost his wife in July 1918. Whatever his feelings about Fisher himself, the King, who remembered Lady Fisher as far back as 1885 when he was training as a young officer in the *Excellent*, sent the following telegram on 19 July:

The Queen and I are deeply grieved to hear of your irreparable loss. Personally I had in Lady Fisher a dear old friend whom I have known for more than thirty years and whose kindness I shall never forget. We offer you and your family our heartfelt sympathy in your sorrow.

George R. I.[5]

[1] F.P. 1368a.   [2] *D.S.* iv, 177.
[3] He became Viscount Jellicoe of Scapa on 15 Jan. 1918.
[4] *F.G.* iii, 577.   [5] Kilv. MSS, Pkt. 3.

In fact, Fisher had caused his wife a good deal of unhappiness by the amount of time that he spent, after his resignation in May 1915, with the Duke and Duchess of Hamilton. In his unresting search for a way back to power, Fisher came to repose special value on the lively partisanship of the comparatively youthful Duchess.[1] But Fisher was in patient attendance on his wife during her last days (at the house of their daughter, Beatrix Neeld, near Malmsbury) and some of the memorial which he composed at her death should be quoted here:

Today, July 18th, 1918, there passed blissfully away, without pain or anguish and a smile in Death on her face, with her husband and children with her in her last days, a woman of whom Solomon spoke when he wrote:

'The Path of the Just is as the Shining Light that shineth more and more unto the perfect day.'

And such was Katharine Delves Broughton, for fifty-two years the wife of Admiral of the Fleet Lord Fisher of Kilverstone, having married him as a young lieutenant without friends or money or prospects, and denied herself all her life long for the sake of her husband and children—to them she was ever loyal, faithful and steadfast, and to such as contemned them she was a Dragon! . . .

. . . A Farm Waggon with the lovely horses she so admired brought her from the station to Kilverstone, and four of the principal men on the estate who she well knew carried her[2] to her grave covered with her husband's Flag of Admiral of the Fleet (the Union Jack), and it was buried with her, and her children, having gathered themselves in Kilverstone Garden the roses she loved, gave to the mother ever mindful of them her last bouquet! Solomon indeed portrayed her!

'Her children shall rise up and call her blessed; her husband also, and he praiseth her.'[3]

Fisher remained 'Radical Jack' and an *enfant terrible* to the end. He turned up in Paris with the Duchess of Hamilton during the peace conference in April 1919, regaled Lloyd George's lunch-parties with endless strings of anecdotes, and (at the age of seventy-eight) waltzed at high speed round the dance floor of the Majestic.[4] During the first half of 1920 he underwent four operations for cancer—though he does not seem to have known the

---

[1] Hough, pp. 354–6, is informative on F.'s connexion with the Hamiltons.

[2] More precisely, her ashes—'for she was cremated as she desired'.

[3] *Some Notes by Lord Fisher for his Friends*, privately printed 1918 (325 pp.), 'Postscript', pp. i–iii.

[4] Frances Lloyd George, *The Years That Are Past*, London, 1967, pp. 157–8.

nature of his illness—and still summoned up enough energy to persist with his 'sack-the-lot' letters to *The Times*. The following example, published on 2 February 1920, testifies to his continuing exuberance and vitality:

Sir,

Quite nice people are quite shocked that the common herd (the unvoiced ones), who invariably control every General Election, have thrown in their lot with the Labour Party . . .

Ireland in rebellion . . . We alienate America and all our sister nations in not allowing Ireland to be as free as they are. The simple and so obvious plan of getting rid of industrial unrest by the working man sharing in the profits is carped at and denied . . . Aviation is practically ignored, and we go fossilizing and bankrupting with weapons of war by sea and land as extinct as bows and arrows . . .

Are you surprised at the universal determination to sack the lot? . . .[1]

On 7 July he dictated what was probably his last letter. Not inappropriately, it was addressed to Arnold White. It was written at Ferne, a property of the Hamiltons' near Salisbury.

I grieve to say that I am leaving here tomorrow, Thursday morning, for London, again to be under the hands of the surgeon, as there is something not going properly in the cure. We hope it will not be for long, but these persistent sets-back tell on one, and the sleepless nights are the very devil. I so wish you could get down here when we return, as the roses are in splendour, and we also have the Fisher sweet-pea, sent accidentally to the gardener.

White here wrote in the margin: 'I sent them. A.W.'[2]

Fisher underwent his last operation on 9 July. The next day, with the Duchess of Hamilton in watchful attendance, 'the dark angel' of the Navy died. He was aged seventy-nine.

On 13 July a public funeral was held in Westminster Abbey.

It was a sight which none that saw it can ever forget. Only the funeral of King Edward, Lord Fisher's devoted friend, could match it. From the west side of St. James's Square, where the coffin, draped with the Union Jack, was placed on the guncarriage, eastwards along Pall Mall, then westward down the great Mall, under the windows of the Royal lady [Queen Alexandra] whom Fisher served with knightly devotion, past the Admiralty and under the triumphal Admiralty Arch, coiling itself within hail of the column of Fisher's

---

[1] *F.G.* iii, 617.   [2] F.P. 3717.

earthly god, Lord Nelson . . . and so through Parliament Square . . . and up to the great West Door of Westminster Abbey, the slow-pacing foot procession—with Marines, arms reversed, in the van, then the band of the Marines, with proudly wailing instruments and the drum beating on our ear like distant guns at sea, and then the blue-jackets drawing the gun-carriage, and the famous admirals walking along-side it—was flanked at every yard, every inch of the long way, by crowds upon crowds of the English people, bareheaded, still, silent, reverently paying their inarticulate homage to the great man, the great child, the ruthless foe, the whole-hearted friend, the dark schemer, the open fighter, the 'ruthless, relentless, remorseless' tyrant, the perfect playfellow, who had spent his huge strength and his genius in their service, and whom they had learned to trust, to love and to mourn.[1]

Before these ceremonials, Fisher's coffin lay in a room at the Hamiltons' house at 19 St. James's Square. In view of Fisher's recent unfriendliness, to say nothing of his own habitual self-containment, no great display of emotion was to be expected from the principal pall-bearer, Admiral Jellicoe. But as he stood waiting by the coffin of the man who had loomed so large in his career since 1884, the Viscount Jellicoe of Scapa freely and unmistakably wept.[2]

Like his wife, Fisher was cremated. His ashes were placed near hers in the churchyard at Kilverstone.

In retrospect, Hankey characterized Fisher—perhaps a shade unkindly—as 'a crank'; but he also thought him 'probably the most remarkable man of his day.'[3] If, as Garvin thought, Fisher was quite unlike his contemporaries in general, he certainly contrasted with the stereotype of the naval officer, whether Victorian or modern. In a sense peculiar unto himself, he was unique.

---

[1] Reprinted from *The Times* of 14 July 1920 in Bacon, ii, 311–12.
[2] Information from F.'s great-niece, Mrs. Marjorie Frances Wentworth Reeve, an eyewitness.
[3] Chalmers, p. 382; Hankey, i, 145.

BIBLIOGRAPHY

NOTE. See also the List of Abbreviations on pp. xv–xvi, above. Attention is drawn to the fine bibliography in Marder's *From the Dreadnought to Scapa Flow*, vol. v, and to the relevant chapters in *A Guide to the Sources of British Military History*, edited by Robin Higham (Berkeley, University of California Press, 1971; and London, Routledge and Kegan Paul, 1972).

A. UNPUBLISHED PAPERS

Admiralty Records (P.R.O.). As may be inferred from the footnotes, the classes Adm. 1 and Adm. 116 were of prime importance. IND. is the reference for a digest or index in the Admiralty archives.

Arnold-Forster Papers (Add. MSS.). Includes typed copies of H. O. Arnold-Forster's outgoing letters.

Asquith MSS. (Dept. of Western MSS., Bodleian Library, Oxford).

Balfour Papers (Add. MSS.). Of major importance for Fisher and defence policy in general, especially 1903–5.

Battenberg Papers (Broadlands Archives Trust). The originals of the main items for Fisher are in F.P. and Kilv. MSS.

Bonar Law Papers (Beaverbrook Library).

Cabinet Papers (P.R.O.). Very important for Fisher and the naval history of his period. (There is a separate handbook for the records of the C.I.D. to 1914.)

Campbell–Bannerman Papers (Add. MSS.).

Corbett's Diary (Mr. Richard Corbett).

De Robeck Papers (Churchill College, Cambridge).

Esher Papers (Churchill College, Cambridge). Much of the material has been published, but several useful items remained.

Fisher Papers (Duke of Hamilton). A great collection for Fisher and the Navy, especially 1900–15. Many prints.

Foreign Office Papers (P.R.O.). Useful for Hague Conference (1899).

Haldane Papers (National Library of Scotland).

Hankey Papers (Churchill College, Cambridge). Only Fisher's letters to Hankey were made available, but these were of much value.

Jellicoe Papers (Add. MSS.).

Kilverstone MSS. (Lord Fisher). Personal and family materials germane to the Admiral's life.

Lloyd George Papers (Beaverbrook Library).

McKenna MSS (Churchill College, Cambridge).

National Maritime Museum. The following important collections of naval officers were used (the letters in brackets being the references used by the N.M.M.). The papers of:

Adl. Sir Cyprian Bridge (BRI).
Adl. of the Fleet Sir Geoffrey Phipps Hornby (PHI).
Adl. of the Fleet Sir William H. May (MAY).
Adl. of the Fleet Sir Gerard Noel (NOE).
Adl. of the Fleet Sir Henry Oliver. (On extended loan.)
Adl. Sir Herbert Richmond (RIC).
Adl. Sir Edmond Slade (microfilm). Valuable diary for 1908.
The papers of the journalist Sir James R. Thursfield (THU) were also used.

Naval Library, Ministry of Defence. Naval prints dating from 1885 were used, including *Notes for Navy Debates,* 1896–97—not available in F.P. or elsewhere; and see Tweedmouth Papers below.

Tweedmouth Papers (Naval Library). Whereas the Library's collections for Selborne and Cawdor consist almost entirely of prints, many of them available elsewhere, the Tweedmouth Papers comprise the First Lord's correspondence for 1906–8, as well as prints.

War Office Records (P.R.O.). Important for documents relating to the pre-war amphibious projects.

B. UNPUBLISHED THESES

D'Ombrain, Nicholas J., 'The Military Departments and the Committee of Imperial Defence, 1902–1914', Oxford D. Phil., 1969. (A revised version is to be published as an Oxford Historical Monograph.)

Moon, Howard R., 'The Invasion of the United Kingdon: Public Controversy and Official Planning, 1888–1918', London Ph.D., 1968.

Summerton, Neil W., 'The Development of British Military Planning for a War against Germany, 1904–1914', London Ph.D., 1970.

Willmott, Hedley P., 'The Navy Estimates, 1906–1909', Liverpool M.A., 1970.

C. PUBLISHED WORKS

This list is largely restricted to books referenced by the author's name in the footnotes.

Appleyard, Rollo, *Charles Parsons: His Life and Work,* London, 1933
Asquith, H. H.: see Oxford and Asquith.
Bacon, Adl. Sir Reginald, *The Life of Lord Fisher of Kilverstone,* London, 1929, 2 vols.
——, *From 1900 Onward,* London, 1940.
Barnaby, K. C., *The Institution of Naval Architects, 1860–1960,* London, 1960.

Barnes, Eleanor C., *Alfred Yarrow: His Life and Work*, London, 1924.
Bell, A. C., *A History of the Blockade of Germany and of the Countries Associated with Her in the Great War*, London, 1961.
Bennett, Geoffrey, *Charlie B: a biography of Admiral Lord Beresford of Metemmeh and Curraghmore*, London, 1968.
Beresford, Lord Charles, *The Betrayal*, London, 1912.
——, *The Memoirs of Lord Charles Beresford*, London, 4th ed., 1916.
Blake, Robert, *The Unknown Prime Minister: the Life and Times of Andrew Bonar Law, 1858–1923*, London, 1955.
Bonham-Carter, Violet, *Winston Churchill As I Knew Him*, London, 1965.
Bonner-Smith, D.: see Navy Records Society.
Bowden-Smith, Adl. Sir Nathaniel, *Naval Recollections, 1852 to 1914*, London, 1914.
Bradford, Adl. Sir Edward E., *Life of Admiral of the Fleet Sir Arthur Knyvet Wilson*, London, 1923.
Brett, M. V.: see Esher.
Callwell, Major-General Sir C. E., *Field-Marshal Sir Henry Wilson*, London, 1927, 2 vols.
Chalmers, Rear-Adl. W. S., *The Life and Letters of David, Earl Beatty*, London, 1951.
Chatfield, Adl. of the Fleet Lord, *The Navy and Defence*, London, 1942. (Autobiography, 1873–1933.)
Churchill, Randolph S., *Winston S. Churchill*, London, 1967, 2 vols.; and the companion volume (documents) relating to vol. ii (published 1969).
Churchill, Winston S., *The World Crisis*, London, 1923–31, 5 vols. in 6.
Clowes, Sir William Laird, *The Royal Navy: a History from the Earliest Times to the Present*, London, 1897–1903, 7 vols.
Colomb, Vice-Adl. Philip H., *Memoirs of Sir Astley Cooper Key*, London, 1898.
Cowie, Captain J. S., *Mines, Minelayers and Minelaying*, London, 1949.
Dewar, Vice-Adl. K. G. B., *The Navy from Within*, London, 1939.
Dorling, Captain Taprell, *Men o' War*, London, 1929.
Dugdale, E. T. S. (ed.), *German Diplomatic Documents, 1871–1914*, London, 1930, 4 vols.
Dunlop, John K., *The Development of the British Army, 1899–1914*, London, 1938.
Egerton, Mrs. E., *Admiral of the Fleet Sir Geoffrey Phipps Hornby*, London, 1896.
Ensor, R. C. K., *England, 1870–1914*, Oxford, 1936.
Esher, Viscount, *Journals and Letters of Reginald, Viscount Esher* (ed. M. V. Brett and Oliver, Viscount Esher), London, 1934–8, 4 vols.

Fisher, Adl. of the Fleet Lord, *Memories*, London, 1919.

——, *Records*, London, 1919.

Gardiner, A. G., *Pillars of Society*, London, 1916.

Gilbert, Martin, *Winston S. Churchill*, vol. iii, London, 1971.

Gollin, Alfred M., *The Observer and J. L. Garvin, 1908–1914*, London, 1960.

Halévy, Elie, *The Rule of Democracy, 1905–1914*, London, 1961.

Hamer, W. S., *The British Army: Civil Military Relations, 1885–1905*, Oxford, 1970.

Hamilton, Lord George, *Parliamentary Reminiscences and Reflections, 1886–1906*, London, 1922.

Hammond, J. L., *C. P. Scott of the Manchester Guardian*, London, rev. ed., 1934.

Hankey, Lord, *The Supreme Command*, London, 1961, 2 vols.

Higham, Robin, *The British Rigid Airship, 1908–1921*, London, 1961.

Hough, Richard, *First Sea Lord: an Authorized Biography of Admiral Lord Fisher*, London, 1969.

James, Adl. Sir William, *A Great Seaman: the Life of Admiral of the Fleet Sir Henry F. Oliver*, London, 1956.

Jameson, Rear-Adl. Sir William, *The Most Formidable Thing*, London, 1965.

Kemp, Lieutenant-Commander Peter K.: see Navy Records Society and Nowell-Smith.

Kerr, Adl. Mark, *Prince Louis of Battenberg: Admiral of the Fleet*, London, 1934.

Keyes, Adl. of the Fleet Sir Roger, *Naval Memoirs*, London, 1934–5, 2 vols.

King-Hall, Louise (ed.), *Sea Saga: Being the Naval Diaries of Four Generations of the King-Hall Family*, London, 1935.

Lee, Sir Sidney, *King Edward VII: a Biography*, London, 1927, 2 vols.

Lewis, Michael, *The Navy of Britain*, London, 1948.

Lloyd George, David, *War Memoirs*, London, 1933–6, 6 vols.

Lumby, E. W. R.: see Navy Records Society.

Manning, Frederic, *The Life of Sir William White*, London, 1923.

Manning, Captain T. D., *The British Destroyer*, London, 1961.

March, Edgar J., *British Destroyers, 1892–1953*, London, 1966.

Marder, Arthur J., *The Anatomy of British Sea Power: a History of British Naval Policy in the Pre-Dreadnought Era, 1880–1905*, Hamden, Conn. 1964; distributed in Britain by Cass. (Same as original ed. of 1940, published in Britain as *British Naval Policy, 1880–1905*.)

——, (ed.), *Fear God and Dread Nought: the Correspondence of Admiral of the Fleet Lord Fisher of Kilverstone*, London, 1952–9, 3 vols.

——, *From the Dreadnought to Scapa Flow: the Royal Navy in the Fisher Era, 1904–1919*, London, 1961–70, 5 vols.

——, *Portrait of an Admiral: the Life and Papers of Sir Herbert Richmond*, London, 1952.

Meynell, Esther, *A Woman Talking*, London, 1940.

Monger, George, *The End of Isolation: British Foreign Policy, 1900–1907*, London, 1963.

Navy Records Society:
>   *Russian War, 1855, Baltic: Official Correspondence*, ed. by D. Bonner-Smith, 1944.
>
>   *The Second China War, 1856–60*, ed. by D. Bonner-Smith and E. W. R. Lumby, 1954.
>
>   *The Papers of Admiral Sir John Fisher*, ed. by P. K. Kemp, 1960 and 1964, 2 vols.
>
>   *The Jellicoe Papers*, ed. by A. Temple Patterson, 1966 and 1968, 2 vols.
>
>   *Policy and Operations in the Mediterranean, 1912–14*, ed. by E. W. B. Lumby, 1970.

Nicolson, Harold, *King George the Fifth*, London, 1952.

Nowell-Smith, Simon (ed.), *Edwardian England, 1901–1914*, London, 1954.

Oliver, R. D., *H.M.S. Excellent, 1830–1930*, Portsmouth, 1930.

Oxford and Asquith, Earl of, *Memories and Reflections, 1852–1927*, London, 1928, 2 vols.

Pack, Captain S. W. C., *Britannia at Dartmouth*, London, 1966.

Padfield, Peter, *Aim Straight: a Biography of Admiral Sir Percy Scott*, London, 1966.

Parkes, Oscar, *British Battleships*, London, rev. ed., 1966.

Patterson, A. Temple, *Jellicoe: a Biography*, London, 1969.

——, see Navy Records Society.

Penn, Commander Geoffrey, *'Up Funnel, Down Screw!': the Story of the Naval Engineer*, London, 1955.

Ponsonby, Sir Frederick, *Recollections of Three Reigns*, London, 1951.

Preston, Anthony, and Major, John, *Send a Gunboat*, London, 1967.

Repington, Lt.-Colonel Charles à Court, *The First World War, 1914–1918*, London, 1920, 2 vols.

Roskill, Stephen, *Hankey: Man of Secrets*, London, 1970–2, 2 vols.

Sayer, G. B., *H.M.S. Vernon: a History*, Portsmouth, 1930.

Schurman, D. M., *The Education of a Navy: the Development of British Naval Strategic Thought, 1867–1914*, London, 1965.

Scott, Adl. Sir Percy, *Fifty Years in the Royal Navy*, London, 1919.

Searle, G. R., *The Quest for National Efficiency*, Oxford, 1971.

Jonathan, Steinberg, 'The Copenhagen Complex' in *Journal of Contemporary History* (1966), vol. I, no. 3.

Sueter, Commander Murray F., *The Evolution of the Submarine Boat, Mine, and Torpedo from the Sixteenth Century to the Present*, Portsmouth, 1907.

Sulivan, H. N., *The Life and Letters of Admiral Sir Bartholomew Sulivan,*
    1810–1890, London, 1896.
Sydenham of Combe, Lord, *My Working Life,* London, 1927.
Walker, Sir Charles, *Thirty-Six Years at the Admiralty,* London, 1934.
Wester Wemyss, Lady, *The Life and Letters of Lord Wester Wemyss,*
    London, 1935.
Whyte, Frederic, *The Life of W. T. Stead,* London, 1925, 2 vols.
Williamson, Samuel R., Jr., *The Politics of Grand Strategy: Britain and
    France Prepare for War, 1904–1914,* Cambridge, Mass., 1969.
Yexley, Lionel, *Our Fighting Sea Men,* London, 1911.
——, *The Inner Life of the Navy,* London, 1908.

INDEX

As far as possible, the highest rank attained by officers is given.

DATE DUE
